The Beverage Testing Institute's

Buying Guide to Wines of North America

Other Publications from the Beverage Testing Institute
and Sterling Publishing Co., Inc.

Buying Guide to Imported Wines

Buying Guide to Spirits

Buying Guide to Inexpensive Wines

Buying Guide to Beers

The Beverage Testing Institute's

Buying Guide to Wines of North America

Edited by Charles Laverick

Sterling Publishing Co., Inc.
New York

Library of Congress Cataloging-in-Publication Data Available

10 9 8 7 6 5 4 3 2 1

Published by Sterling Publishing Company, Inc.
387 Park Avenue South, New York, N.Y. 10016
© 1999 by the Beverage Testing Institute
Distributed in Canada by Sterling Publishing
c/o Canadian Manda Group, One Atlantic Avenue, Suite 105
Toronto, Ontario, Canada M6K 3E7
Distributed in Great Britain and Europe by Cassell PLC
Wellington House, 125 Strand, London WC2R 0BB, England
Distributed in Australia by Capricorn Link (Australia) Pty Ltd.
P.O. Box 6651, Baulkham Hills, Business Centre, NSW 2153, Australia

Sterling ISBN 0-8069-2857-3

Acknowledgements

Wine ratings produced by Marc Dornan and Charles Laverick of BTI, with the help of regular guest panelists Bob Bansberg (Ambria), Kevin Cahoon (Langdon & Shiverick), Alan Dikty (Applied Beverage Technologies), Tom Hyland (North Shore Wine News), Phil Matievic (Frugal Wine Co.), and Tim Wermerling (Wermerling & Co.). Tasting notes written by Marc Dornan and Charles Laverick. Introductory material and AVA information written by Charles Laverick with the exception of Canada and certain AVA tracts, which were written by Marc Dornan. Editing by Jim Clark, Alan Dikty, Marc Dornan, and Charles Laverick. Graphic design and layout was done by Kelley Witzemann of Jokerman Studio in Chicago with assistance from Jeff Bowes. Special thanks to Jon Winsell of BTI for his tireless technical assistance and able coordination between all involved (He deserves a vacation and some time at home with his daughter, Julia). Also, thanks to Richard Cooper of BTI for his general support and the simple fact that he acquires our samples. No Coop, no book.

BTI is a team effort. Further thanks must go to Debra Bernstein and Rochelle Calhoun for their administrative support and Gary Nei, Pat Welsh, and Burt Eisenberg, members of the board who have put their money where our mouths are. By purchasing this book, you have moved us ever closer to repaying them. Consider buying another one, wine books make great stocking-stuffers.

Finally, last but certainly not least, we are all indebted to Craig Goldwyn, founder and longtime president of BTI, who has made the rather unusual transition from wine critic to webmaster. It was he who had the guts to start BTI (in his basement) in 1981, despite the advice of pundits long forgotten. Through the lean years he stuck it out, only recently to realize the fruits of his sacrifices. His stubborn nature and determination are reflected in all that BTI does today. He is one of a kind—give him a bump.

Contents

The Beverage Testing Institute's
Buying Guide to Wines of North America

Introduction

This book would have been impossible to write 30 years ago. Even 20 years ago it would have been pretty thin. The intervening years, however, have seen exponential growth in the North American wine industry. This growth is not just limited to California. New regions are being developed, and states like Oregon and Washington are poised on the brink of stardom in their own right. What will the next ten years hold with New York, Virginia, and even parts of Canada continuing to develop apace? Of course, just as few could have foreseen today's market or the rise of these new appellations 30 years ago, will today's Texas or New Mexico become tomorrow's Washington? The dawn of the new century finds a newly awakened and powerful American wine industry, capable of making wines that compete with the finest in the world.

The statistics in this book are staggering—nearly 800 producers representing over 3,500 individual wines. There are over 900 Cabernets alone, and these are all very recent reviews, the figures haven't been padded by the inclusion of ten year-old Sauvignon Blancs. We review thousands of American wines each year, and were actually forced to trim current reviews for space considerations. For that reason, non-recommended wines are not included, and wines scoring 82 points or less are not printed with their tasting notes. This information can be found on our website, Tastings.com. The fact that there are just so many American wines out there these days says something about the vast array of choices available to the American wine consumer. This is where a book like this comes in handy. It is not only a great reference to almost every commercially significant wine produced in North America, but contains all sorts of handy information that allows you, the consumer, to make a more informed buying decision.

The first part of the book is arranged in chapters by state (or country in the case of Canada) and contains all wine reviews listed alphabetically by producer. This allows you to look up a specific producer or wine and to peruse reviews from New York State for instance. These sections also carry introductions that explain some of what is or has been going on in each of these areas. The second half of the book is arranged by grape varietal and wine style. Each of these chapters contains introductions to the wines in question, lists the top wines of that style reviewed in the first half of the book, and contains "Best Producer" lists. These lists are compiled with three quality tiers that tell you which wineries have a proven track record for producing the best wines of a given type. Best Producer lists are extremely useful, as it is sometimes difficult to find the exact wine you might be looking for. Should that be the case you can search for wines from a producer who is proven to be consistently excellent with the type of wine in question.

Finally, a number of the varietal sections contain information about what U.S. appellations (or regions where the grapes come from) are producing the best wines of a given grape—Chardonnay or Merlot for example. These "AVA" sections also tell you how wines produced in different regions may differ from each other. This means that instead of just letting me say which wine I like better, you can find an appellation that looks interesting, or makes wines to your taste, and start from there. This is a useful tool for the consumer to use in order to "whittle down the field." An in-depth explanation of the concept is to be found in Chapter Eight.

The various features allow you to approach what could otherwise be a fairly complex subject from a number of different simplifying angles. It has been designed with ease of use in mind, but also contains essential information that is easy to reference—all you wanted to know about U.S. Merlot in a snap, for instance. This, in combination with general information such as how to become a wine expert in ten easy steps (page 16), will have you off and running in no time. Never again should you be disappointed by an American wine purchase or intimidated by a restaurant wine list or a snooty sommelier.

About BTI

The Beverage Testing Institute (BTI) was founded in 1981, with a mission to create fair and reliable reviews. This led to the institute publishing a well-respected magazine, *International Wine Review*, from 1984 through 1990. Subsequently, the results of BTI tastings were featured first in *Wine & Spirits* magazine, and then in *Wine Enthusiast* magazine as an independently produced buying guide. Other publications, including the *Chicago Tribune* and the *Washington Post*, have showcased BTI reviews over the years.

In 1994, BTI began to review beer and spirits in addition to wine. Today, we are the largest full-time beverage review body in the world. In 1999 BTI will review more than 10,000 wines, beers, and spirits. We produce a bimonthly publication, *Tastings, the Journal*, which carries up-to-the-minute reviews and insight from the world of wine, beer, and spirits. *Tastings, the Journal* is supported by our website, Tastings.com, which contains hundreds of articles, links to all things gustatory, including thousands of winery and brewery listings, and a database of over 30,000 of our recent reviews, linked to retailers around the country so that you don't have to pull your hair out looking for that hard to find wine. Additionally, Tastings.com features the Insiders Club, a subscription service that alerts consumers to highly rated products from upcoming issues of the Journal. This puts you ahead of the crowd, before those products sell out. To subscribe, or to get more information about either *Tastings, the Journal* or the Insiders Club at Tastings.com, email us at journal@tastings.com; write to us at Beverage Testing Institute, 310 South Peoria Street, Suite 504A, Chicago, IL 60607; or phone us at 312-226-7857.

In addition to these endeavors, BTI produces a range of books. These include *Buying Guide to the Wines of North America, Buying Guide to Imported Wines, Buying Guide to Inexpensive Wines from Around the World, Buying Guide to Beer,* and *Buying Guide to Spirits.* They are all published by Sterling Publishers. Other publications that currently carry our reviews and musings include *Restaurant Hospitality* magazine, *All About Beer* magazine, Epicurious—the website of *Bon Appetit* and *Gourmet* magazines, AOL at keyword "Drinks," and Foofoo.com, to name a few.

BTI employs eight people on a full-time basis. BTI, in no particular order, is: Craig Goldwyn-web guy/guru, Jon Winsell-operations/man of databases, Richard Cooper-marketing/man of cigars, Charles Laverick-wine/outdoorsman, Marc Dornan-wine/beer/resident alien, Catherine Fallis-Journal/woman of words, Debra Bernstein-whip cracker/chef, Rochelle Calhoun-teamster/Latin dance instructor and Señor Alan Dikty-man of letters/spirits. As a group, we spend lots of time listening to Devo.

How BTI Reviews Are Created

My name is Charles Laverick. I am responsible for wine reviews at the Beverage Testing Institute, but I don't do it alone, and that is the difference between a BTI review and a review from a wine critic who is working alone. My colleague, Marc Dornan, sits in on nearly all reviewing sessions, as does an invited guest panelist chosen specifically for expertise in a given region. This panel of three convenes on a daily basis at 9:30 a.m. to conduct our wine reviews, and uses a proprietary methodology, which insures that BTI reviews are both consistent and meaningful.

The Quality Question

There are two widely used scales in the product-testing universe. These are the qualitative assessment scale and the consumer acceptance scale. While a consumer scale asks the taster whether or not they like a particular product and if so to what degree, a qualitative scale is focused on a given product's quality vis-à-vis its peers (i.e., Qualitative: "In the world of Cabernet is this a world class product?" Consumer: "Do you personally care for Cabernet or the flavors of this Cabernet in particular?").

Other critics don't fit neatly into either category, but tend to put a great deal of weight on their personal wine preferences, regardless of style. After some experimentation, we have come to the conclusion that a strict qualitative scale does the job better, as it more accurately reflects the consumer's understanding of the 100-point scale to which our reviews are ultimately translated. A 90 score signifies an excellent wine in the wider context of the wines of the world. Do consumers, or even professionals, like the flavors caused by malolactic fermentation in Chardonnay? Herbal Sauvignons? Oak-driven reds? We think these questions are best left to marketing professionals. Instead a BTI panelist will look at any style of wine as valid. We are not in an endless quest for thick wines with lots of oak or any other uniform wine style. We believe diversity should be celebrated and endeavor not to set out on any stylistic crusades or frame qualitative decisions along purely stylistic guidelines. A BTI panelist will set aside any personal prejudices about particular wine styles (oaked Chablis, modern Barolo, New Zealand Sauvignon, etc.) and judge wines solely on their own merits. Using this challenging set of criteria necessitates a small, well-trained cadre of tasting professionals.

Three's Company

While a consumer approach requires a broad base of panelists to get an accurate sample size, a qualitative approach requires a small number of professionals who specialize in whatever varietal or region is being addressed, and have demonstrated expertise as such. A BTI panel will most always contain exactly three panelists. Why three? Relying on a single taster carries with it a certain risk. After all everyone has a bad day. However, panels have their faults as well. Chief among them is the "law of averages." Two panelists give a product low marks while two give a product high marks—the net result? The data "averages" to describe a middle-of-the-road product, what none of the four originally thought. Borrowing an approach from the Australian show system (clever, those Antipodeans), we use a panel of three. This eliminates the inherent problem of averaging; helping to guarantee that what we print is what we meant to say. That's not to say that we won't on occasion have an extra individual in the room. Unlike some reviewers, we make a point of being transparent, welcome qualified visitors, and are happy to have them "audit" a session. Additionally, new panelists, or those without depth of experience in the category du jour will always "audit" the tasting (meaning their scores won't count) until such time as they are deemed ready. In order to achieve and maintain the desired level of consistency, the panel of three contains our two in-house tasting directors and one specifically invited expert for the "guest slot." This allows us to review very large categories with most panelists seeing the majority, if not all wines in that category. Finally, all panelists undergo a rigorous warm-up exercise that is not only educational, but allows each individual to determine whether or not they are "up to snuff" for the day's tasting. If there is the slightest doubt, that panelist is expected to disqualify himself before the tasting, and be replaced by one of the other trained in-house tasters whom we have on hand.

A Banded Approach

The scoring system that our panelists use is quite narrow, and hence our scoring tends to be highly repeatable. A score is given only after a thorough, objective assessment of a wine's qualities. We have devised a system based on the bands in the 100-point scale, which are widely recognized and roughly correspond to a five-star style system. These bands are:

96-100	Superlative
90-95	Exceptional
85-89	Highly Recommended
80-84	Recommended
<80	Not Recommended

After this thorough assessment of a wine's characteristics, a panelist is asked to place it in one of four quality bands in each of two rounds. All wines are initially tasted under "first round" parameters using a qualitative assessment that does not assess points for certain elements that are then added, but instead looks at overall quality. The first round scale is as such:

Round One

1 - A wine that one would not recommend in the wider context of today's global wine market (<80 points)

2 - A wine of sound commercial quality, though not overly exciting (80-84)

3 - A very good wine showing style and character, yet probably not of the highest merit (85-89)

4 - A wine that may be at the highest quality levels (potentially 90+)

Those wines that receive at least two scores of 4 are sent to the "merit round" whose scale is as follows:

Round Two

3 - A very good wine, yet upon comparison with examples of the highest quality, not of the highest merit (88-89 points)

4 - A truly excellent wine, of style and distinction (90-92)

5 - An outstanding wine, though not quite one of the world's finest (93-95)

6 - A world-class wine, providing one of the world's great wine experiences (96-100)

This banded approach allows our tasters to think in broad terms of general quality without getting mixed up in the minutiae of adding up points for "ageability," "color," or "aftertaste." We, just like the consumer, are addressing the wine in question only in its totality. Further, individual tasters do not have to concern themselves with what constitutes the differences between an 88 or an 86 or a 90 and a 91. Finally, one of the chief advantages of this system is the large percentage of wines tasted more than once. To witness, wines scoring over the critical 90 point barrier are without exception tasted twice, a virtual guarantee that a wine rated as such will be deserving of the accolades. Also, after the first round, all wines that show a wide disparity in scoring between panelists (controversial) are re-tasted at a later date under first round parameters, as are many low scoring wines.

A Novel Permutation

Final scores are reached using a novel mapping process that does not average the three scores but instead uses the mode, a statistic much closer to what the panelists, as a group, are really saying. If, for instance, a wine in the first round receives three scores of "3," it is placed in the upper center of the (85-89) band and given a final score of 88 points. Should the third score be a 4 or a 2, the wine in question would be given an 89 or an 86, respectively. The third score is used to move the final score up or down within the same band. Again, permutations that are controversial will be re-tasted. While the need to further narrow down scores within bands is a topic of some debate in the industry, we have taken the position that it is still in the consumer's interest to do so for the top four recommended bands: 80-84, 85-89, 90-95, and 96-100. Wines falling in the lowest band (<80) are simply noted as not recommended (NR) and no further breakdown is attempted. We realize that there are many conflicting views about the 100-point scale, but feel that we have devised the fairest system going for reaching individual points on that scale.

Description Is Key

In our continued attempt to lead the consumer "beyond the scores," we have been putting ever-greater emphasis on our descriptive evaluations. In order to continue this process, and also to insure thorough and consistent assessments, we use a comprehensive evaluation form in our tasting room. These forms translate directly to the final "tasting notes" that we try to print with every recommended wine (In instances where space doesn't permit this, all notes can be found on our website, www.tastings.com.) This form places an emphasis on objective structural information from color through intensity of finish. It covers several vital parameters and is amended with a final qualitative comment. This insures that all of our tasting notes are consistent in style, yet readable, while accurately conveying stylistic information to the consumer.

In order to make this descriptive information as consistent as possible (not to mention our qualitative assessments) we continue to rely heavily on our state-of-the-art tasting facility in Chicago. This room was specially designed to minimize external factors, and maximize our panelists concentration. Tasting at the same time of day, blind, under the same conditions, our panel continually works under ideal conditions. Hand in hand with our scorecard, we have specially designed tasting aids in order to standardize our tasting vocabularies. To this end we have even gone to the length of installing a state-of-the-art natural lighting system, paired with a standardized color palate for ever greater consistency. If all this sounds fanatical, it's because we are fanatical. Our institute is unique in the world of wine. We provide the world's only full-time professional reviewing service. This is not a contest, and couldn't be further from your typical "set 'em up and knock 'em down" wine fair. We take what we do seriously and train rigorously; both out of respect for producers and with an eye to providing the most trustworthy reviews a consumer can find.

Special Reports

Occasionally, we must travel to a wine region in order to cover it in a timely fashion. The best example would be Bordeaux, where we taste the new vintage from barrel on an annual basis, because the wine is sold in the futures market before it is bottled. These field tastings are referred to as "Special Reports," and an "SR" next to the tasting note designates reviews created in this fashion. This is to tell the reader that the review was not created under the ideal circumstances that we have established at our tasting lab in Chicago. Further, if the wine being reviewed was a barrel sample (a wine that has not finished aging or undergone the rigors of bottling), the score will be shown as a range—for instance 90-95. This is to make it clear to the reader that wines at this stage of evolution are tricky to evaluate, and that we are only aiming to put it into a general qualitative range based on its potential. Even when in the field, however, we strive to maintain as much of our methodology as possible, including a penchant for tasting blind. Lamentably, this is not always possible and that is why we do the vast majority of our tastings in Chicago where we can control all external factors.

Ten Things You Need to Know about Buying, Storing, and Serving Wine

1. Drink what you like.

Don't be intimidated. If you like a bit of sweetness to your wine, revel in it. If you just don't like red wine no matter what Morley Safer has to say, don't sweat it. Figure out what type of wine you like and get on with it. There are great examples of wine made in all styles. You pay for it and it should make you happy. If someone who presumes to know more than you do about wine gives you a hard time, get rid of them by referring to them as "cork dork" repeatedly or tell them that their Cabernet would be better on the rocks (see point ten).

2. Find a good retailer.

There are tons of wine shops around the country, both large and small, with people who are genuinely interested in wine waiting to answer your questions. If no one is willing to answer your questions, it is not a good wine shop. If they tell you what you should buy without asking you some fundamental questions—like what you like—it is not a good wine shop. In the end this person can steer you in the right direction and prevent the condition known as "overwhelming choice panic." Making a friend at a wine shop also may give you access to the allocated stuff that never hits the shelves. Your chances of getting a better wine for your money at a wine specialist (with assistance) as opposed to a grocery store (without assistance) are pretty good—plus you don't have to wait for an adult to come over and ring you up.

3. Pull from the bottom.

When in the wine shop, you will often notice that the wine is displayed vertically with a bottle on top and more of the same kind underneath it. Don't take the bottle on top; pull one from underneath. There are two reasons for this. One is that wine is sensitive to light, and fluorescent light in particular (hence the added protection of green or brown bottles). If your wine has been sitting there for a long time it may not be in quite the same condition as those that are a little more sheltered. Second, your new friend the retailer will have to come over and put one of the bottles from underneath in the display spot so that the next person knows what's there. This may endanger your chances of getting free samples and other handouts.

4. Beware the window and the vertical bottle.

Wine is not only sensitive to light; it is also sensitive to heat. If the wine shop in question is 90 degrees Fahrenheit in the summer or the wine is sitting on a shelf in front of a window, it is not a good wine shop. The heat will degrade the wine rather quickly, while constant temperature swings provided by exposure to sun, followed by cooler temperatures at night will accelerate the wine's demise at an alarming rate. Heat damaged wines can sometimes be spotted by the fact that the wine will have expanded and popped the cork up out of the bottle a half inch or so. In bad cases, there may even be a bit of "seepage." Finally, wines that don't have a high turnover rate should be stored horizontally, not upright. This is because when upright, the cork is no longer in contact with the wine. After some time the cork will dry out and contract, losing its seal. If the wine is then stored horizontally for a long period of time the wine may seep out the side. A sign of seepage (a sticky residue or stain) on the neck of the bottle under the capsule is not a good sign. If it is an old or rare wine, a cool, constant temperature over the years and horizontal storage should be prerequisites. If it seems like an unbelievable deal, there may be a reason. Show restraint.

5. Thou shalt not put wine near furnace.

When you bring wine home, don't forget everything you just learned. Wine does not like light, heat, temperature swings, or vibration. If you intend to keep it for a while don't put it next to the furnace. If it's a bottle for tonight, or next week, or next month, don't worry (real extremes excluded). If you intend to keep some wine around for a while though, find a decent spot for it. Storage doesn't have to be expensive. Put it on its side in a cool basement, or in a cooler part of the house that is usually dark, such as a closet. Though you may hear that ideal storage conditions are 55 degrees and about 70% humidity (to keep the cork moist and maintain the seal—very dry climates can dry a cork from the outside over a very extended period of time), the reality is that wine stored at a constant temperature of even 70 or 72 degrees Fahrenheit should be just fine. Remember that wild swings in temperature are worse. That being said, if you are a big shooter who invests lots of money, a cooling unit that also controls humidity is probably in order, especially if you are likely to have wine sitting around for a long time. It becomes a sickness, trust me. Plus, when you go to auction wine because you realize that your grandchildren will still be well provisioned with what you have left, the auction house will check "provenance." Has the wine been well stored over its lifetime? Poor cellar conditions will translate to lower bids. Seepage or popped corks probably mean rejection.

6. The myth of food pairing.

Cork dorks (see point one) like nothing better than to prattle on about food pairing. These inane people have given the average consumer the idea that they can't drink a particular wine without this or that type of food. Serving wine can lead to agitation and a condition known as corkophobia, whereby a wine's owner is afraid to pop the cork because they have been incapacitated by the thought of making a food pairing blunder. Here's the scoop. Drink what you like with food you like. While it is true that certain combinations may heighten the qualities of both food and wine, it is an impractical nightly ritual, and most wine is not meant to be a special occasion beverage. Rarely will a combination prove truly disastrous, and if you don't notice anyway does it really matter? One final inside secret. I am a wine critic. At home I drink red wine 95% of the time. I usually have wine with dinner. I do not have a breast of Muscovy duck sliced razor thin, dressed with a compote of rare Moroccan cherries and served on a melange of juvenile central Asian grains to go with a specific wine because it worked for someone else who is paid to come up with this drivel. Sometimes I have fish. Sometimes I have cheeseburgers. I then have a glass of red and never give it a second thought.

7. Get a grip on the glass.

Glassware has become a hot topic recently. There are companies that have designed specific glasses for every conceivable type of wine, from Napa Valley

Chardonnay to Chianti between two and three point five years of age grown on young vines and harvested on a Thursday under a waxing moon. Simple really, once the evil crystal cartels have their claws in you, you will have to buy a glass for every bottle you bring home. Where will you put them after a while? Also, with the profits they will be making from your initial purchases, they will design ever more perfect and riveting glasses, compelling you to buy them, always in search of glass-wine nirvana. The result of this spiraling descent into the fluffy cloud that is wine crystal? You will be penniless and on the street, with only a bottle, a paper bag, and your MD 20/20 super-sommelier 6450 glass to console you. To avoid this fate get yourself a set of simple glasses. Ideally, they should be tulip shaped and stemmed, with a slight taper inward toward the rim. This is so that when you give the wine a little swirl and put your nose to the top of the glass, the aromas will be right there for you. Don't fill the glass beyond a half to a third full for the simple reason that when you give it a little swirl you will spill it on yourself, or your date. If you like to drink your wine out of pewter tankards and it makes you happy, that's okay too, otherwise clear glass is a good idea, not these funny colored things that don't let you see the color of your wine. Since we actually evaluate wine for a living, we have researched glassware quite thoroughly. After lots of experimentation, we settled on the Riedel red wine glass from their "Overture" series. It works well for all types of wine, even Champagne, as the winemaker of Dom Perignon was amused to learn when visiting our office.

8. To decant or not to decant?

Rich red wines or ports that have been aged for five years or so—sometimes a little less, sometimes a lot more—can throw a sediment. This happens when some of the "stuffing" (technical term) falls out of solution as a dark-colored sandy-type substance, and settles on the bottom of the bottle. The problem is that when the bottle is shaken the wine turns cloudy and takes on a sort of gritty astringency when you drink it. The same effect can be had when the unshaken sediment from the bottom of the bottle is poured into your glass. How to solve this problem? Decanting. Get a carafe, or a decanter, or a water pitcher—anything that can hold the contents of the bottle. Light a candle or place the container over some other source of light. Take the bottle, which has been resting on its side or placed upright a couple of days before to allow "sedimental relocation" (hint), and open it while resisting the urge to shake it violently. Slowly pour from the bottle into the container with the neck of the bottle strategically positioned over the light source. It will look dark at first but don't panic. When about half the wine is poured out you will note the red color of the wine and be able to see clearly through to the light. Keep pouring, slowly tilting the bottle, and near the end you will notice a dark curl of sediment creeping up the bottle. Before it hits the neck, stop pouring. Congratulations, you have "decanted." Throw the little bit that's left out or cook with it. Decanting can also be done when drinking a youthful, full-bodied red that is muted and tannic. The interchange with oxygen helps to "open" the wine, simulating years of age in an hour or two. Be warned the cork dork who says that a wine bottle should be opened, then left on the table to "breathe." How much oxygen do you think 750 ml of wine gets from a dime-sized air space over an hour? Rather less than it will get from the act of pouring it into your glass I can assure you.

9. Don't serve it too cold.

Now that you are about to drink the wine that you have bought, stored, decanted, and generally fussed over—or not—do yourself a favor. Don't leave it on ice or in the arctic reaches of the refrigerator until it is so cold that you wouldn't want to put your tongue on the bottle. You are drinking a nice wine because good wine smells and tastes like something. If you don't like the taste of wine, however, over-chilling is a good tactic. It has the effect of dulling the wine's aromas and flavors. To chill, but not over-chill, an hour in the fridge is fine. In a restaurant, if the wine has been on ice for a while or a waiter brings you an arctic bottle and sets it back in the ice bucket, just pull it out and put it on the table. It will warm throughout the meal and open up in a few minutes time. While cold temperatures are something to watch with whites, Champagne is a bit of an exception. Champagne, due to its carbonation, has a tendency to be a bit rough at warmer temperatures, sort of like warm Coca-Cola. Bubbly needs a pretty good chill. If it is a really good Champagne (usually, but not always expensive is key here) don't over chill it for the same reasons as with whites, it will usually have a bit of age to it that has dulled the carbonation anyway. You paid the extra money because you think it tastes better than Cold Duck. Don't treat it like Cold Duck.

10. Or too hot.

You may have heard that red wines are best served at room temperature. This is true, but only partially. The adage meant European room temperature, and that usually referred to Britain. If you haven't been in a typical English home, take my word for it, it's chilly. There are Eskimos in Alaska who keep warmer igloos. The fact of the matter is a rich, high-alcohol (anything over 13%) red takes on a hot, rather aggressive profile where the alcohol dulls the aromas, at temperatures much above 70 or 72 degrees Fahrenheit. This is particularly true of the big, rich, ripe reds being produced in California, Australia, and other warm climate regions. When we taste reds at BTI, we serve them at about 67 or 68 degrees. When talking about something like Zinfandel, the difference is like night and day. At home I keep wines at cellar temperature, but if I have something that seems a bit warm, I'll throw the bottle in the fridge for ten minutes or so. Try heavy reds both ways, you'll be instantly converted. I even find that an ice cube can rescue a heavy red from being served too warm, particularly at a cocktail party or in the heat of summer. Many restaurants have the nasty habit of chilling the whites beyond recognition and then storing the reds somewhere above the grill, particularly in the United States. Even in France, however, they have not quite got the hang of it. At one particularly well-known French restaurant that shall remain nameless, I was subjected to a Cote-Rotie that had been stored near the restaurant's exquisite wood burning fire. The remedy, of course, was to ask for an ice bucket on which the decanter could rest for a few minutes and an ice cube for the wine in my glass. The inverse came later in the meal, with an old bottle of Sauternes that was being subjected to the polar treatment. The bottle was pulled and allowed to rest on the table. I gave no speeches and never treat such instances as a big deal, but that is how these wines show best. Even if it gave the sommelier something to snicker at for months on end, it made my dining companions and me happy. In the end, with wine, that's all that matters.

Section One: Regional Information and Reviews

one

The Wines
of California

The Wines of California

California is on a roll. It seems as though people just can't get enough wine from the Golden State. The sunny, consistent, Mediterranean climate makes for big, ripe, fruity styles of wine with lots of alcohol and intensity. Producers are selling all they can make and planting vineyards on a grand scale to address the seemingly insatiable demand. Grape prices have never been higher for those who don't own their own vineyards, and land prices in glamour appellations such as the Napa Valley are at stratospheric levels. All of this adds up to one thing: It's a seller's market. California wine is getting more and more expensive at all levels. It is not unheard of for wines to double in price over two or three vintages. It has gone well beyond inflation in many instances and is getting into a "keeping up with the Joneses" situation. If a producer's neighbor raises prices, then why shouldn't he?

Cult Wine Mayhem

Industry insiders refer to an entire segment of new wineries and labels that seem to be popping up on a daily basis as "ego wineries," particularly in the more glamorous appellations where current land prices would never justify a land investment in pure business terms. These outfits are often started by someone who has made a fortune somewhere else. Fortunate, as the quickest way to make a small fortune in the wine business under the current terms is to start with a large one. Nonetheless, these enterprises are often started not to make money, but to create something. The goal is usually a "great" wine and everyone knows that great wine is expensive, right?

This leads us to the uniquely Californian phenomenon of wines with one or two vintages under the belt being sold for over $100 a bottle. A few people get together, make a bit of wine, it gets a favorable review, and before you can say "Screaming Eagle" someone is actually writing a check for something like $500, $600, do I hear $700 a bottle—sight unseen? What's a Ridge, or Stag's Leap, or Opus One to do? One can't blame these top shelf estates for taking modest 10% to 30% increases and gettin' while the gettins' good. At least they show breed and have a track record.

While this is the strangest wine market anyone has seen, there is one thing certain, it won't last. The Californians will find out what the Bordelaise have known for some time. Fine wine is a commodity and the market is cyclical. The next downturn in the stock market or the economy will bring with it a downturn in the super-premium wine market. These $50 and up wines are now just another commodity. They are not as much drunk as bought, sold, auctioned, and traded. When the party stops, the Opus Ones of the world will be fine, thank you very much. Their wines are great and they have built a loyal following over the last decade or three. As for some of the meteoric, flash-in-the-pan ego wineries? People will not be lining up to buy anymore, if that which they already bought is now worth a fraction of what they paid for it last year. Oh, by the way, how does it taste? These wines are more frequently admired than consumed. In the high-end California wine market today, as in the stock market, buyer beware, on the whole it is grossly overvalued.

Scale: Superlative (96-100), Exceptional (90-95), Highly Recommended (85-89),
Recommended (80-84), Not Recommended (Under 80)

Stylistic Trends

There are also some worrying stylistic trends in California. Foremost among them is the retro-flashback to 1970s style, late harvest, high alcohol reds. I, and other people that actually drink wine in addition to just rating it, thought that these styles had been relegated to the back of the closet with pet rocks and platform heels. Come to think of it, platforms have come back haven't they? Perhaps Helen Turley owns a pair? Anyway, while the Californians spent much of the late '80s and early '90s admirably toiling away on concepts such as tannin management and soft extraction techniques that resulted in softer, better balanced, more accessible wines, the corresponding push for ever greater levels of ripeness, often in the name of "ripe tannins" and "flavor development" is now approaching the outer limits.

There are now a bevy of California reds over 15% alcohol, while 17% and up is not even uncommon anymore. Have you ever sat down to enjoy a bottle of red wine with a meal when that wine has 17% alcohol? How about a sweet, porty character due to the extreme ripeness? I will let these winemakers in on a secret. Only the British drink very high alcohol wines in warm climates—and they can't help it, they're British; they do it while wearing woolies and tweed. Yes, by the way, most of the country is warm much of the time. Even if we were in Alaska, however, overly alcoholic, porty reds are still too tough for most people to drink.

The insidious undercurrent here is that some would say these wines are made not to be drunk, but to be noticed—to reach out and grab the unsuspecting critic at a blind tasting—to jump out and say "Hey, look at me, I'm impressive." After all, critics spit, they don't actually try to drink a bottle or anything. No, that is up to the consumer who has just written a large check to acquire some of this massive, tannic, impenetrable elixir with the motor oil-like viscosity and the appropriately high rating. Once again, buyer beware, there is sometimes a difference between an impressive wine and a drinkable wine. Think about how you intend to use it before you buy it and when you read the tasting note, think about it again.

California at a Glance

Wines Reviewed:

2398

Producers/Brands Represented:

533

California Wine Is Good

Just so that no one gets the wrong impression so far, I would like to set the record straight. I like California wine. California wine is good. It is rich and flavorful and comes in a myriad of styles. The climate is forgiving and temperate and the wines are consistent. A number of producers are actually trying to hold the line on prices, and at the low end, say $8 or less per bottle, California still makes some of the world's best wine values. While the aforementioned wines that no one ever tastes grab the headlines, it is these more tangible California wines that bring a little sunshine to peoples' lives. California has the unique ability to make great wine at all levels, but sometimes gets caught up in its own sense of fashion. Perhaps that's the way it always is with California, just when you're ready to write it off as too crazy or far out, they seem to right the ship. For some reason, California always seems to make the most of its potential and make the rest of the world jealous in the process. For that reason, I think California wine will emerge better than ever in the next few years, but in the meantime, you will forgive me if I forego the expensive, but trendy motor oil, and keep buying from the vast majority of California producers who make delicious, balanced, reasonably priced wines.

Reviews

Acacia

1997 Chardonnay, Carneros $19.50. **84**

Bright straw cast. Moderately full-bodied. Full acidity. Highly extracted. Minerals, citrus. Reined-in aromatically, with a lean and angular impression in the mouth. Firm and intense through the toasty finish.

1996 Chardonnay, Reserve, Carneros $30. **82**

1995 Pinot Noir, Carneros $16. **87**

Full cherry red. Medium-bodied. Moderately extracted. Moderately oaked. Mildly tannic. Rounded sweet and tart red fruit flavors have a vanilla oak edge that runs through the finish. Easygoing and straightforward.

1996 Pinot Noir, Reserve, Carneros $30. **84**

Pale violet-ruby color. Medium-bodied. Moderately extracted. Mildly tannic. Red berries, minerals. Soft berry aromas lead a rounded mouthful of red berry flavors that concludes with some tannic grip. Acids are on the softer side, though this has some intensity and structure.

Acorn

1996 Dolcetto, Alegria Vineyards, Russian River Valley $18. **87**

Bright purple. Medium-bodied. Full acidity. Highly extracted. Mildly oaked. Mildly tannic. Mint, dried herbs, black fruits. Pleasantly aromatic, with a full though lean palate feel. Finishes on an angular note.

Adastra

1996 Chardonnay, Carneros, Napa Valley $22. **87**

Yellow-straw hue. Moderately full-bodied. Balanced acidity. Moderately extracted. Yellow apples, butter. Markedly buttery, toasty aromas. A full, rounded mouthfeel with juicy flavors that finish dryly. A generous, textured style.

Scale: Superlative (96-100), Exceptional (90-95), Highly Recommended (85-89), Recommended (80-84), Not Recommended (Under 80)

Adelaida

1996 Chardonnay, San Luis Obispo County $21.   **86**

Bright yellow-gold. Moderately full-bodied. Low acidity. Subtly extracted. Heavily oaked. Coconut, nuts. Generous flavors are dominated by sweet wood notes and a slight hint of maturity. Shows a broad low-acid mouthfeel and a lengthy oak-dominated finish.

1994 Cabernet Sauvignon, San Luis Obispo County $21.   **86**

Deep red-violet. Medium-bodied. Highly extracted. Moderately tannic. Black cherries, briar fruits, oak spice. Ripe, fleshy aromas show dark Cabernet fruit flavors complemented by chewy tannins. Not overly tough, but should soften with another year or two in the bottle.

1994 Calitage, San Luis Obispo County $27.   **89**

Bright ruby red. Medium-bodied. Moderately extracted. Moderately tannic. Red berries, vanilla. High-toned, fruity aromas follow through well on a particularly juicy palate, with elevated acids leaving the mouth refreshed. Tannins are supple and soft.

1995 Pinot Noir, HMR Vineyards, Paso Robles $24.   **80**

1995 Sangiovese, San Luis Obispo County $24.   **90**

Ruby purple. Medium-bodied. Balanced acidity. Highly extracted. Mildly oaked. Moderately tannic. Earth, red fruits. Dirty nose. Rustic, dry flavors finish with some grainy tannins. Very deep and concentrated, with great structure and plenty of new oak influence. Very ripe flavors.

1996 Zinfandel, San Luis Obispo County $19.   **88**

Bright cherry red. Medium-bodied. Balanced acidity. Moderately extracted. Moderately tannic. Pepper, red berries, minerals. Full, spicy, juicy fruit flavors have a big dash of pepper to complement them on the finish. Decent structure.

Adler Fels

1997 Chardonnay, Sonoma County $14.   **82**

1997 Chardonnay, Coleman Reserve, Sonoma County $16.   **81**

1997 Gewürztraminer, Sonoma County $11.   **92**

Deep yellow-gold. Penetrating, opulent lychee, spice, and melon aromas show great varietal intensity. A rich entry leads a full-bodied palate, with vibrant acidity and a glycerous texture. Extremely lengthy, flavorful finish. Drink now.

Aficionado Cellars

1996 Cabernet Sauvignon, Il Cuore, California $13.99.   **83**

Deep cherry red. Medium-bodied. Moderately extracted. Moderately oaked. Moderately tannic. Red fruits, cassis. Ripe berry fruit aromas lead solid, jammy flavors, with structure showing dry, fine-grained tannins that dry the mouth. A touch tough—better in a year or two.

Ahlgren

1996 Cabernet Franc, Bates Ranch, Santa Cruz Mountains $18.   **89**

Bright ruby purple. Medium-bodied. Balanced acidity. Moderately extracted. Mildly oaked. Mildly tannic. Red fruits, minerals, mint. Pleasantly aromatic, with a supple and generous quality to the palate. Smooth, harmonious, and well balanced, showing a sense of delicacy to the finish.

1993 Cabernet Sauvignon, Bates Ranch Reserve,
Santa Cruz Mountains $24.   **80**

Alban

1996 Grenache, Alban Estate Vineyard, Edna Valley $29.   **92**

Rich, opaque violet red to the rim. Powerful black fruit and vanilla aromas show a generous wood influence. A supple attack leads a moderately full-bodied palate, with velvety tannins. Lush, flavorful finish. Hedonistic and well balanced. Drink now.

1996 Reva Syrah, Edna Valley $23.   **92**

Deep purple, opaque to the rim. Intense blackberry, spicy oak, and olive flavors. Hefty wood tones. Firm entry. Full-bodied. Abundant grainy tannins. A rich, heavyweight style, with plenty of structuring tannin. Complex, intense varietal expression. Persistent rich finish. Drink within five years.

1996 Lorraine, Syrah, Edna Valley $29.   **89**

Deep purple, opaque, and luminous to the rim. Intense, fantastic oak, plum, blackberry, and coffee flavors. Hefty wood tones. Firm entry. Full-bodied. Plentiful grainy tannins. A heavyweight, with plenty of dry extract and spicy oak, and Rhone-like intensity. Lingering finish. Drink within five years.

Albertoni

1996 Barbera, California $13.99.   **81**

1996 Sangiovese, California $13.99.   **86**

Bright cherry red. Medium-bodied. Balanced acidity. Moderately extracted. Mildly tannic. Cherries, minerals, vanilla. Sweet berry aromas. Engaging and straightforward, with a soft, lingering finish.

Alderbrook

1997 Sauvignon Blanc, Dry Creek Valley $11.   **84**

Pale yellow-gold. Medium-bodied. Balanced acidity. Moderately extracted. Citrus, minerals. Yeasty, restrained aromas lead austere, tart citrus flavors with some mild dryness on the finish.

1997 Viognier, Russian River Valley $18.   **81**

1996 Cabernet Sauvignon, Sonoma County $16.   **87**

Deep purple. Moderately full-bodied. Balanced acidity. Highly extracted. Moderately oaked. Moderately tannic. Brown spices, game, earth. Forward and generous aromatics feature an unusual earthy touch. Quite firmly structured in the mouth, with hearty tannins that rear up on the finish.

1997 Pinot Noir, Russian River Valley $18.   **81**

1996 Zinfandel, OVOC, Sonoma County $16.   **84**

Deep blackish purple. Moderately full-bodied. Full acidity. Moderately extracted. Mildly oaked. Mildly tannic. Briar fruits, minerals, pickle barrel. Quite aromatic, with a fruit-centered palate feel. Crisp acidity lends a sense of vibrancy to the palate. Crisp through the finish.

Alexander Valley Vineyards

1997 Chardonnay, Wetzel Family Reserve, Alexander Valley $24.   **83**

Bright straw hue. Unusual blanched almond aromas seem to show a hint of oxidation. A rich entry leads a full-bodied palate with bright acidity and a mild sensation of sweetness. Brisk, vibrant finish. Drink now.

1996 Cabernet Franc, Wetzel Family Estate, Alexander Valley $20.   **83**

Bright ruby purple. Medium-bodied. Balanced acidity. Moderately extracted. Mildly tannic. Earth, minerals. Unusual aromatics lead a lighter-styled mouthfeel. Finishes on a lean, minerally note. Interesting, almost Old World in style.

1995 Cabernet Sauvignon, Alexander Valley $17.   **85**

Dark red. Medium-bodied. Moderately extracted. Mildly tannic. Blackberry, cassis, oak spice. Ripe black fruit aromas lead a plush, fruity palate, with some dry oak accents on the finish. Generously proportioned.

1996 Cabernet Sauvignon, Alexander Valley $17.50.   **86**

Bright ruby red with a slight fade. Medium-bodied. Balanced acidity. Moderately extracted. Moderately oaked. Mildly tannic. Earth, leather, black fruits. Distinctive, earthy aromatics lead a lean palate. Finishes with a slight note of bitterness.

1997 Syrah, Wetzel Family Estate, Alexander Valley $20.   **81**

Altamura

1995 Cabernet Sauvignon, Napa Valley $40.   91
Very deep purple-red hue. Intense, aromatic berry fruit and cordial aromas carry a slight oak influence. A lush entry leads to a moderately full-bodied palate with a stylish, lively mouthfeel, and velvety tannins. Supple and very lengthy flavorful finish. Exceptionally well balanced. Drink now or later.

1994 Sangiovese, Napa Valley $28.   90
Deep blackish ruby hue. Full-bodied. Balanced acidity. Highly extracted. Heavily oaked. Mildly tannic. Vanilla, black fruits. Quite aromatic and very modern in style, with a large-scaled, harmonious wave of dark fruit and toasty oak flavors. Rich and firmly structured, with exceptional length.

Amador Foothill Winery

1996 Fumé, Shenandoah Valley $8.   82

1996 Semillon, Shenandoah Valley $9.   86
Bright golden yellow. Medium-bodied. Full acidity. Moderately extracted. Kiwi, minerals, lemons. Clean tropical aromas follow through on a fresh, vibrant palate with a rounded mouthfeel. Well balanced.

1995 Sangiovese, Shenandoah Valley $12.   87
Deep ruby cast. Moderately full-bodied. Balanced acidity. Highly extracted. Mildly oaked. Moderately tannic. Overripe red fruits, herbs, wood. Shows a slightly Port-like quality and a touch of heat throughout. Rustic and full-framed, with tannins that bite down on the finish.

Anapamu

1996 Chardonnay, Central Coast $14.   90
Bright yellow-gold. Moderately full-bodied. Balanced acidity. Moderately extracted. Moderately oaked. Smoke, cream, tropical fruits. Aromatic and intense, with forward smoky flavors and a ripe creamy quality in the mouth. Shows fine balance through the lengthy finish.

1994 Cabernet Sauvignon, Monterey County $10.   83
Bright ruby red. Medium-bodied. Moderately extracted. Mildly tannic. Cherries, bell pepper, cedar. Rounded, plush, and soft, with a juicy character and very supple tannins that invite immediate drinking.

1996 Pinot Noir, Central Coast $14.   83
Pale cherry red. Moderately light-bodied. Subtly extracted. Mildly tannic. Red fruits, herbs, vanilla. Light, high-toned fruit aromas follow through on a lightly framed palate with subtle flavors that finish quickly.

S. Anderson

1997 Chardonnay, Carneros $22.   84
Bright pale gold. Generous aromas of honey and tropical fruits are rather unusual. A bright, fruity attack leads a moderately full-bodied palate with extravagant fruit intensity that follows through on the finish. A hedonistic, well-balanced style, though quite distinctive. Drink now.

1997 Chardonnay, Stags Leap District $22.   86
Pale yellow-straw hue. Aromatically restrained with an oaky note. A juicy attack is followed by a medium-bodied palate with moderate apple and pear flavors. The finish is clean, with good persistent acidity. Cleanly flavored and nicely textured.

1994 Cabernet Sauvignon, Richard Chambers Vineyard, Stags Leap District $54.   95
Opaque ruby hue with purple highlights. Medium-bodied. Highly extracted. Moderately tannic. Red fruits, brown spice, cinnamon, chocolate. Bright, exotically spiced aromas. Elegant mouthfeel with concentrated red fruit flavors on entry that expand on the palate. The finish shows dry, textured tannins. This has cellaring structure.

1995 Cabernet Sauvignon, Richard Chambers Vineyard,
Stags Leap District $65.   **94**

Saturated blood-ruby red. Moderately full-bodied. Highly extracted. Moderately tannic.
Spice, tobacco, black fruits. Dusty, exotic nose. Concentrated flavors show depth and a
minerally edge persisting through a long finish that turns austere. Sublimely balanced
and very approachable now.

1995 Merlot, Reserve, Stags Leap District $32.   **89**

Inky ruby color with purple highlights. Moderately full-bodied. Balanced acidity.
Moderately extracted. Moderately oaked. Mildly tannic. Briar fruits, vanilla, minerals.
Fruit centered with an aromatic and flavorful character. Light, bright, and well
balanced on the palate. Some mildly astringent tannins pop up on the finish.

1996 Merlot, Reserve, Stags Leap District $40.   **94**

Bright purple-red, well saturated. Juicy, bright attack with plush, ripe flavors that are
carried nicely by juicy acids. The tannins are particularly velvety and smooth on the
finish. An elegant and concentrated style, which is drinking wonderfully. Drink now.

Anderson's Conn Valley Vineyards

1996 Chardonnay, Fournier Vineyard, Carneros $40.   **86**

Deep gold-straw color. Moderately full-bodied. Balanced acidity. Highly extracted.
Moderately oaked. Butterscotch, pineapple. Thick, concentrated, and flavorful. This
does veer toward the heavy buttery style, making for a rich finish.

1994 Cabernet Sauvignon, Estate Reserve, Napa Valley $40.   **90**

Very deep purple. Medium-bodied. Highly extracted. Mildly tannic. Vanilla, brown
spice, plums. Sweet vanilla oak aromas. The tightly wound palate does not show much
generosity in the middle at present. Fine-grained dry tannins dominate the finish.

1995 Cabernet Sauvignon, Estate Reserve, Napa Valley $48.   **86**

Bright ruby purple. Moderately full-bodied. Full acidity. Highly extracted. Mildly oaked.
Moderately tannic. Vanilla, minerals, red fruits. Aromatically reserved, with a firm and
linear mouthfeel. Firm tannins bite down on the finish. Needs time.

1993 Eloge, Napa Valley $60.   **84**

Deep ruby hue. Full-bodied. Full acidity. Highly extracted. Mildly oaked. Moderately
tannic. Minerals, red fruits. Reserved and quite firm, with sturdy acidity and elevated
tannins. Angular and quite lean through the finish. Needs time.

Angeline

1996 Zinfandel, Old Vine Cuvée, Mendocino County $11.   **82**

Antares

1996 Cabernet Sauvignon, California $30.   **83**

Bright purple red hue. Very ripe black fruit aromas with a note of anise. A firm entry
leads to a moderately full-bodied palate with very flavorful black cherry and dry oak
accents. Sturdy and well gripped through the finish.

1995 Merlot, California $24.99.   **90**

Deep ruby to the rim with brilliant clarity. Medium-bodied. Balanced acidity. Moderately
extracted. Heavily oaked. Mildly tannic. Pencil shavings, plums, cedar. Pleasantly aromatic
with a decided wood accent. In the mouth, this wine has the stuffing to balance out the
oak, and all elements combine for an elegant, well-integrated finish.

Arciero

1995 Cabernet Franc, Paso Robles $10.50.   **84**

Pale ruby cast with a slight fade. Moderately light-bodied. Full acidity. Subtly extracted.
Mildly oaked. Mildly tannic. Vanilla, citrus, red fruits. Lean and angular, with tart acidity
through the finish. Flavors are wood driven and drying.

1995 Cabernet Sauvignon, Paso Robles $12.   82

1994 Nebbiolo, Paso Robles $9.95.   80

1995 Sangiovese, Paso Robles $14.99.   83

Bright ruby-garnet cast. Medium-bodied. Balanced acidity. Moderately extracted. Mildly oaked. Mildly tannic. Overripe red fruits, sweet herbs. Quite aromatic, with a slight Port-like note. Light and soft in the mouth, with some edgy acidity that props up the finish. Interesting.

Arrowood

1997 Chardonnay, Sonoma County $24.   82

1996 Chardonnay, Réserve Spéciale, Cuvée Michel Berthoud,
Sonoma County $38.   92

Bright straw hue. Elegant, yeasty, toasty aromas show a degree of complexity and a harmonious oak accent. A rich entry leads a moderately full-bodied palate with rounded acidity. The finish is creamy and persistent. A well-balanced and elegant style that is not overly weighty or flashy. Drink now.

1995 Cabernet Sauvignon, Sonoma County $35.   90

Bright ruby-purple hue. Generous red fruit and mineral aromas are concentrated and intense. A supple entry leads to a ripe, moderately full-bodied mouthfeel with velvety tannins. Forward, lengthy finish. Harmonious and elegant with exceptional balance and finesse. Drink now or later.

1994 Cabernet Sauvignon, Réserve Spéciale, Sonoma County $50.   92

Opaque ruby cast. Full-bodied. Balanced acidity. Moderately extracted. Mildly oaked. Mildly tannic. Minerals, chocolate, earth. Generous aromas are complex and forward. Full yet well structured in the mouth, with a supple, harmonious quality. Seamless through the lengthy finish.

Atlas Peak Vineyards

1997 Chardonnay, Atlas Peak, Napa Valley $16.   86

Bright pale yellow-gold. Moderate aromas of very subtle toasty oak and ripe citrus. A crisp entry leads a moderately full-bodied palate with ripe flavors and generous alcohol that combine with oak spice on the finish. Generous though well balanced by acids. Drink now.

1994 Cabernet Sauvignon, Atlas Peak, Napa Valley $18.   88

Deep ruby hue. Medium-bodied. Full acidity. Moderately extracted. Heavily oaked. Moderately tannic. Brown spices, cedar, red fruits. Exotic aromas feature a hefty wood accent. Firm and angular in the mouth, with a lean core of flavors. Crisp finish with some grip. Well balanced.

1995 Cabernet Sauvignon, Atlas Peak, Napa Valley $18.   80

1995 Cabernet Sauvignon, Consenso Vineyards, Atlas Peak,
Napa Valley $30.   83

Bright ruby with a slight fade. Forward, meaty, earthy, vanilla aromas show an oak accent and seem to be reductive. May blow off with aeration. A firm attack leads to a medium-bodied palate with grainy tannins. Subdued finish. Interesting, but could use a bit more grip through the finish. Drink now or later.

1995 Sangiovese, Reserve, Atlas Peak, Napa Valley $24.   86

Deep ruby red. Medium-bodied. Full acidity. Highly extracted. Moderately oaked. Moderately tannic. Bitter cherries, earth, minerals. Not very aromatic. Solid, flavorsome palate has bitter red fruit flavors and a large dose of spice in the finish. Quite an austere style.

Au Bon Climat

1997 Chardonnay, Santa Barbara County $18.   89

Medium yellow-straw hue. Smoky, yeasty aromas with ripe apple fruit. A fruity entry leads a moderately full-bodied palate with a glycerous, rich mouthfeel and juicy fruit acids persisting through the finish. Rather stylish. Drink now or later.

1996 Chardonnay, Le Bouge D'à Côte, Santa Barbara County $19. **89**

Bright yellow-straw cast. Moderately full-bodied. Full acidity. Moderately extracted. Moderately oaked. Smoke, tart citrus. Striking smoky, yeasty aromas lead a tart citrus entry with a linear, bright follow-through showing bright acids and a youthful structure. Taut and young now.

1997 Chardonnay, Reserve Talley, Arroyo Grande Valley $25. **84**

Bright yellow-straw hue. Restrained citrus, yeast, and mineral aromas. A crisp entry leads a moderately full-bodied palate with balanced acidity. Mildly buttery, stylish finish. Drink now.

1997 Chardonnay, Alban Vineyard, Edna Valley $35. **93**

Deep straw hue. Exotic yeast, tropical fruit, and vanilla aromas show a harmonious oak influence. A zesty attack leads a moderately full-bodied palate with racy acidity. Intense, refreshing finish. Drink now or later.

95/96 Pinot Noir, Central Coast $19. **90**

Pale garnet with a fading rim. Medium-bodied. Moderately extracted. Moderately oaked. Mildly tannic. Strong and exotic earthy, minerally nose. Plenty of herbal complexity, with crisp red fruit and a nice mouthfeel. Deceptively long finish with good varietal character. Drinking nicely now.

1996 Pinot Noir, La Bauge Au-Dessus, Santa Barbara County $25. **85**

Pale ruby cast. Moderately full-bodied. Full acidity. Moderately extracted. Mildly oaked. Mildly tannic. Earth, minerals, dried herbs. Unusual earthy aromas lead a firm, intense mouthfeel that has spritzy acidity. Lean through the finish. Rather disjointed but perhaps just suffering from the pangs of youth.

1996 Pinot Noir, Sanford & Benedict Vineyard, Santa Ynez Valley $35. **90**

Bright cherry-ruby cast. Moderately full-bodied. Full acidity. Moderately extracted. Mildly oaked. Mildly tannic. Minerals, spice. Quite aromatic, with complex minerally flavors throughout. Lean and zesty in the mouth, with a precise linear quality. Firm and intense through the lengthy finish.

1996 Pinot Noir, Piccho and Rincon, Arroyo Grande Valley $40. **92**

Pale cinnamon-ruby cast. Moderately full-bodied. Full acidity. Highly extracted. Moderately oaked. Mildly tannic. Iron, minerals, spice. Intense, complex aromatics are a dead ringer for a first rate Vosne-Romanée. Firm and lean in the mouth, with an intensely minerally backbone. Finishes with fine grip and intensity. Should age well.

1996 Pinot Noir, Isabelle, California $50. **90**

Violet red with a pale rim. Medium-bodied. Moderately extracted. Mildly oaked. Flowers, red berries, vanilla. Classically perfumed Pinot Noir aromas lead a mouthwatering, succulent palate with just a hint of dry astringency on the finish. Textbook.

Audubon

1996 Chardonnay, Sangiacomo Vineyards, Carneros, Sonoma $14. **81**

1996 Merlot, Hopper Creek Vineyard, Napa Valley $20. **89**

Deep ruby red with a fading rim. Earthy, herbal, spicy aromas have a woody character. Medium-bodied with a soft attack and developed, mature flavors. Moderately tannic with a powdery texture through the finish. This is near its optimum maturity. Drink now.

1997 Late Harvest Chardonnay, Trio C Vineyard, Napa Valley $12/375 ml. **84**

Deep gold-straw hue. Forward honey and spice aromas. A sweet entry leads a medium-bodied palate. Soft, lush, and rounded. Drink now.

Babcock

1996 Pinot Noir, Santa Ynez Valley $30. **86**

Full cherry red. Medium-bodied. Moderately extracted. Moderately oaked. Moderately tannic. Cherries, vanilla, minerals. Sweet, fleshy fruit aromas follow through on the palate. Has some grip on the finish, making for a solid style.

Scale: Superlative (96-100), Exceptional (90-95), Highly Recommended (85-89), Recommended (80-84), Not Recommended (Under 80)

32

1997 Pinot Noir, Santa Barbara County $20.　　　**89**

Bright ruby hue with a violet rim. Medium-bodied. Moderately extracted. Cherries, minerals, vanilla. Sweet, ripe red fruit flavors are complemented by vanilla oak accents that linger through the finish. Stylish, though acids are a tad low, making for a soft, easy-drinking style.

1996 Sangiovese, Eleven Oaks, Santa Ynez Valley $18.　　　**85**

Deep blackish ruby cast. Moderately full-bodied. Balanced acidity. Moderately extracted. Moderately oaked. Mildly tannic. Leather, brown spices, earth. Quite aromatic, with a distinctive, gamey flavor profile. Rich, supple, and velvety in the mouth, with firm structure through the lengthy finish.

Baileyana

1997 Chardonnay, Edna Valley $17.　　　**89**

Bright gold-straw hue. Restrained butter and orange marmalade aromas. A crisp entry leads a moderately full-bodied palate with vibrant acidity. Lengthy, oak-kissed finish. Drink now or later.

Baily

1997 Montage, Temecula $11.　　　**81**

1997 Merlot, Temecula $15.95.　　　**81**

Bandiera

1997 Chardonnay, Coastal California $9.　　　**83**

Pale straw cast. Medium-bodied. Balanced acidity. Moderately extracted. Pears, melon. Features an agreeable fruit accent to the nose. Crisp and light in the mouth with a vibrant finish.

1997 Cabernet Sauvignon, Coastal, California $9.　　　**83**

Deep purple-red hue. Forward vanilla, black fruit, and mineral aromas belie a generous oak accent. A lush attack leads to a medium-bodied palate with velvety tannins and just enough acidity to lend a sense of buoyancy on the palate. Soft, flavorful finish. Drink now.

1995 Cabernet Sauvignon, Reserve 5, Napa Valley $14.　　　**84**

Saturated red-purple. Moderately full-bodied. Highly extracted. Moderately tannic. Spice, black fruits, licorice. Very ripe, generous aromas follow through on the palate, with a fruit-forward entry that concludes with a dry, short finish.

1996 Merlot, California $9.　　　**81**

Barefoot

1997 Chardonnay, Reserve, Sonoma County $9.99.　　　**83**

Bright yellow-straw hue. Unusual, subdued citrus and mineral aromas show a touch of heat. A lean entry leads a medium-bodied palate with rounded acidity. Quick buttery finish. Drink now.

NV White Zinfandel, California $3.99.　　　**80**

Bargetto

1997 Chardonnay, Regan Vineyards, Santa Cruz Mountains $18.　　　**86**

Pale straw hue. Subdued citrus and mineral aromas. A crisp entry, a medium-bodied palate, vibrant acidity. The finish is clean and racy. Drink now.

1997 Pinot Grigio, Central Coast $15.　　　**87**

Bright platinum cast. Moderately full-bodied. Balanced acidity. Moderately extracted. Smoke, citrus, minerals. Aromatic and flavorful, with a ripe melange of smoky flavors. Full in the mouth yet well balanced, with angular acidity. Shows fine grip and intensity on the finish.

1995 Cabernet Sauvignon, Santa Cruz Mountains $18. 88
Deep saturated ruby cast. Medium-bodied. Balanced acidity. Highly extracted. Mildly oaked. Moderately tannic. Spice, minerals. Pleasantly aromatic, with real complexity to the minerally flavors. Firm, lean, and angular through the precise finish.

1993 Cabernet Sauvignon, Bates Ranch, Santa Cruz Mountains $18. 86
Rich ruby red. Medium-bodied. Moderately extracted. Mildly tannic. Dill, brown spice, plums, earth. Outstanding spicy, earthy aromas reveal a supple, rounded palate with exotic brown spice notes through the finish. Attractive and juicy, but with a certain earthy note. Very approachable now.

1996 Merlot, California $18. 86
Deep ruby red to the rim with brilliant clarity. Moderately full-bodied. Balanced acidity. Highly extracted. Mildly oaked. Mildly tannic. Black fruits, sweet herbs, vanilla, earth. Though aromatically restrained, this wine is deeply flavored and lush on the palate. Well balanced and rich, with a pleasant herbal accent that adds complexity to the fruit flavors.

1996 Merlot, Santa Cruz Mountains $25. 86
Bright ruby red to the rim. Aggressive tea, herb, and mint aromas carry a slight oak accent. A soft attack is followed by a medium-bodied palate with juicy acidity and grainy tannins. Fades toward the finish. Unusual but interesting. Drink now.

1996 Merlot, Regan Vineyard, Santa Cruz Mountains $24. 84
Deep ruby hue with brilliant clarity. Medium-bodied. Full acidity. Moderately extracted. Moderately oaked. Moderately tannic. Red fruits, vanilla, minerals. Quite crisp, with buoyant acidity that turns sharp on a lighter-styled palate. Astringent tannins mark the finish.

1994 Pinot Noir, Santa Cruz Mountains $20. 88
Pale cherry red. Medium-bodied. Moderately extracted. Mildly tannic. Tart red berry and vanilla aromas show complexity. Crisp cherry flavors have a solid mineral note, with toasty oak spice on the finish.

Chaucers Mead, $9. 86
Deep yellow-straw cast. Moderately full-bodied. Low acidity. Moderately extracted. Honey, cream, vanilla. Fragrant and extremely pure in flavor, with a balanced, rounded mouthfeel. Finishes with fine length and mild sweetness.

Chaucers Raspberry Wine, $9/500 ml. 86
Deep ruby cast. Moderately full-bodied. Full acidity. Highly extracted. Raspberries, minerals. Pleasantly aromatic, with definitive red fruit overtones and a flavorful palate. Firm and concentrated, with vibrant acidity making for a tart finish. The sweetness provides a sense of roundness in the mouth. Lengthy and intense.

Barnett
1994 Cabernet Sauvignon, Spring Mountain District, Napa Valley $35. 87
Dark cherry red. Medium-bodied. Highly extracted. Quite tannic. Black cherries, currants, minerals, toasted oak. Solid and immensely dry through the finish, with mouthcoating tannins. Has some nice toasty qualities and black fruit flavors, though it needs time before it is approachable.

1995 Cabernet Sauvignon, Spring Mountain District, Napa Valley $35. 92
Deep ruby hue with a slight purple cast. Moderately full-bodied. Balanced acidity. Highly extracted. Moderately tannic. Anise, minerals, sweet herbs. Features an enticing and exotic high-toned array of flavors. Well structured and deep in the mouth, with firm tannins through the finish. Needs time.

Bartholomew Park
1996 Cabernet Sauvignon, Desnudos Vineyard, Sonoma Valley $35. 90
Deep purple-red hue. Intense plum, mineral, and herb aromas jump from the glass. A supple entry leads to a moderately full-bodied palate with excellent acidic grip and silky tannins. Lengthy, complex finish. Exquisitely balanced and harmonious. Drink now or later.

Scale: Superlative (96-100), Exceptional (90-95), Highly Recommended (85-89), Recommended (80-84), Not Recommended (Under 80)

34

1996 Merlot, Alta Vista Vineyards, Sonoma Valley $32.   **94**

Bright purple with a subtle fade. Intense red cherry and herb aromas. A supple attack leads a moderately full-bodied palate with velvety tannins and juicy acids. The lingering finish is flavorful and fruity. Drink now or later. Can improve with more age.

1995 Pinot Noir, Sonoma Valley $23.   **82**

Beaucanon

1997 Chardonnay, Reserve, Napa Valley $12.   **89**

Pale straw cast. Moderately full-bodied. Balanced acidity. Moderately extracted. Minerals, melon, citrus. Forward aromas feature a subtle spicy accent. Rich and fruity on entry, with a weighty midpalate. Finishes with lingering zesty acids.

1997 Chardonnay, Jacques de Coninck, Napa Valley $30.   **87**

Bright yellow-gold. Richly aromatic with full smoky, tropical accents. A lush entry leads a full-bodied palate with rich, rounded texture and generous alcohol. Finishes with a toasty oak accent and a note of warmth. Drink now.

1994 Cabernet Sauvignon, Napa Valley $14.   **89**

Medium cherry red. Medium-bodied. Moderately extracted. Moderately tannic. Red fruits, minerals, tea. Bright but rather lean, with a firm minerally backbone through to the finish. Solid, with well-extracted flavors and some firm tannins.

1995 Cabernet Sauvignon, Napa Valley $14.   **86**

Bright ruby violet. Medium-bodied. Highly extracted. Moderately tannic. Black fruits, brown spice. Lighter and crisp, showing a hint of very dry tannin on the finish. A fruit-centered, supple style that shows Cabernet flavors in a very balanced package. Suited to current drinking.

1996 Cabernet Sauvignon, Reserve, Napa Valley $14.   **86**

Bright crimson-red hue with a subtle fade to the rim. Muted aromas show oak spice and dark fruits. A crisp entry leads a medium-bodied palate with moderate cassis fruit flavors and a minerally, tannic grip through the finish. A lighter style with lively acids. Drink now.

1995 Merlot, Napa Valley $15.   **81**

1996 Merlot, Reserve, Napa Valley $15.   **83**

Full ruby-violet hue with a subtle fade. Crisp, fragrant aromas show red fruits and vanilla. Smooth on the attack, with a moderately full body and lush black cherry flavors. Finishes with fine-grained tannins and vanilla oak. Drink now or later. Can improve with more age.

Beaulieu

1997 Chardonnay, Coastal, California $9.99.   **81**

1997 Chardonnay, BV Carneros, Carneros $12.99.   **83**

Yellow-straw color. Medium-bodied. Balanced acidity. Moderately extracted. Moderately oaked. Lime zest, minerals. Straightforward citrus zest flavors with a minerally finish. An undemanding, easy-drinking style.

1996 Sauvignon Blanc, Napa Valley $10.95.   **80**

1996 Viognier, BV, Napa Valley $16.   **84**

Deep yellow-gold. Full-bodied. Low acidity. Moderately extracted. Mildly oaked. Toast, butter, oranges. Extremely full and ripe with a fat and unctuous palate feel. Has an oak accent with a buttery finish, making for an opulent style suited for near-term drinking.

1997 Pinot Noir Vin Gris, Signet Collection, Carneros $8.   **84**

Very pale russet hue. Generous strawberry and herb aromas. A lush entry leads a medium-bodied palate showing supple acidity. The finish is flavorful and stylish. Quite light, but showing interesting flavors. Drink now.

1994 Cabernet Sauvignon, Georges de Latour Private Reserve, Rutherford $50.　　92

Dark cherry red. Medium-bodied. Highly extracted. Moderately tannic. Cassis, cherries, brown spice. Full toasty nose leads a dusty mouthful of concentrated, layered red fruit flavors, with generous oak spice notes lingering in the finish. Not fleshy, but still very generous and structured in its proportions. This should have good cellar potential.

1995 Cabernet Sauvignon, Georges de Latour Private Reserve, Rutherford $59.99.　　92

Very deep, saturated ruby cast with a purple edge. Moderately full-bodied. Balanced acidity. Moderately extracted. Moderately oaked. Mildly tannic. Cassis, brown spices, minerals. Classic black currant aromas are intense and forward. Full, generous, and rich, with supple and abundant tannins lending a seamless quality through the finish. An elegant and refined wine.

1995 Grenache, Signet Collection, San Benito $8.　　81

1994 Tapestry Reserve, Napa Valley $20.　　90

Deep crimson red with purple highlights. Medium-bodied. Moderately extracted. Moderately tannic. Vanilla, toasted oak, black fruits. Harmonious, generous Cabernet fruit aromas. Solid midpalate with curranty fruit flavors and toasty notes throughout. Fine-grained, textured tannins through the finish.

1995 Tapestry Reserve, Napa Valley $24.99.　　89

Saturated dark red. Moderately full-bodied. Highly extracted. Moderately tannic. Brown spice, black fruits, licorice. Spicy, dark fruit aromas have a dusty quality. Lush mouthfeel with cordial-like flavors up front, turning dry and spicy through the finish. Quite a classic structure.

1994 Merlot, Napa Valley $12.99.　　85

Deep ruby red to the rim with brilliant highlights. Medium-bodied. Balanced acidity. Moderately extracted. Mildly tannic. Red fruits, dried herbs, minerals. Pleasant and well integrated, with firm structure and an angular presence on the palate. Finishes with dusty, drying tannins and lingering flavors.

1997 Pinot Noir, Carneros $16.　　81

1995 Pinot Noir, Reserve, Carneros $29.95.　　87

Full pinkish-tinged red. Medium-bodied. Moderately extracted. Heavily oaked. Mildly tannic. New oak dominates on the nose. Crisp blackberry and blueberry fruit flavors show through plenty of new oak on the palate. Some astringency on the finish. Quite high toned.

1996 Pinot Noir, Reserve, Carneros $30.　　93

Deep violet red. Moderately full-bodied. Moderately extracted. Mildly tannic. Chocolate, vanilla, cherries. Perfumed, oak-accented aromas lead a full-flavored chocolatey mouthfeel, with a dusting of dry tannins through the finish. An elegant and flavorful style.

1996 Beauzeaux, Signet Collection, California $20.　　87

Deep ruby red to the rim. Generous red fruit and mineral aromas. A supple attack leads a full-bodied palate showing dark fleshy fruits and chocolate flavors, with drying tannins. Clipped, deeply flavored finish. Well extracted and youthful, with a bit of an edge to the finish. Drink now or later. Can improve with more age.

1996 Ensemble, Signet Collection, California $25.　　90

Deep ruby red to the rim. Generous red fruit and chocolate aromas. A supple attack leads a moderately full-bodied palate with silky tannins. Attractive, velvety finish. Quite stylish, and eminently drinkable. Drink within five years.

1995 Sangiovese, Signet Collection, Napa Valley $16.　　83

Dark ruby red with a lightening rim. Medium-bodied. Balanced acidity. Moderately extracted. Moderately oaked. Moderately tannic. Earth, minerals. Austere aromas show some maturity. Uncompromisingly dry, assertive palate shows fine-grained tannins through the finish.

1995 Syrah, Signet Collection, Dry Creek Valley $25.   **92**
Deep ruby red to the rim. Forward spice box, tobacco, and earth aromas show a hefty wood accent. A firm attack leads a moderately full-bodied palate with tannic grip and buoyant acidity. Lingering, flavorful, edgy finish. Quite stylish, with fine cool-climate varietal intensity. Drink now or later. Can improve with more age.

1996 Syrah, Signet Collection, North Coast $25.   **87**
Dark ruby red to the rim. Forward, overripe red fruit and mineral aromas show a judicious oak accent. A firm attack leads a medium-bodied palate that shows drying tannins. Angular, snappy finish. Compact and reserved. Drink now.

1996 Zinfandel, BV, Napa Valley $14.   **84**
Bright cherry red. Medium-bodied. Balanced acidity. Moderately extracted. Mildly oaked. Moderately tannic. Vanilla, black fruits. Ripe berry aromas lead a rounded palate with aggressive tannins drying the finish.

NV Muscat de Beaulieu, California $10.99/375 ml.   **90**
Deep tawny hue with orange highlights. Forward, spirity butterscotch and orange peel aromas. A rich entry leads a moderately full-bodied palate that has warm, spicy flavors. Liqueur-like. Showing fine intensity. Drink now.

Bel Arbor

1997 Chardonnay, California $5.99.   **81**
1997 White Zinfandel, California $5.99.   **84**
Very pale pink. Subdued citrus and berry aromas. A crisp entry leads a medium-bodied palate with a nice balance between sweetness and acidity. Shows decent intensity of flavor with a lengthy finish. Drink now.

1997 Merlot, California $6.99.   **81**

Bell

1994 Cabernet Sauvignon, Baritelle Vineyard, Rutherford $50.   **86**
Light, bright brick red. Moderately light-bodied. Moderately extracted. Mildly tannic. Bramble fruit, cherries, minerals. Rounded red fruit flavors, with a minerally, earthy, dry finish. Not fleshy, but it does show some structure and length in an austere manner.

1995 Cabernet Sauvignon, Baritelle Vineyard, Jackson Clone, Rutherford $50.   **84**
Bright brick red hue. Classic dusty, cedary aromas. A flavorful entry leads a medium-bodied palate with juicy mature fruit flavors and elegant cedary, dusty character. Evolved, softer tannins make this very attractive now. Drink now.

Bella Vigna

1997 Merlot, Twin Creeks Vineyard, Lodi $12.   **86**
Full ruby red with a subtle fade. Generously spicy aromas show a toasty oak accent with ripe fruity notes. A soft entry lead a medium-bodied palate with powdery, elegant tannins. Finishes with notably fine oak spice and fruit persistence. Very well balanced and varietally expressive. Drink now.

Belvedere

1997 Chardonnay, Sonoma County $10.   **84**
Bright straw hue. Muted citric aromas carry a very slight oak accent. A crisp entry is followed by a moderately full-bodied palate with creamy acidity. Rounded, buttery finish. Drink now.

1994 Cabernet Sauvignon, Dry Creek Valley $13.50.   **89**
Bright reddish purple. Medium-bodied. Highly extracted. Moderately tannic. Tobacco, plums, brown spice. Rich toasty aromas lead a ripe, rich mouthful of plummy fruits showing great texture and integration. Soft, rounded tannins linger through the finish.

1995 Cabernet Sauvignon, Dry Creek Valley $16.   89
Saturated blood red. Moderately full-bodied. Highly extracted. Moderately tannic. Currant, minerals. Jammy, ripe fruit aromas follow through on the palate. Chewy and rich, with a minerally note on the finish.

1996 Merlot, Dry Creek Valley $16.   88
Dark violet-red with a slight fade. Rich oaky aromas with black fruit accents. A lush attack leads a moderately full-bodied palate with fine-grained dry tannins and soft juicy acids. Short-term cellaring may help, but don't wait too long. Drink now or later.

1995 Merlot, Preferred Stock, Dry Creek Valley $24.   86
Very deep blackish ruby hue. Moderately full-bodied. Full acidity. Highly extracted. Heavily oaked. Moderately tannic. Vanilla, black fruits, menthol. Quite aromatic, with a big palate feel accented by mouthwatering acidity. Has a very deep core of fruit flavors but maintains a sense of lightness. Tannins grip down on the finish. It's a bit tough at present; mid-term (3-6 years) aging may make it more accessible.

1996 Pinot Noir, Anderson Valley $12.   88
Bright pale ruby cast. Medium-bodied. Full acidity. Moderately extracted. Mildly tannic. Iron, red fruits. Fragrant and intense, with an exotic minerally quality. Angular and zesty in the mouth, with bright flavors and a clean finish.

1995 Zinfandel, Dry Creek Valley $12.   84
Bright ruby purple to rim. Medium-bodied. Balanced acidity. Highly extracted. Moderately tannic. Briar fruits, chocolate, dried herbs. Fairly aromatic, with a firm and somewhat angular mouthfeel. Showing solid grip, but a little ungenerous.

Benziger
1996 Chardonnay, Carneros $13.   86
Bright yellow-gold. Medium-bodied. Balanced acidity. Moderately extracted. Moderately oaked. Coconut, yeast, apples. Sweet oak aromas follow through on a ripe, juicy palate, with a hint of dryness and spice on the finish.

1995 Tribute White, Sonoma Mountain $17.   91
Brilliant yellow-gold. Medium-bodied. Balanced acidity. Moderately extracted. Mildly oaked. Vanilla, citrus, butter. Toasty, zesty aromas. On the palate, a lovely overlay of vanilla with a hint of butter. Fine grip, concentration, and length, and drinking well now.

1996 Pinot Blanc, Imagery Series, Bien Nacido Vineyard, Santa Maria Valley $18.   81

1996 Fumé Blanc, Sonoma County $10.   90
Bright medium straw cast. Medium-bodied. Balanced acidity. Moderately extracted. Moderately oaked. Vanilla, smoke, citrus. Oak accents are pronounced on the nose. Spicy and oaky on the palate, with brisk citrus flavors elevated by racy acids.

1996 Cabernet Franc, Imagery Series, Rancho Salina & Blue Rock Vineyards, Sonoma County $22.   89
Bright ruby purple. Medium-bodied. Balanced acidity. Moderately extracted. Moderately oaked. Mildly tannic. Vanilla, red fruits, minerals. Extremely aromatic, with an expensive oak overlay and a seamless core of red fruit flavors. Well balanced and harmonious, displaying a sense of delicacy. Refined and crisp through the lengthy, flavorful finish.

1995 Cabernet Sauvignon, Sonoma County $16.   90
Full dark red with bright highlights. Medium-bodied. Moderately extracted. Mildly tannic. Cassis, mint, black fruits, vanilla. Ripe, juicy berry aromas have sweet vanilla accents that are confirmed on the palate. Very rounded and open-knit in an accessible style. Plenty of sweet varietal Cabernet flavors.

1996 Cabernet Sauvignon, Sonoma County $17.   89
Dark ruby cast. Moderately full-bodied. Balanced acidity. Highly extracted. Moderately oaked. Mildly tannic. Black fruits, vanilla. Ripe and generous, with a fruit-forward personality and a lash of sweet vanilla oak. Generous on the palate, with mouthwatering acidity and angular tannins lending structure to the flavorful finish.

Scale: Superlative (96-100), Exceptional (90-95), Highly Recommended (85-89), Recommended (80-84), Not Recommended (Under 80)

38

1995 Cabernet Sauvignon, Ash Creek Vineyards Reserve,
Alexander Valley $25.   86

Dark purple. Full-bodied. Balanced acidity. Highly extracted. Moderately oaked. Moderately tannic. Vanilla, black fruits. Generous aromas lead a dense and chunky palate feel. Ripe and flavorful throughout, with big tannins on the lengthy oak-tinged finish.

1995 Cabernet Sauvignon, Rancho Salina Vineyard, Sonoma Valley $28.   89

Bright red-purple. Moderately full-bodied. Moderately extracted. Moderately tannic. Black fruits, toasted oak. Bright berry aromas follow through on a vibrant palate that finishes with a toasty note and dry, fine-grained tannins. High-toned style.

1995 Cabernet Sauvignon, Reserve, Sonoma Mountain $35.   90

Saturated cherry red. Medium-bodied. Moderately extracted. Mildly tannic. Cassis, vanilla, spice. Rich, spicy, fleshy aromas lead a supple, textured palate with opulent fruit flavors and very supple tannins. Weighty and solid nonetheless.

1994 Tribute Red, Sonoma Mountain $25.   88

Deep reddish purple. Medium-bodied. Highly extracted. Moderately tannic. Cassis, vanilla, tobacco. Lots of chewy Cabernet fruit. Well-extracted dry tannins linger on the finish with sweet cedary notes. Very rounded and supple in the middle. Quite attractive now.

1995 Tribute Red, Sonoma Mountain $25.   91

Saturated dark ruby hue. Medium-bodied. Moderately extracted. Mildly tannic. Black fruits, coffee. Ripe, fleshy aromas follow through on an open-knit palate, with charred brown spice notes on the finish. Very supple.

1995 Merlot, Reserve, Sonoma County $32.   92

Deep blackish ruby hue. Moderately full-bodied. Balanced acidity. Highly extracted. Heavily oaked. Mildly tannic. Vanilla, black fruits, mint. Almost Australian in style, with a huge overlay of oak and a deep core of vibrant fruit flavors. Well integrated nonetheless, with solid grip and fine balance. Lingering flavorful finish.

1995 Pinot Noir, California $18.   88

Medium cherry red with purple highlights. Medium-bodied. Moderately extracted. Moderately oaked. Mildly tannic. Rounded, ripe berry flavors have a mild sweetness. A smooth, textured mouthfeel gives a polished feel. Plenty of sweet oak flavors make this very accessible.

Beringer

1997 Chardonnay, Founders' Estate, California $9.99.   82

1996 Chardonnay, Napa Valley $15.   86

Bright yellow-gold. Medium-bodied. Balanced acidity. Moderately extracted. Green apples, brown spice, vanilla. Typical aromas of oak spice and butter follow through with a textured, rounded palate feel, and a finish that shows spicy persistence.

1997 Chardonnay, Appellation Collection, Napa Valley $16.   83

Brilliant yellow-gold. Quite aromatic, showing browned butter and green apple aromas with a subtle oak accent. A crisp entry leads a medium-bodied palate with tart flavors and subtle oak spice. The finish is clean and quick. Rather lean. Drink now.

1996 Chardonnay, Private Reserve, Napa Valley $30.   90

Deep golden hue. Moderately full-bodied. Balanced acidity. Moderately extracted. Moderately oaked. Yeast, brown spices, bread dough. Ripe and opulent, with forward oak-accented aromatics and a big yeasty component. Weighty on the palate, yet balanced by appropriate acidity. Fine length and intensity on the finish.

1997 Chardonnay, Private Reserve, Napa Valley $36.   92

Brilliant golden yellow. Rich smoky, toasty oak aromas with yeast notes. A firm attack leads a moderately full-bodied palate with vibrant citrus flavors and lingering vanilla notes. Impressively concentrated. Drink now or later.

1996 Chardonnay, Sbragia-Limited Release, Napa Valley $35.   **94**

Bright yellow-gold. Moderately full-bodied. Full acidity. Moderately extracted. Moderately oaked. Yeast, yellow apples, brown spice. Rich butter and spice aromas follow through on the palate. Very spicy and direct, with a big up-front rush of flavors that taper through the finish. Extravagant yeasty qualities are a standout.

1996 Alluvium Blanc, Knights Valley $16.   **82**

1996 Sauvignon Blanc, Napa Valley $9.   **90**

Deep yellow-gold. Moderately full-bodied. Balanced acidity. Moderately extracted. Heavily oaked. Vanilla, brown spices, oranges. A hefty overlay of oak is supported by a core of ripe fruit flavors. Lush and rich in the mouth with a pleasant smoky finish.

1996 Viognier, Napa Valley $25.   **87**

Deep golden hue. Full-bodied. Balanced acidity. Moderately extracted. Moderately oaked. Toasted coconut, vanilla, tropical fruits. Wood accented, with a flavor profile dominated by oak. Attractive nonetheless, with a ripe palate feel that is rich yet well balanced by acidity through the finish. Made like a California Chardonnay.

1998 White Zinfandel, California $6.   **81**

1997 Rosé de Saignée, California $16.   **89**

Pale russet hue. Generous, rich bread dough and red fruit aromas. A soft entry leads a rich, moderately full-bodied palate that has great flavor intensity. Supple and stylish. Drink now.

1994 Cabernet Sauvignon, Knights Valley $20.   **88**

Bright crimson purple. Medium-bodied. Moderately extracted. Mildly tannic. Black cherries, vanilla. Bright dried fruit flavors on entry conclude with gentle tannins and vanilla sweetness, giving this a lighter note through the finish. Very attractive and well balanced. Drinking nicely now.

1995 Cabernet Sauvignon, Appellation Collection, Knights Valley $22.   **86**

Dark violet hue. Generous aromas of black cherry and vanilla. A fruity entry leads a medium-bodied palate with lush black fruits and soft tannins that fade quickly on the finish. Very user friendly. Drink now.

1993 Cabernet Sauvignon, Private Reserve, Napa Valley $65.   **94**

Opaque dark red-purple. Moderately full-bodied. Highly extracted. Quite tannic. Toasted oak, plums, cassis, pepper. Toasted oak and black fruit aromas. Tons of chewy black Cabernet fruit, with solid dry tannins through the finish. Assertive and structured, this should do well in the cellar.

1994 Cabernet Sauvignon, Private Reserve, Napa Valley $75.   **97**

Brilliant deep ruby red hue. Richly aromatic with generous vanilla oak accents and plush ripe cherry fruits. A silky entry leads a moderately full-bodied palate with plush, silky tannins and rich fruit flavors. Seamless and smooth through the finish. Drink now.

1996 Gamay Beaujolais, California $7.   **81**

1995 Alluvium Red, Knights Valley $30.   **86**

Saturated deep ruby-red hue. Generously aromatic with deeply fruited aromas of plums and dark fruits. Shows a toasty wood influence. A rich entry leads a moderately full-bodied palate with lush, supple fruit flavors and excellent mouthfeel. Tannins are fine grained and powdery. Harmonious, very approachable. Drink now or later.

1994 Merlot, Bancroft Ranch, Howell Mountain $45.   **92**

Deep blackish ruby hue. Full-bodied. Full acidity. Highly extracted. Heavily oaked. Quite tannic. Black fruits, cedar, earth. Extremely full and deep in style, with a hugely extracted core of complex flavors. Muscular throughout, though seemingly in balance, with very big, skillfully extracted tannins. Unapproachable now, this is a long-term (7–10 years) cellar candidate.

1995 Merlot, Bancroft Ranch, Howell Mountain $50.   **90**

Saturated dark purple-violet. Very woody aromas, with black cherry notes. A rich attack shows a marked oak influence, with fleshy fruit flavors in a tightly wound frame that concludes with a lingering dry oak finish. Drink within five years.

1996 Pinot Noir, Founders Estate, California $9.99.   **86**

Brilliant red-violet hue. Medium-bodied. Moderately extracted. Mildly tannic. Red fruits, vanilla. Generous and vibrant floral, fruity flavors explode on the palate and are supported by restrained, soft tannins. A fine, easy-drinking style.

1996 Pinot Noir, North Coast $16.   **89**

Pale ruby red with a subtly fading rim. Medium-bodied. Moderately extracted. Moderately oaked. Mildly tannic. Red fruits, vanilla, minerals. Bright, crisp aromas follow through on the palate with a sense of delicacy and fruit sweetness.

1995 Pinot Noir, Stanly Ranch, Los Carneros, Napa Valley $30.   **91**

Dark ruby cast. Medium-bodied. Highly extracted. Moderately tannic. Black fruit cordial, spice, tea. Rich, brooding aromas lead a solid, dry mouthful of flavors with fruit standing up to dry tannins and oak spice. Fine grip through the finish. This is showing solid, ageworthy structure.

1995 Zinfandel, Appellation Collection, North Coast $12.   **84**

Dark cherry red. Moderately light-bodied. Balanced acidity. Moderately extracted. Mildly oaked. Mildly tannic. Minerals, black fruits, pepper. A toasty nose with tarlike notes leads a lighter palate with black fruit focus, and a firm, minerally undernote that comes through on the finish.

1994 Port of Cabernet Sauvignon, Napa Valley $20.   **88**

Opaque blackish purple. Full-bodied. Balanced acidity. Highly extracted. Heavily oaked. Mildly tannic. Vanilla, cassis. Extraordinarily aromatic, with a melange of wood-accented black fruit flavors. Rich and deep in the mouth, with some drying wood tannins through the finish. Interesting.

1994 Botrytized Sauvignon Blanc-Semillon, Nightingale,
Private Reserve, Napa Valley $22/375 ml.   **95**

Deep yellow-gold. Full-bodied. Balanced acidity. Moderately extracted. Heavily oaked. Toasted coconut, vanilla, tropical fruits. Outrageously toasty, with a hefty oak profile and a raft of botrytis-accented fruit flavors. Luxurious and complex in the mouth, with a supple, spicy finish. Hedonistic.

Bernardus

1996 Chardonnay, Monterey County $18.   **88**

Bright yellow-straw hue. Moderately full-bodied. Balanced acidity. Moderately extracted. Mildly oaked. Minerals, brown spices, citrus. Carries a judicious oak accent and a firm core of citric flavors. Vibrant and juicy, with oak spice lingering through the finish.

1994 Marinus, Carmel Valley $28.   **91**

Deep dark red. Medium-bodied. Moderately extracted. Moderately tannic. Cassis, tobacco, toasted oak. Elegantly structured, with fine integration of flavors that unfold on a solid palate. Some balanced tannins come through on the finish. Claret-like in character.

Bianchi

1996 Cabernet Sauvignon, Proprietor's Reserve, California $6.95.   **81**

Blackstone

1996 Merlot, California $10.   **85**

Dark ruby to the rim with brilliant clarity. Medium-bodied. Balanced acidity. Moderately extracted. Mildly tannic. Red fruits, vanilla. Straightforward and flavorful, with a well-integrated palate feel. Pleasantly structured through the finish.

1997 Merlot, California $10.   **84**

Pale ruby red with a bright cast. Sweet berry aromas follow through to a medium-bodied palate with sweet fruit and oak flavors. Acids are quite low and tannins are soft through the finish. An easy-drinking quaffer for near-term consumption.

1996 Merlot, Napa Valley $14.   82

Blossom Hill
1997 Chardonnay, California $4.99.   81
1996 Merlot, California $5.99.   80

Bogle
1997 Chardonnay, California $8.   81
1997 Sauvignon Blanc, California $7.   81
1997 Cabernet Sauvignon, California $10.   88
Saturated purple hue. Generous cassis and vanilla aromas with a judicious oak accent.
A supple attack leads to a moderately full-bodied palate with lush tannins on the finish.
Very fruit centered and well structured. Drink now or later.
1997 Merlot, California $9.   83
Brilliant violet with a bright cast. Aromas of cordials and vanilla oak. Medium-bodied,
with clean black fruit flavors and sweet oak and juicy acids through the finish. Drink now.
1997 Petite Sirah, California $10.   92
Dark ruby purple. Moderately full-bodied. Highly extracted. Quite tannic. Plums,
chocolate. Floral, bright fruity aromas follow through on the palate, with substantial
tannins not turning too dry on the finish. This could use a few years, although is
approachable now.
1995 Zinfandel, Old Vine Cuvée, California $11.   88
Bright blackish ruby hue. Moderately full-bodied. Full acidity. Moderately extracted.
Mildly oaked. Mildly tannic. Vanilla, black fruits. Pleasant spicy oak nuances combine
with a solid core of dark fruit flavors on the palate. Approachable, but showing solid
concentration through the finish.

Bommarito
1997 Merlot, Napa Valley $12.   82

Bonny Doon
1996 Le Cigare Volant, California $22.   90
Bright, limpid purple-red to the rim. Powerful herb, red fruit, and vanilla aromas show
a subtle wood accent. A soft attack leads a moderately full-bodied palate, with crisp acidity
and mild tannic grip. The lingering finish is clean and flavorful. Bright, modern, and
stylish. Drink now or later. Can improve with more age.
1997 Muscat Vin de Glacière, California $15/375 ml.   90
Pale yellow-copper hue. Forward, nutty apricot and tropical fruit aromas. A rich entry
leads a moderately full-bodied palate featuring tons of sweetness. Flavorful and complex.
Enticing in small measures. Drink now.

Bonterra
1997 Chardonnay, Mendocino County $12.   84
Bright yellow-straw hue. Subtle brown spice and citrus aromas carry a slight oak accent.
A clean entry leads a medium-bodied palate that has decent acidity. Well balanced,
flavorful finish. Drink now.
1995 Cabernet Sauvignon, North Coast $12.99.   87
Bright crimson red. Moderately light-bodied. Moderately extracted. Mildly tannic. Tart
cassis, vanilla, cedar. Sweet fruit aromas. Crisp black fruit flavors keep the palate lively.
Not particularly deep, though very accessible and good for early drinking.
1996 Cabernet Sauvignon, North Coast $13.   86
Saturated ruby blood-red hue. Lean, crisp aromas of tart black fruits and vanilla. A lean
attack leads to a moderately full-bodied palate with vibrant acids and crisp, leaner fruit
flavors. Finishes cleanly and quickly. A little ungenerous. Drink now or later.

Scale: Superlative (96-100), Exceptional (90-95), Highly Recommended (85-89),
Recommended (80-84), Not Recommended (Under 80)

1996 Merlot, Mendocino County $17.   **86**

Bright ruby red. Unusual, high-toned anise, sweet herb, and mineral aromas. A crisp attack is followed by a lean, medium-bodied palate with juicy acidity and a bright, flavorful finish. A stylish lightweight. Drink now.

1996 Syrah, Mendocino County $25.   **91**

Deep, bright purple-red hue to the rim. Forward, perfumed, floral red fruit aromas. A supple attack leads a medium-bodied palate showing velvety tannins. Mouthwatering acidity lends a sense of buoyancy. Clean, flavorful finish. Stylish and elegant. Drink now.

Bonverre

1996 Chardonnay, California $8.   **81**

Bouchaine

1996 Chardonnay, Carneros $18.   **86**

Pale straw hue. Medium-bodied. Full acidity. Moderately extracted. Moderately oaked. Butter, minerals, lemon. Subtly smoky, buttery aromas lead a vibrant, crisp mouthful of tart fruit flavors that finish cleanly with minimal oak influence.

1995 Chardonnay, Estate Reserve, Carneros, Napa Valley $24.   **83**

Pale straw cast. Medium-bodied. Full acidity. Moderately extracted. Mildly oaked. Butter, vanilla, citrus. Stylishly textured, with a rounded, full mouthfeel and crisp acids lingering through the finish. Oak flavors are subtle.

1996 Cabernet Franc, Limited Release, Napa Valley $18.   **81**

1996 Pinot Noir, Carneros $19.   **84**

Pale violet hue. Medium-bodied. Moderately extracted. Mildly tannic. Vanilla, minerals, red fruits. Subtle fruity aromas lead a delicate, minerally palate that shows soft tannins and light berry fruit flavors.

1994 Pinot Noir, Reserve, Carneros $27.   **92**

Full cherry red. Medium-bodied. Moderately extracted. Moderately oaked. Moderately tannic. The rich, complex nose has a leathery accent. The gamey, supple, rounded palate is nicely textured. A long, complex finish has leather and earth notes with subtle oak spice. Drinking very well now.

1995 Pinot Noir, Reserve, Carneros $30.   **84**

Bright pale violet hue. Moderately light-bodied. Subtly extracted. Mildly tannic. Dried herbs, minerals, red fruits. Pronounced floral, dried herbal aromas lead a lightly framed palate with mild tannins and a quick finish.

Brophy Clark

1996 Pinot Noir, Arroyo Grande Valley $18.   **83**

Pale ruby cast. Medium-bodied. Balanced acidity. Moderately extracted. Mildly tannic. Minerals, dried herbs. Quite light in style with a decided herbal overtone. Lean and angular through the finish.

David Bruce

1997 Chardonnay, Santa Cruz Mountains $NA.   **85**

Bright yellow-straw hue. Pleasant earth and mineral aromas. A firm entry leads a medium-bodied palate, with crisp acids. Clipped finish. Drink now.

1994 Cabernet Sauvignon, Reserve, Santa Cruz Mountains $20.   **90**

Deep reddish purple. Medium-bodied. Highly extracted. Moderately tannic. Black fruits, dill, brown spice. Exotic pickled spice aromas. Rich, concentrated, and mouthfilling, with youthful vigor that does not mask its pure, ripe primary fruit flavors. Dry oak notes come through on the finish. Rather appealing now.

1996 La Rusticana d'Orsa, Santa Cruz Mountains $32.   **90**

Deep ruby purple to the rim. Generous spice, red fruit, and sweet herb aromas carry a hefty oak influence. A firm entry leads a moderately full-bodied palate, with robust tannins. Chewy, rich, and extracted, with a flavorful finish. Drink now or later.

1997 Petite Syrah, Central Coast $16. 88

Opaque purple. Moderately full-bodied. Highly extracted. Quite tannic. Black cherries, vanilla. Rich, peppery, explosively fruity aromas follow through to a thick, flavorsome palate with a textured mouthfeel and relatively supple finish, despite the impressive tannin levels.

1997 Petite Syrah, Ranchita Canyon, Paso Robles $18. 85

Very dark, opaque violet red. Brooding black fruit and mineral aromas show a generous oak influence. A hard entry leads a full-bodied palate that has big, robust tannins. An absolute monster; thick and rich with a tannic bite. Mid-term cellar candidate (3–6 years).

1996 Pinot Noir, Central Coast $16. 91

Deep cherry red. Medium-bodied. Moderately extracted. Mildly tannic. Black cherries, vanilla. Ripe black fruit aromas lead a smooth fruity palate. Bright primary flavors and soft tannins result in an opulent style. Supple and rounded, drinking well now.

1997 Pinot Noir, Central Coast $NA. 88

Rich ruby red with a slight fade. Generous red fruit, mineral, and dried herb aromas. A firm entry leads a moderately light-bodied palate that has drying tannins. Lingering, flavorful finish. Drink now.

1996 Pinot Noir, Sonoma County $NA. 89

Luminous, saturated ruby red. Fantastic flower and red fruit aromas carry a hefty oak accent. A firm entry leads a medium-bodied palate, with drying tannins. Structured, aromatic, and flavorful. Drink now or later.

1996 Pinot Noir, Russian River Valley $NA. 90

Bright, saturated ruby purple. Generous berry and mineral aromas show a big oak accent. A firm entry leads a moderately full-bodied palate, with crisp acids and drying tannins. A full, rich style. Drink now or later.

1995 Pinot Noir, Chalone $32. 94

Deep crimson purple. Medium-bodied. Highly extracted. Heavily oaked. Moderately tannic. Cocoa and berry aromas. Exotic, rich, deep black cherry and chocolate flavors expand on the palate and linger through a finish showing soft powdery tannins. A plush, ripe, rounded style that has the stuffing to keep and improve for a few years, though it is drinking nicely now.

1996 Pinot Noir, Chalone $32. 95

Dark cherry red. Moderately full-bodied. Highly extracted. Moderately tannic. Black cherries, anise, chocolate. Impressively rich, spicy aromas follow through on the palate, with solid tannins making for a structured style that will benefit from some cellar age. An intense and powerful style of New World Pinot.

1996 Pinot Noir, Santa Cruz Mountains $35. 86

Very dark ruby cast. Moderately full-bodied. Balanced acidity. Moderately extracted. Moderately oaked. Mildly tannic. Spice, minerals, black fruit. Forward aromas show depth and complexity. Ripe fruit flavors carry a spicy oak accent throughout. Firm and intense through the finish.

1995 Pinot Noir, Reserve, Russian River Valley $26. 92

Dark purple-red. Moderately full-bodied. Highly extracted. Moderately oaked. Moderately tannic. Sweet raspberry and vanilla aromas lead a juicy full palate, with chocolatey richness and a textured, generous mouthfeel. The finish is dominated by dry, fine-grained tannins. Excellent structure and weight.

1994 Pinot Noir, Estate Reserve, Santa Cruz Mountains $35. 91

Full ruby color. Medium-bodied. Highly extracted. Moderately oaked. Mildly tannic. Dark fruit aromas. Rich earthy, toasty character, with spicy black plum and cherry fruit flavors through a wonderful dry finish. Drinking nicely now.

Scale: Superlative (96-100), Exceptional (90-95), Highly Recommended (85-89), Recommended (80-84), Not Recommended (Under 80)

44

1995 Zinfandel, Ranchita Canyon Vineyard, Paso Robles $15.   **91**

Deep blackish purple. Moderately full-bodied. Balanced acidity. Highly extracted. Moderately oaked. Mildly tannic. Vanilla, black fruits, mint. Quite aromatic, with a very full, focused palate feel. Firmly structured, intense, and lengthy, with a vibrant finish. Great grip and depth.

1996 Zinfandel, Ranchita Canyon Vineyard, Paso Robles $15.   **88**

Deep blackish purple. Full-bodied. Balanced acidity. Highly extracted. Heavily oaked. Mildly tannic. Brown spices, cedar, black fruits. Quite aromatic, with a hefty overlay of wood spice and a deep core of fruit flavors. Full and rich on the palate, with enough acidity to maintain a sense of balance.

Brutocao

1997 Chardonnay, Bliss Vineyard, Reserve, Mendocino $22.   **80**

1996 Sauvignon Blanc, Mendocino $10.50.   **82**

1995 Merlot, Hopland Ranch, Mendocino $18.   **85**

Deep blackish ruby hue. Moderately light-bodied. Balanced acidity. Moderately extracted. Mildly oaked. Mildly tannic. Red fruits, mint, sweet herbs. Lighter in style, showing straightforward crisp fruit flavors and a relatively firm structure. Oak becomes more and more apparent on the finish.

1995 Zinfandel, Hopland Ranch, Mendocino $14.   **84**

Bright ruby-garnet cast. Moderately full-bodied. Balanced acidity. Moderately extracted. Moderately oaked. Mildly tannic. Chocolate, minerals. Pleasantly aromatic, with a soft, supple palate feel. Finishes on a generous note with velvety tannins and fine length.

Buehler

1995 Cabernet Sauvignon, Estate, Napa Valley $35.   **85**

Saturated deep ruby-brick red hue. Generously aromatic with an oak-spiced character and ripe dark fruits. A firm attack leads a moderately full-bodied palate with generous cassis flavors and solid gripping tannins. Impressively concentrated and ripe with a big tannic kick through the finish. Soundly structured. Drink now or later.

Buena Vista

1996 Chardonnay, Carneros $14.   **84**

Pale straw hue. Medium-bodied. Full acidity. Moderately extracted. Crisp apples, tart citrus. Clean and bright, with tart fruity flavors and vibrant acids playing out on the finish. Very refreshing, with no oak flavors present.

1994 Cabernet Sauvignon, Carneros $16.   **85**

Deep reddish purple. Medium-bodied. Moderately extracted. Mildly tannic. Red berries, vanilla. Full herbaceous berry-accented aromas follow through on the palate. Concentrated and focused, with a bright-fruit profile that extols its cool climate origins.

1995 Cabernet Sauvignon, Carneros $16.   **83**

Saturated dark red with purple highlights. Moderately full-bodied. Highly extracted. Quite tannic. Cassis, minerals. Angular, with bright fruit flavors up front that give way to brief, minerally tannins. Showing some tannic grip on the finish.

1993 Cabernet Sauvignon, Grand Reserve, Carneros $26.   **88**

Medium ruby red. Medium-bodied. Highly extracted. Moderately tannic. Red fruits, vanilla, black tea. Concentrated on the entry with some rich fruity character. Solid finish shows assertively dry tannins. Plenty of grip and authority through the finish.

1994 Cabernet Sauvignon, Grand Reserve, Carneros $28.95.   **86**

Saturated dark red. Moderately full-bodied. Highly extracted. Moderately tannic. Cassis, vanilla, oak spice. Deep oak spice aromas follow through on the palate, with lush black fruit flavors deferring to oak character. Tannins are ample and powdery, though not too overbearing for current consumption.

1995 Merlot, Carneros $19.   **86**

Rich cherry red. Lean mineral aromas. A firm attack leads a medium-bodied palate with drying, angular tannins. Lean through the finish. This one walks on the tougher side of Merlot. Drink within 5 years.

1996 Pinot Noir, Sonoma Valley, Carneros $14.   **80**

1995 Pinot Noir, Grand Reserve, Carneros $26.   **89**

Cherry red with a pinkish hue. Medium-bodied. Moderately extracted. Mildly oaked. Moderately tannic. Perfumed vanilla oak aromas with fresh, crisp raspberry notes. Concentrated red fruit flavors on the palate, with some dry astringency through the finish. Has some cellaring structure.

1996 Zinfandel, The Celebration, Sonoma $19.50.   **84**

Bright ruby purple. Moderately full-bodied. Balanced acidity. Moderately extracted. Mildly tannic. Pepper, minerals, briar fruits. Somewhat reserved aromatically, with subtle peppery overtones. Ripe fruit flavors emerge on the compact palate. Finishes with some drying tannins.

Burgess

1994 Cabernet Sauvignon, Vintage Selection, Napa Valley $22.   **87**

Full crimson red with bright highlights. Medium-bodied. Moderately extracted. Mildly tannic. Vanilla, raspberries, red fruits. Attractive ripe berry aromas have vanilla oak accents. Fleshy forward flavors are rounded and accessible now. Hints of dry toasted character on the palate linger through the finish.

1995 Cabernet Sauvignon, Vintage Selection, Napa Valley $24.   **86**

Bright ruby purple. Moderately full-bodied. Balanced acidity. Moderately extracted. Heavily oaked. Moderately tannic. Vanilla, black fruits, earth. Pleasantly aromatic, with a hefty oak accent and a firm core of fruit flavors. Weighty and rich, with chunky tannins through the finish.

Buttonwood

1997 Sauvignon Blanc, Santa Ynez Valley $10.   **84**

Pale yellow-straw cast. Moderately light-bodied. Balanced acidity. Moderately extracted. White citrus, dried herbs. Very straightforward, showing simple citrus flavors in a very clean frame, leaving the palate refreshed.

1994 Cabernet Sauvignon, Santa Ynez Valley $16.   **86**

Dark garnet red. Medium-bodied. Highly extracted. Mildly tannic. Earthy, tobacco-scented aromas. Solid black Cabernet fruit on the palate gives way to a balanced dry finish showing cedary nuances. Quite dry overall, even slightly austere.

1995 Merlot, Santa Ynez Valley $18.   **83**

Very deep blackish ruby hue. Moderately full-bodied. Balanced acidity. Moderately extracted. Moderately oaked. Mildly tannic. Earth, cedar, black fruits. Profoundly earthy in style. Rich, well-structured mouthfeel. Some drying tannins on the flavorful finish.

Byington

1993 Cabernet Sauvignon, Bates Ranch, Santa Cruz Mountains $20.   **89**

Dark ruby red. Medium-bodied. Moderately extracted. Mildly tannic. Vanilla, red berries, anise, pepper. A somewhat toasty, spicy nose leads a bright red fruit entry that expands on the midpalate. Balanced astringency through the finish. Approachable now, with good acids keeping it lively.

1994 Cabernet Sauvignon, Smith Reichel Vineyard, Alexander Valley $18. **89**

Dark brick red. Medium-bodied. Moderately extracted. Moderately tannic. Cooked fruit, brown spice, toasted oak. Jammy aromas lead a warm, generous palate, with dry assertive tannins through the finish. Angular and flavorsome.

Scale: Superlative (96-100), Exceptional (90-95), Highly Recommended (85-89), Recommended (80-84), Not Recommended (Under 80)

1994 Cabernet Sauvignon, Twin Mountains, Santa Cruz Mountains $14.50. 91
Full brick red. Medium-bodied. Highly extracted. Moderately tannic. Mint, brown spice, earth, red fruits. Exotic spicy, earthy aromas. A smooth but dry palate shows a seamless earthy quality through the finish. Seems to have mature flavors already, though it is still vigorous. Austere in a sophisticated manner.

1995 Merlot, Bradford Mountain, Sonoma County $20. 89
Very deep blackish ruby hue. Full-bodied. Full acidity. Highly extracted. Heavily oaked. Moderately tannic. Black fruits, lacquer. Quite aromatic, with a deep and brooding character. The dense core of flavor has a big overlay of oak notes. Still quite firm and tannic but well balanced. A candidate for mid-term (3–6 years) to long-term (7–10 years) aging.

1995 Pinot Noir, Central Coast $18. 86
Pale garnet red. Medium-bodied. Moderately extracted. Moderately oaked. Mildly tannic. Toasty, earthy nose with black cherry notes. Solid earthy backbone, with a minerally finish showing plenty of oak spice. A dry, assertive style that will show best with food.

1995 Pinot Noir, Willamette Valley $20. 89
Medium ruby red. Medium-bodied. Moderately extracted. Moderately oaked. Moderately tannic. Leather, earth, and black bramble fruit aromas are expressed well on the dry palate, with a lingering tobacco note on the finish. Quite austere.

Byron

1996 Pinot Blanc, Santa Maria Valley $16. 87
Bright golden hue. Moderately full-bodied. Full acidity. Moderately extracted. Mildly oaked. Toast, minerals, vanilla. Oak influences prevail on the nose and palate. In the mouth this wine is full though angular, with solid acidity.

1996 Pinot Gris, Santa Maria Valley $16. 84
Deep straw hue. Moderately full-bodied. Full acidity. Moderately extracted. Talc, oranges, lacquer. Marked aromas, with a distinctive high-toned note. Full on the palate, with racy acidity that balances out the finish.

1996 Pinot Noir, Santa Maria Valley $18. 93
Saturated dark ruby cast. Moderately full-bodied. Full acidity. Moderately extracted. Moderately oaked. Mildly tannic. Red fruits, dill pickle, wood. Generous aromas are in the classic Pinot range. Lush and supple on the palate, yet with a firm minerally backbone that lends a sense of balance.

1994 Pinot Noir, Reserve, Santa Barbara County $24. 86
Medium ruby red. Medium-bodied. Moderately extracted. Heavily oaked. Mildly tannic. Bright cherry fruit flavors up front, with plenty of toasted oak flavors coming through. Some warmth on the finish.

Cafaro

1995 Cabernet Sauvignon, Napa Valley $34. 89
Bright violet purple hue. Youthful crisp fruity aromas with a good overlay of new vanilla oak. A rich entry leads to a moderately full-bodied palate with crushed berry flavors and toasty new oak accents through the finish. Well stuffed and very youthful at present. Drink within 5 years.

1995 Merlot, Napa Valley $30. 88
Bright violet red. Sweet vanilla and red fruit aromas indicate generous oak accents. Moderately full-bodied with a bright attack, a midpalate with accents of crisp fruit, and velvety tannins through the finish. Drink now or later. Can improve with more age.

Cain

1996 Sauvignon Blanc, Musque, Ventana Vineyard, Monterey $16.   **94**

Bright yellow-gold. Medium-bodied. Balanced acidity. Moderately extracted. Earth, citrus, asparagus. Full citrus zest aromas follow through on a palate distinguished by its concentration, mouthfeel, and length. Very pure, cool climate Sauvignon Blanc flavors, with plenty of stuffing and earthy complexity.

1994 Cain Cuvée, Napa Valley $19.   **85**

Dark ruby purple. Medium-bodied. Moderately extracted. Mildly tannic. Tobacco, cassis. Varietally expressive aromas lead a straightforward palate with a certain lightness to the mouthfeel. Dry, fine-grained tannins on the finish.

1995 Cain Cuvée, Napa Valley $22.   **86**

Bright ruby cast. Moderately full-bodied. Balanced acidity. Moderately extracted. Mildly oaked. Mildly tannic. Chocolate, spice, minerals. Pleasantly aromatic, with a rich but firm palate feel. Turns lean and angular through the finish.

1994 Cain Five, Napa Valley $50.   **91**

Deep saturated ruby hue. Moderately full-bodied. Balanced acidity. Highly extracted. Mildly oaked. Moderately tannic. Minerals, cassis. Youthful and tightly wound with reined-in aromatics, but impressively structured. Shows breeding and elegance. Should gain complexity with mid- to long-term cellaring.

1995 Cain Five, Napa Valley $50.   **87**

Deep saturated ruby hue. Moderately full-bodied. Balanced acidity. Highly extracted. Mildly oaked. Moderately tannic. Minerals, brown spices, cassis. Aromas show oak spice and black fruits, with a firm, minerally backbone and a lean and taut structure. Built for the long haul.

Cakebread

1997 Chardonnay, Napa Valley $26.   **84**

Brilliant yellow-gold. Shows a very buttery nose. A tart attack leads a moderately full-bodied palate with strong butter and apple flavors that persist through the lengthy finish.

1996 Sauvignon Blanc, Napa Valley $14.   **90**

Bright straw cast. Moderately full-bodied. Full acidity. Moderately extracted. Mildly oaked. Brown spices, yeast, citrus. A hefty oak influence is backed up by a solid frame of fruit-derived flavors. Lush but well structured, with a zesty finish.

1994 Cabernet Sauvignon, Napa Valley $25.   **88**

Bright purple. Moderately light-bodied. Moderately extracted. Mildly tannic. Raspberries, cassis. Ripe raspberry and cassis aromas follow through on the juicy, open-knit palate. Very accessible, drink now.

1995 Cabernet Sauvignon, Napa Valley $30.   **90**

Bright ruby purple. Moderately full-bodied. Balanced acidity. Moderately extracted. Mildly oaked. Mildly tannic. Red fruits, minerals. Bright, fruit-centered aromatics are forward and generous. Supple and tasty in the mouth, with a gentle, velvety structure. Drinking very well.

1994 Cabernet Sauvignon, Reserve, Napa Valley $50.   **91**

Deep ruby purple. Moderately full-bodied. Balanced acidity. Moderately extracted. Moderately oaked. Mildly tannic. Black fruits, minerals, toast. Aromatic and generous, with a high-toned, fruit-centered quality. Supple and elegant in the mouth, with fine concentration and grip.

1995 Cabernet Sauvignon, Three Sisters, Napa Valley $75.   **93**

Deep ruby purple. Full-bodied. Balanced acidity. Highly extracted. Mildly oaked. Moderately tannic. Mint, red fruits, earth. Forward and distinctive aromatics lead a ripe and weighty mouthfeel. Concentrated and precise, with firm tannins. Fine length and intensity. Should develop beautifully.

Scale: Superlative (96-100), Exceptional (90-95), Highly Recommended (85-89), Recommended (80-84), Not Recommended (Under 80)

1995 Cabernet Sauvignon, Benchland Select, Napa Valley $75. **94**

Bright ruby purple. Moderately full-bodied. Balanced acidity. Moderately extracted. Moderately oaked. Mildly tannic. Vanilla, minerals, red fruits. Bright and aromatic, with a juicy, fruit-centered quality accented by judicious use of oak. Supple and flavorful through the lengthy finish.

1995 Merlot, Napa Valley $28.50. **88**

Very deep ruby red to the rim with a purplish cast. Moderately full-bodied. Full acidity. Highly extracted. Mildly tannic. Briar fruits, sweet herbs, minerals. Fruit driven, with jammy, vibrant flavors. Brightly textured in the mouth with snappy acidity. Quite accessible now, though it should gain complexity with mid-term (3–6 years) aging.

Calera

1997 Chardonnay, Central Coast $16. **89**

Deep straw cast. Moderately full-bodied. Balanced acidity. Moderately extracted. Bananas, minerals. Aromatically reserved, with subtle malolactic flavors and a firm core of steely acidity. Crisp through the finish.

1997 Viognier, Mount Harlan $30. **85**

Bright yellow-gold. Full-bodied. Balanced acidity. Moderately extracted. Tropical fruits, butter, minerals. Rather reserved aromatically, but big, ripe, and flavorful on the palate, with a rich buttery finish showing enough acidity to balance the weight.

1997 Pinot Noir, Central Coast $16. **86**

Very pale violet hue. Moderately light-bodied. Moderately extracted. Mildly tannic. Dried herbs, red fruits, vanilla. Berry fruit and crisp herbal aromas follow through on the palate. A light structure makes this very approachable now.

1994 Pinot Noir, Jensen, Mount Harlan $38. **86**

Medium cherry red. Medium-bodied. Moderately extracted. Moderately oaked. Moderately tannic. Ripe raisiny, cherry aromas. Exotically scented with great persistence throughout. Delicate yet full flavored. Dry tannins provide some grip on the finish, but this is nice now.

1994 Pinot Noir, Mills, Mount Harlan $35. **86**

Bright cherry red. Medium-bodied. Moderately extracted. Moderately tannic. Red berries, brown spice, minerals. Ripe, generous aromas lead a solidly flavorsome palate with dry tannins giving a firm impression on the finish.

1995 Pinot Noir, Selleck, Twentieth Anniversary Vintage, Mount Harlan $38. **91**

Cherry red with a violet rim. Medium-bodied. Moderately extracted. Moderately tannic. Berry fruits, minerals, vanilla. Richly aromatic, with oak influences that come through on the palate. Vibrant acids and good berry fruit flavors play on the finish. Shows some dry tannins and will probably age well.

Callaway

1998 Chenin Blanc, California $7.50. **83**

Very pale straw cast. Pleasantly aromatic with white peach nuances. Juicy and flavorful on the entry. Medium-bodied, with good flavor concentration following through to the finish. Drink now.

1997 Pinot Gris, Temecula $12. **86**

Bright copper cast. Moderately full-bodied. Balanced acidity. Moderately extracted. Dried herbs, minerals, gooseberries. Distinctively aromatic, with a big earthy, herbal streak. Full and rich in the mouth with some racy acidity through the smoky finish.

1997 Sauvignon Blanc, Temecula $8. **84**

Pale platinum-straw hue. Medium-bodied. Balanced acidity. Moderately extracted. Tropical fruits, dried herbs. Aromatic, with a juicy tropical character and an herbal note that follows through on the finish.

1995 Cabernet Sauvignon, California $11.   83

Bright cherry red. Moderately light-bodied. Subtly extracted. Mildly tannic. Red fruits. Soft, candied aromas follow through, with candied fruit flavors and soft tannins on the finish.

1996 Dolcetto, Temecula $15.   81

1994 Nebbiolo, California $15.   81

Cambria

1996 Chardonnay, Reserve, Santa Maria Valley $36.   88

Bright yellow-straw cast. Moderately full-bodied. Balanced acidity. Moderately extracted. Moderately oaked. Yeast, cream, citrus. Ripe and impressive flavors show a complex yeasty note. Full and rounded in the mouth, with a distinct impression of fruit sweetness through the finish.

1995 Pinot Noir, Julia's Vineyard, Santa Maria Valley $27.   89

Dark red with a garnet rim. Moderately full-bodied. Highly extracted. Moderately oaked. Mildly tannic. Full-throttled spicy, mature aromas. Rich flavors of stewed cherries and berries with a distinctly earthy quality throughout. Tannins are grainy but not excessive for current drinking. Substantial style.

1996 Pinot Noir, Reserve, Santa Maria Valley $42.   94

Deep ruby cast. Moderately full-bodied. Balanced acidity. Moderately extracted. Moderately oaked. Mildly tannic. Vanilla, red fruits, minerals. Ripe and aromatic, with a core of lush fruit flavors and a hedonistic overlay of oak. Supple and generous through the finish. Exquisitely proportioned.

1996 Sangiovese, Tepusquet Vineyard, Santa Maria Valley $18.   86

Bright cherry red with a youthful rim. Medium-bodied. Balanced acidity. Moderately extracted. Moderately oaked. Mildly tannic. Raspberries, vanilla. Sweet, fleshy red fruit aromas follow through on the palate, with vanilla sweetness and juicy acids making this very approachable.

1996 Syrah, Tepusquet Vineyard, Santa Maria Valley $18.   89

Deep ruby purple, limpid and brilliant to the rim. Generous, sound vanilla and black fruit flavors. Firm entry. Moderately full-bodied. Moderate drying tannins. Bright, succulent fruit is not obscured by heavy oak. Lingering rich finish. Drinkable now, but can improve with more age.

Camelot

1997 Chardonnay, California $13.   82

Canyon Road

1997 Sauvignon Blanc, California $6.99.   86

Pale yellow-gold. Medium-bodied. Balanced acidity. Moderately extracted. Dried herbs, minerals, citrus. High-toned, zesty aromas. A dry citrusy attack, with some nice varietal character that lingers through the finish. This is very clean and racy with no distracting oak influences.

1995 Cabernet Sauvignon, Reserve, Sonoma County $18.   88

Dark saturated ruby to the rim. Moderately full-bodied. Full acidity. Moderately extracted. Mildly tannic. Black fruits, chocolate, minerals. Youthful and tightly wound, with a pleasant nose and deep, brooding flavors. Acidity lends structure through the angular finish.

Cardinale

1996 Royale, California $20.   91

Bright golden cast. Full-bodied. Balanced acidity. Moderately extracted. Heavily oaked. Smoke, yeast, cream. Quite heavily oaked, with a big smoky flavor profile. Luxuriant and rich, with yeasty complexity and enough acidity to maintain a sense of balance through the finish.

1995 Red Wine, California $70.   **89**

Saturated dark ruby hue. Moderately full-bodied. Moderately extracted. Moderately
oaked. Moderately tannic. Anise, brown spice, black fruits. Chocolatey aromas show
plummy, spicy accents that follow through on the palate. Finely wrought and flavorsome,
with a long, dry finish. This has plenty of ripe, developed Cabernet flavors.

Carmenet

1997 Chardonnay, Sangiacomo Vineyard, Carneros, Sonoma Valley $18.   **83**

Deep gold. Fat, oaky aromas. A rich, concentrated attack leads a moderately full-bodied
palate with solid flavors that seem closed in at present. Finishes tight and austere with
good acids and a touch of phenolic dryness. Drink now or later.

1997 Gewürztraminer, Sonoma Valley $14.   **82**

1996 Reserve White Meritage, Paragon Vineyard, Edna Valley $15.   **86**

Full golden yellow. Medium-bodied. Balanced acidity. Moderately extracted. Butter,
lemon, oak spice. Soft aromas with mild lemon cream notes. Good mouthfeel, and quite
flavorful, though lacking grip and intensity though the short finish.

1995 Cabernet Franc, Moon Mountain Vineyard, Sonoma Valley $25.   **84**

Deep, saturated ruby red hue. Subdued earth and red fruit aromas. A lush attack leads
to a moderately full-bodied palate with chunky tannins and decent acidic grip. Firm,
rich finish. Shows good weight and intensity but a little closed in at present. Drink now
or later.

1993 Moon Mountain Estate Reserve Meritage, Sonoma Valley $27.50.   **91**

Ruby color with a pale rim. Medium-bodied. Moderately extracted. Moderately tannic.
Dust, earth, red fruits. Dusty, earthy nose. Quite dry and austere, yet the tannins are
rounded. Not many primary fruit sensations here. Well integrated and smooth through
the finish. Exotic.

1995 Moon Mountain Estate Reserve Meritage, Sonoma Valley $40.   **87**

Bright ruby red. Medium-bodied. Moderately extracted. Moderately tannic. Black fruits,
spice. Bright, black berry fruit aromas follow through on a dry, oaky palate with a lean
finish. Tasty now, though it will be better in a year or so. Elegant.

1996 Merlot, Sangiacomo Vineyard, Carneros, Sonoma Valley $20.   **89**

Saturated, bright violet red. Generously aromatic with rich fruity aromas and toasted oak
accents. A lush entry leads a moderately full-bodied palate with smooth tannins and lush
fruity flavors. Very supple and lengthy, with plenty of toasty oak spice on the finish. Drink
now or later.

Carmody McKnight

1996 Cadenza, Paso Robles $22.50.   **86**

Saturated dark ruby hue. Ripe cordial-like aromas. A firm entry leads a moderately
full-bodied palate with a thick mouthfeel and generous dark fruit flavors. Finishes with
tough, gripping tannins. Solidly structured. Drink now or later.

Carneros Creek

1996 Pinot Noir, Fleur de Carneros, Carneros $12.   **82**

1997 Pinot Noir, Fleur de Carneros, Carneros $12.   **82**

1996 Pinot Noir, Carneros $18.   **88**

Bright cherry red. Medium-bodied. Moderately extracted. Heavily oaked. Moderately
tannic. A toasty, oak-accented nose leads bright raspberry and cherry fruit flavors. Rich
oak and rounded berry fruit flavors linger through a long toasty, smoky finish. Generous.

Maurice Carrie

1998 Johannisberg Riesling, California $7.95.   **83**

Bright pale straw cast. Ripe tropical fruit aromas have a zesty, minerally note. A lean
attack leads a medium-bodied palate showing sweet citrus flavors. Low in acid, with a
clipped finish. Drink now.

1996 Sauvignon Blanc, Temecula $7.95.   **84**

Bright pale straw hue. Medium-bodied. Balanced acidity. Moderately extracted. Lemon, yeast. Straightforward lemony aromas follow through on the palate with little complexity but reasonable acid balance and length.

Case

1994 Pinot Noir, Sleepy Hollow Vineyards, Monterey $26.   **89**

Medium garnet red. Medium-bodied. Moderately extracted. Mildly oaked. Mildly tannic. Rich, smoky red berry fruit aromas have a perfumed character. The elegant, focused palate has well-integrated flavors and a clean finish. Drinking nicely now.

Castle

1997 Chardonnay, Sonoma Valley $18.   **84**

Bright straw cast. Moderately full-bodied. Balanced acidity. Highly extracted. Yeast, citrus, nuts. Pleasantly aromatic, with a ripe and rounded mouthfeel. Finishes with an attractive nutty accent.

1997 Chardonnay, Los Carneros $22.   **81**

1997 Viognier, Ripken Vineyard, California $18.   **81**

1996 Cabernet Sauvignon, Nicolas Vineyard, Sonoma Valley $25.   **84**

Deep ruby red hue with a slight fade. Subdued and brooding mineral, earth, and red fruit aromas. A firm attack leads to a lean, medium-bodied mouthfeel with mildly astringent tannins. Firm, drying finish. Drink within five years.

1997 Cinsault, Dry Creek Valley $19.   **86**

Bright pale purple-red hue to the rim. Clean, forward berry and mineral aromas. A firm attack leads a medium-bodied palate, with drying tannins. Snappy, clean finish. A lighter style and tasty. Drink now.

1996 Merlot, Sonoma Valley $18.   **88**

Bright violet with a subtle fade. Crisp berry, herb, and vanilla aromas. A bright attack leads a medium-bodied palate with fine-grained tannins and juicy acids. Drink now.

1996 Merlot, Sangiacomo Vineyard, Carneros $25.   **89**

Deep, saturated purple-red. Generous mint and red fruit aromas carry a mild wood accent. A lush attack is followed by a medium-bodied, supple palate with crisp tannins and juicy acidity. The finish is lively and flavorful. Quite buoyant, with fine grip and intensity. Drink within 5 years.

1997 Pinot Noir, Los Carneros $22.   **84**

Bright violet red. Medium-bodied. Moderately extracted. Mildly tannic. Vanilla, red fruits. Toasty vanilla aromas lead a bright mouthful of tart red fruit flavors. A bite of dry tannins linger on the finish, giving this a note of astringency and solidity.

1997 Pinot Noir, Durell Vineyard, Los Carneros $30.   **87**

Brilliant violet cast. Medium-bodied. Moderately extracted. Moderately tannic. Berry fruits, minerals, oak spice. Intriguingly spiced and generous berry fruit aromas follow through on the palate in an expressive jammy manner, giving a sense of power and depth, with toasted spicy oak making a statement. Finishes with smooth, ripe tannins.

1997 Pinot Noir, Sangiacomo Vineyard, Los Carneros $30.   **89**

Bright violet hue. Medium-bodied. Moderately extracted. Mildly tannic. Vanilla, minerals, berry fruits. Toasted oak and berry fruit aromas follow through well on a lighter-framed palate, with bright, gripping acids making for a lively character. Acidity is marked and impressive.

1996 Syrah, Sonoma Valley $20.   **83**

Dark crimson color, limpid with a slight fade. Oak-influenced aromas. Generous, sound mineral, brown spice, and coffee flavors. Hefty wood tones. Firm entry. Moderately full-bodied. Moderate, drying tannins. Persistent finish. Rather distinctive and unusual. Drink now.

1996 Zinfandel, Sonoma County $16.   **88**

Bright blackish ruby cast. Medium-bodied. Full acidity. Moderately extracted. Mildly oaked. Mildly tannic. Briar fruits, wood. Pleasantly aromatic, with a fruit-accented palate feel. Lean and vibrant in the mouth, showing crisp acidity through the finish.

Castoro

1997 Chardonnay, Central Coast $12.   **84**

Bright yellow straw hue. Ripe green apple and butter aromas with vanilla. Ripe fruity on the entry, with a medium-bodied palate and nice notes of butter and oak matched by crisp acids. Well balanced and versatile. Drink now.

1995 Cabernet Sauvignon, Paso Robles $11.50.   **85**

Bright reddish purple. Medium-bodied. Moderately extracted. Mildly tannic. Red currant, dried herbs. Bright red fruit entry. A juicy palate has an herbal, toasty note through the finish. Quite straightforward, with some nice astringency running through it.

1996 Cabernet Sauvignon, Paso Robles $15.   **86**

Bright purple hue. Markedly ripe, jammy aromas. A fat entry leads a moderately full-bodied palate with a ripe core of fleshy fruit flavors and firm tannins clamping down on the medium-length finish. Rich and thick, though acids are rather soft. This should be better in a few years. Drink now or later.

1996 Zinfandel, Paso Robles $12.95.   **86**

Deep blackish purple cast. Moderately full-bodied. Full acidity. Moderately extracted. Moderately oaked. Mildly tannic. Black fruits, chocolate. Quite aromatic, with a full, flavorful palate feel. Lush and supple in the mouth, with vibrant acidity making for a bright finish. Big but well balanced.

1996 Zinfandel, Vineyard Tribute, Paso Robles $15.   **81**

Caymus

1994 Cabernet Sauvignon, Napa Valley $35.   **92**

Dark red-purple. Moderately full-bodied. Highly extracted. Moderately tannic. Cassis, plums, cedar. A bright, dense center of pure cassis fruit with good supporting tannins through the finish. Very well balanced. Has the structure to cellar, but it's approachable in youth.

1995 Cabernet Sauvignon, Napa Valley $65.   **93**

Deep blood red. Moderately full-bodied. Highly extracted. Moderately tannic. Lead pencil, cassis, minerals. Outstanding aromas are truly expressive. Rich tannins show exceptional balance with pure Cabernet fruit flavors that persist through a lengthy finish.

1994 Cabernet Sauvignon, Special Selection, Napa Valley $110.   **95**

Very deep ruby hue. Full-bodied. Balanced acidity. Highly extracted. Heavily oaked. Moderately tannic. Smoke, charred wood, black fruits. Quite aromatic, with a forward, smoky, toasted impression to the nose. Firm and full, though amazingly supple. Shows fine length and intensity. Approachable now, but far better to wait for further complexity to develop.

Cecchetti Sebastiani

1993 Cabernet Sauvignon, Napa Valley $30.   **87**

Dark crimson-ruby color. Medium-bodied. Moderately extracted. Moderately tannic. Plums, black fruits, black tea. Ripe black fruit aromas show a toasty note that is confirmed on the palate, with some dry, fine-grained tannins coming through on the finish. This has a meaty, savory quality.

Cedar Brook

1994 Cabernet Sauvignon, California $8.99.   **84**

Bright cherry red. Medium-bodied. Moderately extracted. Mildly tannic. Vanilla, red fruits. Sweet, forward aromas follow through on the open-knit palate and brief finish. Very simple and straightforward.

1996 Merlot, California $8.99.   83

Deep crimson-ruby color with brilliant highlights. Moderately light-bodied. Full acidity. Moderately extracted. Moderately oaked. Mildly tannic. Plums, black fruits, vanilla. Pleasantly aromatic and flavorful with a dark fruit accent. Juicy acidity lends a sense of vibrancy. Subtle oaky overtones come into play on the snappy finish.

1995 Zinfandel, California $8.99.   84

Bright blackish ruby color. Medium-bodied. Balanced acidity. Moderately extracted. Moderately oaked. Mildly tannic. Brown spices, coffee, black fruits. Oak nuances dominate the aromas and play out on the palate. Soft, supple, and velvety in the mouth, with a lingering finish.

Cedar Mountain

1997 Chardonnay, Blanches Vineyard, Livermore Valley $16.   89

Medium straw hue. Moderately full-bodied. Balanced acidity. Heavily oaked. Toasted coconut, brown spice, apples. Assertive yeasty, toasted oak aromas follow through on the palate, with complex yeast and wood accents dominating the finish. Stylish and flavorsome.

1994 Cabernet Sauvignon, Livermore Valley $20.   90

Dark red with purple highlights. Medium-bodied. Highly extracted. Mildly tannic. Black fruits, tobacco. Attractive ripe plum aromas. Concentrated black Cabernet fruit flavors expand on the palate, with dry but textured tannins keeping the finish firm.

1995 Cabernet Sauvignon, Blanches Vineyard, Livermore Valley $22.   88

Very deep blackish ruby hue. Opulent briar fruit and vanilla aromas show a decided wood accent. A lush entry leads to a thick, full-bodied palate with big velvety drying tannins. Ripe, flavorful finish. A big show style. Drink now or later.

1995 Duet, Livermore Valley $22.   88

Deep, saturated blackish ruby hue. Intense brown spice, black fruit, and licorice aromas show a generous oak accent. A rich entry leads to a thick full-bodied palate with robust velvety tannins. Features just enough acidity to maintain a sense of liveliness. Flavorful, persistent finish. A flashy showy style. Drink now or later.

1995 Merlot, Livermore Valley $21.50.   85

Very deep blackish purple hue. Medium-bodied. Full acidity. Highly extracted. Mildly tannic. Black cherries, cordial, sweet herbs, lacquer. Aromatic and fruit driven, with a dense core of very ripe fruit flavors. Vibrant acidity makes for a crisp, mildly astringent finish.

1996 Vintage Port, Amador County $19.50.   92

Opaque blackish ruby cast. Full-bodied. Balanced acidity. Highly extracted. Chocolate, black fruits, flowers. Shows amazing depth of concentration, with a fragrant and immensely flavorful palate feel. Rich and firmly structured, with just a hint of sweetness in the finish. A dead ringer for a high-end Portuguese wine. Intense and impressive.

Chalk Hill

1996 Chardonnay, Chalk Hill, Sonoma County $28.   86

Deep straw cast. Moderately full-bodied. Balanced acidity. Moderately extracted. Mildly oaked. Yeast, cream, smoke. Aromatic and full, with a ripe smoky quality throughout. Shows both complexity and richness, with a generous lengthy finish.

1996 Sauvignon Blanc, Chalk Hill, Sonoma County $19.   93

Deep green-gold. Moderately full-bodied. Balanced acidity. Moderately extracted. Moderately oaked. Vanilla, butter, oranges. Richly aromatic, with luxuriant oak accents. Full, round, and lush on the palate, with a velvety mouthfeel and a core of fruit flavor. Well balanced with fine length.

1994 Cabernet Sauvignon, Chalk Hill, Sonoma County $26.   88

Dark red. Medium-bodied. Moderately extracted. Moderately tannic. Tea, black fruits, brown spice. Sweet herbal notes on the nose lead a solidly flavored palate and a long dry finish showing lingering oak spice flavors. Some alcoholic warmth shows through.

1995 Cabernet Sauvignon, Chalk Hill, Sonoma County $32.   **82**

Chalone
1996 Chardonnay, Chalone $27.   **88**
Bright straw cast. Moderately full-bodied. Balanced acidity. Moderately extracted. Apples, pears, citrus. Ripe varietally pure Chardonnay aromas follow through on the palate. Full and rounded in the mouth, with a lush texture and well-defined, zesty finish.

1997 Chardonnay, The Pinnacles, Chalone $31.   **88**
Pale straw hue. Subdued mineral aromas. A lean entry leads an extracted, moderately full-bodied palate with steely flavors and very little oak influence. Shows clean varietal flavors and solid grip through the finish. May open with moderate age. Drink now or later.

1996 Chardonnay, Reserve, Chalone $45.   **89**
Deep straw cast. Moderately full-bodied. Balanced acidity. Highly extracted. Cream, citrus. Aromatically reserved, featuring a ripe and rounded mouthfeel. Broadly textured in the mouth, and full and rich through the finish.

1996 Chenin Blanc, Reserve, Chalone $20.   **84**
Medium gold hue. Mildly aromatic, with a hint of oak spice and key lime. A juicy entry leads a medium-bodied palate with a firm, structured character. Taut finish. Drink now or later.

1993 Pinot Noir, Reserve, Chalone $35.   **88**
Dark red with a subtle garnet cast. Medium-bodied. Moderately extracted. Moderately tannic. Black fruits, earth, spice. Rich, deep fruity aromas show an earthy note that follows through on the palate. Finishes with lingering astringency. A very sturdy style.

Chameleon
1996 Barbera, Amador County $14.   **89**
Bright pale ruby cast with a purple edge. Moderately light-bodied. Full acidity. Moderately extracted. Mildly oaked. Mildly tannic. Red fruits, minerals. Pleasantly aromatic and lighter in style, with a super-concentrated wave of briar fruit flavors. Vibrant acidity lends brightness throughout, and provides a clean, angular finish.

1996 Sangiovese, North Coast $16.   **88**
Cherry pink. Medium-bodied. Full acidity. Moderately extracted. Mildly tannic. Tart cherries, minerals. A lighter style with crisp, red fruit flavors and a solid, minerally underlay. Clean and fresh, with minimal new oak treatment. Uplifting acids give great grip.

Chappellet
1997 Chardonnay, Estate, Napa Valley $17.   **88**
Pale medium-straw hue. Ripe fruity aromas have a buttery, yeasty accent with obvious toasty oak notes. A smooth entry leads a moderately full-bodied palate with smooth texture and generous fruity flavors. Finishes with a note of yeasty complexity.

1997 Chardonnay, Signature Estate, Napa Valley $26.   **91**
Pale straw hue. Ripe apple and pear aromas. A lush entry leads a moderately full-bodied palate with a rounded mouthfeel and pure fruit flavors that linger through the finish. Particularly lengthy, with well-integrated toasty oak. Elegant.

1997 Dry Chenin Blanc, Napa Valley $11.   **85**
Pale straw hue. Subdued tropical fruit aromas. A rich entry leads a moderately full-bodied palate showing vibrant acidity. Full and intense in style. Drink now.

1997 Old Vine Cuvée, Special Select White Wine, Napa Valley $14.   **88**
Deep yellow-straw hue. Rich cream, pear, and spice aromas. A rich attack leads a concentrated, full-bodied palate, with firm acids and a drying finish. A powerful Chenin. Drink now or later.

1996 Cabernet Franc, Napa Valley $24.   86

Deep, saturated ruby red hue. Subdued red fruit and mineral aromas. A rich entry leads to a moderately full-bodied palate with robust tannins. Firm, flavorful finish. A big, ripe, extracted style. Drink now or later.

1995 Cabernet Sauvignon, Signature, Napa Valley $24.   89

Dark ruby hue. Moderately aromatic with distinct oak accent. A firm entry leads to a moderately full-bodied palate with a deep core of cassis. Finished with solid tannins and fine acidity. Well balanced and structured for further aging. Drink now or later.

1996 Merlot, Napa Valley $22.   89

Brilliant violet red. Generous black cherry aromas with vanilla accents. Bright, lush, and flavorsome on the entry, with a moderately full body and cedar and anise notes through the finish. Tannins are velvety and fine grained. Drink now or later. Can improve with more age.

1995 Sangiovese, Napa Valley $22.   89

Dark ruby red. Medium-bodied. Balanced acidity. Moderately extracted. Mildly oaked. Mildly tannic. Dried cherries, earth, licorice. Brooding, ripe aromas. Solid and mouthfilling, with excellent grip and length. Dry, austere finish.

Chateau Julien

1996 Chardonnay, Private Reserve "Sur Lie," Monterey County $15.   83

Pale straw cast. Medium-bodied. Full acidity. Moderately extracted. Vanilla, blanched almonds. Shows a hefty oak accent and a note of maturity. Lean and angular with a touch of dryness to the finish.

1995 Cabernet Sauvignon, Private Reserve, Monterey County $20.   86

Bright violet-red. Medium-bodied. Moderately extracted. Moderately tannic. Cherries, minerals, dried herbs. Crisp and lively bright red fruit flavors have an herbal note, with a bright, minerally finish showing some grip. Drinking well now.

1996 Cabernet Sauvignon, Private Reserve, Monterey County $25.   82

1996 Merlot, Grand Reserve, Monterey County $9.99.   86

Pale violet hue. Clean aromas of herbs, berry fruit, and vanilla. A soft entry leads a light-bodied palate with very gentle tannins. Easily quaffable. Drink now.

1996 Merlot, Private Reserve, Monterey County $20.   89

Bright violet red. Generous black cherry and vanilla aromas show a generous oak accent. A supple attack leads a medium-bodied palate with light, soft tannins and juicy acids. Drink now.

Chateau Montelena

1996 Chardonnay, Napa Valley $29.   86

Bright yellow-gold. Fresh aromas of ripe citrus with minimal oak influence. A crisp entry leads a medium-bodied palate with lemony flavors persisting through the finish. Well-balanced acidity. For youthful consumption.

1995 Cabernet Sauvignon, Calistoga Cuvée, Napa Valley $18.   87

Dark crimson appearance. Moderately full-bodied. Highly extracted. Moderately tannic. Black cherries, currants, oak spice. Decadent curranty, crushed black fruit flavors give this a strong fruity palate that is balanced by rounded soft tannins and spicy oak on the finish. Quite tight at present.

1996 Cabernet, Calistoga Cuvée, Napa Valley $25.   83

Bright violet red hue. Lighter, perfumed aromas do not show much weight. Rather simple and straightforward with a mildly reductive character.

1993 Cabernet Sauvignon, Montelena Estate, Napa Valley $40.   90

Saturated blood red. Moderately full-bodied. Highly extracted. Quite tannic. Currants, black cherries, black tea. Deep, ripe black fruit aromas follow through on the palate. Solid and dry through the finish. This will need some time to resolve the tannins.

Scale: Superlative (96-100), Exceptional (90-95), Highly Recommended (85-89), Recommended (80-84), Not Recommended (Under 80)

1994 Cabernet Sauvignon, Montelena Estate, Napa Valley $85.　　　92

Bright ruby-violet hue. Spicy oak accented aromas show fleshy dark fruit accents.
A firm entry leads a full-bodied palate with fleshy fruits and bright acids that give
this a well-gripped angular finish. Well structured, this will need a few more years.
Drink now or later.

Chateau Potelle

1995 Chardonnay, Central Coast $16.　　　84

Bright golden cast. Moderately full-bodied. Balanced acidity. Moderately extracted.
Minerals, vanilla. Subdued flavors play out on a soft and rounded palate. Features a
touch of viscosity tempered by acidity in the finish.

1996 Chardonnay, VGS, Mount Veeder, Napa Valley $38.　　　89

Bright gold. Rich buttery aromas with an oak accent. A smooth attack leads a
moderately full-bodied palate with a rounded mouthfeel and a soft finish. Fat
and generous with stylish touches. Drink now.

1996 Sauvignon Blanc, Napa Valley $11.　　　89

Very deep yellow-straw color. Moderately full-bodied. Full acidity. Moderately extracted.
Citrus, minerals, cream. Pleasantly aromatic, with a crisp fruit accent to the flavors that
follows through to a vibrant, snappy, intense finish.

1993 Cabernet Sauvignon, Mount Veeder, Napa Valley $29.　　　92

Deep ruby cast. Moderately full-bodied. Balanced acidity. Highly extracted. Moderately
tannic. Minerals, cassis. Tightly wound and firm, with reined-in flavors. Lean and angular
in the mouth, with a crisp yet weighty structure. Intense. Should open with time.

1994 Cabernet Sauvignon, VGS, Mount Veeder, Napa Valley $39.　　　89

Deep, saturated ruby red hue. Complex game, mineral, and red fruit aromas. A firm
attack leads to a moderately full-bodied palate with robust velvety tannins. Bursts with
flavor. Extremely lengthy concentrated finish. A well-balanced, graceful, and elegant
mountain wine. Drink now or later.

1995 Zinfandel, VGS, Mount Veeder, Napa Valley $35.　　　91

Solid red with purple highlights. Moderately full-bodied. Balanced acidity. Highly
extracted. Moderately oaked. Moderately tannic. Black fruits, chocolate, vanilla.
Rich, oak-forward aromas lead a thick mouthfeel of ripe briar fruits, with textured,
well-integrated tannins on the finish. Very stylish; expensive winemaking is evident.

Chateau Souverain

1997 Chardonnay, Sonoma County, Alexander Valley $13.　　　83

Pale straw cast. Medium-bodied. Balanced acidity. Moderately extracted. Minerals, cream.
Lean and crisp with a firm palate feel, finishing on an angular note.

1996 Chardonnay, Winemaker's Reserve, Russian River Valley $20.　　　87

Deep green-gold. Moderately full-bodied. Full acidity. Heavily oaked. Lemons, brown
spice. Youthful oak spice aromas lead a flavorsome, brashly oak-spiced mouthfeel of
generous fruit flavors with crisp acids. This should be better in a year or two.

1995 Cabernet Sauvignon, Alexander Valley $16.50.　　　89

Dark purple. Moderately full-bodied. Balanced acidity. Highly extracted. Mildly
oaked. Mildly tannic. Black fruits, chocolate. Tightly wound and dense, with restrained
aromatics. Silky mouthfeel. Lush, chewy tannins clamp down on the finish.

1994 Cabernet Sauvignon, Winemaker's Reserve, Alexander Valley $30.　　　90

Dark red with subtle purple highlights. Medium-bodied. Moderately extracted.
Mildly tannic. Earth, black fruits, oak. Rich oaky nose is confirmed on the palate.
Quite concentrated, with a viscous mouthfeel, though currently astringent through
the finish with dry oak character coming through.

1995 Cabernet Sauvignon, Winemaker's Reserve, Alexander Valley $35.　　**86**

Deep, opaque purple red hue. Intense anise, vanilla, and mineral aromas show a forward oak accent. A supple attack leads to a moderately full-bodied palate with firm tannins and shy acidity. Closes up toward the finish. May open with some age. Drink now or later.

1996 Merlot, Alexander Valley $16.50.　　**83**

Deep, dark ruby red. Subdued earth and black fruit aromas. A thick entry leads a full-bodied palate with chewy, velvety tannins and low levels of acidity. Big, fat, supple finish. Could use a bit more grip. Drink now.

Chateau St. Jean

1997 Chardonnay, Sonoma County $13.　　**84**

Bright green-straw cast. Medium-bodied. Balanced acidity. Moderately extracted. Minerals, cream, citrus. Aromatically reserved, with a rounded mouthfeel balanced by zesty acidity. A crisp, clean style.

1997 Chardonnay, Belle Terre Vineyard, Alexander Valley $24.　　**84**

Bright straw hue. Subdued mineral and citrus aromas. A lush entry is followed by a medium-bodied palate with lean acidity. The finish is juicy and mouthwatering, though somewhat austere. Drink now or later.

1996 Chardonnay, Durell Vineyard, Carneros $24.　　**88**

Deep yellow-gold. Moderately full-bodied. Balanced acidity. Highly extracted. Moderately oaked. Brown spice, citrus. A strong impression of oak and citrus on the nose follows through on the palate, with minerally leanness through the finish.

1996 Chardonnay, Robert Young Vineyard, Alexander Valley $24.　　**92**

Bright straw hue. Forward, nutty, yeasty aromas show a degree of complexity. A ripe entry leads a moderately full-bodied palate with balanced acidity. The finish is lush, rounded and harmonious. Drink now.

1996 Fumé Blanc, Sonoma County $9.　　**81**

1996 Fumé Blanc, La Petite Etoile Vineyard, Russian River Valley $13.　　**88**

Bright pale straw cast. Medium-bodied. Balanced acidity. Moderately extracted. Moderately oaked. Brown spice, toasted oak, citrus zest. Generous toasty nose leads a bright spicy palate with toasted oak flavors to the fore. Has enough stuffing, grip, and citrus flavors to make for an assertive style that will stand up to richer foods.

1994 Cabernet Sauvignon, Cinq Cépages, Sonoma County $24.　　**89**

Deep ruby cast. Moderately full-bodied. Balanced acidity. Moderately extracted. Mildly tannic. Chocolate, earth, cassis. Generous aromas have begun to reveal mature nuances. Supple yet firm in the mouth, with a velvety quality through the lengthy finish.

1995 Cabernet Sauvignon, Cinq Cépages, Sonoma County $24.　　**89**

Deep saturated ruby red hue. Deep, brooding black fruit and chocolate aromas show a judicious oak accent. A supple entry leads to a moderately full-bodied palate with grippy tannins and marked acidity that enlivens the fruit flavors and helps to carry the wine's weightiness. Firm, stuffed finish. Drink now or later.

1992 Cabernet Sauvignon, Reserve, Sonoma County $45.　　**94**

Deep ruby cast. Moderately full-bodied. Balanced acidity. Moderately extracted. Mildly oaked. Mildly tannic. Brown spices, red fruits, cedar. Generous aromas feature a well-integrated oak accent that merges with a firm core of fruit-centered flavors. Harmonious and supple, though well structured through the finish. Features fine grip and intensity.

1994 Cabernet Sauvignon, Reserve, Sonoma County $60.　　**88**

Very deep ruby red hue. Intense black fruit and vanilla aromas show a hefty oak influence. A thick entry leads to a full-bodied palate with chewy grainy tannins. Rich, robust finish. A heavyweight, beginning to dry out. Drink within five years.

1996 Merlot, Sonoma County $18.   **88**

Saturated dark red. Oak-accented, generous berry fruit aromas. A flavorful attack leads a moderately full-bodied palate with persistent velvety tannins. Stylish and impressively concentrated. Drink now or later. Can improve with more age.

1994 Merlot, Reserve, Sonoma County $55.   **97**

Deep blood red. Richly aromatic with plummy, oaky aromas. A supple attack leads a moderately full-bodied palate with smooth tannins. The finish is most elegant. Already well developed and showing complexity, a rich, seamless wine with extraordinary finesse.

1995 Pinot Noir, Durell Vineyard, Carneros $30.   **89**

Full ruby red. Medium-bodied. Highly extracted. Moderately oaked. Mildly tannic. Earthy, crisp berry aromas lead a weighty palate that has a solid feel and plenty of tart red fruit flavors lingering through an assertive oaky finish.

1996 Pinot Noir, Durell Vineyard, Carneros $30.   **81**

1995 Johannisberg Riesling, Belle Terre Vineyards,
Special Select Late Harvest, Alexander Valley $25/375 ml.   **92**

Deep copper hue. Exotic petrol and caramel aromas jump from the glass. A lean entry leads a complex, medium-bodied palate. Lots of sweetness balanced by firm acidity. Explodes with flavor. Intense and generous. Drink now.

Chateau Woltner

1996 Chardonnay, Howell Mountain, Napa Valley $13.   **81**

Chimére

1996 Pinot Blanc, Bien Nacido Vineyard, Santa Barbara County $13.   **82**

1996 Pinot Noir, Edna Valley $20.   **84**

Pale ruby-garnet cast. Medium-bodied. Full acidity. Moderately extracted. Heavily oaked. Mildly tannic. Brown spices, minerals. Quite fragrant, with a wood-dominated array of flavors. Rich though firm in the mouth, with an angular, earth-accented finish.

1996 Pinot Noir, Bien Nacido Vineyard-Mosby Vineyard,
Santa Barbara County $23.   **82**

Chimney Rock

1997 Fumé Blanc, Napa Valley $13.   **84**

Pale straw cast. Medium-bodied. Full acidity. Highly extracted. Citrus, apples, minerals. Clean, racy, and austere in style, with precise and well-defined flavors through a vibrant, focused finish.

1994 Cabernet Sauvignon, Napa Valley $26.   **88**

Medium reddish purple. Medium-bodied. Moderately extracted. Mildly tannic. Violets, cassis, plums. Generous floral, ripe aromas lead an open-knit, juicy black fruit palate. Very supple, soft tannins on the finish.

1996 Cabernet Sauvignon, Napa Valley $30.   **94**

Deep violet-purple hue. Richly fruit forward aromas with sweet tobacco notes. A ripe entry leads to a lush fruity, moderately full-bodied palate with a light tannic structure and juicy acids. Very hedonistic. Drink now.

1994 Cabernet Sauvignon, Reserve, Stags Leap District $50.   **90**

Bright purple-red. Medium-bodied. Moderately extracted. Mildly tannic. Dried herbs, cassis, cedar, brown spice. Spicy black fruit aromas. Lively and vibrant on the palate, with full spicy oak flavors on the finish. Tannins are soft and rounded.

1995 Cabernet Sauvignon, Reserve, Stags Leap District $50.   **94**

Bright red with purple highlights. Moderately full-bodied. Highly extracted. Moderately tannic. Black cherries, cedar, vanilla. Scented, perfumed aromas lead a cordial-like array of fruit flavors that linger through the finish, with oak spice coming through. Supple and bright, yet with a pure, minerally intensity.

1994 Elevage, Stags Leap District $40.   **90**

Full reddish purple. Medium-bodied. Highly extracted. Moderately tannic. Cassis, toasted oak, brown spice. Full toasty aromas. Concentrated berry flavors, with generous oaky spice and a dry, fine-grained tannic finish. Showing some solid structure.

1995 Elevage, Stags Leap District $50.   **90**

Brilliant ruby red. Moderately full-bodied. Highly extracted. Moderately tannic. Mint, cassis, raspberries. Soft, supple, and harmonious, with an exotically bright and pure fruit center accented by leafy notes and oak spice. Tannins show great finesse, making for very attractive drinking now.

Christopher Creek

1996 Syrah, Russian River Valley $18.   **83**

Medium purple, brilliant with a slight fade. Generous tart berry fruit flavors. Subtle wood tones. An acidic entry leads a medium-bodied palate. Crisply acidic, lean, and dry, with some bright fruit underneath. Moderate, robust tannins and a finish that has grip. Drinkable now, but can improve with age.

Cilurzo

1996 Petite Sirah, Proprietor's Reserve, Temecula $14.95.   **80**

1997 Petite Sirah, Reserve, Temecula $19.95.   **84**

Opaque purple. Moderately full-bodied. Highly extracted. Moderately tannic. Big, generous core of blueberry flavors. Rather soft, low acids do not quite match the dry, powdery tannins.

Cinnabar

1997 Chardonnay, Santa Clara County-Santa Barbara County $16.50.   **88**

Deep green-straw cast. Moderately full-bodied. Full acidity. Highly extracted. Mildly oaked. Vanilla, minerals, citrus. Forward aromas carry a generous oak accent. Firm, rich, and ripe in the mouth, with a crisp, minerally backbone.

1996 Chardonnay, Santa Cruz Mountains $23.   **89**

Pale straw hue. Medium-bodied. Balanced acidity. Moderately extracted. Moderately tannic. Apples, spice. Ripe, spicy aromas lead a bright, fruity mouthful of apple flavors, with a supple, spicy finish that lingers.

1994 Cabernet Sauvignon, Saratoga Vineyard, Santa Cruz Mountains $25.   **94**

Bright brick red. Medium-bodied. Moderately extracted. Mildly tannic. Minerals, red fruits, earth, brown spice. An attractive minerally, earthy nose leads a solid minerally palate with crisp fruity flavors and a lingering astringent finish. Fine, powdery tannins distinguish this wine. Austere in a sophisticated manner. Nice now, it should develop character with more age.

1995 Cabernet Sauvignon, Saratoga Vineyard, Santa Cruz Mountains $25.   **87**

Deep ruby red with a slight fade. Medium-bodied. Balanced acidity. Moderately extracted. Moderately oaked. Mildly tannic. Brown spices, red fruits, minerals. Pleasantly aromatic, with a forward accent of spicy oak. Supple and velvety in the mouth, with fine length and smooth tannins.

1996 Xcellence, California $16.50.   **81**

1997 Merlot, Central Coast $18.   **87**

Medium, bright brick red. Sound ripe, evolved fruity aromas with plenty of oak spice accents. A mellow attack leads a medium-bodied palate with gentle tannins. A clean finish shows vanilla notes. Structured for near-term drinking.

Claudia Springs

1996 Pinot Noir, Anderson Valley $16.   **90**

Deep ruby-garnet hue. Moderately light-bodied. Balanced acidity. Moderately extracted. Mildly tannic. Dried herbs, minerals. Shows an herbal edge throughout. Quite light in style, yet broadens out somewhat on the finish. Stylish.

1996 Pinot Noir, Reserve, Anderson Valley $18.   91

Deep ruby purple. Medium-bodied. Full acidity. Moderately extracted. Mildly oaked. Mildly tannic. Minerals, berries, spice. High-toned aromas lead a lean and crisp palate. Bright fruit flavors linger through a complex spicy finish.

1996 Zinfandel, Vessar Vineyard, Redwood Valley $18.   89

Bright purple-red. Medium-bodied. Balanced acidity. Moderately extracted. Moderately oaked. Mildly tannic. Raspberries, vanilla. Very pure red berry aromas follow through on the palate, with some ripe tannins on the finish. Drinking very nicely now. Fruity and hedonistic.

Cline

1996 Marsanne, Los Carneros $20.   91

Bright golden cast. Full-bodied. Full acidity. Highly extracted. Mildly oaked. Tropical fruits, yeast, citrus. Exotically aromatic, with a huge range of complex flavors on the palate. Extremely full and rich in the mouth, yet there is quite racy acidity, and a zesty, spicy finish.

1996 Carignane, Ancient Vines, Contra Costa County $18.   91

Red-purple hue with slight fade. Moderately full-bodied. Highly extracted. Moderately tannic. Crisp cherries, coal tar, herbs. An impressive medicinal note on the nose, with faintly herbal and crisp fruit aromas that follow on the palate. Balanced dry tannins. Very complex.

1996 Mourvedre, Ancient Vines, Contra Costa County $18.   93

Blackish ruby hue. Medium-bodied. Highly extracted. Moderately tannic. Oak spice, mint, cherries. Fine eucalyptus aromas with a big blast of oak spice. Rich, fully extracted flavors and a generous mouthfeel are impressive. This will improve with a few years in the cellar.

1996 Mourvedre, Small Berry Vinyard, Contra Costa $28.   95

Bright ruby hue with a purple cast. Medium-bodied. Moderately extracted. Moderately tannic. Toasted oak spice, black fruits. Classy oak-accented aromas follow through on the palate, with solidly extracted flavors and firm tannins giving this a cellarworthy structure.

1996 Syrah, Caneros $18.   86

Rich purple, limpid and brilliant, with a slight fade. Generous, pleasant bramble fruit and vanilla flavors. Generous wood tones. Smooth entry. Moderately full-bodied with crisp acidity. Moderate silky tannins. Soft, supple extraction with plenty of balancing fruit acids. Subtle rich finish. Drink now.

1996 Zinfandel, Ancient Vines, Contra Costa County $18.   89

Deep blackish purple. Moderately full-bodied. Full acidity. Moderately extracted. Moderately oaked. Mildly tannic. Briar fruits, coffee, chocolate. Spicy oak notes emerge on the nose, and translate well to the fruit-centered palate. Vibrant acidity makes for a zesty, uplifting finish.

1996 Zinfandel, Big Break Vineyard, Contra Costa County $24.   97

Deep blackish purple. Full-bodied. Full acidity. Moderately extracted. Moderately oaked. Mildly tannic. Mint, black fruits, vanilla. Quite aromatic, with a full-throttled, flavorful character on the palate. Shows great richness and depth through the vibrant finish. Excellent grip and intensity.

1996 Zinfandel, Bridgehead Vineyard, Contra Costa County $24.   91

Deep blackish ruby hue. Full-bodied. Balanced acidity. Moderately extracted. Mildly oaked. Mildly tannic. Eucalyptus, chocolate, minerals. Extremely aromatic, with a rich, flavorful palate feel. Big but well balanced, with solid acidity making for a clean finish. Intense and lengthy.

1996 Zinfandel, Live Oak Vineyard, Contra Costa County $24.   95

Deep blackish purple. Full-bodied. Full acidity. Highly extracted. Moderately oaked. Mildly tannic. Vanilla, black fruits, minerals. Quite aromatic, with a flavorful, racy character on the palate. Deep and extracted, with vibrant acidity through the finish. Well balanced and intense.

1995 Muscat Canelli, Sonoma Valley $14/375 ml.   **88**

Deep yellow-straw hue. Generous caramel, orange, and spice aromas. A soft entry leads a moderately full-bodied palate showing lots of sweetness. Rich and rounded, with an attractive nutty complexity. Drink now.

Cloninger

1997 Chardonnay, Monterey $13.   **81**

1994 Cabernet Sauvignon, Monterey $13.   **87**

Saturated blackish red. Medium-bodied. Highly extracted. Mildly tannic. Dried herbs, blackberries. Full aromas have deep fruit accents with herbaceous notes. A solid and angular palate, with concentrated black fruit flavors showing a distinct herbal character through the finish

1996 Cabernet Sauvignon, Quinn Vineyard, Carmel Valley $14.   **89**

Opaque violet red. Moderately full-bodied. Moderately extracted. Moderately oaked. Mildly tannic. Dill, menthol, black fruits. Strong oak-accented aromas lead a crisp mouthful of tart fruit flavors, with spice emerging on the finish. Tannins are marginal.

Clos du Bois

1997 Chardonnay, Sonoma County $14.   **83**

Bright straw hue. Subdued mineral aromas carry a subtle tropical fruit accent. A lean entry leads a medium-bodied palate with angular acidity. Crisp finish. Well structured but not overly flavorful. Drink now.

1997 Chardonnay, Alexander Valley $15.   **83**

Pale straw hue. Medium-bodied. Full acidity. Moderately extracted. Citrus, minerals, vanilla. Tart and lean in flavors, though it has a sense of citric brightness and a clean finish that make for a very user-friendly style.

1997 Chardonnay, Calcaire Vineyard, Alexander Valley $18.   **86**

Bright yellow-gold. Moderately full-bodied. Balanced acidity. Moderately extracted. Mildly oaked. Vanilla, butter, green apples. A smooth mouthfeel with vanilla notes through the finish. Has a nice acidic cut that maintains a sense of balance.

1996 Chardonnay, Flintwood Vineyard, Dry Creek Valley $18.   **84**

Pale straw cast. Moderately full-bodied. Full acidity. Moderately extracted. Mildly oaked. Toasted oak, citrus. Pronounced smoky, buttery aromas lead an angular, citrus zest palate with a glycerous, full mouthfeel. Restrained, mildly smoky oak influences.

1995 Cabernet Sauvignon, Sonoma County $15.   **81**

1996 Cabernet Sauvignon, Sonoma County $15.   **83**

Deep cherry red with a slight fade. Generous spice and vanilla aromas show a hefty oak influence. A supple attack leads to a medium-bodied palate with ripe tannins. Soft, rounded finish. Pleasant, but lacks a bit for grip and intensity. Drink now.

1995 Cabernet Sauvignon, Alexander Valley Selection, Alexander Valley $21.   **83**

Bright ruby cast. Medium-bodied. Balanced acidity. Moderately extracted. Mildly tannic. Dried herbs, red fruits, brown spices. Pleasantly aromatic, with a lively, lighter-styled mouthfeel. Juicy and angular through the finish.

1994 Cabernet Sauvignon, Briarcrest Vineyard, Alexander Valley $21.   **83**

Bright ruby red with a slight fade. Medium-bodied. Full acidity. Moderately extracted. Moderately tannic. Minerals, cassis. Lean, angular, and minerally, with a firm, linear quality. Picks up some mild astringency through the finish.

1995 Cabernet Sauvignon, Briarcrest Vineyard, Alexander Valley $30.   **83**

Deep garnet red hue. Subdued berry and mineral aromas. A soft entry leads to a moderately light-bodied palate with subtle tannins. Zesty acidity enlivens the palate. Clean, lean finish. Drink now.

1995 Cabernet Sauvignon, Winemaker's Reserve, Alexander Valley $50.   **88**

Deep garnet hue. Pronounced minty aromas carry an herbal overtone. A lush entry leads to a medium-bodied palate with lean tannins and zesty acidity. Flavorful, complex finish. Lighter in style, but well balanced and harmonious. Drink now.

1994 Marlstone Vineyard, Alexander Valley $25.   **84**

Bright ruby red with a slight fade. Medium-bodied. Full acidity. Moderately extracted. Mildly oaked. Mildly tannic. Brown spices, minerals. Aromatically reserved, with a lighter-styled palate feel. Bright acids lend an angular, juicy quality. Pleasant, angular finish.

1996 Merlot, Sonoma County $17.   **84**

Pale ruby red with a subtle fade. Aromas of herbs and red fruits. A subtle entry leads a light-bodied palate with gentle tannins and quick, clean finish. Drink now.

1995 Merlot, Selection, Alexander Valley $20.   **91**

Deep ruby hue to the rim with brilliant clarity. Medium-bodied. Full acidity. Moderately extracted. Moderately oaked. Mildly tannic. Chocolate, black fruits, sweet herbs. Quite rich in style, with a mouthfilling velvety palate feel. The tannins are very well integrated, and the use of oak has been judicious. Lengthy chewy mouthfeel.

1996 Merlot, Alexander Valley $20.   **86**

Bright ruby red to the rim. Subdued herb and red fruit aromas. A soft entry is followed by a moderately full-bodied, supple palate with low levels of acidity and chewy tannins. Soft, fleshy finish.

1995 Zinfandel, Sonoma County $14.   **83**

Bright ruby-garnet cast. Medium-bodied. Balanced acidity. Subtly extracted. Mildly oaked. Mildly tannic. Dried herbs, vanilla. Quite aromatic, with distinctive herbal overtones. Soft and lush on the palate, with a supple finish.

Clos du Lac

1997 Zinfandel Blanc, Sierra Foothills $8.   **82**

1996 Cabernet Franc, Sierra Foothills- Amador County $15.   **83**

Bright ruby purple. Medium-bodied. Full acidity. Moderately extracted. Moderately oaked. Moderately tannic. Minerals, cassis, chocolate. Generous aromas lead a ripe and flavorful palate that shows complexity. Toughens a bit on the finish, where the tannins rear up.

1997 Muscat Vin Doux Naturel, Sierra Foothills $12/375 ml.   **84**

Deep straw hue with a slight greenish cast. Moderately full-bodied. Full acidity. Highly extracted. Flowers, sweet herbs, citrus. Quite forward in aromatics, with a touch of heat. Full and round in the mouth, with a finish enlivened by buoyant acidity.

Clos du Val

1993 Cabernet Sauvignon, Napa Valley $24.   **87**

Dark ruby hue with purple highlights. Medium-bodied. Moderately extracted. Moderately tannic. Black currants, black cherry. Dusty black fruit aromas. Rich black fruit flavors on entry turn quite dry. Solid, dry, tealike, fine-grained tannins on the finish give this authority and structure.

1995 Cabernet Sauvignon, Napa Valley $24.   **87**

Bright violet hue. A soft entry leads a medium-bodied palate with juicy acids and a lighter fruit-centered palate. Finishes quickly and cleanly. Drink now.

1993 Cabernet Sauvignon, Reserve, Napa Valley $50.   **91**

Deep ruby hue with purple highlights. Medium-bodied. Highly extracted. Mildly tannic. Chocolate, brown spice, black fruits. Rich black fruit aromas. Smooth, textured mouthfeel shows great elegance. Clean lengthy finish shows persistent fruity nuances. Fine balance, with complex flavors persisting.

1994 Cabernet Sauvignon, Reserve, Napa Valley $53. 92

Deep ruby hue with a slight purple cast. Moderately full-bodied. Full acidity. Highly extracted. Moderately oaked. Moderately tannic. Red fruits, vanilla, minerals. Generous aromas lead a firm and intense palate feel. Bright and juicy, with a sense of angularity. Focused and well balanced. Should age well.

1996 Merlot, Napa Valley $28. 84

Medium ruby red with a subtle fade. Pleasant herbal aromas. Moderately full-bodied with a supple attack and a rich texture giving way to firm tannins that grip the finish. Drink now or later. Can improve with more age.

1995 Pinot Noir, Carneros $20. 85

Cherry red with a pinkish tinge. Medium-bodied. Moderately extracted. Moderately oaked. Moderately tannic. Toasty, tart aromas lead tart red cherry flavors. Plenty of tart acids and astringent tannin through the finish. Quite tight and angular now, it should soften with a little time.

1995 Zinfandel, California $15. 85

Bright ruby-garnet cast. Medium-bodied. Balanced acidity. Moderately extracted. Mildly tannic. Tea, minerals. An interesting melange of earthy aromas plays out well on the palate, which is firm and well structured, in a rather reserved style. Fine grip and intensity; a Claret style.

Clos La Chance

1997 Chardonnay, Napa Valley $17. 91

Medium yellow-gold. Aromatically rich with buttery, smoky character and lots of ripe fruit. A rich entry leads a full-bodied palate with ripe fruit flavors and creamy texture. Lush through the finish.

1997 Chardonnay, Santa Cruz Mountains $19. 83

Bright straw hue. Unusual wool and earth aromas. A crisp entry leads a medium-bodied palate with vibrant acidity. Lean finish. Drink now.

1996 Chardonnay, Vintner's Reserve, Santa Cruz Mountains $27. 84

Brilliant yellow-straw hue. Intense buttery aromas. A rich entry leads a moderately full-bodied palate with creamy acidity. Generous lactic finish. Drink now.

1994 Cabernet Sauvignon, Santa Cruz Mountains $22. 90

Bright cherry red. Medium-bodied. Moderately extracted. Mildly tannic. Mint, toasted oak, cranberry. Pronounced minty, vanilla-kissed aromas. Lively red fruit flavors marry with assertive oak in a lightly framed palate showing clean astringency through the finish.

1995 Cabernet Sauvignon, Santa Cruz Mountains $21. 86

Bright ruby red with a slight fade. Medium-bodied. Balanced acidity. Moderately extracted. Moderately oaked. Mildly tannic. Spice, minerals, sweet herbs. Quite aromatic, showing a hefty oak accent. Light in the mouth, with a lean and angular finish.

1996 Cabernet Sauvignon, Santa Cruz Mountains $22. 86

Bright cherry garnet hue. Forward dried herb and brown spice aromas show a judicious oak accent. A lush entry leads to a moderately full-bodied palate with velvety tannins and a clean acidic cut. Ripe rounded finish.

1996 Merlot, Central Coast $18. 81

1996 Pinot Noir, Santa Cruz Mountains $24. 84

Bright ruby-garnet cast. Medium-bodied. Balanced acidity. Moderately extracted. Moderately oaked. Mildly tannic. Sandalwood, dill pickle. Generous aromas feature an exotic spicy quality. Lush and seamless in the mouth with a silky palate feel. The finish is lengthy and flavorful.

Scale: Superlative (96-100), Exceptional (90-95), Highly Recommended (85-89), Recommended (80-84), Not Recommended (Under 80)

64

Clos Pegase

1995 Cabernet Sauvignon, Napa Valley $22.99.　　　　89

Deep ruby hue. Forward leather, berry, and mineral aromas. A lush entry leads to a moderately full-bodied palate with rich chewy tannins. Supple and persistent through the finish with classic dusty cherry flavors. Elegant but focused. Drink now or later.

1994 Cabernet Sauvignon, Hommage Reserve, Napa Valley $40.　　　93

Deep cherry red. Medium-bodied. Moderately extracted. Mildly tannic. Toasted oak, concentrated red berries. Elegant oaky aromas are well integrated, with some floral accents. Bright, plush fruit flavors show refinement and suppleness. Very attractive now, it is hard to see this tasting better with extended aging.

B.R. Cohn

1994 Cabernet Sauvignon, Olive Hill Vineyard, Sonoma Valley $32.　　　92

Deep reddish purple. Medium-bodied. Highly extracted. Moderately tannic. Cassis, vanilla, brown spice. Youthful, vibrant aromas that show vanilla and cassis notes. The solid, tightly wound palate has good depth of flavors and dense tannins that make this backward at present.

1995 Cabernet Sauvignon, Olive Hill Vineyard, Sonoma Valley $75.　　　94

Dark blood red. Moderately full-bodied. Highly extracted. Moderately tannic. Ripe black fruits. Rich cassis aromas follow through on a supple palate, with voluptuous flavors and impressive length. Very classic.

Concannon

1997 Chardonnay, Selected Vineyard, Central Coast $10.95.　　　86

Pale yellow-straw hue. Mildly aromatic with apricot character. A smooth attack leads a medium-light body with subtle oak flavors. Clean, rather short finish. Very user friendly.

1996 Chardonnay, Reserve, Livermore Valley $18.95.　　　83

Bright medium gold. Moderately aromatic with citrus and oak accents. A crisp entry leads a medium-bodied palate with straightforward citrus flavors. The persistent finish has full spicy oak notes. Drink now.

1997 Gewürztraminer, Limited Bottling, Arroyo Seco-Monterey $9.95.　　　83

Deep old-gold hue. Fat, overripe melon aromas show a slight herbal accent. A rich entry leads an oily, moderately full-bodied palate. Lean through the finish. Drink now.

1996 Marsanne, Santa Clara Valley $13.95.　　　84

Deep golden cast. Moderately full-bodied. Full acidity. Highly extracted. Oranges, blanched almonds, cream. Quite ripe aromatically. The entry is viscous, but it turns rather lean in the mouth with a sense of angularity and some mild bitterness to the finish.

1996 Assemblage White Reserve, Livermore Valley $12.95.　　　83

Bright straw cast. Moderately full-bodied. Balanced acidity. Moderately extracted. Citrus, toast, butter. Pleasantly aromatic, with a lush presence on the palate. Zesty acidity lends a counterpoint to the buttery finish.

1997 Orange Muscat, Limited Bottling, Yolo County $10.95.　　　84

Brilliant yellow-straw hue. Generous pear and ripe tropical fruit aromas jump from the glass. A lush entry leads a medium-bodied palate with moderate sweetness and zesty acidity. Rich, flavorful finish. Drink now.

1997 Johannisberg Riesling, Arroyo Seco-Monterey $9.95.　　　85

Bright yellow-gold. Distinctive minerally, mildly honeyed aromas seem to show a touch of botrytis. A heavy attack leads a moderately full-bodied palate with concentrated flavors and low acids. Mildly bitter notes through the finish. Interesting. Drink now.

1996 Sauvignon Blanc, Livermore Valley $7.95.　　　82

1996 Cabernet Sauvignon, Selected Vineyard, Central Coast $11.45. **82**

1995 Cabernet Sauvignon, Reserve, Livermore Valley $19.95. **83**

Bright cherry red with a garnet rim. Forward mineral, herb, and red fruit aromas. A lush entry leads to a medium-bodied palate with grippy tannins. Clipped, angular finish. Drink now.

1994 Assemblage Red Reserve, Central Coast $15.95. **86**

Bright ruby red. Medium-bodied. Moderately extracted. Mildly tannic. Red berries, dried herbs, mild toasted oak. Ripe berry aromas have subtle toasty hints with herbaceous overtones. Open-knit, lively flavors make for an accessible style with a clean finish. Drink now.

1995 Assemblage Red Reserve, Livermore Valley $18.95. **81**

1996 Mourvedre, Contra Costa County $16.95. **84**

Ruby red, with a pale cast. Moderately extracted. Mildly tannic. Medium-bodied. Ripe fruits. Cooked, spicy, and jammy. Rather weak in acids, with dry, powdery tannins on the finish. The soft character suggests near-term drinking.

1996 Petite Sirah, Selected Vineyard, California $11.45. **83**

Opaque purple-blue color. Full-bodied. Highly extracted. Quite tannic. Well-extracted flavors with dark, fleshy fruit character following through on the finish. Dry, thick tannins linger. Monolithic and intense.

1995 Petite Sirah, Reserve Vineyard, Central Coast $22.95. **84**

Bright purple. Moderately full-bodied. Balanced acidity. Moderately extracted. Complex aromas show herbal, medicinal, briar fruit aromas. Lush, textured, and well proportioned, with tannins not drying the finish excessively.

1995 Zinfandel, Late Harvest, Limited Bottling, Livermore Valley $16.95. **86**

Bright ruby cast. Medium-bodied. Full acidity. Moderately extracted. Mildly tannic. Dried herbs, red fruits. Fairly aromatic, with bright herbal overtones. Lean and crisp, with a hint of sweetness.

Conn Creek

1994 Cabernet Sauvignon, Limited Release, Napa Valley $22. **82**

1994 Anthology, Napa Valley $44. **88**

Deep red-violet. Moderately full-bodied. Highly extracted. Moderately tannic. Cassis, black fruits, brown spice. Fleshy, ripe fruit aromas follow through on a silky, textured, and rounded palate, with oak spice and velvety tannins defining the finish.

1995 Anthology, Napa Valley $44. **92**

Deep ruby hue. Generous and exceptionally attractive vanilla and red fruit aromas carry a big sweet oak accent. A lush entrance leads to a moderately full-bodied palate that bursts with ripe fruit flavors. Rich velvety tannins and a juicy note of acidity provide support. Lengthy, attractive finish. Well balanced and eminently drinkable but structured to hold. Drink now or later.

Cook's

NV Spumante, American $4.29. **82**

Cooper-Garrod

1996 Chardonnay, Santa Cruz Mountains $18. **80**

1996 Cabernet Franc, Santa Cruz Mountains $18. **81**

1994 Cabernet Sauvignon, Santa Cruz Mountains $25. **90**

Bright crimson red with purple highlights. Medium-bodied. Moderately extracted. Mildly tannic. Plums, fresh herbs, earth. Exotic herbal-accented nose leads a fleshy, plummy palate with a very forward juicy character that makes this inviting to drink now.

Scale: Superlative (96-100), Exceptional (90-95), Highly Recommended (85-89), Recommended (80-84), Not Recommended (Under 80)

66

1995 Cabernet Sauvignon, Santa Cruz Mountains $28. **93**

Deep ruby purple. Moderately full-bodied. Balanced acidity. Moderately extracted. Mildly tannic. Cassis, black fruits, minerals. Extraordinarily aromatic, showing a pure, fruit-centered flavor profile. Intense and lively, with fine length and grip. Harmony and elegance dominate.

1995 Cabernet Sauvignon, Proprietor's Reserve, Santa Cruz Mountains $35. **89**

Deep ruby purple. Moderately full-bodied. Balanced acidity. Moderately extracted. Mildly tannic. Red fruits, minerals. Intense and pure, with fruit-centered flavors and very little oak influence. Racy and lean, with fine intensity and grip.

Corbett Canyon

1997 Chardonnay, Reserve, Santa Barbara County $10. **82**

1996 Sauvignon Blanc, Reserve, California $9. **84**

Pale golden yellow. Medium-bodied. Balanced acidity. Moderately extracted. Mildly oaked. Lime, smoke, minerals. Aromatic buttery aromas. A brisk attack, with citrus flavors and a buttery malolactic note. Rather soft through the finish; it could use more grip and persistence.

1995 Cabernet Sauvignon, Reserve, Sonoma County $10. **85**

Medium ruby-red hue. Moderately aromatic with dusty, soft cherry accents. A supple attack leads a medium-bodied palate with bright, soft fruity flavors showing development. Tannins are evolved and supple. Drink now.

Corison

1994 Cabernet Sauvignon, Napa Valley $35. **89**

Bright reddish purple. Medium-bodied. Highly extracted. Moderately tannic. Cherries, eucalyptus, lead pencil. Full, complex aromas lead a crisp, astringent, full-flavored palate, with firm dry tannins on the finish. This has good focus and grip.

Cornerstone

1993 Cabernet Sauvignon, Beatty Ranch, Howell Mountain $32. **91**

Deep blackish ruby color. Moderately full-bodied. Highly extracted. Moderately tannic. Cassis, plums, loam, toasted oak. A fine earthiness runs through the palate and is well supported by concentrated toasty black fruit flavors that persist through the finish. This has great length and balance. Good now, though cellaring can only help. Huge but elegant.

Cosentino

1997 Chardonnay, Napa Valley $18. **87**

Bright straw cast. Moderately full-bodied. Full acidity. Highly extracted. River pebbles, tropical fruits, minerals. Focused aromatics have a pure fruit-driven quality throughout. Lean and intense through the zesty finish. Excellent grip and focus.

1997 Chardonnay, "The Sculptor" Reserve, Napa Valley $30. **89**

Pale straw cast. Moderately full-bodied. Full acidity. Moderately extracted. Mildly oaked. Toast, minerals. Aromatically reserved, with an understated toasty accent. A generous mouthfeel reveals subtle flavors. Finishes with crisp, persistent fruit flavors.

1996 Cabernet Franc, Napa Valley $25. **88**

Bright ruby cast. Medium-bodied. Balanced acidity. Moderately extracted. Heavily oaked. Mildly tannic. Spice, dill pickle, minerals. Oak-driven aromatics lead a lean and precise palate feel. Lengthy and flavorful through the finish. Weighty, yet well balanced.

1995 Cabernet Sauvignon, Napa Valley $18. **85**

Bright ruby hue with subtle purple highlights. Medium-bodied. Moderately extracted. Moderately tannic. Cassis, cedar, tobacco. Soft black currant and cedar aromas follow through very nicely on the palate, with texture and a sense of elegance imparted by the velvety tannins. Delicious ripe varietal expression.

1996 Cabernet Sauvignon, Napa Valley $20. **84**
Bright ruby red. Medium-bodied. Moderately extracted. Mildly tannic. Vanilla, red berries, minerals. A hint of herbal quality on the nose and palate. Lively and straightforward, for current drinking.

1994 Cabernet Sauvignon, Reserve, Napa Valley $40. **90**
Bright cherry red. Medium-bodied. Moderately extracted. Moderately tannic. Toasted oak, vanilla, red berries. Rich, sweet oak-accented aromas follow through on the palate, with juicy berry flavors giving way to a firm spicy oak finish. Persistent toasty note.

1995 Cabernet Sauvignon, Reserve, Napa Valley $40. **88**
Bright cherry red. Medium-bodied. Moderately extracted. Mildly tannic. Vanilla, cedar, red fruits. Oak-scented aromas lead a bright, juicy palate, with mildly chunky tannins playing on the finish. A firm, oaky style.

1994 The Poet Meritage, Napa Valley $30. **90**
Dark ruby red. Medium-bodied. Highly extracted. Moderately tannic. Cassis, black fruits, subtle spice, eucalyptus. Fleshy, ripe aromas lead a smooth and textured palate that shows generous Cabernet fruit flavors and well-integrated soft tannins throughout. Plush, very harmonious, and forward drinking. Nice now.

1995 The Poet Meritage, Napa Valley $38. **89**
Deep ruby hue with a pale rim. Moderately full-bodied. Highly extracted. Moderately tannic. Cedar, vanilla, cassis. Full oaky aromas lead a fleshy mouthful of ripe fruit flavors, with layers of silky tannins and oak spice through the finish. Very hedonistic and textured throughout.

1995 M. Coz Meritage, Napa Valley $75. **94**
Dark violet red. Medium-bodied. Highly extracted. Moderately tannic. Toasted oak, brown spice, cassis. Scented, oak-driven aromas have complementary plush dark fruit flavors, with velvety tannins helping make this accessible. Has a fine mineral note through the finish. Very textured and stylish.

1996 Merlot, Reserve, Napa Valley $34. **92**
Deep ruby-violet red with a subtle fade. Raspberry, herbal, and vanilla aromas. Moderately full-bodied. Lush and fruity on the attack, with a moderately full body, and bright acids lifting the lush tannins through the finish. Elegant and complex. Drink now.

1996 Merlot, Oakville, Napa Valley $60. **90**
Bright cherry red. Very aromatic with outstandingly complex oaky accents and raspberry and violet scents. Moderately full-bodied with a big complement of exotic cherry flavors that conclude with a lingering, flavorful oak-accented finish. Drink now.

1996 Pinot Noir, Carneros $30. **86**
Bright purple-tinged pale red. Medium-bodied. Moderately extracted. Heavily oaked. Mildly tannic. Plenty of cedar and vanilla aromas lead a palate of light, delicate red fruit flavors, with a nice mouthfeel. Vanilla oak flavors take over on the finish.

1996 Pinot Noir, Russian River Valley $50. **89**
Bright cherry red with purple highlights. Medium-bodied. Moderately extracted. Moderately oaked. Mildly tannic. Floral, vanilla, and cedar aromas lead a bright, juicy palate, with concentrated raspberry and cherry flavors on the midpalate and plenty of vanilla oak dominating the finish. Somewhat youthful and angular.

1996 Zinfandel, The Zin, California $22. **81**

Costa de Oro
1996 Chardonnay, Gold Coast Vineyards, Santa Maria Valley $18. **82**
1997 Chardonnay, Gold Coast Vineyards, Santa Maria Valley $18. **81**

Cottonwood Canyon
1994 Chardonnay, Santa Barbara County $24. **82**

1994 Chardonnay, Barrel Select, Santa Barbara County $29.   **86**

Bright yellow-gold. Moderately full-bodied. Balanced acidity. Moderately extracted. Heavily oaked. The color and aroma hint at maderization. Turns extremely woody on the palate, with a wave of sweet coconut flavors.

1994 Cabernet Sauvignon, Central Coast $24.50.   **90**

Pale ruby red. Moderately light-bodied. Moderately extracted. Mildly tannic. Red berries, chocolate, brown spice. High-toned oak-accented aromas show peppery notes. Elegant berry flavors on entry give way to a toasty, chocolatey finish. Well balanced and drinking well now. Subtlety and complexity evident.

1994 Synergy Classic, Central Coast $28.   **84**

Full garnet red. Medium-bodied. Moderately extracted. Mildly tannic. Brown spice, licorice. Mature, spicy aromas lead a ripe, soft palate with a mildly stewed-fruit flavor profile. Finishes with a minerally note. Not for further cellaring.

1995 Merlot, Central Coast $26.   **88**

Dark ruby with a garnet cast. Moderately light-bodied. Full acidity. Moderately extracted. Heavily oaked. Mildly tannic. Brown spices, cherries, minerals. Lighter in style and oak driven, this wine is both aromatic and flavorful. Relatively austere on the palate, with fine structural acidity and good length.

Coturri

1996 Zinfandel, Sonoma Mountain $21.   **84**

Deep blackish ruby color. Full-bodied. Balanced acidity. Moderately extracted. Mildly oaked. Mildly tannic. Chocolate, overripe fruits. Features a Port-like aromatic note, and carries the overripe theme through the palate. Thick and dense in the mouth, with an overtone of sweetness. Interesting, but not for everyone.

1996 Zinfandel, Freiberg Vineyards, Sonoma Valley $23.   **84**

Deep blackish purple. Full-bodied. Balanced acidity. Highly extracted. Moderately tannic. Dates, chocolate, earth. Deeply aromatic, with slight notes of overripeness and dark, brooding flavors. Thick and viscous in the mouth, showing an overtone of sweetness. Finishes with some chunky tannins.

1996 Zinfandel, P. Coturri Family Vineyards, Sonoma Valley $23.   **85**

Opaque blackish ruby hue. Moderately full-bodied. Balanced acidity. Highly extracted. Moderately tannic. Chocolate, black fruits. Aromatic, with deep, chocolatey flavors. Full, ripe, and thick, with chunky tannins through the finish. A mouthful.

Robert Craig

1994 Affinity, Napa Valley $33.   **90**

Saturated opaque reddish purple. Medium-bodied. Moderately extracted. Moderately tannic. Plums, black tea, licorice. Generous plummy aromas lead a full-flavored palate with weight and depth of flavors. Has a rounded mouthfeel, with some solidity to the tannins on the finish.

1995 Affinity, Napa Valley $35.   **89**

Saturated red-purple. Medium-bodied. Moderately extracted. Mildly tannic. Violets, chocolate, black fruits. Vibrant, fruity aromas lead a bright, juicy entry that gives way to slight tannins, with a mild, drying quality. A lighter-framed wine with firm structural elements that will allow it to age.

Creston

1995 Merlot, Paso Robles $16.   **82**

1995 Zinfandel, Paso Robles $13.   **83**

Bright ruby cast. Medium-bodied. Full acidity. Moderately extracted. Mildly tannic. Briar fruits. Quite aromatic, featuring a fruit-centered quality. Lighter in the mouth, with juicy acidity making for a vibrant finish.

Crichton Hall

1996 Chardonnay, Napa Valley $22.   88
Bright yellow-gold. Medium-bodied. Balanced acidity. Moderately extracted. Mildly oaked. Ripe apples, citrus, butter. Rich, generous aromas of ripe fruits follow through on the palate, with a smooth, buttery texture and full and broad flavors. Well balanced and flavorful.

1996 Merlot, Napa Valley $26.   86
Bright ruby red. Herbal, minerally aromas. Medium-bodied with a lean attack and crisp black fruit flavors that finish in a subtle manner. Drink now.

1995 Pinot Noir, Napa Valley $25.   87
Pale pink-tinged red. Moderately light-bodied. Moderately extracted. Moderately oaked. Mildly tannic. Sweet, florally accented fruit aromas. Delicate strawberry and raspberry flavors unfold on the palate, with a dry oak-accented finish.

Cronin

1996 Chardonnay, Stuhlmuller Vineyard, Alexander Valley $18.   83
Bright yellow-straw hue. Unusual blanched almond and mineral aromas. A lush entry is followed by a medium-bodied palate with lively bright acidity and a crisp, intense finish. Drink now.

Curtis

1997 Syrah Rosé, Santa Ynez Valley $8.   88
Pale cherry red. Intense briar fruit and herb aromas jump from the glass. A fat entry leads a weighty, moderately full-bodied palate with rounded acidity. A full, rich, flavorful Rosé for the table. Drink now.

1997 Heritage, Old Vines Red, California $10.   85
Bright purple-red hue to the rim. Generous red fruit, sweet herb, and mineral aromas. A crisp attack leads a medium-bodied palate that shows drying, astringent tannins. Clipped, snappy finish. Youthful and compact. Drink now or later. Can improve with more age.

1996 Syrah, Ambassador's Vineyard, Santa Ynez Valley $18.   87
Medium cherry red, limpid, with a slight fade. Mild, sound herb, jammy black fruit, and olive flavors. Subtle wood tones. Soft entry. Medium-bodied. Soft, jammy fruit flavors dissipate quickly on a subtle, short finish. Delicate Rhone-like qualities. Drink now.

Cuvaison

1997 Chardonnay, Carneros $NA.   89
Rich straw hue. Generous butter, citrus, and yeast aromas. A firm entry leads a moderately full-bodied palate. Features deep citrusy flavors with plenty of vanilla. Flashy, with a touch of phenolic dryness through the finish. Drink now.

1996 Chardonnay, Reserve, Napa Valley $NA.   92
Bright yellow-gold. Generous leesy, ripe citrus, and roasted nut aromas. A soft entry leads a full-bodied palate, with balanced acidity. Nutty, ripe, and rich. A blowsy style, but well balanced. Drink now.

1994 Cabernet Sauvignon, Napa Valley $24.99.   93
Dark reddish purple. Moderately full-bodied. Highly extracted. Moderately tannic. Cassis, currant, anise. Rich, concentrated black fruit flavors have supple integrated tannins giving this a rich center. Young and tight at present, though with plenty of attractive qualities.

1995 Cabernet Sauvignon, Napa Valley $NA.   88
Dark, saturated ruby purple. Generous cassis and oak spice aromas. A firm entry leads a moderately full-bodied palate, with grainy tannins. Classic, varietal, and well gripped. Should age well. Mid-term cellar candidate (3–6 years).

1996 Merlot, Carneros, Napa Valley $NA.   **90**

Deep ruby red with a slight fade. Vanilla and ripe black fruit aromas show a pleasant
wood accent. A firm entry leads a moderately full-bodied palate, with drying, well-
gripped tannins. Good structure and fine, uplifting acidity. Well fruited and flavorful
through the finish. Drink now or later.

1995 Pinot Noir, Eris, Carneros $18.99.   **87**

Dark red. Medium-bodied. Moderately extracted. Moderately oaked. Mildly tannic.
Toasted oak aromas with bramble fruit accents. On the palate, crisp black fruit flavors
with a mineral edge and crisp acids. Spicy, toasty finish with some subtle gamey notes.

1996 Pinot Noir, Eris, Carneros $20.   **82**

Dalla Valle

1993 Cabernet Sauvignon, Napa Valley $40.   **90**

Saturated garnet-cherry red. Moderately full-bodied. Highly extracted. Moderately
tannic. Plums, cassis, mineral. The solid, full-flavored palate has ripe black fruit flavors
and generous minerally complexity that linger through the finish. This has the structure
to cellar, though it is nice now.

Dark Star

1996 Cabernet Sauvignon, Paso Robles $19.   **88**

Very deep saturated ruby cast. Full-bodied. Balanced acidity. Highly extracted. Moderately oaked. Moderately tannic. Black fruits, minerals, spice. Aromatically reserved, with a
firm, concentrated, intense palate feel. Tannins clamp down on the finish.

1996 Ricordati, Paso Robles $20.   **87**

Bright violet-red. Medium-bodied. Moderately extracted. Mildly tannic. Black fruits, mint,
cedar. Mildly toasty, ripe, fleshy aromas follow through on the palate, with bright, spicy
fruit flavors and soft tannins on the finish. A very accessible style.

Davis Bynum

1994 Cabernet Sauvignon, Hedin Vineyard, Russian River Valley $24.   **87**

Bright ruby purple. Moderately full-bodied. Full acidity. Moderately extracted. Mildly
tannic. Minerals, lead pencil, red fruits. Generous aromas are complex and unusual.
Firm and angular in the mouth, with a bright, linear quality and vibrant acidity.

1994 Eclipse, Sonoma County $28.   **87**

Bright ruby purple. Full-bodied. Full acidity. Highly extracted. Mildly tannic. Lead pencil,
minerals, red fruits. Unusual aromas are complex and generous. Firm and angular in the
mouth, with a clean, linear quality. Solid acidity says this is a good match for foods.

1995 Merlot, Laureles Estate Vineyard, Russian River Valley $24.   **89**

Saturated dark violet red. Oaky, black raspberry, lead pencil aromas. A firm entry leads a
full-bodied palate with plentiful chewy dry tannins and bright acidity marking the finish.
Impressive and stylish with a hugely wrought, thickly textured mouthfeel, and a snappy,
high-toned finish. Drink within 5 years.

1995 Pinot Noir, Limited Edition, Russian River Valley $28.   **91**

Full, dark cherry red. Medium-bodied. Highly extracted. Moderately oaked. Mildly
tannic. Dried herbs, leather, and black cherries on the nose lead a complex, flavorsome
palate, with tobacco and cedar notes on the long finish. Dry, powdery tannins give some
grip on the finish.

1996 Pinot Noir Limited Edition, Limited Edition,
Russian River Valley $28.   **86**

Bright ruby cast. Moderately full-bodied. Full acidity. Highly extracted. Mildly oaked.
Moderately tannic. Red fruits, minerals. Dark, minerally aromas lead a firm and extracted
mouthfeel. Angular and intense through the finish.

De Loach

1993 Cabernet Sauvignon, OFS, Russian River Valley $25.   **92**

Bright, rich cherry red. Medium-bodied. Moderately extracted. Mildly tannic. Cassis, red fruits, dried herbs. Bright primary fruit aromas with subtle herbal notes. Harmonious and well integrated, with lots of bright red berry flavors expanding through the midpalate. Very attractive, giving lots of pleasure now.

1994 Cabernet Sauvignon, OFS, Russian River Valley $27.50.   **90**

Bright reddish purple. Medium-bodied. Highly extracted. Mildly tannic. Black tea, plums, brown spice. Generous spicy, curranty aromas lead rich, ripe flavors that expand on the silky palate and persist through a spicy finish. Very supple. Nice now, though a few years will only improve it.

1997 Pinot Noir, OFS, Russian River Valley $30.   **81**

1996 Zinfandel, Russian River Valley $18.   **86**

Deep blackish purple. Moderately full-bodied. Balanced acidity. Moderately extracted. Mildly oaked. Mildly tannic. Minerals, black fruits. Rather reserved aromatically, with a firm, taut, highly structured palate feel. Lean and angular through the finish. Could use a bit more time.

1996 Zinfandel, Barbieri Ranch, Russian River Valley $20.   **94**

Deep blackish purple. Moderately full-bodied. Balanced acidity. Moderately extracted. Moderately oaked. Mildly tannic. Black fruits, vanilla. Aromatic and flavorful, with a lush, velvety mouthfeel. Quite hedonistic, with velvety tannins through the finish.

1996 Zinfandel, Gambogi Ranch, Russian River Valley $20.   **84**

Bright blackish purple. Moderately full-bodied. Balanced acidity. Moderately extracted. Moderately oaked. Mildly tannic. Earth, briar fruits. Quite aromatic, with a distinctive earthy edge. Lush and velvety in the mouth, with a supple finish.

1996 Zinfandel, Papera Ranch, Russian River Valley $20.   **89**

Deep blackish purple. Moderately full-bodied. Balanced acidity. Moderately extracted. Moderately oaked. Mildly tannic. Black fruits, vanilla. Quite aromatic, with a fruit-centered palate that features harmonious oak overtones throughout. Lush, velvety, and supple, with a deep, intense finish.

1996 Zinfandel, Pelletti Ranch, Russian River Valley $20.   **86**

Bright blackish purple. Moderately full-bodied. Balanced acidity. Highly extracted. Mildly oaked. Moderately tannic. Minerals, black fruits. Rather reserved aromatically, with a firm, well-structured palate feel. Deeply flavored and intense, with tannins that bite down on the finish.

1996 Zinfandel, Saitone Ranch, Russian River Valley $20.   **93**

Deep blackish purple. Full-bodied. Full acidity. Highly extracted. Moderately oaked. Moderately tannic. Earth, chocolate, black fruits. Quite aromatic, with distinctive minerally overtones. Firm, deep, and focused, with an angular, juicy finish. Could use a bit more time to resolve itself.

1996 Zinfandel, OFS, Russian River Valley $27.50.   **93**

Deep blackish purple. Moderately full-bodied. Balanced acidity. Moderately extracted. Moderately oaked. Mildly tannic. Vanilla, black fruits. Quite aromatic, with a pleasant interplay between fruit and wood nuances. Lush and supple in the mouth, with an exceptionally lengthy finish.

de Lorimier

1996 Chardonnay, Alexander Valley $16.   **86**

Medium straw hue. Moderately full-bodied. Full acidity. Mildly oaked. Vanilla, green apples. Rich and zesty, with angular acids and broad flavors that give it a solid character. The finish is austere.

Scale: Superlative (96-100), Exceptional (90-95), Highly Recommended (85-89), Recommended (80-84), Not Recommended (Under 80)

72

1996 Spectrum, Alexander Valley $14.   84

Full golden hue. Medium-bodied. Low acidity. Moderately extracted. White peach, citrus.
Floral aromas reveal a soft, rounded palate with much warmth on the finish. With a
touch more acidity this would have perfect balance.

1994 Mosaic Meritage, Alexander Valley $20.   90

Dark crimson red. Medium-bodied. Moderately extracted. Moderately tannic. Pepper,
black fruits, plums, toasted oak. Rich plummy flavors unfold on the palate. The finish is
bright and peppery. Fine acids give this a lively character and keep the finish fresh.

1995 Mosaic Meritage, Alexander Valley $24.   89

Deep ruby purple. Full-bodied. Balanced acidity. Highly extracted. Mildly oaked.
Moderately tannic. Minerals, black fruits. Aromatically reserved, with a firm and tightly
wound palate feel. Aggressive tannins bite down on the finish.

1996 Merlot, Alexander Valley $18.   89

Bright, opulent purple-red to the rim. Forward red fruit and vanilla aromas show a
judicious oak accent. A generous, supple attack leads a moderately full-bodied palate
with firm tannins. Flavorful and extremely lengthy through the finish. Well balanced
and lush. Drink now.

De Rose

1997 Chardonnay, Cienega Valley $13.99.   81

1996 Viognier, Cienega Valley $15/375 ml.   89

Bright golden cast. Moderately full-bodied. Balanced acidity. Moderately extracted.
Orange blossom, tropical fruits, yeast. Very aromatic, revealing tropical flavors along
classic Viognier lines. Full and rich in the mouth, yet vibrant acidity gives fine balance
through the finish.

1996 Cabernet Sauvignon, De Rose Family Vineyard,
Dryfarmed Old Vines, Cienega Valley $17.95.   82

1994 Zinfandel, Dry Farmed Old Vines, Cedolini Vineyards,
Cienega Valley $19.95.   88

Deep blackish ruby cast. Moderately full-bodied. Balanced acidity. Highly extracted.
Heavily oaked. Moderately tannic. Red fruits, Bourbon. Quite aromatic, with a pervasive
oak influence. Big and rich in the mouth, with a lengthy, drying finish.

1995 Zinfandel, Dry Farmed Old Vines, Cedolini Vineyards, Cienega Valley
$19.95.   89

Deep blackish ruby cast. Full-bodied. Low acidity. Highly extracted. Mildly oaked. Mildly
tannic. Overripe black fruits. Fruit-centered aromatics carry a slight Port-like note
through a thick, rich palate. Low acidity makes for a heavy finish.

1996 Zinfandel, Dry Farmed Old Vines, Cedolini Vineyards,
Cienega Valley $19.95.   89

Dark blackish purple. Full-bodied. Low acidity. Moderately extracted. Heavily oaked.
Mildly tannic. Stewed fruits, chocolate, cedar. Extremely ripe, with a stewed note to the
nose and a wave of toasty oak accents. The mouthfeel is thick and rich, with low acidity.
Fat, generous, and flavorful through the finish.

Deaver

1997 Chardonnay, Sierra Foothills $11.99.   86

Pale straw hue with a greenish tint. Mild aromas show a muted green apple note.
A crisp entry leads a medium-bodied palate with bright acids and juicy apple flavors.
Oak influence is very subtle. Drink now.

1996 Sangiovese, Amador County $16.   86

Pale cherry red. Medium-bodied. Low acidity. Moderately extracted. Mildly tannic. Dried
cherries. Oak-accented aromas follow through on the palate, with dried red fruit flavors
lingering well through the finish.

1995 Zinfandel, Amador County $15.   86

Deep blackish ruby cast. Moderately full-bodied. Balanced acidity. Highly extracted.
Mildly oaked. Mildly tannic. Black fruits, chocolate, minerals. Somewhat reserved
aromatically, but rich, ripe, and concentrated on the palate. Full and intensely flavored,
with a thick though well-balanced finish.

1994 Zinfandel, Old Vines, Amador County $12.99.   89

Deep blackish purple. Full-bodied. Balanced acidity. Highly extracted. Heavily oaked.
Moderately tannic. Port, vanilla. Carries a slightly overripe note to the nose. Extremely
full and rich on the palate, with a firm structure and hefty oak accents. The overall
impression is of drinking a dry Port.

Deer Valley

1996 Sauvignon Blanc, Monterey County $3.99.   80

1995 Cabernet Sauvignon, California $5.99.   81

1996 Merlot, California $5.99.   80

Dehlinger

1997 Chardonnay, Russian River Valley $25.   83

Bright golden yellow. Restrained aromas show an oaky accent. Austere on the attack with
a medium-bodied palate and subdued flavors. The finish seems tight and dry. Youthful,
but has the stuffing to improve.

1995 Cabernet Sauvignon, Russian River Valley $28.   88

Deep ruby red hue with purple highlights. Bright briar fruit and mineral aromas. A soft
attack leads to a medium-bodied palate with lean tannins and solid fruit ripeness. Clean
through the finish with velvety fruit extract. Drink within five years.

1995 Syrah, Russian River Valley $35.   91

Dark purple, opaque, and brilliant to the rim. Intense, fantastic black cherry and
blueberry flavors. Hefty wood tones. Smooth entry. Full-bodied. Plentiful drying
tannins. Dense and richly extracted, with dry oak accents. Lingering rich finish.
Intensely flavorful and hedonistic. Drink now or later. Can improve with more age.

1996 Syrah, Goldridge Vineyard, Russian River Valley $28.   91

Deep purple, opaque, and brilliant to the rim. Intense, fantastic ripe black cherry flavors.
Generous wood tones. Supple entry. Moderately full-bodied. Moderate drying tannins.
Fully extracted, deep, and rich through the lingering finish. Succulent, mildly overripe,
and hedonistic. Drink now or later. Can improve with more age.

Delicato

1997 Cabernet Sauvignon, California $4.99.   84

Bright ruby-purple hue. A juicy attack leads to a medium-bodied palate with black
cherry fruit flavors and mildly gripping tannins on the finish. Drink now.

1997 Merlot, California $4.99.   83

Bright violet hue. Herbal, berry fruit aromas have a vanilla accent. Medium-bodied, lush,
and smooth through the finish with mild velvety tannins lingering. Straightforward and
unchallenging. Drink now.

1997 Syrah, California $5.99.   81

Diamond Creek

1994 Cabernet Sauvignon, Red Rock Terrace, Napa Valley $50.   88

Bright, deep cherry red. Medium-bodied. Moderately extracted. Moderately tannic.
Cassis, toasted oak, vanilla. Attractive toasty aromas lead a juicy, ripe Cabernet fruit
palate, with some fine-grained tannins closing up the finish. Excellent acids and
ripeness should allow this to develop in the cellar.

1995 Cabernet Sauvignon, Red Rock Terrace, Napa Valley $75.   **93**

Deep ruby purple. Moderately full-bodied. Balanced acidity. Moderately extracted. Mildly oaked. Mildly tannic. Red fruits, spice, minerals. Attractive aromas feature a ripe core of fruit flavors with a spicy oak accent. Firm and lean in the mouth, with a crisp but elegant structure. Finishes with some grainy tannins. Approachable, but worthy of cellaring.

1994 Cabernet Sauvignon, Volcanic Hill, Napa Valley $50.   **90**

Deep opaque purple. Moderately full-bodied. Highly extracted. Moderately tannic. Minerals, flint, black fruits. Lean and steely, with an outstandingly long and dry palate showing firmness through the finish. Fine acids and tightly wound flavors indicate this will take some years to show its potential.

1995 Cabernet Sauvignon, Volcanic Hill, Napa Valley $75.   **93**

Deep ruby purple. Moderately full-bodied. Balanced acidity. Moderately extracted. Mildly tannic. Minerals, cassis. Aromatic and elegant, with an emphasis on terroir, not winemaking. Lean and minerally, with exceptional balance and finesse. Fine grip and intensity.

Dolce

1995 Late Harvest Dessert Wine, Napa Valley $50/375 ml.   **97**

Very deep yellow-gold. Moderately full-bodied. Balanced acidity. Moderately extracted. Moderately oaked. Vanilla, figs, apricots. Heavily botrytized, with a wave of toasty oak and ripe tropical flavors. Lush, rich, velvety mouthfeel and fine acids. Intense, it should develop with further age.

Domaine Carneros

1993 Brut, Carneros $19.   **91**

Medium yellow-straw cast. Medium-bodied. Biscuit, ripe citrus, minerals. Fine toasty, biscuity aromas lead a richly flavored palate showing nutty development through the finish. Crisp, fine-beaded carbonation gives a vibrant mousse. Very stylish.

1992 Le Reve, Blanc de Blancs, Carneros $35.   **93**

Bright green-straw cast. Moderately full-bodied. Full acidity. Biscuits, cream, toast. Classic biscuity aromas lead a refined and generous, though still quite youthful, mouthfeel. Shows fine balance and length, and a very satisfying degree of maturity now, though this has the vibrancy and weight to improve further with bottle age.

1995 Pinot Noir, Carneros $20.   **86**

Bright magenta. Medium-bodied. Moderately extracted. Mildly tannic. Crisp, bright red berry fruit flavors are complemented by vanilla oak notes and a pleasing hint of astringency. Some weight is evident on the palate.

1996 Pinot Noir, Carneros $23.99.   **83**

Pale ruby red. Medium-bodied. Moderately extracted. Mildly tannic. Strawberries, vanilla. Soft berry fruit aromas follow through on the palate, with vanilla oak accents lingering on the finish. Soft acids make for an easy-drinking style. This is not structured for aging.

Domaine Chandon

NV Blanc de Noirs, Carneros $18.   **86**

Pale copper cast. Moderately full-bodied. Full acidity. Highly extracted. Minerals, toast, red fruits. Subtle aromas lead a big, forceful, well-balanced mouthfeel. Vibrant, crisp, and weighty through the substantial finish.

NV Brut Cuvée, Napa County $18.   **88**

Pale straw hue with a brilliant cast. Medium-bodied. Yeast, bread, citrus. A creamy mouthfeel shows vibrant, fine-beaded carbonation. The flavors have a clean citrusy streak through the finish, though there are hints of smoky yeast complexity.

1998 25th Anniversary Reserve Cuvée, Napa County $24.   **89**

Medium green-straw color. Medium-bodied. Burnt coffee, mocha, citrus. Smoky aromas. Generously proportioned and structured, showing a creamy mouthfeel and fine concentration of flavors. Nice now, though this should be smokier in a year or two.

1996 Pinot Noir, Carneros $28.95.   87

Dark ruby cast. Medium-bodied. Moderately extracted. Moderately tannic. Leather, earth, black fruits. Some classic aromas and flavors are present, though this is generously proportioned and weighty. Complex and stylish.

Domaine de la Terre Rouge

1994 Noir, Grande Année, Sierra Foothills $20.   83

Deep brick red with a fading rim. Lean aromas of herbs, minerals, and earth. A supple attack leads a medium-bodied palate, with drying tannins. Clipped, linear finish. Drink now.

1997 Tête-à-Tête, Sierra Foothills $12.   81

1996 Syrah, Sentinel Oak Vineyard, Pyramid Block,
Shenandoah Valley $25.   86

Deep, opaque ruby color, with a slight fade. Chocolate and black fruit flavors. Medium-bodied. Well extracted, with dry, grainy tannins. Tough and structured but impressively flavorsome. Drink within five years.

Domaine Napa

1996 Chardonnay, Sonoma County $13.99.   81

1996 Chardonnay, Napa Valley $15.99.   84

Burnished gold hue. Delicate floral nose. Medium-bodied lemon-dominated palate with weight and richness of mouthfeel yet showing an acid spike through the finish. Rather a strange style.

1996 Fumé Blanc, Napa Valley $9.99.   87

Very deep straw hue. Moderately full-bodied. Balanced acidity. Moderately extracted. Minerals, citrus. Aromatically reserved, with a full but soft mouthfeel. Picks up some nice grip through the finish.

Domaine Saint George

1997 Chardonnay, Select Reserve, California $5.99.   83

Pale straw cast. Medium-bodied. Balanced acidity. Moderately extracted. Minerals, citrus, pears. Aromatically reserved, with a crisp yet rounded structure. Shows a lingering citric finish.

1996 Fumé Blanc, Select Reserve, California $7.   83

Bright golden yellow. Medium-bodied. Balanced acidity. Moderately extracted. Moderately oaked. Vanilla, toasted oak, ripe citrus. Full toasty oak aromas lead a buttery, ripe citrus palate with smoky oak overtones through the finish. A softer, appealing style.

1997 Cabernet Sauvignon, Select Reserve, California $10.   83

Bright cherry purple hue. Decidedly berry-like, vanilla aromas. A crisp attack leads to a medium-bodied palate with a fruity center and mild tannins. Finishes in a lean, brief manner. Drink now.

1995 Cabernet Sauvignon, STG, Russian River Valley $15.   81

Dominus

1992 Napanook Vineyard, Napa Valley $50.   88

Deep ruby to the rim. Moderately full-bodied. Balanced acidity. Highly extracted. Moderately oaked. Quite tannic. Dry. Reminiscent of tea, herbs, cassis. Distinctive herbal aromatics are overshadowed by a wave of tannins on the palate of this Bordelaise-styled wine. Focused in structure, this is relatively inaccessible. Seems rather heavy on the tannins without requisite stuffing to balance, but this may be resolved with cellaring.

1994 Napanook Vineyard, Napa Valley $75. **95**

Opaque blood red. Moderately full-bodied. Highly extracted. Quite tannic. Bitter chocolate, black fruits, earth. An exotic, powerfully earthy nose reveals a big dry mouthful of concentrated mineral and earth, with tightly wound fruit flavors showing through. This has impressive structure, with firm dry tannins and an austere feel throughout.

1995 Cabernet Sauvignon, Napanook Vineyard, Napa Valley $95. **95**

Deep ruby red with a slight fade. Moderately full-bodied. Balanced acidity. Moderately extracted. Mildly oaked. Moderately tannic. Minerals, pencil shavings, earth. A Francophilic style, with restrained and complex mineral and earth-accented flavors. Supple on entry, with a lush quality up front and firm tannins on the finish. Needs time.

Douglass Hill

1997 Chardonnay, Napa Valley $15.99. **81**

1995 Cabernet Franc, Napa Valley $16. **84**

Bright garnet hue. Unusual mint and vanilla aromas show a big oak accent. A crisp attack leads to a medium-bodied palate with drying tannins and zesty acidity. Features a cedary, mature quality to the finish. Lighter styled but interesting. Drink now.

1995 Cabernet Sauvignon, Napa Valley $16. **81**

Dover Canyon

1997 Chardonnay, Cougar Ridge Vineyard, Central Coast $16. **84**

Pale golden cast. Moderately full-bodied. Full acidity. Moderately extracted. Mildly oaked. Toast, cream, citrus. Generous aromas show a pleasant leesy note that adds a measure of complexity to a firm core of wood-accented fruit flavors. Zesty and stylish, with good grip to the finish.

1996 Cabernet Sauvignon, Paso Robles $18. **86**

Deep, saturated ruby purple. Moderately full-bodied. Balanced acidity. Highly extracted. Mildly oaked. Moderately tannic. Licorice, wood, minerals. Unusual aromatics lead a firm and flavorful palate. Firm tannins bite down on the finish.

1995 Ménage, Paso Robles $22. **88**

Bright violet-red. Medium-bodied. Moderately extracted. Mildly tannic. Cassis, leaves, vanilla. Leafy, ripe aromas lead a soft, lush palate of berry flavors, with silky tannins giving a forward, accessible structure. Drinking very well now.

1996 Ménage, Paso Robles $28. **88**

Bright violet-ruby hue. Generously aromatic with a ripe nose of cassis aromas. A firm entry leads a moderately full-bodied palate with a ripe core of black currant flavors and solid, gripping tannins that clamp down on the finish. A solidly structured wine with plenty of youthful character. Drink now or later.

1996 Merlot, Reserve, Central Coast $24. **89**

Saturated crimson red. Distinctive aromas of blackberries and spice. A firm attack leads a moderately full-bodied palate with tough, chunky tannins and crisp acids. Finishes with flavors and grip. Well structured and solid, best to give it a year or two. Drink now or later. Can improve with more age.

Dry Creek Vineyard

1997 Chardonnay, Sonoma County $16. **87**

Deep yellow-straw hue. Generous tropical fruit and citrus aromas show a judicious oak accent. A lush entry leads a full-bodied palate with rounded acidity. Weighty, rich finish. Drink now.

1997 Chardonnay, Reserve, Sonoma County $20. **90**

Deep yellow-straw hue. Forward brown spice and citrus aromas show a hefty oak accent. A lush attack leads a full-bodied palate with rounded, creamy acidity and generous yeasty flavors. Ripe, lengthy finish. Rich but well balanced. Drink now.

1996 Fumé Blanc, Reserve, Dry Creek Valley $15.75.   **87**

Medium yellow-straw hue. Medium-bodied. Balanced acidity. Moderately extracted.
Mildly oaked. Dried herbs. Smoky, citrusy aromas follow through well on the palate.
Ripe, smoothly textured mouthfeel. Finishes with lingering smoke and oak spice notes.

1995 Cabernet Franc, Vintner's Selection, Dry Creek Valley $25.   **83**

Bright ruby purple. Medium-bodied. Balanced acidity. Moderately extracted. Mildly
tannic. Green herbs, minerals, earth. Carries a green streak through to the lighter-styled
palate. Lacks somewhat for grip or intensity. Overcropped and vapid.

1996 Cabernet Sauvignon, Dry Creek Valley $18.75.   **93**

Bright red-purple. Medium-bodied. Highly extracted. Mildly tannic. Black cherries, anise,
dried herbs. A very ripe, plummy nose follows through on the palate, with dry, powdery
tannins clamping down on the finish.

1995 Cabernet Sauvignon, Reserve, Dry Creek Valley $27.   **94**

Saturated red-purple. Moderately full-bodied. Highly extracted. Moderately tannic. Black
cherries, licorice. Fleshy, ripe aromas lead an intense mouthful of dark fruit flavors, with
firm tannins giving a dry, angular finish at present.

1995 Meritage, Dry Creek Valley $25.   **88**

Bright red-purple. Moderately full-bodied. Highly extracted. Moderately tannic. Black
cherries, brown spice, anise. A dusty nose leads an intense burst of ripe black fruits, with
powdery tannins drying the finish. Impressive, but needs time.

1996 Meritage, Sonoma County $25.   **84**

Bright violet-purple hue. Perfumed aromas of cedar, vanilla and berry fruits. A fruity
attack leads a medium-bodied palate with silky tannins and juicy red cherry flavors.
Very attractive and fruit forward. Drink now.

1996 Merlot, Sonoma County $18.75.   **81**

1995 Merlot, Reserve, Dry Creek Valley $30.   **81**

1995 Zinfandel, Old Vines, Sonoma County $16.   **86**

Deep blackish ruby hue. Moderately full-bodied. Balanced acidity. Moderately extracted.
Mildly oaked. Mildly tannic. Mint, dried herbs, red fruits. Quite aromatic, with distinctive
herbal overtones. A lush but well-structured palate feel, with solid grip through the finish.

1995 Zinfandel, Reserve, Sonoma County $25.   **89**

Bright ruby-garnet hue. Moderately full-bodied. Balanced acidity. Moderately extracted.
Heavily oaked. Mildly tannic. Vanilla, black fruits. Spicy oak notes emerge on the nose
and dominate the palate. Lush and velvety in the mouth, with a supple quality. Picks up
some very mild tannins on the finish.

Duckhorn

1997 Sauvignon Blanc, Napa Valley $14.   **83**

Bright yellow-gold. Medium-bodied. Full acidity. Moderately extracted. Tart tropical
fruits, lemons. Quite ripe, with a full complement of flavors. Angular acidity follows
through on the short finish.

1994 Cabernet Sauvignon, Napa Valley $35.   **88**

Solid blackish red. Medium-bodied. Highly extracted. Moderately tannic. Plums, earth,
black tea. Rich spicy, plummy nose leads an assertive entry, with impressive austere, dry
tannins on the finish. Angular and structured, this will be better in a few years.

1995 Cabernet Sauvignon, Napa Valley $32.   **82**

1995 Paraduxx, Napa Valley $20.   **93**

Deep blackish purple. Full-bodied. Balanced acidity. Highly extracted. Heavily oaked.
Mildly tannic. Vanilla, black fruits. Pleasantly aromatic, with a bright, fruit-centered
overtone and generous oak seasoning. Full, but well structured on the palate, with a
lean finish.

1996 Decoy Migration, Napa Valley $15.   81

1993 Merlot, Howell Mountain, Napa Valley $30.   90

Very deep blackish ruby hue to the rim. Moderately full-bodied. Balanced acidity. Highly extracted. Mildly oaked. Moderately tannic. Chocolate, black fruits, minerals. Deep and well extracted, this is a very dense wine. A rich core of flavor is ensconced in a notably firm structure, with a wave of velvety tannins at the finish. Solid balance bodes well for mid-term (3–6 years) to long-term (7–10 years) aging.

1995 Merlot, Napa Valley $28.   90

Deep ruby to the rim with a slight purplish cast. Moderately full-bodied. Balanced acidity. Highly extracted. Moderately oaked. Mildly tannic. Brown spices, dusty cherries, minerals. Quite aromatic, with a firm and concentrated character on the palate. Flavorful throughout, with dusty tannins and a lingering finish.

1996 Merlot, Napa Valley $32.   88

Saturated violet hue. Aromas show a youthful, oaky character with dark fleshy fruit accents. A crisp entry leads a moderately full-bodied palate with ample fine-grained tannins and an impressive concentration of fruit flavors. Dense and well structured. Drink now or later.

Dunn

1993 Cabernet Sauvignon, Napa Valley $35.   92

Opaque dark purple. Moderately full-bodied. Highly extracted. Quite tannic. Cassis, blackberries, earth, black tea. Very impressive tightly wound flavors have all the classic hallmarks of the variety. Tight midpalate and great supporting tannins through the finish suggest the possibility of a long cellar life.

Dunnewood

1996 Sauvignon Blanc, Coastal Series, Vintner's Select, Mendocino $5.99.   86

Pale green-gold. Medium-bodied. Balanced acidity. Moderately extracted. Lemon, mineral. A clean herbaceous, mildly buttery nose delivers faithfully on the palate. A little light in flavors but the mouthfeel is a plus point.

1997 White Zinfandel, California $5.99.   80

1996 Cabernet Sauvignon, Coastal Series, North Coast $7.99.   80

1994 Cabernet Sauvignon, Dry Silk, Napa Valley $9.99.   87

Brilliant violet-red hue. Generously aromatic with a spicy, pickle note and well-defined crisp fruits. A bright entry leads to a medium-bodied palate with sensational bright acids and deep black cherry flavors that finish cleanly with a lingering note of oak subtlety. Solid, in a more reserved, classical style. Drink now or later.

1996 Merlot, North Coast $8.99.   81

1996 Pinot Noir, North Coast $7.99.   83

Medium dark ruby hue. Medium-bodied. Moderately extracted. Moderately tannic. Minerals, earth. Austere earthy aromas lead a tight, somewhat lean mouthful of flavors with a touch of fruit generosity.

Durney

1993 Cabernet Sauvignon, Carmel Valley $20.   85

Deep ruby red. Medium-bodied. Moderately extracted. Moderately tannic. Earth, brown spice, tomato. Rustic aromas of leather and earth follow through on the palate. The flavors manage to be both ripe and austere. Not for keeping.

Eberle

1997 Chardonnay, Paso Robles $15. 84

Bright yellow-straw hue. Generous spice and tropical fruit aromas carry a slightly unusual honeyed quality. A crisp entry leads a medium-bodied palate with zesty acidity. Ripe, intense finish. Drink now.

1997 Counoise Rose, Lauridsen Vineyard, Paso Robles $11. 84

Pale cherry-garnet hue. Forward spice and berry aromas. A rich entry leads a moderately full-bodied palate, with a wave of exotic, smoky fruit flavors. Acidity is on the low side, making for a big, heavy Rosé. Drink now.

1996 Cabernet Sauvignon, Paso Robles $20. 86

Pale ruby-red hue with a fading rim. Very aromatic with a spice box quality and a suggestion of ripe berry fruits. A ripe, juicy entry leads a medium-bodied palate with attractive sweet cherry and toasty oak flavors. Finishes with very gentle tannins. Very supple and forward, this is drinking well now. Drink now.

1996 Côtes-du-Rôbles, Paso Robles $13. 83

Pale orange-red hue. Subdued herb and mineral aromas. Moderately light-bodied. A crisp attack leads a light-bodied palate with drying tannins. The finish is clipped and clean. A lightweight with grip. Drink now.

1996 Zinfandel, Sauret Vineyard, Paso Robles $18. 82

1998 Muscat Canelli, Paso Robles $11. 83

Bright yellow-straw hue. Attractive orange blossom and honeyed citrus aromas. A rich entry leads a medium-bodied palate showing mild sweetness. Soft and lush. Drink now.

Echelon

1997 Chardonnay, Central Coast $12.50. 81

Edgewood

1997 Chardonnay, Napa Valley $18. 88

Bright yellow-gold. A rich smoky, leesy nose shows toasty oak influences. A spicy attack leads a moderately full-bodied palate with glycerous smoothness and a lingering yeasty finish. Very elegant and rich. Drink now.

1995 Cabernet Sauvignon, Napa Valley $20. 86

Saturated red-purple. Moderately full-bodied. Highly extracted. Moderately tannic. Back fruits, licorice. Solid, tightly wound, concentrated fruit flavors and impressive structural tannins that give a firm, reserved note to the finish.

1996 Cabernet Sauvignon, Napa Valley $20. 83

Deep purple red hue. Lean, brooding mineral and black fruit aromas carry an earthy edge. A firm attack leads to a medium-bodied palate with big, astringent tannins. Clipped finish. On the tough side.

1996 Malbec, Napa Valley $18. 83

Rich ruby purple hue. Generous vanilla and briar fruit aromas show a judicious oak accent. A lush attack leads to a moderately full-bodied palate with big supple tannins. Rich, intense finish. Drink now.

1993 Cellarette Cuvée, Napa Valley $22.50. 87

Full red-purple. Medium-bodied. Moderately extracted. Moderately tannic. Cassis, black fruits, brown spice. Soundly structured, with attractive toasty oak notes lingering through the finish. Tart and juicy, with vanilla oak notes throughout.

1994 Merlot, Napa Valley $19.99. 82

1995 Petite Sirah, Napa Valley $14. 81

1995 Zinfandel, Napa Valley $14. 86

Opaque dark red. Medium-bodied. Balanced acidity. Highly extracted. Moderately oaked. Ripe black fruits, vanilla. Ripe nose reminiscent of Port. Solid and compact palate, with dry, dusty tannins on the finish. Rather structured, and lacking midpalate stuffing.

Edmeades

1996 Chardonnay, Anderson Valley $18.   **89**

Rich gold. Very ripe tropical aromas have a citrus zest quality and spicy oak influence. A rich attack leads a full-bodied palate with concentrated ripe fruit flavors, bright acids, and well-balanced oak flavors. Quite a powerful style, yet well structured. Drink now or later.

1996 Petite Sirah, Eagle Point Vineyard, Mendocino $20.   **87**

Opaque blackish red. Full-bodied. Highly extracted. Quite tannic. An extremely chewy texture shows the massive extract of this wine. Monolithic and tough, with a mild, cooked-fruit character.

1995 Pinot Noir, Anderson Valley $20.   **86**

Bright cherry red. Medium-bodied. Moderately extracted. Moderately oaked. Moderately tannic. Brown spice nuances on the nose. Crisp, focused cherry and berry flavors have plenty of firm oak in support, with dry tannins coming through on the finish.

1996 Pinot Noir, Anderson Valley $20.   **93**

Deep ruby cast. Moderately full-bodied. Balanced acidity. Moderately extracted. Mildly oaked. Mildly tannic. Spice, minerals, tomato vine. Quite aromatic, with real complexity. Generous yet firm in the mouth, with an angular, spicy finish. Shows fine persistence and intensity.

Edmunds St. John

1996 Syrah, California $18.   **93**

Rich, hazy garnet red with a slight fade. Intense, powerful medicinal, old-vine, spice cabinet, and game aromas. A supple attack leads a moderately full-bodied palate that has tannic grip. Lengthy, flavorful finish. Individualistic, but not everyone's cup of tea. Drink now or later. Can improve with more age.

Edna Valley Vineyard

1997 Chardonnay, Paragon Vineyard, Edna Valley $18.   **83**

Deep yellow-straw hue. Restrained mineral aromas show a slightly earthy edge. A rich entry leads a full-bodied palate with angular acidity. Well structured but not overly flavorful. Drink now.

Ehlers Grove

1997 Chardonnay, Winery Reserve, Carneros, Napa Valley $30.   **86**

Bright golden yellow. Ripe subtly honeyed aromas. A crisp attack leads a moderately full-bodied palate with bright acids and deep flavors. Well balanced and structured. Drink now or later.

El Molino

1995 Pinot Noir, Napa Valley $41.95.   **90**

Full ruby hue with a lightening rim. Medium-bodied. Moderately extracted. Moderately tannic. Minerals, black fruits, leather. A distinctively minerally, oak-spiced nose leads a solid, well-gripped palate, with structuring tannins showing well through the finish. Elegant yet firm.

Elkhorn Peak

1997 Chardonnay, Fagan Creek Vineyard, Napa Valley $18.   **89**

Medium straw hue. Generously aromatic with pure ripe fruit and smoky oak aromas. A juicy attack leads a moderately full-bodied palate with a succulent fruity character and judicious oak accents. A big, ripe, lush style.

1995 Pinot Noir, Fagan Creek Vineyard, Napa Valley $26.   **89**

Pale cherry red. Medium-bodied. Moderately extracted. Moderately oaked. Mildly tannic. Perfumed new oak aromas have a dill accent, leading a rounded palate with good weight. Full cherry fruit flavors are complemented by toasty notes through the finish.

1996 Pinot Noir, Fagan Creek Vineyard, Napa Valley $26. **86**

Pale ruby red. Medium-bodied. Moderately extracted. Mildly oaked. Mildly tannic. Red berries, dried herbs, vanilla. Soft red fruit aromas follow through well on a generous palate, with light, gripping tannins and relatively soft acids making for an accessible style.

Eos

1996 Zinfandel, Paso Robles $15.99. **82**

Equinox

NV Harmony Cuvée Brut, Santa Cruz Mountains $27. **90**

Bright yellow-gold. Medium-bodied. Full acidity. Charred yeast, roasted coffee. Complex smoky, yeasty aromas lead a taut, concentrated palate, with bright acids and fine toasty yeast notes. The lengthy dry finish has an assertive character. Shows soft carbonation, with a fine bead.

1992 Cuvée de Chardonnay, Blanc de Blanc, Santa Cruz Mountains $33. **92**

Bright yellow-straw cast. Moderately full-bodied. Full acidity. Smoke, toast, blanched almonds. Outstandingly complex, highly smoky yeast aromas. Forceful and intense palate, with vibrant carbonation and intense Chardonnay character that makes for a very bright and flavorful mouthful.

Estancia

1997 Chardonnay, Pinnacles, Monterey County $11. **83**

Deep golden yellow. Aromas show a marked oak accent. A rich entry leads a full-bodied palate that does not show matching fruit generosity on the midpalate. Alcohol, wood, and glycerine are the key elements.

1997 Chardonnay, Reserve, Monterey $19. **83**

Bright golden yellow. Moderately aromatic with toasted oak character making an impression. An angular entry leads a moderately full-bodied palate with glycerine and alcohol outdoing fruit flavors. Finishes with a lean note.

1996 Fumé Blanc, Pinnacles, Monterey County $10. **94**

Deep golden luster. Moderately full-bodied. Balanced acidity. Highly extracted. Moderately oaked. Dried herbs, toasted oak, citrus. Assertive oak aromas with a strong dried herbal accent. Rich, mouthfilling herbal flavors with a fine smoky oak note through the finish. Very hedonistic, though this is not for the cellar—drink it now.

1995 Cabernet Sauvignon, California $12. **86**

Full ruby red. Medium-bodied. Balanced acidity. Moderately extracted. Moderately tannic. Lead pencil, cassis, minerals. Bright, varietally correct aromas show an oak spice note that follows through on the palate. Firm yet generous, this is drinking nicely now.

1996 Cabernet Sauvignon, California $12. **80**

1996 Duo, Alexander Valley $18. **83**

Bright blackish ruby cast. Moderately full-bodied. Full acidity. Highly extracted. Mildly tannic. Black fruits, minerals. Rather reserved aromatically, but the deep fruit flavors are highlighted by racy acidity. Finishes with a mildly bitter note.

1994 Red Meritage, Alexander Valley $18. **91**

Bright cherry red. Medium-bodied. Highly extracted. Mildly tannic. Chocolate, toasted oak, cinnamon. A gorgeously rich and generous nose leads a full-flavored toasty palate, with an outstanding lingering chocolatey finish. Very harmonious and balanced.

1995 Red Meritage, Alexander Valley $22. **86**

Bright ruby with a slight fade. Medium-bodied. Balanced acidity. Moderately extracted. Moderately oaked. Mildly tannic. Brown spices, cedar. Quite aromatic, with a definite oak accent. Lighter-styled but lush through the wood-driven finish.

Scale: Superlative (96-100), Exceptional (90-95), Highly Recommended (85-89), Recommended (80-84), Not Recommended (Under 80)

82

1996 Merlot, Sonoma County $14.   88

Bright violet-ruby hue. Black fruit and herb aromas. A supple attack leads a moderately
full-bodied palate with firm, dry tannins. Finishes with an angular tannic grip. Drink now
or later. Can improve with more age.

1997 Pinot Noir, Monterey $12.   84

Pale cherry red. Medium-bodied. Moderately extracted. Mildly tannic. Fruit cordial,
vanilla. Ripe, cordial-like aromas follow through on the palate with a range of jammy
flavors. Finishes with soft tannins.

1996 Pinot Noir, Pinnacles, Monterey $12.   80

1996 Pinot Noir, Reserve, Monterey $18.   87

Deep cherry red. Medium-bodied. Moderately extracted. Cherries, dried herbs, vanilla.
Ripe red fruit aromas lead a generous palate, with crisp fruity flavors that show a marked
oak impression through the finish. Opulently fruity, with fine length.

Estate Cellars

NV Cabernet Sauvignon, California $7.99.   80

Estrella

1997 Chardonnay, California $5.99.   81

1995 Sauvignon Blanc, Proprietor's Reserve, California $9.99/1.5 L.   83

Pale straw. Medium-bodied. Balanced acidity. Moderately extracted. Mildly oaked. Dried
herbs, citrus. Nice herbal suggestion on the nose follows through on a rounded, crisp
palate with a lively acid balance.

1998 White Zinfandel, California $4.99.   80

1996 Cabernet Sauvignon, Proprietor's Reserve, California $5.99.   81

1996 Pinot Noir, Proprietor's Reserve, California $9.99/1.5 L.   81

1996 Zinfandel, Proprietor's Reserve, California $9.99/1.5 L.   82

Etude

1995 Pinot Noir, Carneros $33.50.   89

Bright cherry red. Medium-bodied. Highly extracted. Moderately oaked. Mildly tannic.
Full red fruit and vanilla aromas. Concentrated flavors, with a fine, weighty palate that
is not hugely fruity. Fine-grained tannins on the dry finish. This has some structure for
cellaring.

1996 Pinot Noir, Carneros $30.   83

Dark violet hue. Medium-bodied. Moderately extracted. Mildly tannic. Blackberries,
minerals. Crisp, tart black fruit flavors. The rather ripe black fruit flavors are backed up
with oak spice and very mild tannins.

Falconer

1983 Blanc de Blancs RD, San Luis Obispo County $19.95.   90

Deep gold. Moderately full-bodied. Full acidity. Highly extracted. Bread dough, almonds,
caramel. Forward, toasty aromas indicate an attractive level of maturity. Surprisingly
youthful in the mouth, with sturdy acidity and aggressive, refreshing carbonation.
Balanced and flavorful, in a rustic style.

Fanucchi

1996 Zinfandel, Fanucchi Wood Road Vineyard, Old Vine,
Russian River Valley $33.75.   84

Opaque blackish purple. Full-bodied. Balanced acidity. Highly extracted. Mildly oaked.
Moderately tannic. Lacquer, black fruits. Reserved aromatically, with a hugely extracted,
dense mouthfeel. Brooding flavors are tightly wrapped in the highly structured palate.
Finishes with a lash of tannin. Impressive, but perhaps a bit too tough.

Far Niente

1997 Chardonnay, Napa Valley $40.   86

Pale yellow-straw hue. Oaky, blanched almond aromas. A tart entry leads a medium-bodied palate with spiky acidity and phenolic dryness through the finish.

1994 Cabernet Sauvignon, Napa Valley $55.   90

Full dark red. Medium-bodied. Highly extracted. Moderately tannic. Plums, dried herbs, minerals. Bright black fruit flavors on entry. Good viscous mouthfeel with some earthy qualities and solid dry tannins on the finish. Herbal notes add complexity.

1995 Cabernet Sauvignon, Napa Valley $70.   91

Very deep ruby hue. Generous brown spice and red fruit aromas show a refined oak accent and a complex gamey edge. A lush attack leads to a moderately full-bodied palate with ripe velvety tannins. Rich, flavorful finish. A big but well-balanced style. Drink now or later.

Farella-Park

1994 Cabernet Sauvignon, Napa Valley $28.   87

Deep dark red with purple highlights. Medium-bodied. Moderately extracted. Moderately tannic. Black fruits, black tea, brown spice. Solid dark fruit flavors are matched by some tough tannins that make for an assertive finish. This should be better in a few years.

1995 Cabernet Sauvignon, Napa Valley $32.   85

Saturated, opaque red-purple. Moderately full-bodied. Highly extracted. Quite tannic. Cassis, minerals, oak spice. Very pure, cordial-like fruit aromas lead a concentrated mouthfeel, with dense, fine-grained tannins drying the finish. Heavily extracted and firm, this will need years of cellaring.

1995 Merlot, Napa Valley $24.   88

Deep ruby hue to the rim. Moderately full-bodied. Balanced acidity. Highly extracted. Mildly oaked. Mildly tannic. Black fruits, earth, minerals. Quite firm in style, with a dense and highly extracted mouthfeel. Robust tannins clamp down on the palate, but its balance is such that it should mellow nicely with mid-term (3–6 years) aging.

Gary Farrell

1996 Chardonnay, Allen Vineyard, Russian River Valley $28.   94

Brilliant yellow-gold. Moderately full-bodied. Balanced acidity. Peach, apples, yeast, vanilla. Fruit-laden aromas are a standout. Generously textured, with full juicy flavors showing impressive persistence through the finish. Some oaky character remains as a well-integrated background component, adding to the complexity.

1995 Cabernet Sauvignon, Hillside Selection, Sonoma County $24.   86

Saturated bright purple. Medium-bodied. Full acidity. Moderately extracted. Mildly tannic. Minerals, black fruits. Aromatically reserved, with a core of primary fruit on the palate. Bright and zesty, with acidity to the fore and an angular, crisp finish.

1996 Merlot, Russian River Valley $22.   91

Saturated bright purple. Crisp berry fruit and vanilla aromas. A vibrant attack leads a medium-bodied palate with velvety, supple tannins. Finishes with a lingering fruit persistence. Drink now.

1995 Merlot, Ladi's Vineyard, Sonoma County $22.   86

Very deep blackish ruby hue with a slight purplish cast. Medium-bodied. Full acidity. Highly extracted. Mildly oaked. Moderately tannic. Black fruits, black pepper, menthol. Quite youthful and a bit closed. Features a tightly wound core of dark flavors and juicy acidity. Tannins close in on the finish.

1995 Pinot Noir, Anderson Valley $30.   90

Dark ruby red. Medium-bodied. Highly extracted. Quite tannic. Nice leathery, meaty aromas. Dry dark fruit flavors have a tar and licorice note, with tealike tannins on the finish. Rather tough now. Austere style.

1996 Pinot Noir, Russian River Valley $22.50. **88**

Bright pale ruby cast. Moderately light-bodied. Full acidity. Moderately extracted. Mildly oaked. Mildly tannic. Cherries, raspberries, vanilla. Fruit centered and delicate, with a flavorful, zesty quality and a light frame. Crisp and racy finish.

1995 Pinot Noir, Allen Vineyard, Russian River Valley $40. **90**

Bright purple-red. Medium-bodied. Highly extracted. Moderately oaked. Moderately tannic. Bright raspberry fruit aromas with vanilla accents follow through on the palate, with up-front juicy acids highlighting dry, tealike tannins on the finish. Sound structure.

1996 Pinot Noir, Bien Nacido Vineyard, Santa Barbara County $28. **87**

Pale ruby purple. Medium-bodied. Full acidity. Moderately extracted. Mildly oaked. Moderately tannic. Raspberries, minerals. Restrained berryish aromas lead a firm and intense mouthfeel with excellent fruit persistence. Vibrant and zesty finish. Lighter in style but packed with flavor.

1995 Pinot Noir, Rochioli Vineyard, Russian River Valley $50. **89**

Deep ruby cast. Medium-bodied. Full acidity. Moderately extracted. Mildly oaked. Mildly tannic. Iron, earth, berries. Generous aromatics show a degree of minerally complexity. Fine depth of flavor in the mouth, with a lingering and intense finish.

1996 Zinfandel, Old Vine Selection, Sonoma County $22.50. **91**

Bright purple. Moderately full-bodied. Full acidity. Moderately extracted. Mildly oaked. Mildly tannic. Briar fruits, vanilla. Quite aromatic, with a vibrant, fruit-centered mouthfeel. Lush and generous, with a lengthy finish.

Fenestra

1996 Semillon, Livermore Valley $9.50. **89**

Bright full-gold hue. Moderately full-bodied. Balanced acidity. Moderately extracted. Moderately oaked. Vanilla, oak spice, tropical fruits. Rich, toasty aromas lead a rounded, glycerous mouthfeel with juicy tropical flavors. Acids give this fine structure and it should improve with further age.

1995 Cabernet Franc, Santa Lucia Highlands $12.50. **81**

1994 Cabernet Sauvignon, Livermore Valley $13.50. **83**

Bright ruby hue with a slight garnet cast. Moderately full-bodied. Balanced acidity. Highly extracted. Heavily oaked. Moderately tannic. Brown spices, minerals. Quite aromatic, with a hefty oak accent. Thick and rich in the mouth. Tannins bite down on the finish.

1992 Cabernet Sauvignon, Smith & Hook Vineyard,
Santa Lucia Highlands $14. **84**

Bright brick red. Medium-bodied. Moderately extracted. Mildly tannic. Loam, minerals, spice. Mature aromas are showing through. A refined palate of minerals and faded fruit flavors conveys a sense of elegance and maturity.

Ferrari-Carano

1996 Chardonnay, Alexander Valley $21. **93**

Yellow-gold. Moderately full-bodied. Balanced acidity. Moderately extracted. Vanilla, smoke, lemon, quince. Rich smoky aromas. Sweetly fruity and generous, with a supple, creamy mouthfeel. Shows a persistent, fine, juicy, flavorful finish.

1995 Chardonnay, Reserve, 87%Napa County, 13%Sonoma County $34. **94**

Bright yellow-gold. Moderately full-bodied. Balanced acidity. Moderately extracted. Moderately oaked. Smoke, yeast, crisp apples. Outstanding bright acids perfectly frame this intensely fruity style that shows extravagant texture and well-balanced oak spice. Outstanding Champagne-like smoky yeast complexity.

1993 Cabernet Sauvignon, Sonoma County $22.50. **90**

Dark red with purple highlights. Medium-bodied. Highly extracted. Moderately tannic. Olive, vanilla, cedar, cassis. Generous aromas reveal ripe, fleshy Cabernet fruit on the palate, with balanced powdery tannins through the finish. Solidly structured with plenty of stuffing.

1994 Cabernet Sauvignon, Sonoma County $28.   91

Dark ruby cast. Moderately full-bodied. Balanced acidity. Moderately extracted.
Moderately oaked. Mildly tannic. Chocolate, earth, black fruits. Pleasantly aromatic,
with a full, rich mouthfeel. Supple, lush, and velvety, showing a firm structure through
the finish. Well balanced.

1995 Siena, Sonoma County $28.   86

Deep blackish ruby hue. Moderately full-bodied. Balanced acidity. Moderately extracted.
Mildly oaked. Mildly tannic. Red fruits, minerals, spice. Pleasantly aromatic, with a lush,
though well-structured palate feel. Picks up a pleasant angular note on the finish.

1992 Reserve Red, Sonoma County $47.   91

Bright reddish purple. Medium-bodied. Highly extracted. Moderately tannic. Black
cherry, mint, cassis. Elegant perfumed nose of mint and cassis leads a concentrated
palate of black cherry fruits with ample supple tannins showing great integration.
Soundly structured, this should be worth holding on to.

1993 Tresor Reserve, Sonoma County $55.   94

Deep blackish ruby cast. Moderately full-bodied. Balanced acidity. Moderately extracted.
Mildly tannic. Earth, black fruits, mushrooms. Generous aromas have an exotic and
complex quality beginning to hint at maturity. Large scaled and firm in the mouth,
with a lengthy finish. Shows fine grip and intensity.

1995 Merlot, Sonoma County $25.   83

Saturated dark red. Deeply woody, oak spice aromas. A firm attack leads a moderately
full-bodied palate with firm fine-grained tannins. Drink now.

1995 Zinfandel, Sonoma County $18.   86

Dark blackish ruby hue with a purple edge. Moderately full-bodied. Balanced acidity.
Moderately extracted. Mildly oaked. Mildly tannic. Chocolate, black fruits, vanilla.
Pleasantly aromatic, with deep fruit flavors throughout. Full and lush on the palate,
but well structured, with chunky tannins through the finish.

Gloria Ferrer

NV Blanc de Noirs, Carneros $15.   86

Pale copper hue with a subtle pinkish overtone. Full-bodied. Full acidity. Highly
extracted. Minerals, red fruits. Aromatically reserved, with a forceful and austere
mouthfeel featuring vibrant carbonation. Intense and racy through the finish.

NV Brut, Sonoma County $15.   83

Bright pale gold hue. Medium-bodied. Full acidity. Grapefruit, yeast. Steely, bright
citrus aromas have a fresh yeasty note that follows through on the flavor-packed palate
and persistent finish. Shows lively medium-beaded carbonation.

1989 Carneros Cuvée Brut, Carneros $28.   92

Brilliant yellow-gold. Moderately full-bodied. Full acidity. Nuts, spice, baked fruit. Rich,
complex aromas show a toasty, nutty character, indicating maturity that is confirmed on
the palate. Concentrated, fine-beaded carbonation supplies a tight mousse. This shows
persistence of flavors.

1990 Royal Cuvée Brut, Vintage Reserve, Carneros $20.   88

Medium straw cast. Medium-bodied. Full acidity. Spice, toast, citrus zest. Generous bready
aromas. Full carbonation with a frothy mouthfeel. Very lively and concentrated, with a
long, zesty finish.

1996 Pinot Noir, Carneros $19.   83

Pale ruby-violet hue. Medium-bodied. Low acidity. Subtly extracted. Red fruits, vanilla.
Soft, perfumed aromas lead a rounded, fat, pleasant mouthful of flavors. This lacks
structure to develop further in the bottle.

Fetzer

1997 Chardonnay, Sundial, California $7.99.   81

Scale: Superlative (96-100), Exceptional (90-95), Highly Recommended (85-89),
Recommended (80-84), Not Recommended (Under 80)

1997 Chardonnay, Barrel Select, Mendocino County $11.99.   81

1996 Chardonnay, Reserve, Mendocino County $20.   88

Rich yellow-straw hue. Generous brown spice and pear aromas show a judicious oak accent. A fat entry leads a moderately full-bodied palate with shy acidity. Rounded, buttery finish. Hedonistically attractive but will not keep. Drink now.

1997 Gewürztraminer, California $5.99.   82

1997 Johannisberg Riesling, California $6.99.   88

Medium yellow-straw color. Rich aromas of ripe stone fruits and petrol are classic, pure Riesling. A rich attack follows through well on the medium-bodied palate, with oily flavors through the finish. Drink now.

1997 White Zinfandel, California $5.99.   80

1996 Cabernet Sauvignon, Valley Oaks, California $8.99.   81

1995 Cabernet Sauvignon, Barrel Select, North Coast $14.99.   87

Saturated dark ruby hue. Elegant aromas of lavish oak and rich cassis and plum. A lush entry leads to a moderately full-bodied palate with velvety, abundant tannins and sweet cedary oak flavors that persist through the finish. Very supple and mouthfilling. Drink now.

1994 Cabernet Sauvignon, Reserve, Napa Valley $28.   93

Dark ruby hue. Markedly ripe, oak-accented aromas have a sweet vanilla note. A soft entry leads a moderately full-bodied mouthfeel with clean acidity and ripe black fruit flavors that give way to a dark chocolate note on the finish. A thicker, rich style. Drink now or later.

1997 Merlot, Eagle Peak, California $8.99.   83

Bright violet-ruby hue. Moderately aromatic with weedy and oak accents and plummy fruit. A supple entry leads a medium-bodied palate with berry fruit flavors matched by supple tannins and lingering oak flavors. Well balanced with fine acidity and good grip on the finish. Drink now.

1995 Merlot, Barrel Select, Sonoma County $13.99.   85

Deep blackish ruby hue with brilliant clarity. Moderately light-bodied. Balanced acidity. Moderately extracted. Mildly oaked. Mildly tannic. Red fruits, vanilla. Lighter in style, with a soft mouthfeel. Straightforward fruit flavors are accented by a kiss of oak.

1996 Merlot, North Coast $14.99.   85

Bright ruby red to the rim. Clean cherry and mineral aromas. A lean attack leads a medium-bodied palate with firm tannins and juicy acidity, and a crisp, clipped finish. Racy and refreshing. Drink now.

1995 Merlot, Reserve, North Coast $22.   88

Bright ruby red to the rim. Attractive red fruit and vanilla aromas show an attractive wood accent. A crisp attack leads a medium-bodied palate with vibrant acidity and subdued tannins. Flavorful, ripe, wood-accented finish. Lighter in style but well balanced and tasty. Drink now.

1996 Pinot Noir, California $12.99.   84

Bright ruby cast. Medium-bodied. Balanced acidity. Moderately extracted. Mildly tannic. Minerals, red fruits. Lean aromas lead a firm and grippy mouthfeel. Full yet lean through the finish.

1995 Pinot Noir, Bien Nacido Vineyard Reserve,
Santa Barbara County $24.   88

Bright cherry red. Medium-bodied. Moderately extracted. Moderately oaked. Mildly tannic. Full, generous, rounded cherry and raspberry fruit flavors fill the palate. Nice bright acids with a hint of herbal character on the finish.

1993 Port, Mendocino County $18.99.   82

Ficklin

Tinta Port, California $12.   **86**

Deep ruby-garnet cast. Medium-bodied. Balanced acidity. Moderately extracted. Brown spices, toast. Pleasantly aromatic, with a gentle woody note and a touch of heat. Ripe and full in the mouth, with a lingering, flavorful finish.

1988 Vintage Port, California $25.   **91**

Deep ruby-garnet cast. Moderately full-bodied. Balanced acidity. Moderately extracted. Overripe red fruits, tea, minerals. Quite aromatic and complex, with a mature, flavorful palate feel. Full but well structured, with a sense of leanness through the finish, provided by buoyant acidity.

10 Year Old Tawny Port, California $22.   **92**

Opaque mahogany cast with a greenish fade to the rim. Full-bodied. Full acidity. Highly extracted. Salted pecans, rancio, treacle. Extraordinarily flavorful, with a well-aged, Oloroso Sherry edge to the complex flavors. Thick, rich, and concentrated on the palate, with great intensity and style.

Fife

1995 Merlot, Napa Valley $20.   **80**

1996 L'Attitude 39, Mendocino $18.   **84**

Deep ruby red to the rim. Generous earth, herb, and spice aromas show a moderate wood accent. A soft attack leads a medium-bodied palate that has tannic grip. The finish is supple and flavorful. Well balanced. Drink now.

1996 Max Cuvée, Napa Valley $30.   **88**

Very dark, opaque violet red to the rim. Brooding, intense black fruit, vanilla, and mineral aromas show a generous wood accent. A firm attack leads a full-bodied palate, with abundant robust, chunky tannins. The finish is flavorful and tannic. A monster show style, displaying extract, color, and tannin galore, it is not for the faint of heart. Good for long-term (7–10 years) cellaring.

1995 Zinfandel, Redhead Vineyard, Redwood Valley $18.50.   **84**

Bright blackish ruby cast. Moderately full-bodied. Balanced acidity. Highly extracted. Mildly oaked. Moderately tannic. Minerals, red fruits, black pepper. Somewhat reserved aromatically, with a firm, compact palate feel. Lean and austere through the concentrated finish.

J. Filippi

Fondante Ciello, Chocolate Port, California $18/500 ml.   **80**

Firestone

1997 Chardonnay, Santa Ynez Valley $13.   **83**

Bright straw hue. Forward mineral and spice aromas show a restrained oak accent. A crisp entry leads a medium-bodied palate with racy acidity. Sharp, cleansing finish. Drink now.

1997 Gewürztraminer, Carranza Mesa Vineyard, Santa Ynez Valley $9.   **82**

1997 Riesling, Santa Barbara County $7.   **89**

Medium green-gold hue. Exotic aromas of petrol and minerals. A rich entry leads a medium-bodied palate with a glycerous mouthfeel, peach flavors, and an oily texture that sets this apart. Lingering, rich finish. An excellent match with pork or other white meats. Drink now or later.

1993 Reserve Red, Santa Ynez Valley $30.   **89**

Dark red. Moderately full-bodied. Moderately extracted. Mildly tannic. Plums, toasted oak, chocolate. Attractive rich black fruit aromas have tobacco accents. The rounded mouthfeel has generous ripe flavors and sweet, spicy, chocolatey notes on the finish. Drinking nicely now.

Scale: Superlative (96-100), Exceptional (90-95), Highly Recommended (85-89), Recommended (80-84), Not Recommended (Under 80)

1995 Merlot, Santa Ynez Valley $14.   **83**

Deep blackish ruby hue. Medium-bodied. Balanced acidity. Moderately extracted. Mildly tannic. Earth, black fruits. Aromatics are quite earthy. Compact palate feel. Features some mild astringency and an herbal note to the finish.

1995 Port, Santa Ynez Valley $20.   **82**

Fisher

1997 Chardonnay, Coach Insignia, Sonoma County $25.   **82**

1997 Chardonnay, Whitney's Vineyard, Sonoma County $40.   **89**

Bright straw hue. Restrained, youthful yeasty aromas. A lush entry leads a full-bodied palate with rounded yet vibrant acidity. Features a substantial, harmonious mouthfeel and a crisp finish. Should open with age. Midterm cellar candidate.

1995 Cabernet Sauvignon, Coach Insignia, Napa Valley $25.   **91**

Bright ruby purple. Moderately full-bodied. Balanced acidity. Highly extracted. Moderately tannic. Minerals, cassis, earth. Pleasantly aromatic, with a firm and intense palate feel. Crisp, lean, and angular through the finish.

1996 Coach Insignia Red, Napa County $30.   **84**

Deep ruby-violet hue. Rich, ripe aromas show a deeply fruited character, somewhat reserved. A lush entry leads a moderately full-bodied palate with dense dark fruit flavors and finely wrought grainy tannins. Stuffed, well-gripped, and flavorful. This has cellarable structure. Drink now or later.

1994 Cabernet Sauvignon, Lamb Vineyard, Napa Valley $50.   **95**

Opaque red with bright purple highlights. Full-bodied. Highly extracted. Moderately tannic. Currants, black fruit, tea. Weighty and massively full on the palate. Dense and chewy, with assertive dry tannins making it backward at present. Excellent structure for long-term (7–10 years) cellaring.

1995 Cabernet Sauvignon, Lamb Vineyard, Napa Valley $50.   **92**

Deep, saturated ruby hue. Moderately full-bodied. Balanced acidity. Highly extracted. Moderately tannic. Black fruits, minerals. Features a youthful, minerally array of flavors. Tight and firm, but showing great depth and intensity. Firm tannins rise on the finish. A long-term (7–10 years) cellar candidate.

1994 Cabernet Sauvignon, Wedding Vineyard, Sonoma County $50.   **92**

Very deep ruby hue with a slight purple cast. Full-bodied. Balanced acidity. Highly extracted. Moderately tannic. Currants, black fruit, tea. Aromatically reserved, with a powerful, tightly wound palate feel. Dense and brooding, though not thick or heavy, with excellent structure. Tannins clamp down on the finish, though this should open with long-term (7–10 years) aging.

1996 Merlot, RCF Vineyard, Napa Valley $30.   **89**

Bright violet red. Generous cherry fruit aromas are appealing, with a minerally note. Lush on the attack, with a moderately full-bodied palate that shows concentrated black cherry flavors lifted by juicy acids. Fine-grained tannins supply some grip on the minerally finish. Drink now or later. Can improve with more age.

Flora Springs

1997 Chardonnay, Reserve, Napa Valley $24.   **88**

Full golden yellow. Very aromatic with rich, ripe smoky aromas. A lush entry is followed by a full-bodied palate with tropical ripeness and oaky accents that linger on the finish. A big, bold style.

1995 Cabernet Sauvignon, Cypress Ranch, Napa Valley $40.   **90**

Opaque purple. Full-bodied. Highly extracted. Quite tannic. Pepper, licorice, black fruit. Heavyweight, dry, and big-shouldered, with drying, earthy tannins clamping down on the finish. This will need rare meaty fare for near-term consumption.

1994 Trilogy, Napa Valley $30.   **90**

Dark cherry red. Medium-bodied. Highly extracted. Moderately tannic. Earth, black fruits, brown spice. Rich earthy, minty nose with toasty accents leads a solid, mouthfilling palate, with some assertive structure giving authority and grip through the finish.

1995 Trilogy, Napa Valley $40.   **93**

Deep ruby cast. Moderately full-bodied. Balanced acidity. Moderately extracted. Moderately oaked. Mildly tannic. Mint, red fruits, vanilla. Aromatic and harmonious, with a lush, supple entry. Exquisitely made, with gentle extraction making for a velvety mouthfeel. Flavorful and generous through the lengthy finish.

1996 Trilogy, Napa Valley $45.   **90**

Saturated dark violet red hue. Intensely aromatic with bright cassis and tobacco notes. A rich entry leads a full-bodied palate with a deep core of lushly extracted fruit flavors with waves of spice and licorice through the lengthy finish.

1995 Merlot, Napa Valley $16.   **87**

Very deep ruby hue to the rim. Medium-bodied. Balanced acidity. Highly extracted. Mildly oaked. Mildly tannic. Black fruits, chocolate, minerals. Somewhat perfumed in character, with a dense mouthfeel. Chewy tannins come out on the lingering finish.

1995 Merlot, Windfall Vineyard, Napa Valley $32.   **93**

Deep, opaque blackish ruby hue. Moderately full-bodied. Balanced acidity. Highly extracted. Moderately oaked. Mildly tannic. Black fruits, brown spices, mint. Quite aromatic, with a big, rich mouthfilling character. Features a chewy texture with velvety tannins, and a lengthy flavorful finish.

1996 Merlot, Windfall Vineyard, Napa Valley $40.   **92**

Saturated dark ruby hue. Dense aromas of oak, dark fruits, and earth. A firm entry leads a full-bodied palate with very dense flavors showing great depth of fruit and a heavy oak accent that lingers on the finish. Tannins are dry and dusty. A big, dense wine with a thick mouthfeel. Drink now or later.

1996 Pinot Noir, Lavender Hill Vineyard, Carneros $20.   **82**

Thomas Fogarty

1997 Chardonnay, Monterey $17.50.   **80**

1997 Chardonnay, Santa Cruz Mountains $19.   **80**

1996 Chardonnay, Estate Reserve, Santa Cruz Mountains $28.   **84**

Bright yellow-gold. Moderately full-bodied. Full acidity. Highly extracted. Moderately oaked. Nuts, spice, citrus. Reserved nutty aromas lead a weighty, solid mouthful of broad flavors held together by firm acids that stretch out through the finish.

1997 Gewürztraminer, Monterey $12.50.   **89**

Deep yellow-straw hue. Bold, generous flower and spice aromas. A lush entry leads a moderately full-bodied palate, with mild sweetness offset by vibrant acidity. Ripe, flavorful finish. Drink now.

1996 Cabernet Sauvignon, Napa Valley $25.   **89**

Saturated deep violet hue. Aromatically reserved with cherry fruit and vanilla. A crisp entry leads a medium-bodied palate with bright cherry fruit flavors and mild but dry fine-grained tannins. Youthful and angular with fine varietal flavors. Drink now or later.

1996 Cabernet Sauvignon, Santa Cruz Mountains $25.   **90**

Deep ruby hue. High-toned anise, vanilla, and brown spice aromas carry a big oak accent. A lush attack leads to a moderately full-bodied palate with velvety tannins and bright acidity. Supple, harmonious, wood-accented finish. A very stylish wine, drinking beautifully now. Drink now.

1996 Merlot, Santa Cruz Mountains $23.   **85**

Bright, saturated ruby red. High-toned red fruit and mineral aromas. A crisp attack, and a moderately light-bodied palate with zesty acidity and subtle tannins. Bright, fruit-forward finish. Drink now.

Scale: Superlative (96-100), Exceptional (90-95), Highly Recommended (85-89), Recommended (80-84), Not Recommended (Under 80)

90

1996 Pinot Noir, Santa Cruz Mountains $27. **86**

Deep ruby cast. Moderately full-bodied. Low acidity. Moderately extracted. Mildly tannic. Anise, black fruits. Forward aromas carry an unusual high-toned quality. Broad in the mouth, with low acidity levels fleshing out the finish.

1995 Pinot Noir, Estate Reserve, Santa Cruz Mountains $30. **89**

Full cherry red. Medium-bodied. Highly extracted. Moderately oaked. Moderately tannic. Full oak and red fruit aromas. Concentrated raspberry and cherry flavors have plenty of dry oak accents in support. Youthful and tight at present.

1996 Sangiovese, Estate Reserve, Santa Cruz Mountains $27.50. **91**

Saturated ruby purple. Medium-bodied. Balanced acidity. Highly extracted. Moderately oaked. Moderately tannic. Vanilla, red fruits. Solid, tight palate of red fruits, with a heavy influence of new oak barrels that give it a strong vanilla note and a dry finish. Quite silky and stylish.

Foley

1996 Chardonnay, Barrel Select, Santa Barbara County $25. **94**

Deep straw cast. Moderately full-bodied. Full acidity. Moderately extracted. Moderately oaked. Citrus, vanilla, brown spices. Generous aromas feature a big oak component and join a core of zesty citrus flavors in the mouth. Sumptuous and flavorful, with a fine acid backbone that make for a firm and lengthy finish.

1997 Chardonnay, Barrel Select, Santa Barbara County $28. **98**

Deep gold. Nutty, generously oaky aromas are very Burgundian. Very fruity on the attack, leading a moderately full-bodied palate with vibrant acids to match the rich fruity center. Persistent fruit character through the finish. Very impressively concentrated, with lavish winemaking. Drink now or later.

1997 Chardonnay, Bien Nacido Vineyard, Santa Maria Valley $24. **95**

Deep yellow-straw hue. Opulent tropical fruit and toasted coconut aromas indicate a sweet wood influence. A crisp entry leads a moderately full-bodied palate with racy acidity. Shows great intensity of flavor and excellent grip, and a complex, stylish finish. Drink now.

1996 Sauvignon Blanc, Santa Barbara County $14. **93**

Yellow-straw hue. Medium-bodied. Balanced acidity. Highly extracted. Lemon, limes, minerals. Forceful and intense on the palate. This has a smoky theme through the finish. Showing no shortage of character, this is an exuberant California interpretation of the Pessac style.

1995 Cabernet Sauvignon, La Cuesta Vineyard, Santa Ynez Valley $27. **88**

Full cherry red with subtle purple highlights. Medium-bodied. Moderately extracted. Mildly tannic. Plums, cassis, licorice, earth. Bright black fruit flavors reveal smoky Cabernet fruit character. The lingering finish has plenty of complexity. Well balanced and full of character.

1996 Pinot Noir, Santa Maria Hills Vineyard, Santa Maria Valley $25. **87**

Dark ruby purple. Full-bodied. Full acidity. Highly extracted. Moderately tannic. Anise, chocolate, tea. Aromatic and complex, with an unusual array of flavors. Full, firm, and zesty in the mouth, showing great intensity. Finishes with a hint of bitterness.

1997 Pinot Noir, Santa Maria Hills Vineyard, Santa Maria Valley $32. **89**

Bright saturated ruby purple. Moderately full-bodied. Full acidity. Highly extracted. Moderately tannic. Dried herbs, tea, iron. Forward aromas are complex and distinctive. Full throttled in the mouth, with real intensity and depth of flavor. Lengthy and persistent.

Folie à Deux

1993 Fantaisie Brut, Napa Valley $18. **85**

Bright yellow-straw hue. Medium-bodied. Full acidity. Yeast, minerals, citrus. Developed, yeasty aromas are distinctive. Crisp and bright on the palate, with an angular, drying finish that could use another year to resolve.

1995 Cabernet Sauvignon, Napa Valley $18.   87

Medium ruby red. Medium-bodied. Moderately extracted. Mildly tannic. Red berries, brown spice. Vanilla and spice nose shows berry fruit accents that are confirmed on the palate. God oak spice flavors through the finish. Balanced and appealingly straightforward.

1995 Cabernet Sauvignon, Reserve, Napa Valley $22.   88

Dark ruby center with purple highlights. Medium-bodied. Moderately extracted. Mildly tannic. Plums, pepper, brown spice. An assertively spicy, peppery nose is confirmed on the palate, with full black fruit flavors giving a sense of depth.

1996 Sangiovese, Amador County $16.   85

Bright blackish garnet cast. Moderately full-bodied. Low acidity. Moderately extracted. Mildly tannic. Overripe red fruits, dried herbs. Extremely ripe, with a hint of Port. Soft and flabby in the mouth, this could use a bit more grip.

1996 Zinfandel, Old Vine, Amador County $18.   86

Deep blackish ruby cast. Medium-bodied. Balanced acidity. Moderately extracted. Mildly oaked. Mildly tannic. Chocolate, minerals. Reserved aromatically, with a lighter-styled though flavorful mouthfeel. Soft and velvety through the finish.

1996 Zinfandel, Eschen Vineyard Old Vine, Fiddletown $22.   87

Bright blackish ruby hue. Moderately full-bodied. Balanced acidity. Highly extracted. Mildly oaked. Mildly tannic. Black fruits, minerals. Somewhat reserved aromatically, with a full, ripe mouthfeel. Highly structured, with lean tannins and a lengthy finish.

Foppiano

1996 Petite Sirah, Russian River Valley $16.   83

Opaque, saturated purple-red hue. Restrained spicy wood and black fruit aromas. A lush attack leads a very full-bodied palate, with robust astringent tannins. The finish is thick, with grip. Lots of stuffing but rather shy of flavor. Drink now or later. Can improve with more age.

Forest Glen

1997 Chardonnay, California $9.99.   90

Rich golden yellow. Powerful toasted wood, citrus, and cream aromas show a hefty oak accent. A ripe attack leads a moderately full-bodied palate with juicy acidity. Flavorful, lengthy finish. Shows a lot of style. Drink now or later.

1996 Cabernet Sauvignon, California $9.99.   84

Bright crimson-purple hue. Markedly toasty oak-accented aromas with ripe cassis notes. A firm entry leads to a medium-bodied wine with plenty of dry oaky flavors and a bright fruity backdrop with grainy tannins. Drink now.

1997 Merlot, California $9.99.   83

Full violet ruby hue. Oak-accented aromas follow through on the medium-bodied palate with up-front brambly fruit flavors and an earthy dry note coming through on the finish.

1996 Sangiovese, California $9.99.   87

Bright cherry red. Moderately light-bodied. Balanced acidity. Moderately extracted. Moderately oaked. Mildly tannic. Red berries, vanilla. Soft, rounded, and supple. Finishes with velvety tannins and vanilla flavors.

1996 Shiraz, California $9.99.   84

Medium red-purple. Red currants, vanilla, and mineral flavors. Hint of wood tones. A firm entry leads a medium-bodied palate. Moderate, drying tannins. Fruit flavors are rather muted. Subtle, short finish. Dry and lean, this will work best with food. Drink now.

Forest Hill

1995 Chardonnay, Private Reserve, Napa Valley $60.   81

Scale: Superlative (96-100), Exceptional (90-95), Highly Recommended (85-89), Recommended (80-84), Not Recommended (Under 80)

Forest Ville

1997 Chardonnay, California $5.99.   83

Bright yellow-straw hue. Subtle mineral and citrus aromas. A creamy entry leads a
medium-bodied palate with rounded acidity. The finish is clean and weighty. Drink now.

1997 Gewürztraminer, California $5.99.   86

Deep yellow-straw hue. Generous spice, citrus, and orange rind aromas. A lush entry
leads a moderately full-bodied palate, with marked sweetness offset by solid acidity.
Flavorful and intense. Drink now.

1996 Johannisberg Riesling, California $5.99.   81

1995 Sauvignon Blanc, California $5.99.   83

Bright pale yellow. Medium-bodied. Balanced acidity. Moderately extracted. Mildly oaked.
Vanilla, citrus. Faintly smoky aromas lead a simple palate, with faint varietal flavors and a
hint of oak influence on the finish.

1997 White Zinfandel, California $4.99.   81

1998 White Merlot, California $5.99.   82

1996 Cabernet Sauvignon, California $5.99.   81

1997 Merlot, California $5.99.   86

Bright violet red. Attractive vanilla and cherry fruit aromas. Medium-bodied, open-knit
style with generous red fruit and oak accents through the clean finish. Very user friendly
and supple.

1997 Shiraz, California $5.99.   84

Pale cherry-purple color, limpid and brilliant, with a slight fade. Subtle, pleasant herb,
black fruit, and vanilla flavors. Hint of wood tones. A soft entry and a medium-bodied
palate. Light, drying tannins. Subtle, short finish. This is a jammy, lighter style to drink
now.

Forman

1996 Chardonnay, Napa Valley $28.   81

1994 Cabernet Sauvignon, Napa Valley $38.   88

Bright crimson red. Medium-bodied. Moderately extracted. Moderately tannic. Cherries,
berries, vanilla. Bright aromas lead tightly wound cherry fruit flavors. Solid, though not
a heavyweight in style. Oak flavors are in fine balance. Has a youthful character.

1995 Cabernet Sauvignon, Napa Valley $40.   91

Deep violet purple. Medium-bodied. Highly extracted. Moderately tannic. Cassis, spice.
Bright through the finish, which has some grip and a dusting of fine-grained tannins.
The mouthfeel is rich and deep.

Fox Hollow

1997 Chardonnay, California $8.99.   83

Deep yellow-straw hue. Subdued citrus and spice aromas. A full entry is followed by a
moderately full-bodied palate with edgy acidity and a subtle finish. Drink now.

1995 Cabernet Sauvignon, California $8.99.   86

Bright cherry red with subtle purple cast. Ripe fruit-centered aromas show cassis and
subtle oak influence. A lush entry leads to a medium-bodied palate with lush, supple
tannins and generous, ripe fruit flavors that linger on the finish. Drink now.

1997 Merlot, California $8.99.   86

Bright violet red. Faintly fleshy aromas lead a soft attack with vanilla oak and black
fruit flavors on a medium-bodied palate. Finishes with mild, grainy tannins. A soft, lush
easy-drinking style. Drink now.

1997 Pinot Noir, Monterey County $8.99.   83

Bright violet red. Cherries, vanilla. Crisp, vibrant, fruity aromas follow through on a
supple palate with precise black cherry flavors.

1996 Shiraz, California $8.99.   **86**

Pale purple, limpid, and brilliant, with a slight fade. Subtle, pleasant cherry and vanilla flavors. Hint of wood tones. Smooth entry. Moderately light-bodied. Very mild, silky tannins. Structurally light, with up-front bright fruit flavors carried by fruit acidity. Subtle, short finish. Straightforward and quaffable. Drink now.

Foxen

1995 Pinot Noir, Sanford & Benedict Vineyard, Santa Ynez Valley $28.   **89**

Bright ruby red. Medium-bodied. Moderately extracted. Moderately oaked. Mildly tannic. Elegant, complex aromas. Rich black and red berry fruit flavors, with lingering sweet tobacco and vanilla notes.

Foxridge

1997 Chardonnay, Carneros $9.99.   **86**

Pale straw hue. Medium-bodied. Balanced acidity. Moderately extracted. Citrus, apples. Clean, fruity aromas. Bright, lively, and juicy, with a crisp finish that does not show much oak influence.

Franciscan

1995 Chardonnay, Oakville Estate, Cuvée Sauvage, Napa Valley $30.   **91**

Deep yellow-gold. Full-bodied. Balanced acidity. Highly extracted. Moderately oaked. Lanolin, minerals, spices. Forward and aromatic, with complex and enticing flavors. Rich, lush, and opulent in the mouth. Acidity provides a backbone, though this is rich through the finish.

1996 Chardonnay, Oakville Estate, Cuvée Sauvage, Napa Valley $30.   **94**

Full gold. Generous aromas of toasted oak, yeast, ripe fruits, and butter. An opulent attack leads a moderately full body with rich flavors that taper to an oaky, leesy finish. Very stylish and decadent. Some bottle age should help this settle down. Drink now or later.

1997 Chardonnay, Oakville Estate, Napa Valley $15.   **86**

Bright gold. Moderate aromas of browned butter and tropical fruits. A rich entry leads a full-bodied palate with opulent texture, though the fruit flavors are somewhat restrained. The finish is clean. Drink now.

1994 Cabernet Sauvignon, Oakville Estate, Napa Valley $17.   **90**

Deep red. Moderately full-bodied. Highly extracted. Mildly tannic. Plums, cassis, toasted oak. Ripe, faintly Port-like nose. Rich, supple black fruit flavors unfold on the palate and linger through the toasty finish. Very plush and generously fruity style.

1995 Cabernet Sauvignon, Oakville Estate, Napa Valley $17.   **86**

Deep ruby red with a slight fade. Moderately full-bodied. Balanced acidity. Moderately extracted. Mildly oaked. Mildly tannic. Cassis, minerals, spice. Pleasantly aromatic, with a firm palate feel. Focused and angular through the finish, with a big, chunky character.

1994 Oakville Estate, Magnificat Meritage, Napa Valley $25.   **91**

Dark blood red. Medium-bodied. Moderately extracted. Moderately tannic. Toasted oak, black currants, plums. Full berry fruit aromas have a toasty accent. Ripe, bright black fruit flavors fill the palate and linger through the finish. Delicious, with lots of primary fruit flavors making it irresistible.

1995 Oakville Estate, Magnificat Meritage, Napa Valley $30.   **89**

Deep ruby hue with a slight fade to the rim. Moderately full-bodied. Balanced acidity. Moderately extracted. Heavily oaked. Mildly tannic. Brown spices, leather, red fruits. Generous aromas are largely oak driven, with a big spicy overlay of flavor throughout. Soft and supple in the mouth, with a well-structured, somewhat angular finish.

Scale: Superlative (96-100), Exceptional (90-95), Highly Recommended (85-89), Recommended (80-84), Not Recommended (Under 80)

1996 Merlot, Napa Valley $17.   **84**

Dark ruby hue with a slight fade. Generous fruit and vanilla aromas. Medium-bodied, with a lush, ripe attack that follows through on the midpalate with fine-grained tannins and vanilla oak. Drink now or later. Can improve with more age.

Franus

1994 Cabernet Sauvignon, Napa Valley $25.   **86**

Solid, opaque blackish red. Moderately full-bodied. Highly extracted. Moderately tannic. Earth, plums, black fruits. Full meaty aromas lead a deeply textured palate, with lots of integrated dry, fine-grained tannins providing excellent grip. Plenty of fleshy fruit flavors here. Medium-term cellaring.

Freemark Abbey

1996 Chardonnay, Napa Valley $20.   **81**

1996 Chardonnay, Carpy Ranch Vineyard, Napa Valley $26.   **84**

Deep straw cast. Moderately full-bodied. Balanced acidity. Moderately extracted. Minerals, citrus, butter. Aromatically reserved, with a lean and zesty presence on the palate. Crisp and angular through the finish.

1994 Cabernet Sauvignon, Napa Valley $19.99.   **88**

Bright reddish purple. Medium-bodied. Moderately extracted. Moderately tannic. Plums, cassis, cedar. Generous, rounded, plush, bright Cabernet fruit flavors unfold on the silky palate. The tannins are still quite dry and youthful through the finish.

1995 Cabernet Sauvignon, Napa Valley $24.   **87**

Bright ruby hue. Interesting mint, earth, and mineral aromas. A lean attack leads to a medium-bodied palate with earthy flavors and supple tannins. A ripe, fruity quality emerges on the finish. Stylish and flavorful. Drink now.

1992 Cabernet Sauvignon, Bosché Estate, Napa Valley $27.99.   **92**

Deep ruby red. Medium-bodied. Moderately extracted. Moderately tannic. Black cherries, toasted oak. Expressive, integrated aromas have a toasty accent. Rich but supple entry shows a velvety character, with plenty of vigorous tannins coming through on the finish. Nice now, but this will soldier on in the cellar.

1994 Cabernet Sauvignon, Bosché Estate, Napa Valley $44.   **92**

Bright ruby hue to the rim. Opulent red fruit and mineral aromas carry a subtle oak accent. A crisp entry leads to a moderately full-bodied palate with lush, chewy tannins. Zesty acidity lends buoyancy to the flavors. Ripe, racy finish. Approachable and well balanced with the structure to age beautifully. Drink now or later.

1992 Cabernet Sauvignon, Sycamore Vineyard, Napa Valley $26.49.   **90**

Full ruby red. Medium-bodied. Moderately extracted. Mildly tannic. Black bramble fruits, lead pencil, chalk. Lead pencil aromas lead a velvety palate, with fine chalky tannins coming through on the finish. Balanced and very well integrated. Drinking nicely now.

1993 Cabernet Sauvignon, Sycamore Vineyard, Napa Valley $28.99.   **89**

Deep ruby cast. Moderately full-bodied. Balanced acidity. Moderately extracted. Moderately oaked. Mildly tannic. Vanilla, red fruits, minerals. Generous aromas lead a supple and harmonious palate feel. Gentle and velvety, though quite flavorful, with fine length.

Freestone

1994 Cabernet Sauvignon, Napa Valley $15.   **89**

Ruby-red center with a pale rim. Medium-bodied. Moderately extracted. Mildly tannic. Vanilla, black cherries, brown spice. Straightforward red and black fruit flavors with a rounded mouthfeel and a tart spicy edge running through the finish. Very accessible and drinking well now.

Frey

1997 Cabernet Sauvignon, Butow Vineyards, Redwood Valley $10.50. **89**

Bright purple-red hue. Intense black fruit and vanilla aromas show a sweet oak accent. A ripe attack leads to a moderately full-bodied palate with juicy acidity and lush tannins. Flavorful, lengthy finish. Shows excellent cut and integration. Well balanced and stylish. Drink now or later.

Frick

1994 Zinfandel, Dry Creek Valley $15. **84**

Bright blackish purple. Medium-bodied. Full acidity. Highly extracted. Mildly tannic. Briar fruits, minerals. Quite aromatic, with a high-toned quality. Light, juicy, and angular in the mouth. Finishes on a tart note.

Gabrielli

1995 Pinot Noir, Floodgate Vineyard, Anderson Valley $17. **88**

Full cherry red. Medium-bodied. Moderately extracted. Moderately oaked. Moderately tannic. Ripe berry and vanilla aromas lead a sweet berry fruit entry that turns quite dry and assertive through the finish. Plenty of depth of flavor and a solid structure, with well-balanced oakiness.

Gainey

1996 Chardonnay, Limited Selection, Santa Barbara County $28. **87**

Bright straw cast. Medium-bodied. Full acidity. Moderately extracted. Toast, yeast, citrus. Fine toasty aromas. Light on the palate, with delicate yet complex flavors. Crisp and stylish through the zesty finish.

1998 Riesling, Central Coast $10. **83**

Pale straw hue. Tart citrus aromas with a floral note. Crisp on entry, leading a medium-bodied palate with leaner citrus flavors lingering on the finish. Drink now.

1996 Cabernet Franc, Limited Selection, Santa Ynez Valley $20. **86**

Rich ruby hue with a slight fade. Generous wood and black fruit aromas. A lush entry leads to a moderately full-bodied palate with firm tannins. Rich, tannic finish. Big, but rather tough at present. Drink now or later.

1996 Merlot, Santa Ynez Valley $16. **87**

Deep, saturated ruby red. Forward cedar, black fruit, and vanilla aromas show a big oak accent. A soft attack leads a full-bodied, lush mouthfeel with robust powdery tannins. The finish is rich and flavorful. Shows depth and intensity on a generous frame. Drink now or later. Can improve with more age.

1996 Pinot Noir, Limited Selection, Santa Maria Valley $28. **89**

Deep ruby-garnet cast. Moderately full-bodied. Full acidity. Moderately extracted. Moderately oaked. Mildly tannic. Spice, red fruits, sweet wood. Generous aromas feature ripe fruit and sweet oak overtones. Lush and flavorful in the mouth, yet underpinned by a firm, minerally backbone and zesty acidity. Finishes with fine length and intensity.

Gallo Sonoma

1997 Chardonnay, Russian River Valley $14. **88**

Bright yellow-gold. Generous ripe citrus aromas with judicious oak and yeast accents. A generous, lush attack leads a moderately full-bodied palate with broad, full fruit flavors that persist through the finish. Hedonistic. Drink now.

1996 Chardonnay, Estate, Northern Sonoma $38. **94**

Deep yellow-straw hue. Forward, flashy aromas show a buttery, yeasty opulence and a big oak accent. A rich entry leads a full-bodied palate with racy acidity lending balance. Big and intensely flavored with fine grip and a lengthy, persistent finish. A great show style. Drink now or later.

1996 Chardonnay, Laguna Ranch Vineyard, Russian River Valley $20.   87

Bright yellow-gold. Moderately full-bodied. Balanced acidity. Highly extracted. Moderately oaked. Smoke, toast, citrus. Aromatically complex, with a pleasant toasty accent and a core of citric flavors. Rich and ripe through the finish.

1996 Chardonnay, Stefani Vineyard, Dry Creek Valley $18.   86

Bright straw cast. Moderately full-bodied. Balanced acidity. Moderately extracted. Mildly oaked. Cream, brown spices, citrus. Ripe and opulent, with a lush, rounded texture offset by zesty acidity. Rich and lengthy through the finish.

1994 Cabernet Sauvignon, Sonoma County $12.   87

Deep garnet hue. Generous cedar and brown spice aromas show a mellow oak accent. A rich entry leads to a full-bodied palate with silky tannins and excellent acidic structure. Firm, flavorful finish. A harmonious and very elegant wine. Drink now or later.

1994 Cabernet Sauvignon, Barrelli Creek Vineyard, Alexander Valley $20.   90

Deep ruby hue. Moderately full-bodied. Balanced acidity. Moderately extracted. Heavily oaked. Mildly tannic. Toasted coconut, plums. Quite fragrant, with a hefty oak overlay and a dense, chewy palate feel. Lush and supple through the lengthy finish.

1993 Cabernet Sauvignon, Frei Ranch Vineyard, Dry Creek Valley $18.   91

Blackish red. Moderately full-bodied. Highly extracted. Moderately tannic. Brown spice, black fruits, earth. Exotic, spicy nose shows dark fruit flavors. The concentrated, assertively full-flavored palate has rich earthy qualities, with exotic spices lingering on the dry finish. Tannins are quite dry and authoritative.

1994 Cabernet Sauvignon, Frei Ranch Vineyard, Dry Creek Valley $18.   93

Saturated dark red. Moderately full-bodied. Highly extracted. Moderately tannic. Briar fruits, anise, toasted coconut. Powerful spicy aromas lead expressive black fruit flavors, with ripe tannins that conclude with a touch of dryness. Very flavorsome and drinking well now.

1993 Cabernet Sauvignon, Stefani Vineyard, Dry Creek Valley $18.   88

Opaque black cherry hue. Moderately full-bodied. Highly extracted. Quite tannic. Black fruits, black tea, earth, brown spice. Ripe plummy flavors on entry expand on the midpalate giving a fleshy quality. Assertively dry, with strapping tannins through the finish.

1994 Cabernet Sauvignon, Stefani Vineyard, Dry Creek Valley $18.   86

Very deep ruby red hue. Intensely fragrant brown spice and licorice aromas show a dominant wood influence. A lush attack leads to a full-bodied palate with big grainy tannins. Firm, flavorful finish. A big showy style, drinking well now, but lacking long term acidity. Drink within five years.

1993 Cabernet Sauvignon, Estate, Northern Sonoma $45.   90

Dark blackish red. Moderately full-bodied. Highly extracted. Quite tannic. Black tea, black fruits, cinnamon, brown spice, plums. Enticing spicy nose. Vigorous and youthful, with ripe extracted flavors on entry turning dry and assertive through the finish.

1994 Cabernet Sauvignon, Estate, Northern Sonoma $54.99.   93

Deep ruby hue. Subdued mineral and earth aromas show a slight oak influence. A firm attack leads to a medium-bodied palate with strong tannins and shy acidity. Firm, intense finish. Drink within five years.

1994 Valdigue, Barrelli Creek Vineyard, Alexander Valley $13.   89

Deep cherry red. Medium-bodied. Moderately extracted. Mildly tannic. Briar fruit, chocolate. Mature, earthy aromas lead a deeply flavored, fleshy mouthful of mature-tasting fruit with dark chocolatey notes through the finish.

1996 Merlot, Sonoma County $11.   87

Deep, saturated purple-red. Subdued overripe red fruit aromas. A firm attack followed by a medium-bodied palate with robust tannins. The finish is lean and flavorful. Overall, on the firm side. Drink now.

1996 Pinot Noir, Russian River Valley $11.99.   84

Light ruby red with a slight fade. Moderately full-bodied. Balanced acidity. Moderately extracted. Mildly tannic. Minerals, chocolate. Aromatically reserved, with a weighty impression on the palate. Tasty, but somewhat lacking in finesse.

1995 Zinfandel, Barrelli Creek Vineyard, Alexander Valley $14.   87

Opaque blackish cast. Full-bodied. Balanced acidity. Moderately extracted. Moderately oaked. Mildly tannic. Chocolate, black fruits. Quite aromatic, deep, and brooding. Lush, rich, and flavorful on the palate, with a thick, velvety quality. Supple and well balanced through the finish.

1995 Zinfandel, Frei Ranch Vineyard, Dry Creek Valley $14.   84

Deep blackish purple. Medium-bodied. Balanced acidity. Moderately extracted. Mildly oaked. Mildly tannic. Black fruits, minerals. Somewhat reserved aromatically, with a lighter-styled, minerally palate feel. Firm and compact through the finish, with solid grip. A lean and elegant style.

Gan Eden

1997 Black Muscat, San Joaquin County $14.   85

Pale cherry red. Exotic rose and black cherry aromas spring from the glass. A crisp entry leads a moderately light-bodied palate that has mild sweetness. Snappy and flavorful. Drink now.

1997 Gewürztraminer, Late Harvest, Monterey County $14.   80

Geyser Peak

1994 Shiraz-Cabernet, Sparkling, Alexander Valley $19.99.   84

Full cherry red. Medium-bodied. Vanilla, plums. Red wine aromas have an oak-aged Shiraz impression that follows through in a lighthearted manner on the palate. For those who like their red wine with bubbles; or possibly the ideal barbecue wine.

1997 Chardonnay, Sonoma County $14.   82

1996 Chardonnay, Reserve, Alexander Valley $23.   90

Bright yellow-straw hue. Opulent brown spice and tropical fruit aromas show a sweet oak influence. A rich attack leads a full-bodied palate with vibrant acidity. Juicy, intense finish. Drink now.

1997 Sauvignon Blanc, Sonoma County $8.50.   82

1996 Cabernet Franc, Winemaker's Selection, Alexander Valley $20.   83

Bright ruby purple hue. Subdued mineral and anise aromas. An angular entry leads to a medium-bodied palate with austere, mildly astringent tannins. Firm, flavorful finish. On the tough side. Drink within 5 years.

1994 Cabernet Sauvignon, Reserve, Alexander Valley $28.   88

Saturated, deep crimson red. Medium-bodied. Highly extracted. Moderately tannic. Cassis, black fruits, brown spice, tea. Toasty aromas have black fruit accents. Compact on the midpalate, with some angular tannins on the finish. A solid wine with good structure.

1995 Cabernet Sauvignon, Reserve, Alexander Valley $24.99.   89

Dark purple. Full-bodied. Balanced acidity. Highly extracted. Heavily oaked. Moderately tannic. Oriental spices, lacquer, minerals. Outrageously aromatic, with a huge oak accent. Firm, concentrated, and tightly wound in the mouth, with a wallop of tannins through the finish. Needs time.

1996 Malbec, Winemaker's Selection, Alexander Valley $20.   85

Deep, brilliant purple red hue. Unusual, high-toned anise and mineral aromas. A crisp attack leads to a rich, moderately full-bodied mouthfeel, with zesty acidity. Vibrant, flavorful finish. Well balanced and carries its weight well. Drink within five years.

Scale: Superlative (96-100), Exceptional (90-95), Highly Recommended (85-89), Recommended (80-84), Not Recommended (Under 80)

1994 Reserve Alexandre Meritage, Alexander Valley $28.   **88**

Full cherry red with a bright cast. Medium-bodied. Moderately extracted. Mildly tannic.
Red berries, cassis, dried herbs, toasted oak. Rounded, soft, and supple on entry, with
bright fruity flavors lingering on the finish. Excellent balance and an appealing juicy
character make for pleasurable early drinking.

1995 Reserve Alexandre Meritage, Alexander Valley $24.99.   **88**

Deep ruby purple. Moderately full-bodied. Balanced acidity. Highly extracted. Moderately
oaked. Mildly tannic. Vanilla, cassis, licorice. Pleasantly aromatic, with intertwined wood
and fruit flavors. Well balanced and lean through the finish, with crisp acidity.

1996 Reserve Alexandre Meritage, Alexander Valley $32.   **84**

Bright purple red hue. Forward berry and mineral aromas carry a slight oak accent.
A lighter entry leads to a moderately light-bodied palate with subtle tannins. Shows some
grip to the finish. Almost a quaffer. Lacks intensity or depth. Drink now.

1996 Merlot, Reserve, Alexander Valley $32.   **88**

Deep, saturated purple-red. Intense anise and vanilla aromas show a dominant oak
accent. A rich entry leads a moderately full-bodied, chunky palate with big drying
tannins. Firm, structured finish. Could use a bit more time to resolve its structure.
Good for long-term cellaring.

1996 Petite Sirah, Winemaker's Selection, Alexander Valley $20.   **88**

Saturated purple. Moderately full-bodied. Highly extracted. Quite tannic. Significantly
oaky aromas follow through on the palate, with black cherry flavors. Dry, astringent
tannins have a chalky character on the finish.

1996 Petite Verdot, Winemaker's Selection, Alexander Valley $20.   **86**

Opaque, saturated purple red hue. Subdued anise and mineral aromas carry a big oak
accent. A thick entry leads to a full-bodied palate with big firm tannins. Shows breadth of
flavor before the tannins bite into the finish. Impressively extracted. Drink now or later.

1996 Shiraz, Sonoma County $16.   **86**

Medium purple color, limpid and brilliant, with a slight fade. Generous, pleasant
aromas of vanilla, black fruits, flowers. Generous wood tones. A firm entry leads a
medium-bodied palate, with crisp acidity. Moderate, drying tannins. Crisp and lean
on the midpalate, with bright fruit. Lingering finish. Drink now.

1996 Shiraz, Reserve, Sonoma County $32.   **87**

Deep purple, opaque, and brilliant. Generous, pleasant blackberry and mineral flavors.
Generous wood tones. Firm entry. Moderately full-bodied, with crisp acidity and plentiful
grainy tannins. Dry, lean, and angular, though well extracted. Lingering finish. Fine
American oak accents.

1995 Zinfandel, Sonoma County $15.   **83**

Bright blackish purple. Moderately full-bodied. Full acidity. Moderately extracted.
Mildly oaked. Mildly tannic. Red fruits, minerals. Fruit-centered and relatively high-toned
aromas. Full, but quite lively on the palate, with well-balanced acidity.

1995 Henry's Reserve Shiraz Port, Alexander Valley $15/375 ml.   **87**

Opaque dark cherry red. Medium-bodied. Moderately extracted. Reminiscent of
blackberries, plums, black tea. Rich, plummy black fruit aromas open up on the
midpalate. Finishes with a dry, solid layer of tannins that suggest this will soften with
some age. Good balance.

Girard

1994 Cabernet Sauvignon, Napa Valley $25.   **90**

Dark crimson center with purple highlights. Moderately full-bodied. Moderately
extracted. Moderately tannic. Cassis, cedar. Toasty oak nose shows black fruit accents.
Pure, focused black Cabernet fruit is supple and generous, with textured, rounded
tannins on a very persistent fruity finish.

1995 Cabernet Sauvignon, Napa Valley $28.   **92**
Bright ruby purple. Moderately full-bodied. Balanced acidity. Moderately extracted.
Moderately oaked. Mildly tannic. Licorice, mint. Unusual, high-toned aromatics are
stylish and complex. Lean and angular in the mouth, with a focused and well-defined
personality. Crisp, lengthy finish.

1994 Cabernet Sauvignon, Reserve, Napa Valley $40.   **91**
Full purple-red. Medium-bodied. Highly extracted. Moderately tannic. Cassis, toasted
oak. The tight, focused fruity nose shows generous oaky accents. Great concentration and
fine-toasted character, with good tannic grip through the finish. Youthful and vigorous,
this will need time to show its best.

Glen Ellen

1995 Viognier, Expressions, San Benito County $11/375 ml.   **87**
Bright golden cast. Full-bodied. Balanced acidity. Moderately extracted. Mildly oaked.
Cinnamon, orange peel, pine. Outrageously aromatic, with a huge and complex
bouquet. The exotic flavors are well translated onto a rich and supple palate. Good
grip and fine length.

1996 Cabernet Sauvignon, Proprietor's Reserve, California $6.   **81**

1997 Gamay Beaujolais, Proprietor's Reserve, California $5.   **81**

Grand Cru

1996 Gewürztraminer, California $7.99.   **80**

1996 Johannisberg Riesling, California $7.99.   **83**
Gold-straw hue. Aromatically intense, with petrol and mineral accents. Concentrated
flavors on the attack, leading a moderately full-bodied palate, with sweetness up front
giving way to leaner, dryer flavors on the finish. Rather unusual. Drink now.

1995 Sauvignon Blanc, California $7.99.   **83**
Brilliant pale yellow-gold. Medium-bodied. Balanced acidity. Moderately extracted.
Heavily oaked. Vanilla, smoke, ripe citrus. Assertive French oak aromas. A heavy smoky
note pervades the palate and lingers through the finish. Solid weight and mouthfeel.
Some will like the oak dominance and others will hate it.

1996 Cabernet Sauvignon, Premium Selection, California $7.99.   **83**
Bright cherry red hue. Aromas show toasted oak, vanilla, and black fruits. A light,
fruity attack leads to a medium-bodied palate with smooth tannins and a lively finish.
Drink now.

1997 Merlot, California $7.99.   **86**
Violet purple with a bright cast. Bright fruity aromas have cherry and vanilla accents.
Medium-bodied, flavorful, and fruity on the attack, showing fine grip and grainy tannins
through the finish. Drink now or later. Can improve with more age.

1995 Pinot Noir, Premium Selection, California $7.99.   **80**

1997 Syrah, California $7.99.   **83**
Medium crimson purple, limpid and brilliant, with a slight fade. Subtle, sound cherry,
berry fruit, and vanilla flavors. Subtle wood tones. Smooth entry. Medium-bodied.
Moderate, velvety tannins. Lingering rich finish. Peppery, jammy, youthful, and supple.
Drink now.

1996 Zinfandel, Premium Selection, California $7.99.   **84**
Deep blackish purple. Medium-bodied. Balanced acidity. Moderately extracted. Heavily
oaked. Moderately tannic. Vanilla, black fruits. Hefty oak notes dominate the nose and
join ripe berry flavors on the palate. Lighter in style and relatively soft, with a pleasant,
lingering finish.

Granite Springs

1995 Zinfandel, El Dorado $11.50.   **86**

Bright blackish ruby cast. Moderately full-bodied. Balanced acidity. Moderately extracted. Moderately oaked. Mildly tannic. Chocolate, black fruits. Quite aromatic, with a firm and flavorful mouthfeel. Well balanced and deep through the finish.

Green & Red

1996 Zinfandel, Chiles Valley Vineyards, Napa Valley $18.   **84**

Bright blackish ruby cast. Medium-bodied. Balanced acidity. Subtly extracted. Mildly tannic. Red fruits, minerals. Rather reserved aromatically, with a lighter-styled, lean palate feel. Focused and angular through the finish.

Grey Wolf

1995 Cabernet Sauvignon, Paso Robles $20.   **83**

Deep ruby cast. Moderately full-bodied. Balanced acidity. Moderately extracted. Moderately oaked. Mildly tannic. Brown spices, red fruits, minerals. Shows a spicy oak accent throughout. Lean and firm in the mouth. Acidity makes for a bright, juicy finish.

1994 Barton Family Reserve Meritage, Paso Robles $19.   **87**

Deep crimson red. Moderately full-bodied. Highly extracted. Moderately tannic. Cassis, licorice, mint. Solid, structured style. Features a full-flavored, viscous mouthful of dark fruit flavors that linger through the finish. Impressively proportioned wine in a classic style. A heavyweight.

1995 Barton Family Reserve Meritage, Paso Robles $22.   **89**

Dark violet red with a subtle fade. Medium-bodied. Moderately extracted. Moderately tannic. Tobacco, earth, black fruits. Ripe dark fruit aromas with earthy overtones. Weighty and flavorsome, though open-knit in structure. Earthy tannins on the finish ride lightly on the palate. Best consumed when still relatively young.

1995 Merlot, Reserve, Paso Robles $17.   **83**

Deep ruby purple. Medium-bodied. Balanced acidity. Moderately extracted. Mildly oaked. Mildly tannic. Earth, licorice, black pepper. Slightly funky aromatics, with a lighter-styled, crisp palate. Finishes with some wood notes and mild astringency.

Grgich Hills

1997 Chardonnay, Napa Valley $30.   **88**

Bright golden yellow. Moderately aromatic with subtle butter, vanilla, and ripe fruits. A juicy entry leads a moderately full-bodied palate with ripe, generous citrus flavors and a subtle oak impression on the finish. Drink now.

1996 Fumé Blanc, Napa Valley $18.   **87**

Deep straw cast. Moderately full-bodied. Full acidity. Highly extracted. Citrus, minerals. Aromatic, with a firm and angular though flavorful mouthfeel. Crisp through the finish with a hint of bitterness.

1994 Cabernet Sauvignon, Napa Valley $30.   **91**

Saturated, deep reddish purple. Medium-bodied. Highly extracted. Moderately tannic. Cassis, black fruits, minerals. Very aromatic nose. The compact palate has a crisp edge. Solid dry tannins are accentuated by fine acids. Very well structured and lively, though not yet showing its best.

1995 Cabernet Sauvignon, Napa Valley $45.   **93**

Bright ruby red hue. Generous red fruit and vanilla aromas carry a sweet oak accent. A crisp entry leads to a medium-bodied palate buoyed by juicy acidity. Flavorful, vibrant finish. Stylish and well balanced with particularly admirable acidity. Drink now or later.

1994 Cabernet Sauvignon, Yountville Selection, Napa Valley $85.   93

Bright purple-red hue. Intense and exotic spice, floral, and anise aromas. A lean entry leads to a medium-bodied palate with grippy tannins. Shows admirable restraint and finesse in these days of high alcohol show monsters. Lively, buoyant finish. Well balanced and showing excellent grip and intensity through the finish. Drink now or later.

1995 Zinfandel, Sonoma County $18.   88

Dark ruby purple. Moderately full-bodied. Balanced acidity. Moderately extracted. Mildly oaked. Mildly tannic. Chocolate, black fruits. Reserved in style, with a firm, focused mouthfeel. Rich nonetheless, with deep fruit and mineral flavors. More of a Claret style.

1995 Violetta, Late Harvest, Napa Valley $40/375 ml.   90

Deep tawny amber hue. Exotic toffee and caramel aromas show a touch of rancio. A lush entry leads a medium-bodied palate with lean acids and mild sweetness. Well balanced, with complex, Sherried flavors. Drink now.

Groth

1995 Cabernet Sauvignon, Napa Valley $30.   89

Deep ruby cast. Medium-bodied. Balanced acidity. Moderately extracted. Mildly oaked. Mildly tannic. Minerals, red fruits. Elegant and reserved, with firm and focused flavors. Crisp and lean through the angular finish.

Guenoc

1997 Chardonnay, North Coast $15.50.   84

Pale straw cast. Medium-bodied. Full acidity. Moderately extracted. Minerals, citrus zest, dried herbs. Lean and angular, with an herbal cast. Firm and zesty through the finish.

1996 Chardonnay, Reserve, Genevive Magoon Vineyard, Guenoc Valley $25.   90

Full yellow-straw hue. Moderately full-bodied. Balanced acidity. Highly extracted. Moderately oaked. Yeast, smoke, ripe citrus. Smoky aromas follow though on a structured, firm palate, with nutty depth and a spicy finish. Still youthful and tight, this should improve.

1997 Chardonnay, Reserve, Genevive Magoon Vineyard, Guenoc Valley $25.   89

Pale yellow-straw color. Moderately full-bodied. Balanced acidity. Highly extracted. Vanilla, smoke, green apples. A tart and vibrant core of crisp fruit and a good dollop of oak spice through the finish give this a lingering complexity.

1996 Chardonnay, "Unfiltered" Reserve, Genevive Magoon Vineyard, Guenoc Valley $30.   91

Yellow-straw hue. Moderately full-bodied. Full acidity. Moderately extracted. Mildly oaked. Citrus, vanilla, spice. Perfumed vanilla and spice aromas. Vibrant and angular on the palate, with racy citric acids and oak spice vying for attention through the finish.

1997 Chardonnay, "Unfiltered" Reserve, Genevive Magoon Vineyard, Guenoc Valley $30.   92

Bright yellow-straw color. Medium-bodied. Full acidity. Moderately extracted. Moderately oaked. Vanilla, yeast, apples. Attractive yeasty aromas. Vibrant and racy, with crisp flavors complemented by smoke and vanilla notes that emerge on the finish along with notable yeast complexity.

1996 Sauvignon Blanc, North Coast $13.50.   84

Pale straw cast. Medium-bodied. Balanced acidity. Moderately extracted. Mildly oaked. Smoke, citrus zest. Smoky tropical aromas lead a rounded fruit-centered palate. Not weighty, but delightful in flavor intensity and purity.

1996 Cabernet Sauvignon, California $12.   84

Bright cherry red. Medium-bodied. Moderately extracted. Mildly tannic. Red fruits, vanilla, minerals. Plush fruit-centered aromas follow through on the palate, with a brief, dry finish.

Scale: Superlative (96-100), Exceptional (90-95), Highly Recommended (85-89),
Recommended (80-84), Not Recommended (Under 80)

102

1995 Cabernet Sauvignon, North Coast $15.50.   **84**

Dark, saturated ruby hue. Medium-bodied. Full acidity. Moderately extracted. Mildly tannic. Minerals, red fruits. Firm and minerally, with a zesty palate feel. Vibrant, mouthwatering acidity makes for a bright if slightly austere finish.

1994 Cabernet Sauvignon, Beckstoffer IV Reserve, Napa Valley $40.50.   **88**

Bright purple. Moderately full-bodied. Full acidity. Moderately extracted. Moderately oaked. Mildly tannic. Vanilla, black fruits, minerals. Aromatic and intense, with a bright, fruit-centered quality. Crisp and lean through the juicy finish.

1995 Cabernet Sauvignon, Beckstoffer IV Reserve, Napa Valley $40.50.   **86**

Bright purple. Moderately full-bodied. Full acidity. Moderately extracted. Mildly oaked. Mildly tannic. Licorice, red fruits, minerals. Bright, zesty, angular, and crisp, in a high-toned, fruit-accented style. The finish is lean and flavorful.

1994 Cabernet Sauvignon, Bella Vista Reserve, Napa Valley $30.50.   **85**

Deep ruby purple. Moderately full-bodied. Highly extracted. Moderately tannic. Beets, minerals. Earthy, austere aromas. Fleshy dark fruit flavors are overtaken by lean, slightly bitter notes on the finish.

1995 Cabernet Sauvignon, Bella Vista Reserve, Napa Valley $30.50.   **89**

Dark ruby-brick red. Medium-bodied. Highly extracted. Heavily oaked. Moderately tannic. Vanilla, chocolate, berry fruits. Strong oak accents on the nose. Deep and voluptuous dark fruit flavors, with a full complement of earthy, chocolatey notes persisting through the finish. Very supple up front, though oak tannins dry the finish.

1995 Meritage, California $18.50.   **86**

Bright violet-red. Medium-bodied. Moderately extracted. Moderately tannic. Brown spice, red cherries, minerals. Dusty, oak-spiced aromas follow through on a crisp, minerally palate, with dry, minerally tannins highlighted by the vibrant acids. Firm and dry.

1995 Petite Sirah, California $15.50.   **84**

Dark purple. Moderately full-bodied. Highly extracted. Moderately tannic. Succulent dark cherry fruit aromas. Well gripped and solidly extracted, with dry tannins on the finish.

1996 Zinfandel, California $11.   **86**

Deep blackish purple. Medium-bodied. Full acidity. Highly extracted. Moderately tannic. Black fruits, minerals. Rather unyielding aromatically, with a firm, highly structured, intense palate feel. Features a core of brooding black fruit flavors, and finishes with solid tannins.

1994 Vintage Port, California $25.   **87**

Dark cherry red with a ruby cast. Medium-bodied. Balanced acidity. Moderately extracted. Moderately oaked. Moderately tannic. Reminiscent of tobacco, lacquer, brown spice, baked raspberry tart. Compact texture. A brawny style, with youthful tannins up front. Sweet berry notes are nicely accented by soft, plush earthy components. A polished style, if a bit coarse at the present. Should cellar well.

Guglielmo

1997 Chardonnay, Vineyard Selection Series, Monterey County $9.95.   **81**

1997 Chardonnay, Private Reserve, Monterey County $14.   **86**

Emphatic deep gold. Butter and oak-spiced aromas show a subdued fruity character. A lean entry leads a moderately full-bodied palate with lush buttery qualities. Fruit flavors are faint through the finish. Drink now.

Gundlach Bundschu

1997 Chardonnay, Rhinefarm Vineyards, Sonoma Valley $16.   **83**

Bright straw hue. Lean minerally aromas. A crisp entry leads a moderately light-bodied palate with racy acidity. Shows little if any oak influence. Clean, tart finish. Drink now.

1997 Chardonnay, Sangiacomo Ranch, Sonoma Valley $18.   **80**

1997 Gewürztraminer, Rhinefarm Vineyards, Sonoma Valley $12.　　**81**

1996 Cabernet Sauvignon, Rhinefarm Vineyards, Sonoma Valley $24.　　**87**

Deep purple red hue. Intense and unusual floral, anise, and mineral aromas. A supple entry leads to a ripe and rounded moderately full-bodied palate. Rich, herb-tinged finish shows complexity. A well-balanced, well-structured style. Drink now or later.

1996 Merlot, Rhinefarm Vineyards, Sonoma Valley $21.　　**89**

Deep ruby-violet red. Generous, spicy oak-accented aromas show dill and cedar notes. A rich attack is followed by a moderately full-bodied palate with chewy tannins and softer acids. Drink now or later. Can improve with more age.

Hacienda

1997 Chardonnay, Clair de Lune, California $6.99.　　**82**

1996 Cabernet Sauvignon, Clair de Lune, California $6.99.　　**86**

Bright cherry red hue. Attractive cedar, vanilla, and cassis aromas. A rich entry leads to a moderately full-bodied palate with lush, velvety tannins and generous cassis fruit flavors. Drink now.

1997 Merlot, Clair de Lune, California $6.99.　　**84**

Deep, dark violet hue. Brambly, ripe fleshy aromas. Medium-bodied, with bright blackberry and cherry flavors up front, and subtle velvety tannins and obvious vanilla oak flavors lingering on the finish. Drink now.

1996 Pinot Noir, Clair de Lune, California $6.99.　　**86**

Pale violet red. Moderately light-bodied. Moderately extracted. Mildly tannic. Vanilla, red berries. Perfumed, sweetish aromas lead a bright and fruity palate with lively acids providing solid grip.

1996 Shiraz, Clair de Lune, California $6.99.　　**84**

Medium cherry red, limpid and brilliant to the rim. Generous, sound cedar and cherry flavors. Generous wood tones. Smooth entry. Medium-bodied. Moderate velvety tannins. Oak dominated, with brown spice notes. Subtle finish. Drink now.

Hagafen

1997 Chardonnay, Napa Valley $13.50.　　**83**

Pale straw cast. Moderately full-bodied. Full acidity. Moderately extracted. Citrus, minerals. Aromatically reserved, with lean, crisp, focused flavors. Ripe and zesty through the finish.

1997 Chardonnay, Reserve, Napa Valley $18.　　**87**

Bright straw cast. Moderately full-bodied. Balanced acidity. Moderately extracted. Mildly oaked. Spice, melon, minerals. Forward aromas carry a spicy oak overlay. Bright and crisp in the mouth, with an angular, zesty finish.

1998 Johannisberg Riesling, Napa Valley $12.　　**86**

Pale straw hue. A lean attack leads a medium-bodied palate with stone fruit flavors and subtle herbal notes through the finish. Mildly off-dry style. Drink now.

1996 Cabernet Franc, Napa Valley $18.　　**87**

Bright ruby cast. Medium-bodied. Balanced acidity. Moderately extracted. Moderately oaked. Moderately tannic. Red fruits, vanilla. Aromatic and deeply flavored, with a core of ripe fruit flavors and a generous oak accent. Firm and intense in the mouth, with a lengthy finish. Approachable, but should continue to improve.

1995 Cabernet Sauvignon, Napa Valley $20.　　**85**

Opaque, deep purple-red. Medium-bodied. Highly extracted. Moderately tannic. Black fruit, plums, brown spice. Violets and spice in the nose follow through on the palate. Concentrated flavors, with a tart edge and plenty of soft tannins that give texture. A bit young and aggressive.

1996 Cabernet Sauvignon, Napa Valley $24. **80**

1996 Pinot Noir, Napa Valley $13. **86**
Strawberry red. Moderately light-bodied. Moderately extracted. Moderately oaked. Mildly tannic. Vanilla and strawberry aromas are well conveyed on the palate. Crisp and juicy through the finish. Well balanced, very drinkable.

Hahn Estates

1997 Chardonnay, Monterey $11. **83**
Deep straw cast. Moderately full-bodied. Balanced acidity. Moderately extracted. Mildly oaked. Lychee, spice, butter. Generous flavors carry an aromatic varietal overtone. Ripe and rounded, with a buttery note to the finish.

1996 Cabernet Franc, Santa Lucia Highlands $10. **83**
Bright ruby cast. Moderately light-bodied. Balanced acidity. Subtly extracted. Mildly tannic. Vegetables, minerals. Shows a green streak throughout. Light though firmly structured in the mouth, with a lean finish.

1996 Red Meritage, Santa Lucia Highlands $15. **87**
Saturated dark ruby red hue. Very ripe fruit with an herbal streak. A tart entry leads a moderately full-bodied palate with bright fruit flavors and racy tart acids that give this great cut through the finish. Finishes very cleanly. Drink now.

Hallcrest

1991 Cabernet Sauvignon, Covington Vineyards,
El Dorado County $22.50. **85**
Dark blackish red. Medium-bodied. Moderately extracted. Moderately tannic. Plums, black tea, earth. Leafy, earthy aromas are confirmed on the palate. Bright acids keep this lively and accentuate the tough tannins that make for an assertive finish.

Handley

1993 Brut, Anderson Valley $22. **84**
Bright yellow-gold. Medium-bodied. Full acidity. Baked bread, ripe citrus. Bright, lively, and clean, with a high-toned, fruity accent. Flavors show impressive concentration through the finish.

1997 Chardonnay, Anderson Valley $18. **81**

1997 Chardonnay, Dry Creek Valley $18. **83**
Medium gold. Moderate aromas show alcohol. A bright, tart entry is followed by a medium-bodied palate that has straightforward tart fruit flavors that finish quickly, with mild oak influences. Drink now.

1997 Pinot Gris, Anderson Valley $18. **83**
Bright platinum cast. Medium-bodied. Full acidity. Moderately extracted. Smoke, minerals. Reserved aromatically, with a lean, racy, vibrant palate feel. Finishes with a telltale smoky richness.

Hanna

1996 Chardonnay, Russian River Valley $16. **83**
Brilliant yellow-gold. Moderately full-bodied. Balanced acidity. Moderately extracted. Mildly oaked. Honey, apples, spice. Curiously honeyed, rich aromas lead a juicy, fruity mouthful of flavors with a clean, mouthwatering finish. Rather distinctive.

1995 Cabernet Sauvignon, Alexander Valley $20. **90**
Bright ruby purple. Medium-bodied. Balanced acidity. Moderately extracted. Moderately oaked. Mildly tannic. Black fruits, brown spices, minerals. Generous aromatics lead a lean and pure mouthfeel, with precise fruit flavors. Crisp and angular, with excellent definition to the lengthy finish.

1995 Merlot, Alexander Valley $21. **89**

Deep ruby with a slight purplish cast. Medium-bodied. Balanced acidity. Moderately extracted. Mildly oaked. Mildly tannic. Plums, minerals, sweet herbs. Still a little reined in aromatically, with a youthful, compact palate. Fruit driven and very dense in flavor through the finish. Has some chunky tannins that should be mitigated with mid-term (3–6 years) cellaring.

Harmony

1997 Chardonnay, San Luis Obispo County $14.50. **85**

Deep yellow-straw hue. Opulent vanilla, citrus, and cream aromas show a hefty oak accent. A firm entry leads a moderately full-bodied palate with rounded acidity. Extremely lengthy buttery finish. Rather wood dominated, but hedonistically interesting.

1997 Johannisberg Riesling, Paso Robles $9. **84**

Medium gold hue. Classical aromas of petrol and green apples. A bright attack leads a medium-bodied palate, with rich flavors and an oily note through the finish. Fine, pure Riesling character. Drink now.

Harrison

1994 Cabernet Sauvignon, Napa Valley $33. **89**

Dark crimson with subtle purple highlights. Medium-bodied. Moderately extracted. Mildly tannic. Cassis, plums, cedar. Rich, ripe Cabernet aromas. Smooth and velvety, with textured black fruit flavors and supple tannins on the finish. Quite a polished style that is very accessible for current drinking.

Hartford Court

1996 Chardonnay, Seascape Vineyard, Sonoma Coast $35. **89**

Deep golden cast. Full-bodied. Balanced acidity. Highly extracted. Moderately oaked. Brown spices, tropical fruits, yeast. Generous aromatics lead a rich mouthfeel buttressed by firm acidity. Ripe and intense yet well balanced, with complex flavors.

1995 Pinot Noir, Dutton Ranch-Sanchietti Vineyard, Russian River Valley $29. **84**

Medium reddish purple. Medium-bodied. Moderately extracted. Moderately oaked. Moderately tannic. An oak-dominated nose leads a mild black cherry and pepper palate, with bitter notes on the finish.

1995 Pinot Noir, Arrendell Vineyard, Russian River Valley $34. **87**

Dark reddish purple. Medium-bodied. Highly extracted. Moderately oaked. Moderately tannic. Generous black cherry and raspberry aromas have a chocolate richness through the finish. Plenty of stuffing, but also lots of toasted oak through the finish.

1996 Pinot Noir, Arrendell Vineyard, Russian River Valley $42. **88**

Bright saturated ruby purple. Moderately full-bodied. Balanced acidity. Highly extracted. Mildly oaked. Moderately tannic. Minerals, chocolate, black fruits. Bright aromas lead a weighty and intense mouthfeel. Competent, but seems to lack that extra dimension and ends up seeming a tad hollow.

Hartwell

1997 Chardonnay, Stags Leap District, Napa Valley $39.99. **84**

Bright yellow-gold. Moderate aromas of citrus zest and oak spice. A crisp entry leads a medium-bodied palate with bright citrus flavors. Finishes with a note of dryness and oak spice. Well balanced, with bright acids. Drink now.

1994 Cabernet Sauvignon, Sunshine Vineyard, Stags Leap District $45. **85**

Garnet-brick red. Medium-bodied. Moderately extracted. Mildly tannic. Earth, black fruit, currant. Minty accents on the nose. An austere, earthy palate has toasty, spicy flavors lingering on the finish. Nice now, this does not need further cellaring.

Scale: Superlative (96-100), Exceptional (90-95), Highly Recommended (85-89), Recommended (80-84), Not Recommended (Under 80)

1995 Cabernet Sauvignon, Sunshine Vineyard, Stags Leap District $80.   **94**

Opaque blood red. Moderately full-bodied. Highly extracted. Quite tannic. Cassis, licorice, earth. Deep, fleshy aromas have an earthy accent that follows on a rich, spicy mouthful of flavors, concluding firmly with assertive tannins.

Havens

1994 Bourriquot, Napa Valley $28.   **88**

Deep reddish purple. Medium-bodied. Highly extracted. Moderately tannic. Plums, black fruits, bitter chocolate, brown spice. Full, assertive, and rich, with deep savory flavors that linger through a chalky, bitter-chocolate finish. Approachable now, though this should be better in a few years.

1996 Merlot, Napa Valley $20.   **84**

Bright ruby hue with a subtle fade. Clean cherry fruit and vanilla aromas. Soft on the attack, with a medium-bodied palate and ripe berry flavors that finish with soft tannins. Drink now.

Hawk Crest

1997 Chardonnay, California $10.   **81**
1996 Sauvignon Blanc, Stag's Leap Wine Cellars, California $8.   **82**
1996 Cabernet Sauvignon, California $12.   **81**

Haywood

1997 Chardonnay, Vintner's Select, California $7.99.   **81**
1996 Cabernet Sauvignon, California $8.50.   **81**
1997 Merlot, California $7.99.   **86**

Bright violet-ruby red. Perfumed, fruity aromas have a berry fruit quality. Medium-bodied, lush on the attack with velvety tannins and juicy berry fruit flavors. Finishes with soft, lush tannins. Well stuffed and flavorsome. Drink now.

1995 Zinfandel, Los Chamizal Vineyard, Sonoma Valley $18.   **84**

Dark ruby purple. Moderately full-bodied. Balanced acidity. Moderately extracted. Mildly tannic. Black fruits. Pleasantly aromatic, with a ripe, luxuriant array of fruit-centered flavors on the palate. Lush in texture and well balanced, with a focused finish.

1995 Zinfandel, Rocky Terrace, Los Chamizal Vineyard,
Sonoma Valley $25.   **87**

Dark ruby purple to the rim. Moderately full-bodied. Balanced acidity. Moderately extracted. Moderately oaked. Mildly tannic. Brown spices, black fruits, chocolate. Quite aromatic, with a hefty oak accent and a flavorful palate feel. Lush and deep in the mouth, with a velvety quality. Finishes with some mild, dusty tannins.

Heartswood

1995 Chardonnay, Private Reserve, Monterey $9.99.   **86**

Deep yellow-straw cast. Moderately full-bodied. Balanced acidity. Moderately extracted. Flowers, spice. Forward, generous aromas show an opulent spicy accent. Lush, generous, and rounded in the mouth, with a note of viscosity.

Heiss

1997 Chardonnay, Santa Clara Valley $25.   **88**

Pale yellow-green. Medium-bodied. Full acidity. Moderately extracted. Moderately oaked. Lemon, minerals. Clean, bright primary fruit flavors with a considerable overlay of spicy, nutty oak accents that make for a complex finish.

Heitz

1997 Chardonnay, Cellar Selection, Napa Valley $18.   84

Medium yellow-gold. Melon and pear aromas have a buttery accent. A thick entry leads a full-bodied palate with a heavy malolactic character. Finishes in a thick alcoholic manner. Very generous.

1992 Cabernet Sauvignon, Napa Valley $20.   89

Bright brick red. Medium-bodied. Moderately extracted. Mildly tannic. Cassis, mineral, mint, dried herbs. Subtle herbal, minty aromas lead a solid, full-flavored palate, with a firm minerally backbone and a hint of firm tannins on the finish. Plenty of character.

1993 Cabernet Sauvignon, Napa Valley $21.   86

Deep ruby-garnet cast. Moderately full-bodied. Balanced acidity. Moderately extracted. Mildly oaked. Moderately tannic. Mint, earth, chocolate. Forward aromas have a high-toned accent and a deep, earthy quality. Rich in the mouth, with an angular, structured finish.

1994 Cabernet Sauvignon, Napa Valley $25.   86

Dark ruby hue. Plummy, very ripe aromas. A heavy entry leads a full-bodied palate with a thick mouthfeel and low acidity. Big shouldered and chocolatey with very tough tannins that dry the finish. This will need much more time. Drink now or later.

1993 Cabernet Sauvignon, Bella Oaks Vineyard, Napa Valley $28.   86

Deep ruby cast. Moderately full-bodied. Balanced acidity. Moderately extracted. Mildly tannic. Red fruits, mint, minerals. Light in style, with a pure, focused palate feel. Crisp and intense through the flavorful finish.

1994 Cabernet Sauvignon, Bella Oaks Vineyard, Napa Valley $35.   83

Fading ruby with a garnet rim. Weak, mildly herbal aromas seem rather tired. A weak entry leads a medium-bodied palate with dilute flavors and a dull woody finish. Not showing much concentration or the ability to age any further. Drink now.

1992 Cabernet Sauvignon, Martha's Vineyard, Napa Valley $68.   93

Dark blood red. Medium-bodied. Moderately extracted. Moderately tannic. Cassis, plums, mint, minerals, tea. A ripe, somewhat earthy nose shows minty accents. Very attractive bright black fruit flavors have a solid underlying minerally base, with astringent tannins keeping the finish dry. Very impressive now, though this can only improve.

1992 Cabernet Sauvignon, Trailside Vineyard, Napa Valley $48.   87

Bright blood red. Medium-bodied. Highly extracted. Moderately tannic. Cassis, mint, minerals. A very particularly eucalyptus nose. Rich, supple Cabernet fruit flavors unfold on the palate, with dusty tannins lingering on the minty finish.

1993 Cabernet Sauvignon, Trailside Vineyard, Napa Valley $48.   91

Deep ruby hue with a slight purple edge. Moderately full-bodied. Balanced acidity. Moderately extracted. Mildly oaked. Mildly tannic. Licorice, mint, minerals. Aromatic and complex, with an emphasis on pure fruit flavors showing terroir, not winemaking. Supple and gentle in the mouth, with fine intensity through the finish.

1996 Grignlino Port, Napa Valley $18.   83

Deep blackish purple. Medium-bodied. Low acidity. Moderately extracted. Black fruits, licorice. Pleasantly aromatic and solidly fruit centered, with a touch of heat. Ripe, flavorful, and straightforward on the palate, with a decidedly sweet finish.

Helena View

1995 Cabernet Franc, Johnston Vineyards, Napa Valley $30.   84

Bright ruby-garnet cast. Medium-bodied. Balanced acidity. Moderately extracted. Heavily oaked. Mildly tannic. Spice, cherries. Quite aromatic, with oak-driven flavors throughout. Light in the mouth, with a lean, angular finish.

1992 Cabernet Sauvignon, Napa Valley $20.   **90**

Full brick red. Medium-bodied. Moderately extracted. Mildly tannic. Vanilla, toasted oak. Minty, mature nose is well expressed on the palate. Very toasty through the finish. Oaky style with astringency running through the finish. Drinking very well now.

1994 Cabernet Sauvignon, Napa Valley $32.50.   **86**

Pale cherry red. Medium-bodied. Moderately extracted. Mildly tannic. Oak spice, red fruits. Supple and juicy, in a very straightforward, early-drinking manner. Harmonious, if lighter in style.

1995 Cabernet Sauvignon, Napa Valley $32.50.   **84**

Pale cherry red. Medium-bodied. Moderately extracted. Mildly tannic. Dill, red fruits. An aromatic, oaky nose follows through on a lightweight palate with straightforward berry flavors. Nicely balanced, drinking well now.

1995 Cabernet Sauvignon, Tradition, Napa Valley $38.   **85**

Mature pale garnet red. Medium-bodied. Moderately extracted. Mildly tannic. Leather, spice, black fruits. Showing perfumed, mature character on the palate, with light, leathery flavors and a touch of tannic bite. Not for further keeping.

Hendry

1993 Cabernet Sauvignon, Block 8, Napa Valley $22.   **93**

Opaque blackish red. Medium-bodied. Highly extracted. Moderately tannic. Sweet herbs, black cherries, mint, brown spice. Exotic, fresh herbal aromas. Rich and concentrated black fruit flavors on the palate have a minty accent that lingers through a solid finish. Very attractive now, though it has sound structure for cellaring.

1995 Cabernet Sauvignon, Block 8, Napa Valley $24.   **90**

Bright ruby cast. Medium-bodied. Balanced acidity. Moderately extracted. Mildly oaked. Mildly tannic. Mint, red fruits. Forward, distinctive aromatics feature a decidedly minty accent. Lighter in style, with a supple quality and a juicy, flavorful finish.

1995 Zinfandel, Block 7, Napa Valley $18.   **89**

Deep ruby cast. Medium-bodied. Balanced acidity. Moderately extracted. Moderately oaked. Mildly tannic. Brown spices, mint, red fruits. Shows a flashy, spicy oak accent to the nose, with a core of bright fruit flavors in the mouth. Well balanced and lively, with an uplifting, lengthy finish.

Herzog

1997 Chardonnay, Baron Herzog, California $12.95.   **88**

Brilliant yellow-straw hue. Generous brown spice and pear aromas show a hefty oak accent. A rich entry leads a moderately full-bodied palate with rounded acidity. The finish is ripe and stylish. Drink now.

1996 Chardonnay, Special Reserve, Russian River Valley $19.99.   **86**

Bright pale gold. Medium-bodied. Balanced acidity. Moderately extracted. Brown spice, citrus, butter. Smoky, zesty aromas lead a smooth, spicy mouthful of flavors with a rounded texture through the finish.

1998 White Zinfandel, Baron Herzog, California $6.95.   **80**

1995 Cabernet Sauvignon, Baron Herzog, California $13.99.   **86**

Bright crimson red with a purple rim. Medium-bodied. Moderately extracted. Mildly tannic. Cassis, black fruits, currant, oak spice. Soft, rounded berry fruit flavors unfold on the palate. A ripe, fruity style with nice oak spice on the finish.

1996 Cabernet Sauvignon, Baron Herzog, California $13.99.   **86**

Bright cherry red. Medium-bodied. Moderately extracted. Mildly tannic. Vanilla, cassis. Clean, fruity accents follow through on the palate, with a supple character and a mild note of minerally astringency through the finish.

1994 Cabernet Sauvignon, Special Reserve, Alexander Valley $26.69.   **91**

Dark crimson with subtle purple highlights. Medium-bodied. Highly extracted. Mildly tannic. Vanilla, tobacco, black fruits. Sweet, ripe fruity aromas. Rich, flavor-packed palate has ripe chocolatey accents and a lingering toasty finish. Very attractive and forward.

1995 Cabernet Sauvignon, Special Reserve, Alexander Valley $25.99.　　　**91**

Very deep ruby hue. Moderately full-bodied. Balanced acidity. Moderately extracted. Moderately oaked. Mildly tannic. Vanilla, spice, black fruits. A toasty nose melds seamlessly with a firm core of fruit flavors on the palate. Balance and elegance are key, with a focused and well-structured though supple finish. Fine length and intensity.

1997 Gamay, Baron Herzog, Paso Robles $7.95.　　　**83**

Pinkish red. Moderately light-bodied. Subtly extracted. Mildly tannic. Herbs, flowers, citrus. Crisp herbaceous aromas lead a taut, vibrant palate with a cleansing finish.

1996 Zinfandel, Baron Herzog, California $12.99.　　　**86**

Bright ruby purple. Medium-bodied. Full acidity. Moderately extracted. Moderately oaked. Mildly tannic. Vanilla, briar fruits. Toasty oak nuances emerge on the nose and join a wave of bright, fruit-centered flavors in the mouth. Lighter in style, with a sense of liveliness brought forth by buoyant acidity.

Hess Collection

1996 Chardonnay, Napa Valley $15.　　　**89**

Bright yellow-gold. Medium-bodied. Balanced acidity. Moderately extracted. Mildly oaked. Yeast, citrus. Smooth, rounded mouthfeel has a ripe core of fruit flavors with restrained oak spice not overwhelming the ensemble. Very appealing and direct, with a nice mouthfeel.

1993 Cabernet Sauvignon, Mount Veeder, Napa Valley $20.　　　**94**

Bright dark red. Medium-bodied. Highly extracted. Moderately tannic. Vanilla, toasted oak, cassis, plums. Delicious toasty oak aromas lead an elegantly fruity palate, with juicy ripe accents and firm oak spice flavors on the finish. A little too vigorous now, it should settle with a few years aging.

1994 Cabernet Sauvignon, Mount Veeder, Napa Valley $19.75.　　　**91**

Deep ruby purple. Moderately full-bodied. Balanced acidity. Moderately extracted. Moderately oaked. Moderately tannic. Vanilla, red fruits, minerals. Forward, fruit-centered flavors feature a spicy oak accent. Rich and firm in the mouth, with abundant ripe tannins. Lengthy finish.

1995 Cabernet Sauvignon, Mount Veeder, Napa Valley $24.75.　　　**92**

Deep, saturated ruby red hue. Powerful briar, brown spice, and mineral aromas. A lush entry leads to a moderately full-bodied palate with complex gamey flavors and velvety tannins. Generous and supple finish with fine length. Approachable, but has the extract to age. Drink now or later.

1995 Merlot, Mount Veeder, Napa Valley $22.50.　　　**84**

Bright ruby red. Generous mocha and plum aromas have an oaky accent. Full-bodied, with a firm attack and solidly structured palate firmly gripped by tannins and showing complex, evolved flavors. Judiciously oaked. Drink now or later. Can improve with more age.

Hidden Cellars

1996 Chauche Gris, Mendocino $11.　　　**84**

Bright golden hue. Full-bodied. Balanced acidity. Moderately extracted. Cream, oranges. Rather reserved aromatically, but quite full and rich on the palate, with a mouthfilling character. Snappy acidity lends a sense of balance to the finish. A big wine for rich food, and consumption over the near term.

1996 Sauvignon Blanc, Mendocino $13.　　　**84**

Bright golden yellow. Medium-bodied. Balanced acidity. Moderately extracted. Mildly oaked. Butter, yeast, brown spice. Soft, vanilla-accented aromas lead a textured mouthfeel, with buttery character balanced by zesty acids on the mildly oak-spiced finish.

Scale: Superlative (96-100), Exceptional (90-95), Highly Recommended (85-89), Recommended (80-84), Not Recommended (Under 80)

1996 Sorcery Red, Mendocino $28.   **86**

Bright blackish ruby cast. Medium-bodied. Balanced acidity. Highly extracted. Moderately oaked. Quite tannic. Vanilla, briar fruits. Very aromatic, with a lighter-styled mouthfeel. Finishes with impressively firm tannins. Rather tough at present.

1995 Zinfandel, Mendocino Heritage, Hildreth Ranch, Mendocino $25.   **86**

Deep blackish ruby cast. Moderately full-bodied. Balanced acidity. Moderately extracted. Mildly oaked. Mildly tannic. Chocolate, black fruits, forest floor. Quite aromatic, with a soft, supple, flavorful palate feel. Crisp and focused through the finish.

1996 Zinfandel, Mendocino Heritage, Ford-Hitzman Vineyards,
Mendocino $32.   **89**

Deep blackish ruby cast. Moderately full-bodied. Balanced acidity. Moderately extracted. Moderately oaked. Mildly tannic. Brown spices, chocolate, black fruits. Quite aromatic, with a hefty wood accent to the core of bright fruit flavors. Supple and rich in the mouth, with velvety tannins through the finish.

1996 Zinfandel, Old Vines, Mendocino $18.   **85**

Bright blackish ruby cast. Moderately full-bodied. Balanced acidity. Highly extracted. Moderately oaked. Quite tannic. Stewed red fruits, wood. Intensely aromatic, with a hint of overripeness and a touch of heat. Firm and compact in the mouth, with a tannic finish.

William Hill

1997 Chardonnay, Napa Valley $14.50.   **86**

Bright yellow-gold. Restrained yeasty and buttery aromas. A rich entry leads a moderately full-bodied palate with ripe, full fruit flavors and judicious oak. Generous alcohol gives this a degree of warmth on the finish.

1997 Chardonnay, Reserve, Napa Valley $20.   **86**

Medium straw cast. Moderately full-bodied. Balanced acidity. Moderately extracted. Mildly oaked. Apples, melon, butter. Floral, fruity aromas. Weighty, buttery smooth, and very conventional, with reserved fruit expression and glycerous texture.

1995 Cabernet Sauvignon, Napa Valley $16.   **82**

1996 Cabernet Sauvignon, Napa Valley $18.   **86**

Deep violet-red hue. Very ripe fleshy fruit aromas. A lush attack leads a moderately full-bodied palate with a rich center of cassis fruits and softer acids. Finishes with textured, supple tannins. A hedonistic style. Drink now.

1994 Cabernet Sauvignon, Reserve, Napa Valley $27.   **90**

Deep red-purple with a lightening rim. Medium-bodied. Moderately extracted. Moderately tannic. Vanilla, violets. Floral aromas. Tight and angular, with grainy, aggressive tannins drying the finish. This has all the attributes of a very youthful wine that will need time.

1995 Cabernet Sauvignon, Reserve, Napa Valley $27.   **88**

Saturated dark violet hue. Generously aromatic black cherry and vanilla aromas. A fruity attack leads a moderately full-bodied palate with bright fruit forward flavors and judicious, supple tannins. Very generous and fruity. Drink now.

1996 Merlot, Napa Valley $19.   **84**

Bright violet purple. Generous raspberry aromas. Medium-bodied, with a supple attack and a rounded, ripe mouthful of red fruit flavors with soft acids and mild tannins. Drink now.

HMR Winery

1997 Muscat Canelli, Paso Robles $11.   **80**

Hop Kiln

1996 Zinfandel, Sonoma County $16.   90

Dark ruby purple. Moderately full-bodied. Balanced acidity. Moderately extracted. Mildly tannic. Briar fruits, chocolate. Quite aromatic, with a deep, fruit-centered character. Lush, but well structured on the palate. Shows good grip and intensity through the finish.

1996 Primitivo Zinfandel, Sonoma County $22.   90

Deep blackish purple. Moderately full-bodied. Full acidity. Highly extracted. Mildly tannic. Red fruits, chocolate, black pepper. Quite aromatic, with a deep, fruit-centered character. Firmly structured and tight on the palate, with excellent grip through the finish. Should evolve nicely.

Robert Hunter

1992 Brut de Noirs, Sonoma Valley $25.   85

Deep straw cast. Full-bodied. Full acidity. Highly extracted. Yeast, toast, minerals. Forward aromas feature an intense, mature, yeasty quality. Full-throttled and rich in the mouth, with vibrant carbonation and a generous, lengthy finish.

Huntington

1997 Chardonnay, Sonoma County $9.99.   84

Deep straw cast. Medium-bodied. Full acidity. Moderately extracted. Minerals, citrus. Aromatically reserved, with a ripe and rounded mouthfeel. Shows some zesty acidity and a touch of spice through the finish.

1997 Chardonnay, Cairns Cuvée, Alexander Valley $16.   89

Bright straw hue. Attractive pear and apple aromas show varietal intensity and subdued oak influence. A brisk entry leads a full-bodied palate with racy, vibrant acidity. Shows grip and intensity through the juicy finish. Structured to improve with moderate age. Midterm cellar candidate (3–6 years).

1996 Cabernet Sauvignon, California $10.   81
1996 Merlot, California $10.   84

Bright ruby red. Attractive red fruit aromas. A crisp attack is followed by a moderately light-bodied palate with juicy acidity and modest tannins. Lean finish. A bright quaffer to be consumed in the near term.

Husch

1997 Chardonnay, Mendocino $12.50.   84

Pale yellow-straw hue. Pleasant citrus and toast aromas carry a slight oak accent. A firm entry leads a medium-bodied palate with racy acidity. Crisp, flavorful finish. Relatively light in style and well structured. Drink now or later.

1997 Chardonnay, La Ribera Vineyards, Mendocino $16.   83

Pale straw hue. Restrained biscuit and toast aromas. A crisp entry leads a ripe, medium-bodied palate that shows zesty acidity. Subtle, well-structured finish. A clean, racy style. Drink now.

1996 Chardonnay, Special Reserve, Anderson Valley $22.   87

Full golden yellow. Heavy buttery, ripe aromas show a pear and yeast character. A rich attack leads a moderately full-bodied palate with oak spice and butter flavors. The fruit flavors are muted. Rather thick, though the acids show through.

1998 Chenin Blanc, Mendocino $8.50.   84

Pale straw hue. Moderately aromatic, showing sweet apple and peach nuances. A juicy entry leads a medium-bodied palate, with clean, fruity flavors that linger on the finish. Drink now.

Scale: Superlative (96-100), Exceptional (90-95), Highly Recommended (85-89), Recommended (80-84), Not Recommended (Under 80)

1998 Gewürztraminer, Anderson Valley $11. 86

Pale straw hue. Lean aromas are youthful and undeveloped, with a sulfurous note that should diminish with further bottle age. A crisp entry leads a medium-bodied palate that has a touch of sweetness and vibrant acidity. The finish is clean and crisp. Could use a few more months to come together. Drink now or later.

1996 Sauvignon Blanc, La Ribera Vineyard, Mendocino $10.50. 88

Deep straw cast. Moderately full-bodied. Full acidity. Moderately extracted. Mildly oaked. Yeast, oranges, spice. Very aromatic, with a full range of flavors and a toasty oak influence. Crisp and vibrant finish. Smoky aromas lead a bright, citrus-centered palate with smoky overtones. Finishes assertively with snappy acidity.

1995 Cabernet Sauvignon, Mendocino $16.50. 84

Violet-ruby hue with a fading rim. Medium-bodied. Moderately extracted. Mildly tannic. Red fruits, minerals. Crisp, minerally aromas, with bright red fruit flavors that fade quickly. A straightforward, snappy style with a leaner character that invites current drinking.

1996 Cabernet Sauvignon, Mendocino $16.50. 86

Bright saturated ruby hue. Generous briar fruit, sour cherry, and vanilla aromas show a pleasant wood accent. A crisp attack leads to a medium-bodied palate with lean grippy tannins and zesty acidity. Racy finish. Lighter in style, but flavorful and intense. Drink now.

1994 Cabernet Sauvignon, La Ribera Vineyard, Mendocino $15. 88

Bright crimson red. Medium-bodied. Moderately extracted. Mildly tannic. Black cherries, dried herbs. Lively black fruit aromas are confirmed on the palate and accentuated by bright acids that give this a lean feel through the finish. Quite lengthy. Very attractive for early drinking.

1995 Pinot Noir, Anderson Valley $16. 88

Pale cherry red. Medium-bodied. Moderately extracted. Mildly oaked. Mildly tannic. Supple, rounded red cherry flavors have good weight and depth. Lingering astringency reveals some dry tannins. Nice now, with the appropriate food.

1995 Pinot Noir, Reserve, Anderson Valley $29. 81

1998 Muscat Canelli, Mendocino $14. 83

Bright straw hue with a slight spritz. Subdued mineral and talc aromas. A zesty entry leads a moderately light-bodied palate, with mild sweetness offset by racy acidity. Rather light in style, but clean and refreshing. Drink now.

1998 Gewürztraminer, Late Harvest, Anderson Valley $14/375 ml. 85

Deep straw hue. Subdued spicy aromas show a varietal Gewürztraminer accent. A lean entry leads a medium-bodied palate that shows sharp acidity and moderate sweetness. Very clean, with a well-cut finish. Drink now.

Indigo Hills

1997 Chardonnay, Mendocino County $11. 88

Bright straw cast. Medium-bodied. Full acidity. Moderately extracted. Minerals, apples, citrus. Crisp, zesty aromas lead a firm mouthful of bright flavors that remain pure, vibrant, and crisp through the finish, with a subtle toasty accent lingering.

1995 Cabernet Sauvignon, Paso Robles $9. 83

Deep ruby-purple hue. Dark berry fruit and herbal notes on the nose. Shows a marked oak accent. A rich attack leads a moderately full-bodied palate with ripe berry flavors up front and lingering supple tannins on the finish. Not structured for cellaring, this is nice now.

1996 Pinot Noir, Mendocino County $12. 84

Full cherry red. Medium-bodied. Moderately extracted. Mildly tannic. Red fruits, minerals, brown spices. Jammy fruit aromas lead a fleshy, rounded palate with soft tannins lingering on the finish.

Iron Horse

1993 Brut, Sonoma County $23.50.   90

Brilliant pale gold hue. Moderately full-bodied. Full acidity. Minerals, yeast, citrus. Firm, yeasty aromas. Bright and lively, with full acids highlighting the clean citrus and mineral flavors. Youthful at present, this has the structure to benefit from further cellaring.

1993 Russian Cuvée, Sonoma County $23.50.   89

Brilliant pale gold hue. Medium-bodied. Full acidity. Bread, citrus, tart tropical fruits. Soft, leesy aromas lead a concentrated, juicy, bright mouthful of flavors that persist well through the finish. Soundly structured, this will benefit from extra bottle age.

1993 Vrais Amis, Sonoma County $28.   89

Bright yellow-gold. Medium-bodied. Full acidity. Bread, ripe citrus. Vibrant, lively carbonation. Well-defined, bright, fruity flavors are lifted by lively acids. A fine aperitif style, though quite tight at present; another year or two of cellaring will be rewarded.

1993 Brut Rose, Sonoma County $28.   90

Deep pinkish salmon cast. Full-bodied. Full acidity. Highly extracted. Red fruits, minerals, toast. Ripe, toasty aromas lead a forceful and intense palate. Tightly wound and firm, though bursting with flavor. Probably best with food now, though this has the stuffing to cellar well.

1991 Blanc de Blancs, Sonoma County $30.   91

Bright pale golden cast. Full-bodied. Full acidity. Highly extracted. Bread dough, cream, toast. Tight and youthful, with a forceful and powerful structure. Firm and intense in the mouth, with classic but reserved flavors. Impressive now, though this will blossom with mid-term (3–6 years) cellaring.

1989 Brut LD, Sonoma County Green Valley $45.   92

Straw color. Medium-bodied. Full acidity. Reminiscent of biscuit, minerals, stone fruits. Rich aromas lead a tightly wrought, complex, flavorsome palate with a strong impression of yeast on the midpalate through the finish. Should cellar well.

1990 Blanc de Blancs LD, Sonoma County, Green Valley $45.   92

Bright pale yellow-gold. Medium-bodied. Full acidity. Moderately extracted. Lemons, roasted coffee, minerals. Pronounced smoky, roasted coffee aromas lead a tight, concentrated palate and a lingering finish. Very focused citrus flavors. This is probably a few years away from optimum maturity, although it is drinkable now.

1997 Chardonnay, Sonoma County, Green Valley $22.   83

Pale straw cast. Medium-bodied. Balanced acidity. Moderately extracted. Dried herbs, minerals. Lean and crisp, with brisk acidity lending a sense of balance. Nicely textured and well balanced, if light on flavors.

1997 Sauvignon Blanc, Cuvée Joy, Alexander Valley $18.   84

Pale golden yellow. Medium-bodied. Balanced acidity. Moderately extracted. Citrus zest, minerals. Bright citrus aromas are followed by straightforward citrus flavors that could use more clarifying acidity on the warm finish.

1997 Fumé Blanc, Alexander Valley $18.   83

Pale yellow-straw hue. Medium-bodied. Low acidity. Moderately extracted. White citrus, dried herbs. Acids are quite soft; this has a very rounded, almost glycerous mouthfeel, though the flavors are straightforward.

1997 Viognier, Alexander Valley $18.   86

Bright yellow-gold. Full-bodied. Balanced acidity. Highly extracted. Mildly oaked. Melon, tropical fruits, talc. Quite aromatic, with a ripe and complex array of flavors. Full and rich on the palate, but balanced by a zesty note of acidity. Finishes with a slight wood accent.

1994 Cabernet Sauvignon, Alexander Valley $20.   86

Saturated, deep reddish purple. Medium-bodied. Moderately extracted. Mildly tannic. Black fruits, cassis, brown spice, chocolate. Ripe spicy aromas lead a velvety palate and a powdery tannic finish. Some firm astringency runs through this.

1995 Cabernet Sauvignon, Alexander Valley $22.   **82**

1996 Pinot Noir, Green Valley, Sonoma County $23.   **89**

Bright cherry red with pink highlights. Medium-bodied. Moderately extracted. Moderately oaked. Mildly tannic. Floral, candied cherry aromas. Very full, with a juicy mouthfeel and a nice glycerous touch through the finish. Fine concentration of smooth cherry flavors with plenty of vanilla oak notes in support.

1997 Pinot Noir, Green Valley, Sonoma County $24.   **84**

Pale ruby-garnet cast. Moderately light-bodied. Full acidity. Subtly extracted. Mildly oaked. Mildly tannic. Red fruits, minerals. Features a grapey, primary fruit quality to the nose. Light and zesty in the mouth with a hint of wood spice. Drying fruity finish.

1995 Sangiovese, Alexander Valley $16.   **86**

Bright cherry red. Moderately light-bodied. Balanced acidity. Moderately extracted. Mildly tannic. Cherries, earth, oak. Hints of floral, high-toned fruits. Lively dried fruit flavors are well focused, with a minerally, lean backbone through the finish.

J Wine Co.

1994 J Brut, Sonoma County $28.   **90**

Pale yellow-straw hue. Medium-bodied. Full acidity. Tart apples, citrus, yeast. Bright, fruity, doughy aromas. Clean, crisp flavors with fine-beaded carbonation and subtle yeast complexity. This is a not a heavyweight style, but is characterized by finesse and poise.

Marcus James

NV White Zinfandel, Special Reserve, $6.99.   **80**

Jarvis

1996 Chardonnay, Napa Valley $38.   **90**

Bright straw cast. Moderately full-bodied. Balanced acidity. Moderately extracted. Minerals, green apples, butter. Aromatically reserved, yet with a focused and precise set of flavors on the palate. Rich but well structured, with a lengthy spicy finish.

1996 Chardonnay, Reserve, Napa Valley $48.   **90**

Bright gold. Aromatically generous with a fine smoky, toasted-oak note and buttery richness. A smooth entry leads a moderately full-bodied palate with a rich, rounded mouthfeel showing some intensity. Very stylish.

1996 Cabernet Franc, Napa Valley $44.   **93**

Deep ruby purple. Moderately full-bodied. Balanced acidity. Highly extracted. Moderately oaked. Mildly tannic. Black fruits, minerals, spice. Aromatic and rich, with a weighty core of ripe fruit flavors and a judicious oak accent. Supple and harmonious in the mouth, with a very lengthy, exotically flavored finish.

1993 Cabernet Sauvignon, Napa Valley $55.   **93**

Deep red. Medium-bodied. Highly extracted. Mildly tannic. Red fruits, cassis, toasty oak spice. Very attractive spicy aromas. Distinguished by a silky mouthfeel with concentrated plush flavors that linger through the finish. Beautifully integrated flavors leave a luxurious impression.

1994 Cabernet Sauvignon, Napa Valley $58.   **98**

Opaque red with a brick rim. Moderately full-bodied. Highly extracted. Moderately tannic. Mineral, chocolate, black fruits. Dusty, spicy aromas lead a solid, mineral-packed mouthful of flavors through a long, drying finish. Has a pleasing note of austerity that makes for a classic, highly sophisticated character. Drinking very well now.

1993 Cabernet Sauvignon, Reserve, Napa Valley $75.   **97**

Saturated dark red. Moderately full-bodied. Highly extracted. Moderately tannic. Cassis, oak spice, lead pencil. Fleshy, minerally aromas follow through on the palate with a sense of concentration and austerity through the finish. Very classy and reserved, in a Claret-like manner.

1993 Lake William, Napa Valley $45. **92**

Deep ruby hue with a pale purple-tinged rim. Medium-bodied. Moderately extracted. Mildly tannic. Pepper, spice, black bramble fruits. High-toned aromas show complexity. Spicy, almost pickled red berry fruit flavors through the finish are highlighted by bright acids. Very nice now, and full of exotic spicy flavors.

1996 Lake William, Napa Valley $48. **94**

Saturated red-purple. Moderately full-bodied. Highly extracted. Moderately tannic. Vanilla, smoke, red fruits. Rich, smoky aromas have high-toned fruity accents that follow through on the palate, showing concentration and vibrancy through a spicy finish.

1996 Merlot, Napa Valley $46. **86**

Deep violet-ruby hue. Generously aromatic with chocolate and ripe black cherry aromas. Medium-bodied, with a lively attack that develops into bright fleshy fruit flavors that linger through the supple finish. Drink now.

Jekel

1997 Chardonnay, FOS Reserve, Monterey $22. **85**

Medium golden yellow. Richly aromatic with a heavy dose of oak spice and yeasty character. A fat entry leads a full-bodied palate with glycerine and alcohol to the fore. Tart apples, butter, and spice flavors. Moderately short finish. Drink now.

1998 Johannisberg Riesling, Monterey $10. **84**

Bright pale gold hue. Generous apple and tropical fruit aromas. A juicy, moderately sweet attack leads a medium-bodied palate, with clean, straightforward flavors through the finish. Drink now.

1996 Cabernet Franc, Sanctuary Estate Reserve, Monterey $18. **84**

Bright ruby red hue. Forward mineral and red fruit aromas. A crisp attack leads to a medium-bodied palate with lean tannins. Firm, angular finish. Rather austere but well structured. Drink within 5 years.

1996 Malbec, Sanctuary Estate Reserve, Monterey $18. **82**

1994 Sanctuary Estate Meritage, Monterey $16. **80**

1995 Sanctuary Estate Meritage, Monterey $25. **87**

Saturated dark ruby-red hue. Aromatically reserved. A firm entry leads a medium-bodied palate with fine-grained tannins and racy, bright fruit flavors. Medium-length finish shows a minerally quality. Wood flavors are well integrated. Drink now or later.

1996 Merlot, California $12. **84**

Brickish ruby hue with a subtle fade. Spicy, woody aromas. A crisp attack followed by mildly astringent tannins on the medium-bodied palate. Well gripped by tannins and acids on the finish. Drink now.

1996 Merlot, Sanctuary Estate Reserve, Monterey $18. **88**

Bright violet-crimson hue. Generous rich aromas of black fruits and brown spice. A supple, smooth attack leads a moderately full-bodied palate with velvety, drying tannins. Generously fruity and deep, with a persistent finish. Drink now or later. Can improve with more age.

1996 Petit Verdot, Sanctuary Estate Reserve, Monterey $18. **84**

Deep ruby red hue. Forward herb and cola aromas. A lean attack leads to a moderately light-bodied palate with grippy tannins. Crisp, zesty finish. An interesting but very light interpretation of Petite Verdot. Drink now.

1996 Pinot Noir, Gravelstone, Monterey $13. **83**

Pale cherry red. Medium-bodied. Moderately extracted. Mildly tannic. Red berry fruits, minerals. Perfumed aromas follow through on the palate, with lean flavors showing a minerally edge on the finish.

1997 Late Harvest Johannisberg Riesling, Monterey $25/375 ml.   **83**

Deep bronze hue. Lean brown spice and lacquer aromas show a nutty, buttery note.
A lush entry leads a medium-bodied palate that has marked sweetness. Straightforward,
nutty, toffee-flavored finish. Drink now.

Jepson

1994 Blanc de Blanc, Burnee Hill Vineyard, Mendocino County $19.   **80**

1996 Chardonnay, Mendocino County $15.   **89**

Bright yellow-gold. Medium-bodied. Full acidity. Moderately extracted. Citrus, lemons,
vanilla. Crisp and lively on the palate, with a lemony firmness running through the finish
that stands up to the buttery, oaky character. A flavorful and firm style.

1997 Sauvignon Blanc, Mendocino County $10.   **81**

1997 Viognier, Mendocino County $15.   **81**

1995 Pinot Noir, Sonoma County $15.   **80**

Jessandra Vittoria

1995 Cabernet Sauvignon, Sonoma Valley $30.   **88**

Opaque blackish red. Medium-bodied. Highly extracted. Moderately tannic. Black fruits,
allspice. Full aromas of dust and spice are rather distinctive. A full, concentrated palate
follows the aromas with a marked spicy, tangy, tart note on the finish. Not to everyone's
liking, perhaps, but bursting with character.

Jordan

1994 Cabernet Sauvignon, Alexander Valley $34.   **88**

Bright ruby purple. Medium-bodied. Full acidity. Moderately extracted. Mildly oaked.
Mildly tannic. Red fruits, minerals, brown spices. Pleasantly aromatic, with a core of ripe
fruit flavors. A lighter style, with a sense of crispness through the finish. Well balanced.

Jory

1997 Chardonnay, El Nino, Central Coast $15.   **81**

*1997 Chardonnay, Lion Oaks Ranch, Selected Clone,
Santa Clara Valley $30.*   **84**

Bright yellow-straw hue. Medium-bodied. Full acidity. Moderately extracted. Mildly oaked.
Minerals, grape skins. Muted aromas lead a clean, bright, angular palate with dry notes
lingering on the finish.

1996 Black Hand, Mano Nera Red, California $13.   **83**

Deep ruby purple. Moderately full-bodied. Balanced acidity. Highly extracted. Mildly
oaked. Mildly tannic. Briar fruits, vanilla. Lighter in style, with vibrant fruit flavors. Juicy,
with a clean edge of acidity to the finish.

Joullian

1996 Chardonnay, Monterey $15.50.   **88**

Pale straw cast. Medium-bodied. Full acidity. Moderately extracted. Minerals, citrus, toast.
Toasty, zesty aromas precede generous yet precise flavors highlighted by crisp and zesty
acids that persist through the finish.

1996 Sauvignon Blanc, Family Reserve, Carmel Valley $16.50.   **83**

Pale straw. Medium-bodied. Balanced acidity. Moderately extracted. Apples, lemons.
Very straightforward, bright, clean fruity flavors give way to a warm alcohol finish
showing a touch of oak spice.

1996 Zinfandel, Sias Cuvée, Carmel Valley $16.   **80**

Judd's Hill

1995 Cabernet Sauvignon, Napa Valley $28.　89

Saturated violet red. Moderately full-bodied. Highly extracted. Moderately tannic. Violets, cassis, vanilla. Solid, gripping tannins with highlighted fruit flavors showing great intensity. Rich and well structured, this will be better in a few years.

Justin

1997 Chardonnay, Native Yeast, Paso Robles $18.50.　82

1997 Chardonnay, Reserve, Paso Robles $18.　86

Bright straw hue. Subdued mineral and coconut aromas show a slight wood accent. A lush entry is followed by a medium-bodied palate with rounded acidity, and a crisp, buttery finish. Drink now.

1995 Cabernet Sauvignon, Paso Robles $20.　84

Deep ruby cast. Moderately full-bodied. Balanced acidity. Moderately extracted. Mildly tannic. Minerals, black fruits. Aromatically reserved, but full and flavorful in the mouth. Angular through the finish.

1996 Cabernet Sauvignon, Paso Robles $20.　84

Full ruby red hue. Aromas are jammy and herbal. A crisp entry leads a medium-bodied palate with chewy cassis fruit flavors and moderate tannins that take a greenish turn through the finish. Rather angular. Drink now.

1995 Justification, Paso Robles $22.50.　81

1994 Isosceles, Paso Robles $32.50.　88

Saturated dark blackish red with purple highlights. Moderately full-bodied. Highly extracted. Quite tannic. Toasted oak, cassis, blackberries, brown spice. Ripe, brooding nose. Dense, mouthfilling Cabernet fruit flavors. The textured mouthfeel shows richness and a chewy character through the richly tannic finish. Solidly structured and backward, it needs three to four years to show at its best.

1995 Isosceles, Paso Robles $36.50.　84

Medium ruby-red hue with a subtle fade. Subtle aromas have a lean character, showing red fruits and herbs. A bright entry leads a medium-bodied palate with racy acids and tart red fruit flavors. Finishes with a note of green tannins. Drink now.

1996 Merlot, Reserve, Paso Robles $25.　86

Bright, deep purple-red. Intense mint, plum, and overripe black fruit aromas. A crisp attack leads a medium-bodied palate with vibrant acidity and firm tannins. The finish is on the light side, but juicy and flavorful. A racy, cheerful style. Drink now.

1995 Nebbiolo, San Luis Obispo County $22.50.　84

Bright blackish ruby cast. Moderately full-bodied. Low acidity. Moderately extracted. Mildly tannic. Red fruits, minerals. Rather reserved aromatically, with austere minerally flavors on the palate. Low acidity levels make for a lush entry. Could use a bit more grip.

1995 Sangiovese, San Luis Obispo County $22.50.　83

Cherry red with a subtle fade. Medium-bodied. Balanced acidity. Moderately extracted. Mildly tannic. Red berries. Soft red berry flavors, with mild oak/spice notes on the finish. A rounded, easy-drinking style.

1996 Obtuse, Paso Robles $22.50.　86

Opaque blackish purple. Full-bodied. Balanced acidity. Highly extracted. Mildly tannic. Black fruits, minerals. Quite aromatic, with a full and flavorful palate feel. Round and rich, though well structured through the finish.

Kautz Ironstone

1997 Chardonnay, Kautz, Library Collection, California $14.99.　81

Robert Keenan

1997 Chardonnay, Napa Valley $18.   84
Bright straw cast. Moderately full-bodied. Full acidity. Moderately extracted. Minerals, green apples. Aromatically reserved, with precise and focused flavors. Firm and quite lean, with mouthwatering acidity making for a clean, refreshing finish.

1993 Cabernet Sauvignon, Hillside Estate, Spring Mountain District, Napa Valley $23.   89
Saturated, opaque dark purple. Moderately full-bodied. Highly extracted. Quite tannic. Black fruits, black tea, tobacco, earth. Inky, solid palate has tightly wound flavors with firm, dry tealike tannins making it a little mean at present. A structural monster.

1994 Cabernet Sauvignon, Hillside Estate, Spring Mountain District, Napa Valley $24.   92
Deep saturated ruby purple. Full-bodied. Balanced acidity. Highly extracted. Heavily oaked. Quite tannic. Vanilla, black fruits, minerals. All systems go, in a full-throttled, hearty, chunky wine with very modern, fruit-centered, wood-accented flavors. Finishes with a wallop of tannin. A show style that needs a lengthy tour of duty in the cellar.

1996 Merlot, Napa Valley $30.   89
Dark violet red. Ripe fruit aromas. A soft, fruity attack leads a generously fruity midpalate with mild powdery tannins on the finish. Drink now.

Kendall-Jackson

1996 Chardonnay, Camelot Vineyard, Santa Maria Valley $19.   85
Bright yellow-straw cast. Moderately full-bodied. Low acidity. Moderately extracted. Heavily oaked. Brown spices. A big, oaky style with forward oaky aromas and substantial texture on the palate, though it lacks grip on the finish.

1996 Chardonnay, Paradise Vineyard, Arroyo Seco $18.   85
Deep yellow-straw cast. Moderately full-bodied. Full acidity. Highly extracted. Minerals, citrus. Crisp, lean, and intense, with a subtle yeasty overtone. The finish is vibrant.

1997 Chardonnay, Vintner's Reserve, California $16.   83
Bright yellow-gold. Medium-bodied. Balanced acidity. Moderately extracted. Spicy, yeasty aromas show an oak influence that comes through on the palate. Bright sweet lemon flavors provide a lively note.

1996 Chardonnay, Grand Reserve, California $26.   80
1997 Chardonnay, Grand Reserve, California $26.   90
Brilliant golden yellow. Generous toast, yeast, and cream flavors show a judicious oak accent. A smooth attack is followed by a moderately full-bodied palate with balanced acidity. The finish is persistent and flavorful. Overall, a rich and intense wine. Drink now or later.

1997 Chenin Blanc, Vintner's Reserve, California $11.   83
Medium yellow-gold. Moderately aromatic, with a sweet citrus note. A juicy entry leads a medium-bodied palate, with fine concentration and some glycerous richness. Finishes with a note of citrus zest. Drink now.

1997 Johannisberg Riesling, Vintner's Reserve, California $11.   86
Deep yellow-gold. Aromatically generous, with big ripe fruit character. A rich, moderately sweet entry leads a medium-bodied palate. Pure green apple flavors linger through the finish. A soft, juicy style. Drink now.

1995 Cabernet Franc, Buckeye Vineyard, Alexander Valley $20.   86
Very deep ruby hue. Medium-bodied. Balanced acidity. Moderately extracted. Mildly tannic. Licorice, minerals. High-toned aromas lead a weighty but firm and angular mouthfeel that fades toward the finish.

1995 Cabernet Franc, Grand Reserve, California $18.   83
Deep, saturated ruby garnet hue. Subdued mineral and black fruit aromas. A rich attack leads to a moderately full-bodied palate with robust chunky tannins. Big, firm finish. Full throttle but rather monolithic. Drink now or later.

1994 Cabernet Sauvignon, Buckeye Vineyard, Alexander Valley $24.   89

Deep crimson red with purple highlights. Moderately full-bodied. Moderately extracted. Moderately tannic. Toasted oak, black currants, brown spice. Generous oak-accented, rich black fruit aromas are confirmed on the palate. Well-balanced tannins are plush and rounded on the palate with good texture through the finish. Quite structured.

1995 Cabernet Sauvignon, Buckeye Vineyard, Alexander Valley $27.   88

Deep ruby purple. Moderately full-bodied. Balanced acidity. Moderately extracted. Mildly oaked. Moderately tannic. Minerals, black fruits, vanilla. Aromatically reserved, but flavorful and rich on the palate. Firm structure throughout, with tannins clamping down on the finish.

1994 Cabernet Sauvignon, Vintner's Reserve, California $18.   88

Full brick red. Medium-bodied. Moderately extracted. Mildly tannic. Black fruits, earth, brown spice. Dusty black fruit aromas reveal a well-balanced palate with generous ripe flavors and a spicy accent through the finish.

1995 Cabernet Sauvignon, Vintner's Reserve, California $18.   83

Bright cherry red. Medium-bodied. Moderately extracted. Moderately tannic. Cassis, tea. Jammy, black fruit aromas lead ripe, fruity flavors with a streak of powdery, dry tannins on the finish. Backward now.

1994 Cabernet Sauvignon, Grand Reserve, California $41.   89

Deep reddish purple. Medium-bodied. Highly extracted. Mildly tannic. Mint, vanilla, black fruits. Attractive mint-nuanced aromas. Solid, chewy Cabernet fruit on the palate gives way to dry, powdery tannins through the finish. Good acids give this a tart edge.

1995 Cabernet Sauvignon, Grand Reserve, California $42.   87

Saturated dark red-purple hue. Brooding black fruit, toasted oak aromas. A tough entry leads to a full-bodied palate with well-extracted fruit flavors and whopping, chewy, drying tannins that grip the finish. Very dry and tough at present. Drink within five years.

1995 Merlot, Buckeye Vineyard, Alexander Valley $29.   84

Deep, saturated ruby hue. Interesting, high-toned anise, chocolate and red fruit aromas show a hearty oak accent. A lush entry leads a rounded, medium-bodied palate with drying tannins and low levels of acidity. The finish is fat and rich. Eminently drinkable. Drink now.

1996 Merlot, Vintner's Reserve, California $19.   83

Full ruby red. Oak-dominated aromas with brambly accents. Medium-bodied, with a lush entry and an oaky palate showing dry, powdery tannins on the finish. Relatively low acids make for a softer, rounded style.

1995 Merlot, Grand Reserve, California $42.   86

Full ruby red. Distinctly oak-accented aromas. Dry and well gripped on the medium-bodied palate with oak dominating the ripe, plummy black fruit flavors. Finishes in a dry cedary manner.

1997 Pinot Noir, Vintner's Reserve, California $30.   82

1996 Pinot Noir, Grand Reserve, California $30.   88

Pale violet red. Moderately light-bodied. Moderately extracted. Mildly tannic. Vanilla, berry fruits, cherry. Bright berry and vanilla aromas lead a supple, brightly fruity palate with a clean, crisp finish.

1996 Syrah, Vintner's Reserve, California $16.   86

Dark purple, limpid, and brilliant to the rim. Sound black cherry and bitter chocolate flavors. Mild wood tones. A firm entry leads a medium-bodied palate with balanced acidity. Moderate, drying tannins. Sweet fruit, chocolate, and wood notes work well through the subtle bitter finish. Drink now or later. Can improve with more age.

1995 Syrah, Grand Reserve, California $20.   86

Medium cherry red, limpid with a slight fade. Subtle, pleasant berry fruit and cedar flavors. Hint of wood tones. A smooth entry and a medium-bodied palate. Moderate drying tannins on a subtle finish. Fleshy black fruit flavors make this attractive. Spicy, oak-accented style. Drink now.

1996 Zinfandel, Vintner's Reserve, California $16.　　　　**84**

Bright blackish purple. Moderately full-bodied. Balanced acidity. Moderately extracted. Mildly oaked. Moderately tannic. Black fruits, vanilla. Carries an oaky nuance on the nose, and merges with a nice fruit-centered core of flavors. Lighter in style, with some hefty tannins toward the finish.

1997 Chardonnay, Select Late Harvest, California $40/375 ml.　　　　**89**

Brilliant deep gold. Rich apricot and honey aromas. A lush attack leads a medium-bodied palate with attractive, intensely juicy tropical flavors. Acids and sugars strike a fine balance. Subtly botrytized.

Kathryn Kennedy

1994 Cabernet Sauvignon, Santa Cruz Mountains $75.　　　　**95**

Opaque reddish purple. Moderately full-bodied. Highly extracted. Moderately tannic. Black cherries, brown spice, anise. A spicy pickled nose leads a pure, concentrated palate with very focused primary fruit flavors on entry that dominate the midpalate. Acid levels are impressively high. Still a little tight.

1995 Cabernet Sauvignon, Santa Cruz Mountains $110.　　　　**94**

Saturated ruby purple. Moderately full-bodied. Full acidity. Highly extracted. Moderately tannic. Cherry cordial, minerals. Pure fruit aromas are defined with great intensity and focus. Terroir is magnified in the form of a ripe, minerally character, with little if any wood influence. Admirably restrained. Approachable, but should become more complex with age.

1996 Lateral, California $35.　　　　**83**

Bright ruby with a pale rim. Moderately light-bodied. Moderately extracted. Mildly tannic. Dried herbs, raspberry, red berries. Perfumed, fruity, and lighter in style, with bright red berry flavors and a dusting of mineral through the finish.

1996 Syrah, Maridon Vineyard, Santa Cruz Mountains $38.　　　　**93**

Very dark purple, opaque and brilliant to the rim. Generous, fantastic plum and vanilla flavors. Generous wood tones. Supple entry. Full-bodied, with plentiful velvety tannins. Lingering rich finish. A lush, supple, well-extracted style showing great varietal character. Drink now or later. Can improve with age.

Kenwood

1997 Chardonnay, Sonoma County $15.　　　　**81**

1997 Chardonnay, Reserve, Sonoma Valley $22.　　　　**83**

Pale straw hue. Medium-bodied. Balanced acidity. Moderately extracted. Mildly oaked. Vanilla, apples, minerals. An oak-spiced nose leads a crisp appley palate of flavors with a light, clean finish. Very quaffable.

1996 Sauvignon Blanc, Sonoma County $10.　　　　**84**

Deep green-straw cast. Moderately full-bodied. Full acidity. Moderately extracted. Dried herbs, minerals. Quite aromatic, with a distinctive herbal Sauvignon Blanc personality. Full but zesty in the mouth, with vibrant acidity through the finish.

1996 Sauvignon Blanc, Reserve, Sonoma Valley $15.　　　　**86**

Medium yellow-straw hue. Medium-bodied. Balanced acidity. Moderately extracted. Mildly oaked. Vanilla, citrus zest, oak spice. Pleasant smoky nose. Rounded, somewhat soft mouthfeel, with a faintly oak-spiced finish. Easy going, open-knit style.

1994 Cabernet Sauvignon, Sonoma Valley $18.　　　　**87**

Full reddish purple. Medium-bodied. Moderately extracted. Mildly tannic. Blackberry, cassis, cedar. Vanilla-scented nose leads a chewy mouthful of black Cabernet fruit, with finely balanced powdery tannins on the finish. Attractive now.

1995 Cabernet Sauvignon, Sonoma Valley $18.　　　　**88**

Bright red with a pale ruby rim. Medium-bodied. Moderately extracted. Moderately tannic. Mineral, red fruits. Earthy, ferric nose seems odd. Brisk berry flavors pass quickly, leaving a minerally, dry finish.

1994 Cabernet Sauvignon, Jack London Vineyard, Sonoma Valley $25. **91**

Dark garnet red. Medium-bodied. Moderately extracted. Mildly tannic. Earth, licorice, black fruits, brown spice. Deep, rich earthy nose leads a supple palate with black fruit and licorice flavors. Austere yet soft on the finish. Very approachable now, probably not for long-term (7–10 years) cellaring.

1995 Cabernet Sauvignon, Jack London Vineyard, Sonoma County $25. **90**

Dark ruby red. Medium-bodied. Moderately extracted. Moderately tannic. Cassis, mineral, brown spice. Dark, fleshy aromas lead a tight, minerally palate showing good grip, with generous Cabernet fruit flavors showing through. A lighter style whose tannins are in fine balance.

1995 Cabernet Sauvignon, Yulupa, Sonoma County $25. **83**

Bright ruby hue. Medium-bodied. Balanced acidity. Moderately extracted. Mildly tannic. Minerals, red fruits. Subtle aromas point to a more reserved style, with a lighter-styled palate feel and crisp flavors that follow through on the finish. Drinking well now.

1995 Merlot, Sonoma County $20. **89**

Deep blackish ruby color with brilliant clarity. Medium-bodied. Balanced acidity. Highly extracted. Mildly oaked. Mildly tannic. Black fruits, vanilla. Bright and forceful, with a juicy quality to the dark fruit flavors. Well integrated and nicely balanced. There is a kiss of oak on the finish.

1995 Merlot, Jack London Vineyard, Sonoma Valley $25. **89**

Deep ruby with a purplish cast. Moderately full-bodied. Full acidity. Moderately extracted. Mildly tannic. Black fruits, earth, black olives. A little reserved aromatically and somewhat tight on the palate. Still, it features a very deep core of dark flavors and a veil of velvety tannins. Well balanced. Should open with mid-term (3–6 years) cellaring.

1995 Merlot, Massara, Sonoma Valley $25. **89**

Very deep blackish ruby hue with a purple cast. Moderately full-bodied. Full acidity. Highly extracted. Mildly tannic. Black fruits, earth, dried herbs. Still quite closed, though very deep and extracted. Features a vibrant note of acidity and rich tannins through the finish. Will need time to open up more fully.

1995 Pinot Noir, Russian River Valley $17. **84**

Pale garnet red. Moderately light-bodied. Subtly extracted. Mildly oaked. Mildly tannic. A pleasant mouthful of dried red fruits and minerals with a touch of tobacco through the finish. Has nice varietal character, though it is quite light.

1995 Pinot Noir, Olivet Lane, Russian River Valley $22. **88**

Pale garnet red. Moderately light-bodied. Moderately extracted. Mildly oaked. Mildly tannic. Strawberry aromas lead a well-balanced palate with crisp cherry flavors, and fine powdered tannins and minerals through the finish.

1995 Zinfandel, Sonoma Valley $15. **86**

Bright blackish ruby cast. Medium-bodied. Balanced acidity. Moderately extracted. Mildly tannic. Black fruits, minerals. Reserved aromatically, with a firm, well-structured palate feel. Though tightly wound, a core of dark fruit flavors emerges here and there. Shows fine grip on the finish. Well balanced; should open in the near term.

1995 Zinfandel, Jack London Vineyard, Sonoma Valley $20. **82**

1995 Zinfandel, Upper Weise Ranch, Sonoma Valley $20. **86**

Bright blackish ruby cast. Moderately full-bodied. Balanced acidity. Moderately extracted. Mildly oaked. Mildly tannic. Black fruits, spice. Lighter in style, with a high-toned, lively presence on the palate. Flavorful throughout, however, with a crisp, balanced finish.

Kistler

1993 Cabernet Sauvignon, Kistler Vineyard, Sonoma Valley $30. **85**

Deep dark ruby red. Moderately full-bodied. Highly extracted. Moderately tannic. Earth, blackberry, black tea, black fruits. Exotically earthy nose with herbal accents. The deeply layered palate shows an austere character, with plenty of tealike notes through the finish. Rich and savory.

Scale: Superlative (96-100), Exceptional (90-95), Highly Recommended (85-89), Recommended (80-84), Not Recommended (Under 80)

122

Korbel

NV Chardonnay Brut, California $12.99.   83

Medium yellow-straw cast. Medium-bodied. Spice, tropical fruits. Yeasty, spicy aromas lead a generously flavored palate showing weight and some citrus length. The flavors are very attractive, though the bubbles are rather large.

NV Natural Sparkling Wine, California $12.99.   83

Pale yellow-gold. Medium-bodied. Citrus zest, canned pears. Powdery, zesty aromas follow through on the palate, with a dry finish that has an authoritative grip. Full, crisp carbonation.

NV Rouge Sparkling Wine, California $12.99.   84

Pale cherry red. Medium-bodied. Rose petals, cherries. A floral, dark fruit impression is conveyed on the nose and palate, with the very slightest suggestion of dry tannin on the finish. Novel, but undeniably appealing.

1994 Cabernet Sauvignon, Alexander Valley $18.99.   90

Medium cherry red. Medium-bodied. Moderately extracted. Mildly tannic. Black pepper, brown spice, bright black fruits. Wonderfully spiced aromatics lead a well-balanced palate with supple character and generous flavors. Very bright, with good acids lingering through the finish.

Charles Krug

1996 CK Mondavi Zinfandel, California $7.   81

1995 Cabernet Sauvignon, Napa Valley $16.   84

Bright brick red. Medium-bodied. Moderately extracted. Mildly tannic. Mint, berries. Bright oak and berry aromas lead a succulent and juicy mouthful of flavors, with oak playing a prominent role. Drink now.

1994 Peter Mondavi Family, Generations, Napa Valley $30.   85

Bright ruby red with a distinct fade on the rim. Medium-bodied. Highly extracted. Moderately tannic. Allspice, vanilla, red fruits. Dusty, spicy aromas lead a similar flavor profile, with dusty tannins lingering on the finish. The finish falls off quickly.

1994 Cabernet Sauvignon, Vintage Selection, Napa Valley $47.   88

Deep ruby hue with a fading rim. Medium-bodied. Moderately extracted. Moderately tannic. Brown spice, black fruits, caramel. Very ripe black fruit aromas are complemented by a toasted oak note that comes through on the finish. Ripe and full, this is drinking well now.

1994 Merlot, Reserve, Napa Valley $21.50.   89

Deep crimson red with a slight fade to the rim. Medium-bodied. Balanced acidity. Moderately extracted. Heavily oaked. Mildly tannic. Red fruits, dill pickle, brown spices. Quite aromatic, with well-extracted fruit flavors mingling with complex oak accents. Nicely integrated, with some dusty tannins and a lingering drying finish.

1996 Pinot Noir, Carneros $16.   81

1995 Sangiovese, Reserve, Napa Valley $16.   83

Browning garnet hue. Medium-bodied. Moderately extracted. Moderately oaked. Mildly tannic. Earth, brown spice. Mature spicy aromas. Rather rustic and dry, with little primary fruit character showing.

1995 Zinfandel, Napa Valley $11.   81

Kunde

1996 Chardonnay, Kinneybrook Vineyard, Sonoma Valley $20.   86

Medium yellow-gold. Moderately full-bodied. Balanced acidity. Moderately extracted. Mildly oaked. Yeast, vanilla, apples. Rich yeasty aromas follow through on a generous mouthfeel, with a pleasant doughy quality throughout that should develop further with a few months of cellaring.

1996 Chardonnay, Wildwood Vineyard, Sonoma Valley $20.   87

Bright pale straw color. Medium-bodied. Balanced acidity. Moderately extracted. Mildly oaked. Vanilla, apple. Shows a light touch of oak on the nose, with clean appley flavors on a brief finish. Balanced and flavorful, with a supple texture that stands out.

1996 Chardonnay, Reserve, Sonoma Valley $22.   84

Bright yellow-gold. Moderately full-bodied. Balanced acidity. Moderately extracted. Moderately oaked. Vanilla, apples, yeast. Doughy aromas seem reserved now. A weighty, generous mouthfeel has a spicy persistence, with acids rearing up on the finish.

1997 Viognier, Sonoma Valley $18.   83

Bright yellow-gold. Moderately full-bodied. Balanced acidity. Moderately extracted. Citrus, minerals. Citrus zest aromas lead a full, ripe palate that is well balanced by structural acidity. Could use a little more intensity of flavor.

1994 Cabernet Sauvignon, Sonoma Valley $17.   90

Dark red with subtle purple highlights. Medium-bodied. Highly extracted. Moderately tannic. Loam, cinnamon, vanilla, dark fruits. Toasty nose shows a singular earthy note that follows through on the assertively flavored palate. Good acids give this a lively feel through the finish. Well balanced and harmonious.

1995 Cabernet Sauvignon, Sonoma Valley $20.   93

Saturated dark red. Medium-bodied. Moderately extracted. Moderately tannic. Black fruits, minerals, vanilla. Reserved, fleshy aromas lead a chunky yet bright mouthful of flavors, with dry, powdery tannins through the finish. Well balanced and noble, with poise and elegance.

1997 Merlot, Sonoma Valley $17.   86

Bright violet purple. Warm, very ripe berry fruit aromas. A juicy attack leads a moderately full-bodied palate with powdery tannins and some alcohol warmth. Firm dry tannins on the finish. Drink within five years.

La Crema

1997 Chardonnay, Cold Coast Vineyards, Sonoma Coast $19.   91

Bright yellow-straw hue. Generous yeast and vanilla aromas carry a hefty oak accent. A lush entry leads a moderately full-bodied palate buoyed by crisp acidity. The finish is intense and flavorful. Drink now or later.

1996 Chardonnay, Reserve, Sonoma Coast $27.   82

1995 Pinot Noir, Sonoma Coast $21.   86

Medium cherry red. Moderately light-bodied. Moderately extracted. Moderately oaked. Mildly tannic. Red berry fruit aromas. Cranberry and strawberry flavors have an astringent backbone, with sweet tobacco notes lingering on the finish.

1996 Pinot Noir, Sonoma Coast $20.   83

Pale ruby cast. Moderately light-bodied. Full acidity. Subtly extracted. Mildly tannic. Sweet herbs, minerals, red fruits. Lean and stylish, with varietal Pinot aromas and a clean, angular finish. Crisp and tasty.

1995 Pinot Noir, Reserve, Sonoma Coast $26.   87

Bright pale cherry red with purple highlights. Medium-bodied. Moderately extracted. Moderately oaked. Mildly tannic. Bright, tart cherry flavors have tobacco and spice accents. Lengthy astringent finish. Dry and somewhat austere. Some complex chocolate notes.

1996 Pinot Noir, Reserve, Sonoma Coast $27.   86

Bright saturated ruby cast. Medium-bodied. Full acidity. Moderately extracted. Mildly tannic. Minerals, black fruits. A racy, fruit-driven nose leads a firm and intense palate feel. Crisp, lean, and vibrant through the finish.

1996 Zinfandel, Reserve, Sonoma County $22.   86

Bright purple. Moderately full-bodied. Full acidity. Moderately extracted. Mildly oaked. Mildly tannic. Briar fruits, vanilla. Aromatic, with a pleasant interplay between fruit and oak nuances. Well balanced and lively, with subtle tannins through the finish.

Scale: Superlative (96-100), Exceptional (90-95), Highly Recommended (85-89), Recommended (80-84), Not Recommended (Under 80)

La Jota

1995 Cabernet Sauvignon, Howell Mountain Selection, Howell Mountain, Napa Valley $30.   93

Saturated ruby cast. Moderately full-bodied. Balanced acidity. Highly extracted. Moderately oaked. Moderately tannic. Mint, plums, cedar. Pleasantly aromatic, with a deep black fruit core accented by spicy oak nuances. Deep and full in the mouth, with robust yet velvety tannins. Exceptional balance and depth. Should be more approachable in five to ten years.

1996 Cabernet Sauvignon, Howell Mountain Selection, Howell Mountain, Napa Valley $34.   87

Deep ruby hue. Generous vanilla and mineral aromas show a decided oak accent. A rich entry leads to a moderately full-bodied palate with grippy tannins. Firm, authoritative finish. Quite rich and stylish, but could use a bit more acidity toward the finish. Drinking well now. Drink now or later.

1996 Cabernet Sauvignon, 15th Anniversary, Howell Mountain, Napa Valley $58.   96

Deep, opaque purple-red hue. Intense and attractive vanilla, black fruit, and mineral aromas. A lush attack leads to a full-bodied, mouthfilling palate with velvety, chewy tannins. Outstanding, lengthy finish. Big and rich, but carries its weight seamlessly. Approachable now but exquisitely balanced and quite age worthy.

Laetitia

1993 Elegance Brut Rose, San Luis Obispo County $23.   87

Pale salmon cast. Full-bodied. Full acidity. Highly extracted. Charred yeast, minerals. Forward, charred-yeast nuances feature prominently in the flavor profile. Full-throttled and firm in the mouth, with aggressive carbonation and a rich, zesty finish. This will show best with food.

1993 Elegance Brut, California $23.   88

Deep yellow-gold. Moderately full-bodied. Full acidity. Mature, faintly maderized aromas. Broad flavors show plenty of black grape character, with a mouthfilling presence and lengthy finish. A forceful, big-shouldered style that will match with food.

1996 Chardonnay, Reserve, San Luis Obispo County $18.   86

Deep yellow-straw hue. Intense vanilla, citrus, and mineral aromas show judicious oak influences and a slightly earthy overtone. A firm entry leads a moderately full-bodied palate with crisp acidity. Subtle nutty finish. Drink now.

1996 Pinot Blanc, Reserve, San Luis Obispo County $17.   88

Deep golden cast. Moderately full-bodied. Full acidity. Moderately extracted. Heavily oaked. Smoke, tropical fruits, butter. Quite aromatic, with heavily toasted oak and ripe fruit flavors. This is a full-throttled style with a flavorful palate and vibrant acidity making for a brisk finish.

1996 Pinot Blanc, La Colline Vineyard Designated Reserve, $25.   88

Bright golden hue. Moderately full-bodied. Full acidity. Moderately extracted. Moderately oaked. Toasted coconut, butter, tropical fruits. Oak influence is readily apparent on the nose and plays out on the palate with a bevy of ripe tropical flavors. Quite full and weighty, with vibrant acidity through the finish.

1996 Pinot Noir, San Luis Obispo County $29.   82

1996 Pinot Noir, Laetitia Vineyard, San Luis Obispo County $29.   93

Deep ruby purple. Full-bodied. Balanced acidity. Highly extracted. Moderately oaked. Mildly tannic. Vanilla, red fruits, sweet herbs. Lavish oak accents are prominently featured, with a lush core of berry flavors lending balance in the mouth. Big and supple, with fine weight and intensity through the finish.

1996 Pinot Noir, Les Galets Vineyard, San Luis Obispo County $29.   **91**

Dark blackish ruby cast. Moderately full-bodied. Balanced acidity. Highly extracted. Moderately oaked. Moderately tannic. Vanilla, black fruits, minerals. Fragrant and intense, with a linear minerally quality featuring fruit and sweet wood accents. Extracted and intense, showing a very firm structure, yet it seems to have the requisite stuffing to balance everything out in the end.

1996 Pinot Noir, Reserve, San Luis Obispo County $18.   **86**

Deep ruby cast. Moderately full-bodied. Full acidity. Highly extracted. Moderately tannic. Earthy, herbal aromas lead a deep and extracted palate with a firm minerally core. Angular through the finish with a hint of bitterness.

Lake Sonoma

1995 Zinfandel, Heck Cellar Selection, Dry Creek Valley $17.   **84**

Deep ruby hue with a slight fade. Moderately full-bodied. Balanced acidity. Highly extracted. Mildly oaked. Moderately tannic. Cedar, earth, red fruits. Aromatically reserved, with a touch of heat. Firm and flavorful on the palate, with chunky tannins through the finish.

Lakespring

1996 Chardonnay, California $11.99.   **83**

Deep straw hue. Forward tropical fruit and melon aromas. A vibrant entry is followed by a full-bodied mouthfeel with crisp acidity and a clean finish. Drink now.

Lambert Bridge

1997 Chardonnay, Sonoma County $18.   **88**

Pale straw hue. Generous yeast and toast aromas. A lush entry leads a moderately full-bodied palate with crisp acidity. Elegant, flavorful, and well-structured finish. Drink now.

1997 Chardonnay, Abbe Vineyard, Dry Creek Valley $24.   **84**

Intense deep gold. Impressive aromas of toasted oak, yeast, and lush fruit. Forceful on the attack with a moderately full body and a big oaky influence on the palate. Bright acids give good structure. Finishes with an assertive oaky note. Bottle age should help. Drink now or later.

1994 Crane Creek Cuvée, Dry Creek Valley $28.   **92**

Dark blackish red with purple highlights. Moderately full-bodied. Highly extracted. Moderately tannic. Plums, anise, brown spice. Rich, well-extracted flavors show plenty of chewy Cabernet fruit character, with fine-textured tannins on the finish. Well balanced and solidly structured.

1995 Crane Creek Cuvée, Dry Creek Valley $32.   **85**

Very deep, saturated purple-red hue. Deep, brooding anise and mineral aromas. A firm entry leads to a ripe and intense mouthfeel with big chewy tannins. Firm, concentrated finish. Somewhat reserved at present but strikes an admirable balance between structure and extract. Good for long-term cellaring.

1996 Merlot, Sonoma County $20.   **88**

Bright violet red. Generous berry and earth aromas. A rich attack leads a moderately full-bodied palate with balanced velvety tannins. Drink now.

1996 Zinfandel, Dry Creek Valley $20.   **91**

Deep ruby purple. Moderately full-bodied. Full acidity. Moderately extracted. Mildly oaked. Mildly tannic. Vanilla, briar fruits. Quite aromatic, with a lush, concentrated, fruit-centered palate feel. Lengthy and vibrant through the finish, with dusty tannins.

Lamborn Family

1995 Zinfandel, The French Connection, Unfiltered, Howell Mountain, Napa Valley $22.50. **93**

Full dark cherry cast. Moderately full-bodied. Highly extracted. Moderately tannic. Pepper, black fruits, red fruits. Good glycerous mouthful. Concentrated and intense, with great acid balance and finesse. Very structured, with ripe tannins giving an astringent finish. Quite classy.

Landmark

1997 Chardonnay, Overlook, Sonoma County/Santa Barbara County/Monterey County $22. **89**

Yellow-gold. Medium-bodied. Balanced acidity. Moderately extracted. Sweet citrus fruits, oak spice, yeast. Sweetly aromatic, with subtle smoky accents and a bright, zesty core of flavors. Very supple and silky texture makes for a refined style.

1996 Chardonnay, Damaris Reserve, Sonoma County $32. **88**

Deep yellow-gold. Moderately full-bodied. Balanced acidity. Moderately extracted. Cream, citrus, toast. Ripe and full yet tightly wound, with a big, weighty mouthfeel that shows a creamy, well-toasted character that remains rich through the finish.

1995 Pinot Noir, Grand Detour, Sonoma County $30. **82**

Lang

1995 Zinfandel, Twin Rivers Vineyards, El Dorado $14. **80**

Langtry

1996 White Meritage, Guenoc Valley $21. **87**

Deep straw cast. Moderately full-bodied. Balanced acidity. Moderately extracted. Moderately oaked. Toasted coconut, cream. Luxuriant oaky notes are readily apparent on the nose and translate well to the palate. Rich and lush in style with solid acidity through the finish.

1994 Red Meritage, Napa Valley $41. **87**

Bright reddish purple. Medium-bodied. Moderately extracted. Moderately tannic. Cassis, black tea, tobacco. Rich, pure cassis fruit aromas lead a tight mouthful of dark fruit flavors that linger through a fine-grained tannic finish. This has some solidity and structure. Very classic style.

1995 Red Meritage, North Coast $41. **87**

Bright red-purple. Medium-bodied. Moderately extracted. Moderately tannic. Black fruits, minerals, brown spice. Youthful aromas. Angular and tough, with alcohol showing on the finish. Hard to appreciate at present.

Latcham Vineyards

1995 Zinfandel, El Dorado $10. **83**

Deep blackish ruby cast. Moderately full-bodied. Balanced acidity. Moderately extracted. Mildly oaked. Mildly tannic. Minerals, black fruits. Rather reserved aromatically, with a firm, structured palate feel. Compact and flavorful, with a bit of tannic bite to the finish.

1995 Zinfandel, Special Reserve, El Dorado $14. **84**

Deep blackish purple. Moderately full-bodied. Balanced acidity. Highly extracted. Mildly oaked. Moderately tannic. Plums, minerals. Quite aromatic, with a decidedly minerally note. Firm and dense on the palate, though well structured, with a precise and focused finish.

Laurel Glen

1994 Cabernet Sauvignon, Sonoma Mountain $38.   **90**

Opaque reddish purple. Moderately full-bodied. Highly extracted. Quite tannic.
Green olive, eucalyptus, earth, bright fruits. Bright fruity flavors on entry are quickly
overwhelmed by huge dry, firm tannins through the finish. This is a densely structured
wine that will need years to resolve its tannins. Impressive but not showing its paces yet.

1995 Cabernet Sauvignon, Sonoma Mountain $38.   **90**

Opaque, saturated purple. Full-bodied. Highly extracted. Quite tannic. Black fruits, tea.
Inky, deep, and impenetrable at present. Plenty of dark fruit flavors and big tannins. Not
a pleasure to drink now; needs years in the cellar.

Domaine Laurier

1996 Chardonnay, Reserve, Sonoma County $16.   **91**

Deep yellow-straw hue. Pungent lemon and vanilla aromas show a powerful oak
influence. A crisp entry leads a moderately full-bodied palate balanced by vibrant
acidity. Persistent, intense finish. Perhaps a tad manipulated, but impressive. Drink now.

Laurier

1996 Chardonnay, Sonoma County $15.   **88**

Bright yellow-gold. Generous citrus and vanilla aromas show an integrated wood accent.
A lush entry is followed by a moderately full-bodied palate with creamy acidity and a soft,
gentle finish. Stylish. Drink now.

1996 Pinot Noir, Sonoma County $16.99.   **84**

Deep saturated ruby cast. Medium-bodied. Balanced acidity. Moderately extracted.
Moderately oaked. Mildly tannic. Vanilla, minerals, red fruits. Fragrant and intense,
though rather light in frame. Finishes on an intense, angular note. Shows fine grip.

Daniel Lawrence

1997 Chardonnay, Ricci Vineyard, Carneros $12.   **81**

1996 Chardonnay, Vineyard Reserve, Santa Cruz Mountains $15.   **89**

Bright golden yellow. Moderately full-bodied. Balanced acidity. Highly extracted.
Moderately oaked. Green apples, vanilla, butter. Generously aromatic, with a leesy,
ripe character coming through on a deeply flavored palate that shows opulent fruity
flavors, texture, and length. Very stylish.

1997 Chardonnay, Reserve, Santa Cruz Mountains $15.   **84**

Pale yellow-gold. Medium-bodied. Balanced acidity. Moderately extracted. Moderately
oaked. Apples, white peach, vanilla. Fragrant, almost floral aromas lead a juicy, crisp
palate with judicious oak accents on the finish. Very bright and fresh.

1997 Merlot, Kathleen's Cuvée, Alexander Valley $11.99.   **83**

Bright purple-red. Lean mineral and red fruit aromas. A crisp attack leads a light-bodied
palate with gentle tannins. The finish is light and fruity. A quaffer. Drink now.

Lazy Creek

1995 Pinot Noir, Anderson Valley $16.   **86**

Pale ruby red. Medium-bodied. Moderately extracted. Mildly oaked. Mildly tannic.
Slightly warm aromas have mild vanilla and cherry notes. Crisp, simple cherry-berry
flavors linger through a mildly astringent finish. Shows some good varietal character.

Le Ducq

1994 Cabernet Sauvignon, Sylviane, Napa Valley $30.   **89**

Deep reddish purple. Medium-bodied. Moderately extracted. Moderately tannic. Cassis,
bramble fruits, toasted oak, brown spice. Good toasty nose with suggestive dark fruit
notes. Solid, textured mouthfeel, with tight black Cabernet fruit flavors and good dry
tannins through the finish. Time will improve this.

1995 Cabernet Sauvignon, Sylviane, Napa Valley $30. 88

Deep ruby purple. Moderately full-bodied. Balanced acidity. Highly extracted. Mildly oaked. Moderately tannic. Black fruits, minerals. Rather reserved in style, but showing a ripe, fruit-centered quality. Firm, chunky tannins bite into the finish.

1993 Meritage, Napa Valley $91. 92

Deep ruby cast. Full-bodied. Balanced acidity. Moderately extracted. Mildly oaked. Mildly tannic. Earth, red fruits, minerals. Aromatically subdued, but rich and flavorful in the mouth. Ripe and seductive, with a velvety quality through the finish.

1994 Meritage, Napa Valley $99. 93

Saturated ruby cast. Moderately full-bodied. Balanced acidity. Moderately extracted. Moderately oaked. Mildly tannic. Brown spices, red fruits, minerals. Forward, generous aromas lead a rich and supple palate, buttressed by ripe tannins. Well balanced and built for aging, though this can be enjoyed now.

1995 Meritage, Napa Valley $65. 89

Deep ruby cast. Moderately full-bodied. Balanced acidity. Highly extracted. Moderately oaked. Mildly tannic. Chocolate, red fruits, minerals. Aromatically reserved, with a weighty, chunky quality. Big tannins bite down on the finish.

1994 Merlot, Sylviane, Napa Valley $30. 90

Very deep blackish ruby hue. Moderately full-bodied. Balanced acidity. Mildly oaked. Moderately tannic. Black fruits, chocolate, minerals. Beautifully textured, with a rich, lush mouthfeel and dense, dark flavors. Well balanced, with a cascade of velvety tannins at the finish. Approachable now, it should mellow nicely with near-term to mid-term (3–6 years) aging.

1995 Merlot, Sylviane, Napa Valley $30. 86

Deep blackish ruby hue. Moderately full-bodied. Balanced acidity. Highly extracted. Mildly oaked. Quite tannic. Black fruits, vanilla, lacquer. Assertive dark flavors are plentiful on a very firmly structured palate. Tannins really rear up on the finish, making this wine a bit tough and compact.

Lewis Cellars

1997 Chardonnay, Reserve, Napa Valley $34.99. 90

Bright pale gold. Reserved, tight aromas have a subtle yeasty accent. A bright entry leads a medium-bodied, flavor-packed palate, with subtle oaky notes and intense citrus zest character. An opulently textured style. Drink now or later.

Limerick Lane

1996 Zinfandel, Collins Vineyard, Russian River Valley $24. 88

Bright blackish purple. Moderately full-bodied. Low acidity. Moderately extracted. Moderately oaked. Mildly tannic. Vanilla, overripe red fruits, roasted nuts. Quite aromatic, with a lighter-styled and vibrant mouthfeel. Flavorful and lean through the zesty finish.

LinCourt

1997 Chardonnay, Santa Barbara County $14. 89

Deep gold. Rather developed oak spice aromas. Possibly a touch maderized. A rich entry leads a full-bodied palate with mature flavors and a thick alcoholic mouthfeel. Interesting now, but maybe not for cellaring.

1996 Syrah, Santa Barbara County $14. 90

Opaque, brilliant dark crimson hue to the rim. Intense black fruit cordial, briar, oak spice, and pickle flavor elements. Hefty wood tones. Supple entry. Full-bodied with plentiful velvety tannins. Lots of everything here in a supple, well-extracted style. Lingering, rich finish. Intense, concentrated, and stuffed. Drinkable now, but can improve with age.

Liparita

1997 Chardonnay, Carneros $24.   85

Full gold. Aromatically restrained with oaky notes. A soft entry leads a full-bodied palate with a generous texture and restrained acids, but dulled flavors. Finishes quickly. Drink now.

Livingston

1995 Cabernet Sauvignon, Stanley's Selection, Napa Valley $24.   89

Dark ruby cast. Moderately full-bodied. Balanced acidity. Highly extracted. Moderately oaked. Mildly tannic. Cassis, licorice, minerals. Aromatic and complex, with an emphasis on terroir, not winemaking. Firm though supple in the mouth, with a sense of brightness to the lengthy finish. Seamless.

Lockwood

1997 Chardonnay, Monterey $14.99.   86

Medium-full yellow-gold. Generous aromas of sweet wood and tart fruits. A bright entry leads a moderately full-bodied palate with angular acids. Fruit flavors are generous and ripe with judicious oak accents through the finish.

1996 Chardonnay, Partners' Reserve, Monterey $19.99.   80

1994 Cabernet Sauvignon, Partners' Reserve, Monterey $21.   87

Deep purple-tinged red. Medium-bodied. Highly extracted. Mildly tannic. Red berries, spice, vanilla. Spicy aromas lead a somewhat lean though reasonably concentrated mouthful of red berry fruit flavors through a long minerally finish. Well balanced and harmonious.

1996 Cabernet Sauvignon, Partners' Reserve, Monterey $19.99.   83

Full dark ruby-purple hue. Toasty black cherry and toasted oak aromas. A rich entry leads a moderately full-bodied palate with a rich center of dark fruits and chewy dry tannins that grip the finish. Solidly structured, ripe style. Drink now or later.

1995 Merlot, Monterey County $18.   90

Deep blackish ruby hue with purple highlights. Moderately full-bodied. Balanced acidity. Moderately extracted. Moderately oaked. Mildly tannic. Plums, vanilla, green herbs. Aromatic and quite flavorful, with real complexity. Quite snappy on the palate, with good grip and a lengthy oak-accented finish.

1996 Merlot, Monterey County $17.99.   86

Bright crimson-ruby hue. Good aromas of herbs with minerally edges. A crisp attack leads a medium-bodied palate with lean, dry tannins and lively acids. Drink now.

1995 Merlot, Partners' Reserve, Monterey County $24.   92

Very deep, opaque blackish ruby hue with purple highlights. Moderately full-bodied. Balanced acidity. Highly extracted. Heavily oaked. Mildly tannic. Black fruits, vanilla, minerals. Quite deeply flavored, with a pure expression of dark fruit flavors intertwined with wood and mineral notes. Well structured on the palate, with a hint of austerity and a lengthy finish.

1996 Merlot, Partners' Reserve, Monterey $24.99.   91

Bright purple-red. Attractive toasty vanilla and berry aromas. A supple attack leads a moderately full-bodied palate with generous ripe tannins and juicy acids. Finishes with lingering toasty notes and bright fruits. Drink now or later. Can improve with more age.

1996 Syrah, Monterey $16.   83

Dark ruby color, limpid with a slight fade. Coal tar, herbs, black fruits. Medium-bodied. Pruney, ripe, and soft, with a flabby finish. Drink now or later. Can improve with age.

Scale: Superlative (96-100), Exceptional (90-95), Highly Recommended (85-89), Recommended (80-84), Not Recommended (Under 80)

J. Lohr

1997 Chardonnay, Cypress, California $10.   84

Bright yellow-straw hue. Powerful banana and vanilla aromas show a big sweet oak accent. A rich entry leads a full-bodied palate that has creamy acidity. Rounded, opulent finish. Drink now.

1997 Chardonnay, Riverstone, Monterey $14.   91

Medium golden yellow. Quite aromatic with butter and apple aromas marked by vanilla oak influence. A rich entry leads a moderately full-bodied palate with nutty oak flavors coming through on the persistent finish. Excellent match with lobster, crab, or any rich white fish. Drink now or later.

1996 Merlot, Cypress, California $10.50.   87

Deep ruby purple with brilliant highlights. Moderately full-bodied. Balanced acidity. Highly extracted. Mildly oaked. Moderately tannic. Cherry cordial, licorice, bacon. Aromatic and deeply flavored, with a sturdy, well-structured palate feel. Velvety tannins bite into the finish, but the stuffing indicates that near-term cellaring should help open up this wine.

1996 Syrah, South Ridge, Paso Robles $14.   88

Dark black cherry color, limpid and brilliant. Generous, sound bramble fruit and vanilla flavors. Subtle wood tones. Smooth entry. Moderately full-bodied with crisp acidity. Moderate drying tannins. Chunky, rich, and fruity. Lengthy finish. Drinkable now, but can improve with age.

Lokoya

1995 Chardonnay, Wild Yeast, Napa Valley $30.   80
1995 Cabernet Sauvignon, Diamond Mountain, Napa Valley $100.   89

Deep, saturated blackish ruby hue. Intense chocolate, herb, and mineral aromas show judicious oak usage. A lush entry leads to a thick, full-bodied mouthfeel with big velvety tannins. Firm, grippy finish. A real heavyweight in every respect. A very ripe style that is rather fatiguing at present. Good for long-term cellaring.

1995 Cabernet Sauvignon, Mount Veeder, Napa Valley $100.   87

Deep, saturated purple-red hue. Brooding, intense red fruit and mineral aromas show a firm oak accent. A structured entry leads to a full-bodied palate with a big tannic wallop. Clipped, tannic finish. Quite tough at present. May come around with years of cellaring. Seems to have the fruit to hold out but rather shy of acidity. Good for long-term cellaring.

1995 Cabernet Sauvignon, Rutherford, Napa Valley $100.   95

Very deep, intense ruby hue. Powerful brown spice, cedar, and berry aromas carry a hefty wood accent. A lush entry leads to an extraordinarily flavorful palate with cordial-like intensity. Chewy tannins are buttressed by sturdy acidity. Intense flavorful finish. Lots of wood to be sure, but has the fruit extract to carry the day. Drink now or later.

Lolonis

1996 Chardonnay, Private Reserve, Redwood Valley, Mendocino $25.   88

Bright green-gold. Medium-bodied. Full acidity. Moderately extracted. Mildly oaked. Vanilla, white peach. Warm, smoky aromas lead a silky, rounded palate featuring sweet citrus flavors. Broad texture makes for a substantial style.

1996 Cabernet Sauvignon, Redwood Valley $17.   81
1994 Cabernet Sauvignon, Private Reserve, Mendocino County $25.   89

Deep, saturated ruby-red hue. Perfumed brown spice and black fruit aromas carry a pronounced wood accent. A lush attack leads to a moderately full-bodied palate with integrated tannins. Harmonious and well balanced with the structure to contain the ripeness. Flavorful, grippy finish. Developing beautifully. Drink now or later.

1996 Merlot, Private Reserve, Redwood Valley $25.   84

Bright purple-red. Generous overripe berry fruit and chocolatey aromas. A lush entry leads a thick, full-bodied palate with comparatively low acidity levels and chunky tannins. Big, rich finish. This is a heavier style in need of food. Drink now.

1995 Zinfandel, Redwood Valley $17.   89

Deep blackish purple. Moderately full-bodied. Balanced acidity. Moderately extracted. Moderately oaked. Mildly tannic. Chocolate, black fruits. Quite aromatic, with a rich, supple mouthfeel. Ripe and velvety through the long, flavorful finish.

1995 Zinfandel, Private Reserve, Redwood Valley $25.   86

Deep blackish purple. Moderately full-bodied. Balanced acidity. Moderately extracted. Moderately oaked. Mildly tannic. Chocolate, black fruits. Pleasantly aromatic, with well-integrated oak and fruit flavors. Rich and supple in the mouth, with chunky tannins through the finish.

Longoria

1995 Cabernet Franc, Blues Cuvée, Santa Ynez Valley $21.   81

1997 Pinot Noir, Bien Nacido Vineyard, Santa Maria Valley $32.   82

Lyeth

1995 Meritage, North Coast $9.   81

MacRostie

1997 Chardonnay, Carneros $17.99.   84

Medium-bright gold. Mild aromas of butter with heavy oak accents. A dull entry leads a moderately full-bodied palate with dry flavors that come through on the finish. Not very generous. Drink now.

1996 Merlot, Carneros $26.   86

Saturated ruby red. Muted, minerally, floral aromas. A stern attack leads a moderately full-bodied palate with drying tannins. The finish is tannic, though flavorful. Well structured, and rather tight at present. Drink now or later. Can improve with more age.

1995 Pinot Noir, Carneros $17.75.   88

Pale bright cherry red. Medium-bodied. Moderately extracted. Mildly oaked. Mildly tannic. Rich perfumed red fruit aromas show nice varietal character. Crisp and fruity on the palate, with supple berry flavors. A hint of tannin and toasted oak on the finish.

1995 Pinot Noir, Reserve, Carneros $25.   91

Bright translucent blood red. Medium-bodied. Moderately extracted. Moderately oaked. Mildly tannic. Excellent rich Pinot Noir fruit aromas show great varietal character, with eucalyptus notes. Supple, rounded, and delicate through the lingering finish. A toasty chocolate note adds appeal. Drinking nicely now.

Maddalena

1996 Cabernet Sauvignon, Central Coast $9.95.   81

1996 Merlot, San Simeon Reserve, Central Coast $14.95.   82

Madroña

1993 Quintet, El Dorado $15.   86

Deep ruby-violet hue Moderately full-bodied. Highly extracted. Quite tannic. Leather, earth, minerals. Austere dark fruit aromas lead a dry, minerally mouthful of flavors, with an earthy finish. Tannins are quite demanding and tough at present.

1996 Zinfandel, Reserve, El Dorado $16.   86

Deep blackish purple. Full-bodied. Balanced acidity. Moderately extracted. Moderately oaked. Moderately tannic. Black fruits, chocolate. Rather reserved aromatically, but supple and rich, with a chunky, generous mouthfeel. Deeply flavored through the finish.

Marcelina

1996 Chardonnay, Napa Valley $20.   83

Bright yellow-straw cast. Moderately full-bodied. Balanced acidity. Highly extracted. Minerals, citrus peel. Bright and aromatic, with a full impression in the mouth and a firm, pithy finish. Solid and flavorful.

1993 Cabernet Sauvignon, Napa County $20.   85

Medium ruby red with ripe aromas. A thick entry leads a moderately full-bodied palate with ripe, mature fruit flavors and tough chewy tannins. Seems rather old fashioned. Drink now.

Marietta

1996 Cabernet Sauvignon, Sonoma County $17.   89

Saturated dark ruby hue. Ultra ripe primary fruit-forward aromas. A juicy entry leads a moderately full-bodied palate of jammy ripe fruit flavors with supple, silky tannins lingering on the finish. Low acids give a thickish mouthfeel. Drink now.

1996 Syrah, California $16.   89

Deep dark red, limpid, and brilliant to the rim. Generous, appealing blackberry, bramble fruit, and cinnamon flavors. Generous wood tones. Smooth entry. Moderately full-bodied. Plentiful velvety tannins. Very bright flavors. Lingering rich finish. Fruit forward, fleshy, and hedonistic. Drink now or later. Can improve with more age.

Markham

1994 Cabernet Sauvignon, Napa Valley $15.49.   89

Deep reddish purple. Medium-bodied. Highly extracted. Mildly tannic. Black cherries, chocolate, brown spice. Rich, mouthfilling, and textured, with full, rounded flavors and ample soft tannins through the finish. Very polished and plush. Attractive for current drinking.

1995 Cabernet Sauvignon, Napa Valley $19.   88

Bright violet-red. Medium-bodied. Moderately extracted. Moderately tannic. Black fruits, minerals. Juicy, supple, and well balanced. This is well suited for current drinking, with a fine finish of powdery tannins giving grip.

1995 Merlot, Napa Valley $18.   88

Very deep ruby to the rim with brilliant clarity. Moderately full-bodied. Balanced acidity. Subtly extracted. Moderately tannic. Licorice, plums, earth. Still reined in aromatically, this youthful wine opens up on the palate with fruit-driven flavors. Chewy tannins bite into the finish.

1996 Merlot, Napa Valley $19.   86

Deep, saturated ruby red. Bright candied red fruit aromas show a subtle oak accent. A crisp attack leads a medium-bodied palate with vibrant acidity and mild tannins. The finish is generous, soft, and flavorful. An effusively clean and fruity effort. Drink now.

1995 Merlot, Reserve, Napa Valley $38.   89

Deep, saturated ruby red. Generous red fruit and vanilla aromas show a modest oak accent. A lush attack leads a medium-bodied palate with drying, woody tannins. The finish is supple and rounded. A mellow style, but well balanced and structured. Drink now.

1995 Zinfandel, Napa $16.   92

Blood red with a subtle purple note. Medium-bodied. Balanced acidity. Moderately extracted. Moderately oaked. Mildly tannic. Black fruits, bittersweet chocolate. Rich, ripe fruit flavors reveal some depth and persistence on the palate, with a good dose of vanilla oak seasoning. Pleasantly chewy, with great balance.

Martin Brothers (Renamed Martin & Weyrich, Spring 1999)

1995 Cabernet Sauvignon, Etrusco, Paso Robles $18.   **89**

Medium ruby red. Medium-bodied. Moderately extracted. Mildly tannic. Red berry fruits, chocolate, minerals. Developed aromas show an earthy generosity that is confirmed on the palate, with brisk acids and ripe fruit flavors. Seasoned with a dose of oak spice that emerges on the finish.

NV Insieme Red, Central Coast $10.   **81**

1996 Nebbiolo, Central Coast $11.   **81**

1995 Nebbiolo, Vecchio, Central Coast $20.   **84**

Bright blackish ruby cast. Moderately full-bodied. Full acidity. Highly extracted. Mildly oaked. Mildly tannic. Red fruits, flowers, earth. Quite aromatic, with a distinctive earthy, herbal edge. Finishes on a lean note, with angular acidity.

1996 Sangiovese, Il Palio, Central Coast $12.   **80**

1998 Moscato Allegro, California $10.   **86**

Bright golden hue with a slight spritz. Forward melon and pear aromas. A vibrant entry leads a flavorful palate displaying juicy acidity and mild sweetness. Lively and refreshing. Drink now.

Martinelli

1996 Chardonnay, Gold Ridge, Russian River Valley $20.   **95**

Deep, saturated yellow-straw hue. Powerful yeast, cream, and spice aromas show a hefty oak accent. A rich entry leads a full-bodied but balanced palate. Extremely flavorful and big; this is a showy, opulent style. Drink now.

1996 Chardonnay, Charles Ranch, Sonoma Coast $30.   **86**

Deep, saturated yellow-straw hue. Generous cream and hazelnut aromas carry a toasty oak influence. A supple entry leads a moderately full-bodied palate. A big, rich style with shy acidity. On the fat side, but flavorful and opulent, with a touch of wood. Drink now.

1997 Gewürztraminer, Russian River Valley $12.   **93**

Deep, saturated green-gold hue. Powerful, varietally intense lychee, spice, and sweet citrus aromas. A rich entry leads a full-bodied palate, with crisp acidity and a hint of sweetness. Big, intense, and rich, with great power. Drink now.

1996 Pinot Noir, Martinelli Vineyard, Russian River Valley $25.   **88**

Pale ruby-garnet cast. Moderately full-bodied. Balanced acidity. Moderately extracted. Moderately oaked. Mildly tannic. Green herbs, spice, minerals. Unusual aromatics lead a full and flavorful impression in the mouth. Ripe and zesty through the warming finish.

1997 Zinfandel, Louisa & Giuseppe, Russian River Valley $18.   **91**

Opaque, saturated violet red. Powerful, brooding black fruit, anise, and spice aromas. A jammy entry leads a full-bodied palate, with shy acidity and velvety tannins. Hedonistic and rich, with hefty ripeness, but there is a dry, savory edge to the finish. Drink now.

1996 Zinfandel, Jackass Vineyard, Russian River Valley $25.   **96**

Deep blackish ruby hue with a slight haze. Full-bodied. Balanced acidity. Highly extracted. Heavily oaked. Mildly tannic. Pickle barrel, black fruits, pomegranate, spice cabinet. Redolent of wood seasoning, with a distinctive pickled note often associated with American oak. Full and rich on the palate, with a thick, velvety texture. Lengthy and supple through the finish. Exotic and intense.

1997 Muscat Alexandria, Jackass Hill, Russian River Valley $18/375 ml.   **90**

Bright straw hue. Perfumed flower, peach blossom, and Muscat aromas. A rich entry leads a moderately sweet, full-bodied palate. Extremely flavorful, with an unctuous, viscous texture. Drink now.

Scale: Superlative (96-100), Exceptional (90-95), Highly Recommended (85-89), Recommended (80-84), Not Recommended (Under 80)

Louis Martini

1997 Chardonnay, North Coast $10.   83

Pale straw cast. Medium-bodied. Full acidity. Moderately extracted. Flowers, citrus.
Vibrant aromas have an unusual overtone. Lean, crisp, and zesty through the finish.

1996 Chardonnay, Reserve, Russian River Valley $18.   82

1996 Sauvignon Blanc, Napa Valley $9.   80

1994 Barbera, Heritage Collection, Lake County $12.   87

Bright blackish ruby cast. Medium-bodied. Full acidity. Moderately extracted. Mildly
tannic. Red fruits, minerals. Rather reserved aromatically, but flavorful and very well
structured on the palate. Finishes on an austere, minerally note, and shows admirable
restraint. Will be excellent at the table.

1994 Cabernet Sauvignon, Reserve, Napa Valley $18.   91

Bright red-purple. Moderately full-bodied. Highly extracted. Moderately tannic. Cassis,
minerals, vanilla. Rich, spiced black fruit aromas follow through on the palate, with fine
grip and balance making for an approachable style that will age well.

*1994 Cabernet Sauvignon, Monte Rosso Vineyard Selection,
Sonoma Mountain $30.*   92

Dark blackish red with purple highlights. Medium-bodied. Moderately extracted. Mildly
tannic. Vanilla, black fruits, brown spice, earth. Oak-accented aromas lead an earthy but
rounded palate with assertive and complex flavors and soft tannins through the finish.
Harmonious and very forward.

*1995 Cabernet Sauvignon, Monte Rosso Vineyard Selection,
Sonoma Valley $35.*   87

Saturated blood red. Moderately full-bodied. Highly extracted. Moderately tannic.
Jammy black fruits, brown spice. Dusty, ripe aromas lead a firm palate, with gripping
tannins and fine persistence through the finish. Tannins have a dry, powdery quality.
A more old-fashioned style.

1995 Merlot, Reserve, Russian River Valley $18.   88

Blood red with a brick-red rim. Leathery, extravagantly spiced black fruit aromas show
a distinct oak influence. A bright entry leads a medium-bodied palate with slight but
powdery dry tannins. The lingering, spicy finish shows complex flavors. Very evolved
and mature tasting. Drink now.

1993 Zinfandel, Heritage Collection, Sonoma Valley $12.   86

Bright ruby cast. Moderately full-bodied. Balanced acidity. Moderately extracted. Mildly
tannic. Minerals, red fruits. Reserved aromatically, with distinctive minerally nuances.
Features an elegant, balanced character with a firm, focused finish. Artfully crafted for
those who tire of "Zin monsters."

Martini & Prati

1996 Pinot Bianco, Monterey $10.   84

Deep golden cast. Moderately full-bodied. Balanced acidity. Moderately extracted.
Flowers, citrus, tropical fruits. Quite aromatic, with some complexity to the flavors.
Full though angular on the palate, with steely acidity through the finish.

1996 Vino Grigio, California $12.50.   88

Bright golden cast. Moderately full-bodied. Full acidity. Moderately extracted. Tropical
fruits, spice, cream. Ripe aromas follow through on the palate, with a sense of richness
to the fruit-accented flavors. Full and lush, with zesty acidity providing good grip.

1993 Fuoco di Sant Elmo, California $20.   82

1995 Zinfandel, California $15.   82

1996 Zinfandel, Reserve, Russian River Valley $18.   90

Deep blackish purple. Full-bodied. Balanced acidity. Moderately extracted. Heavily oaked.
Mildly tannic. Vanilla, black fruits. Extremely aromatic, with real intensity to the dark
fruit flavors and a hedonistic wave of toasty oak accents. Lush and exotic on the palate,

with velvety tannins. Intense and charming, not unlike a top Aussie Shiraz.

Paul Masson
Rich Ruby Port, California $5.99.   82

Matanzas Creek
1996 Chardonnay, Sonoma Valley $30.   88

Brilliant yellow-straw hue. Subdued mineral and citrus aromas. A crisp entry leads a moderately full-bodied palate with firm acidity and fine intensity. The finish is creamy and generous. A well-structured wine that should open with some aging. Midterm cellar candidate (3–6 years).

1995 Chardonnay, Journey, Sonoma Valley $95.   94

Deep straw hue. Opulent vanilla, yeast, and orange aromas show an attractive leesy quality and generous oak influence. A firm entry leads a full-bodied palate that has lean, intense acidity. Flavorful and complex through the racy finish. Drink now.

1996 Sauvignon Blanc, Sonoma County $18.   91

Bright golden yellow. Medium-bodied. Balanced acidity. Moderately extracted. Moderately oaked. Lime zest, brown spice, minerals. Toasty tart citrus aromas lead a solid palate, with a minerally backbone and toasty oak spices on the finish. Well structured, with a good mouthfeel. This would be a good food partner.

1996 Merlot, Sonoma Valley $47.   88

Dark ruby red. Muted aromas show a mild oaky character. A soft entry leads a moderately full-bodied palate with plenty of fine-grained tannins and dark fruit flavors. Rather heavily extracted flavors make for a leaner style with a drying finish.

1994 Merlot, Journey, Sonoma Valley $155.   94

Saturated dark violet-ruby hue. Impressively powerful, dense oak-accented black fruit and olive aromas show great complexity. A firm attack leads a full-bodied palate with fine-grained gripping tannins and powerful, concentrated flavors. Rather a dry finish with spice and minerals lingering. Good for long-term cellaring.

Maxus
1991 Midnight Cuvée, California $19.99.   90

Deep salmon cast. Full-bodied. Red fruits, toast. Generous aromas show a complex character with oak nuances. Rich, ripe, and rounded in the mouth, with fine weight and intensity. Subtle red fruit flavors linger on the finish.

1991 Brut, California $19.99.   90

Full yellow-gold. Moderately full-bodied. Nuts, apples. Developed nutty, bready aromas follow through on a soft yet generous palate showing good maturity and length. Plush, rich, and full-flavored. For those who like mature styles.

1991 English Cuvée, California $29.99.   91

Full golden yellow. Moderately full-bodied. Bread, nuts, baked apples. Profoundly rich, developed aromas show a powerful yeast accent that comes through on the palate, with rich flavors and soft acids. A very hedonistic and voluptuous style.

Mayacamas
1992 Cabernet Sauvignon, Napa Valley $30.   89

Deep ruby red with a slight fade. Medium-bodied. Balanced acidity. Moderately extracted. Mildly tannic. Mushroom, minerals, licorice. Aromatic and intense, with a high-toned, earthy quality throughout. Lean and angular on the palate, with a crisp finish.

1993 Cabernet Sauvignon, Napa Valley $38.   86

Deep cherry red with a garnet rim. Interesting and mature forest, earth, and herb aromas. A lush entry leads to a medium-bodied palate with grippy tannins and a well-balanced structure. Angular, flavorful finish. Showing some mature complexities and

Scale: Superlative (96-100), Exceptional (90-95), Highly Recommended (85-89), Recommended (80-84), Not Recommended (Under 80)

drinking well now. Drink within five years.

1993 Sauvignon Blanc, Late Harvest, Napa Valley $16/375 ml.   **86**

Deep bronzed golden hue. Moderately full-bodied. Balanced acidity. Moderately extracted. Mildly oaked. Petrol, rancio, tropical fruits. Quite complex aromas, with a rich, lush, viscous palate feel. Carries an almost Alsatian tone of exoticism. A touch of acidity keeps the finish lively. Individualistic style.

Peter McCoy

1996 Chardonnay, Clos de Pierres, Knights Valley $39.   **90**

Yellow-straw hue with a slight haze. Moderately full-bodied. Balanced acidity. Highly extracted. Mildly oaked. Yeast, cream, citrus. Forward aromas are quite complex, showing a big yeasty, creamy accent. Full and rich in the mouth with an opulent and rounded character. Flavorful through the finish.

McDowell

1996 Viognier, Mendocino $15.   **84**

Deep straw cast. Full-bodied. Full acidity. Moderately extracted. Minerals. Rather reserved aromatically, with a generous mouthfeel buttressed by vibrant and racy acidity. Well structured, but neutral in the flavor department.

1997 Grenache Rosé, Mendocino $9.   **83**

Very pale pinkish salmon hue. Subdued berry and citrus aromas. A crisp entry leads a taut, moderately light-bodied palate that has vibrant acidity. The finish is clean and flavorful. Drink now.

1997 Syrah, Mendocino $12.   **85**

Bright purple-red hue to the rim. Subdued earth, herb, and red fruit aromas. A firm attack leads a moderately full-bodied palate, with aggressive astringent tannins. Lacks somewhat for acidic grip. Tannic, earthy finish. Rather tough at present, with a funky edge that should blow off. Drink within five years.

McIlroy

1996 Zinfandel, Porter-Bass Vineyard, Russian River Valley $18.   **86**

Bright blackish ruby cast. Moderately full-bodied. Balanced acidity. Moderately extracted. Mildly oaked. Mildly tannic. Black fruits, minerals. Pleasantly aromatic, with a deep fruit core. Lush but firm in the mouth, with chunky tannins through the finish.

McKeon-Phillips

1996 Chardonnay, Reserve, Santa Barbara County $21.33.   **88**

Deep yellow-straw cast. Moderately full-bodied. Balanced acidity. Moderately extracted. Moderately oaked. Vanilla, spice, citrus. Generous aromas feature a hefty wood accent that follows through on a ripe, rounded mouthfeel. The finish is crisp and flavorful.

Mer et Soleil

1993 Chardonnay, Central Coast $30.   **94**

Moderately full-bodied. Lots of acid. Lots of fruit. Lots of oak. Dry. Reminiscent of baking bread, citrus, pears, butterscotch. Rich, piquant fruit is swamped by layers of aromatic oak. Rounded in the mouth, immensely proportioned, and chock full of succulent, stunningly complex flavors. This is a big-boned Chardonnay, kept in balance by its fabulous lingering acidity.

1994 Chardonnay, Central Coast $31.99.   **93**

Very deep gold. Medium-bodied. Balanced acidity. Moderately extracted. Heavily oaked. Dry. Reminiscent of citrus, brown spice. Big flavors reveal a strongly oak-influenced palate with some bright citrus fruit underneath. Generous, slightly oily texture is kept lively by some good acidity.

1995 Chardonnay, Central Coast $35.   **93**

Bright yellow-gold. Medium-bodied. Highly extracted. Heavily oaked. Full vanilla oak aromas lead an oak-accented palate with plenty of tropical nuances, and spice and smoke on the finish. The acid balance is zippy, making this a powerful yet polished style.   137

1996 Chardonnay, Central Coast $34.99.   92

Bright yellow-straw hue. Forcefully aromatic with oaky, nutty accents. A flavorful attack leads a moderately full-bodied palate with complex flavors of yeast, toasted oak, and tart apples. Well structured and assertive through the finish. This would be an excellent match with lobster, crab, or any rich white fish. Drink now.

Meridian

1997 Chardonnay, Santa Barbara County $11.   84

Bright green-straw hue. Medium-bodied. Balanced acidity. Vanilla, sweet citrus. Appealing vanilla and sweet fruit aromas lead a direct, juicy mouthful of fruit flavors that linger through the finish.

1996 Chardonnay, Coastal Reserve, Edna Valley $15.   89

Bright yellow-gold. Moderately full-bodied. Balanced acidity. Moderately extracted. Mildly oaked. Cream, minerals, citrus. Forward aromas feature a complex yeasty note. Big and ripe in the mouth, with an opulent, creamy texture. Lengthy flavorful finish.

1997 Sauvignon Blanc, California $8.50.   83

Bright yellow-gold. Medium-bodied. Balanced acidity. Moderately extracted. Mildly oaked. Butter, vanilla, citrus. Rich buttery aromas with a smoky note. Rounded, mouthfilling flavors with plenty of glycerin and alcohol. Well proportioned, showing Chardonnay structure and character.

1995 Cabernet Sauvignon, California $12.   86

Bright ruby hue to the rim. Moderately full-bodied. Balanced acidity. Moderately extracted. Moderately oaked. Mildly tannic. Cedar, red fruits. Pleasantly aromatic, with a well-integrated oak accent and a core of ripe fruit flavors. Understated, elegant, and well balanced.

1994 Cabernet Sauvignon, Coastal Reserve, California $20.   86

Deep ruby red to the rim. Moderately full-bodied. Balanced acidity. Moderately extracted. Moderately oaked. Mildly tannic. Cherry cordial, vanilla. Generous aromas feature a hefty oak accent. Firm and flavorful in the mouth, with angular tannins through the finish.

1995 Merlot, California $13.   83

Very deep red with brilliant highlights. Medium-bodied. Balanced acidity. Subtly extracted. Mildly tannic. Red fruits, vanilla, black tea. Lighter in style, with straightforward fruit-driven flavors and an accent on acidity at the finish.

1997 Pinot Noir, Santa Barbara $14.   85

Bright pale ruby cast. Moderately light-bodied. Full acidity. Moderately extracted. Moderately tannic. Minerals, red fruits. Lean, minerally aromas lead a firm and tightly wound palate feel. Angular through the finish, with a hint of bitterness.

1996 Pinot Noir, Coastal Reserve, Santa Barbara County $20.   88

Deep ruby cast. Moderately full-bodied. Balanced acidity. Moderately extracted. Moderately oaked. Mildly tannic. Spice, minerals, red fruits. Forward aromatics carry a prominent oak accent. Ripe and full in the mouth, with a sense of richness. Finishes with grainy tannins.

1996 Syrah, Paso Robles $14.   88

Deep purple-red, limpid, and brilliant to the rim. Generous, fantastic cedar and red currant flavors. Firm entry. Medium-bodied with crisp acidity. Moderate, grainy tannins. Well gripped through the finish, with fine structuring acids. Lingering finish. Bright and lively, with a nice oak overlay. Drink now.

1996 Zinfandel, Paso Robles $12.   86

Deep blackish ruby cast. Medium-bodied. Balanced acidity. Moderately extracted. Heavily oaked. Mildly tannic. Vanilla, black fruits. A fragrant oak influence is readily apparent on the nose, and joins a restrained core of fruit flavors in the mouth. Well balanced and elegant, in a sturdy Claret style.

Scale: Superlative (96-100), Exceptional (90-95), Highly Recommended (85-89), Recommended (80-84), Not Recommended (Under 80)

138

Merryvale

1997 Chardonnay, Starmont, Napa Valley $20.   83
Deep straw cast. Moderately full-bodied. Full acidity. Moderately extracted. Minerals, flint, butter. Unusual high-toned aromas are focused and precise. Turns full and rich in the mouth, with a tapering finish.

1996 Chardonnay, Reserve, Napa Valley $30.   85
Bright yellow-straw cast. Medium-bodied. Full acidity. Moderately extracted. Mildly oaked. Smoke, toast, citrus. Shows a forward toasty oak accent throughout. Light in the mouth, with a bright, zesty texture. Crisp and vibrant finish.

1996 Vignette, Napa Valley $22.   93
Deep green-gold. Moderately full-bodied. Balanced acidity. Moderately extracted. Mildly oaked. Figs, lanolin, toast. Features classic nutty Semillon aromas with a judicious overlay of oak. Rich and flavorful in the mouth, and well balanced through a very lengthy finish. A decidedly harmonious style.

1996 Sauvignon Blanc, Napa Valley $17.   89
Deep yellow-gold. Full-bodied. Full acidity. Highly extracted. Mildly oaked. Butter, vanilla, citrus. Full and toasty on the nose with very ripe overtones. Mouthfilling and vibrant through the lengthy finish. A well-structured, assertive Fumé style.

1996 Cabernet Sauvignon, Hillside, Napa Valley $18.   86
Saturated violet red. Medium-bodied. Highly extracted. Moderately tannic. Red berries, minerals. Bright, juicy, and somewhat cordial-like flavors, with a mild note of green tannins on the finish. Acids remain quite lively, accentuating a dry, tannic finish.

1994 Cabernet Sauvignon, Napa Valley $27.   87
Dark saturated ruby appearance. Medium-bodied. Highly extracted. Moderately tannic. Cassis, plums, licorice, chocolate, black tea. Generous black fruit aromas lead a solid palate with deep flavors. Solid tannins on the finish. Well structured, this should improve with some maturity.

1995 Cabernet Sauvignon, Reserve, Napa Valley $30.   91
Dark blood-violet red. Moderately full-bodied. Highly extracted. Quite tannic. Cassis, cedar, mineral. A concentrated, fruit-packed palate with toasty overtones. Firm-edged tannins show on the finish. This will need some time to resolve its firm structure.

1993 Profile, Napa Valley $48.   88
Opaque garnet red. Moderately full-bodied. Highly extracted. Quite tannic. Licorice, brown spice, black fruits. A brooding nose leads a full-flavored palate that is tightly wound. Firm dry finish. This needs cellaring to show its potential.

1994 Profile, Napa Valley $55.   96
Saturated, opaque blood red. Moderately full-bodied. Highly extracted. Quite tannic. Nutmeg, oriental spice, cassis. Exotic, oriental-spiced aromas are intriguing. Solidly extracted, with very tight, grainy tannins. This is a wine for long-term (7–10 years) cellaring; needs more bottle age to show its best.

1995 Profile, Napa Valley $66.   91
Bright ruby-violet hue. Ripe plummy aromas with a dusty, spiced accent. A firm entry leads a medium-bodied palate with very tight tannins and good fruit concentration. Well gripped and dry through the finish. Drink now or later.

1995 Merlot, Reserve, Napa Valley $32.   90
Very deep blackish ruby hue to the rim. Moderately full-bodied. Balanced acidity. Highly extracted. Moderately oaked. Moderately tannic. Chocolate, black fruits, licorice. Deep and flavorful with a dense core of extract. Though firmly structured, this wine is well balanced, with a lingering finish. Approachable now but will improve with mid-term (3–6 years) aging.

1996 Merlot, Reserve, Napa Valley $32.   86
Saturated dark ruby hue. Restrained aromas show a woody character with muted fruit. A lean entry leads a full-bodied palate with tough, drying tannins masking fruit flavors. Finishes in a rustic, dry manner. This seems to be drying out.

Peter Michael

1996 Chardonnay, "Clos du Ciel," Napa County $38.   90

Bright yellow-gold. Moderately full-bodied. Full acidity. Moderately extracted. Lime, lemon zest, spice. Bright, zesty fruit flavors have a piercing purity that is not dulled by considerable oak spice and yeasty notes. This is bright and youthful at present, with a very distinctive character.

1996 Chardonnay, "Belle Côte," Knights Valley $42.   89

Bright yellow-straw cast. Moderately full-bodied. Full acidity. Mildly oaked. Cream, citrus, yeast. Forward aromatics carry a complex yeasty quality throughout. Bright and firm in the mouth with zesty acidity through the finish.

1996 Sauvignon Blanc, L'Apres-Midi, Napa County $20.   91

Full bright yellow-gold. Moderately full-bodied. Full acidity. Highly extracted. Moderately oaked. Toasted oak, ripe citrus. Very aromatic, with distinct oak and smoky yeast influences. Rich, heavily toasted flavors with fine concentration and grip through the finish. Nice now, though this should develop further with short-term (1–2 years) cellaring.

1994 Les Pavots Red, Knights Valley $35.   90

Saturated red. Medium-bodied. Highly extracted. Moderately tannic. Black cherries, plums, vanilla, tobacco. Chewy Cabernet fruit flavors lead cigar box notes on the finish, which is quite dry from the assertive tannins. Shows some good structure; quite a heavyweight.

Michel-Schlumberger

1993 Cabernet Sauvignon, Dry Creek Valley $19.50.   86

Deep purple-red. Medium-bodied. Moderately extracted. Mildly tannic. Tart red fruits, minerals. Rather crisp and tart, with focused cherry fruit flavors up front that give way to lemony acids and minerally notes on the finish.

1994 Cabernet Sauvignon, Dry Creek Valley $20.   90

Saturated red-purple. Moderately full-bodied. Highly extracted. Quite tannic. Red fruits, minerals. Youthful and tannic, showing a floral nose and deep palate with firm tannins and vibrant berry fruit flavors. This needs time.

1995 Cabernet Sauvignon, Dry Creek Valley $22.   81

1993 Cabernet Sauvignon, Schlumberger Reserve, Dry Creek Valley $35.   86

Black cherry red. Medium-bodied. Moderately extracted. Moderately tannic. Black cherries, mineral, spice. Aromas of mineral and black fruits follow on the palate. The finish turns dry, with a mildly bitter note. A lean, taut style.

1996 Merlot, Sonoma County $21.   83

Bright ruby-violet red. Lean herbal and red fruit aromas. A mild attack leads a medium-bodied palate with slight drying tannins and low acids. Drink now.

1996 Syrah, Coastal California $20.   86

Deep ruby red, opaque and brilliant, with a slight fade. Medium-bodied. Tart berry, raspberry, and mineral flavors. Lively acids make for an aggressive, puckering mouthful. Flavorsome and youthful. Drinkable now, but can improve with more age.

Midnight Cellars

1996 Chardonnay, Central Coast $19.   84

Deep straw cast. Medium-bodied. Full acidity. Highly extracted. Mildly oaked. Brown spices, minerals. Subdued aromas carry a pleasant oak accent. Crisp, lean, and very zesty through the finish.

1995 Cabernet Franc, Crescent, Paso Robles $15.   87

Bright ruby purple. Medium-bodied. Balanced acidity. Moderately extracted. Mildly oaked. Mildly tannic. Red fruits, brown spices, minerals. Aromatic, with a flavorful palate. Lean and angular through the finish, showing a firm structure on a lighter frame.

1995 Cabernet Sauvignon, Nocturne, Paso Robles $15.   **84**

Bright ruby purple. Moderately full-bodied. Balanced acidity. Highly extracted. Heavily oaked. Moderately tannic. Black cherries, vanilla. Quite aromatic, with a hefty oak overlay and an intense, cordial-like fruit accent. Ripe and flavorful, with decent acidity and firm tannins on the finish.

1995 Merlot, Eclipse, Paso Robles $19.   **89**

Deep ruby red with a blackish hue. Moderately full-bodied. Balanced acidity. Highly extracted. Heavily oaked. Mildly tannic. Plums, vanilla, cordial. Fruit driven and quite aromatic, with a sense of sweetness to the flavors. Velvety, lush, and quite supple in the mouth, with a lengthy oak-tinged finish.

Mietz

1995 Merlot, Sonoma County $21.   **89**

Deep blackish ruby with a slight purplish cast. Moderately full-bodied. Balanced acidity. Highly extracted. Mildly oaked. Mildly tannic. Black fruits, vanilla, sweet herbs. Aromatic and flavorful with a sense of richness to the palate. Vibrant acidity lends some buoyancy to the dark fruit flavors. Tannins are still a bit chunky in the finish. Should integrate nicely in the near term.

Milano

1995 Zinfandel, Sanel Valley Vineyard, Mendocino County $12.   **82**

Mill Creek

1996 Merlot, Dry Creek Valley $17.50.   **84**

Bright violet hue with a slight fade. Anise and black plum aromas. A smooth attack leads a medium-bodied palate with soft tannins and juicy acids. Drink now.

Mirassou

1997 Chardonnay, Family Selection, Monterey County $11.95.   **83**

Pale straw cast. Medium-bodied. Full acidity. Moderately extracted. Minerals, bread dough. Firm, lean, and crisp, with a measure of austerity throughout. Angular, brisk finish.

1996 Pinot Blanc, Harvest Reserve, Monterey County $15.95.   **81**

1998 Riesling, Family Selection, Monterey County $7.50.   **84**

Pale straw hue. Aromas of butter, flowers, and tart apple, with an herbal twist. A soft entry leads a medium-bodied palate, with juicy fruit flavors lingering on the finish. Drink now.

1998 White Zinfandel, Family Selection, California $6.95.   **80**

1993 Cabernet Sauvignon, Monterey County $11.95.   **85**

Bright cherry red. Moderately light-bodied. Moderately extracted. Mildly tannic. Mint, cranberry, minerals. Attractive minty nose leads a crisp, clean palate, with bright red fruit flavors and a mildly astringent finish. Quite light in style but well balanced.

1994 Cabernet Sauvignon, Harvest Reserve, Napa Valley $17.95.   **86**

Bright purple-red. Moderately light-bodied. Moderately extracted. Mildly tannic. Tart cherries, raspberries. High-toned red fruit flavors give this wine a bright feel through the finish. Though the flavors are not especially deep, there is an appealingly accessible balance with plenty of bright fruity character.

1995 Cabernet Sauvignon, Harvest Reserve, Napa Valley $17.95.   **87**

Bright violet-red with a weak rim. Medium-bodied. Moderately extracted. Mildly tannic. Red fruits, vanilla. Bright berry fruit aromas follow through on a juicy, bright palate, with clean flavors and lively acids making for an easy-drinking style. Best drunk in its youth.

1990 Petite Sirah, Monterey County $35.   **84**

Full brick red with a subtly fading rim. Moderately full-bodied. Moderately extracted. Moderately tannic. Tobacco and currant aromas follow through on the palate, with a heavy spice and coffee character coming through on the finish. Very interesting and complex, showing marked maturity.

1996 Petite Sirah, Monterey County $11.95.   83

Opaque purple. Moderately full-bodied. Highly extracted. Quite tannic. Herbal and blueberry aromas follow through on a palate that shows a thick, textured mouthfeel. Impressive grainy tannins on the finish.

1995 Pinot Noir, Family Selection, Central Coast $10.95.   89

Pale ruby hue. Moderately light-bodied. Moderately extracted. Mildly oaked. Mildly tannic. Crisp red berry fruit aromas have gamey notes. Lean and crisp, with subtle astringency through the finish. Nice oak spice notes linger. Well balanced and drinking well now.

1996 Pinot Noir, Family Selection, Monterey County $10.95.   83

Very pale red. Moderately light-bodied. Subtly extracted. Red fruits, dried herbs, minerals. Crisp fruity aromas lead a lightly framed palate with lean, bright flavors and a clean finish.

1995 Pinot Noir, Harvest Reserve, Monterey County $15.95.   85

Bright cherry red. Medium-bodied. Moderately extracted. Mildly oaked. Mildly tannic. Smooth spicy cherry and berry flavors linger through the finish, with pleasing hints of tannin and vanilla oak.

1996 Pinot Noir, Harvest Reserve, Monterey County $15.95.   86

Bright violet purple. Medium-bodied. Moderately extracted. Vanilla, cherries. Sweet oak-driven aromas follow through well on the palate with supple fruity flavors. Clean finish.

1988 Zinfandel, Harvest Reserve, Santa Clara Valley $32.50.   86

Fading garnet with browning pale rim. Moderately light-bodied. Low acidity. Subtly extracted. Mildly tannic. Spice, stewed fruits. Very mature aromas have a stewed character that is either interesting or off-putting, depending on your tastes. The flavors follow the aromas, with dusty spice and stewed flavors. Graceful and mellow, with a soft mouthfeel. Unrecognizable as Zinfandel.

1995 Zinfandel, Harvest Reserve, Santa Clara Valley $15.95.   80

1997 Johannisberg Riesling, Late Harvest, San Vicente Ranch,
Monterey County $15.95.   89

Deep straw hue. Attractive honeyed pineapple and tropical fruit aromas. A rich entry leads a moderately full-bodied palate that has an oily texture and complex petrol overtones. Sweet, but well balanced and extremely flavorful. Drink now.

Mission View

1995 Cabernet Franc, Paso Robles $13.50.   85

Bright ruby purple. Medium-bodied. Balanced acidity. Highly extracted. Moderately oaked. Mildly tannic. Bacon fat, vanilla, minerals. Oak-driven flavors play out on a lighter-styled palate. Lean and drying through the finish.

1996 Cabernet Sauvignon, Paso Robles $12.75.   84

Pale crimson with a purple fading rim. Sweet vanilla aromas with a note of cherry fruits. A bright entry leads a medium-bodied palate with sweet fruit flavors and rather slight tannins. Finishes with a note of warmth. Drink now.

1995 Merlot, Limited Release, Paso Robles $14.50.   81

1996 Merlot, Midnight Mischievous, Paso Robles $15.   81

1996 Zinfandel, Eastside Ecstasy, Paso Robles $13.50.   86

Bright ruby cast. Moderately full-bodied. Balanced acidity. Highly extracted. Moderately tannic. Briar fruits. The generous fruit flavors carry a slight sense of overripeness. Firm and compact on the palate, with an overtone of sweetness, and hefty tannins through the finish.

Robert Mondavi

1996 Chardonnay, Napa Valley $19.   87

Bright yellow-gold. Medium-bodied. Balanced acidity. Moderately extracted. Vanilla, tart apple, spice. Crisp and bright, with citrus flavors and mild buttery texture; an elegant style. Shows good grip through the finish.

1996 Chardonnay, Carneros $25.   81

1996 Chardonnay, Reserve, Napa Valley $30.   92

Bright golden yellow. Moderately full-bodied. Balanced acidity. Moderately extracted. Moderately oaked. Ripe apples, vanilla, brown spice. Ripe toasty, spicy aromas. Broad and textured, with generous apple flavors and toasted oak accents throughout, and a flavorful finish.

1996 Sauvignon Blanc, Coastal, North Coast $8.   81

1996 Fumé Blanc, Napa Valley $12.   83

Deep yellow-straw hue. Moderately full-bodied. Full acidity. Moderately extracted. Mildly oaked. Vanilla, citrus, yeast. Oak influence is readily apparent on the nose and combines with a pleasant yeasty note to add a measure of complexity to the palate. Well balanced, with good intensity.

1994 Fumé Blanc, To-Kalon Vineyard Reserve, Napa Valley $20.   89

Deep yellow-gold. Moderately full-bodied. Full acidity. Moderately extracted. Moderately oaked. Brown spices, citrus, minerals. Quite aromatic, with a hefty note of barrel influence balanced by crisp fruit flavors. Full though vibrant on the palate, with a snappy finish.

1995 Fumé Blanc, To-Kalon Vineyard Reserve, Napa Valley $22.   87

Bright yellow-gold. Moderately full-bodied. Full acidity. Moderately extracted. Citrus, minerals. Youthful, with reserved aromatics and a tightly wound palate feel. Good intensity, with a firm structure through the finish. Should develop further with near-term cellaring.

1995 Cabernet Sauvignon, Coastal, North Coast $10.95.   84

Deep ruby hue to the rim. Medium-bodied. Balanced acidity. Moderately extracted. Mildly tannic. Dried herbs, earth, red fruits. Somewhat light in style, with an earthy quality throughout. Lean and angular through the finish.

1994 Cabernet Sauvignon, Napa Valley $22.   87

Dark reddish purple. Medium-bodied. Highly extracted. Moderately tannic. Cassis, plums, brown spice. Rather dry and austere at present, with some lean fruit flavors on the midpalate and solid tannins through the finish. Decently structured, this could happily take more cellar time.

1995 Cabernet Sauvignon, Napa Valley $21.   91

Saturated red with violet highlights. Medium-bodied. Highly extracted. Moderately tannic. Cassis, earth, brown spice. Rich black fruit aromas follow through on the palate, with earthy tannins giving grip. Solid and flavor-packed; nice both now and a few years hence.

1994 Cabernet Sauvignon, Oakville, Napa Valley $28.   87

Dark red. Medium-bodied. Moderately extracted. Moderately tannic. Black fruits, plums, cedar. Robustly flavorful, with chewy black fruit flavors and rich tannins on the finish. This is approachable and enjoyable now, but will benefit from one to two more years in bottle.

1995 Cabernet Sauvignon, Oakville, Napa Valley $27.   87

Deep ruby cast. Moderately full-bodied. Balanced acidity. Moderately extracted. Moderately oaked. Mildly tannic. Brown spices, cassis, minerals. Pleasantly aromatic, with a lush and supple mouthfeel that is buttressed by a firm, minerally backbone. Showing complexity and a sense of terroir. Well balanced and lengthy.

1995 Cabernet Sauvignon, SLD, Napa Valley $27.　　88

Saturated red-purple. Moderately full-bodied. Highly extracted. Moderately tannic. Cassis, mint, cedar. Crisp yet full fruit-laden aromas follow through on the palate, with plenty of mineral stuffing and some hard-edged tannins that will need a few years to resolve.

1994 Cabernet Sauvignon, Reserve, Napa Valley $75.　　89

Dark reddish purple. Moderately full-bodied. Highly extracted. Quite tannic. Cassis, black fruits, minerals. Somewhat meaty aromas. Well structured and proportioned, with impressive tannins drying out the finish. Solidly extracted flavors make for an assertive style that would benefit from some extra fleshiness on the midpalate.

1995 Cabernet Sauvignon, Reserve, Napa Valley $75.　　93

Saturated dark red. Moderately full-bodied. Highly extracted. Quite tannic. Earth, mineral. Rich aromas, hinting of dark fruits and earth. Dense, gripping palate of fleshy dark fruits and granular tannins. Big-shouldered and rather young at present, though drinkable.

1997 Merlot, Coastal, Central Coast $14.　　84

Bright crimson red. Clean aromas of minerals and herbs. A crisp attack leads a medium-bodied palate with light drying tannins and lively acids that provide some grip. There are nice fruit accents throughout. The finish is clean and quick. Drink now.

1995 Merlot, Napa Valley $26.　　87

Deep blackish ruby hue. Medium-bodied. Balanced acidity. Moderately extracted. Moderately oaked. Mildly tannic. Dried herbs, black fruits, leather. Pleasantly aromatic with a hefty oak accent. The core of fruit flavors gains complexity from an herbal streak. Relatively supple in structure, with some dusty tannins on the finish.

1996 Merlot, Napa Valley $26.　　86

Deep ruby red. Pleasant aromas show an oaky quality. Medium-bodied, with a ripe, lush entry and plummy flavors that conclude with a dry cedary note. Drink now or later. Can improve with more age.

1996 Pinot Noir, Coastal, Central Coast $10.95.　　80

1995 Pinot Noir, Napa Valley $18.　　88

Medium cherry red. Medium-bodied. Moderately extracted. Moderately oaked. Moderately tannic. Rich cherry pie aromas with vanilla accents lead a rounded palate with some depth of fruit flavors. A hint of astringent tannins gives some authority to the finish.

1996 Pinot Noir, Napa Valley $19.　　84

Pale violet red. Medium-bodied. Moderately extracted. Mildly oaked. Mildly tannic. Red fruits, minerals. A note of herbal greenness shows on the nose and follows through on the palate, with tart berry flavors and a dry, astringent finish. Good grip, though not great depth.

1995 Pinot Noir, Carneros $26.　　88

Medium cherry red with a pale rim. Medium-bodied. Moderately extracted. Moderately oaked. Mildly tannic. Perfumed vanilla and red fruit aromas. Crisp, juicy raspberry and strawberry flavors with just a hint of tannin on the finish. Nice now, this has some weight and structure.

1996 Pinot Noir, Carneros $26.　　84

Full ruby red with a lightening rim. Medium-bodied. Moderately extracted. Mildly tannic. Minerals, vanilla. Rustic aromas with a red fruit accent lead a lean, minerally palate with some grip on the finish. Probably best over the near term.

1995 Pinot Noir, Reserve, Napa Valley $31.　　89

Cherry red with subtle purple highlights. Medium-bodied. Moderately extracted. Moderately oaked. Moderately tannic. Complex, rich, rounded aromas of toast and ripe cherry fruit. The solid palate has tightly wound flavors, with a veneer of dry tannin throughout.

1996 Pinot Noir, Reserve, Napa Valley $36.   **90**

Pale violet red. Medium-bodied. Moderately extracted. Mildly tannic. Red berry fruits, vanilla. Subtly perfumed, fruity aromas lead a linear and precise palate with red fruit flavors and oak spice. Finishes with fine minerally persistence.

1995 Zinfandel, Coastal, North Coast $10.   **81**

1996 Zinfandel, Napa Valley $18.   **87**

Deep blackish ruby cast. Moderately full-bodied. Balanced acidity. Moderately extracted. Mildly oaked. Mildly tannic. Red fruits, brown spices. Somewhat reserved aromatically, with a flavorful, rich palate feel. Made in a Claret style with a well-integrated oak nuance woven throughout. Firm and well structured through the finish.

La Famiglia di Robert Mondavi

1996 Tocai Friulano, California $18.   **89**

Deep golden cast. Moderately full-bodied. Full acidity. Moderately extracted. Petrol, minerals, lime peel. Almost Riesling-like aromatically, with a full and rich palate feel. Angular acidity makes for a very lean and focused finish. An unusual though extremely interesting wine.

1996 Pinot Grigio, California $16.   **86**

Bright golden hue. Moderately full-bodied. Balanced acidity. Moderately extracted. Smoke, citrus, cream. Pleasantly aromatic, with a full, rich mouthfeel. Buoyant acidity enlivens the palate and makes for a zesty finish.

1995 Barbera, California $18.   **83**

Bright ruby purple. Moderately full-bodied. Full acidity. Moderately extracted. Mildly tannic. Black pepper, dried herbs, overripe black fruits. Unusual aromatics, with a slight Port-like note. Full but lean on the palate, with a concentrated finish.

1995 Sangiovese, California $22.   **82**

Monterey Peninsula Winery

1996 Pinot Noir, Sleepy Hollow Vineyard, Monterey County $16.99.   **81**

1995 Zinfandel, Naraghi Vineyard, Monterey County $14.99.   **85**

Bright ruby-garnet cast. Medium-bodied. Low acidity. Moderately extracted. Mildly tannic. Cherry tomatoes, stewed fruits. Engaging, mildly overripe notes in the nose. Light on the palate, with low acidity through the finish. A distinctive style, though very quaffable.

Monterey Vineyard

1996 Sauvignon Blanc, Monterey County $5.50.   **82**

Monterra

1997 Chardonnay, San Bernabé Ranch, Monterey County $8.99.   **86**

Pale straw hue. Yeasty, yellow apple aromas. A juicy entry leads a medium-bodied palate with judicious oak flavors and subtle yeasty notes. The subtle, lingering finish shows some juicy acidity. Drink now.

1995 Cabernet Sauvignon, Monterey County $9.99.   **84**

Bright violet-purple. Medium-bodied. Moderately extracted. Mildly tannic. Black fruits, flowers. Floral aromas lead a simple array of berry fruit flavors that finish with soft tannins. Quaffing style.

1996 Cabernet Sauvignon, Promise, Monterey County $9.99.   **87**

Deep purple red hue. Generous black fruit and vanilla aromas show a judicious oak component. A lush attack leads to a medium-bodied palate with soft, velvety tannins. Supple, harmonious finish. Rather shy of acidity, but very tasty in the near term. Drink now.

1995 Merlot, Monterey County $9.99. 85

Deep blackish ruby hue to the rim. Medium-bodied. Balanced acidity. Moderately extracted. Mildly tannic. Currants, minerals, black fruits. Clean and forceful, with a lighter-styled palate and solid structure. Features a hint of astringency on the snappy finish.

1996 Merlot, Promise, Monterey $9.99. 84

Bright crimson-violet hue, well saturated. Ripe, jammy black fruit aromas. The medium-bodied palate shows low acidity, and thick tannins come forward on an earthy finish. Drink now.

1996 Syrah, Monterey County $9.99. 86

Rich purple, limpid and brilliant, with a slight fade. Medium-bodied. Blueberry and vanilla flavors. A soft, round fruit-forward style with fine persistence of fruit flavors. Supple and easy drinking. Drink now.

Montevina

1997 Nebbiolo, Rosato, Amador County $7.50. 86

Bright pink. Medium-bodied. Full acidity. Moderately extracted. Minerals, citrus, red fruits. Pleasantly aromatic, with a clean, green edge. Ripe and full in the mouth, with an uplifting finish and a hint of sweetness.

Monthaven

1996 Chardonnay, Monterey $10. 84

Bright yellow-straw cast. Moderately full-bodied. Full acidity. Highly extracted. Moderately oaked. Yeast, brown spices, minerals. Shows a big oak accent to the firm backbone of minerally flavors. Aggressive in the mouth, with a forceful angular quality and a dry note on the finish.

1997 Chardonnay, Napa Valley $9.99. 87

Bright green-gold. Extravagant toasted coconut, smoke, and ripe fruit aromas. A sumptuous attack leads a full-bodied palate with impressive buttery richness and glycerous smoothness. Impressive depth of fruit flavors. Finishes with leesy complexity.

1995 Cabernet Sauvignon, Napa Valley $9.99. 86

Blood red. Medium-bodied. Moderately extracted. Moderately tannic. Black fruits, earth. Reserved aromas lead a chunky, broad palate of flavors, with powdery tannins. Pleasantly rustic, with a spicy finish.

1995 Carignane, California $14. 83

Brick red with a slight fade. Medium-bodied. Moderately extracted. Mildly tannic. Anise, black fruits. Lean and firmly structured, with dusty tannins and black fruit flavors lingering through the finish. A flavorful, rustic style.

1996 Syrah, California $9.99. 81

1995 Zinfandel, Napa Valley $9.99. 87

Full dark cherry red. Medium-bodied. Balanced acidity. Moderately extracted. Mildly oaked. Mildly tannic. Black fruits. Very straightforward; a burst of solid black fruit flavors tapers off with indecent haste. Quite generous.

1996 Zinfandel, California $9.99. 80

Monticello

1996 Chardonnay, Wild Yeast Corley Reserve, Napa Valley $32.50. 88

Deep yellow-straw cast. Moderately full-bodied. Full acidity. Moderately extracted. Mildly oaked. Bread dough, vanilla, citrus. Spicy aromas feature a distinctive doughy note. Rich but angular in the mouth, and lean through the finish.

1995 Cabernet Sauvignon, Jefferson Cuvée, Napa Valley $22.   **84**

Medium ruby red. Medium-bodied. Moderately extracted. Mildly tannic. Lead pencil, black fruits. Restrained, elegant, oak-spiced aromas lead a harmonious, supple mouthful of attractive Cabernet fruit flavors, with drying tannins on the finish. Nice now.

1994 Cabernet Sauvignon, Corley Reserve, Napa Valley $35.   **88**

Deep violet-red color. Medium-bodied. Moderately extracted. Mildly tannic. Oak spice, black fruits. Bright, oaky aromas lead crisp berry fruit flavors with a vanilla and spice theme through the finish.

1994 Merlot, Corley Reserve, Napa Valley $28.   **90**

Deep ruby red to the rim with brilliant highlights. Moderately full-bodied. Balanced acidity. Highly extracted. Moderately oaked. Moderately tannic. Red fruits, minerals, vanilla. Quite aromatic, with a firmly structured mouthfeel and a deep core of flavor. Well-integrated oak accents add complexity to the minerally fruit notes. Solid acidity rounds out the package.

1996 Pinot Noir, Napa Valley $22.   **84**

Pale ruby cast. Medium-bodied. Moderately extracted. Mildly tannic. Oak spice, berry fruits. Spicy, fruity aromas lead a soft, fruit-forward palate, with a generous amount of oak spice lingering on the finish.

Montpellier

1997 Chardonnay, California $6.99.   **81**

1997 White Zinfandel, California $5.99.   **80**

1996 Cabernet Sauvignon, California $6.99.   **84**

Bright ruby red with a slight fade. Unusual aromas of tart berries and dust. A crisp entry leads a moderately full-bodied palate with hollow fruit flavors and firm, drying tannins. Drink now.

1997 Merlot, California $6.99.   **84**

Bright violet hue with a fading rim. Floral, vanilla oak aromas. Jammy flavors on the attack with a soft, fruity character through the finish. A lighter-bodied wine with easy drinkability.

1997 Syrah, California $6.99.   **84**

Medium purple, limpid and brilliant, with a slight fade. Mild, pleasant black cherry and vanilla flavors. Mild wood tones. Smooth entry, moderately light-bodied with balanced acidity. Mild, silky tannins. Bright fruity accents throughout. Structurally light. Subtle, short finish. Appealingly straightforward, with a soft, fruity character. Drink now.

1996 Zinfandel, California $6.99.   **80**

Morgan

1997 Chardonnay, Monterey $20.   **84**

Rich gold. Aromas show a degree of smoky development/maderization. A viscous entry leads a full-bodied palate with warming alcohol coming through. Drink now.

1996 Chardonnay, Reserve, Monterey $25.   **91**

Medium yellow-gold. Smoky, vanilla-scented aromas with yeasty accents. A bright entry leads a medium-bodied palate with a taut structure and fine depth of fruit and oak flavors. Finishes with lingering smoky complexity. Drink now or later.

1997 Sauvignon Blanc, Sonoma-Monterey $13.   **85**

Full golden yellow. Medium-bodied. Full acidity. Moderately extracted. Lime, lemon zest, minerals. High-toned, zesty aromas lead a full, rounded mouthfeel with good citrus flavors and a minerally finish. Fresh and lively style.

1996 Pinot Noir, Monterey $20.   **83**

Pale cherry red. Moderately light-bodied. Moderately extracted. Mildly tannic. Vanilla, berries. Floral, oaky aromas follow through on the palate, with soft tannins through the finish.

1995 Pinot Noir, Reserve, Monterey $28.   87

Medium cherry-garnet hue. Medium-bodied. Moderately extracted. Moderately oaked. Mildly tannic. Tomato vine, brown spice, and sour cherry flavors abound, with bright acids through the finish. Quite complex and flavorsome. This has a minerally feel throughout. Well balanced and nice to drink now.

1996 Pinot Noir, Reserve, Monterey $32.   88

Bright violet red. Medium-bodied. Moderately extracted. Mildly tannic. Red berries, flowers, vanilla. Bright perfumed aromas lead juicy, vibrant fruit flavors, with a generous vanilla oak influence coming through on the finish.

1996 Syrah, Monterey $20.   84

Rich, limpid, brilliant ruby purple with a slight fade. Medium- to light-bodied. Bramble fruit and vanilla aromas. Juicy and immediate, and lifted by good fruit acids. Drink now.

Moshin

1995 Pinot Noir, Russian River Valley $16.   86

Medium cherry red. Moderately light-bodied. Moderately extracted. Mildly tannic. Leathery, raspberry-accented aromas. Well-concentrated, focused raspberry flavors on the palate with an oaky backnote. Dry, powdery tannins give a dry finish.

Mount Eden

1997 Chardonnay, MacGregor Vineyard, Edna Valley $17.99.   84

Deep golden yellow. Forward smoke, yeast, and charred oak aromas carry a big wood accent. A lean entry leads a moderately full-bodied palate with rounded acidity. Lean, buttery finish. Drink now.

1995 Cabernet Sauvignon, Santa Cruz Mountains $20.   88

Deep ruby purple. Medium-bodied. Balanced acidity. Moderately extracted. Mildly tannic. Licorice, minerals, flowers. High-toned aromatics are forward and intense. Somewhat light in the mouth, with a lean and angular impression. Crisp and bright through the finish.

1993 Cabernet Sauvignon, Old Vine Reserve, Santa Cruz Mountains $35.   94

Deep blackish red with purple highlights. Moderately full-bodied. Highly extracted. Moderately tannic. Brown spice, toasted oak, licorice, black fruits. Brooding dark fruit aromas. Thick, chewy black Cabernet fruit dominates the palate. An assertively dry finish shows fine-grained tannins and rich oak spice flavors. A big-shouldered wine in need of cellaring.

*1995 Cabernet Sauvignon, Old Vine Reserve, Santa Cruz Mountains $39.99.*88

Very deep blackish ruby hue. Intense chocolate and anise aromas show a pronounced oak influence. A firm entry leads to a full-bodied palate with lush thick tannins and a marked note of acidity that enlivens the flavors. Firm, intense finish. A big brooding style, rather awkward at present, but with the stuffing to blossom with age. Good for long-term cellaring.

Mount Palomar

1996 Cortese, Castelletto, Temecula $16.   93

Bright golden cast. Moderately full-bodied. Balanced acidity. Moderately extracted. Blanched almonds, cream, oranges. Attention-grabbing aromas, with lush and exotic flavors. Rich and rounded in the mouth with buoyant acidity that enlivens a flavorful finish.

1997 Rey Sol Le Mediterrane Blanc, Temecula $16.   87

Deep golden cast. Full-bodied. Balanced acidity. Moderately extracted. Honey, yeast, tropical fruits, butter. Aromatic, with big, ripe, honeyed flavors. Full and rich in the mouth, though well balanced with juicy acidity.

1997 Roussane, Rey Sol, Temecula $18.   **86**

Deep golden cast. Full-bodied. Low acidity. Moderately extracted. Bananas, cream.
Extremely fat and ripe, with a buttery accent. Full and tropical in flavor with a weightiness that is accentuated by low levels of acidity.

1997 Viognier, Rey Sol, Temecula $18.   **84**

Very deep golden hue. Full-bodied. Low acidity. Moderately extracted. Mildly oaked.
Oranges, vanilla. Aromatic, with extremely ripe fruit notes offset by subtle oak accents.
Full and rich in the mouth with low levels of acidity.

1996 Rey Sol Le Mediterrane Old Vines Selection Red, South Coast $10.   **85**

Bright garnet red with a slight fade. Forward earth and leather aromas. A soft attack
leads a medium-bodied palate that lacks tannic grip. The finish is flat and earthy. This
wine is in search of a bit more structure. Drink now.

1994 Sangiovese, Castelletto, Temecula $18.   **84**

Dark ruby red with a subtle fade. Medium-bodied. Balanced acidity. Moderately
extracted. Moderately oaked. Mildly tannic. Red fruits, oak spice. Powerfully aromatic,
spicy aromas. Good weight and roundness to the mouthfeel, with crisp red fruit flavors
that turn dry and spicy through the finish.

Mount Veeder Winery

1995 Cabernet Sauvignon, Napa Valley $30.   **91**

Deep ruby hue. Moderately full-bodied. Balanced acidity. Moderately extracted.
Mildly oaked. Mildly tannic. Red fruits, brown spices, minerals. Forward aromas reveal
well-integrated fruit and wood flavors. Soft and supple, with generosity and elegance.
Well balanced and lengthy.

1993 Reserve, Napa Valley $40.   **95**

Dark blood red. Medium-bodied. Highly extracted. Moderately tannic. Red currants,
cassis, cedar. Ripe berry aromas reveal bright, high-toned fruit flavors that show a ripe
juicy character up front. Firm tannins clamp down on the finish, though this is quite
approachable now with rich food.

1995 Reserve, Napa Valley $50.   **92**

Deep, saturated ruby purple hue. Brooding brown spice, mineral, and leather aromas.
A firm attack leads to a moderately full-bodied palate with grippy tannins and solid
acidity for balance. Lengthy, flavorful finish. Approachable now but well balanced and
built for age. Carries its weight admirably. Drink now or later.

Mumm Cuvée Napa

NV Blanc de Noir, Napa Valley $15.95.   **88**

Bright pale pink cast. Moderately full-bodied. Full acidity. Red fruits, minerals, citrus.
Forward, attractive aromas carry a pleasant fruity overtone. Soft and generous in the
mouth, with crisp acidity and fine balance.

NV Brut Prestige, Napa Valley $15.95.   **87**

Bright pale gold hue. Medium-bodied. Citrus, minerals. Juicy, bright, clean, fruity aromas
follow through well on the palate, with crisp carbonation and moderate bead size.

Murphy-Goode

1997 Chardonnay, Sonoma County $15.   **84**

Bright straw hue. Subdued aromas carry a crisp appley note. A lean entry leads a
moderately light-bodied palate with crisp acidity. Crisp, clipped finish. Drink now.

1996 Chardonnay, Island Block Reserve, Alexander Valley $24.   **89**

Deep yellow-straw hue. Generous pear and tropical fruit aromas. A crisp entry leads a
medium-bodied palate that shows zesty acidity. The finish is clean and snappy. Drink now.

1996 Chardonnay, J&K Murphy Vineyard Reserve, Russian River Valley $24.   89

Full yellow-gold. Spicy, yellow apple aromas. A fresh entry leads a medium-bodied palate with crisp fruity flavors that persist through the finish. Shows good varietal flavors. Drink now.

1996 Pinot Blanc, Sonoma County $13.50.   85

Bright golden cast. Medium-bodied. Full acidity. Moderately extracted. Moderately oaked. Toasted coconut, minerals. Marked oak spice on the nose also dominates the flavors on the palate. Clean and brisk in structure, with vibrant acidity making for a snappy finish.

1997 Fumé Blanc, Sonoma County $11.50.   86

Bright yellow-gold. Medium-bodied. Full acidity. Moderately extracted. Citrus zest, minerals. Bright, zesty aromas follow through on the palate with lively acids playing through the finish. Shows some clean varietal character in the herbal notes.

1996 Fumé, Reserve, Alexander Valley $16.50.   92

Full yellow-gold. Moderately full-bodied. Balanced acidity. Moderately extracted. Moderately oaked. Brown spice, ripe citrus fruits. Nice toasty oak accents on the nose lead a spicy, flavorsome palate, showing a structured character and some dryness on the finish. Nice now, this should be better in a year or two.

1996 Fumé II, The Deuce, Alexander Valley $24.   93

Bright yellow-straw color. Medium-bodied. Balanced acidity. Moderately extracted. Mildly oaked. Toasted oak, butter, peach. Smoky, vanilla aromas lead a rounded mouthfeel with buttery character and a pronounced spicy finish. An extravagant texture with exotic smoky flavors are the keynotes of this hedonistic wine. Sublimely balanced.

1995 Cabernet Sauvignon, Alexander Valley $20.   89

Medium cherry red. Medium-bodied. Moderately extracted. Mildly tannic. Dried herbs, red fruits, chocolate. Crisp herbal aromas show an oak influence. Crisp fruity flavors give way to dry oaky and herbal notes through the finish. A subtle, elegant style.

1996 Cabernet Sauvignon, Alexander Valley $19.   81

1994 Cabernet Sauvignon, Murphy Ranch, Alexander Valley $25.   88

Medium-dark cherry red. Medium-bodied. Moderately extracted. Mildly tannic. Brown spice, red fruits. An elegant spicy nose leads a supple palate, with nice crisp fruity flavors that finish cleanly. Distinguished by some subtlety of flavors, a good mouthfeel, and bright acids.

1994 Cabernet Sauvignon, Brenda Block, Alexander Valley $30.   91

Full dark cherry red. Medium-bodied. Highly extracted. Moderately tannic. Brown spice, chocolate, berry fruits. The smooth, velvety mouthfeel has generous and rich flavors through the finish. Quite concentrated. Elegant and structured, with ample soft tannins. Nice now but can cellar.

1996 Zinfandel, Sonoma County $16.   87

Bright ruby cast. Moderately full-bodied. Balanced acidity. Moderately extracted. Mildly oaked. Mildly tannic. Black fruits. Aromatic, with a lovely interplay between fruit and oak notes. Soft and lush through the finish.

Mystic Cliffs

1997 Chardonnay, California $8.   81

1995 Cabernet Sauvignon, California $6.99.   88

Bright cherry red. Medium-bodied. Moderately extracted. Mildly tannic. Toasted oak, vanilla, red fruits. A bright, fruity nose leads a juicy, open-knit palate with a hint of oak spice and astringency on the finish.

Nalle

1996 Zinfandel, Dry Creek Valley $20.   86

Bright blackish purple. Moderately full-bodied. Balanced acidity. Highly extracted.
Mildly oaked. Moderately tannic. Black fruits, minerals. Quite aromatic, with a pure,
fruit-centered flavor profile. Lean and well structured through the finish. Rather
tough at present.

Napa Creek

1997 Chardonnay, Lodi $8.99.   81
1996 Cabernet Sauvignon, Lodi $8.99.   81
1996 Merlot, Lodi $8.99.   80

Napa Ridge

1997 Chardonnay, Coastal Vines, North Coast $9.   81
1995 Chardonnay, Reserve, Napa Valley $15.   81
1996 Cabernet Sauvignon, Central Coast $10.   89

Bright crimson red hue. Generous aromas show black cherry fruit and sweet oak accents.
A flavorful, fruity entry leads a medium-bodied palate with fleshy, ripe fruit flavors and
rounded tannins. Finishes with lingering fruit persistence and well-integrated oak flavors.
Drink now or later.

1995 Cabernet Sauvignon, Coastal Reserve, Napa Valley $15.   84

Bright violet-purple hue. Fruit-forward, ripe aromas have a nice vanilla oak accent.
A firm entry leads a medium-bodied palate with cherry fruit flavors and dry tannins.
Flavors dissipate quickly. Drink now.

1996 Pinot Noir, Coastal, North Coast $19.   85

Pale cherry red with a pink tinge. Moderately light-bodied. Moderately extracted.
Moderately oaked. Mildly tannic. Mildly jammy, vanilla-accented aromas lead a bright
sweet fruit mouthful, with a lingering fruity, vanilla oak finish. Very pleasant and
straightforward.

Newlan

1997 Chardonnay, Napa Valley $16.   83

Bright yellow-gold. Subtle oak aromas with ripe buttery accents. A soft entry leads a
moderately full-bodied palate with generous texture and mouthfeel, though fruit flavors
are restrained. Finishes with a note of oak and alcohol. Drink now.

1995 Cabernet Sauvignon, Napa Valley $20.   88

Saturated ruby-violet hue. Moderately full-bodied. Highly extracted. Moderately tannic.
Vanilla, spice, black fruits. Lively, high-toned fruit flavors, bright and well gripped by
tannins through the finish.

1995 Pinot Noir, Napa Valley $19.   90

Bright red with purple hints. Medium-bodied. Moderately extracted. Moderately oaked.
Mildly tannic. Floral, aromatic fruity nose has violet accents. Bright and fruity, with a
mineral accent. Crisp acids keep the palate fresh. Tannins on the finish are slight.

1995 Pinot Noir, Reserve, Napa Valley $28.   88

Pale garnet red. Medium-bodied. Moderately extracted. Mildly oaked. Mildly tannic.
Baked cherries with a spicy accent make for complex aromas. Full flavored on the palate,
with good weight. Very spicy oak finish. A dry style.

1996 Zinfandel, Napa Valley $18.   83

Deep blackish purple. Moderately full-bodied. Full acidity. Moderately extracted. Mildly
oaked. Moderately tannic. Briar fruits, earth. Quite aromatic, showing distinct earthy
overtones. Full and rich in the mouth, with elevated acidity making for a crisp finish.

Newton

1997 Chardonnay, Napa County $25.   94

Bright yellow-gold. Moderately full-bodied. Balanced acidity. Highly extracted. Vanilla, toasted oak, ripe citrus. Aromatically complex, with assertive yeasty accents. A rich, creamy mouthful shows plush texture with balanced oak spice, vanilla, and ripe fruit components. The finish is very lush and generous.

1995 Cabernet Sauvignon, Napa Valley $36.99.   89

Deep purple red hue. Brooding mineral and berry cordial aromas. A firm entry leads to a full-bodied palate with robust grippy tannins and a real structural edge. Firm, angular finish. Has all the components to age beautifully, and needs it. Good for long-term cellaring.

1996 Merlot, Napa Valley $32.   87

Saturated dark ruby hue. Moderately full-bodied with concentrated black cherry flavors and a lush, tannic structure that grips the finish. Drink now or later. Can improve with more age.

Neyers

1997 Chardonnay, Carneros $27.99.   85

Dark gold. Very ripe aromas have a tropical note. A lush entry is followed by a full-bodied palate with rounded texture and concentrated flavors that linger on the finish. This is a rich, leesy style with impressive weight. Drink now or later.

1995 Cabernet Sauvignon, Napa Valley $40.   89

Deep red-violet. Moderately full-bodied. Moderately extracted. Moderately tannic. Brown spice, black fruits, licorice. Oak spice shows strongly on the nose, with a restrained, dry palate finishing quickly. Quite an austere style.

1996 Merlot, Napa Valley $28.   91

Pale ruby hue with a fading rim. Intriguing earthy, oak-accented aromas. Medium-bodied with a crisp attack and understated, complex flavors on the midpalate. The tannins are subtle and evolved. The finish lingers, with complex, mature flavors. Drink now.

Nichols

1997 Chardonnay, Edna Ranch Vineyard, Edna Valley $32.   86

Bright straw cast. Moderately full-bodied. Low acidity. Moderately extracted. Mildly oaked. Earth, vanilla, butter. Generous aromas carry a slightly unusual quality. Ripe and full in the mouth with a fat texture. Balanced by a hint of acidity in the finish.

1996 Chardonnay, Paragon Vineyard, Edna Valley $32.   87

Bright yellow-straw cast. Moderately full-bodied. Balanced acidity. Moderately extracted. Mildly oaked. Yeast, toast, citrus. Forward aromas carry a complex yeasty accent. Vibrant and crisp in the mouth, with zesty citric flavors through a snappy finish.

1996 Pinot Noir, Cottonwood Canyon Vineyard,
Santa Barbara County $33.   90

Very pale ruby red. Moderately light-bodied. Moderately extracted. Mildly oaked. Mildly tannic. Lean, herbal, meaty aromas. A smooth, glycerous mouthfeel, with some bitter cherry flavors through the minerally finish. Quite sophisticated and seamless. More flavorful and intense than it first seems.

1996 Pinot Noir, Pisoni Vineyard, Monterey County $42.   91

Very deep black cherry color. Medium-bodied. Highly extracted. Moderately oaked. Moderately tannic. Rich dark fruit aromas have cedar and tobacco notes. Rich, concentrated fruit flavors linger through a long, complex finish with nice toasty character. Drinking well now, though it could be cellared.

Scale: Superlative (96-100), Exceptional (90-95), Highly Recommended (85-89), Recommended (80-84), Not Recommended (Under 80)

1996 Pinot Noir, Reserve, Central Coast $45. **90**

Full cherry red with slight purple highlights. Medium-bodied. Moderately extracted. Moderately oaked. Mildly tannic. Hints of tar, black fruit, and tobacco. Complex, ripe aromas. Smooth, elegant texture, with ripe plum flavors through a complex, lengthy finish. Nice now, this should improve with one to two years of cellaring.

1996 Zinfandel, Cienega Valley Vineyards, Central Coast $24. **80**

Niebaum-Coppola

1997 Chardonnay, Napa Valley $20. **88**

Bright green-straw cast. Medium-bodied. Balanced acidity. Moderately extracted. Mildly oaked. Ripe lemons, apples. Very sweet, juicy fruit flavors are clean and direct, with a subtle vanilla oak influence that lingers through the finish.

1996 Cabernet Franc, Napa Valley $20. **90**

Bright ruby purple. Moderately full-bodied. Balanced acidity. Moderately extracted. Moderately oaked. Mildly tannic. Licorice, black fruits, coffee. Showing some aromatic complexity, with well-integrated fruit and wood flavors. Firm and well balanced, with deep flavors and acidity making for a buoyant finish. Stylish.

1997 Cabernet Sauvignon, Francis Coppola Diamond Series Black Label Claret, North Coast $17. **80**

1992 Rubicon, Rutherford, Napa Valley $45. **91**

Nearly opaque dark blood red. Medium-bodied. Highly extracted. Moderately tannic. Plums, cassis, black tea, chocolate. A plummy nose leads a dense, tight palate with concentrated, tightly wound flavors that linger through the finish. Still quite closed, this should cellar well.

1994 Rubicon, Rutherford, Napa Valley $65. **92**

Deep ruby purple. Moderately full-bodied. Balanced acidity. Moderately extracted. Moderately oaked. Mildly tannic. Black fruits, chocolate, brown spices. Enticingly aromatic, with a large-framed though supple mouthfeel. Shows great intensity of flavor, with fine depth. Exceptional length, with acidity lending balance to the finish. Approachable, but structured for long-term (7–10 years) aging.

1995 Rubicon, Rutherford, Napa Valley $65. **93**

Saturated dark ruby hue. Exotically spicy aromas show dark fruits and rich oak spice. A rich entry leads to a moderately full-bodied palate with a fleshy core of cordial-like fruit and well-integrated lush oak spice that comes through strongly on the finish. Hedonistic and drinking well now. Drink now.

1995 Merlot, Francis Coppola Family Wines, Napa Valley $32. **92**

Very deep ruby to the rim with a purplish cast. Medium-bodied. Balanced acidity. Moderately extracted. Mildly oaked. Mildly tannic. Licorice, black fruits, sweet herbs. Flavorful and extremely well integrated, with a real sense of depth to the palate. Solid acidity enlivens the lengthy finish.

1996 Merlot, Napa Valley $32. **89**

Saturated violet purple. Generously aromatic with an oaky character. Full-bodied, with a lush, velvety mouthfeel, broad fleshy cherry fruit flavors, and plenty of vanilla oak accents through the finish. Drink now or later. Can improve with more age.

1996 Zinfandel, Edizione Pennino, Napa Valley $26. **88**

Dark cherry red. Medium-bodied. Balanced acidity. Moderately extracted. Moderately tannic. Tobacco, plums. Forward, attractive aromas lead a seductive, richly wrought palate, with ample tannins providing structure and grip on the finish.

Norman

1995 Cabernet Sauvignon, Paso Robles $17.   81

1996 No Nonsense Red, Claret, Paso Robles $15.   82

1995 Pinot Noir, William Cain Vineyard, Paso Robles $18.   87

Cherry red with a garnet rim. Medium-bodied. Moderately extracted. Moderately oaked. Mildly tannic. Fragrant brown spice aromas have a cinnamon accent. Nice soft Pinot fruit flavors on entry have plenty of plum, chocolate, and toast flavors through the finish. Drinking nicely now, with just a hint of dry tannins.

Oakville Ranch

1996 Chardonnay, ORV, Oakville $32.   85

Bright straw cast. Medium-bodied. Balanced acidity. Moderately extracted. Minerals, butter. Aromatically subdued, with subtle flavors. Ripe and lush in the mouth with a textured quality. Buttery through the finish.

1996 Chardonnay, Vista Vineyard, California $26.   84

Bright straw cast. Moderately full-bodied. Balanced acidity. Moderately extracted. Green apples, melon, cream. Ripe and forward, with fruit-centered flavors and an opulent texture. Shows generosity through the well-balanced buttery finish.

1994 Cabernet Sauvignon, Napa Valley $30.   87

Dark blackish purple. Moderately full-bodied. Highly extracted. Moderately tannic. Cassis, plums, black tea. Pure cassis aromas lead a fleshy, bright palate, with chewy fruit flavors and ample soft tannins through the finish. Attractive now, but this will be better with some age.

1995 Cabernet Sauvignon, Napa Valley $35.   89

Very deep ruby purple. Moderately full-bodied. Balanced acidity. Highly extracted. Mildly oaked. Quite tannic. Minerals, cassis. Aromatically reserved, with a tightly wound, dense mouthfeel. Aggressive tannins merge with a firm, minerally backbone to suggest long-term (7–10 years) cellaring.

1994 Robert's Blend, Napa Valley $45.   91

Opaque blackish purple. Medium-bodied. Highly extracted. Moderately tannic. Cassis, black fruits, tobacco. Ripe cassis aromas with cedary notes are fully expressed on the palate. Bright Cabernet fruit flavors linger through a tobacco-accented finish. Very plush and generous style.

1995 Robert's Blend, Napa Valley $45.   89

Saturated ruby purple. Moderately full-bodied. Balanced acidity. Highly extracted. Moderately oaked. Moderately tannic. Vanilla, minerals, briar fruits. Pleasantly aromatic, with a firm and intense mouthfeel. Firm tannins bite down on the finish. Needs time.

1995 Merlot, Napa Valley $35.   90

Saturated dark violet red with purple highlights. Rich, brooding aromas have a lush dark-fruit character with oaky accents. Rich and lush on entry with fantastic grip and fine-grained tannins. Mouthfilling fruity flavors with excellent structure. Good for long-term cellaring.

1996 Zinfandel, Napa Valley $20.   82

Obester

1996 Sauvignon Blanc, Mendocino $9.95.   84

Medium straw hue. Moderately light-bodied. Balanced acidity. Moderately extracted. Dried herbs, vanilla, citrus. Bright zesty aromas have a subtle smoky accent. Crisp and flavorful on the palate, this finishes cleanly with an acid snap and a hint of dryness.

1995 Sangiovese, 20th Anniversary, Mendocino County $13.95.   87

Bright ruby hue with a pink rim. Medium-bodied. Full acidity. Moderately extracted. Moderately oaked. Mildly tannic. Red fruits, bitter cherries, vanilla. High-toned fruity aromas lead a brisk, minerally palate with dry oak notes on the finish. Lively style.

Scale: Superlative (96-100), Exceptional (90-95), Highly Recommended (85-89),
Recommended (80-84), Not Recommended (Under 80)

154

Ojai

1996 Chardonnay, Talley Vineyard, Arroyo Grande Valley $24.   **83**

Bright straw cast. Medium-bodied. Full acidity. Moderately extracted. Minerals, citrus. Aromatically reserved, with a crisp and angular presence in the mouth. Acidity turns tart on the finish.

Opus One

1992 Oakville, Napa Valley Red $65.   **97**

Moderately full-bodied. Medium acid. Lots of fruit. Medium oak. Lots of tannin. Dry. Reminiscent of earth, cassis, black fruits, cherry tobacco. Displays stunning depth and breadth of flavor. Dark, luscious black fruit is surprisingly approachable, but fine acidity and a firm lattice of tannins insure long-term aging potential. Deep, elegantly structured, and very complex.

1993 Oakville, Napa Valley Red $85.   **96**

Deep ruby to the rim with purplish highlights. Moderately full-bodied. Balanced acidity. Highly extracted. Highly oaked. Moderately tannic. Dry. Reminiscent of vanilla, black cherries, leather. Attractive aromatic qualities play out on a solidly crafted and balanced framework. Quite deep with impressive length, it is slightly more closed than recent vintages but should cellar beautifully.

1994 Oakville, Napa Valley Red $90.   **94**

Opaque dark red. Medium-bodied. Highly extracted. Quite tannic. Cassis, black cherries, mint, black tea. Rich plummy aromas lead a focused, tight palate, with concentrated black Cabernet fruit flavors and stern tannins on the finish. Solidly structured, this wine needs cellaring to reveal its potential.

1995 Oakville, Napa Valley Red $100.   **99**

Deep ruby cast. Moderately full-bodied. Balanced acidity. Moderately extracted. Heavily oaked. Moderately tannic. Leather, earth, black fruits. Aromatic and concentrated, with complexity to the flavors throughout. Lush, supple, and harmonious, showing velvety tannins and a lengthy finish. Almost approachable, but best in a few years.

Orfila

1997 Chardonnay, Ambassador's Reserve, San Diego & San Luis Obispo Counties $14.98.   **81**

1995 Merlot, Coastal, California $16.   **86**

Deep ruby red with a slight fade to the rim. Medium-bodied. Full acidity. Moderately extracted. Heavily oaked. Mildly tannic. Dusty cherries, toasted coconut, vanilla. A heavy wood accent with a drying palate feel. Nonetheless, it features a core of dusty fruit flavors that support the oak and lead to an angular, well-defined finish. A little bit like a Rioja in style. Attractive and interesting.

1995 Merlot, Ambassador's Reserve, San Diego County $25.   **82**

1996 Merlot, Ambassador's Reserve, San Diego County $25.   **84**

Medium ruby hue with a slight fade. Berry fruit and generous oak accents on the nose. A supple entry leads a medium-bodied palate with soft jammy fruit flavors and pleasant oak spice through the rounded finish. Drink now.

Tawny Port, California $14.98/500 ml.   **83**

Deep orange-copper cast with a definite haze. Medium-bodied. Balanced acidity. Moderately extracted. Caramel, toffee. Pleasantly aromatic, with a gentle woody tone throughout. Light and straightforward on the palate. Finishes with a touch of heat.

The Organic Wine Works

1997 Merlot, California $16.   **80**

Page Mill

1997 Chardonnay, Bien Nacido Vineyard, Santa Maria Valley $18.   **81**

1997 Chardonnay, Garbett Vineyard, Matadero Valley,
Santa Clara County $20.   86

Bright yellow-straw color. Moderately full-bodied. Balanced acidity. Highly extracted. Moderately oaked. Smoke, butter, lemons. Forceful burnt butter aromas lead a firm, tart mouthful of flavors with mineral and oak spice character gripping the finish.

1997 Sauvignon Blanc, French Camp Vineyard, San Luis Obispo $11.   85

Medium yellow-straw color. Medium-bodied. Balanced acidity. Moderately extracted. Grapefruit, smoke. Ripe, smoky, citrusy aromas follow through well on a textured palate, with a smooth and flavorful finish.

1993 Cabernet Sauvignon, Napa Valley $20.   82

1995 Macaire, Napa Valley $32.   89

Bright ruby cast. Moderately full-bodied. Balanced acidity. Moderately extracted. Moderately oaked. Mildly tannic. Minerals, red fruits, dried herbs. Pleasantly aromatic, with real complexity to the range of flavors. Soft and supple in the mouth, with a leafy quality that is very Merlot-like. Well balanced.

1996 Pinot Noir, Bien Nacido Vineyard, Santa Maria Valley $20.   81

Pahlmeyer

1995 Red, Napa Valley $60.   94

Deep ruby cast. Moderately full-bodied. Balanced acidity. Highly extracted. Moderately oaked. Moderately tannic. Cedar, black fruits, earth. Forward aromas show breeding and complexity. Firm and deep in the mouth, with fine concentration and length. Balanced for long-term (7–10 years) aging.

Paradise Ridge

1995 Blanc de Blanc, Private Reserve, Sonoma County $19.   81

1997 Chardonnay, Nagasawa Vineyard, Sonoma County $15.95.   84

Bright yellow-straw hue. Unusual, high-toned blanched almond and mineral aromas. A lean entry leads a medium-bodied palate with firm extraction and angular acidity. Finishes with a phenolic, mildly astringent quality. Drink now.

1997 Chardonnay, Barrel Select, Nagasawa Vineyard,
Sonoma County $17.95.   89

Bright straw hue. Generous vanilla and spice aromas show an integrated oak accent. A firm entry is followed by a moderately full-bodied palate with lush acidity and a rounded, ripe finish. Well balanced. Drink now.

1996 Cabernet Sauvignon, North Coast $18.95.   83

Pale ruby-purple hue. Cedar, vanilla aromas. A bright entry leads to medium-bodied palate with vibrant red fruit flavors and light but dry gripping tannins. Drink now.

Paraiso Springs

1997 Chardonnay, Santa Lucia Highlands $16.   89

Pale yellow-straw hue. Moderate vanilla, smoke, and clean apple aromas. A fruity entry leads a medium-bodied palate with a ripe fruity center and judicious oak accents. Drink now.

1997 Gewürztraminer, Santa Lucia Highlands $9.   87

Bright straw hue. Clean, intense mineral and honeyed tropical fruit aromas. A lean entry leads a medium-bodied palate that has an assertive acidic edge. Firm through the dry finish. Taut and stylish. Drink now.

1997 Riesling, Santa Lucia Highlands $9.   90

Bright yellow-gold. Intense varietally pure aromas of petrol, minerals, and peach. A flavorful attack leads a medium-bodied palate, with mild sweetness and good acid balance through the finish. Quite stylish. Drink now.

1995 Pinot Noir, Santa Lucia Highlands $18.　　　　　　　　　　**86**

Dark garnet red. Medium-bodied. Moderately extracted. Moderately tannic. Faintly stewed red fruit aromas have an earthy accent. Interesting cherry and tomato flavors linger through an herbal finish. Plenty of character, though maybe not everyone's preference.

1996 Pinot Noir, Santa Lucia Highlands $22.50.　　　　　　　　　**89**

Pale red with a subtle garnet rim. Medium-bodied. Moderately extracted. Mildly tannic. Game, red berries. Elegant perfumed aromas follow through well on the palate, with sweet fruit flavors and subtle tannins. Gamey flavors linger on the finish.

1996 Syrah, Santa Lucia Highlands $22.50.　　　　　　　　　　**86**

Dark purple, limpid and brilliant to the rim. Plentiful drying tannins. Medium-bodied. Juicy, fleshy fruit flavors with a supple finish. A touch of game and berries in a soft structure make for attractive early drinking.

Parducci

1996 Chardonnay, Carneros Bighorn Ranch, Reserve, Napa Valley $20.　　**86**

Pale straw hue. Medium-bodied. Balanced acidity. Moderately extracted. Moderately oaked. Butterscotch, blanched almonds. Heavy buttery aromas follow through on the palate, which shows an oaky accent. Citrusy flavors stay in the background.

1995 Cabernet Sauvignon, Mendocino $10.　　　　　　　　　　**86**

Bright reddish purple. Medium-bodied. Moderately extracted. Mildly tannic. Black berry fruits, vanilla. Ripe, deep fruit flavors have a juicy feel on the palate, with a clean lingering finish showing very soft tannins. Lots of primary fruit flavors make this very accessible and forward.

1996 Cabernet Sauvignon, Vineyard Select, North Coast $10.　　　　**86**

Bright purple-red hue. Attractive toasted oak and cassis aromas. A smooth entry leads to a moderately full-bodied palate with lively, bright fruit flavors and very fine grippy tannins on the finish. Well balanced and flavorsome. Drink now or later.

1997 Merlot, California $10.　　　　　　　　　　　　　　　**81**

1997 Syrah, Mendocino $10.　　　　　　　　　　　　　　　**83**

Bright ruby red to the rim. Generous herb, red fruit, and vanilla aromas show a subtle wood accent. A soft attack leads a medium-bodied palate, with supple tannins. The angular finish has some grip. A lighter-styled quaffer. Drink now.

Fess Parker

1997 Chardonnay, Santa Barbara County $16.　　　　　　　　　**87**

Bright green-gold. Smoky, yeasty aromas show subtle, well-integrated oak. A fruity entry leads a moderately full-bodied palate with a lush center of ripe Chardonnay fruit and complex leesy notes persisting through the finish.

1997 Chardonnay, American Tradition Reserve,
Santa Barbara County $22.　　　　　　　　　　　　　　　**88**

Rich gold-straw hue. Intense yeast, mineral, and vanilla aromas show a harmonious oak accent. A lush entry leads a full-bodied palate with angular acidity and complex, intense flavors. Powerful, assertive finish. Drink now.

1997 Chardonnay, American Tradition Reserve, Marcella's Vineyards,
Santa Barbara County $24.　　　　　　　　　　　　　　　**89**

Deep golden yellow. Intense tropical fruit, cream, and yeast aromas show judicious wood influence. A ripe entry is followed by a full-bodied palate with balanced acidity and a rich, flavorful finish. A big, weighty, intense style. Drink now.

1996 Viognier, Santa Barbara County $22.　　　　　　　　　　**91**

Bright golden hue. Moderately full-bodied. Balanced acidity. Moderately extracted. Flowers, citrus, minerals. Perfumed aromas, with a complex array of flavors. Well structured and zesty on the palate, with vibrant acidity that does not mask the ripeness. Has the hallmarks of classic Viognier.

1996 Pinot Noir, Santa Barbara County $18.   **85**

Pale ruby-garnet cast. Medium-bodied. Balanced acidity. Moderately extracted. Mildly oaked. Mildly tannic. Minerals, dried herbs. Aromatically reserved, with a lean and angular palate feel. Finishes with some mild bitterness.

1995 Pinot Noir, American Tradition Reserve, Santa Barbara County $28. **90**

Dark red. Medium-bodied. Highly extracted. Moderately oaked. Mildly tannic. Earthy black fruit aromas. Licorice, earth, and black cherries come through on the palate. Long finish. Plenty of character here.

1996 Pinot Noir, American Tradition Reserve, Santa Barbara County $26. **86**

Pale ruby-garnet cast. Moderately full-bodied. Full acidity. Moderately extracted. Heavily oaked. Moderately tannic. Sweet wood, red fruits, minerals. Aromatic and distinctive, though largely wood driven in flavor. Lean and angular in the mouth, with a lengthy spicy finish.

1996 Syrah, Santa Barbara County $18.   **88**

Deep, dark red, limpid to the rim. Hefty wood tones. Firm entry. Moderately full-bodied. Moderate, grainy tannins. Chewy and flavorsome, with muted, unusual black fruit, spice, and earth flavors. Lingering rich finish. Well structured, concentrated, and youthful. Drink now.

1996 Syrah, American Tradition Reserve, Rodney's Vineyard, Santa Barbara County $30.   **89**

Dark brick red, limpid and dull to the rim. Hefty wood tones. Firm entry. Full-bodied. Plentiful, drying tannins. Shows a developed, woody character with rather muted, unusual brown spice, fruit, and earth flavors. Short finish. Drink now.

Patz & Hall

1997 Chardonnay, Napa Valley $30.   **91**

Brilliant pale yellow-gold. Stylish yeasty, smoky aromas. A smoky entry leads a medium-bodied palate with great focus of flavors. The acid balance is notably good. Finishes with a crisp, toasty note. Drink now or later.

1997 Chardonnay, Carr Vineyard, Mount Veeder $42.   **89**

Full gold. Rich buttery aromas. A lush attack leads a full-bodied palate with a rounded, generous mouthfeel. Acids come through on the finish. A weighty, fat style although the acids are in balance. Drink now.

1997 Chardonnay, Hyde Vineyard, Carneros $36.   **92**

Bright yellow-gold. Buttery, smoky aromas. A rich attack leads a moderately full-bodied palate with tart acids. Rich, opulent style with classy notes of oak and lees balanced by good acidity through the finish. Drink now.

1996 Pinot Noir, Russian River Valley $30.   **86**

Pale ruby-garnet cast. Medium-bodied. Balanced acidity. Moderately extracted. Mildly tannic. Dried herbs, minerals. Aromatically reserved, with a lean, minerally quality throughout. Lingering dusty finish.

Peachy Canyon

1995 Zinfandel, Dusi Ranch, Paso Robles $22.   **81**

Robert Pecota

1998 Dry Chenin Blanc, Monterey County $11.   **84**

Pale straw hue. Sweet pineapple and mineral aromas. A juicy entry leads a medium-bodied palate, with good tropical fruit flavor concentration and a zesty finish. Very pleasant.

1997 Sauvignon Blanc, California $11.   **83**

Pale platinum-gold. Medium-bodied. Balanced acidity. Moderately extracted. Citrus, minerals. Restrained smoky aromas. Straightforward flavors are carried by lively acids through a reasonably clean finish. Lacks only some flavor intensity on the midpalate.

Scale: Superlative (96-100), Exceptional (90-95), Highly Recommended (85-89), Recommended (80-84), Not Recommended (Under 80)

1995 Cabernet Sauvignon, Kara's Vineyard, Napa Valley $25.　　　**83**

Bright red-purple. Moderately full-bodied. Moderately extracted. Moderately tannic. Black fruits, minerals. Pickled and bright on the palate, with crisp acids and powdery tannins that dry the finish.

1996 Cabernet Sauvignon, Kara's Vineyard, Napa Valley $29.　　　**84**

Bright violet-red hue. Youthful primary fruit aromas show a cherry fruit and vanilla. A bright, fruity entry leads a moderately full-bodied palate with dry, grainy tannins that grip the finish. Youthful. Well structured. Drink now or later.

1995 Merlot, Steven Andre Vineyard, Napa Valley $25.　　　**87**

Very deep ruby red with a purplish cast. Moderately full-bodied. Full acidity. Moderately extracted. Mildly tannic. Red fruits, minerals. Lighter in style, with acidity to the fore on the bright palate. Quite minerally throughout, with a crisp, angular finish.

1996 Merlot, Steven Andre Vineyard, Napa Valley $29.　　　**86**

Bright purple-red to the rim. Generous berry and mineral aromas show a spicy oak accent. A firm attack leads a lean, medium-bodied palate with tannic grip. The finish is tart and angular. Surprisingly light in style, but structured and snappy, clean and precise. Drink now or later. Can improve with more age.

1998 Muscat Canelli, Moscato d'Andrea, Napa Valley $11/375 ml.　　　**86**

Bright yellow-straw hue. Generous nutty pear and honey aromas. A lush entry leads a medium-bodied palate showing mild sweetness offset by lean acids. Lighter in style, but well flavored. Drink now.

Pedroncelli

1997 Chardonnay, F. Johnson Vineyard, Dry Creek Valley $13.　　　**88**

Medium yellow-gold. Mild aromas of yellow apples and heavily charred oak. Crisp on the attack with a moderately full body and tart fruit flavors standing up to the alcohol. Rather angular through the finish. Drink now.

1998 Zinfandel Rosé, Vintage Selection, Sonoma County $8.　　　**92**

Very deep raspberry pink. Intense, grapey, red fruit aromas. A firm entry leads a medium-bodied palate that has tons of flavor and great acidity. A powerful, stylish Rosé. Drink now.

1995 Cabernet Sauvignon, Morris Fay Vineyard, Alexander Valley $13.　　　**86**

Bright ruby cast. Medium-bodied. Balanced acidity. Moderately extracted. Mildly tannic. Minerals, dried herbs. Lighter in style, with a slightly herbal character. Lean flavors linger through the finish.

1995 Cabernet Sauvignon, Three Vineyards, Dry Creek Valley $12.50.　　　**88**

Deep cherry red. Medium-bodied. Highly extracted. Moderately tannic. Earth, black fruits, tobacco. Brooding, earthy nose with smoky notes leads a rich, chewy, impressively proportioned palate. Textured tannins linger on the finish.

1996 Cabernet Sauvignon, Three Vineyards, Dry Creek Valley $12.　　　**88**

Bright red-purple. Medium-bodied. Highly extracted. Moderately tannic. Red fruits, mineral. Mineral and red fruit aromas lead a dry palate, with fine-grained tannins showing on the finish. A youthful, vibrant style.

1996 Pinot Noir, F. Johnson Vineyard, Dry Creek Valley $13.　　　**83**

Pale ruby cast. Moderately light-bodied. Full acidity. Subtly extracted. Mildly tannic. Sweet herbs, minerals, meat. Unusual aromas lead a very light palate. Crisp through the finish.

1995 Pinot Noir, Single Vineyard Selection, Dry Creek Valley $13.　　　**84**

Very pale ruby hue with a light rim. Moderately light-bodied. Moderately extracted. Mildly oaked. Mildly tannic. Strawberry and vanilla-scented aromas lead a light, somewhat delicate palate with a minerally finish. Well balanced and very drinkable, with plenty of varietal character.

1996 Zinfandel, Mother Clone, Special Vineyard Selection, Dry Creek Valley $12. **90**

Deep blackish ruby color with a brilliant cast. Moderately full-bodied. Low acidity. Moderately extracted. Mildly oaked. Mildly tannic. Briar fruits, minerals, chocolate. Quite aromatic, with a flavorful palate feel. Soft and generous in the mouth, with low acidity. Finishes with mild astringency.

1996 Zinfandel, Pedroni-Bushnell Vineyard, Single Vineyard Selection, Dry Creek Valley $13. **86**

Deep blackish ruby hue with a purple edge. Moderately full-bodied. Balanced acidity. Moderately extracted. Mildly tannic. Black fruits, earth, chocolate. Aromatic and quite deeply flavored, with brooding, dark fruit notes. Surprisingly soft and supple on entry, with some mild astringency through the finish.

Peirano

1997 Cabernet Sauvignon, Lodi $8.99. **83**

Bright ruby hue. Subdued mineral and anise aromas. A crisp attack leads to a medium-bodied palate with crisp acidity and grippy tannins. Fades toward the finish. Drink now.

1997 Merlot, Six Clones, Lodi $9.99. **81**

Peju Province

1997 Chardonnay, Napa Valley $18. **92**

Bright yellow-gold. Medium-bodied. Balanced acidity. Moderately extracted. Moderately oaked. Coconut, green apples, oak spice. Very appealing toasted oak aromas show a bright citrus accent that comes through on the palate. Outstanding lingering smoky finish.

1997 Chardonnay, HB Vineyard, Napa Valley $26. **88**

Bright yellow-straw hue. Moderately full-bodied. Balanced acidity. Moderately extracted. Mildly oaked. Butter, spice, yellow apples. Complex yeasty aromas have a forceful character. Generously fruity, textured, and supple, this strikes all the right notes and finishes cleanly.

1997 Provence-A California Table Wine, California $16.50. **86**

Brilliant, saturated pale purple. Lean herb and cherry aromas. A zesty entry leads a medium-bodied palate with vibrant acidity. Deep fruit flavors roll through the finish. Powerful, but a tad austere. Should open with a few more months of aging. Drink now or later.

1995 Cabernet Franc, Napa Valley $25. **84**

Bright ruby hue with a garnet rim. Forward vanilla and spice aromas show a dominant oak influence. A lush entry leads to a medium-bodied palate with velvety tannins and a core of chocolatey flavors. Rich, generous, flavorful finish. Lower acidity levels make for a lush attractive wine, but not a keeper. Drink now.

1995 Cabernet Sauvignon, Napa Valley $28. **93**

Bright saturated ruby cast. Moderately full-bodied. Balanced acidity. Moderately extracted. Heavily oaked. Mildly tannic. Briar fruits, coconut, vanilla. Outrageously aromatic, with a forward and intense flavor profile. Shows great definition despite a supple, open-knit structure. Velvety and stylish.

1994 Cabernet Sauvignon, H.B. Vineyard, Napa Valley $55. **94**

Opaque dark crimson appearance. Moderately full-bodied. Highly extracted. Moderately tannic. Sweet herbs, black currant, brown spice, chocolate. Exotic spicy nose has sweet herbal overtones. A concentrated center of generous black juicy fruits is kept in check by firm dry tannins. Very structured and powerful.

Scale: Superlative (96-100), Exceptional (90-95), Highly Recommended (85-89), Recommended (80-84), Not Recommended (Under 80)

1995 Cabernet Sauvignon, Estate Bottled, Napa Valley $55.   **95**

Deep ruby purple. Moderately full-bodied. Balanced acidity. Moderately extracted.
Moderately oaked. Mildly tannic. Oriental spices, cassis, ginger. Exotically aromatic,
with complexity throughout. Supple and generous in the mouth. Carries its weight
effortlessly, with great refinement and style.

1995 Merlot, Napa Valley $35.   **90**

Bright cherry red, well saturated. Generous ripe aromas have a toasty oak accent.
Moderately full-bodied with a firm attack and concentrated black fruit flavors that are
well matched by ripe, chewy dry tannins that clamp down on the finish. Drink now or
later. Can improve with more age.

1997 Chardonnay, Late Harvest, Napa Valley $35/375 ml.   **80**

Robert Pepi

1997 Malvasia Bianca, Central Coast $14.   **88**

Deep yellow-straw hue. Enticing flower and herb aromas are perfumed and exotic.
A rich entry leads a moderately full-bodied palate showing crisp, juicy acidity. Drying
finish. A real flavor bomb with a lean structure; an antidote for Chardonnay. Drink now.

1996 Barbera, Sonoma County $19.   **84**

Deep blackish purple. Medium-bodied. Full acidity. Moderately extracted. Mildly oaked.
Mildly tannic. Earth, dried herbs, black fruits. Forward, interesting aromatics lead a lush
palate feel buoyed by crisp acidity. Lean, focused finish.

1995 Sangiovese, Colline di Sassi, Napa Valley $25.   **84**

Dark ruby hue. Medium-bodied. Balanced acidity. Highly extracted. Moderately oaked.
Mildly tannic. Earth, black fruits, brown spice. Spicy, earthy aromas lead a solid mouthful
of earthy black fruits that turns dry on the finish. Rather ripe and chewy.

Pepperwood Grove

1997 Cabernet Sauvignon, California $7.   **83**

Pale cherry-red hue. Vanilla and red cherry aromas show a marked sweet oak influence.
A soft attack leads to a medium-bodied palate with a juicy cherry fruit flavors and mild
velvety tannins. Drink now.

1997 Merlot, California $7.   **81**

1997 Pinot Noir, California $6.99.   **83**

Very pale violet hue. Moderately light-bodied. Subtly extracted. Mildly tannic. Cherries,
vanilla. Vibrant, sweet, fruity aromas follow through on the palate, with a crisp finish that
makes for a fresh style.

1996 Zinfandel, California $6.99.   **81**

Perry Creek

1997 Chardonnay, El Dorado $12.   **84**

Pale straw hue. Clean aromas of mild apple fruit with very subtle oak. A clean attack leads
a medium-bodied palate with bright fruit flavors that have refreshing varietal character.
Acids are crisp through the finish. Drink now.

1996 Cabernet Sauvignon, El Dorado $12.50.   **83**

Deep garnet hue. Generous spice and mineral aromas. A lush entry leads to a
moderately full-bodied palate with mildly astringent tannins. Ripe, rounded finish.
Decent, but lacking grip and intensity. Drink now.

1996 Merlot, El Dorado $12.   **81**

1996 Sangiovese, El Dorado $15.   **81**

1996 Zinfandel, Zin Man, Sierra Foothills $12.   **81**

Pesenti

1995 Cabernet Sauvignon, Paso Robles $20.   **80**

1996 Cabernet Sauvignon, Paso Robles $15.   **86**
Deep ruby-purple hue. Moderate aromas show a sweet oak accent and ripe berry fruits. A fruity entry leads a medium-bodied palate with broad cherry fruit flavors and soft tannins lingering on the finish. Generously fruity with some underlying structure. Drink now.

1995 Zinfandel, Paso Robles $16.   **84**
Deep blackish ruby cast. Moderately full-bodied. Full acidity. Moderately extracted. Mildly oaked. Moderately tannic. Minerals, stewed fruits, wood. Quite aromatic, with a full but lean palate feel. Elevated acidity makes for an angular, juicy finish.

1996 Zinfandel, Paso Robles $16.   **84**
Deep blackish purple. Moderately full-bodied. Balanced acidity. Moderately extracted. Moderately oaked. Mildly tannic. Black fruits, brown spices. Pleasantly aromatic, with a solid interplay between fruit and wood nuances. Soft and supple on the palate, and well structured through the finish.

1997 Zinfandel Port, Second Estate Reserve, Paso Robles $20/500 ml.   **84**
Opaque blackish purple. Full-bodied. Full acidity. Highly extracted. Moderately tannic. Briar fruits, minerals. Extremely aromatic and wholly fruit-centered, with a ripe, jammy quality throughout. Full-throttled and intense, this wine is really showing its youth. Not for the faint of heart.

Peterson

1996 Cabernet Sauvignon, Bradford Mountain Vineyard,
Dry Creek Valley $25.   **88**
Very deep, saturated purple red hue. Intense vanilla and red fruit aromas show a big oak accent. A supple attack leads to a medium-bodied palate with ripe, supple tannins. Rich, rounded finish. A ripe and generous style. Drink within five years.

1996 Merlot, Dry Creek Valley $22.50.   **87**
Bright, saturated purple-red. Subdued mineral, chocolate, and red fruit aromas. A lean entry leads a medium-bodied palate with mildly astringent tannins and a firm, clipped finish. Rather austere but shows depth. Drink now.

1995 Zinfandel, Dry Creek Valley $14.   **84**
Deep blackish ruby cast. Moderately full-bodied. Balanced acidity. Highly extracted. Moderately oaked. Moderately tannic. Spice, chocolate, dried herbs. Somewhat reined in aromatically, with a firm, austere palate feel. Rather lean through the finish.

Pezzi King

1997 Chardonnay, Sonoma County $21.   **91**
Bright straw hue. Forward citrus and vanilla aromas show a pleasant oak accent. A crisp entry leads a moderately full-bodied palate with rounded acidity. Vibrant, persistent finish. Rich, but well balanced. Drink now.

1995 Cabernet Sauvignon, Dry Creek Valley $25.   **89**
Saturated cherry red. Moderately full-bodied. Highly extracted. Moderately tannic. Black cherries, minerals, brown spice. Deep, concentrated flavors are tightly wound, with fine-grained tannins clamping down on the finish. This will be better in a year or two.

1996 Cabernet Sauvignon, Dry Creek Valley $26.   **84**
Bright ruby red hue to the rim. Generous red fruit and vanilla aromas show a judicious oak accent. A soft entry leads to a medium-bodied palate with velvety tannins. Fruit-centered, ripe finish. Supple and eminently drinkable. Drink now.

Scale: Superlative (96-100), Exceptional (90-95), Highly Recommended (85-89),
Recommended (80-84), Not Recommended (Under 80)

Joseph Phelps

1996 Chardonnay, Los Carneros $22.   84
Bright pale straw cast. Medium-bodied. Full acidity. Moderately extracted. Moderately oaked. Menthol, vanilla, minerals. Assertively oaky aromas lead a lean palate, with vanilla flavors lingering through the finish. The creamy texture is a plus.

1996 Chardonnay, Ovation, Napa Valley $40.   89
Bright straw cast. Moderately full-bodied. Balanced acidity. Moderately extracted. Mildly oaked. Tropical fruits, minerals, yeast. Ripe and opulent, with complex if understated flavors. A weighty mouthfeel is balanced by zesty acidity. Lean through the finish.

1996 Viognier, Vin du Mistral, Napa Valley $28.   90
Deep straw cast. Full-bodied. Balanced acidity. Moderately extracted. Apples, minerals, flowers. Quite aromatic, with a complex array of flavors. Full and rich on the palate, showing a buttery character that is well balanced by acidity.

1994 Cabernet Sauvignon, Napa Valley $24.   90
Opaque dark purple-red. Medium-bodied. Highly extracted. Moderately tannic. Vanilla, brown spice, plums. Rich, spicy ripe fruit aromas lead a solid-textured palate with a powdery mouthfeel and impressive ripe flavors. Well integrated and quite plush. Lively high-toned fruity character.

1995 Cabernet Sauvignon, Napa Valley $27.   90
Deep ruby cast. Moderately full-bodied. Balanced acidity. Moderately extracted. Moderately oaked. Moderately tannic. Licorice, black fruits, earth. Big and weighty in style, with a rich and lush mouthfeel. Chunky tannins rear up on the finish.

1996 Cabernet Sauvignon, Napa Valley $30.   91
Saturated ruby-violet hue. Generously aromatic with big plummy fruit aromas and toasty vanilla notes. A rich attack leads a full-bodied palate with a thick, chewy mouthfeel and lush ripe cherry fruit flavors complimented by generous, supple tannins. A big, chewy wine that has the structure to age further. Drink now or later.

1994 Cabernet Sauvignon, Backus Vineyard, Napa Valley $70.   92
Opaque dark red-purple. Moderately full-bodied. Highly extracted. Moderately tannic. Cassis, plums, black tea. Ripe, brooding fleshy fruit aromas lead a thick, concentrated palate. Tight tannins envelope the finish. Needs some years to resolve the tannins. Structurally impressive.

1995 Cabernet Sauvignon, Backus Vineyard, Napa Valley $70.   93
Saturated ruby purple. Full-bodied. Balanced acidity. Highly extracted. Moderately oaked. Moderately tannic. Black fruits, minerals, mint. Aromatically reserved, with a dense and youthful palate feel. Tightly wound and stuffed with flavor. Shows excellent grip and intensity through the finish. Needs time to show its best.

1994 Insignia, Napa Valley $70.   93
Solidly opaque dark purple. Moderately full-bodied. Highly extracted. Moderately tannic. Violets, cassis, tobacco, cedar. Violet-edged dark berry fruit aromas. A solid, layered palate has fruity depth and richness, with a long, flavorful finish showing ample soft tannins. Still youthful, though very accessible now.

1995 Insignia, Napa Valley $75.   92
Dark ruby purple. Full-bodied. Balanced acidity. Highly extracted. Heavily oaked. Moderately tannic. Cocoa, earth, black fruits. Powerfully aromatic, displaying great depth and intensity. Complex throughout, with a weighty, extracted quality buttressed by firm tannins. A long-term (7–10 years) cellar candidate.

1995 Merlot, Napa Valley $26.   90
Deep blackish ruby hue with a slight purple cast. Moderately full-bodied. Balanced acidity. Moderately extracted. Moderately oaked. Mildly tannic. Black fruits, chocolate, minerals. Aromatic and complex, with a range of dense flavors and a judicious oak accent. Lush and chewy in the mouth with a firm structure. Velvety tannins rise on the finish.

1996 Merlot, Napa Valley $30.   **89**

Saturated dark ruby-violet hue. Rich, generous aromas show a chocolatey, toasty oak accent with dark fruits. A rich entry leads a full-bodied palate with deep fruit flavors and lush, textured tannins through the finish. Impressively dense, with chocolatey and plum flavors. Drink now or later.

1996 Le Mistral, California $25.   **92**

Deep purple-red hue to the rim. Forward perfumed red fruit, earth, and vanilla aromas with a mild wood accent. A smooth attack leads a full-bodied palate with abundant velvety tannins. Persistent, flavorful finish. Rich, elegant, and wonderfully made with the latest in soft extraction techniques. Drink now or later. Can improve with more age.

Philippe-Lorraine

1995 Cabernet Sauvignon, Napa Valley $17.50.   **80**

1996 Cabernet Sauvignon, Napa Valley $18.50.   **92**

Bright ruby with a slight garnet cast. Intense kirsch, vanilla, and cordial-like aromas show a big wood accent. A lush attack leads to a medium-bodied palate with ripe tannins. Exceptionally flavorful and attractive, fruit-centered finish. Unusual but hedonistic. Drink within five years.

1996 Merlot, Napa Valley $21.   **91**

Dark ruby-violet hue. Well-developed oaky, earthy, black fruit aromas. Firm on the attack with lushly extracted flavors and dry tannins through the finish. Quite complex and evolved, though it could use some cellar time and would improve with more age. Drink now or later.

R.H. Phillips

1997 Chardonnay, Barrel Cuvée, Dunnigan Hills $8.   **80**

1997 Sauvignon Blanc, Night Harvest, Dunnigan Hills $7.   **81**

1996 Syrah, EXP, Dunnigan Hills $12.   **86**

Dark ruby color, limpid with a slight fade. Medium-bodied. Cooked fruit flavors. Crisp, fruity, and well supported by grainy tannins and bright acids. Fruit-centered and relatively firmly structured. Drink now.

Pietra Santa

1996 Sangiovese, San Benito County $20.   **82**

Pine Ridge

1997 Chardonnay, Knollside Cuvée, Napa Valley $17.50.   **86**

Pale green-straw hue. Moderately full-bodied. Balanced acidity. Moderately extracted. Moderately oaked. Apples, butter, minerals. Soft vanilla and butter aromas follow through on the palate, with a lush mouthfeel and sweet, bright apple flavors that linger on the finish.

1997 Chardonnay, Dijon Clones, Napa Valley, Carneros $24.   **84**

Greenish gold. Medium-bodied. Full acidity. Moderately extracted. Lime, lemon. Bright citrus zest aromas. Crisp and tart, with a firm citrus edge that turns dry on the finish.

1994 Cabernet Sauvignon, Howell Mountain, Napa Valley $35.   **91**

Opaque blackish red. Moderately full-bodied. Highly extracted. Quite tannic. Earth, minerals, black fruits, black tea. Austere, closed-up nose. The tightly wound palate is not showing much generosity, though concentrated black fruit flavors are evident and hugely impressive. Tough through the finish. Needs long-term cellaring.

1995 Cabernet Sauvignon, Howell Mountain, Napa Valley $37.50.   **94**

Dark ruby purple. Full-bodied. Balanced acidity. Highly extracted. Moderately oaked. Quite tannic. Chocolate, licorice, brown spices. Exotic aromas show breeding and complexity. Deep and profound in the mouth, with a wave of brooding flavors. Firm tannins clamp down on the rich finish. Needs time.

Scale: Superlative (96-100), Exceptional (90-95), Highly Recommended (85-89), Recommended (80-84), Not Recommended (Under 80)

1996 Cabernet Sauvignon, Howell Mountain, Napa Valley $40.   **97**

Deep, opaque purple-red hue. Forward, intense vanilla and cordial-like blackberry aromas. A lush concentrated entry leads to a full-bodied supple palate feel with robust velvety tannins. Flavorful, stylish finish. Concentrated and impressive, yet very well balanced. Drink now or later.

1994 Cabernet Sauvignon, Stags Leap District, Napa Valley $35.   **86**

Full raspberry red. Medium-bodied. Moderately extracted. Mildly tannic. Raspberries, cassis, anise. Crisp, high-toned aromas. Bright, juicy raspberry and black fruit flavors expand vibrantly on the palate, with soft tannins through the finish and attractive minerally accents. Nice now.

1995 Cabernet Sauvignon, Stags Leap District, Napa Valley $37.50.   **93**

Saturated violet red. Moderately full-bodied. Highly extracted. Moderately oaked. Moderately tannic. Licorice, black fruits, earth. Toasty, dark fruit aromas follow through on the palate, with a vibrant, fruity center and dry, earthy notes through the lean finish. Impressively structured, though this is giving pleasure now.

1996 Cabernet Sauvignon, Stags Leap District, Napa Valley $40.   **95**

Brilliant ruby hue. A rich entry leads a moderately full-bodied palate with forcefully intense dark fruit flavors and voluptuous supple tannins that linger through the finish. Very hedonistic and persistent. Drink now or later.

1995 Cabernet Sauvignon, Rutherford, Napa Valley $24.   **90**

Deep ruby hue with a slight purple cast. Moderately full-bodied. Balanced acidity. Moderately extracted. Mildly oaked. Mildly tannic. Cassis, vanilla. Pleasantly aromatic, with a soft, supple, and harmonious palate feel. Gentle and well balanced, and quite flavorful through the finish.

1996 Cabernet Sauvignon, Rutherford, Napa Valley $25.   **90**

Medium ruby-violet hue. Attractively aromatic with deep cordial-like aromas. A richly fruity entry leads a moderately full-bodied palate with fantastic fruit intensity with cordial-like flavors that persist through a long finish. Drink now or later.

1994 Andrus Reserve, Napa Valley $85.   **94**

Dark reddish purple. Moderately full-bodied. Highly extracted. Moderately tannic. Black fruits, loam, minerals. Austere minerally nose leads a concentrated minerally palate with austere black fruit flavors that show amazing persistence on the finish. This wine impresses with its weight and persistence.

1995 Andrus Reserve, Napa Valley $85.   **91**

Deep ruby purple. Moderately full-bodied. Balanced acidity. Moderately extracted. Moderately oaked. Mildly tannic. Licorice, minerals, cassis. High-toned aromas lead a precise and well-defined palate feel. Crisp and intense through the angular finish. Shows fine grip and very judicious use of wood.

1996 Merlot, Crimson Creek, Napa Valley $25.   **89**

Bright violet-ruby hue. Lean, restrained aromas have a minerally, black fruit quality Moderately full-bodied, with a firm attack, minerally backbone, and some tough tannins. Rather angular through the finish, but well structured. Drink now or later. Can improve with more age.

1996 Merlot, Carneros $35.   **94**

Semi-saturated dark ruby hue. Generous dark chocolate and plum aromas. A rich attack leads a moderately full-bodied palate with chunky, soft tannins and a deeply flavorful finish. Drink now or later. Can improve with more age.

1993 Black Diamond Port, Napa Valley $16/375 ml.   **80**

Piper Sonoma

NV Brut, Sonoma $14.   **87**

Bright straw cast. Medium-bodied. Full acidity. Toast, citrus peel. Forward aromas feature a subtle yeast accent. Crisp, bright, and austere through the finish, yet showing fine biscuity nuances.

NV Blanc de Noir, Sonoma $15.   **90**

Deep straw cast. Moderately full-bodied. Yeast, toast, bread dough. Forward, mature aromatics are complex and yeasty. Smooth and supple in the mouth, with a silky texture. This seems very generous and developed, with signs of extended bottle age.

Plam

1994 Cabernet Sauvignon, Vintner's Reserve, Napa Valley $30.   **90**

Dark garnet-red center. Medium-bodied. Highly extracted. Moderately tannic. Cassis, earth, chocolate, brown spice. Deep spicy aromas suggest concentrated black fruit flavors that are confirmed on the palate. The solid, chewy mouthfeel concludes with an assertive finish.

1995 Cabernet Sauvignon, Vintner's Reserve, Napa Valley $30.   **94**

Saturated, opaque purple. Full-bodied. Highly extracted. Quite tannic. Spice, cassis, chocolate. Rich, deep, fruity aromas show a heavy oak spice accent. Weighty, heavily wrought texture and flavors convey power and structure. This needs time.

1995 Merlot, Vintner's Reserve, Napa Valley $25.   **93**

Deep blackish ruby color. Moderately full-bodied. Balanced acidity. Highly extracted. Heavily oaked. Mildly tannic. Cedar, cherry cordial, brown spices. Supple on the entry and extremely aromatic and flavorful on the palate, with some dusty tannins. Very lengthy finish. Quite solid and well balanced.

Prager Winery & Port Works

1993 Petite Sirah, Royal Escort LBV Port, Napa Valley $38.50.   **88**

Deep blackish ruby cast. Moderately full-bodied. Full acidity. Highly extracted. Mildly tannic. Brown spices, black fruits, chocolate. Oaky aromas, with spicy flavors throughout. Full though drying on the palate, with a deep core of dark fruit flavors. Finishes with a touch of heat.

Noble Companion 10 Year Old Tawny Port, Napa Valley $45.   **89**

Deep mahogany cast. Moderately full-bodied. Full acidity. Highly extracted. Mildly tannic. Salted nuts, treacle, brown spices. Carries a fiery impression on the nose. Full throttled and flavorful on the palate, with some Sherry-like complexities. The lengthy finish is a touch hot.

Pride Mountain

1996 Cabernet Franc, Sonoma County $25.   **89**

Deep ruby purple. Moderately full-bodied. Balanced acidity. Highly extracted. Moderately oaked. Moderately tannic. Vanilla, black fruits. Aromatic and modern, with a forward, fruit-and-wood flavor profile. Full and round in the mouth, with a drying, flavorful finish. Well balanced.

1996 Cabernet Sauvignon, Napa Valley $29.99.   **98**

Saturated black-ruby hue. Chocolate and anise aromas are quite distinctive. A rich entry leads to a full-bodied palate showing enormous density of flavors and a rich, rounded mouthfeel that finishes with toasty oak accents. A voluptuous style that is very approachable now. Drink now or later.

Quady

Batch 88 Starboard, California $11.50.   **89**

Deep ruby-garnet cast. Full-bodied. Balanced acidity. Highly extracted. Chocolate, tea, black fruits. Aromatic and quite complex, with a wide range of flavors throughout. Lush, rounded, and well balanced on the palate, with a lengthy finish.

1993 LBV Port, Amador County $12.   **91**

Deep blackish garnet cast. Moderately full-bodied. Balanced acidity. Highly extracted. Chocolate, brown spices, black fruits. Carries a generous wood accent throughout, with a deeply flavored, supple palate feel. Shows fine grip and intensity, with excellent length.

Scale: Superlative (96-100), Exceptional (90-95), Highly Recommended (85-89), Recommended (80-84), Not Recommended (Under 80)

1989 Frank's Vineyard Vintage Starboard, California $19.   **90**

Deep ruby cast with a brick rim. Moderately full-bodied. Balanced acidity. Moderately extracted. Mild sweetness. Reminiscent of black fruits, earth, dried apricots. Rich earthy aromas introduce this full-flavored Port with a firm, woody character. The sweetness is subsumed by well-balanced acidity and wood influences. Finishes with complex, Sherry-like tones.

1990 Frank's Vineyard Vintage Starboard, California $19.   **89**

Black-ruby hue with brickish rim. Moderately full-bodied. Balanced acidity. Highly extracted. Medium sweetness. Reminiscent of black fruits, vanilla, butterscotch. Rich and ripe tasting, and very nicely textured, with grainy tannins lingering in a long, flavorful finish. Evolving nicely and destined for further improvement.

1990 Vintage Starboard, Amador County $21.50.   **93**

Opaque blackish garnet cast. Moderately full-bodied. Balanced acidity. Moderately extracted. Minerals, black fruits, olives. Quite aromatic, with pleasant mature nuances throughout. Rich, supple, and velvety in the mouth, with a very lengthy finish. Classic and stylish.

1997 Black Muscat, Elysium, California $12.   **86**

Saturated pale cherry-garnet hue. Generous herb and red fruit aromas carry a spiritish accent. A lush entry leads a full-bodied palate that has lots of sweetness and lean acidity. Perfumed through the finish. Full throttled. Drink now.

1997 Orange Muscat, Essensia, California $12.   **86**

Deep copper hue. Exotic, spiritish orange peel and mineral aromas. A lush entry leads a moderately full-bodied, sweet palate with a pithy finish. This vintage of Essensia is moving toward the rustic side, with an herbal overtone. Drink now.

Quail Ridge

1996 Sauvignon Blanc, Reserve, Rutherford River Ranch,
Napa Valley $14.99.   **82**

1994 Cabernet Sauvignon, Napa Valley $14.99.   **85**

Pale purplish red. Moderately light-bodied. Moderately extracted. Moderately tannic. Crisp berries, minerals. Quite lean in style, with some juicy flavors up front, and astringency running through the palate to give a somewhat compact finish.

1995 Cabernet Sauvignon, Napa Valley $15.99.   **86**

Pale, bright cherry red with purple highlights. Moderately light-bodied. Moderately extracted. Mildly tannic. Raspberries, cherries, cedar. Crisp fruity aromas follow through on an open-knit palate with accessible flavors. Nice now, but not for the long haul.

1996 Cabernet Sauvignon, Napa Valley $22.   **84**

Medium violet-purple hue. Restrained sweet herbal aromas. A light entry leads to a lighter-bodied palate with subtle flavors and a minerally grip through the finish. Rather restrained in style. Drink now.

1993 Cabernet Sauvignon, Volker Eisele Vineyard Reserve,
Napa Valley $39.99.   **92**

Full cherry red with a subtle brick cast. Medium-bodied. Moderately extracted. Moderately tannic. Violets, black currants, spice. Hugely perfumed with enticing violet hints. An elegant and delicate palate shows well-integrated, noble, fine-grained tannins and great persistence of flavors through the finish. Attractive now, though more age will probably improve it.

1995 Cabernet Sauvignon, Volker Eisele Vineyard Reserve,
Napa Valley $40.   **88**

Medium ruby hue. Leaner, reserved aromas show a minerally overtone. A firm entry leads to a medium-bodied palate with firm flavors and a tannic structure and acidity that makes for a well-gripped finish. Fruit flavors are tightly focused, bright, and cherry-like. Drink now or later.

1995 Merlot, California $19.99.   **82**

Quatro
1997 Chardonnay, Sonoma County $9.99.   **81**
1996 Merlot, Sonoma County $12.   **89**
Brilliant violet red. Generous cherry fruit and vanilla aromas. A vibrant attack leads a medium-bodied palate with balanced fine-grained tannins. Finishes with juicy, fruity persistence. This is a concentrated, stylish wine to be consumed now or later. Can improve with more age.

Quinta da Sonora
1996 Vinho Tinto, Sierra Foothills $18.   **87**
Deep blackish purple. Moderately full-bodied. Balanced acidity. Highly extracted. Mildly oaked. Mildly tannic. Blueberries, minerals, vanilla. Exotically aromatic, with a lush, flavorful mouthfeel. Full and lean through the finish. Intense and well balanced.

Quintessa
1995 Red, Rutherford $75.   **90**
Bright ruby-garnet hue. Mature coffee and oak spice aromas show a developed, tertiary character. A firm entry leads to a moderately full-bodied palate with rounded fruit flavors and plenty of spicy oak notes through the finish. Elegant, and drinking very nicely now.

Qupé
1997 Chardonnay, Bien Nacido Vineyard, Santa Barbara County $18.   **93**
Pale straw hue. Mildly aromatic with apple character. A crisp entry leads a medium-bodied palate with zesty citrus flavors and no oak influences. The finish is clean. This would be an excellent match with sole or delicate fish.

1996 Chardonnay, Bien Nacido Reserve, Santa Barbara County $25.   **90**
Medium yellow-gold. Generous aromas of toasty oak and ripe fruit. A juicy entry leads a moderately full-bodied palate with bright acids to match the full citrus fruits. Alcohol seems a bit on the high side. Finishes with judicious oak spice flavors. Drink now or later.

1996 Los Olivos Red Cuvée, Ibarra, Young, and Stolpman Vineyards, Santa Barbara County $18.   **90**
Bright purple-red to the rim. Forward black fruit, earth, and spice aromas show a subtle wood influence. A soft attack leads a medium-bodied palate showing velvety tannins. Supple, lengthy, flavorful finish. Harmonious and complete. Drink now.

1997 Syrah, Central Coast $13.50.   **84**
Pale purple, limpid, with a fading rim. Subtle, clean flower and crisp berry flavors. Firm entry. Moderately light-bodied with crisp acidity. Has a relatively light frame. The finish is clipped and short. Drink now.

1996 Syrah, Bien Nacido Reserve, Santa Barbara County $25.   **89**
Dark ruby purple, limpid and brilliant, with a slight fade. Generous, sound black fruit, cherry, and vanilla flavors. Generous wood tones. Smooth entry. Moderately full-bodied. Moderate thick tannins. Lingering finish. Thick, chewy, and fruity. Drink now.

1996 Syrah, Bien Nacido Hillside Estate, Santa Barbara County $35.   **92**
Dark crimson purple, limpid and brilliant to the rim. Generous, ripe, juicy berry fruit and jammy black fruit flavors. Soft entry. Moderately full-bodied. Moderate drying tannins. Rather weak on the finish. Drink now.

Ramey
1996 Chardonnay, Hyde Vineyard, Carneros, Napa Valley $45.   **91**
Bright gold. Smoky, buttery aromas with obvious oak influence. A bright attack leads a moderately full-bodied palate with impressive flavor concentration. Finishes with persistent flavors and lingering oak spice. Drink now or later.

Ramspeck

1995 Cabernet Sauvignon, Napa Valley $18.   **85**

Blackish red. Medium-bodied. Highly extracted. Moderately tannic. Earth, pencil lead, brown spice, black fruits. Quite an austere style, with a solid minerally presence on the midpalate. Good grip through the finish, with a firm chalky feel. Time will probably help this one.

Rancho Sisquoc

1994 Cabernet Sauvignon, Santa Maria Valley $18.   **88**

Bright purple-crimson color. Medium-bodied. Highly extracted. Moderately tannic. Cigar box, black cherries. Cedar and tobacco in the nose. Concentrated black cherry flavors on entry linger through a well-balanced finish showing fine soft tannins that provide a supple character.

1996 Cabernet Sauvignon, Santa Maria Valley $20.   **90**

Deep ruby-red hue. Generous aromas show chocolate and dark fruit accents. A rich entry leads a full-bodied palate with fully extracted flavors and plenty of spicy oak flavors that linger through a persistent finish. Very well balanced with plenty of structure and flavor concentration to allow this to improve.

1995 Merlot, Santa Maria Valley $18.   **89**

Deep blackish ruby color. Medium-bodied. Balanced acidity. Moderately extracted. Moderately oaked. Mildly tannic. Red fruits, minerals, vanilla. Aromatic and focused, with concentrated red fruit flavors. Firmly structured, with cleansing acidity in the lengthy oak-tinged finish. Well balanced.

1996 Merlot, Santa Maria Valley $20.   **86**

Deep, saturated purple-red. Unusual, high-toned earth and mineral aromas show a reductive note, but seem to blow off with aeration. A lean entry leads a medium-bodied palate with racy acidity and tannic grip. The finish is crisp and linear. Well structured. Drink now or later. Can improve with more age.

Kent Rasmussen

1996 Petite Sirah, Ramsay, Napa Valley $20.   **84**

Bright purple. Moderately full-bodied. Highly extracted. Floral, bright black fruit aromas. Tannins are very dry and fine grained, making this rather tough at present.

1995 Pinot Noir, Carneros $26.   **81**

1996 Pinot Noir, Carneros $27.   **80**

1996 Syrah, Ramsay Reserve, Napa Valley $20.   **89**

Deep purple, opaque, and brilliant, with a slight fade. Generous, pleasant briary bramble fruit and oak spice flavors. Hefty wood tones. Firm entry. Moderately full-bodied. Angular, with plentiful hard-edged tannins through the clipped bitter finish. Good structure, though tough now. Drink within five years.

Ravenswood

1994 Rancho Salina Vineyards Red, Sonoma Valley $30.   **89**

Dark ruby color. Medium-bodied. Moderately extracted. Moderately tannic. Earth, brown spice, black fruits. Exotic dark fruit and spice aromas lead a solid, full-flavored palate, with well-balanced dry tannins on the finish. Quite complex though harmonious in its flavors.

1995 Rancho Vineyards Red, Sonoma Mountain $30.   **91**

Blood red with a subtle garnet cast. Medium-bodied. Moderately extracted. Moderately tannic. Earth, brown spice, black fruits. Dusty, spicy aromas follow through on the palate, with ripe black fruit flavors and a bite to the dry tannins.

1995 Pickberry Vineyards Red, Sonoma Mountain $35.   **90**

Bright blood red. Moderately full-bodied. Highly extracted. Moderately tannic. Bramble fruits, cedar, sage. Smoky, ripe aromas lead a fleshy entry, with fine-grained, angular tannins drying the finish. A well-balanced, generous style that will need a few more years.

1996 Zinfandel, Sonoma County $15.25. 88

Deep blackish ruby hue. Medium-bodied. Full acidity. Moderately extracted. Mildly oaked. Mildly tannic. Black fruits, minerals. Quite aromatic, with a high-toned, fruit-centered palate feel. Crisp, vibrant, and tasty in a lighter style, with a lengthy finish.

1996 Zinfandel, Dickerson Vineyard, Napa Valley $24. 91

Bright blackish ruby cast. Moderately full-bodied. Balanced acidity. Highly extracted. Moderately oaked. Mildly tannic. Black fruits, minerals, vanilla. Quite aromatic, with a firm, angular palate feel. Shows fine depth and length, with a taut finish. Intense and "well gripped."

1996 Zinfandel, Monte Rosso, Sonoma Valley $24. 95

Deep blackish ruby hue. Full-bodied. Full acidity. Highly extracted. Moderately oaked. Moderately tannic. Minerals, black fruits. Pleasantly aromatic, with a concentrated, angular palate feel that shows great depth. Firmly structured and intense, with a lengthy finish.

1996 Zinfandel, Old Hill Vineyard, Sonoma Valley $26. 91

Bright blackish ruby cast. Moderately full-bodied. Balanced acidity. Moderately extracted. Mildly oaked. Mildly tannic. Red fruits, black pepper, licorice. Quite aromatic, with a velvety, lush palate feel. Deeply flavored and very well balanced, with lean tannins through the finish.

1996 Zinfandel, Wood Road Belloni, Russian River Valley $24. 94

Bright blackish purple. Full-bodied. Balanced acidity. Highly extracted. Moderately oaked. Moderately tannic. Chocolate, sweet herbs, black fruits. Quite aromatic, with great complexity to the range of flavors. Deep and intense, with a lush, velvety texture. Firm through the finish.

Martin Ray

1996 Chardonnay, Mariage, California $20. 86

Bright yellow-gold. Medium-bodied. Balanced acidity. Moderately extracted. Toasted oak, citrus, brown spice. Nutty, yeasty aromas lead a rich, rounded mouthfeel, with lush citrus fruit flavors and spicy oak on the finish. A generous style.

1997 Chardonnay, Marriage, California $20. 88

Bright straw hue. Generous brown spice aromas carry an intense oak accent. A firm attack leads a rounded, moderately full-bodied mouthfeel with creamy acidity. Generous, flavorful finish. Drink now.

1995 Cabernet Sauvignon, Santa Cruz Mountains $25. 89

Deep saturated ruby cast. Moderately full-bodied. Balanced acidity. Highly extracted. Heavily oaked. Moderately tannic. Dill pickle, spice, minerals. Quite aromatic, with a flavor profile dominated by American oak. Ripe and full in the mouth, with grainy tannins through a drying finish.

1994 Cabernet Sauvignon, Saratoga Cuvée, California $35.50. 89

Deep red. Medium-bodied. Highly extracted. Moderately tannic. Black fruits, earth, minerals. An earthy, assertive nose leads a rather young and tight palate, with plenty of firm spicy oak flavors on the finish. Quite austere, and with sound structure and some depth, this will be best with richer foods.

1995 Cabernet Sauvignon, Saratoga Cuvée, California $25. 89

Saturated blood red. Medium-bodied. Moderately extracted. Heavily oaked. Moderately tannic. Black fruits, brown spice. Dense black fruit aromas follow through on the palate, with plentiful soft tannins. The balanced finish shows some firmness, yet this is drinking well now. Very oak-influenced style.

1995 Cabernet Sauvignon, Diamond Mountain, Napa Valley $45. 93

Deep ruby cast. Moderately full-bodied. Balanced acidity. Highly extracted. Moderately oaked. Moderately tannic. Brown spices, minerals, pencil shavings. Quite aromatic, with a big toasty oak accent. Firm, lean, and tightly wound in the mouth, with very robust tannins. Needs time.

1995 Pinot Noir, California $36.   **90**

Full cherry-garnet red with a light rim. Medium-bodied. Moderately extracted. Moderately oaked. Mildly tannic. Vanilla and cherry aromas. Full berry flavors are defined by crisp acids that give this a lively and generous palate presence with impressive concentration of flavors. Vanilla notes linger on the finish.

1996 Pinot Noir, California $19.   **86**

Bright ruby cast. Medium-bodied. Balanced acidity. Moderately extracted. Moderately oaked. Mildly tannic. Brown spices, minerals, red fruits. Bright aromas carry a ripe berry quality. Oak spice makes for a drying quality through the finish.

Raymond

1997 Chardonnay, Amberhill, California $10.   **83**

Deep yellow-straw hue. Generous spice, mineral, and vegetable aromas. A rich attack leads a ripe, moderately full-bodied palate with rounded acidity. The finish is rich and flavorful. Drink now.

1997 Chardonnay, Monterey $13.   **86**

Bright yellow-gold. Ripe buttery aromas. A vibrant entry leads a moderately full-bodied palate with a bright, lush, citrus center and full alcohol to match the acids. Finishes with lingering fruit acids. Very flavorful.

1997 Chardonnay, Reserve, Napa Valley $15.   **83**

Dark yellow-straw hue. Toast, green apple, and yeast aromas. A juicy entry leads a moderately full-bodied palate with a juicy, fruity center and a lingering oak spice finish. Drink now.

1996 Chardonnay, Generations, Napa Valley $27.   **88**

Full yellow-straw hue. Rich smoky aromas with a toasty oak accent. A rich attack leads a moderately full-bodied palate with a rounded mouthfeel and alcohol heat showing on the finish. Drink now.

1996 Sauvignon Blanc, Valley Reserve, Napa Valley $11.   **86**

Deep yellow-gold. Moderately full-bodied. Full acidity. Highly extracted. Mildly oaked. Yeast, minerals, citrus. Quite aromatic, with complex flavors and a distinctive yeasty note. Crisp and vibrant through the snappy finish.

1996 Cabernet Sauvignon, Amberhill, California $10.   **81**

1995 Cabernet Sauvignon, Napa Valley $15.   **84**

Violet-red with a lightening rim. Medium-bodied. Moderately extracted. Mildly tannic. Brown spice, black fruits. Spicy oak aromas lead soft black fruit flavors. Supple, with generous alcohol showing on the finish. For current drinking.

1994 Cabernet Sauvignon, Reserve, Napa Valley $20.   **86**

Bright reddish purple. Medium-bodied. Moderately extracted. Mildly tannic. Cassis, plums, tobacco. Rather full, ripe aromas show fleshy cassis-like notes. Supple, rounded, and attractive, with soft tannins on the finish and tobacco notes. Drink now.

1995 Cabernet Sauvignon, Reserve, Napa Valley $20.   **86**

Bright violet-purple with a lightening rim. Moderately full-bodied. Moderately extracted. Moderately tannic. Blueberries, spice. Ripe and smooth, with fine-textured tannins in a supple, friendly style that has enough juicy acidity to provide focus.

1996 Cabernet Sauvignon, Reserve, Napa Valley $23.   **87**

Bright ruby hue. Subdued mineral and berry aromas. A crisp attack leads to a medium-bodied palate with acidic vibrancy and grippy tannins. Clean, stylish finish. Straightforward and attractive. Drink now.

1994 Cabernet Sauvignon, Generations, Napa Valley $35.   **88**

Deep reddish purple. Medium-bodied. Highly extracted. Mildly tannic. Toasted oak, vanilla, cassis. Rich toasted oak aromas. Elegant, smooth, and supple, with fine concentration and full toasty oak components that linger through the finish. Nice now.

1995 Cabernet Sauvignon, Generations, Napa Valley $50. **90**

Deep purple-red hue. Vibrant berry and oak aromas show a typical Australian show wine accent. A lean entry leads to a moderately full-bodied palate with vibrant acidity and gripping tannins. Firm, vibrant, flavorful finish. Quite modern, with direct flavors, but a well-crafted and tasty style. Drink now or later.

Reliz Canyon

1997 Chardonnay, Arroyo Seco $14. **83**

Pale straw cast. Medium-bodied. Full acidity. Moderately extracted. Minerals, citrus peel. Lean and quite austere, with a pithy, citric quality. Firm and intense through the finish.

1996 Merlot, Monterey $13.95. **86**

Violet red. Lean aromas of minerals, red fruits, and herbs. A bright attack, a medium-bodied palate, vibrant acids and light, gripping tannins. Drink now.

Renaissance

1995 Chardonnay, Reserve, North Yuba $19.99. **89**

Bright gold-straw hue. Medium-bodied. Full acidity. Moderately extracted. Mildly oaked. White citrus, vanilla. Clean citrusy aromas lead a bright, lively mouthful of flavors that turn firm and minerally through the finish, with subtle oak spice emerging. A crisp and lean style.

1998 Riesling, Demi-Sec, North Yuba $11.99. **81**

1997 Sauvignon Blanc, North Yuba $10. **87**

Bright yellow-gold. Medium-bodied. Balanced acidity. Moderately extracted. Minerals, dried herbs, citrus fruits. Wet wool aromas similar to Loire Sauvignon Blanc. A bright citrus streak through the palate gives this a vivacious character.

1996 Sauvignon Blanc, Barrel Select, North Yuba $12. **84**

Bright yellow-gold. Medium-bodied. Low acidity. Moderately extracted. Mildly oaked. Butter, citrus. Rich buttery aromas are followed by similar flavors on the palate. A hint of smoky oak comes through on the finish.

1995 Cabernet Sauvignon, North Yuba $13.99. **82**

1994 Cabernet Sauvignon, Reserve, North Yuba $19.99. **86**

Deep ruby red to the rim. Moderately full-bodied. Balanced acidity. Highly extracted. Moderately tannic. Earth, chocolate, minerals. Carries an earthy accent throughout. Full, but firmly structured, with firm tannins through the finish.

1995 Sauvignon Blanc, Late Harvest, North Yuba $19.99. **84**

Deep yellow-gold. Medium-bodied. Full acidity. Moderately extracted. Mildly oaked. Yeast, toast, vanilla. Heavily toasted in the nose, with a distinctive yeasty character. Thick and sweet yet extremely vibrant acidity gives a mouthwatering finish.

Renwood

1996 Viognier, Amador County $21.95. **82**

1996 Barbera, Amador County $18.95. **81**

1994 Vintage Port, Shenandoah Valley $21.95/500 ml. **84**

Deep blackish garnet cast. Moderately full-bodied. Balanced acidity. Moderately extracted. Minerals, earth, black fruits. Fragrant and flavorful, with a deep and brooding array of flavors. Well balanced, with measured sweetness to the finish.

1996 Zinfandel, Amador Ice, Amador County $9.95/375 ml. **81**

Richardson

1995 Cabernet Sauvignon, Horne Vineyard, Sonoma Valley $18. **89**

Opaque dark red with bright purple accents. Moderately full-bodied. Highly extracted. Moderately tannic. Mint, vanilla, and red and black fruits. Very aromatic cedary, minty nose shows oak accents. Big minty mouthful, with a solid structured feel through a balanced but astringent finish.

1996 Cabernet Sauvignon, Horne Vineyard, Sonoma Valley $22.   **94**
Saturated red-purple. Moderately full-bodied. Moderately extracted. Moderately oaked. Moderately tannic. Bright black fruits, mint, minerals. Abundant fruit-forward aromas jump out of the glass. Bright and vibrant, with a chewy, textured character and supple tannins that are nice now.

1994 Synergy, Sonoma Valley $17.   **85**
Medium cherry red. Medium-bodied. Moderately extracted. Mildly tannic. Tea, red fruits, vanilla. Simple berry and vanilla aromas. Straightforward, with crisp fruity flavors on a simple palate. Does not show extravagant weight or concentration, though the balance is good.

1996 Synergy, Sonoma Valley $20.   **92**
Bright red-purple. Moderately full-bodied. Moderately extracted. Moderately oaked. Mildly tannic. Red fruits, vanilla. Fleshy red fruit aromas. Velvety fruit-centered flavors have a supple, polished character with great persistence through the finish.

1996 Pinot Noir, Sangiacomo Vineyard, Carneros $19.   **89**
Bright cherry red with a pinkish tinge. Medium-bodied. Moderately extracted. Mildly tannic. Bright perfumed, fruity aromas have dill note. Racy, well-defined fruit flavors on the palate show a crisp vanilla accent through the finish. Very fruity and lively.

1997 Syrah, Sonoma Valley $22.50.   **86**
Rich purple, limpid, and brilliant to the rim. Subtle, sound leather, spice, and black fruit flavors. Generous wood tones. Firm entry. Moderately full-bodied. Plentiful drying tannins. Dry and lean, with some leathery overtones. Clipped finish. Nice briar and minty notes, though a little dirty. Flavorsome. Drink now.

Ridge

1997 Chardonnay, California $NA.   **91**
Deep, saturated yellow-straw hue. Generous citrus, cream, and spice aromas. A supple entry leads a moderately full-bodied but well-balanced palate. Rounded and rich, with great persistence. Drink now.

1996 Chardonnay, Santa Cruz Mountains $25.   **92**
Bright golden luster. Moderately full-bodied. Full acidity. Highly extracted. Honeysuckle, peaches, apples. Rich honeyed aromas lead a bright, vibrantly fruity mouthful with a degree of generosity that follows through the engagingly honeysuckle-like finish.

1997 Coast Ridge Red, California $NA.   **86**
Brilliant, saturated ruby purple. Generous red fruit, mineral, and flower aromas. A crisp entry leads a medium-bodied palate, with drying tannins. Bright fruity finish. Drink now.

1995 Cabernet Sauvignon, Santa Cruz Mountains $22.   **93**
Opaque reddish purple. Moderately full-bodied. Highly extracted. Quite tannic. Black plums, toasted oak, black tea. The nose is muted but suggestively rich, with toasty accents. Extraordinarily thick and viscous mouthfeel. Whopping tannins on the finish make this tough at present. Fruit flavors are immensely concentrated and bright. This wine needs cellaring.

1993 Cabernet Sauvignon, Monte Bello, Santa Cruz Mountains $55.   **96**
Opaque blackish red. Moderately full-bodied. Highly extracted. Moderately tannic. Toasted oak, ripe plums, minerals, allspice. Toasty, dill-accented nose with suggestive dark fruit notes. Rich, dense, concentrated, and chewy. Hugely proportioned, with great depth of flavors. Tannins are rather dry and constraining on the finish at present. Densely structured.

1994 Cabernet Sauvignon, Monte Bello, Santa Cruz Mountains $65.   **95**
Deep, saturated ruby purple. Moderately full-bodied. Balanced acidity. Moderately extracted. Mildly oaked. Moderately tannic. Cassis, minerals, toast. Very aromatic, with a firm, minerally backbone to the fruit-forward flavors. Oak seems to play a minor supporting role. Elegant and exceptionally well balanced, with a crisp finish. Not a show wine, but a style that blossoms with age.

1995 Cabernet Sauvignon, Monte Bello, Santa Cruz Mountains $70.   92

Deep, saturated ruby purple. Full-bodied. Full acidity. Highly extracted. Moderately oaked. Moderately tannic. Vanilla, black fruits, minerals, flowers. Extremely aromatic, with a ripe core of intense fruit flavors bolstered by judicious use of oak. Deep, impressive, and intense, with a firm but velvety palate feel. Very approachable, but cellaring will undoubtedly bring out a great measure of complexity.

1995 Merlot, Santa Cruz Mountains $40.   90

Very deep blackish ruby hue with a slight purple cast. Moderately full-bodied. Full acidity. Moderately extracted. Mildly oaked. Moderately tannic. Red fruits, dried herbs, minerals. Still a bit reserved aromatically, this youthful wine fills out on the palate. Flavors are complex, with a hefty mineral accent. Full acidity and a firm structure are in balance with the level of extract. Will need some aging to fully reveal itself. Elegant.

1996 Merlot, Monte Bello Ridge, Santa Cruz Mountains $40.   93

Saturated purple-red. Deep, profound black fruit and vanilla aromas show a judicious oak accent. A firm attack leads a moderately full-bodied palate with firm tannins and juicy acidity, followed by a crisp finish. The wine literally bursts with flavor. Drink now or later. Can improve with more age.

1997 Mataro, Bridgehead, Contra Costa County $NA.   88

Bright, saturated ruby purple. Generous red fruit, earth, and mineral aromas. A firm entry leads a medium-bodied palate, with velvety tannins. Quite stylish. Drink now.

1996 Petite Sirah, York Creek, Spring Mountain, Napa Valley $NA.   90

Deep, saturated ruby purple. Generous black fruit and wood aromas show a hefty oak influence. A firm entry leads a full-bodied palate, with robust tannins. Aromatic and stuffed, with a big tannic finish. Needs time. Mid-term cellar candidate (3–6 years).

1996 Zinfandel, Dusi Ranch, Paso Robles $25.   95

Deep blackish ruby cast. Moderately full-bodied. Balanced acidity. Moderately extracted. Mildly oaked. Mildly tannic. Chocolate, black fruits. Somewhat reserved aromatically, but rich and flavorful on the palate. Amazingly lush, with a supple, velvety texture. Quite well balanced; should gain in complexity with age.

1997 Zinfandel, Late Picked, Paso Robles $NA.   89

Dark, saturated violet-red. Fantastic black fruit and chocolate aromas carry distinctive floral overtones. A firm entry leads a moderately full-bodied palate with velvety tannins. Big and rich with a sweetish edge, but balanced by solid acidity. Drink now.

1995 Zinfandel, Geyserville, Sonoma County $22.   92

Deep blackish ruby cast. Moderately full-bodied. Balanced acidity. Moderately extracted. Heavily oaked. Mildly tannic. Brown spices, sandalwood, black fruits. Quite aromatic, with a hefty overlay of spicy wood notes, and a firm core of ripe fruit flavors. Lush and generous through the lengthy finish.

1996 Zinfandel, Lytton Springs, Dry Creek Valley $25.   92

Deep blackish purple. Moderately full-bodied. Balanced acidity. Highly extracted. Moderately tannic. Black fruits, chocolate, pepper. Rather reserved aromatically, with a firm, focused palate feel. Elegant in the mouth, showing a seamless texture and a lean finish. Should reward mid-term (3–6 years) aging.

1995 Zinfandel, Pagani Ranch, Late Picked 100 Year Old Vines, Sonoma Valley $22.   91

Deep blackish purple. Full-bodied. Balanced acidity. Moderately extracted. Mildly oaked. Mildly tannic. Black pepper, briar fruits, licorice. Quite aromatic, with a rich, opulent texture. Extremely ripe and lush, with a weighty, flavorful mouthfeel. Carries a hint of Port throughout. Finishes with some mild astringency.

1996 Zinfandel, Sonoma Station, Sonoma County $18.   88

Bright blackish purple. Medium-bodied. Balanced acidity. Moderately extracted. Mildly oaked. Mildly tannic. Briar fruits, vanilla. Quite aromatic, with a lighter-styled, fruit-centered palate feel. Nicely textured, featuring solid grip through the lengthy, flavorful finish.

1997 Zinfandel, Sonoma Station, Sonoma County $NA.　　　**89**

Brilliant, saturated purple. Forward briar fruit and mineral aromas. A crisp entry leads a medium-bodied palate, with marked acidity and grainy tannins. Lots of fruit, with a great acidic cut. Drink now.

1995 Zinfandel, York Creek, Spring Mountain $22.　　　**88**

Bright blackish ruby hue. Moderately full-bodied. Balanced acidity. Highly extracted. Mildly oaked. Moderately tannic. Minerals, chocolate. Made in a reserved Claret style. Taut and firm in structure, with a minerally backbone. Finishes with mild astringency.

River Run

1996 Carignane, Wirz Vineyard, Cienega Valley $15.　　　**86**

Crimson hue with a pale, fading rim. Medium-bodied. Moderately extracted. Mildly tannic. Raspberry notes. Generous berry fruit aromas show a ripe, jammy character. Well gripped and lively on the palate with a fruit center. Supple tannins on the finish.

1997 Malbec, Mannstand Vineyard, Santa Clara County $18.　　　**82**

1996 Merlot, California $15.　　　**87**

Very deep purplish ruby hue. Moderately full-bodied. Full acidity. Highly extracted. Mildly oaked. Mildly tannic. Black fruits, plums, vanilla. Deep and brooding, with a rich, chewy texture. Attractive fruit flavors are highlighted by vibrant acidity. Clean through the finish, with velvety tannins.

Rochioli

1995 Chardonnay, Estate, Russian River Valley $25.　　　**93**

Medium straw hue. Clean citrus, mineral, and hazelnut aromas. A firm entry leads a medium-bodied palate showing crisp acids. A vibrant style with some grip and leesy complexity. Quite flavorful, with great balance. Opulent yet restrained. Meursault-like. Drink now or later.

1997 Sauvignon Blanc, Russian River Valley $16.　　　**86**

Pale straw cast. Medium-bodied. Balanced acidity. Moderately extracted. Apple, gooseberry. High-toned aromas. A hint of sweetness with high-toned tropical fruit flavors on the palate. Clean, simple, and juicy, showing some intriguing varietal character.

1995 Pinot Noir, Russian River Valley $34.99.　　　**89**

Medium red-purple. Medium-bodied. Moderately extracted. Moderately oaked. Mildly tannic. Floral and vanilla aromas. Bright vanilla-edged raspberry and cherry fruit flavors. Light, fine-grained tannins on the finish. Still a little tight.

1996 Pinot Noir, Russian River Valley $35.　　　**86**

Pale ruby cast. Medium-bodied. Full acidity. Moderately extracted. Mildly tannic. Minerals, red fruits, vanilla. Unusual aromas lead a brisk and angular palate feel. Lean but flavorful through the finish.

1997 Pinot Noir, Sonoma Valley $25.　　　**90**

Pale cherry red with a slight fade. Interesting dusty cherry and herb aromas carry a mild oak accent. A supple entry leads a medium-bodied palate, with velvety tannins. Well balanced and elegant, with crisp Pinot flavors. Light but elegant. Drink now.

Rocking Horse

1994 Cabernet Sauvignon, Garvey Family Vineyard, Rutherford $25.　　　**88**

Dark reddish purple. Medium-bodied. Moderately extracted. Moderately tannic. Black cherry, cassis, black tea, brown spice. Solid, chewy black Cabernet fruit flavors turn dry, with fine-grained tannins dominating the finish. Soundly structured.

1996 Zinfandel, Lamborn Vineyard, Howell Mountain $18.　　　**94**

Bright cherry red. Medium-bodied. Balanced acidity. Moderately extracted. Moderately tannic. Cherries, minerals, vanilla. Intense, pure, black cherry aromas follow through on the palate, with elegant, concentrated flavors. Tightly wound yet still very stylish. Cellar.

Roederer Estate

NV Brut, Anderson Valley $17.   89

Pale yellow-straw hue. Medium-bodied. Full acidity. Smoke, citrus, minerals. Aromas are smoky, yet they have a piercing citrus note. The aromas follow through on the palate, with concentrated flavors and bright acids. Fine-beaded, pinpoint bubbles are a standout. Sound structure and persistence indicate that this could gain more complexity in a year or two.

NV Brut Rose, Anderson Valley $21.   92

Pale copper hue with a pinkish overtone. Moderately full-bodied. Minerals, citrus, red fruits. Reserved and elegant, with classic flavors. Well-balanced carbonation adds a refreshing note and elegant mousse to the silky mouthfeel. Very stylish and refreshing, and drinking well now.

1992 L'Ermitage, Anderson Valley $35.   93

Brilliant yellow-gold. Medium-bodied. Full acidity. Smoke, ripe citrus. Profoundly complex, smoky aromas. Rich, round, and flavorsome, with fine-beaded bubbles and complex yeasty accents that persist through the finish. Very elegant and classic, showing the refinement of tête de cuvée Champagne.

Rombauer

1997 Chardonnay, Carneros $25.75.   87

Brilliant yellow-gold. Moderately full-bodied. Balanced acidity. Highly extracted. Moderately oaked. Vanilla, smoke, tropical fruit. Plenty of sweet tropical fruit and toasty oak flavors compete for attention right through the lengthy finish. Shows a concentrated character.

Rosenblum

1997 Chardonnay, Edna Valley $23.   86

Bright yellow-straw cast. Moderately full-bodied. Full acidity. Moderately extracted. Earth, citrus. Shows a slightly unusual earthy note on the nose. Crisp and linear in the mouth. Finishes with a vibrant wood-accented note.

1996 Semillon-Chardonnay, Livermore Valley $11.   86

Bright yellow-gold. Moderately light-bodied. Full acidity. Moderately extracted. Figs, dried herbs, lemons, minerals. Bright and vibrant, with a nice figgy twist through a racy and flavorsome finish.

1997 Viognier, Santa Barbara County $15.   91

Bright straw cast. Moderately full-bodied. Full acidity. Moderately extracted. Tropical fruits, oranges, flowers. Quite aromatic, with an extremely ripe and complex fruit-centered flavor profile. Vibrant acidity balances the weightiness of the wine through a fine and intense finish.

1995 Cabernet Sauvignon, Hendry Vineyard, Reserve, Napa Valley $40.   87

Deep blood-brick red. Moderately full-bodied. Highly extracted. Moderately oaked. Mildly tannic. Eucalyptus, black fruits, brown spice. Rich, minty aromas, with an earthy backnote that follows through on the palate. Lengthy, powdery tannins, yet a very flavorful finish.

1995 Holbrook Mitchell Trio, Napa Valley $35.   89

Bright violet-red. Medium-bodied. Moderately extracted. Mildly tannic. Licorice, minerals, cassis. Earthy notes on the nose come through on the palate, with good minerally grip, fine acids, and bright black fruit flavors.

1996 Holbrook Mitchell Trio, Napa Valley $35.   87

Bright red-purple. Medium-bodied. Moderately extracted. Moderately oaked. Mildly tannic. Cassis, licorice, oak spice. Warm, spicy aromas lead a bright, lively palate, with great balance evident. Oak accents play a substantial role.

Scale: Superlative (96-100), Exceptional (90-95), Highly Recommended (85-89), Recommended (80-84), Not Recommended (Under 80)

1995 Merlot, Lone Oak Vineyard, Russian River Valley $20.   **90**
Blackish ruby hue. Medium-bodied. Full acidity. Highly extracted. Moderately oaked.
Mildly tannic. Vanilla, black fruits, mint. Quite racy in style, with vibrant acidity that
makes the fruit flavors seem juicy. Features a well-integrated oak overlay and a clean,
snappy finish with some mild astringency. Fine length.

1997 Mourvedre, Chateau La Paws, Côte du Bone,
Contra Costa County $9.50.   **86**
Pale ruby red with a slight fade. Medium-bodied. Moderately extracted. Mildly tannic.
Raspberry, cola, vanilla. Soft, berryish, and fruit centered, with a supple lingering finish.
Very high drinkability factor.

NV Zinfandel, Vintners Cuvée XVI, California $9.50.   **85**
Deep ruby purple. Moderately full-bodied. Balanced acidity. Moderately extracted. Mildly
tannic. Red berries, minerals. Bright, fruit-centered aromatics lead a lighter-styled, lively
palate feel. Precocious and tasty, with good grip to the finish. Well balanced.

1996 Zinfandel, Contra Costa County $15.   **82**

1996 Zinfandel, Annette's Reserve, Rhodes Vineyard, Redwood Valley $20. **95**
Deep reddish purple. Medium-bodied. Highly extracted. Moderately oaked. Mildly
tannic. Coffee, chocolate, raspberries. Exotically ripe, expressive aromas follow through
well on the explosively fruity palate. A fine dusting of tannins gives this some needed grip
through the finish. Exciting.

1996 Zinfandel, Ballentine Vineyard, Napa Valley $19.   **83**
Bright cherry purple. Medium-bodied. Balanced acidity. Moderately extracted. Mildly
oaked. Mildly tannic. Briar fruits, vanilla. Juicy, supple sweet fruit flavors. This is a softer
style with low acids.

1996 Zinfandel, Continente Vineyard, Old Old Vine,
Contra Costa County $20.   **86**
Deep blackish ruby cast. Full-bodied. Balanced acidity. Moderately extracted. Moderately
oaked. Mildly tannic. Black fruits, brown spices, chocolate. Quite aromatic, with a spicy
oak overlay and a lush palate feel featuring solid fruit concentration. Rich and ripe
through the finish.

1996 Zinfandel, Harris Kratka Vineyard, Alexander Valley $22.   **91**
Deep blackish ruby cast. Full-bodied. Balanced acidity. Moderately extracted. Heavily
oaked. Mildly tannic. Chocolate, black fruits. Quite aromatic, with a big, lush, chocolatey
character in the mouth. Smooth and supple, with a thick, velvety texture. Intense
and enticing.

1996 Zinfandel, Reserve, Hendry Vineyard, Napa Valley $22.   **88**
Bright cherry red. Medium-bodied. Balanced acidity. Moderately extracted. Mildly oaked.
Mildly tannic. Plums, berry fruits, chocolate. The smooth, rich, textured mouthfeel shows
plenty of hedonistic fruit flavors and vanilla oak nuances.

1996 Zinfandel, Richard Sauret Vineyard, Paso Robles $17.   **90**
Bright blackish purple. Moderately full-bodied. Balanced acidity. Moderately extracted.
Mildly oaked. Mildly tannic. Chocolate, black fruits. Intensely aromatic, with a supple
and deeply flavored mouthfeel. Well balanced and seductive through the finish.

1996 Zinfandel, Rockpile Vineyard, Dry Creek Valley $22.   **91**
Dark ruby purple to the rim. Moderately full-bodied. Full acidity. Moderately extracted.
Mildly oaked. Mildly tannic. Briar fruits, vanilla. Quite aromatic, with a solid interplay
between oak and fruit flavors. Lush and rich in the mouth, with buoyant acidity that
keeps everything lively through the finish. Well balanced and intense.

1996 Zinfandel, Samsel Vineyard, Maggie's Reserve, Sonoma Valley $28.   **95**
Bright ruby purple. Moderately full-bodied. Full acidity. Moderately extracted. Mildly
oaked. Mildly tannic. Briar fruits. Quite aromatic, with a big, fruit-centered flavor profile.
Lush and rich in the mouth, yet with the requisite acidity to keep things lively. Quite
pure, finishing with excellent grip.

1996 Zinfandel, White Cottage Vineyard, Howell Mountain $21.   **95**

Dark cherry red. Medium-bodied. Balanced acidity. Moderately extracted. Moderately tannic. Plums, black fruits. A deep, fleshy, fruit-centered style with an underlying concentration of flavors backed by some fine tannins. Very ripe, almost soft, this is currently drinking well. May not have the stuffing to cellar extensively. Hedonistic.

1994 Zinfandel, Late Harvest, Sonoma County $15/375 ml.   **89**

Opaque blackish ruby hue. Moderately full-bodied. Balanced acidity. Moderately extracted. Mildly oaked. Mildly tannic. Chocolate, black fruits. Quite aromatic, with a fruit-centered, Portlike mouthfeel. Rich and dense through the finish. Quite flavorful; made for chocolate.

1994 Port, California $10/375 ml.   **82**

1991 Late Harvest Sauvignon Blanc, Concento d'Oro,
Napa Valley $15/375 ml.   **81**

Stephen Ross

1997 Chardonnay, Edna Ranch, Edna Valley $18.50.   **88**

Deep straw hue. Reserved mineral, wool, and citrus aromas. A lean entry leads a medium-bodied palate with angular acidity. Firm, phenolic finish. Drink now.

1997 Chardonnay, Bien Nacido Vineyard, Santa Maria Valley $20.   **90**

Bright yellow-straw hue. Restrained and stylish yeast, toast, and mineral aromas. A firm entry is followed by a medium-bodied palate with crisp acidity and a ripe, persistent finish. Exceptionally well balanced. Drink now.

1996 Pinot Noir, La Colline Vineyard, Arroyo Grande Valley $20.   **86**

Pale cherry red with subtle purple highlights. Medium-bodied. Moderately extracted. Moderately oaked. Mildly tannic. Crisp and well-defined red cherry and berry flavors have an herbal, minerally theme through the finish. Very bright.

1996 Pinot Noir, Edna Ranch, Edna Valley $22.   **86**

Reddish purple with a bright rim. Medium-bodied. Moderately extracted. Moderately tannic. Crisp candied cherry flavors up front turn very dry and minerally through the finish. Tight, fine-grained tannins make this tough at present, though the structure is impressive.

1996 Pinot Noir, Bien Nacido Vineyard, Santa Maria Valley $24.   **87**

Bright purple. Medium-bodied. Moderately extracted. Moderately oaked. Mildly tannic. Clean, smooth, and juicy, with sweet cherry flavors through the finish highlighted by herbal notes and mild citrus acidity. Tannins are very soft, with subtle oak accents.

Round Hill

1997 Chardonnay, California $8.   **84**

Pale green-gold. Medium-bodied. Full acidity. Moderately extracted. Tart citrus, flowers. Tart yet floral aromas lead a vibrant, angular palate with straightforward flavors that finish quickly.

1995 Cabernet Sauvignon, California $9.   **80**

1992 Cabernet Sauvignon, 20th Anniversary Release, Napa Valley $24.   **84**

Deep ruby-violet hue. Medium-bodied. Moderately extracted. Moderately tannic. Minerals, anise, earth. Lean, dry aromas lead a tough, dry mouthful of flavors, with green tannins making for a dry finish.

1996 Merlot, California $8.   **81**

J. Runquist

1995 Zinfandel, Z, Massoni Ranch, Amador County $18.   **81**

Scale: Superlative (96-100), Exceptional (90-95), Highly Recommended (85-89), Recommended (80-84), Not Recommended (Under 80)

Rust Ridge

1995 Cabernet Sauvignon, Napa Valley $24.   **89**

Deep brick red. Medium-bodied. Moderately extracted. Moderately tannic. Licorice, black fruits, cherries. Ripe, earthy, developed aromas indicate a harmony that follows through on the palate. Broad, softer flavors come together well. Finishes with good grip. Excellent for current drinking.

1996 Zinfandel, Napa Valley $18.   **86**

Bright cherry red. Medium-bodied. Balanced acidity. Moderately extracted. Moderately oaked. Mildly tannic. Vanilla, cherries, raspberries. Attractive vanilla and berry aromas follow through on a balanced palate, showing stylish winemaking. Very drinkable, succulent, and lush.

Rutherford Grove

1995 Merlot, Napa Valley $9.99.   **80**

Rutherford Hill

1995 Merlot, Reserve, Napa Valley $40.   **90**

Deep opaque ruby to the rim with a slight purplish cast. Moderately full-bodied. Balanced acidity. Highly extracted. Heavily oaked. Moderately tannic. Brown spices, mint, red fruits. Oak-driven aromatics lead a well-integrated, finely wrought mouthfeel with a deep core of fruit flavors. Well balanced and nicely crafted, with chewy tannins and a lengthy finish buoyed by juicy acidity.

1996 Merlot, Reserve, Napa Valley $44.   **94**

Saturated bright ruby red with violet highlights. Fabulously fruity aromas. Full-bodied and rich on the attack with lush fruit flavors and velvety tannins that are well integrated and carry through the lengthy finish. A rich and hedonistic style. Drink now or later. Can improve with more age.

1995 Sangiovese, 21st Anniversary, Napa Valley $30.   **91**

Ruby red. Medium-bodied. Full acidity. Moderately extracted. Moderately oaked. Mildly tannic. Mint, vanilla, tart cherries. Bright and lively, with juicy acids and bright flavors underscored by minerally austerity and dried red fruit flavors. Very tasty.

Rutherford Ranch

1997 Chardonnay, Napa Valley $10.   **81**

1993 Cabernet Sauvignon, Napa Valley $12.   **89**

Medium brick-cherry color. Medium-bodied. Moderately extracted. Mildly tannic. Red fruits, toasted oak, minerals. Subtle toasty nose. Juicy red fruit flavors on the palate linger on the finish. Good balance for early drinking, but not for extended keeping.

1995 Cabernet Sauvignon, Napa Valley $12.   **80**

1995 Merlot, Napa Valley $13.   **80**

Rutherford Vintners

1997 Chardonnay, Stanislaus County $8.99.   **85**

Pale straw hue. Faint melony aromas. A clean entry leads a medium-bodied palate with peach and apple flavors that linger on the medium-length finish. No oak influence. Drink now.

1995 Fumé Blanc, Barrel Select, North Coast $8.99.   **86**

Very deep golden hue. Moderately full-bodied. Full acidity. Moderately extracted. Mildly oaked. Brown spice, menthol, lime, lemons. Minty aromas and toasty oak spice make a strong impression, with a bright center of zesty fruit flavors filling the palate. Well structured, with good grip.

1997 White Zinfandel, Lodi $5.99.   **84**

Saturated raspberry pink. Generous talc and berry aromas. A lush entry leads a medium-bodied palate that has good flavor intensity. Decent acid-sugar balance through the finish. Drink now.

1996 Cabernet Sauvignon, Lodi $8.99. **84**

Ruby hue with a pale violet rim. Moderately light-bodied. Moderately extracted. Mildly tannic. Black fruits, flowers. Aromas of dark Cabernet fruit with floral accents. Juicy, straightforward, and light in style.

1997 Merlot, Stanislaus County $8.99. **84**

Light violet hue. Light fruit-scented, floral aromas are quite fragrant. A juicy attack reveals a lighter-bodied palate with crisp acidity and a clean finish. Drink now.

1997 Shiraz, Stanislaus County $8.99. **83**

Dark ruby color, with a fading rim. Cherry and vanilla flavors. Medium-bodied. Tart aromas lead crisp fruit flavors through a drying finish. Drink now.

1996 Zinfandel, Lodi $8.99. **84**

Bright red-purple. Medium-bodied. Balanced acidity. Moderately extracted. Mildly tannic. Red berries. Superripe, fleshy berry aromas follow through on the palate. Generous and round, with soft tannins. Easy drinking.

Rutz

1996 Chardonnay, Russian River Valley $20. **81**

1996 Chardonnay, Dutton Ranch, Russian River Valley $30. **85**

Bright yellow-gold. Moderately full-bodied. Full acidity. Apples, vanilla, spice. Vibrant and intense, this has a tight core of bright Chardonnay flavors and a weighty mouthfeel that features oak spice on the finish. It should be better in a year.

1996 Pinot Noir, Sleepy Hollow Vineyard, Monterey $30. **81**

Saddleback

1997 Pinot Blanc, Napa Valley $13.50. **86**

Deep straw cast. Medium-bodied. Full acidity. Highly extracted. Mildly oaked. Butter, minerals, tropical fruits. Quite buttery aromas and flavors, with a lean and angular palate feel that still conveys a sense of ripeness. Good lengthy finish.

1996 Cabernet Sauvignon, Napa Valley $32. **87**

Saturated dark ruby hue. Dark fruit aromas with earth and anise. A flavorful entry leads a medium to moderately full-bodied palate with rich black cherry and wood flavors. Tannins are well balanced and moderately supple through the finish. Drink now.

Saintsbury

1996 Chardonnay, Reserve, Carneros $28. **84**

Brilliant yellow-gold. Moderately full-bodied. Balanced acidity. Moderately extracted. Moderately oaked. Smoke, green apples. The toasty, smoky nose shows a crisp fruity accent that comes through on the palate with a decidedly crisp mouthfeel.

1995 Pinot Noir, Reserve, Carneros $28. **91**

Dark cherry red. Medium-bodied. Highly extracted. Moderately oaked. Moderately tannic. Black cherry and bramble fruit aromas lead a mouthful of dark fruit flavors, with an earthy licorice note through the finish. Plenty of flavors and structure here.

1996 Pinot Noir, Reserve, Carneros $34. **86**

Dark violet red with a lightening rim. Medium-bodied. Moderately extracted. Moderately oaked. Moderately tannic. Raspberries, oak spice, minerals. Perfumed sweet aromas show an oaky note. Full-flavored and fruity on the palate, with a firm, lingering spicy finish. Flavorful and varietally faithful.

Salmon Creek

1996 Chardonnay, Los Carneros, Sonoma County $16. **86**

Bright yellow-gold. Generous aromas of oak and crisp citrus fruits. A bright attack leads a moderately full-bodied palate with zesty flavors and oak spice. Finishes with a note of dryness. Drink now.

San Saba

1997 Chardonnay, Monterey $20.　　　　93

Dark golden cast. Moderately full-bodied. Balanced acidity. Highly extracted. Moderately oaked. Butterscotch, vanilla, ripe citrus. Features a rich, viscous, buttery texture and a strong sensation of yeast and vanilla oak flavors. Decadent, though a softer style.

1994 Cabernet Sauvignon, Monterey $17.　　　　85

Deep garnet red. Medium-bodied. Moderately extracted. Mildly tannic. Bell pepper, stems, red berries. Very distinctively herbal nose leads a soft, rounded mouthfeel with berry flavors that give way to an herbal finish.

1995 Merlot, Monterey $20.　　　　81

Sanford

1997 Chardonnay, Santa Barbara County $18.　　　　85

Pale straw hue. Muted aromas. Rather heavy on the medium-bodied palate with soft acids accentuating the warm finish.

1995 Pinot Noir, Santa Barbara County $20.　　　　90

Rich ruby red. Medium-bodied. Moderately extracted. Moderately oaked. Mildly tannic. Meaty, leathery, dusty cherry aromas lead a smooth, rounded palate. Shows a delightful balance and full Pinot Noir fruit character. Lovely finish with lingering cinnamon notes.

Santa Barbara Winery

1996 Chardonnay, Reserve, Santa Ynez Valley $24.　　　　90

Bright yellow-straw cast. Moderately full-bodied. Balanced acidity. Moderately extracted. Tropical fruits, cream, citrus. Generous aromas feature a rich fruity quality. Opulent and textured in the mouth, with a lengthy, complex finish. Generous and elegant.

Santa Rita Creek

1995 Pinot Noir, Paso Robles $14.50.　　　　85

Pale cherry red with a purple cast. Moderately light-bodied. Moderately extracted. Moderately oaked. Mildly tannic. Crisp, faintly candied cherry flavors lead a very balanced palate, with bright cherry and berry flavors and plenty of vanilla oak through the cleanly astringent finish.

Santino

1997 Harvest White Zinfandel, Shenandoah Valley $4.95.　　　　81

1996 Satyricon, California $11.95.　　　　84

Bright garnet red with a slight fade. Attractive, generous leather, herb, and mineral aromas. A supple attack leads a medium-bodied palate, with drying, mildly astringent tannins. The finish is lean and angular. Rather edgy. Drink now.

1995 Zinfandel, California $10.　　　　84

Deep blackish ruby hue. Full-bodied. Full acidity. Highly extracted. Mildly oaked. Mildly tannic. Brown spices, chocolate. Oak overtones are readily apparent on the nose, and play out on the palate. Thick and chunky, with a drying, dusty finish. A tad rustic.

1996 Muscato del Diavolo, Amador County $9.95/500 ml.　　　　80

V. Sattui

1997 Chardonnay, Napa Valley $16.75.　　　　83

Pale green-straw hue. Subdued yeasty aromas. Clean on the attack, leading a moderately full-bodied palate with a glycerous mouthfeel and short flavors. Drink now.

1997 Chardonnay, Carsi Vineyard, Napa Valley $18.　　　　86

Green-gold. Rich tropical aromas with a toasted coconut note. The attack is rich, leading a full-bodied palate and a glycerous mouthfeel. Flavors of juicy apples and smoky oak persist through the finish. Very elegant and refined.

1997 Chardonnay, Carsi Vineyard, Old Vine, Napa Valley $19.75.   **83**

Full yellow-gold. Ripe aromas of melon, apple, and smoky yeast with obvious wood influence. A rich attack leads a rather thick, full-bodied palate with a glycerous mouthfeel and tropical generosity through the finish. Drink now.

1998 Gewürztraminer, Sonoma County $11.25.   **83**

Bright straw hue. Intense spice and banana aromas jump from the glass. A racy entry leads a medium-bodied palate, with mild sweetness offset by crisp acidity. Refreshing finish. A quaffer. Drink now.

1998 Dry Johannisberg Riesling, Napa Valley $11.25.   **86**

Medium golden hue. Very classic aromas of petrol with herbal, minerally nuances. A soft entry leads a medium-bodied palate, with a rounded mouthfeel and impressive, deep petrol flavors. A streak of acid comes through on the finish. Very stylish. Drink now or later.

1998 Off-Dry Johannisberg Riesling, Napa Valley $11.25.   **83**

Medium gold hue. Very aromatic with a whiff of petrol and some tropical character. A sweet, tropical attack leads a medium-bodied palate, with glycerous richness and off-dry sweetness through the finish. Drink now.

1996 Sauvignon Blanc, Suzanne's Vineyard, Napa Valley $11.25.   **82**

1997 White Zinfandel, California $7.75.   **82**

1997 Gamay Rouge, California $13.75.   **80**

1995 Cabernet Sauvignon, Napa Valley $17.50.   **83**

Saturated ruby purple. Moderately full-bodied. Highly extracted. Quite tannic. Earth, anise. Lean, tough aromas. Tough and heavily wrought tannins give this a formidable structure that is hard to penetrate.

1994 Cabernet Sauvignon, Morisoli Vineyard, Napa Valley $25.   **86**

Opaque dark purple. Medium-bodied. Highly extracted. Mildly tannic. Black plums, brown spice, minerals. Crisp, juicy black fruit flavors seem tight and high toned. Some dry tannins and vigorous acids are restraining this at present.

1995 Cabernet Sauvignon, Morisoli Vineyard, Napa Valley $25.   **89**

Bright ruby purple. Moderately full-bodied. Balanced acidity. Highly extracted. Mildly oaked. Quite tannic. Minerals, black fruits. Aromatically reserved, with a dense and brooding palate feel. Firm, chunky tannins make for a tough and unyielding impression in the mouth. Perhaps it will open after some cellar time.

1994 Cabernet Sauvignon, Preston Vineyard, Napa Valley $30.   **85**

Deep purple. Medium-bodied. Highly extracted. Moderately tannic. Blackberries, plums, brown spice, minerals. Bright, compact red fruit flavors are kept in check by aggressive acids and dry tannins. This is not showing at its best right now, but seems to have all the structural elements to develop with cellaring.

1995 Cabernet Sauvignon, Preston Vineyard, Napa Valley $27.   **89**

Brilliant violet hue. Moderately full-bodied. Balanced acidity. Highly extracted. Mildly oaked. Moderately tannic. Briar fruits, vanilla, minerals. Reined-in aromatics lead a firm and intense palate feel. Fruit centered, with a very sturdy structure. Needs time.

1994 Cabernet Sauvignon, Rosenbrand Family Reserve, Napa Valley $60.   **91**

Brilliant violet cast. Full-bodied. Balanced acidity. Highly extracted. Mildly oaked. Moderately tannic. Flowers, minerals, spice. Intense and unusual aromatics lend a sense of complexity throughout. Generous and supple on the entry, with firm tannins rearing up on the finish. Needs time to mellow; all the components of a long-term (7–10 years) cellar candidate are present.

1994 Cabernet Sauvignon, Suzanne's Vineyard, Napa Valley $20.   **85**

Dark purple. Medium-bodied. Highly extracted. Moderately tannic. Cherries, cassis, minerals, toasted oak. Vibrant toasty aromas show strong oak accents that are confirmed on the bright, juicy, fruity palate. Young and lively, with fine acids and a minerally edge.

1995 Cabernet Sauvignon, Suzanne's Vineyard, Napa Valley $22.50.   **88**

Saturated dark red-purple. Moderately full-bodied. Highly extracted. Quite tannic. Earth, spice, black fruits. Dense and dry, with chunky tannins drying the finish. A powerful style that will need time to resolve its tannins.

1995 Zinfandel, Howell Mountain, Napa Valley $18.   **89**

Opaque center with purple highlights. Medium-bodied. Balanced acidity. Highly extracted. Moderately oaked. Quite tannic. Toasted coconut, black fruits, minerals. An attractive toasty nose leads a solid, tight, minerally palate showing dry, fine-grained tannins. Solidly structured.

1995 Zinfandel, Suzanne's Vineyard, Napa Valley $16.75.   **86**

Blood red. Medium-bodied. Balanced acidity. Moderately extracted. Moderately oaked. Moderately tannic. Red fruits, chocolate, brown spice. Rich and fleshy, with an expansive midpalate and some angular tannins.

1997 Muscat, California $12.   **85**

Brilliant yellow-straw hue. Reserved orange blossom and lacquer aromas. A vibrant entry leads a medium-bodied palate that has crisp acids and moderate sweetness. The finish is clean, flavorful, and refreshing. Drink now.

Saucelito Canyon

1996 Zinfandel, Arroyo Grande Valley $19.   **86**

Opaque red-purple. Moderately full-bodied. Balanced acidity. Highly extracted. Moderately oaked. Moderately tannic. Red fruits. Intensely fleshy red berry aromas. Solid, rather tight palate has plenty of stuffing and a glycerous mouthfeel. Finish has a mildly bitter note.

Savannah-Chanel

1997 Chardonnay, Santa Cruz Mountains $20.   **86**

Bright yellow-straw hue. Moderately full-bodied. Balanced acidity. Highly extracted. Apples, smoke, spice. Markedly floral, oak-spiced aromas follow through on the deeply flavored palate. Finishes with a lingering sense of tartness and spice.

1996 Cabernet Franc, Santa Cruz Mountains $26.   **83**

Bright ruby cast. Medium-bodied. Balanced acidity. Moderately extracted. Mildly oaked. Mildly tannic. Spice, minerals, red fruits. A spicy oak nuance in the nose leads a lighter-styled, angular palate feel. Taut and flavorful through the finish.

1995 Cabernet Franc, Library Selection, Santa Cruz Mountains $35.   **80**

Schramsberg

1994 Blanc de Blancs, Napa Valley $26.   **92**

Bright straw cast. Full-bodied. Full acidity. Minerals, citrus zest. Bright citrus zest and doughy aromas. Firm, concentrated, and lively on the palate. This wine shows a degree of intensity through the finish that bodes well for its cellar life.

1992 Blanc de Noirs, Napa Valley $27.   **91**

Bright pale gold. Full-bodied. Butter, yeast, toast. Developed, toasty, rich aromas lead a rich and ripe mouthfeel. Shows excellent weight and concentration, with fine length and intensity. Complex and attractive now, with a fine, frothy mousse.

1992 J.Schram, Napa Valley $65.   **91**

Full yellow-straw hue. Moderately full-bodied. Smoke, roasted coffee, tropical fruit. Rich, rounded, and leesy, with evident smoky maturity. Very generous and textured, and drinking very well now. This shows outstanding yeast complexity and a finely beaded mousse.

Schuetz Oles

1996 Zinfandel, Napa Valley $12. **84**

Deep blackish ruby cast. Moderately full-bodied. Balanced acidity. Highly extracted. Moderately oaked. Moderately tannic. Tea, brown spices, minerals. Complex aromatics, with a firm, austere palate feel. Astringent tannins clamp down on the finish, but the flavor keeps going. Needs a bit of time.

1996 Zinfandel, Korte Ranch, Napa Valley $18. **88**

Deep blackish ruby hue. Moderately full-bodied. Full acidity. Moderately extracted. Mildly oaked. Mildly tannic. Briar fruits, spice. Pleasantly aromatic, with a firm, flavorful, well-structured palate feel. Angular and clean through the finish.

Schug

1997 Chardonnay, Carneros $18. **86**

Pale yellow-straw color. Moderately full-bodied. Balanced acidity. Moderately extracted. Melon, apple. Clean, ripe Chardonnay aromas lead a mouthful of juicy flavors, with a very light touch of oak. Clean and crisp.

1996 Chardonnay, Heritage Reserve, Carneros $25. **86**

Yellow-straw hue. Medium-bodied. Balanced acidity. Moderately extracted. Moderately oaked. Brown spice, ripe apples, smoke. Decidedly yeasty, smoky aromas strike a pungent note. Flavorful and rounded on the palate, with a brown spice note on the finish.

1995 Cabernet Sauvignon, North Coast $18. **81**

1996 Cabernet Sauvignon, North Coast $18. **82**

1995 Cabernet Sauvignon, Heritage Reserve, Sonoma Valley $40. **89**

Bright red with a lightening purple rim. Moderately full-bodied. Highly extracted. Heavily oaked. Moderately tannic. Dill, spice, black fruits. Powerful oak spice aromas dominate, showing through on the palate along with crisp cassis fruit flavors.

1996 Merlot, North Coast $18. **83**

Bright ruby red to the rim. Lean mineral and red fruit aromas. A crisp entry leads to a medium-bodied palate with tannic grip, followed by an angular finish. Tasty, but it lacks a little stuffing. Drink now.

1996 Merlot, Heritage Reserve, Carneros $30. **84**

Bright ruby red with a subtle fade. Vibrant red berry and herb aromas carry a marked cedary oak accent. A lively attack leads a moderately full-bodied palate with firm tannins. The finish is clean and lightly tannic. Drink now.

1996 Pinot Noir, Carneros $18. **82**

1995 Pinot Noir, Heritage Reserve, Carneros $30. **89**

Medium cherry red with a pale rim. Medium-bodied. Moderately extracted. Moderately oaked. Mildly tannic. Cherry fruit aromas with spicy accents. Assertive and crisp, with bright acids and well-defined fruit flavors. Amazingly persistent on the finish, with concentrated red fruit flavors lingering.

Sea Ridge Coastal

1997 Chardonnay, California $9.99. **84**

Deep yellow-straw hue. Big brown spice and mineral aromas. A full attack leads a moderately full-bodied palate with rounded acidity. Generous, flavorful finish. Drink now.

1995 Cabernet Sauvignon, California $10. **86**

Saturated purple-red hue. Vibrant fruity, cassis aromas with judicious vanilla oak notes. A crisp entry leads to a moderately full-bodied palate with bright fruit-centered character and grainy, gripping tannins. Well structured and varietally expressive.

1996 Pinot Noir, California $10. **81**

Scale: Superlative (96-100), Exceptional (90-95), Highly Recommended (85-89), Recommended (80-84), Not Recommended (Under 80)

184

1996 Shiraz, California $10.   84

Pale red, transparent, with a fading rim. Mild, soundly baked red fruit, vanilla, and cherry flavors. Hint of wood tones. Soft entry. Moderately light-bodied. A lighter style, very quaffable. Drink now.

1996 Zinfandel, California $10.   81

Seavey

1993 Cabernet Sauvignon, Napa Valley $28.   90

Dark crimson-ruby appearance. Medium-bodied. Highly extracted. Moderately tannic. Cooked black fruits, meat, allspice. Full, rich fruity aromas have a savory, meaty accent. Ripe black fruit flavors unfold on the palate, with some dry dusty tannins on the finish.

Seghesio

1996 Zinfandel, Sonoma County $11.   84

Deep blackish purple. Moderately full-bodied. Low acidity. Highly extracted. Mildly oaked. Moderately tannic. Minerals, black fruits, pepper. Rather reserved aromatically, with a lean, firm palate feel. Deeply flavored, with a minerally, austere finish.

Sequoia Grove

1997 Chardonnay, Carneros, Napa Valley $16.99.   81

1995 Cabernet Sauvignon, Napa Valley $22.99.   86

Bright ruby with a slight fade. Generous, high-toned anise, mineral, and red fruit aromas. A crisp entry leads to a supple, medium-bodied palate with grippy tannins and zesty acidity. Vibrant finish. Somewhat lighter in style, but well balanced. Drink now.

1995 Cabernet Sauvignon, Reserve, Napa Valley $35.   89

Deep ruby purple. Moderately full-bodied. Balanced acidity. Moderately extracted. Moderately oaked. Moderately tannic. Brown spices, red fruits. Pleasantly aromatic, with a supple entry quickly backed up by firm tannins. The flavorful finish has grip. Approachable, but needs time.

Sequoia Ridge

1996 Chardonnay, California $8.99.   83

Yellow-straw hue. Medium-bodied. Balanced acidity. Moderately extracted. Vanilla, yeast, sweet lemon. Floral aromas lead a juicy, soft mouthful of flavors, with nice persistence of sweet lemon flavors.

Seven Peaks

1997 Chardonnay, Reserve, Edna Valley $16.   90

Brilliant yellow-straw hue. Zesty vanilla, mineral, and citrus aromas. A lean entry is followed by a medium-bodied palate with angular acidity. The finish is creamy and complex. Drink now.

1996 Cabernet Sauvignon, Central Coast $11.   88

Saturated violet-purple hue. Very rich aromas show a ripe cassis and toasted oak accent. A rich entry leads a full-bodied palate with fleshy flavors with significant new oak character. Very youthful and structured, with dry gripping tannins clamping on the finish. Drink now or later.

1996 Shiraz, Paso Robles $16.   86

Dark ruby color, limpid to the rim. Generous, pleasant tart black fruit, plum, and vanilla flavors. Subtle wood tones. Firm entry. Moderately full-bodied with crisp acidity. Plentiful drying tannins. Solid, angular, and fruity. Lingering dry finish. Drinkable now, but can improve with age.

Shafer

1996 Chardonnay, Red Shoulder Ranch, Carneros, Napa Valley $30.   **93**
Yellow-straw color. Moderately full-bodied. Full acidity. Moderately extracted. Lime, citrus, oak spice. Vibrant, lively, and structured, with impressive concentration and a lingering persistence of citric acids. This should develop more complexity with further bottle age.

1997 Chardonnay, Red Shoulder Ranch, Carneros, Napa Valley $35.   **94**
Brilliant yellow-straw color. Richly aromatic with butter, yeast, and green apple. A rich entry leads a moderately full-bodied palate with a generous oak accent and rich finish showing leesy complexity. The mouthfeel is particularly fine. Drink now or later.

1994 Cabernet Sauvignon, Stags Leap District, Napa Valley $28.   **90**
Opaque bright reddish purple. Medium-bodied. Highly extracted. Moderately tannic. Crisp berries, minerals, brown spice. Assertive, bright fruity aromas. Concentrated and tightly wound flavors on the palate show fruity depth. Plenty of high-toned Cabernet fruit flavors here that will soften with some time in bottle.

1995 Cabernet Sauvignon, Stags Leap District, Napa Valley $30.   **93**
Saturated dark red with violet highlights. Moderately full-bodied. Highly extracted. Moderately tannic. Tobacco, cedar, cassis. Rich, smooth, and supple, with textured, layered tannins and a fruity middle. Elegant, yet weighty.

1996 Cabernet Sauvignon, Stags Leap District, Napa Valley $35.   **89**
Bright violet-purple hue. Ripe cherry aromas with subtle charred accents. A soft entry leads to a moderately full-bodied palate with rich cherry fruit flavors and plush tannins that could use a touch more acidity to keep them in check. Drink now or later.

• *1993 Cabernet Sauvignon, Hillside Select, Stags Leap District, Napa Valley $60.*   **93**
Deep opaque purple. Medium-bodied. Highly extracted. Moderately tannic. Red cherries, cocoa, cedar. Angular and minerally, with some solid tannins contrasting with the crisp red fruit flavors. Shows some structure and depth. This will resolve itself more harmoniously with time.

1994 Cabernet Sauvignon, Hillside Select, Stags Leap District, Napa Valley $85.   **95**
Saturated dark violet-red. Moderately full-bodied. Highly extracted. Moderately oaked. Moderately tannic. Tobacco, black cherries, minerals. Fantastically rich aromas lead a seamlessly smooth mouthful that remains structured yet harmonious through a long, cedary finish. Exotic and very drinkable now, yet will be better in a few years.

1995 Firebreak, Napa Valley $27.   **87**
Deep blackish ruby cast. Moderately full-bodied. Balanced acidity. Moderately extracted. Moderately oaked. Mildly tannic. Black fruits, minerals, spice. Pleasantly aromatic, with a gentle oak overlay and a core of dark fruit flavors. Full and firm on the palate, with an angular quality and lush tannins. Modern in style and well crafted.

1995 Merlot, Napa Valley $28.   **89**
Very deep ruby hue with a slight purplish cast. Medium-bodied. Balanced acidity. Moderately extracted. Moderately oaked. Mildly tannic. Black fruits, cedar, earth. Pleasantly aromatic, with a lighter-styled palate feel that is very well balanced. Quite vibrant through the bright, flavorful finish.

1996 Merlot, Napa Valley $32.   **89**
Well-saturated violet hue. Ripe plum, earth, and tobacco aromas. Moderately full-bodied with a rich, lush attack and velvety, abundant tannins through the finish. Drink now.

Shale Ridge

1997 Chardonnay, Monterey $9.99.   **86**
Pale yellow-straw hue. Apple and pear aromas show no wood influence. A soft entry leads a medium-bodied palate with juicy fruit flavors that linger briefly through the finish. Very easy drinking and versatile. Drink now.

Scale: Superlative (96-100), Exceptional (90-95), Highly Recommended (85-89), Recommended (80-84), Not Recommended (Under 80)

1997 Cabernet Sauvignon, Monterey County $9.99.   **83**

Saturated ruby-purple hue. Aromatically reserved with ripe, jammy notes. A firm entry leads a moderately full-bodied palate with tough, firm tannins that coat the mouth. Rather jammy and structured. Drink now or later.

1997 Merlot, Monterey $9.99.   **83**

Violet-ruby hue with a subtle fade. Unusual aromas of herbs and black fruits. A supple attack, with a moderately full-bodied palate that remains supple despite the chewy tannins. Drink now.

Charles Shaw

1997 Chardonnay, California $8.99.   **85**

Old gold hue. Muted mineral and spice aromas. A lean entry is followed by a medium-bodied palate with angular acidity, and a clean finish. Not overly flavorful, but well structured. Drink now.

1996 Cabernet Sauvignon, California $8.99.   **86**

Bright crimson hue. Herbs and black fruit aromas with mild oak accents. A crisp attack leads to a medium-bodied palate with fine grained grippy tannins through the finish. Drink now.

1997 Merlot, California $8.99.   **88**

Full violet red. Cherry fruit aromas lead a bright, crisp, moderately light-bodied palate with powdery tannins dominating the finish. Good structure and grip, with generous fruit flavors.

1996 Pinot Noir, California $8.99.   **84**

Cherry red with violet highlights. Medium-bodied. Moderately extracted. Mildly tannic. Red fruits, vanilla. Berryish, oak-accented aromas follow through on the palate, with tart fruit flavors and mild astringency lingering on the finish.

1996 Shiraz, California $8.99.   **83**

Medium crimson red, limpid, with a slight fade. Subtle, pleasant cherry, vanilla, and mineral flavors. Hint of wood tones. Soft entry, moderately light-bodied. Mild drying tannins. Subtle, short finish. Jammy and mildly oak spiced. A lighter style. Drink now.

Shenandoah Vineyards

1996 Cabernet Sauvignon, Amador County $11.95.   **86**

Deep ruby-red hue to the rim. Generous brown spice, licorice, and black fruit aromas show a hefty oak accent. A firm entry leads to a moderately full-bodied mouthfeel with big grippy tannins and shy acidity. Big, tannic finish. A flashy style, but without the acidity to age well for the long term. Drink within five years.

1996 Sangiovese, Amador County $12.   **81**

1996 Zinfandel, Special Reserve, Amador County $9.   **84**

Deep blackish ruby cast. Moderately full-bodied. Balanced acidity. Moderately extracted. Mildly oaked. Mildly tannic. Chocolate, black fruits. Pleasantly aromatic, with a core of deep fruit flavors and toasty oak overtones. Thick and rich in the mouth, with a generous, chunky finish.

1996 Zinfandel, Vintners Selection, Shenandoah Valley $15.   **86**

Bright blackish ruby cast. Moderately full-bodied. Balanced acidity. Highly extracted. Heavily oaked. Moderately tannic. Vanilla, red fruits. Quite aromatic, with a hefty wood component and a sturdy core of red fruit flavors. Firm and well structured on the palate, with a lengthy, flavorful, tannic finish.

Siduri

1997 Pinot Noir, Van Der Kamp Vineyards, Old Vines, Sonoma Mountain $40.   **81**

Sierra Vista

1994 Cabernet Sauvignon, Five Star Reserve, El Dorado $24.　　　**90**

Saturated blackish red with purple highlights. Moderately full-bodied. Highly extracted. Moderately tannic. Chocolate, toasted oak, black fruits. Big toasty oak nose reveals a concentrated dry palate with fine fruity flavors that are subordinated to an expressively toasty finish. Quite full throttled.

1997 Syrah, Herbert Vineyard, El Dorado $18.　　　**83**

Deep purple, opaque to the rim. Cooked fruits, berries, mocha flavors. Medium-bodied. Thick and heavy, with ripe, well-extracted flavors not quite matched by the acids. A touch blowsy and ponderous. Drink now.

1996 Syrah, Red Rock Ridge, El Dorado $18.　　　**83**

Rich ruby purple, limpid with a slight fade. Medium-bodied. Ripe berry fruit and chocolate flavors. Fleshy, very ripe, and textured through the finish. Jammy and a touch flabby. Drink now.

1996 Zinfandel, Herbert Vineyard, El Dorado $15.　　　**86**

Deep blackish purple. Moderately full-bodied. Balanced acidity. Moderately extracted. Mildly oaked. Moderately tannic. Brown spices, briar fruits. Aromatic and fruit-centered, with a big, flavorful palate feel. A little rugged through the finish.

1996 Zinfandel, Reeves Vineyard, El Dorado $15.　　　**93**

Deep blackish purple. Moderately full-bodied. Balanced acidity. Moderately extracted. Moderately oaked. Mildly tannic. Black fruits, vanilla. Quite aromatic, with a generous, vanilla-accented core of fruit flavors. Rich and full, though extremely well balanced. It carries its weight effortlessly through the lengthy finish.

Signorello

1997 Chardonnay, Napa Valley $30.　　　**89**

Bright full gold. Aromas show a strong yeasty accent with a heavy oak influence. A flavorful entry leads a moderately full-bodied palate with spicy oak and ripe fruit flavors that finish with alcohol warmth.

1996 Chardonnay, Founder's Reserve, Napa Valley $45.　　　**90**

Deep golden cast. Full-bodied. Balanced acidity. Highly extracted. Moderately oaked. Butter, brown spices, yeast. Ripe and opulent, displaying forward aromatics. Full and rich, with a textured, weighty mouthfeel and vibrant acidity lending balance through the finish.

1996 Chardonnay, Hope's Cuvée, Napa Valley $60.　　　**90**

Bright yellow-straw cast. Moderately full-bodied. Balanced acidity. Moderately extracted. Mildly oaked. Yeast, brown spices. Shows a big, forward toasted yeast note throughout. Ripe and rich in the mouth with a zesty, vibrant finish. Generous and complex.

1997 Chardonnay, Hope's Cuvée, Napa Valley $60.　　　**93**

Bright yellow-gold. Smoky, notably yeasty aromas. An oaky attack leads a moderately full-bodied palate with concentrated ripe fruit flavors and spicy complexity through the finish. The extravagant mouthfeel points to serious pedigree. Has the structure to improve over time. Drink now or later.

1996 Semillon, Napa Valley $20.　　　**87**

Dark golden hue. Moderately full-bodied. Balanced acidity. Highly extracted. Mildly oaked. Vanilla, brown spice, tart tropical fruits. Resinous oak aromas lead a big, full, rich, rounded, glycerous palate. A very ripe, full-blown style, with a warm spicy finish.

1995 Cabernet Franc, Napa Valley $35.　　　**90**

Deep ruby cast. Medium-bodied. Balanced acidity. Moderately extracted. Moderately oaked. Mildly tannic. Spice, minerals, cassis. Perfumed and stylish, with a firm, minerally backbone and a lush, velvety overlay. Supple yet well balanced, with a crisp, flavorful finish.

1994 Cabernet Sauvignon, Napa Valley $30. 90

Dark blood red with subtle purple highlights. Moderately full-bodied. Highly extracted. Moderately tannic. Toasted oak, cassis, plums, brown spice. Rich oaky nose suggests ripe black fruits that are confirmed on the palate. The chewy, ripe palate is full and rounded, with plenty of toasted character on the dry finish.

1995 Cabernet Sauvignon, Napa Valley $30. 92

Saturated dark ruby red. Moderately full-bodied. Highly extracted. Moderately tannic. Toasted oak, brown spice, black fruits. Brooding aromas show oak spice and dark fruits. Rich, finely wrought mineral and earth flavors are well matched with dark fruits. Although drinkable now, this will be better with a few miles in the cellar.

1996 Cabernet Sauvignon, Napa Valley $35. 91

Rich ruby hue with a subtly fading rim. Generously oak spiced aromas. A rich entry leads a moderately full-bodied palate with juicy, bright plummy fruit and generous chocolatey flavors and leathery tannins through the finish. Drinking very well now. Drink now.

1994 Cabernet Sauvignon, Founder's Reserve, Napa Valley $55. 93

Dark crimson red. Moderately full-bodied. Highly extracted. Black pepper, plums, cassis, toasted oak. Rich black fruit in the nose, with toasty overtones. Concentrated curranty flavors are very accessible now. The persistent fruity finish has balanced tannins and toasty oak flavors.

1995 Cabernet Sauvignon, Founder's Reserve, Napa Valley $55. 93

Saturated violet red. Moderately full-bodied. Highly extracted. Moderately tannic. Berry fruits, vanilla, minerals. Youthful, vibrant, concentrated aromas lead a high-toned, bright mouthful of mineral and fruit flavors, with oak spice playing on the finish. Sprightly and young, yet very harmonious.

1996 Cabernet Sauvignon, Founder's Reserve, Napa Valley $75. 92

Bright ruby hue with a subtly fading rim. Generous developed aromas a show marked oak accent. A plush entry leads a moderately full-bodied palate with rich black fruit flavors and grainy tannins that linger on the finish. Has a well-integrated, oaky character and is very approachable now. Drink now or later.

1996 Petite Sirah, 110 Year Old Vines, Napa Valley $25. 88

Opaque dark purple. Full-bodied. Highly extracted. Quite tannic. Fleshy, chunky, and rich, with generous plum and blackberry fruit flavors. Significantly oaky. Tannins do not dominate. A blockbuster to cellar for a few years.

1995 Pinot Noir, Las Amigas Vineyard, Carneros $48. 92

Nearly opaque dark red. Moderately full-bodied. Highly extracted. Moderately tannic. Earthy black fruit aromas lead a fully extracted palate with licorice and black bramble fruit flavors. Solid fine-grained tannins come through on the dry finish, where some mild bitterness and nutmeg notes pop up.

1996 Pinot Noir, Las Amigas Vineyard, Carneros $45. 91

Dark ruby-violet hue. Medium-bodied. Moderately extracted. Moderately tannic. Black fruits, oak spice, minerals. Solid, well-proportioned character, with firm tannins and a core of black fruit flavors. This is approachable now but will be better with age.

1995 Pinot Noir, Martinelli Vineyard, Russian River Valley $48. 88

Very dark reddish purple. Moderately full-bodied. Highly extracted. Moderately oaked. Moderately tannic. Leathery, earthy aromas are very pronounced and complex. Black cherry and licorice flavors on the palate. Very backward and difficult now, this is one for the cellar.

1996 Pinot Noir, Martinelli Vineyard, Russian River Valley $45. 89

Deep ruby red with a slight fade. Moderately full-bodied. Balanced acidity. Highly extracted. Moderately oaked. Mildly tannic. Spice, chocolate, pickle barrel. The deep, complex aromas are pleasantly perfumed. Firm and weighty in the mouth, with an intense, darkly flavored finish.

1996 Syrah, Napa Valley $30.   **93**

Deep ruby red, limpid with a slight fade. Intense toasted oak spice, red fruit, and olive flavors. Hefty wood tones. A firm entry leads a moderately full-bodied palate. Moderate, drying tannins. Well developed and oaky. Lingering finish. Drink now.

1994 Zinfandel, Napa Valley $25.   **88**

Full cherry red. Medium-bodied. Moderately extracted. Moderately oaked. Moderately tannic. Black raspberries, vanilla, pepper. Extroverted, vanilla-scented berry aromas lead a bright, fruity palate; tannins are approachable now, giving the finish some dry authority.

1995 Zinfandel, Napa Valley $25.   **87**

Deep blackish ruby cast. Full-bodied. Full acidity. Moderately extracted. Moderately oaked. Mildly tannic. Vanilla, dried herbs, black fruits. Quite aromatic, with a firm, flavorful palate feel. Deep and intense through the lengthy finish.

1996 Zinfandel, Russian River Valley $25.   **89**

Deep blackish ruby cast. Moderately full-bodied. Balanced acidity. Moderately extracted. Moderately oaked. Mildly tannic. Pepper, black fruits, minerals. Rather reserved aromatically, with a firm, highly structured palate feel. Elegant and well balanced, in more of a Claret style.

Silver Oak

1993 Cabernet Sauvignon, Alexander Valley $38.   **92**

Dark blackish red. Medium-bodied. Highly extracted. Moderately tannic. Toasted oak, licorice, black fruits, brown spice. Exotically rich toasty aromas lead a deep, flavorful, well-extracted palate, with a long toasty finish that has lingering fruit flavors.

1994 Cabernet Sauvignon, Alexander Valley $45.   **91**

Deep ruby hue. Medium-bodied. Balanced acidity. Moderately extracted. Moderately oaked. Mildly tannic. Vanilla, red fruits. Pleasantly aromatic, with a somewhat light palate feel. Toasty oak plays a part throughout, with crisp acidity. Elegant and well balanced. Drinking well.

1993 Cabernet Sauvignon, Napa Valley $50.   **90**

Full brick red. Medium-bodied. Moderately extracted. Moderately tannic. Black cherries, cedar, cinnamon. Generous oak-spiced aromas show some mature accents. Rounded and extravagantly spicy, though not a heavyweight style. This is very approachable now and is not in need of extensive cellaring.

1994 Cabernet Sauvignon, Napa Valley $65.   **90**

Dark ruby hue. Rich, very aromatic spicy oak aromas with fleshy dark fruits. A rich entry leads a supple, moderately full-bodied palate with dark black cherry fruits and elegant powdery tannins that linger. Very well balanced and showing very distinctive flavors of American oak. Drink now or later.

Silver Ridge

1997 Chardonnay, California $9.99.   **88**

Brilliant yellow-straw hue. Generous vanilla and cream aromas carry an attractive oak accent. A rounded entry leads a medium-bodied palate with balanced acidity. Lengthy, flavorful finish. Drink now.

1995 Cabernet Sauvignon, California $9.99.   **81**

1997 Merlot, California $9.99.   **81**

1996 Pinot Noir, California $9.99.   **84**

Pale violet hue. Moderately light-bodied. Subtly extracted. Mildly tannic. Red fruits, vanilla. Smooth yet crisp, with berry fruit flavors and balanced oak notes through the finish. Easy drinking.

1996 Syrah, California $9.99.   **82**

Scale: Superlative (96-100), Exceptional (90-95), Highly Recommended (85-89), Recommended (80-84), Not Recommended (Under 80)

190

Silverado

1994 Cabernet Sauvignon, Napa Valley $22.50.   91
Full reddish purple. Medium-bodied. Moderately extracted. Moderately tannic. Mint, cherries, black fruits. High-toned spicy oak nose has minty notes. The full-flavored palate has a firm overlay of attractive oak flavors that linger through the finish. Nice now, though this will probably come together with a few years of aging.

1995 Cabernet Sauvignon, Napa Valley $25.   88
Saturated deep red-purple. Moderately full-bodied. Highly extracted. Moderately tannic. Mineral, spice, black fruits. Oak-centered aromas lead a crisp black fruit palate, with noble, fine-grained tannins supplying a firm, structured finish.

1994 Cabernet Sauvignon, Limited Reserve, Napa Valley $50.   93
Opaque appearance with bright purple highlights. Moderately full-bodied. Highly extracted. Moderately tannic. Violets, cherries, cedar, tobacco. Vivacious berry fruit aromas follow through on the palate. Rounded, viscous mouthfeel shows great depth and persistence. Quite supple now, though this could profitably use cellar time.

1995 Merlot, Napa Valley $22.50.   94
Very deep ruby hue to the rim. Medium-bodied. Balanced acidity. Moderately extracted. Moderately oaked. Mildly tannic. Mint, red fruits, chocolate. Big, rich, and fruit driven in style, with pleasant mint and barrel accents that add complexity. Well balanced and extremely lush on the palate, with fine length.

Silverado Hill

1995 Cabernet Sauvignon, Napa Valley $13.   80

Simi

1996 Chardonnay, Sonoma County $17.   86
Pale straw cast. Medium-bodied. Full acidity. Moderately extracted. Green apples, minerals. Crisp and clean, with precisely defined flavors and a linear structure. Firm acidity makes for a zesty finish.

1996 Chardonnay, Carneros $21.   84
Deep yellow-straw color. Moderately full-bodied. Balanced acidity. Moderately extracted. Butterscotch, apple. Thick, generous, and flavorful, with a subtle note of vanilla oak. Shows a creamy mouthfeel with yeasty overtones that emerge on the finish.

1995 Chardonnay, Reserve, Sonoma County $29.   88
Bright yellow-gold. Forward aromas show a subtle oak accent and a citric core. The moderately full-bodied palate has flavors of brown spices, citrus and cream, with mild oak notes and assertive acidity. Full yet angular in the mouth with a crisp spicy finish.

1995 Sendal, Sonoma County $20.   85
Deep golden cast. Moderately full-bodied. Balanced acidity. Moderately extracted. Figs, citrus, nuts. Quite aromatic, with a richly luxuriant flavor profile. Solid acidity makes for a racy and buoyant finish.

1996 Sauvignon Blanc, Sonoma County $14.   84
Medium straw hue. Medium-bodied. Balanced acidity. Moderately extracted. White peach, apples. Reserved, perfumed aromas reveal orchard fruit flavors up front, with some alcohol warmth and dryness on the finish.

1994 Cabernet Sauvignon, Alexander Valley $19.   89
Bright reddish purple. Medium-bodied. Moderately extracted. Mildly tannic. Black cherries, plums. Attractive fruity, ripe berry-accented nose leads a smooth, lush palate and with a simple finish. A very fruit-forward style that is drinking well now.

1995 Cabernet Sauvignon, Alexander Valley $22.   87
Bright ruby hue. Moderately full-bodied. Balanced acidity. Moderately extracted. Mildly tannic. Black fruits, minerals. Generous aromas feature a decided fruit accent. Rich and stylish in the mouth, with velvety tannins lending structure. Well balanced and lengthy.

1994 Cabernet Sauvignon, Reserve, Sonoma County $46.　　　**91**

Deep ruby purple. Moderately full-bodied. Balanced acidity. Moderately extracted. Mildly oaked. Mildly tannic. Minerals, black fruits, brown spices. Pleasantly aromatic, with a soft and supple palate feel. Rich and velvety in the mouth, with a seamless quality through the lengthy finish.

1996 Shiraz, Sonoma County $18.50.　　　**84**

Medium purple, limpid and brilliant, with a slight fade. Mild, sound flower, cherry, vanilla, and cedar flavors. Subtle wood tones. Supple entry. Medium-bodied with crisp acidity. Moderately short finish. A light, easy-drinking style with a delicate finish. Drink now.

Smith & Hook

1996 Viognier, Arroyo Seco $18.　　　**87**

Deep golden cast. Full-bodied. Low acidity. Highly extracted. Oranges, cream, talc. Very aromatic, with unusual though complex flavors. Extremely full in the mouth with relatively low acidity. Finishes with an angular, assertive note.

1994 Cabernet Sauvignon, Santa Lucia Highlands $18.　　　**87**

Black cherry red. Medium-bodied. Moderately extracted. Mildly tannic. Dill, black fruits, minerals. Mildly toasty nose and a lean, crisp palate with fine acids give this wine presence on the palate. Rather similar to though lighter than its pricier stablemate.

1995 Cabernet Sauvignon, Santa Lucia Highlands $18.　　　**89**

Bright brick red. Medium-bodied. Moderately extracted. Mildly tannic. Spice, minerals, red fruits. Dusty, spicy, almost meaty aromas lead an elegant mouthful of leaner flavors, with bright acids and mild tannins providing some grip and lending a food-friendly balance. This is an Old World style.

1996 Cabernet Sauvignon, Santa Lucia Highlands $18.　　　**82**

1994 Cabernet Sauvignon, Masterpiece Edition,
Santa Lucia Highlands $35.　　　**90**

Dark black cherry color. Medium-bodied. Highly extracted. Mildly tannic. Dill, black fruits, minerals. Toasty, oak-accented nose leads a deep, fruity palate with full flavors and complex oaky accents through the finish. Shows great balance and harmony. Dry tannins on the lengthy finish.

1995 Cabernet Sauvignon, Masterpiece Edition,
Santa Lucia Highlands $40.　　　**86**

Brick red with garnet highlights. Medium-bodied. Moderately extracted. Mildly tannic. Minerals, earth, brown spice. Mature, oriental spice aromas lead a lighter-styled, fading palate, with subtlety the key word. This has bright acids and a sense of refinement, though not for keeping. Not for those seeking extravagantly fruity Cabernet styles, this is more of an Old World style.

1995 Merlot, Santa Lucia Highlands $19.95.　　　**87**

Deep ruby with a blackish cast. Medium-bodied. Full acidity. Moderately extracted. Moderately oaked. Mildly tannic. Cedar, black fruits, minerals, green herbs. Oak figures prominently in the aromatics. Crisp and angular in the mouth, with complex flavors and an herbal tinge to the clean, snappy finish.

1996 Merlot, Santa Lucia Highlands $19.　　　**81**

Sobon

1997 Roussanne, Shenandoah Valley $15.　　　**82**

1997 Rhone Rose, Shenandoah Valley $9.　　　**88**

Brilliant pale cherry hue. Forward red fruit and mineral aromas have a lean citric edge. A firm entry leads a moderately full-bodied palate showing vibrant acidity. Flavorful, intense, and refreshing. Drink now.

Scale: Superlative (96-100), Exceptional (90-95), Highly Recommended (85-89), Recommended (80-84), Not Recommended (Under 80)

1996 Syrah, Shenandoah Valley, California $15. **84**

Medium ruby color, limpid, with a slight fade. Medium-bodied. Herbal and berry flavors. Light, bright fruity flavors with mild drying tannins. A touch herbal, but juicy and balanced. Drink now.

1996 Zinfandel, Cougar Hill, Shenandoah Valley $15. **84**

Bright ruby-garnet cast. Medium-bodied. Balanced acidity. Moderately extracted. Mildly oaked. Mildly tannic. Black fruits, minerals, vanilla. Reserved aromatically, with gentle, spicy oak overtones. Lush and generous through the finish. Well balanced.

1996 Zinfandel, Lubenko Vineyard, Fiddletown $15. **84**

Bright blackish ruby cast. Moderately full-bodied. Full acidity. Moderately extracted. Mildly oaked. Mildly tannic. Briar fruits, minerals. Quite aromatic, with a full though angular palate feel. Vibrant acidity provides a juicy finish.

1996 Zinfandel, Rocky Top, Shenandoah Valley $15. **80**

Sonoma Creek

1997 Cabernet Sauvignon, Sonoma County $11.95. **84**

Bright ruby red with a slight purple cast. Medium-bodied. Balanced acidity. Moderately extracted. Moderately oaked. Mildly tannic. Bramble fruits, vanilla. Pleasantly aromatic, with a crisp, generous, fruit-centered personality. Clean and angular through the flavorful finish. A cheerful quaffing style.

1995 Cabernet Sauvignon, Reserve, Sonoma Valley $17.95. **92**

Saturated cherry red. Moderately full-bodied. Moderately extracted. Mildly tannic. Black cherries, vanilla. Sweet black fruit aromas follow through on a soft, fleshy palate with soft, rounded tannins through the finish. Very hedonistic.

1995 Cabernet Sauvignon, Rancho Salina Vineyard, Sonoma Valley $28.95. **91**

Saturated ruby purple. Moderately full-bodied. Highly extracted. Moderately tannic. Black cherries, cedar. Rich, luxuriously decadent aromas lead a vibrant palate of fleshy black fruits with complex cedar nuances. Drinking very well now.

1995 Cabernet Sauvignon, Van der Kamp Vineyard,
Sonoma Mountain $28.95. **89**

Saturated red-purple. Moderately full-bodied. Highly extracted. Moderately tannic. Vanilla, cassis. Spicy oak and jammy red fruit aromas follow through on a rounded, fleshy palate, with a good degree of berry intensity.

1995 Meritage, Sonoma Valley $17.95. **89**

Saturated cherry red. Moderately full-bodied. Moderately extracted. Mildly tannic. Black berry fruits, dried herbs. Brash berry fruit flavors leap from the glass. Shows a soft herbal tinge and a good acid cut throughout. Ripe, ample tannins give this cellaring structure, though it is drinkable now.

Sonoma-Cutrer

1997 Chardonnay, Russian River Ranches, Russian River Valley $16.99. **81**

1996 Chardonnay, The Cutrer, Sonoma County $27.99. **91**

Brilliant straw hue. Reserved steely aromas show a slight wood accent. A brisk entry leads a full-bodied palate with flinty, minerally flavors and sharp acidity. Rich, intense finish. Shows fine cut, and has a Chablis-like edge. Drink now or later.

1996 Chardonnay, Les Pierres, Sonoma County $29.99. **92**

Bright straw hue. Subdued mineral and citrus aromas show a subtle leesy quality and mild oak influences. The entry is crisp, followed by a full-bodied palate with brisk acidity. Authoritative, if somewhat austere finish. This needs time to develop and is a midterm cellar candidate.

Sonoma-Loeb

1997 Chardonnay, Sonoma County $20.   83

Bright yellow-straw cast. Medium-bodied. Balanced acidity. Moderately extracted. Minerals, citrus. Aromatically reserved, with a ripe and rounded mouthfeel. Shows a gentle fade to the finish.

1997 Chardonnay, Private Reserve, Sonoma County $30.   84

Deep straw cast. Moderately full-bodied. Balanced acidity. Moderately extracted. Mildly oaked. Minerals, cream, spice. Ripe and rounded, with a soft, creamy texture and subdued flavors. Rich and generous through the finish.

Sonora Winery & Port Works

1996 Zinfandel, Old Vine, Story Vineyard, Amador County $18.   84

Deep blackish ruby cast. Moderately full-bodied. Low acidity. Moderately extracted. Mildly oaked. Mildly tannic. Brown spices, stewed black fruits. Quite aromatic, with a big, full-throttled, flavorful palate feel. Somewhat lacking in acidity. Chunky tannins dominate the finish. Not for the faint of heart.

1996 Zinfandel, Old Vine, TC Vineyard, Amador County $18.   81

1992 Vintage Port, Sierra Foothills $15.99/500 ml.   80

1994 Vintage Port, Sierra Foothills $16/500 ml.   86

Opaque blackish purple. Moderately full-bodied. Low acidity. Highly extracted. Mildly tannic. Minerals, black fruits. Rather reserved aromatically, but opens up on the palate, displaying a lush, rounded mouthfeel. Deep, brooding, and intense, with marked sweetness to the finish. Could use a few more years of age.

Soquel

1994 Cabernet Sauvignon, Santa Cruz Mountains $22.   85

Solid blood red. Medium-bodied. Highly extracted. Moderately tannic. Brown spice, dust, chocolate. Dry, dusty nose has full brown spice accents. The palate is powdery, with well-integrated tannins and a chocolatey note through the finish. Fruit flavors are a little austere.

1994 Cabernet Sauvignon, Partner's Reserve, Santa Cruz Mountains $40.   91

Deep garnet red. Moderately full-bodied. Highly extracted. Moderately tannic. Dill, sage, black plums, anise, earth. An exotically spiced, herbal nose leads a thick, concentrated palate with a chewy mouthfeel and a lengthy finish showing impressive noble tannins. A complex blockbuster.

1995 Cabernet Sauvignon, Partner's Reserve, Santa Cruz Mountains $40.   91

Saturated, opaque red-purple. Moderately full-bodied. Highly extracted. Quite tannic. Cedar, vanilla, cassis. Dense, sweet-edged aromas lead an inky, dry palate that has ample fine-grained tannins, but also a sense of generosity showing through. Impossibly young now.

Sparrow Lane

1996 Zinfandel, Reserve, Beatty Ranch, Howell Mountain $25.   90

Opaque dark red with purple highlights. Moderately full-bodied. Balanced acidity. Highly extracted. Moderately oaked. Moderately tannic. Black fruits. Impressively rich fruit-centered aromas lead a glycerous mouthful of dark fruit flavors, with oak accents coming though. A rather big-shouldered style that is drinkable now.

Spottswoode

1996 Sauvignon Blanc, Napa Valley $18.   89

Bright metallic emerald color. Medium-bodied. Balanced acidity. Moderately extracted. Reminiscent of ripe lemons, pineapple. Clean fruity aromas with some buttery notes. Silky mouthfeel with a hint of zest on the finish. Very refined and elegant.

Scale: Superlative (96-100), Exceptional (90-95), Highly Recommended (85-89), Recommended (80-84), Not Recommended (Under 80)

194

1992 Cabernet Sauvignon, Napa Valley $39.   **92**

Medium-bodied. Medium acid. Medium fruit. Lots of oak. Medium tannin. Dry.
Reminiscent of leather, cassis, vanilla, nutmeg. Dense and well integrated, with a firm
backbone. Wood tones dominate delicately balanced fruit. 94% Cabernet Sauvignon
accented with 6% Cabernet Franc.

1993 Cabernet Sauvignon, Napa Valley $42.   **94**

Deep ruby to the rim with a subtle purplish cast. Moderately full-bodied. Balanced
acidity. Highly extracted. Moderately oaked. Moderately tannic. Dry. Reminiscent of
vanilla, cassis, black cherries. Extremely deep and rich in flavor, this wine has an excellent
level of extraction while maintaining a sense of balance and lushness. Soft tannins come
through in the finish and give a sense of depth and richness. Though accessible now,
it should be even better in five years. A classic California Cabernet.

1994 Cabernet Sauvignon, Napa Valley $45.   **93**

Full bright crimson appearance. Medium-bodied. Moderately extracted. Mildly tannic.
Red berries, cassis, brown spice. Full berry fruit aromas. Bright, juicy primary fruit flavors
expand on the palate. Fine concentration and focus, with a lingering spicy oak finish.
Drinking well now.

1995 Cabernet Sauvignon, Napa Valley $55.   **92**

Deep ruby purple. Moderately full-bodied. Balanced acidity. Highly extracted. Moderately
oaked. Moderately tannic. Vanilla, red fruits, minerals. Quite fragrant, in a modern style,
with a stylish interplay between fruit and wood. Shows fine depth, focus, and structure in
the mouth, with a lengthy finish. Should develop beautifully.

Spring Mountain Vineyard

1993 Miravalle-Alba-Chevalier Red, Napa Valley $28.   **93**

Dark black cherry color. Medium-bodied. Moderately extracted. Moderately tannic.
Earth, minerals, cassis. Toasty, dusty aromas lead a rich chewy palate with great depth
of flavors revealing layers of earthy complexity. The tannins are firm and dry, but do
not dominate totally. Structured for keeping.

1994 Miravalle-Alba-Chevalier Red, Napa Valley $28.99.   **83**

Saturated dark ruby hue. Moderately full-bodied. Highly extracted. Quite tannic. Black
fruits, dark chocolate, brown spice. Rich, spicy aromas follow through well on the palate,
with spicy berry notes playing out through the finish. The tannins are chunky, though
not out of balance.

St. Amant

1995 Vintage Port, Amador County $28.   **85**

Saturated blackish red. Medium-bodied. Highly extracted. Moderately tannic.
Reminiscent of blueberry, chocolate, raspberries. Complex, exotic plummy nose.
Deeply extracted and flavorsome, though somewhat compact on the palate at present,
with dry tannins on the finish. Needs some time.

St. Clement

1997 Chardonnay, Abbots Vineyard, Carneros, Napa Valley $20.   **89**

Rich yellow-gold. Ripe aromas of butter and toasted oak. A spicy attack leads a
moderately full-bodied palate with rich, lush texture and yeasty notes. This is a big,
alcoholic style that maintains reasonable acid balance and shows stylish touches.
Drink now.

1997 Sauvignon Blanc, Napa Valley $13.   **84**

Deep straw cast. Moderately full-bodied. Balanced acidity. Moderately extracted. Minerals,
citrus. Seemingly quite youthful, this wine is rather reserved aromatically, with a lush
entry on the palate, becoming tighter and more angular through the finish.

1994 Cabernet Sauvignon, Napa Valley $25.　　　　　**90**

Full dark red with bright purple highlights. Medium-bodied. Moderately extracted. Mildly tannic. Black fruits, oak spice. Concentrated midpalate, with solid black fruit flavors, and a hint of imposing tannin on a good, long toasty finish. Solid structure, classic style.

1995 Cabernet Sauvignon, Napa Valley $26.　　　　　**87**

Dark ruby-violet hue. Medium-bodied. Highly extracted. Moderately tannic. Cassis, vanilla. Succulent and luxurious, with finely polished tannins and harmoniously ripe flavors. Bursting with textbook Cabernet flavors, in a lighter style.

1994 Cabernet Sauvignon, Howell Mountain, Napa Valley $45.　　**92**

Opaque bright purple. Moderately full-bodied. Highly extracted. Moderately tannic. Crisp cassis, black fruits, chalk. Ripe, high-toned fruity aromas lead a bright fruity entry that expands on the midpalate, with surprisingly accessible tannins coming through on the finish. Youthful and vigorous still.

1995 Cabernet Sauvignon, Howell Mountain, Napa Valley $45.　　**93**

Saturated dark ruby purple. Moderately full-bodied. Balanced acidity. Moderately extracted. Mildly oaked. Mildly tannic. Licorice, minerals, chocolate. Exotic, high-toned aromas lead a supple, smooth palate feel. Concentrated yet elegant, with very fancy extraction resulting in abundant silky tannins. Approachable but ageworthy.

1995 Oroppas, Napa Valley $35.　　　　　**90**

Dark ruby with bright purple highlights. Medium-bodied. Moderately extracted. Mildly tannic. Licorice, cassis, plums, pepper. Generous, ripe black fruit aromas reveal a supple and rounded mouthfeel. The finish is long, with lingering black fruit flavors. A ripe, expressive style.

1996 Oroppas, Napa Valley $35.　　　　　**94**

Bright red-purple. Moderately full-bodied. Highly extracted. Moderately tannic. Cassis, black fruits, vanilla. Very lush, fruit-forward aromas follow through on the palate, with a rounded texture and a silky mouthfeel through the finish. Very hedonistic and supple.

1994 Merlot, Napa Valley $24.　　　　　**87**

Deep ruby red to the rim with brilliant highlights. Medium-bodied. Balanced acidity. Moderately extracted. Mildly oaked. Mildly tannic. Red fruits, chocolate, anise. Still youthful, with a tightly wound dense core of flavor. Rich and thick, but well balanced, with a lingering finish. Should develop some complexity with aging.

1995 Merlot, Napa Valley $24.　　　　　**84**

Deep ruby to the rim with brilliant highlights. Medium-bodied. Balanced acidity. Moderately extracted. Mildly oaked. Mildly tannic. Red fruits, anise, minerals. Lighter in style, with bright flavors. A well-balanced and lingering finish.

1996 Merlot, Napa Valley $24.　　　　　**83**

Well-saturated bright violet hue. Black cherry and herb aromas. Medium-bodied, with a flavorful attack and crisp, generous fleshy fruit flavors that are well balanced by moderate tannic astringency through the finish. Drink now.

1995 Merlot, Columbia Valley $22.　　　　　**90**

Deep blackish ruby hue with brilliant clarity. Medium-bodied. Balanced acidity. Moderately extracted. Moderately oaked. Mildly tannic. Chocolate, minerals, red fruits. Supple and velvety in the mouth, with well-integrated, complex flavors. Quite balanced, this should cellar nicely.

St. Francis

1997 Chardonnay, Sonoma County $12.99.　　　　　**84**

Bright straw hue. Subdued mineral and earth aromas carry a slight oak accent. A lush entry is followed by a medium-bodied palate with rounded acidity and a clean, gentle finish. Drink now.

Scale: Superlative (96-100), Exceptional (90-95), Highly Recommended (85-89), Recommended (80-84), Not Recommended (Under 80)

1997 Chardonnay, Reserve, Sonoma County $22.99.   **91**

Deep yellow-straw color. Opulent toasted-coconut aromas show a dominant oak accent. A crisp entry leads a full-bodied palate with vibrant acidity. Complex, leesy flavors with a slightly buttery quality through the finish. Showy. Drink now.

1995 Cabernet Sauvignon, Sonoma County $10.99.   **87**

Full dark cherry red. Medium-bodied. Moderately extracted. Mildly tannic. Plums, cassis, tobacco. Full-flavored, fleshy dark fruit flavors are forward and attractive, giving an impression of fatness on the midpalate. Soft, supple tannins on the finish. Nice now.

1996 Cabernet Sauvignon, Sonoma County $13.99.   **84**

Bright cherry garnet hue. Subdued mineral, earth, and berry aromas. A soft attack leads to a medium-bodied palate with firm and drying tannins. Lean finish. On the tough side. Drink within five years.

1994 Cabernet Sauvignon, Reserve, Sonoma Valley $30.   **96**

Opaque blackish red. Moderately full-bodied. Highly extracted. Quite tannic. Black fruits, licorice, earth, brown spice. Dark, brooding aromas. The solid, tightly wound palate has an extravagantly concentrated and ripe mouthfeel. Big fine-grained tannins come through on the long finish. Great structure should allow this to cellar for a decade.

1995 Cabernet Sauvignon, Reserve, Sonoma Valley $33.99.   **91**

Opaque, saturated blackish ruby hue. Flashy toasted coconut and chocolate aromas show a huge American oak influence. A thick and supple entry leads to a full-bodied palate with waves of flavor and robust velvety tannins. Very fancy extraction indeed. Soft, very flavorful finish. Without the acidity to be a long-term ager but carries its weight well. A showy hedonistic style. Drink within five years.

1995 Merlot, Sonoma County $18.   **89**

Deep blackish ruby hue. Moderately full-bodied. Balanced acidity. Highly extracted. Moderately oaked. Moderately tannic. Earth, black fruits, incense. Somewhat unusual aromatics, with a slight funky quality. Rich and chewy in the mouth with a thick character and chunky tannins. Lingering perfumed finish. Perhaps it's in a bit of an awkward stage aromatically; give it benefit of the doubt.

1996 Merlot, Sonoma County $23.99.   **92**

Blood red with a garnet cast and a slight fade. Well-developed aromas show leathery, spicy, oaky accents. A crisp attack leads a medium-bodied palate with developed earthy tannins. Finishes with spicy complexity.

1994 Merlot, Reserve, Sonoma Valley $29.   **93**

Very deep blackish ruby hue. Moderately full-bodied. Balanced acidity. Highly extracted. Heavily oaked. Mildly tannic. Brown spices, black fruits, sweet herbs. Deeply aromatic with a big overlay of sweet oak. In the mouth, there is great density of fruit and a chunky texture. Well integrated and well balanced, with velvety tannins.

1995 Merlot, Reserve, Sonoma Valley $33.99.   **93**

Deep brick red. Chocolate and brown spice aromas. A supple attack leads a moderately full-bodied palate with evolved tannins and soft acids, and a solid grip. Complex flavors of minerals and spice linger on the earthy finish. Drink now.

1996 Zinfandel, Old Vines, Sonoma County $20.   **94**

Deep blackish ruby hue. Moderately full-bodied. Balanced acidity. Highly extracted. Moderately oaked. Mildly tannic. Brown spices, black fruits. Toasty oak nuances on the nose merge with a wave of dark fruit flavors in the mouth. Lush, deep, and rich, with a velvety, supple finish. Fine length and intensity.

1996 Zinfandel, Pagani Vineyard Reserve, Sonoma Valley $28.   **95**

Saturated, deep blackish ruby hue. Full-bodied. Balanced acidity. Highly extracted. Moderately oaked. Mildly tannic. Vanilla, black fruits, tar. An opaque color belies this wine's depth and structure, with brooding aromas and a wave of dark flavors on the palate. Rich and forceful, though very well integrated. The toasted coconut nuances of American oak are unmistakable; the combination is reminiscent of a top-flight Aussie Shiraz.

St. Supéry

1996 Chardonnay, Dollarhide Ranch, Napa Valley $12.50.   86

Bright straw cast. Moderately full-bodied. Full acidity. Moderately extracted. Citrus, melon, minerals. Quite aromatic, with bright fruit flavors to the fore. Zesty and intense in the mouth, with a clean, snappy finish.

1996 Meritage, Napa Valley $20.   82

1997 Sauvignon Blanc, Dollarhide Ranch, Napa Valley $9.90.   91

Very deep straw hue. Moderately full-bodied. Full acidity. Highly extracted. Dried herbs, citrus, cream. Ripe and flavorful with marked complexity. Rich and full in the mouth, with a supple texture and a lengthy, herb-tinged finish.

1994 Cabernet Sauvignon, Napa Valley $15.75.   90

Deep cherry red. Medium-bodied. Moderately extracted. Mildly tannic. Currants, cassis, licorice. Rich, ripe berry aromas lead a supple, rounded, ripe palate with some pleasing spice notes and hints of firm tannin on the finish. Very attractive now.

1995 Cabernet Sauvignon, Dollarhide Ranches, Rutherford $16.50.   80

1994 Red Meritage, Napa Valley $40.   89

Bright violet red. Medium-bodied. Moderately extracted. Heavily oaked. Moderately tannic. Vanilla, red fruits. Crisp vanilla, oak-accented aromas lead a lively palate dominated by an oak astringency that grips the midpalate and finish.

1995 Red Meritage, Napa Valley $40.   88

Medium brick red hue. Moderately aromatic with a full oak-spiced nose showing ripe, mature fruits. A firm attack leads a medium-bodied palate with softer acids and lighter tannins. Oak spice flavors come to the fore and linger on the finish. Supple, balanced, and harmonious. Drink now.

1995 Merlot, Dollarhide Ranches, Napa Valley $16.50.   83

Deep ruby red to the rim, with brilliant clarity. Medium-bodied. Balanced acidity. Moderately extracted. Moderately tannic. Dried herbs, earth, red fruits. Veers to the herbal end of the spectrum, with a lighter-styled palate. Tannins clamp down on the lush mouthfeel.

1996 Merlot, Dollarhide Ranches, Napa Valley $16.50.   81

Stag's Leap Wine Cellars

1997 Chardonnay, Napa Valley $26.   84

Bright yellow-gold. Aromatically restrained with subtle oak and yeast notes. A spicy attack leads a moderately full-bodied palate with tart acids and a note of alcohol warmth. Rich, textured mouthfeel.

1996 Chardonnay, Beckstoffer Ranch, Napa Valley $30.   87

Bright straw cast. Medium-bodied. Full acidity. Moderately extracted. Mildly oaked. Minerals, coconut, citrus. Aromatic and forward, showing a definite sweet oak component. Crisp and zesty, with a refreshing vibrant note to the lengthy finish.

1996 Chardonnay, Reserve, Napa Valley $37.   90

Bright straw cast. Moderately full-bodied. Balanced acidity. Moderately extracted. Mildly oaked. Green apples, melon, brown spices. Aromatic and flavorful, with a crisp, focused, and well-defined presence on the palate. Elegant and stylish, with a balanced, lengthy finish.

1995 Cabernet Sauvignon, Napa Valley $26.   89

Dark blood-ruby hue. Medium-bodied. Highly extracted. Moderately tannic. Minerals, cassis, oak spice. Lean, taut, and reserved, with fine structure. This shows plenty of pedigree, though it is not a powerful style. Drinking well now, though it has the structure to age gracefully.

Scale: Superlative (96-100), Exceptional (90-95), Highly Recommended (85-89), Recommended (80-84), Not Recommended (Under 80)

198

1994 Cabernet Sauvignon, Fay, Napa Valley $50.   **94**

Dark ruby red. Medium-bodied. Moderately extracted. Moderately tannic. Plums, cassis, cherries, earth. A big, rich mouthful of black fruit and earth, with black fruit flavors and fine-grained tannins on the finish. This is drinking very well now.

1995 Cabernet Sauvignon, Fay, Napa Valley $70.   **94**

Saturated blood red. Moderately full-bodied. Moderately extracted. Moderately tannic. Toasted oak, cassis, mineral. Charred aromas have a fleshy accent that follows through on the palate. Rich, juicy middle, and layers of ripe tannins that linger through the finish. Has a great mineral accent throughout.

1994 Cabernet Sauvignon, SLV, Napa Valley $50.   **93**

Dark ruby red. Medium-bodied. Moderately extracted. Moderately tannic. Plums, earth, brown spice. Intriguingly earthy spiced aromas. The deeply flavored palate has an earthy richness and smoothness through to its spicy conclusion. Very ripe and supple, and drinking well now.

1995 Cabernet Sauvignon, SLV, Napa Valley $70.   **94**

Saturated blood red. Moderately full-bodied. Highly extracted. Moderately tannic. Mineral, fleshy berries, brown spice. Mineral-rich aromas have plenty of cassis backing. Concentrated flavors show intensity and harmony, with a noble, earthy finish that turns powdery and dry. This is very elegant now, yet will cellar well.

1994 Cabernet Sauvignon, Cask 23, Napa Valley $100.   **96**

Deep ruby hue with purple highlights. Medium-bodied. Highly extracted. Moderately tannic. Plums, black fruits, brown spice. Elegant toasty nose. Deep, chewy black fruit flavors fill the palate, with earthy richness coming through on the long dry finish. Shows some structure, but is very approachable. Exhibits a seemingly strong "gout de terroir."

1995 Cask 23, Napa Valley $120.   **97**

Saturated blood-ruby red. Moderately full-bodied. Highly extracted. Quite tannic. Cassis, oak spice, licorice. Brown spice and expressive Cabernet fruit aromas open up on the palate. Forceful, abrupt dry tannins give a firm finish through which generous fruit is still very marked.

1994 Merlot, Napa Valley $26.   **88**

Very deep ruby red with brilliant highlights. Medium-bodied. Balanced acidity. Moderately extracted. Mildly oaked. Mildly tannic. Currant, minerals, vanilla. Restrained and elegant in style, with a balanced mouthfeel. Complex flavors are buttressed by steely acidity and some tannic grip on the finish. Should open beautifully with mid-term (3–6 years) cellaring. Has more than a little Bordeaux in its overall style.

Staglin

1994 Cabernet Sauvignon, Rutherford, Napa Valley $37.   **88**

Deep cherry red. Medium-bodied. Highly extracted. Quite tannic. Cherries, cassis, chalk. Dusty, spicy nose leads a full mouthful of cherry-accented Cabernet fruit flavors, with firm powdery tannins coming through on the finish.

1995 Cabernet Sauvignon, Rutherford, Napa Valley $42.50.   **92**

Bright ruby purple. Moderately full-bodied. Balanced acidity. Moderately extracted. Moderately oaked. Mildly tannic. Cassis, vanilla. Quite aromatic, with a pure and expressive fruit-centered quality accented by judicious use of oak. Focused and flavorful, displaying fine length and intensity.

1996 Sangiovese, Stagliano, Rutherford, Napa Valley $35.   **90**

Bright reddish purple. Medium-bodied. Balanced acidity. Moderately extracted. Mildly tannic. Raspberries, cherries, chocolate. High-toned red fruit aromas follow through on a clean, lively palate. Quite bright, with great balance.

Stags' Leap Winery

1997 Chardonnay, Napa Valley $21.   **86**

Pale yellow-straw hue. Aromatically subdued with mild green apple and vanilla accents. A clean attack leads a medium-bodied palate with brief fruit flavors and a quick oaky finish. Drink now.

1995 Cabernet Sauvignon, Napa Valley $30.   86

Dark violet-red hue. Dusty, minerally aromas are elegant. A firm entry leads a moderately full-bodied palate with firmer, leaner flavors having a sense of depth and a fine, spicy note. Classically structured and nice now. Drink now or later.

1995 Merlot, Napa Valley $28.   87

Very deep ruby hue to the rim. Moderately full-bodied. Balanced acidity. Highly extracted. Moderately oaked. Mildly tannic. Cassis, dried herbs, brown spices. Quite aromatic, with a complex and flavorful palate to match. Well structured, with drying, dusty tannins through the finish. Fine length.

1996 Merlot, Napa Valley $28.   84

Bright violet hue with a lightening rim. Relatively light floral aromas. Moderately light-bodied with a juicy attack and weaker flavors on the midpalate. Finishes with very subtle tannins and a buttery note. Drink now.

1995 Petite Sirah, Napa Valley $22.   90

Dark crimson purple. Medium-bodied. Moderately extracted. Quite tannic. Solid, well gripped, and dry through the finish. Rich blackberry, mint, and anise flavors show through, giving this a sense of proportion and balance.

Steele

1997 Chardonnay, Steele Cuvée, California $18.   84

Pale green-gold. Medium-bodied. Balanced acidity. Moderately extracted. Mildly oaked. Melon, peach, vanilla. Juicy, ripe tropical flavors linger through the finish. Shows a judicious touch of oak seasoning. An easy-drinking style.

1996 Chardonnay, Bien Nacido Vineyard, Santa Barbara County $26.   91

Bright golden cast. Moderately full-bodied. Balanced acidity. Moderately extracted. Mildly oaked. Yeast, cream, vanilla. Shows a marked leesy accent to the generous aromas. Ripe, rounded, and very flavorful in the mouth, with enough acidity to retain a sense of balance through the finish. Stylish.

1996 Chardonnay, Du Pratt Vineyard, Mendocino County $26.   86

Bright yellow-gold. Medium-bodied. Balanced acidity. Mildly oaked. Green apples, vanilla. Distinctive yeasty aromas with spicy, toasty accents follow through on the palate, with tart fruit flavors and a dry finish.

1996 Chardonnay, Durell Vineyard, Carneros $26.   91

Brilliant golden luster. Medium-bodied. Balanced acidity. Moderately extracted. Smoky oak, tropical fruits. Smoky tropical aromas follow through on a supple, silky palate with marked depth of flavors and a lingering finish showcasing smoky flavors. Very stylish.

1996 Chardonnay, Goodchild Vineyard, Santa Barbara County $26.   84

Bright yellow-gold. Moderately full-bodied. Full acidity. Moderately extracted. Minerals, lanolin. Aromatically reserved, with a lean and racy quality. Angular and austere through the finish.

1996 Chardonnay, Lolonis Vineyard, Mendocino County $28.   84

Bright yellow-straw hue. Moderately full-bodied. Balanced acidity. Moderately extracted. Moderately oaked. Vanilla, pears, apples. Warm, spicy aromas follow through on the palate, with a hot finish showing oak spice and mild drying flavors.

1996 Chardonnay, Parmlee-Hill Vineyard, Sonoma Valley $26.   88

Deep golden yellow. Moderately full-bodied. Balanced acidity. Highly extracted. Moderately oaked. Apples, butter. Big and rounded, with a very buttery texture and flavor. Plush and generous in the mouth, showing a leesy richness. A softer style with low acids.

1996 Chardonnay, Sangiacomo Vineyard, Carneros $24.   84

Bright yellow-gold. Medium-bodied. Balanced acidity. Moderately extracted. Moderately oaked. Vanilla, peach, apple. Firmly structured, with oak spice and smoky accents that emerge in the finish, yet this has a core of ripe Chardonnay flavors that fill the midpalate.

Scale: Superlative (96-100), Exceptional (90-95), Highly Recommended (85-89), Recommended (80-84), Not Recommended (Under 80)

1994 Cabernet Sauvignon, Anderson Valley $28.   89

Saturated reddish purple. Medium-bodied. Highly extracted. Moderately tannic. Plums, black fruits, black tea. Ripe, generous fruity nose has vanilla notes. The solid, compact palate has fine depth of flavors and good acids to balance. Not very forthcoming at present, with firm tannins on the finish. One to two years cellaring?

1995 Pinot Noir, Anderson Valley $23.   90

Full ruby red. Medium-bodied. Moderately extracted. Heavily oaked. Moderately tannic. Rich new oak aromas with ripe berry accents. A solid, flavorsome palate, with plenty of tannic grip and bright fruit flavors. The finish is dry and oaky.

1995 Pinot Noir, Bien Nacido Vineyard, Santa Barbara County $34.   91

Dark reddish purple. Medium-bodied. Highly extracted. Moderately oaked. Moderately tannic. Tarry nose. Toasty, juicy black cherry aromas lead a full, rich mouthful of dark fruits. The toasty finish lingers impressively with black cherry flavors. Nice now, better in a year or two.

1996 Zinfandel, Catfish Vineyard, Clear Lake $18.   95

Deep blackish purple. Moderately full-bodied. Balanced acidity. Moderately extracted. Moderately oaked. Mildly tannic. Vanilla, black fruits. Quite aromatic, with an excellent interplay between fruit and spicy wood notes. Lush though well balanced in the mouth. Intense and lengthy.

1996 Zinfandel, Du Pratt Vineyard, Mendocino $20.   93

Opaque blackish purple. Moderately full-bodied. Full acidity. Moderately extracted. Moderately oaked. Mildly tannic. Blueberries, chocolate. Outrageously aromatic, with a melange of oak-tinged flavors that explode on the palate. Rich, supple, and velvety, with bright acidity making for a lively finish. Excellent grip and intensity.

1996 Zinfandel, Pacini Vineyard, Mendocino $16.   92

Deep blackish ruby cast. Moderately full-bodied. Balanced acidity. Highly extracted. Heavily oaked. Mildly tannic. Vanilla, black cherries. Quite aromatic, with large amounts of attractive oak nuances accenting a rich core of chocolatey fruit. Supple, deep, and rich, with a lengthy finish.

Robert Stemmler

1995 Pinot Noir, Sonoma County $26.   87

Pale cherry red with a pinkish hue. Moderately light-bodied. Moderately extracted. Moderately oaked. Mildly tannic. Crisp and angular, with lean flavors of tart red fruits and a minerally, astringent finish. Earthy, with mild leathery notes.

Sterling

1997 Chardonnay, Napa Valley $15.   88

Bright straw cast. Moderately full-bodied. Balanced acidity. Moderately extracted. Mildly tannic. Citrus, butter, minerals. Creamy citrus aromas lead a smooth-textured mouthful of butter and lemon flavors with fine persistence. Oak character is quite reserved and well integrated.

1996 Sauvignon Blanc, North Coast $10.   84

Pale straw hue. Medium-bodied. Balanced acidity. Moderately extracted. White citrus, dried herbs. Aromatically reserved. Clean and unoaked, with an appropriate herbal note that intensifies on the finish.

1995 Merlot, Napa Valley $14.   86

Very deep ruby hue to the rim. Medium-bodied. Balanced acidity. Moderately extracted. Mildly oaked. Mildly tannic. Red fruits, vanilla, minerals. Straightforward and well craft-ed, with pleasant fruit flavors and oak accents. Nicely structured, though quite drinkable.

Stevenot

1996 Zinfandel, Sierra Foothills $12.   81

Stone Creek

1997 Chardonnay, California $6.89.   **82**

1995 Cabernet Sauvignon, California $6.89.   **89**

Bright cherry red. Medium-bodied. Subtly extracted. Mildly tannic. Berry fruits, vanilla. Jammy, ripe aromas lead soft fruity flavors, with a very ripe accent and quick finish. An open-knit style, this is soft and easy drinking, and will be best in its youth.

1996 Cabernet Sauvignon, Special Selection, California $6.89.   **83**

Pale bright ruby red hue. Muted minerals and red berry aromas. A crisp attack leads to a medium-bodied palate with fine grained tannins and crisp berry fruit flavors. Drink now.

1996 Cabernet Sauvignon, Chairman's Reserve, North Coast $15.50.   **83**

Bright ruby-crimson red hue. Markedly ripe fruit cordial-like aromas with vanilla accents. A light entry leads to a medium-bodied palate with weak fruit flavors that finish quickly, showing very slight tannins. Drink now.

1996 Pinot Noir, Sonoma County $13.50.   **83**

Pale pinkish red. Moderately light-bodied. Moderately extracted. Mildly tannic. Floral, candied red fruit aromas. Simple sweet fruit flavors, with a clean, mildly juicy palate through to a quick finish. Highly quaffable.

Stonegate

1996 Sauvignon Blanc, Napa Valley $9.50.   **88**

Bright yellow-gold. Moderately full-bodied. Full acidity. Highly extracted. Heavily oaked. Brown spices, oranges. Very aromatic with a toasty oak overlay. Extremely vibrant acidity produces a bracing finish. A clean and focused style.

1995 Cabernet Sauvignon, Napa Valley $18.   **86**

Bright violet-red. Medium-bodied. Highly extracted. Moderately tannic. Black berry fruits, licorice. Fruit-centered, bright, and fleshy, with chunky tannins that are not so dry as to prevent pleasure. A solid, fruity style.

1996 Sauvignon Blanc, Late Harvest, Napa Valley $15/375 ml.   **84**

Very deep bronzed golden hue. Full-bodied. Balanced acidity. Moderately extracted. Toasted coconut, figs, smoke. Quite aromatic, with a big oak overlay and a core of figgy Semillon flavors. Lush and viscous in the mouth, but has enough acidity to avoid a cloying finish.

Stonehedge

1997 Chardonnay, California $10.   **83**

Deep straw cast. Moderately full-bodied. Balanced acidity. Moderately extracted. Butter, cream. Aromatically reserved, with a ripe buttery quality in the mouth. A touch of acidity lends some balance to the rich finish.

1996 Sauvignon Blanc, California $10.   **81**

1995 Cabernet Sauvignon, Napa Valley $12.99.   **85**

Bright cherry red. Medium-bodied. Moderately extracted. Moderately tannic. Minerals, black fruits. A straightforward, angular, mineral-dominant style with a dry finish, though it has enough flesh to carry the tougher structural elements. Subtle oak influence.

1994 Malbec, Napa Valley $12.99.   **83**

Deep purple with a lightening rim. Moderately light-bodied. Moderately extracted. Moderately tannic. Vanilla, flowers, red fruit. Solid black fruit aromas follow through on the palate, with licorice-like notes through the finish. Tannins are ripe and chewy, though this tends toward the bland.

1995 Zinfandel, Napa Valley $14.99.   **87**

Opaque dark red. Medium-bodied. Balanced acidity. Highly extracted. Mildly oaked. Moderately tannic. Blackberries. Quite tough and solid, with heavily wrought flavors and no sign of a fruity center. The tannins are rather dry and fine grained.

Scale: Superlative (96-100), Exceptional (90-95), Highly Recommended (85-89), Recommended (80-84), Not Recommended (Under 80)

Stonestreet

1996 Chardonnay, Sonoma County $24.   **81**

1997 Gewürztraminer, Anderson Valley $16.   **88**

Deep yellow-straw hue. Intense spice and lychee aromas jump from the glass. A rich entry leads a full-bodied, oily palate. Fat and weighty, with a rounded, flavorful finish. Drink now.

1994 Cabernet Sauvignon, Alexander Valley $35.   **90**

Opaque deep reddish purple. Medium-bodied. Highly extracted. Mildly tannic. Plums, tobacco, vanilla. Oak-accented aromas show full fruity notes. Rounded, full plummy flavors expand on the palate, with ample soft tannins on the finish. Lovely texture. Approachable now.

1995 Cabernet Sauvignon, Alexander Valley $37.   **88**

Deep ruby hue. Moderately full-bodied. Balanced acidity. Highly extracted. Mildly oaked. Moderately tannic. Black fruits, minerals, chocolate. Firm and concentrated, with a lush but tightly wound palate feel. Tannins rear up on the finish.

1994 Legacy, Alexander Valley $50.   **91**

Bright reddish purple. Medium-bodied. Highly extracted. Moderately tannic. Tobacco, vanilla, cedar, black fruits. Plush, elegant aromas are strikingly attractive, leading a rounded, velvety palate, with textured tannins and a lingering cedary finish. A charmer, drinking nicely now.

1995 Legacy, Alexander Valley $65.   **91**

Dark ruby cast. Full-bodied. Balanced acidity. Highly extracted. Heavily oaked. Moderately tannic. Spice, black fruits. Generous aromas lead a lush, velvety mouthfeel with a very firm structure. Tightly wound through the finish. Tannins clamp down hard. Needs time.

1995 Merlot, Alexander Valley $37.   **82**

1995 Pinot Noir, Russian River Valley $30.   **90**

Full ruby red. Medium-bodied. Moderately extracted. Moderately oaked. Moderately tannic. Rich tobacco and vanilla aromas lead a seductively rounded palate, with well-framed cherry fruit flavors and textured soft tannins showing great integration. Very polished style.

1996 Pinot Noir, Russian River Valley $33.   **83**

Bright ruby-garnet cast. Moderately full-bodied. Balanced acidity. Moderately extracted. Heavily oaked. Mildly tannic. Sandalwood, spice, minerals. Quite aromatic, with a hefty oak overlay. Shows quite a bit of weight in the mouth, but lacks a bit for grip.

Storrs

1997 Chardonnay, Ben Lomond Mountain, Santa Cruz Mountains $24.   **93**

Bright yellow-gold. Moderately full-bodied. Balanced acidity. Highly extracted. Moderately oaked. Smoke, butter, green apples. Exotically rich, generous aromas have a yeasty, spicy character that comes through on an impressively deep and persistent palate with an opulent set of flavors.

1995 Pinot Noir, Sunnyknoll Ranch, Santa Cruz Mountains $20.   **86**

Bright red. Medium-bodied. Balanced acidity. Moderately extracted. Moderately oaked. Mildly tannic. Rich and toasty. French oak aromas have a vanilla theme with bright red fruit accents. Lively berry fruit flavors show sweetness on the entry, then become drier and more oaky through the finish. Drinking well now.

Storybook Mountain

1995 Zinfandel, Eastern Exposures, Napa Valley $19.50.   **90**

Bright reddish purple. Medium-bodied. Balanced acidity. Highly extracted. Quite tannic. Black fruits, tea. This is a thick, extracted monster of a wine, with heavy, dry tannins. Rather tight and not much fruit in the middle yet. Not approachable now, but it has the structure to age well.

1996 Zinfandel, Mayacamas Range, Napa Valley $18.50. **84**

Bright blackish purple. Medium-bodied. Balanced acidity. Moderately extracted. Mildly oaked. Mildly tannic. Pepper, briar fruits, vanilla. Quite aromatic, with a firm, minerally palate feel. Lighter in style, but well structured, with an angular finish.

Stratford

1996 Chardonnay, California $12. **84**

Bright yellow-straw hue. Medium-bodied. Balanced acidity. Moderately extracted. Moderately oaked. Vanilla, menthol, lime. High-toned aromas have a marked menthol note. Crisp, bright citrus flavors with a fine complement of oak spice through the finish.

Rodney Strong

1997 Chardonnay, Chalk Hill, Sonoma County $16. **84**

Bright yellow-green. Moderately full-bodied. Balanced acidity. Moderately extracted. Mildly oaked. Green apples, vanilla. Bright green apple aromas follow through well on a bright, clean, persistently flavorsome palate.

1996 Chardonnay, Chalk Hill Vineyard Reserve, Northern Sonoma $24. **87**

Yellow-straw hue. Medium-bodied. Balanced acidity. Moderately extracted. Mildly oaked. Butter, vanilla, apples. Aromatically reserved, this shows a rounded texture and good weight, with elegant toasty flavors and a soft frame.

1997 Sauvignon Blanc, Charlotte's Home, Northern Sonoma $10. **82**

1995 Cabernet Sauvignon, Sonoma County $13. **86**

Bright ruby cast. Medium-bodied. Balanced acidity. Moderately extracted. Moderately oaked. Mildly tannic. Minerals, brown spices. Pleasantly aromatic, with a spicy oak overlay and a core of red fruit flavors on the palate. Lush and well integrated, with a lengthy finish.

1996 Cabernet Sauvignon, Sonoma County $14. **84**

Medium ruby-violet hue. Smoky, cedary aromas. A supple entry leads a medium-bodied palate with cassis and black cherry fruit flavors. Tannins are supple and smooth through the finish.

1993 Cabernet Sauvignon, Alexander's Crown Vineyard, Northern Sonoma $22. **88**

Bright brick red. Medium-bodied. Moderately extracted. Moderately tannic. Minerals, red fruits, brown spice. Brisk and lively, with a firm, minerally backbone and bright fruit acids through the finish. Quite high toned and elegant.

1995 Cabernet Sauvignon, Alexander's Crown Vineyard, Northern Sonoma $24. **86**

Bright ruby cast. Moderately full-bodied. Balanced acidity. Moderately extracted. Mildly tannic. Minerals, black fruits. Aromatically reserved, with a firm, minerally personality. Well structured and lean through the finish.

1993 Cabernet Sauvignon, Reserve, Northern Sonoma $30. **89**

Full cherry red. Medium-bodied. Moderately extracted. Moderately tannic. Red berries, tea, minerals. Red berry and tea aromas lead a harmonious and balanced palate, with some firm powdery tannins on the finish. Quite lean, with an austere but focused character.

1994 Cabernet Sauvignon, Reserve, Northern Sonoma $35. **89**

Dark ruby hue. Moderately full-bodied. Balanced acidity. Moderately extracted. Moderately oaked. Mildly tannic. Brown spices, black fruits, minerals. Generous aromas feature a pleasant interplay between fruit and wood notes. Harmonious, supple, and velvety in the mouth, with a flavorful, well-structured finish.

1996 Merlot, Sonoma County $16. **88**

Medium ruby hue with a slight fade. Perfumed oaky aromas. A supple attack, a medium-bodied palate and light drying tannins on the finish. Drink now or later. Can improve with more age.

Scale: Superlative (96-100), Exceptional (90-95), Highly Recommended (85-89), Recommended (80-84), Not Recommended (Under 80)

1996 Pinot Noir, Russian River Valley $17.   **84**

Pale ruby-garnet cast. Medium-bodied. Balanced acidity. Subtly extracted. Moderately oaked. Mildly tannic. Spice, licorice. Quite aromatic, with a spicy wood note and an unusual high-toned quality. Full in the mouth, yet lacking somewhat for grip. Unusual.

1995 Zinfandel, Old Vines, Northern Sonoma $16.   **82**

Summerfield
1997 Chardonnay, Vintner's Reserve, California $7.99.   **82**

Summers
1997 Chardonnay, Napa Valley $30.   **80**

Sunstone
1997 Chardonnay, Santa Barbara County $20.   **84**

Bright yellow-gold. Medium-bodied. Balanced acidity. Moderately extracted. Mildly oaked. Apples, spice, butter. Buttery, spicy aromas follow through on a silky smooth palate with a subtle fruity expression and a textural richness through the finish.

1996 Cabernet Sauvignon, Santa Barbara County $20.   **81**

1997 Syrah, Reserve, Santa Barbara County $28.   **83**

Dark crimson, limpid, with a slight fade. Ripe earth, black fruit, and tomato flavors. Generous wood tones. Firm entry. Moderately full-bodied. Plentiful drying tannins. Solidly structured. Lingering rich finish. A strange earthy accent mutes the fruit character. Drink now.

Joseph Swan
1997 Chardonnay, Estate Vineyard, Russian River Valley $22.50.   **89**

Deep, saturated yellow-straw hue. Generous vanilla, brown spice, and citrus aromas show a hefty oak influence. A firm entry leads a moderately full-bodied palate, with crisp acids. A rich, rounded, flavorful style with solid acidity. Drink now or later.

1996 Mourvedre, Russian River Valley $15.   **82**

1997 Pinot Noir, Lone Redwood Ranch, Russian River Valley $10.   **80**

1997 Pinot Noir, Saralee's Vineyard, Russian River Valley $16.   **81**

1996 Pinot Noir, Estate, Russian River Valley $30.   **83**

Bright ruby purple with a slight fade. Briar fruit, spice, and red fruit aromas. A firm entry leads a medium-bodied palate with crisp, drying tannins. A strangely flavored Pinot, but it shows some jammy richness and decent grip toward the finish. Drink now.

Swanson
1998 Sangiovese, Rosato, Napa Valley $14.   **87**

Deep cherry red. Attractive toasty aromas show a subtle oak accent. A lush entry leads a moderately full-bodied palate, with crisp acids and ripe fruit flavors. Angular, edgy finish. Drink now.

1994 Cabernet Sauvignon, Napa Valley $24.   **86**

Dark cherry red. Medium-bodied. Moderately extracted. Mildly tannic. Plums, tobacco. Plummy aromas with tobacco accents follow through on the palate. Soft and almost jammy, with bright acids and soft tannins throughout.

1995 Alexis, Napa Valley $40.   **87**

Saturated violet-ruby hue. Medium-bodied. Moderately extracted. Moderately tannic. Vanilla, brown spice, black currants. Attractive toasty aromas follow through, with spicy, supple flavors showing a fine fruit center, and a silky finish. Nice now.

1995 Merlot, Napa Valley $24.   **91**

Deep ruby red to the rim. Moderately full-bodied. Balanced acidity. Highly extracted. Moderately oaked. Mildly tannic. Mint, brown spices, red fruits. Aromatic and flavorful, with real complexity. In the mouth this wine is chewy and lush, showing solid balance and a firm structure. Velvety tannins rise up in the lengthy finish.

1996 Syrah, $40. 88

Dark red-purple color, limpid, with a slight fade. Generous, sound notes of spicy red berries and currants. Firm entry, moderately full-bodied. Plentiful drying tannins. Well extracted, structured. Lingering rich finish. Well wrought and solidly extracted. Drink within five years.

Sylvester

1995 Cabernet Sauvignon, Kiara Reserve, Paso Robles $13.50. 83

Pale ruby cast. Medium-bodied. Moderately extracted. Moderately oaked. Mildly tannic. Red fruits, vanilla. Pleasantly aromatic, with well-integrated fruit and wood flavors. Firm and angular through the finish.

Tablas Creek

1996 Tablas Hills Cuvée Rouge, Paso Robles $19.99. 88

Bright ruby red to the rim. Generous red fruit, herb, and vanilla aromas show an attractive wood accent. A firm attack leads a medium-bodied palate that has tannic grip. The finish is angular and flavorful. Shows fine grip and intensity. Drink within five years.

Taft Street

1996 Sauvignon Blanc, Russian River Valley $9. 81

Talbott

1996 Chardonnay, Cuvée Cynthia, Monterey $45. 91

Deep straw cast. Medium-bodied. Full acidity. Moderately extracted. Mildly oaked. Yeast, toast, minerals. Outrageously aromatic, with a distinctive yeasty complexity. Surprisingly light in the mouth, showing a sense of delicacy and elegance through the lengthy finish.

1995 Chardonnay, Diamond T Estate, Monterey $45. 90

Deep straw cast. Moderately full-bodied. Full acidity. Highly extracted. Mildly oaked. Toasted coconut, minerals, citrus zest. Aromatic and generous, with a range of complex yeasty flavors. Zesty, vibrant, and extremely intense in the mouth, with excellent acidity through the lengthy finish.

Talley

1996 Chardonnay, Arroyo Grande Valley $20. 81

1997 Chardonnay, Arroyo Grande Valley $22. 87

Medium gold. Generous tropical aromas. A lush attack leads a moderately full-bodied palate with muted fruit flavors and a notably alcoholic mouthfeel. Quite a generous style. Drink now.

Iván Tamás

1997 Chardonnay, Central Coast $8.95. 83

Pale yellow-straw hue. Clean fruity aromas of apples lead a medium-bodied palate with no oak influence obvious. Acids are juicy and fruit flavors are clean through the finish. Drink now.

1996 Chardonnay, Reserve, Central Coast $15. 84

Medium yellow-gold. Straightforward aromas of apples and citrus with subtle oak accents. A crisp entry leads a moderately full-bodied palate with angular acids and a sensation of alcohol on the finish. Drink now.

1994 Cabernet Sauvignon, Reserve, Livermore Valley $15. 81

Scale: Superlative (96-100), Exceptional (90-95), Highly Recommended (85-89), Recommended (80-84), Not Recommended (Under 80)

Temecula Crest

1997 Sauvignon Blanc, Temecula $9.95.   **85**

Pale straw hue. Medium-bodied. Full acidity. Moderately extracted. Tart apples, leaves, grapefruit. High-toned grapefruit aromas lead simple tart apple flavors with a minerally backbone. Zesty, clean character.

1996 Nebbiolo, Temecula $18.   **83**

Bright ruby-garnet cast. Medium-bodied. Full acidity. Highly extracted. Mildly tannic. Minerals, earth. Somewhat reserved in flavor, but structurally quite interesting, with a lean, mildly astringent note. Would make a decent table wine.

Terra d'Oro

1995 Barbera, Montevina, Amador County $18.   **87**

Deep blackish ruby cast. Moderately full-bodied. Balanced acidity. Highly extracted. Moderately oaked. Mildly tannic. Vanilla, black fruits, minerals. Extremely aromatic, with a hefty oak overlay and a sturdy core of dark fruit flavors. Rich, though quite firm through the finish. Well balanced, with fine intensity.

1995 Sangiovese, Montevina, Amador County $16.   **87**

Full ruby red. Medium-bodied. Balanced acidity. Moderately extracted. Moderately oaked. Vanilla, red fruits, earth. Softer juicy red fruit flavors defer to dry, dusty tannins. Acids seem a tad low to allow this to age; drink it soon.

1995 Zinfandel, Montevina, Amador County $16.   **82**

The Terraces

1994 Cabernet Sauvignon, Napa Valley $49.99.   **94**

Bright ruby cast. Moderately full-bodied. Balanced acidity. Moderately extracted. Heavily oaked. Mildly tannic. Vanilla, red fruits, brown spices. Extremely aromatic, with a generous oak accent to a bright core of precisely defined red fruit flavors. Stylish, well integrated, and well balanced, with real distinction. Shows fine grip to the intense finish. Though tasty now, it will be better with further cellaring.

Tessera

1996 Chardonnay, California $10.   **81**

Testarossa

1997 Chardonnay, Santa Maria Valley $26.   **85**

Bright yellow-straw cast. Moderately full-bodied. Balanced acidity. Moderately extracted. Mildly oaked. Brown spices, citrus. Generous aromas show a spicy accent. Ripe and rounded in the mouth, with a crisp, snappy finish.

1996 Chardonnay, Chalone Appellation, Monterey County $29.   **87**

Pale straw cast. Medium-bodied. Full acidity. Moderately extracted. Mildly oaked. Vanilla, citrus, minerals. Light in the mouth though quite flavorful, with an oak-accented, yeasty array of flavors. Bright and zesty through the finish.

1996 Chardonnay, Bien Nacido Vineyard, Santa Maria Valley $29.   **83**

Bright yellow-straw cast. Moderately full-bodied. Balanced acidity. Moderately extracted. Minerals, tropical fruits. Aromatically reserved, and marked by a ripe and rounded texture. Crisp through the finish, with a hint of wood spice lingering.

Thackrey

NV Pleiades VII Old Vines Red, California $28.   **86**

Bright garnet red with a slight fade. Generous medicinal and red fruit aromas. A soft attack leads a medium-bodied palate showing silky tannins. Lengthy, supple finish. Old-vine complexity of flavor is married to easy drinkability. Drink now.

1993 Syrah, Orion, Old Vines Rossi Vineyard, St. Helena, Napa Valley $30. **95**
Opaque purplish black. Full-bodied. Full acidity. Lots of fruit. Moderately oaked. Quite tannic. Dry. Reminiscent of vanilla, black fruits, minerals, passion flowers. This vintage's structure is stunning. Hugely extracted, superripe black fruit is supported by a frame of rugged, lasting tannins. Beautifully integrated acidity results in a lively showstopper, explosive with flavor and exquisitely balanced.

1994 Syrah, Orion, Old Vines Rossi Vineyard, St. Helena, Napa Valley $30. **94**
Blackish ruby purple. Full-bodied. Balanced acidity. Highly extracted. Quite tannic. Dry. Reminiscent of rosemary, eucalyptus, marionberry, lavender, sandalwood. Jammy, rich texture. A potpourri of exotic fragrances beautifully enhanced by succulent, lip-smacking black fruits. Quite tannic at present, this is now in a preview stage of greatness.

1995 Syrah, Orion, Old Vines Rossi Vineyard, St. Helena, Napa Valley $45. **97**
Deep, impenetrable blackish purple. Full-bodied. Balanced acidity. Highly extracted. Quite tannic. Eucalyptus, sweet herbs, black fruits, tar. Inimitable in style, with a signature complex nose that has a medicinal, classic Syrah character. Extremely concentrated with great depth and a lash of tannin. Approachable now only by virtue of its outstanding balance. A show wine, not an everyday drink.

1996 Syrah, Orion, Old Vines Rossi Vineyard, St. Helena, Napa Valley $60. **95**
Very dark purple, opaque and brilliant to the rim. Powerful, fantastic coal tar, black fruit, and oak spice flavors. Hefty wood tones. Smooth entry. Full-bodied. Abundant grainy tannins. Monster extraction with lots of everything in a structured frame. Persistent rich finish. Good for long-term (7–10 years) cellaring.

Thornton

1990 Brut Reserve, California $25.   **84**
Bright yellow-gold. Moderately full-bodied. Baked fruit, spice. Mature, faintly bready aromas lead a rich, moderately alcoholic mouthfeel, with baked fruit flavors predominating.

1998 Grenache Rosé, Collins Ranch, Cucamonga Valley $7.99.   **90**
Saturated, deep raspberry pink hue. Attractive, forward red fruit and licorice aromas. A rich entry leads a moderately full-bodied palate showing rounded acidity. Generous and quite flavorful. Drink now.

1996 Cabernet-Merlot, South Coast, South Coast $17.   **86**
Ruby-garnet hue with a fading rim. Medium-bodied. Moderately extracted. Moderately tannic. Leather, spice. Mature, developed aromas lead a dry palate showing leathery tannins and a silky mouthfeel. Flavors take a meaty character. Not for those seeking a fruit-centered style.

1995 Zinfandel, Old Vine, South Coast $18.   **82**

Titus

1994 Cabernet Sauvignon, Napa Valley $22.   **90**
Saturated dark crimson color. Medium-bodied. Highly extracted. Moderately tannic. Plums, black fruits, brown spice, chocolate. Rich, ripe fruit aromas lead a palate showing solid black Cabernet fruit flavors that are complemented by balanced powdery tannins on the finish.

1996 Zinfandel, Napa Valley $17.   **84**
Bright reddish purple. Medium-bodied. Balanced acidity. Moderately extracted. Mildly oaked. Moderately tannic. Red fruits. Rather brash, with bright red fruits and solid tannins giving an angular structure.

Scale: Superlative (96-100), Exceptional (90-95), Highly Recommended (85-89),
Recommended (80-84), Not Recommended (Under 80)

Topolos

1996 Alicante Bouschet, Old Vines, Sonoma County $18.   **86**

Dark, opaque purple red to the rim. Generous, unusual prune, black fruit, and sandalwood aromas suggest mild wood treatment. A firm attack leads a full-bodied palate that shows marked acidity and drying tannins. Persistent, flavorful, tannic finish. Drink now.

1996 Zinfandel, Bella Lisa, Russian River Valley $16.   **84**

Bright blackish ruby cast. Medium-bodied. Balanced acidity. Moderately extracted. Mildly oaked. Mildly tannic. Stewed fruits, brown spices. Carries a slightly overripe note through a lighter-styled palate feel. Lean through the finish. Lacks intensity.

1995 Zinfandel, Piner Heights, Russian River Valley $16.50.   **86**

Bright blackish ruby cast. Medium-bodied. Balanced acidity. Moderately extracted. Moderately oaked. Mildly tannic. Brown spices, black fruits, sweet herbs. Quite aromatic, with a wave of complex, slightly pruney flavors. Full and ripe on the palate, with some chunky tannins in the finish.

1996 Zinfandel, Rossi Ranch, Sonoma Valley $24.75.   **84**

Deep blackish ruby cast. Full-bodied. Balanced acidity. Highly extracted. Mildly oaked. Moderately tannic. Stewed fruits, minerals. Slightly overripe, with a full, flavorful mouthfeel. Carries a strange salty note through the palate. Unusual.

Marimar Torres

1996 Chardonnay, Don Miguel Vineyard, Sonoma County, Green Valley $25.   **81**

1995 Pinot Noir, Don Miguel Vineyard, Sonoma County, Green Valley $25. **86**

Bright saturated ruby cast. Medium-bodied. Full acidity. Moderately extracted. Mildly oaked. Mildly tannic. Minerals, red fruits. Generous aromas feature a racy fruit-centered note that plays out on the palate. Vibrant and clean in the mouth, with grip and intensity through the finish.

Trefethen

1994 Cabernet Sauvignon, Napa Valley $24.   **86**

Opaque bright purple. Medium-bodied. Highly extracted. Mildly tannic. Flowers, red fruits, minerals. High-toned floral and raspberry aromas. Very bright acids. Concentrated red fruit flavors have great clarity, with a clean minerally finish.

1995 Cabernet Sauvignon, Napa Valley $24.   **84**

Bright violet-red. Medium-bodied. Highly extracted. Moderately tannic. Black cherries, mineral. Lighter styled and juicy, with bright cherry flavors and a supple finish. Drinking well now.

Trentadue

1995 Carignane, Sonoma County $12.   **87**

Dark crimson. Moderately full-bodied. Moderately extracted. Mildly tannic. Plummy, black cherry flavors follow through with a generous palate feel and mouthcoating tannins. Drinking well now, though it will develop in the future. Very modern and well-extracted.

1994 Merlot, Alexander Valley $18.   **85**

Deep ruby with a slight garnet fade and brilliant clarity. Medium-bodied. Full acidity. Moderately extracted. Mildly tannic. Dusty cherries, sweet herbs, mint. Lighter in style, with bright and lively flavors and vibrant acidity on the palate. Some dusty tannins at the finish.

1995 Petite Sirah, Sonoma County $16.   **83**

Dark saturated ruby red. Highly extracted. Medium-bodied. Moderately tannic. Minty, black fruit aromas follow through. Lush fruit flavors with moderate tannins give this a very forward fruit-centered character that invites current drinking.

1995 Sangiovese, Alexander Valley $18.   **89**
Dark ruby color. Medium-bodied. Balanced acidity. Moderately extracted. Moderately oaked. Mildly tannic. Eucalyptus, tart cherries, minerals. Very aromatic. The bright, vibrant palate has tight, minerally focus with high-toned fruit flavors.

1994 Merlot Port, Alexander Valley $20.   **84**
Bright cherry red. Medium-bodied. Balanced acidity. Moderately extracted. Mildly oaked. Mildly tannic. Reminiscent of plums, mint, mocha. Soft, moderately lush texture. A bright plummy nose leads a racy palate with high-toned fruity flavors, delicate brown spice, and some gentle tannins in the finish.

1994 Petite Sirah Port, Alexander Valley $20.   **88**
Opaque reddish purple. Moderately full-bodied. Highly extracted. Reminiscent of cherry, apple, black fruits. Sweet plummy entry expands on the midpalate, with the finish showing tannic grip and spicy notes. A bit unapproachable now, but should soften up beautifully with time.

Tria

1995 Labyrinth Red, California $18.   **86**
Deep ruby hue with a garnet edge. Generous vanilla and red fruit aromas. A lush entry leads to a medium-bodied palate with lean tannins and zesty acidity. Ripe, well-cut finish. Showing some intensity. Drink now.

1996 Pinot Noir, Monterey $20.   **85**
Bright ruby red. Medium-bodied. Moderately extracted. Moderately oaked. Mildly tannic. Leather, black fruits. Spicy, perfumed aromas lead a mouthful of dark fruit flavors, with oak spice rearing up on the finish. Flavorful.

1996 Zinfandel, Dry Creek Valley $18.   **89**
Deep blackish purple. Full-bodied. Balanced acidity. Highly extracted. Mildly oaked. Moderately tannic. Minerals, chocolate. Quite firm and flavorful, with a highly structured palate feel. Rich and intense, with chunky tannins through the finish.

Tribaut

NV Blanc de Blancs Brut, California $9.   **86**
Deep golden cast. Medium-bodied. Full acidity. Subtly extracted. Butter, minerals. Rather overtly mature, with big toasty aromas that follow through on the palate. Shows buttery richness, though not a lengthy finish. Although the maturity is exaggerated, this has attractive character.

NV Blanc de Noirs Brut, California $9.   **80**

M. Trinchero

1996 Chardonnay, Founder's Estate, Napa Valley $25.   **83**
Pale straw hue. Very distinctive aromas show assertive toasted oak and smoky yeast. A woody attack leads a moderately full-bodied, brightly acidic palate dominated by oak-accented flavors.

1995 Cabernet Sauvignon, Founder's Estate, Napa Valley $30.   **84**
Dark violet-red. Medium-bodied. Moderately extracted. Moderately tannic. Earth, licorice, black fruits. Dry and compact, with alcohol supplying a rounded mouthfeel. The finish is rather short and powdery.

1996 Cabernet Sauvignon, Founder's Estate, California $30.   **88**
Intense, saturated neon purple hue. Very aromatic with violet and anise aromas. A firm attack leads to a full-bodied palate with dense, dry tannins drying the palate. Quite tough and unyielding now, but the acids are excellent. Drink within five years.

Scale: Superlative (96-100), Exceptional (90-95), Highly Recommended (85-89),
Recommended (80-84), Not Recommended (Under 80)

Truchard

1996 Chardonnay, Carneros, Napa Valley $24.   91

Pale green-gold. Moderately full-bodied. Full acidity. Moderately extracted. Moderately oaked. Vanilla, spice, lemons. Very aromatic, with plush fruity, smoky aromas following through on the palate. Shows a supple and silky mouthfeel, with a lingering finish.

1995 Cabernet Sauvignon, Carneros, Napa Valley $24.   88

Saturated dark ruby red. Moderately full-bodied. Moderately extracted. Moderately tannic. Spice, crisp berries, cherry tomato. Lively, engaging aromas. Berrylike flavors burst on the palate with balanced, powdery tannins giving some authority on the finish. Very nice now.

1994 Cabernet Sauvignon, Reserve, Carneros, Napa Valley $32.   90

Full ruby hue with violet highlights. Medium-bodied. Moderately extracted. Mildly tannic. Cassis, cedar. Soft, silky, and supple, this has a refined balance with succulent Cabernet fruit flavors. Soft tannins caress the finish, which shows fine persistence. Drinking very nicely now.

1996 Pinot Noir, Carneros, Napa Valley $25.   83

Pale violet-ruby hue. Medium-bodied. Subtly extracted. Mildly tannic. Red fruits, strawberries, vanilla. Perfumed fruity aromas lead a supple, smooth, silky mouthful of flavors with attractive vanilla accents throughout. A delicate style.

1996 Zinfandel, Carneros, Napa Valley $18.   90

Deep blackish ruby cast. Medium-bodied. Full acidity. Moderately extracted. Moderately oaked. Mildly tannic. Mint, brown spices, red fruits. Quite aromatic, with a lively, high-toned array of flavors on the palate. Supple and well balanced, with a lengthy finish. Eminently drinkable.

Tulocay

1997 Chardonnay, Napa Valley $16.   84

Medium yellow-straw color. Aromas show a marked yeasty note that verges on cheesy. Assertively smoky on the attack, with a full body and deep woody flavors, though it is rather short on fruit. Finishes quickly.

1994 Cabernet Sauvignon, Cliff Vineyard, Napa Valley $22.   87

Deep, dark brick red. Moderately full-bodied. Highly extracted. Moderately tannic. Mineral, earth, black plums. The firm, hard-edged palate has deep black fruit flavors up front, with a strong minerally underlay. A little tough now but not impenetrable. Time should resolve this.

1996 Cabernet Sauvignon, Cliff Vineyard, Napa Valley $21.   89

Saturated blackish-ruby hue. Restrained aromas show anise and black fruits. A firm entry leads a moderately full-bodied palate with deeply extracted flavors that finish dryly with a lingering woody note. Rather tough at present. Drink now or later.

1996 Pinot Noir, Haynes Vineyard, Napa Valley $18.   84

Pale ruby red. Moderately light-bodied. Subtly extracted. Mildly tannic. Minerals, oak spice, berry fruits. Lean, high-toned aromas lead a brisk, tart fruit palate with fine grip and a minerally finish. Nice now, it does not have the stuffing for long aging.

Turley

1996 Zinfandel, Old Vines, California $30.   92

Deep blackish ruby hue. Full-bodied. Balanced acidity. Highly extracted. Heavily oaked. Mildly tannic. Black fruits, vanilla. Quite aromatic, with a big, ripe, fruit-centered palate feel. Firm and rich, with a deep, lengthy finish. Weighty but well balanced.

1995 Zinfandel, Moore "Earthquake" Vineyard, Napa Valley $35. 86

Deep ruby-garnet hue with a slight haze. Moderately full-bodied. Low acidity. Moderately extracted. Mildly tannic. Overripe red fruits, brown spices. Quite aromatic, with a full, ripe, rich palate feel. Almost viscous, with a distinct impression of sweetness. Made in a late-harvest style, it features a Port-like note throughout. Soft and luxuriant through the finish, with good length. Surprisingly open-knit, given its weight.

1996 Zinfandel, Hayne Vineyard, Napa Valley $35.   **95**

Deep blackish ruby cast with a slight haze. Full-bodied. Low acidity. Highly extracted. Moderately oaked. Mildly tannic. Black fruits, earth, chocolate. Rather reserved aromatically, with a deep, brooding quality throughout. Dark, firm, and extracted, with a ripe, chocolatey quality. Big and weighty but well balanced, with a highly structured, lengthy finish.

Turnbull

1994 Cabernet Sauvignon, Napa Valley $22.   **88**

Dark garnet-ruby color. Medium-bodied. Highly extracted. Moderately tannic. Plums, ground spice, earth. Deep fleshy aromas with full spicy accents lead a rounded, juicy entry that turns rather earthy and authoritatively dry on the finish.

1995 Cabernet Sauvignon, Napa Valley $20.   **88**

Deep saturated ruby hue. Moderately full-bodied. Balanced acidity. Moderately extracted. Moderately oaked. Mildly tannic. Red fruits, vanilla. Generous aromas reveal a full and well-balanced palate. Firm and angular through the lengthy, flavorful finish.

Turning Leaf

1995 Chardonnay, Reserve, Sonoma County $10.   **84**

Bright yellow-straw cast. Moderately full-bodied. Balanced acidity. Highly extracted. Mildly oaked. Citrus, cream, brown spices. Forward aromas carry an enticing spicy accent and a full mouthfeel but also hint at a degree of maturity. The finish is lean and angular.

1994 Cabernet Sauvignon, Reserve, Sonoma County $10.   **81**
1995 Merlot, Sonoma County $10.   **80**
1996 Merlot, Winemaker's Choice Reserve, Sonoma County $12.   **81**
1995 Pinot Noir, Reserve, Sonoma County $10.99.   **85**

Pale pinkish cherry red. Moderately light-bodied. Moderately extracted. Mildly tannic. Vanilla and raspberry aromas. Simple crisp red fruit palate with dry fine-grained tannins on the finish.

1996 Pinot Noir, Winemaker's Choice Reserve, California $12.   **82**

Twin Hills

1993 Cabernet Sauvignon, Paso Robles $15.   **83**

Deep blackish ruby cast. Moderately full-bodied. Full acidity. Moderately extracted. Mildly oaked. Moderately tannic. Sandalwood, minerals, black fruits. Reined-in, wood-accented aromatics lead a firm and angular palate feel. Crisp through the finish.

1994 Zinfandel, Paso Robles $15.   **80**
Zinfandel Port, Lot XCII, Paso Robles $25.   **89**

Deep garnet cast. Moderately full-bodied. Full acidity. Highly extracted. Roasted salted nuts, rancio, treacle. Extraordinarily aromatic, with an notable Sherry-like quality to the complex flavors. Rich and intense, with a roasted accent and an angular finish provided by juicy acidity.

M.G. Vallejo

1997 Chardonnay, California $6.99.   **81**
1997 White Zinfandel, California $6.   **82**
1996 Pinot Noir, California $6.99.   **82**

Valley of the Moon

1995 Zinfandel, Sonoma Valley $25.   **90**

Bright blackish ruby cast. Moderately full-bodied. Full acidity. Moderately extracted. Mildly tannic. Black fruits, earth. Pleasantly aromatic, with deep, brooding flavors. Rich on the palate, with a finish enlivened by buoyant acidity. Zesty.

Scale: Superlative (96-100), Exceptional (90-95), Highly Recommended (85-89), Recommended (80-84), Not Recommended (Under 80)

Van Asperen

1997 Chardonnay, Napa Valley $12.   81

1994 Cabernet Sauvignon, Napa Valley $15.   84

Bright violet red. Medium-bodied. Moderately extracted. Moderately tannic. Cassis, minerals, vanilla. Bright, crisp aromas follow through on a lively palate with minerally backbone. A leaner style.

1995 Cabernet Sauvignon, Napa Valley $18.   84

Bright cherry red hue. Subdued, lean mineral and earth aromas. A lean entry leads to a moderately light-bodied palate with candied flavors, bright acidity, and grippy tannins. Snappy, flavorful finish. A straightforward but tasty style. Drink now.

1994 Cabernet Sauvignon, Signature Reserve, Napa Valley $28.   86

Bright purple red hue. Pronounced vanilla, mineral, and herb aromas show a judicious oak accent. A lean entry leads to a medium-bodied palate with crisp tannins and vibrant acidity. Generous, flavorful finish. Well balanced. Drink within five years.

1996 Merlot, Napa Valley $15.   83

Bright violet hue with a pale cast. Mildly floral aromas. Medium-bodied, with a soft attack and rounded, lighter flavors and a clean finish. Drink now.

1995 Zinfandel, Napa Valley $10.   82

Van Roekel

1996 Viognier, Temecula $10.95.   82

1997 Rosé of Syrah, Temecula $9.95.   80

1996 Zinfandel, Temecula $13.95.   80

1994 Sweet Salud, Temecula $15.95.   83

Deep golden cast. Medium-bodied. Full acidity. Moderately extracted. Tropical fruits, honey, dried herbs. Aromatic, with a full though angular palate feel. Acidity is extremely vibrant through the finish.

Venezia

1996 Chardonnay, Big River Ranch, Alexander Valley $19.99.   86

Bright yellow-straw cast. Moderately full-bodied. Full acidity. Heavily oaked. Yeast, oak spice, ripe citrus. Complex, toasty aromatics lead a brightly acidic yet full-flavored and weighty palate featuring spicy oak and citrus acids through the finish.

1997 Chardonnay, Regusci Vineyards, Napa Valley $20.   89

Brilliant yellow-gold. Ripe, generous aromas of butter, smoke, and tropical fruits. A rich, fruity entry leads a full- bodied palate with a juicy center and plenty of yeasty, oaky accents emerging on the finish. Drink now.

1995 Cabernet Sauvignon, Meola Vineyards, Alexander Valley $20.   87

Deep crimson red. Medium-bodied. Moderately extracted. Moderately tannic. Toasted oak, vanilla, black fruits. High-toned floral aromas show oaky accents that are confirmed on the palate. Tending toward austere, with tightly wound black fruit flavors and plenty of dry oaky character through the finish.

1996 Cabernet Sauvignon, Meola Vineyards, Alexander Valley $19.99. 88

Very deep ruby purple. Moderately full-bodied. Balanced acidity. Moderately extracted. Moderately oaked. Mildly tannic. Vanilla, cassis, minerals. Generous aromas feature a toasty oak accent. Acidity lends a sense of brightness to the core of fruit flavors. Firm, lengthy finish.

1996 Sangiovese, Alegria Vineyards, Russian River Valley $19.99.   85

Bright purple red. Medium-bodied. Balanced acidity. Moderately extracted. Moderately tannic. Vanilla, black fruits, minerals. A dry, assertive character is imparted by oak influences, with high-toned dried red fruit flavors coming through.

1996 Sangiovese, Nuovo Mondo, North Coast $19.99.   **84**

Bright reddish purple. Moderately light-bodied. Balanced acidity. Moderately extracted. Mildly tannic. Red fruits, vanilla. Rather soft on the finish. Rounded cherry flavors finish quickly.

1996 Sangiovese, Van Noy Vineyards, Russian River Valley $19.99.   **84**

Bright cherry purple. Medium-bodied. Balanced acidity. Moderately extracted. Moderately oaked. Moderately tannic. Red fruits, vanilla. Youthful, high-toned fruity "aromas. Crisp, red fruit flavors elevate a dry oak background that follows through on the finish.

Venge

1996 Sangiovese, Penny Lane Vineyard, Oakville, Napa Valley $20.   **86**

Dark ruby. Medium-bodied. Balanced acidity. Moderately extracted. Mildly oaked. Mildly tannic. Black fruits, earth. Very soft and fleshy, with dark, berry-accented flavors. Velvety tannins. Lush and textured.

Via Firenze

1995 Dolcetto, Napa Valley $14.99.   **84**

Bright ruby cast. Medium-bodied. Full acidity. Moderately extracted. Mildly tannic. Red fruits, minerals. Somewhat reserved aromatically, but turns quite flavorful on the palate. Lean, concentrated, and focused, with a firm, angular finish. Intense and well balanced.

1996 Sangiovese, Tuscan Collection, Mendocino $17.99.   **81**

Viader

1993 Red, Napa Valley $30.   **89**

Full crimson red. Medium-bodied. Moderately extracted. Moderately tannic. Ripe berries, currants, anise. Full, ripe fruity aromas follow through well on the palate, with plush tannins highlighting the finish. Drinking nicely now.

Vigil

1996 A. Nice, Chardonnay, California $12.   **84**

Deep straw cast. Medium-bodied. Full acidity. Moderately extracted. Dried herbs, minerals, butter. Forward high-toned aromas lead a ripe mouthfeel with a textured buttery quality. Crisp acidity makes for a refreshing finish.

1997 Cabernet Franc, Solari Vineyard, Napa Valley $25.   **84**

Deep, saturated purple-red hue. Opulent, unusual ginger and black fruit aromas carry a big oak accent. A lush entry leads to a moderately full-bodied palate with supple velvety tannins. Rich, chocolatey finish. Rather unusual flavors, but not unattractive. Drink now or later.

1995 Valiente Claret, Napa Valley $20.   **86**

Bright reddish purple. Medium-bodied. Moderately extracted. Mildly tannic. Red fruits, minerals, chocolate. Quite light on the midpalate, though the flavors have a juicy quality. Chocolatey flavors and a minerally backbone come through on the finish.

1996 Valiente Claret, Napa Valley $22.   **86**

Bright ruby purple. Medium-bodied. Full acidity. Highly extracted. Moderately oaked. Moderately tannic. Menthol, red fruits, vanilla. Forward aromas carry an overtly minty quality. Racy and lean in the mouth all the way through the flavorful finish, with a firm structure.

1996 Zinfandel, Tres Condados, California $12.99.   **84**

Bright blackish purple. Moderately full-bodied. Balanced acidity. Moderately extracted. Mildly tannic. Black fruits, minerals. Reserved aromatically, but features a solid core of brooding, dark fruit flavors. Well structured and firm, with good grip to the finish.

Villa Mt. Eden

1997 Chardonnay, California $10.   **88**

Bright yellow-gold. Ripe smoky, browned butter aromas. A rich, flavorful entry leads a moderately full-bodied palate with impressively concentrated fruit flavors, juicy acids, and well-integrated oak character. Persistent fruity finish. Drink now or later.

1997 Chardonnay, Grand Reserve, Bien Nacido Vineyard,
Santa Maria Valley $18.   **88**

Bright yellow-gold. Ripe fruity aromas show yeast, butter, and well-integrated oak. A smooth entry leads a medium-bodied palate with good fruit emphasis and a generous mouthfeel. Finishes with a lingering yeasty note. Stylish. Drink now or later.

1996 Chardonnay, Signature Series, Bien Nacido Vineyard,
Santa Maria Valley $30.   **93**

Deep gold. Powerfully aromatic with very ripe fruits, and rich leesy and oaky accents. A sumptuous attack leads a full-bodied palate with a smooth, textured mouthfeel. Flavors are quite concentrated with deep fruity character. Finishes with leesy complexity. Drink now or later.

1995 Cabernet Sauvignon, California $11.   **82**

1995 Cabernet Sauvignon, Grand Reserve, Napa Valley $20.   **89**

Deep brick-violet hue. Ripe fleshy aromas with a woody accent. A smooth attack leads a moderately full-bodied palate with a thickish mouthfeel and softer acidity, allied to supple but richly textured tannins. Generous, rich style. Very approachable now. Drink now.

1994 Cabernet Sauvignon, Signature Series, Mendocino $50.   **90**

Blackish red with purple highlights. Medium-bodied. Highly extracted. Moderately tannic. Plums, black fruits, black tea, brown spice. Oaky aromas have fleshy accents that are confirmed on the palate. Impressively rich and deep, with well-extracted flavors through a dry oaky finish. Short- to medium-term cellaring should round this out.

1995 Cabernet Sauvignon, Signature Series, Mendocino $45.   **90**

Saturated dark red with purple highlights. Moderately full-bodied. Highly extracted. Heavily oaked. Moderately tannic. Vanilla, oak spice, black fruits. Dense oak-dominated aromas follow through on the palate. Deep, rich, and chocolatey, though under the thumb of its oak at present. This should be better in a year or two.

1996 Zinfandel, California $12.   **84**

Bright blackish ruby hue. Moderately full-bodied. Balanced acidity. Highly extracted. Moderately oaked. Moderately tannic. Brown spices, black fruits. Pleasantly aromatic, with a flavorful palate feel. Firm and well structured, with dusty tannins through the finish. Nicely balanced and lengthy.

1996 Zinfandel, Grand Reserve, Monte Rosso Vineyard,
Sonoma Valley $20.   **84**

Deep blackish ruby cast. Full-bodied. Full acidity. Highly extracted. Moderately tannic. Black fruits, pepper. Reserved aromatically but full-throttled on the palate, with prickly acidity and a thick texture. Carries a slightly overripe undercurrent, with a suggestion of sweetness.

Volker Eisele

1995 Cabernet Sauvignon, Napa Valley $30.   **85**

Deep ruby cast. Full-bodied. Balanced acidity. Highly extracted. Mildly oaked. Moderately tannic. Earth, spice, dried herbs. Pleasantly aromatic, showing a firm and chunky palate feel. Rich and weighty, with a wave of tannins that bite into the finish. Needs time.

1996 Cabernet Sauvignon, Napa Valley $30.   **85**

Bright violet-red hue. Aromatically reserved with an herbal note to the nose. A firm entry leads a medium-bodied palate with very tough, youthful tannins gripping the finish. Rather youthful and angular. Drink now or later.

Von Strasser

1994 Cabernet Sauvignon, Diamond Mountain, Napa Valley $32.   **90**

Saturated purple-red. Moderately full-bodied. Highly extracted. Moderately tannic. Red fruits, crisp blackberries, minerals. Bright, high-toned fruit aromas lead a lively, concentrated palate, with minerally austerity coming through on the finish. Promising structure bodes well for keeping.

1995 Cabernet Sauvignon, Diamond Mountain, Napa Valley $36.   **87**

Dark, saturated ruby purple. Full-bodied. Balanced acidity. Highly extracted. Moderately oaked. Quite tannic. Vanilla, minerals, black fruits. Shows a toasty oak accent on the nose, but closes down completely in the mouth, with a wave of astringent tannins. Rather severe, this will need extended cellaring.

Voss

1997 Sauvignon Blanc, Napa Valley $12.50.   **95**

Deep straw cast. Moderately full-bodied. Full acidity. Highly extracted. Dried herbs, pineapple, gooseberries. Markedly pungent, with forceful New Zealand-style herbal flavors. Crisp and extremely vibrant, with a juicy mouthfeel and a lengthy, flavorful finish. Very stylish.

1995 Merlot, Napa Valley $20.   **89**

Deep ruby red to the rim. Medium-bodied. Balanced acidity. Moderately extracted. Mildly oaked. Moderately tannic. Black fruits, earth, minerals. Compact in style, with a youthful core of flavors wrapped in a shroud of velvety tannins. Well balanced, it should mellow with age.

1996 Merlot, Napa Valley $18.   **84**

Bright, pale ruby red. Generous red fruit, vanilla, and herb aromas show an attractive wood accent. A crisp attack is followed by a moderately light-bodied palate with a vibrant, fruity finish. Eminently drinkable and tasty. Drink now.

1995 Shiraz, Napa Valley $16.   **88**

Deep, opaque purple-red hue. Generous sweet wood, vanilla, and berry aromas show a dominant oak accent. A rich, lush attack leads a full-bodied palate, with abundant velvety tannins. Big, chunky finish. Drink within five years.

1996 Botrytis Sauvignon Blanc, Napa Valley $18.50/375 ml.   **89**

Very deep bronzed golden hue. Full-bodied. Full acidity. Moderately extracted. Apricots, honey, vanilla. Heavily botrytized, with a complex wave of flavors on the palate. Though quite viscous, this wine features excellent acidic grip through the finish. An intense style.

Weinstock

1996 Chardonnay, California $10.99.   **83**

Yellow-straw color. Medium-bodied. Balanced acidity. Moderately extracted. Mildly oaked. Vanilla, spice, apples. Light oak spice aromas lead a bright, straightforward mouthful of flavors with buttery texture and enough acid to keep the finish fresh.

1997 Contour, Clarksburg $8.95.   **82**

1998 Contour, Clarksburg $8.95.   **86**

Very pale straw cast. Quite aromatic, with a big floral, fruity character. A lush entry leads a medium-bodied palate, with sweet tropical flavors carrying through to the finish. Drink now.

1997 Sauvignon Blanc, California $8.99.   **81**

1998 White Zinfandel, California $6.95.   **84**

Pale pink. Subdued berry and mineral aromas. A crisp entry leads a medium-bodied palate with sharp fruit acidity balanced by mild sweetness. Very clean and refreshing. Vibrant. Drink now.

Scale: Superlative (96-100), Exceptional (90-95), Highly Recommended (85-89), Recommended (80-84), Not Recommended (Under 80)

1997 Gamay, Paso Robles $7.49.   84

Bright neon violet hue. Medium-bodied. Moderately extracted. Mildly tannic. Black fruits. Grapey and fresh on the nose and through the palate, with clean lightly astringent notes on the finish. Very tasty and balanced.

NV Pinot Noir, Reserve, American $7.99.   80

Wellington

1994 Cabernet Sauvignon, Mohrhardt Ridge Vineyard,
Sonoma County $15.   87

Opaque blackish red-purple. Moderately full-bodied. Highly extracted. Moderately tannic. Plums, cassis, earth, brown spice. Heavyweight black fruit flavors are complemented by a voluptuous mouthfeel, with fine, supple tannins that show a hint of firmness on the finish. Attractive now.

1995 Merlot, Sonoma Valley $16.   89

Deep ruby hue with a purplish cast. Moderately full-bodied. Balanced acidity. Highly extracted. Moderately oaked. Moderately tannic. Red fruits, licorice, vanilla. Aromatic and quite rich in style with a chewy palate feel. Tannins have some grip in the mouth, but the finish is still relatively lengthy. Tasty but serious.

Wente

NV Brut Reserve, Arroyo Seco $14.   81

1997 Chardonnay, Central Coast $11.   83

Pale yellow-straw hue. Generous ripe aromas have a buttery accent. A rich attack leads a moderately full-bodied palate with tropical flavors and judicious oak. The acidity is well balanced and fresh. The finish is persistent, with a touch of oak spice.

1996 Chardonnay, Riva Ranch Reserve, Arroyo Seco, Monterey $16.   86

Pale straw cast. Moderately full-bodied. Full acidity. Moderately extracted. Mildly oaked. Minerals, spice, cream. Generous spicy aromas lead a ripe and creamy mouthfeel. Lushly textured through the zesty finish.

1996 Cabernet Sauvignon, Livermore Valley $11.   80

1994 Cabernet Sauvignon, Charles Wetmore Reserve, Livermore Valley $22.   89

Pale cherry red. Moderately light-bodied. Moderately extracted. Mildly tannic. Red berries, brown spice, minerals. Smooth and juicy mouthfeel, with a soft finish showing lingering brown spice notes. Nicely balanced and very approachable now. A lighter style but well balanced, with a generous character.

1995 Cabernet Sauvignon, Charles Wetmore Reserve,
Livermore Valley $24.   81

1996 Merlot, Crane Ridge Reserve, Livermore Valley $16.   84

Deep, saturated ruby red. Generous dusty cherry and mineral aromas. A soft attack leads a medium-bodied palate, with tannic grip and a structured, flavorful finish. Well balanced and intense. Drink now or later. Can improve with more age.

Mark West

1996 Chardonnay, Russian River Valley $15.   89

Bright yellow-gold. Moderately full-bodied. Full acidity. Moderately extracted. Moderately oaked. Lemons, spice. Bright, zesty aromas show a touch of spice. A crisp, lively mouthful of vibrant flavors grips the palate through the finish.

Whitcraft

1996 Pinot Noir, Bien Nacido Vineyard, Santa Maria Valley $34.99.   88

Dark red with purple highlights. Medium-bodied. Highly extracted. Heavily oaked. Moderately tannic. Brooding, earthy aromas have a ferric note. Fruity black cherry richness up front gives way to a solid, lingering earthy finish that is not too dry. Well structured, and quite distinctive.

Whitehall Lane

1997 Chardonnay, Napa Valley $16.   **84**

Brilliant yellow-gold. Smooth smoky aromas. A spicy entry leads a moderately full-bodied palate with alcohol warmth showing through the tart acids. Drink now.

1996 Cabernet Sauvignon, Napa Valley $22.   **88**

Dark red-violet. Medium-bodied. Highly extracted. Moderately tannic. Ripe berries, vanilla. Very ripe, fruit-laden aromas show rich oak accents that follow through on a rich, softer-styled palate. The finish has ample velvety tannins. Drinking well now.

1994 Cabernet Sauvignon, Morisoli Vineyard Reserve, Napa Valley $36.   **92**

Opaque, dark ruby purple. Medium-bodied. Highly extracted. Moderately tannic. Cassis, black fruits, tobacco. Impressively generous and concentrated black Cabernet fruit flavors are complemented by lovely sweet tobacco and cedar notes through the finish. Mouthfeel is textured and plush.

1995 Cabernet Sauvignon, Morisoli Vineyard Reserve, Napa Valley $40.   **90**

Deep ruby purple. Moderately full-bodied. Balanced acidity. Moderately extracted. Heavily oaked. Mildly tannic. Black fruits, vanilla, spice. Quite aromatic, displaying a hefty oak overlay and a dense core of pure black fruit flavors. Concentrated and harmonious, with an overtone of sweetness to the wood flavors through the finish.

1995 Merlot, Napa Valley $20.   **88**

Deep blackish ruby hue. Balanced acidity. Highly extracted. Moderately oaked. Quite tannic. Chocolate, black fruits, minerals. Deeply flavored though still very tightly wound. Big, aggressive tannins rear up on the finish, but the level of extract should outlast them. Mid-term to long-term (7–10 years) cellaring will help it open up.

1996 Merlot, Napa Valley $22.   **88**

Semi-saturated brick-red hue. Generously aromatic with toasty vanilla accents on the nose. A lush, supple attack shows generous cherry fruit flavors. Quite oaky on the palate, with softer tannins through the finish. Drink now.

1995 Merlot, Leonardini Vineyard Reserve, Napa Valley $36.   **93**

Inky ruby hue with a purple cast. Full-bodied. Balanced acidity. Highly extracted. Heavily oaked. Quite tannic. Toasted coconut, black fruits, minerals. Quite attractive aromatically with a big oak overlay. A dense and focused core of fruit presents itself on the rich and velvety palate. Finishes with a wave of thick tannins. Sturdy but well balanced. Mid-term to long-term (7–10 years) cellaring recommended.

1996 Merlot, Leonardini Vineyard Reserve, Napa Valley $40.   **92**

Well-saturated bright violet red. Ripe fruit-laden aromas with a marked oaky accent. A soft, fruity attack is followed by rounded fruity flavors that fill the midpalate. Finishes with very supple, softer tannins. Drink now.

Wild Horse

1996 Cabernet Sauvignon, Paso Robles $16.   **81**

1997 Valdigue, Paso Robles $13.   **83**

Full purple-red. Medium-bodied. Moderately extracted. Mildly tannic. Jammy red fruits, candied berries. Jammy, ripe aromas lead a mildly overripe mouthful of flavors with very soft tannins on the finish.

1995 Grenache, Cienega Valley $13.   **84**

Pale garnet red with a slight fade. Generous overripe red fruit and mineral aromas. A firm attack leads a moderately light-bodied palate, with mildly astringent tannins. Lean, angular finish. Solid grip but lacks generosity. Drink now.

1995 Merlot, Central Coast $18.   **85**

Deep blackish ruby hue with brilliant clarity. Medium-bodied. Full acidity. Moderately extracted. Mildly tannic. Black fruits, minerals. Straightforward and well structured, with crisp acidity. Clean, angular finish.

Scale: Superlative (96-100), Exceptional (90-95), Highly Recommended (85-89),
Recommended (80-84), Not Recommended (Under 80)

1996 Merlot, Central Coast $16.   **84**

Bright brick red. Lean aromas of minerals and spice. A crisp attack leads a medium-bodied palate with light, grainy tannins. The finish is crisp, with tart fruit flavors persisting nicely. Drink now.

1995 Merlot, Paso Robles $18.   **85**

Deep ruby red with brilliant clarity. Medium-bodied. Balanced acidity. Moderately extracted. Mildly tannic. Black fruits, sweet herbs. Quite focused and very fruit driven. Clean and crisp on the palate, with noticeable acidity and a tart cranberry-accented finish.

1995 Merlot, Unbridled, Paso Robles $28.   **88**

Very deep blackish ruby hue. Moderately full-bodied. Balanced acidity. Moderately extracted. Heavily oaked. Mildly tannic. Leather, black fruits, minerals. Leathery, gamey oak influences mingle with a core of deep fruit flavors. A tad austere on the palate, with a structured, focused mouthfeel. Clean and racy finish.

1996 Mourvedre, James Berry Vineyard, Paso Robles $16.   **86**

Ruby red. Medium-bodied. Moderately extracted. Moderately tannic. Black cherry. Firm and well extracted, with dark fruit flavors giving way to a lengthy finish showing a degree of tannic toughness.

1997 Pinot Noir, Central Coast $19.   **84**

Bright violet red. Medium-bodied. Moderately extracted. Mildly tannic. Flowers, berry fruits, vanilla. Light floral aromas lead a brisk palate, with berry fruit flavors, crisp acids, and subtle vanilla oak notes lingering. Shows a bitter note on the finish.

1996 Syrah, Central Coast $16.   **80**

1996 Syrah, James Berry Vineyard, Paso Robles $18.   **86**

Deep ruby purple, limpid, and brilliant to the rim. Mild, sound herb, mineral, and berry fruit flavors. Subtle wood tones. Firm entry. Moderately full-bodied with crisp acidity. Plentiful grainy tannins. Bright, crisp, and well gripped. Clipped finish. Rather tightly wound, with some tart herbal flavors.

Wildhurst

1996 Sauvignon Blanc, Clear Lake $9.   **81**

1996 Merlot, Clear Lake $14.   **86**

Deep ruby to the rim with brilliant clarity. Medium-bodied. Balanced acidity. Moderately extracted. Mildly tannic. Black fruits, sweet herbs, minerals. Lighter in style, with an angular presence on the palate. The flavors push through some dusty tannins. Pleasant.

1996 Zinfandel, Clear Lake $13.50.   **86**

Bright blackish ruby cast. Moderately full-bodied. Balanced acidity. Moderately extracted. Mildly oaked. Mildly tannic. Black fruits. Fruit-centered and aromatic, with a rich, ripe, lush palate feel. Quite flavorful, with solid length and velvety tannins. Oak nuances come through in the finish.

Windsor

1996 Blanc de Noir, Sonoma County $14.   **82**

1997 Chardonnay, California $10.50.   **81**

1996 Chardonnay, Barrel Fermented, Private Reserve, Russian River Valley $15.   **86**

Bright green-gold. Moderately full-bodied. Full acidity. Moderately extracted. Moderately oaked. Vanilla, spice, lemon zest. Bright lemony aromas show a spicy note that comes through well on the palate with bright citrus-accented flavors.

1997 Chardonnay, Barrel Fermented, Private Reserve, Russian River Valley $16.   **84**

Yellow-gold. Dull nutty aromas show an oak accent. A simple attack leads a medium-bodied palate with subdued apple flavors. Not very clean. Drink now.

1997 Chardonnay, Murphy Ranch, Private Reserve, Alexander Valley $14. **84**
Bright straw hue. Unusual nutty, tropical aromas. A lean entry leads a medium-bodied palate with crisp acidity. The finish is lean and vibrant, with very little oak influence. Well structured. Drink now.

1996 Chardonnay, Preston Ranch, Private Reserve, Russian River Valley $14. **86**
Bright yellow-gold. Moderately full-bodied. Full acidity. Moderately oaked. Apples, vanilla, yeast. Smoky, yeasty aromas lead a rounded mouthfeel showing silky character and bright Chardonnay fruit flavors.

1997 Chardonnay, Preston Ranch, Private Reserve, Russian River Valley $15. **82**

1996 Chardonnay, Shelton Signature Series, Russian River Valley $16. **83**
Deep green-gold. Moderately full-bodied. Full acidity. Moderately extracted. Nutmeg, lemon zest. Forcefully spicy aromas lead a deeply flavored though not hugely fruity palate, with heavy oak accents showing.

1997 Chardonnay, Shelton Signature Series, Russian River Valley $17. **81**

1996 Chardonnay, Private Reserve Estate, Russian River Valley $20. **85**
Deep gold-straw hue. Moderately full-bodied. Balanced acidity. Heavily oaked. Brown spice, vanilla, citrus. Rich, broad aromas accented with oak spice lead a nutty, full-flavored palate that has a rich, smooth texture.

1997 Chardonnay, Private Reserve Estate, Russian River Valley $21. **83**
Deep golden yellow. Oak, butter, and apple aromas. A rounded attack leads a moderately full-bodied palate with generous alcohol providing good mouthfeel. The flavors remain clean throughout. Drink now.

1998 Muscat Canelli, Late Harvest, Murphy Ranch, Alexander Valley $13.50. **85**
Brilliant yellow. Enticing tropical fruit, citrus, and spice aromas. A lush entry leads a rounded, medium-bodied palate showing marked sweetness. Spritzy acidity enlivens the spicy finish. Drink now.

1997 Fumé Blanc, North Coast $9.50. **82**

1997 Fumé Blanc, Private Reserve, Middle Ridge Vineyard, Mendocino County $11. **82**

1997 Semillon, Private Reserve, North Coast $14. **84**
Bright green-gold. Medium-bodied. Balanced acidity. Moderately extracted. Figs, nuts, kiwi fruit. Striking varietal aromas follow through on a lighter palate with good concentration of flavors and juicy acids. Stylish.

1998 Rosé du Soleil, California $12. **81**

1994 Cabernet Sauvignon, Private Reserve, Alexander Valley $20. **89**
Bright dark ruby hue. Moderately full-bodied. Balanced acidity. Moderately extracted. Moderately oaked. Mildly tannic. Cassis, brown spices. Pleasantly aromatic, showing toasty oak nuances. Firm and lean on the palate, with excellent grip. Angular, juicy finish. Well balanced.

1995 Cabernet Sauvignon, Private Reserve, Alexander Valley $21. **82**

1994 Cabernet Sauvignon, Private Reserve, Mendocino County $22. **86**
Dark red with crimson highlights. Medium-bodied. Moderately extracted. Moderately tannic. Crisp berry fruits, minerals. High-toned berry fruit aromas lead a bright and crisp palate, with solid astringency running through the finish.

1994 Cabernet Sauvignon, Private Reserve, Dry Creek Valley $22. **90**
Bright ruby hue. Medium-bodied. Moderately extracted. Mildly tannic. Crisp black cherries, brown spice. Bright fruity aromas lead an understated palate, with crisp juicy fruit flavors expanding on the midpalate, and a solid, astringent finish highlighted by fine acids.

Scale: Superlative (96-100), Exceptional (90-95), Highly Recommended (85-89), Recommended (80-84), Not Recommended (Under 80)

220

1994 Cabernet Sauvignon, River West Vineyard, Russian River Valley $18. 85
Bright ruby red with a slight fade. Medium-bodied. Balanced acidity. Moderately extracted. Mildly tannic. Minerals, dried leaves, herbs. Pleasantly aromatic, with a wave of early-maturing flavors. Crisp and lean in the mouth, with an angular finish.

1995 Cabernet Sauvignon, River West Vineyard, Russian River Valley $18. 82

1994 Cabernet Sauvignon, Shelton Signature Series, Sonoma County $21. 88
Bright ruby cast. Medium-bodied. Balanced acidity. Moderately extracted. Mildly oaked. Mildly tannic. Minerals, red fruits, vanilla. Pleasantly aromatic, with a firm, fruit-centered palate and a generous oak overlay. Lean and angular through the flavorful finish.

1995 Cabernet Sauvignon, Shelton Signature Series, Sonoma County $22. 89
Deep ruby hue. Reserved, unusual anise and berry aromas. A lean entry leads to a medium-bodied palate with supple tannins and bright acidity. Crisp, spicy finish. Drink now.

1996 Carignane, Mendocino County $10. 89
Dark crimson hue with a purple tinge. Moderately full-bodied. Highly extracted. Mildly tannic. Raspberries, cherries. Smooth and fleshy, with a fruit-centered character. Supple tannins on the finish. Very approachable, though chewy tannins come through on the finish.

1993 Private Reserve Meritage, Sonoma County $22. 86
Full cherry red. Medium-bodied. Highly extracted. Moderately tannic. Bitter chocolate, red berries, minerals. A smoky nose leads crisp red fruit flavors showing great elegance through a lingering dry finish. A harmonious integration of flavors distinguishes this wine.

1995 Private Reserve Meritage, Sonoma County $20. 88
Bright ruby cast. Medium-bodied. Balanced acidity. Moderately extracted. Mildly oaked. Mildly tannic. Minerals, red fruits, brown spices. Aromatically generous and quite flavorful on the palate. Crisp acidity makes for a lively, buoyant quality through the finish.

1995 Merlot, Private Reserve, Sonoma County $18. 86
Deep ruby red to the rim. Medium-bodied. Balanced acidity. Moderately extracted. Mildly oaked. Mildly tannic. Black fruits, minerals, vanilla. Straightforward in character with ripe fruit flavors. Minerally accents lend complexity. Soft and fleshy in the mouth, with some velvety tannins on the finish.

1995 Merlot, Shelton Signature Series, Sonoma County $23.50. 90
Deep blackish ruby hue with brilliant clarity. Moderately full-bodied. Balanced acidity. Highly extracted. Moderately oaked. Moderately tannic. Black fruits, vanilla, mint. Deeply flavored and very New World in style, with a big oak overlay and a sense of sweetness to the ripe fruit flavors. Rich though well balanced, with some chewy tannins and a lengthy finish.

1996 Merlot, Shelton Signature Series, Sonoma County $24.50. 88
Bright violet hue. Aromas of cherry fruits and vanilla. A firm attack is followed by a medium-bodied palate with dry tannins that provide grip. Drink now.

1996 Petite Sirah, North Coast $12. 86
Bright red-purple. Moderately full-bodied. Highly extracted. Moderately tannic. Oak spice, red fruits. Heavily oak-accented aromas have a bright fruit underlay that follows through on the palate. Well balanced, and drinking well now.

1995 Pinot Noir, Private Reserve, North Coast $13. 84
Pale cherry red. Moderately light-bodied. Moderately extracted. Moderately oaked. Mildly tannic. Quite straightforward, with bright cherry fruit accents and a short vanilla-kissed finish.

1995 Pinot Noir, Shelton Signature Series, California $16. 88
Pale cherry red with pinkish highlights. Medium-bodied. Moderately extracted. Moderately oaked. Moderately tannic. Nice vanilla and dried herbal nuances on the nose. Bright, crisp raspberry and cherry flavors fill the palate, with some toasty oak notes lingering through the finish. Quite elegant.

1996 Pinot Noir, Shelton Signature Series, Russian River Valley $16.   **80**

1997 Syrah, Private Reserve, Sonoma County $15.   **81**

1996 Zinfandel, Sonoma County $9.75.   **84**

Bright ruby hue. Medium-bodied. Balanced acidity. Subtly extracted. Mildly oaked. Mildly tannic. Black fruits, spice. Fairly aromatic, with a lighter-styled palate feel. Crisp and flavorful through the finish. Good grip.

1996 Zinfandel, Private Reserve, Mendocino County $13.50.   **81**

1996 Zinfandel, Old Vines Private Reserve, Russian River Valley $13.50.   **84**

Bright ruby with a slight garnet cast. Medium-bodied. Balanced acidity. Subtly extracted. Mildly oaked. Mildly tannic. Stewed fruits, vanilla. Carries a slightly overripe note in the aromatics and through the palate. Lighter in style, with a soft character. Tasty, but lacks intensity.

1996 Zinfandel, Shelton Signature Series, Alexander Valley $14.50.   **86**

Bright blackish ruby cast. Medium-bodied. Balanced acidity. Moderately extracted. Mildly oaked. Mildly tannic. Black fruits, brown spices, minerals. Somewhat reserved in style, with a firm, balanced mouthfeel. Made in more of a Claret style, with elegant interplay between fruit and oak nuances. Shows solid grip through the finish.

Rare Port, California $13.   **85**

Deep blackish garnet cast. Moderately full-bodied. Balanced acidity. Moderately extracted. Brown spices, raisins. Made in more of a tawny style, with an obvious wood accent to the flavors. Ripe, thick, and lush. Well-balanced finish with a touch of heat.

1997 Sauvignon Blanc, Murphy Ranch Special Select Late Harvest Private Reserve, Alexander Valley $25.   **87**

Bright yellow-gold. Moderately full-bodied. Full acidity. Moderately extracted. Stone fruits, pears. Very aromatic, with pure and expressive fruit flavors. Thick and viscous in the mouth with solid acidity that helps moderate a very sweet finish.

Windwalker

1996 Barbera, Cooper Vineyard, Amador County $12.50.   **84**

Bright ruby cast. Medium-bodied. Balanced acidity. Moderately extracted. Mildly oaked. Mildly tannic. Vanilla, red fruits. Rather reserved aromatically, with a flavorful, rounded palate feel. Finishes on a lean note.

1996 Merlot, El Dorado $11.25.   **81**

Woodbridge

1996 Chardonnay, Twin Oaks, California $10.   **81**

1997 Merlot, California $10.   **81**

Woodside

1994 Brut, Santa Cruz Mountains $22.   **82**

1993 Cabernet Sauvignon, Santa Cruz Mountains $25.   **90**

Bright raspberry red. Medium-bodied. Highly extracted. Mildly tannic. Raspberries, cherries, dried herbs, sweet tobacco. Concentrated crisp red fruit flavors up front expand on the midpalate, with noble fine-grained tannins coating the mouth on the finish. Balanced and approachable now, but it will be better in a few years.

York Mountain Winery

1994 Pinot Noir, William Cain Vineyard, San Luis Obispo County $14.   **87**

Pale ruby red. Medium-bodied. Moderately extracted. Mildly oaked. Mildly tannic. Perfumed aromas of jasmine. Mellow, well-integrated flavors of floral red fruits and dry minerals through the finish. Has enough grip for richer foods. Stylish and well balanced.

1996 Zinfandel, San Luis Obispo County $14.   **82**

Yorkville

1996 Eleanor of Aquitaine, Randle Hill Vineyard, Mendocino $16.   **86**

Very deep straw cast. Full-bodied. Balanced acidity. Moderately extracted. Moderately oaked. Yeast, toast, citrus, sweet herbs. Aromatic and complex, with a generous yeasty flavor profile. Lush and rich in the mouth, with fine length and intensity.

1997 Semillon, Randle Hill Vineyard, Mendocino $12.   **82**

1996 Cabernet Franc, Rennie Vineyard, Mendocino County $14.   **86**

Bright ruby purple. Moderately light-bodied. Full acidity. Subtly extracted. Moderately oaked. Mildly tannic. Cherries, vanilla. Tart and crisp, with bright vanilla-accented fruit flavors. Lean and zesty through the brisk finish.

1995 Richard the Lion-Heart, Mendocino County $20.   **88**

Saturated bright violet-ruby hue. Medium-bodied. Moderately extracted. Mildly tannic. Minerals, red fruits. Perfumed berry fruit aromas. Linear, angular palate shows a crisp flavor profile, with very spiky, tart acids highlighting the brisk fruit flavors and dusty tannins.

Zabaco

1996 Chardonnay, Russian River Valley $14.   **92**

Rich gold. Aromatically lush with buttery, leesy, and oaky character showing. A lush attack leads a full-bodied palate with hedonistic texture and concentrated flavors. Finishes with an authoritative oaky accent.

1994 Zinfandel, Sonoma County $9.   **85**

Deep blackish ruby cast. Moderately full-bodied. Balanced acidity. Moderately extracted. Mildly oaked. Mildly tannic. Black fruits, wood. Pleasantly aromatic, with a distinct woody note throughout. Firm, lean, and angular through the finish. Features some drying wood tannins.

Zaca Mesa

1996 Roussanne, Zaca Vineyards, Santa Barbara County $16.50.   **86**

Very deep golden cast. Full-bodied. Low acidity. Highly extracted. Mildly oaked. Yeast, toast, minerals. Spicy yeast notes dominate the nose. Quite full on the palate with a rather heavy quality, and a hint of a wood accent on the finish.

1996 Z Cuvée Red, Santa Barbara County $16.50.   **84**

Cherry red with a slight fade. Generous earth and mineral aromas. A firm attack leads a medium-bodied palate, with drying tannins. Compact, flavorful finish. Shows fine grip and intensity. Drink now.

1996 Syrah, Zaca Vineyards, Santa Barbara County $20.   **88**

Deep purple, limpid and luminous to the rim. Generous high-toned, crisp, jammy fruit flavors. Subtle wood tones. Firm entry. Moderately full-bodied with crisp acidity. Moderate grainy tannins. Dry and rather lean on the palate. Subtle finish. Concentrated, well extracted, and rather youthful. Drink now or later. Can improve with more age.

Joseph Zakon

1998 Sweet White Muscat, Muscatini, California $8.50.   **82**

1998 Sweet Red Muscat, Muscatini, California $8.50.   **80**

Zayante

1995 Zinfandel, Santa Cruz Mountains $14.   **87**

Deep blackish ruby color. Full-bodied. Full acidity. Highly extracted. Mildly oaked. Quite tannic. Cigars. A pungent, tobacco-tinged nose leads a full-throttled, tannic, acidic mouthfeel. Tough, bracing finish.

ZD

1997 Chardonnay, California $26.   **88**

Deep straw cast. Moderately full-bodied. Balanced acidity. Moderately extracted. Mildly oaked. Yeast, toast, minerals. Forward aromas carry a distinctive yeasty nuance. Rich in the mouth, yet well balanced by zesty acidity that gives it a solid structure.

1995 Chardonnay, Library Select, California $34.   **86**

Deep golden hue. Full-bodied. Balanced acidity. Moderately extracted. Moderately oaked. Honey, nuts, cream. Ripe and rich, with generous, exotic aromas and a pronounced yeasty quality. Full and weighty in the mouth, with a lengthy, flavorful finish. Showing some maturity.

1994 Cabernet Sauvignon, Napa Valley $30.   **87**

Dark, solid red-purple. Moderately full-bodied. Highly extracted. Quite tannic. Earth, black tea, plums. Earthy, austere nose. The palate is solid and well extracted, with strong fine-grained tannins through the finish. Not showing much generosity now, this is a bit of a dormant monster. Needs time.

1996 Cabernet Sauvignon, Napa Valley $38.   **84**

Saturated dark ruby hue. Generously aromatic with a rich oak accent. A firm entry leads a solid, full-bodied palate with bright acids and firm powdery tannins. Rich and solidly structured, this should improve with age. Drink now.

1993 Cabernet Sauvignon, Reserve, Napa Valley $45.   **90**

Opaque brickish ruby color. Moderately full-bodied. Highly extracted. Quite tannic. Earth, black tea, mineral, plums. Dark, brooding aromas. The weighty palate show serious extracted flavors and an earthy dry character. Needs plenty of time to soften its components.

1995 Pinot Noir, Carneros $24.   **90**

Pale ruby-cherry red. Medium-bodied. Moderately extracted. Moderately oaked. Mildly tannic. Perfumed aromas of vanilla and red berry fruits. Silky smooth, with flavors of coffee, licorice, and black fruits. The textured mouthfeel reveals soft tannins and tobacco and spice flavors on the finish.

two

≈

The Wines
of Washington

≈

An Introduction: The Wines of Washington

In a remarkably brief period of time, Washington State has established itself as one of the nation's premier viticultural regions. Boutique wines such as Leonetti, Andrew Will, and Quilceda Creek have enjoyed remarkable success, and are often under severe allocation. While such specialty wines are indeed worth seeking out, there are also some great Washington wines that enjoy wide distribution and consistent supply, while being sold at attractive price points.

Chateau Ste. Michelle, Hogue, and the Columbia Winery broke new ground in Washington in the '70s and early '80s, paving the way for national consumer acceptance of Washington State wines, and the proliferation of boutique wineries in the last decade. Their success was built largely on their ability to produce excellent wines at very attractive prices. While they all still have wide ranging portfolios with many wines still at attractive price points they have also refined and expanded their production at the top end. Vineyard-designated bottlings from Ste. Michelle and Columbia in particular figure among the finest produced in the state, and often the country, vintage after vintage. Furthermore, with their solid distribution networks, these limited-production wines are available both far and wide.

Chateau Ste. Michelle

Largest and probably best known of the trio is Chateau Ste. Michelle, or more accurately, the wine group known as Stimson Lane. Though tracing its roots back to just after Prohibition, Ste. Michelle came into its own in the early '70s and spun off another winery, Columbia Crest, in the early '80s. Both wineries are owned by parent company, Stimson Lane. Since its inception, Columbia Crest has actually outstripped Chateau Ste. Michelle's own production, becoming the largest winery in the Northwest. While Columbia Crest has focused on moderately priced wines, Ste. Michelle has been largely free to pursue a range of premium wines. This has led to the acquisition of some of the state's best vineyard land and the rapid development of a wide range of vineyard-designated wines. In true Ste. Michelle style, success has been swift and spectacular. Wines from Canoe Ridge, Cold Creek, and Horse Heaven Hills have proven exceptional so far, while new bottlings, such as the recent Chateau Reserve line, are being released every year. This has given Stimson Lane, from Columbia Crest through the specialty wines of Ste. Michelle, one of the widest ranging and highest quality portfolios of wine in the nation.

Columbia Winery

Known as Associated Vintners until 1984, Columbia is Washington's oldest continuously operating premium grape winery, dating to 1962. A psychology professor at the University of Washington and a number of his colleagues, whose subsequent research provided much of the impetus for Washington's grape planting boom, founded it. In 1979 David Lake, a Master of Wine, arrived to take on the winemaking duties, and he has been on board ever since. Lake's wines tend to be quite refined in style, and though long lived, recent vintages have been getting more and more accessible in youth. Of particular note are bottlings from the Red Willow Vineyard, one of the state's finest. This property, owned by respected Washington grower Mike Sauer, has been contracted to Columbia for

Scale: Superlative (96-100), Exceptional (90-95), Highly Recommended (85-89), Recommended (80-84), Not Recommended (Under 80)

several years, and provides a number of limited production wines, including what was the state's first commercial Syrah. Further developments should be interesting as this vineyard now contains recent experimental plantings of such exotic varieties as Sangiovese, Nebbiolo, and even Tempranillo.

Hogue Cellars

In 1949 the Hogue family started a farm in the heart of Washington's Yakima Valley. Hops, asparagus, potatoes, and a number of other crops formed the backbone of the family's production until the late '70s when the patriarch's son, Mike Hogue, decided to plant grapes and make wine. A fortuitous decision, as those early wines, produced in a small concrete shed on the property, won quick acclaim. This began what has been a truly meteoric rise, as Hogue is now among the state's largest wineries. In the late '80s their Riesling gained a national following while Chardonnay and Merlot have followed in the '90s. The year 1989 saw the building of a new winery. For the Hogue family, however, this rapid expansion has not greatly changed their refreshing sense of perspective on what for them is just a special part of the family business. Mike Hogue explains, "We've always had a lot of pride in what we produce, but as soon as the crop was brought in and sold, our identity was lost. With wine it's different. It's our wine, with our pride in it, and the family's name on the label." Something, no doubt, many a consumer understands all to well.

Walla Walla and the Canoe Ridge

While Washington's large wineries have made a splendid reputation for producing high quality wines at reasonable prices, the process has come full circle and paved the way for consumer acceptance of the boutique wineries that have sprung up in the last decade. Much attention in particular should be paid to the exciting wines coming from the Walla Walla Valley and Canoe Ridge. This is true not only of the widely successful Merlot but also of Cabernet and Chardonnay along with some interesting varietals such as Syrah and Semillon.

Washington at a Glance

Wines Reviewed:

319

Producers/Brands Represented:

51

The AVA system in Washington is still underdeveloped, with a huge swath of land entitled to use the Columbia Valley appellation. More recently, however, a continuing recognition of the diversity of the state's wines has led to the creation and pursuit of more precise appellations. The Walla Walla Valley, recently recognized as an official appellation, is one such area.

Long home to a famous onion-producing industry (Walla Walla Sweets), the Walla Walla Valley is in the extreme southeastern portion of the state, and spills over the border into northeastern Oregon. This quirk of political map drawing makes Walla Walla one of the very few cross-state appellations in the country. Lying in the rain shadow of the towering Cascades to the west, the area, like all of eastern Washington, is semi-arid. Agriculture is made possible through the use of irrigation. For most this means precisely controlled drip irrigation that puts the water where it is needed, when it is needed, and in the quantities required. Of the potential vineyard acreage in Walla Walla, only a tiny percentage has been planted thus far, making the area's potential for growth quite exciting. The only limiting factor will be ever-growing demands on the Columbia River and its tributaries for water rights.

Leonetti Cellar, founded in 1977, was Walla Walla's first winery, and foreshadowed the development of the area as a boutique wine haven. Walla Walla wines tend to be lush and endearing with a heavy reliance on oak seasoning. The Merlots of Leonetti, Waterbrook, L'Ecole No. 41, Patrick M. Paul, and the like are highly coveted and eminently accessible. As for Chardonnay, many of the wines swing for the fences, but can always rely on the telltale acidity that Washington wines usually possess for balance. It must be noted that similarities among the area's wines have much to do with winemaking practices, as many of these wineries' bottlings utilize grapes grown outside the Walla Walla Valley. As opposed to offering proof of Walla Walla's supremacy for grape growing, the region's wines actually show how a close-knit winemaking community has helped with the exchange of ideas and allowed the enological equivalent of an artistic colony to develop.

Unlike Walla Walla, the wines of a new micro-appellation (as yet unofficial), Canoe Ridge, owe their startling quality to the region itself, in addition to the skill of the winemakers. Lying well to the west of Walla Walla on the banks of the Columbia River, Canoe Ridge is a 1,000 foot hill rising from the river and looking out over the barren scrub land on the Oregon side. Named by Lewis and Clark on a 19th century expedition through the area, the hill resembles an overturned canoe. It is jointly owned, in its entirety, by Chateau Ste. Michelle and the Canoe Ridge Winery, a member of the prestigious Chalone family of wineries. Planted only in the late '80s, it would be an understatement to say that the initial releases have shown promise. They are already some of the best Merlots in the state and the country, while the Chardonnays have proven exceptional as well. Somewhat more restrained than many Walla Walla wines, Canoe Ridge wines show attractive fruit, while being relatively elegant and restrained. As an added bonus the wines are blessedly devoid of harsh tannins.

With Washington wines on the whole that's much of the idea. Often referred to as one-third California and two-thirds Bordeaux, the region's wines offer the ripe and forward qualities of fine New World wines with the crispness and drinkable structure of the Old. Never overpowering or alcoholic, Washington wines are best defined in one word: balance.

Scale: Superlative (96-100), Exceptional (90-95), Highly Recommended (85-89), Recommended (80-84), Not Recommended (Under 80)

Reviews

Apex

1997 Chardonnay, Columbia Valley $17.99.   **90**

Yellow-straw hue. Spicy oak-accented aromas. A buttery entry leads a moderately full-bodied palate with ripe, fruity flavors. Finishes with a hint of dryness and plenty of spicy oak. This is a well-balanced wine, with fine acids. Drink now or later.

1997 Dry Gewürztraminer, Barrel Fermented, Columbia Valley $13.   **80**

1994 Cabernet Sauvignon, Columbia Valley $35.   **90**

Saturated brick red. Moderately full-bodied. Highly extracted. Moderately tannic. Cassis, oak spice, earth. Chocolatey dark fruit aromas lead a tight, packed palate showing rich, dry tannins and earthy intensity. Well structured, this could improve with further age.

1995 Cabernet Sauvignon, Columbia Valley $35.   **89**

Saturated violet-purple hue. Aromas show a pure cassis fruit expression with marked oak influence. A flavorful, fruity entry leads to a moderately full-bodied palate with supple cabernet tannins gripping the finish. Fruit flavors persist well through the finish. Drink now or later.

1994 Merlot, Columbia Valley $28.99.   **92**

Dark cherry red. Moderately full-bodied. Highly extracted. Moderately oaked. Moderately tannic. Reminiscent of cedar, tobacco, plums. Rich plummy nose leads a fleshy, rounded palate with hugely attractive spice and tobacco notes through the lengthy finish.

1995 Merlot, Columbia Valley $40.   **92**

Deep blackish ruby hue to the rim with brilliant highlights. Medium-bodied. Balanced acidity. Highly extracted. Moderately oaked. Mildly tannic. Red fruits, oriental spice, minerals. Quite aromatic, with an extremely complex array of flavors on the palate. Well integrated, finely wrought, and elegant in style, with solid balance and a pleasant, harmonious finish.

1996 Merlot, Columbia Valley $35.   **87**

Rich ruby red with a slight fade. Powerful cedar and spice aromas show a dominant wood accent. A rich, rounded attack leads a moderately full-bodied palate with chewy, velvety tannins. The finish is supple and flavorful. A generous and mellow wine. Drink within five years.

1995 Pinot Noir, Willamette Valley $20.   **89**

Bright reddish purple. Medium-bodied. Moderately extracted. Mildly tannic. Reminiscent of strawberries, raspberries. Crisp and clean, with bright fruit. Flavors are subtle with a nice but mildly astringent finish. Eminently quaffable.

1996 Pinot Noir, Willamette Valley $20.   **80**

1996 Pinot Noir, Washington $20.   **84**

Bright ruby cast. Medium-bodied. Balanced acidity. Moderately extracted. Mildly oaked. Moderately tannic. Dried herbs, chocolate, earth. Aggressive herbal aromas lead a lush mouthfeel of some substance. Fine-grained tannins on the finish.

1997 Gewürztraminer, Ice Wine, Columbia Valley $35/375 ml.   **92**

Deep yellow-straw hue. Intense, pure tropical fruit and toasted coconut aromas. A rich entry leads a sweet, medium-bodied palate balanced by a firm edge of acidity. Shows great length and intensity through the finish. Drink now.

Arbor Crest

1996 Sauvignon Blanc, Washington $7.25.   **86**

Pale straw hue. Medium-bodied. Balanced acidity. Moderately extracted. White peach, apples. Ripe fruity aromas with a slight tropical edge. Juicy and clean on the palate with decent mouthfeel and no use of oak evident.

1995 Cabernet Sauvignon, Cameo Reserve, Washington $13.   87

Blood red with violet highlights. Moderately full-bodied. Highly extracted. Moderately tannic. Dried herbs, red fruits. Subtle, mildly herbal aromas lead a gently fruity palate. A lean style with mild tannins showing on the finish.

Badger Mountain

1995 Merlot, Columbia Valley $14.   81

Barnard Griffin

1997 Chardonnay, Washington $12.95.   88

Bright golden hue. Moderately full-bodied. Full acidity. Moderately extracted. Moderately oaked. Brown spices, butter, citrus. Generous aromas carry a judicious oak accent. Crisp and zesty, with a vibrant core of minerally, fruity flavors that remain refreshing through the finish.

1996 Chardonnay, Reserve, Columbia Valley $17.95.   86

Deep yellow-straw cast. Moderately full-bodied. Full acidity. Moderately extracted. Mildly oaked. Brown spices, butter, minerals. Forward aromas carry a subtle oak accent to a core of firm citric flavors. Crisp and lean through the finish.

1995 Cabernet Sauvignon, Washington $16.95.   87

Bright cherry red. Medium-bodied. Moderately extracted. Mildly tannic. Black cherries, minerals. Bright, juicy aromas follow through on a velvety palate with elegant tannins. Supremely drinkable.

1996 Cabernet Sauvignon, Columbia Valley $16.95.   91

Saturated bright violet-purple hue. Youthful aromas show primary character of black fruits and oak spice. Bright lively attack leads to a medium-bodied palate with focused cassis fruit flavors and grainy, gripping tannins. A very youthful, somewhat tough wine. Drink now or later.

1995 Merlot, Washington $16.95.   87

Very deep ruby hue to the rim. Medium-bodied. Balanced acidity. Moderately extracted. Mildly oaked. Mildly tannic. Red fruits, minerals, pencil shavings. Well balanced, with complex yet integrated flavors, though a tad austere in the mouth. Lengthy finish. A very solid food wine.

1997 Merlot, Columbia Valley $16.95.   84

Brilliant purple-red to the rim. Perfumed berry and mineral aromas. A crisp attack leads a moderately light-bodied palate with firm tannins. Bright, flavorful, zesty finish. A well-balanced, tasty, lighter-styled wine. Drink within five years.

1997 Merlot, Ciel du Cheval Vineyard, Columbia Valley $39.   89

Bright purple-red to the rim. Attractive floral, spice, and red fruit aromas show a moderate oak accent. A crisp attack leads a medium-bodied palate with lean tannins. The finish is ripe and flavorful. Almost delicate in style, but well balanced and full of flavor. Drink now or later. Can improve with more age.

1994 Merlot, Reserve, Columbia Valley $24.   92

Deep reddish purple. Medium-bodied. Highly extracted. Moderately oaked. Mildly tannic. Reminiscent of raspberries, toasted oak, brown spices. Very distinctive nose of ripe fruits. Nice toasty notes accent the fruity palate, with an elegant finish.

1995 Merlot, Reserve, Columbia Valley $26.95.   90

Very deep blackish ruby color. Medium-bodied. Balanced acidity. Moderately extracted. Moderately oaked. Mildly tannic. Bacon, brown spices, red fruits. Quite aromatic, with a concentrated wave of flavors on the palate. Well-balanced and elegant mouthfeel, with fine length and some dusty tannins on the finish.

Bookwalter

1997 Chardonnay, Columbia Valley $8. 86

Bright straw cast. Medium-bodied. Full acidity. Moderately extracted. Minerals, citrus. Clean and focused, with pure fruit flavors. Zesty, angular, and refreshing through the finish.

1997 Chardonnay, Vintner's Select, Washington $18. 88

Pale straw hue. Ripe apple, smoky aromas. A smooth attack leads a moderately full-bodied palate with a weighty mouthfeel and toasted oak flavors that persist through the finish. Texturally impressive, with a marked oak accent. Drink now.

1998 Chenin Blanc, Washington $6. 81

1998 Johannisberg Riesling, Washington $6. 81

NV Red, Washington $10. 83

Full brick red with a garnet cast. Medium-bodied. Moderately extracted. Moderately tannic. Dried herbs, earth. Herbal, mature aromas follow through on the palate, with dusty, dry tannins making for a lean finish.

1996 Cabernet Sauvignon, Vintner's Select, Washington $39. 84

Deep ruby red hue. Generous spice, mineral, and red fruit aromas. A firm attack leads to a moderately full-bodied palate with robust grippy tannins. Angular, austere finish. Well flavored, but rough. Drink within five years.

1995 Merlot, Washington $15. 80

W.B. Bridgman

1997 Chardonnay, Columbia Valley $10.99. 86

Yellow-straw hue. Aromas of yellow apples and butter. A soft entry leads a moderately full-bodied palate with fruit-centered flavors and soft acids that make for a quick finish. The mouthfeel shows a full buttery quality. Drink now.

1994 Cabernet Sauvignon, Columbia Valley $15. 88

Full cherry red. Medium-bodied. Moderately extracted. Moderately tannic. Juicy red fruits, vanilla, toasted oak. Nice spice and vanilla nose. Crisp and juicy, with a firm, astringent finish. The dry and austere style may not be to everyone's taste, but it is sure to match well with richer foods.

1995 Cabernet Sauvignon, Columbia Valley $13.99. 87

Deep red-violet. Medium-bodied. Highly extracted. Moderately tannic. Mineral, oak spice. Austere aromas show oak spice accents. Dry, lean flavors have some Cabernet fruit character, with minerals defining the finish.

1996 Cabernet Sauvignon, Columbia Valley $14. 86

Brick red with a fading rim. Aromatically reserved with tertiary, mature character. A lean entry leads a moderately full-bodied palate with muted fruit flavors and tart acidity. Drink now.

1994 Merlot, Columbia Valley $14.99. 83

Cherry red. Moderately full-bodied. Moderately extracted. Moderately oaked. Reminiscent of cedar, herbs, black cherry. Crisp herbal-accented nose leads a firm, slightly austere palate with an imposing finish. Fairly assertive.

1995 Merlot, Columbia Valley $14.99. 85

Very dark ruby hue to the rim. Medium-bodied. Balanced acidity. Moderately extracted. Mildly oaked. Mildly tannic. Minerals, red fruits. Still a bit unyielding aromatically, with a youthful character. Well balanced, though somewhat austere on the palate, this wine should work quite well with food.

1996 Merlot, Washington $16. 82

1997 Syrah, Columbia Valley $18. 88

Bright purple-red to the rim. Subdued red fruit and mineral aromas show a mild wood accent. A crisp attack leads a medium-bodied palate, with tannic grip and bright acidity, and a snappy, flavorful finish. Clean and stylish, with cool climate varietal intensity. Drink now.

Canoe Ridge Vineyard

1997 Chardonnay, Columbia Valley $14.   88

Brilliant yellow-gold. Ripe but very subtle oaky aromas. A creamy attack leads a medium-bodied palate that has a lush, textured mouthfeel. Finishes with good fruit persistence. Drink now.

1995 Cabernet Sauvignon, Columbia Valley $22.   90

Dark ruby red with a subtle fade to the rim. Dark fruited aromas with anise notes and a perception of oak. A firm entry leads to a full-bodied palate with firm tannins gripping the finish. Quite structured and gripping on the finish. Drink now or later.

1994 Merlot, Columbia Valley $18.   90

Deep cherry red with a light garnet cast. Moderately full-bodied. Moderately extracted. Moderately tannic. Reminiscent of red fruits, brown spice, dried herbs. Austere nose. Lively ripe fruit on entry with supple tannins through the finish give this a rounded character. Fashioned in a balanced, subtle mold.

1995 Merlot, Columbia Valley $18.   89

Very deep blackish ruby hue to the rim. Moderately full-bodied. Balanced acidity. Highly extracted. Mildly oaked. Mildly tannic. Chocolate, minerals, red fruits. Still a bit closed, with a youthful core of dense, chewy flavors. Pleasantly textured and a bit thick, but well balanced. Should mellow and open with mid-term (3–6 years) aging.

1996 Merlot, Columbia Valley $19.   88

Rich garnet red. Muted spice and mineral aromas show a modest wood accent. A lush attack leads a moderately full-bodied palate with drying, astringent tannins. The finish has plenty of flavor, though it is slightly tough. Drink within five years.

Cascade Ridge

1997 Chardonnay, Columbia Valley $15.   82
1996 Cabernet Sauvignon, Columbia Valley $19.99.   80
1995 Merlot, Columbia Valley $19.99.   80

Caterina

1997 Chardonnay, Columbia Valley $15.   86

Pale yellow-gold. Ripe aromas of butter and yellow apples, showing judicious oak influences. A rich attack leads a moderately full-bodied palate with a glycerous, smooth mouthfeel and juicy apple flavors through the clean finish. Drink now.

1997 Sauvignon Blanc, Columbia Valley $11.   81
1995 Cabernet Sauvignon, Columbia Valley $19.   87

Full blackish red with purple highlights. Medium-bodied. Moderately extracted. Mildly tannic. Tart cherry, currant, minerals. A bright fruity impression on entry is carried by good acids, but the main impression is of minerally concentration and fine austerity through a long finish. Drinking well now.

1995 Cabernet Sauvignon, Wahluke Slope Vineyard Reserve,
Columbia Valley $32.   88

Dark ruby hue with purple highlights. Medium-bodied. Moderately extracted. Moderately tannic. Lemons, red fruits, tobacco. Bright acids give this an assertive palate with crisp, full fruity flavors. Fine concentration and persistence through the finish. Shows a fine earthy "gout de terroir" throughout.

1994 Merlot, Columbia Valley $16.   89

Dark red appearance. Medium-bodied. Highly extracted. Moderately tannic. Reminiscent of black tea, plums, minerals. Dark fruity aromas with some dry accents. A well-structured palate with concentrated flavors and fine astringent tannins through the finish.

1995 Merlot, Columbia Valley $18.   80

Scale: Superlative (96-100), Exceptional (90-95), Highly Recommended (85-89),
Recommended (80-84), Not Recommended (Under 80)

1996 Merlot, Columbia Valley $18.   88

Bright garnet red. Generous spice and red fruit aromas belie a forward wood accent.
A crisp attack is followed by a medium-bodied, substantive palate with firm tannins and
a flavorful, lingering finish. Rather light in style, but it has some grip and is quite tasty.
Drink within five years.

Chateau Ste. Michelle

1996 Chardonnay, Columbia Valley $14.   86

Bright yellow-straw cast. Moderately full-bodied. Balanced acidity. Moderately extracted.
Mildly oaked. Minerals, citrus, cream. Aromatically reserved, with a generous rounded
texture. The finish is crisp.

1996 Chardonnay, Canoe Ridge Estate Vineyard, Columbia Valley $28.   88

Bright yellow-straw cast. Moderately full-bodied. Full acidity. Moderately extracted.
Minerals, yeast, toast. Aromatically reserved, showing lean, minerally flavors in the
mouth. Texturally interesting, with a sense of lushness and a zesty, angular finish.

1996 Chardonnay, Cold Creek Vineyard, Columbia Valley $26.   90

Bright yellow-straw cast. Moderately full-bodied. Balanced acidity. Moderately extracted.
Mildly oaked. Brown spices, minerals, citrus. Generous aromatics feature a hint of oak.
Firm and flavorful in the mouth, with a core of steely fruit flavors that persist through
a lengthy, vibrant finish.

1996 Chardonnay, Indian Wells Vineyard, Columbia Valley $26.   92

Bright yellow-gold. Moderately full-bodied. Full acidity. Moderately extracted. Mildly
oaked. Minerals, brown spices. Aromatically reserved, with a firm and concentrated
palate feel. Opens up toward the finish, with a hint of oak. Should develop further with
some short-term (1–2 years) to mid-term (3–6 years) cellaring.

1996 Chardonnay, Reserve, Columbia Valley $31.   89

Bright straw cast. Medium-bodied. Full acidity. Moderately extracted. Minerals, citrus zest.
Clean, crisp, and angular, with a sense of reserved richness. Firm and weighty through
the steely, angular finish.

1996 Sauvignon Blanc, Barrel Fermented, Columbia Valley $10.   83

Bright pale straw hue. Medium-bodied. Balanced acidity. Moderately extracted. Mildly
oaked. Peach, sweet herbs. Sweet herbal and ripe citrus aromas. Fruity and forward, with
very subtle toasty oak notes that stay in the background.

1996 Sauvignon Blanc, Horse Haven Vineyard, Columbia Valley $15.   84

Pale straw cast. Medium-bodied. Balanced acidity. Moderately extracted. Lime, dried
herbs, minerals. Subtle herbal aromas with high-toned citrus notes. Bright and lively on
the palate, with a clean finish.

1994 Cabernet Sauvignon, Columbia Valley $16.   85

Deep garnet red. Medium-bodied. Moderately extracted. Quite tannic. Plums, currants,
minerals, brown spice. Rich, ripe black fruit aromas are confirmed on the palate. Some
tough angular tannins come through on the finish, giving an assertive character. Best
with rich foods.

1995 Cabernet Sauvignon, Columbia Valley $16.   90

Dark purple-red. Medium-bodied. Moderately extracted. Moderately tannic. Cassis, oak
spice. Generous aromas. Textured and rich, with polished flavors and powdery tannins.
Shows textbook Cabernet character.

1996 Cabernet Sauvignon, Columbia Valley $16.   90

Dark ruby hue with a violet cast. Muted aromas show an anise and dark chocolate note.
A firm entry leads a moderately full-bodied palate with inky, austere flavors. Nice finish.
Should age well.

1995 Cabernet Sauvignon, Cold Creek Vineyard, Columbia Valley $27.   95

Bright violet-red with a subtle fade to the rim. Medium-bodied. Moderately extracted.
Moderately tannic. Cassis, mineral, oak spice. Bright Cabernet fruit aromas show through
on the nose and follow up on the palate, with supple tannins on the finish, and fine,
minerally intensity throughout. Nice now, though this will age further.

1995 Cabernet Sauvignon, Horse Heaven Vineyard, Columbia Valley $27. 94
Bright purple-red. Moderately full-bodied. Highly extracted. Moderately tannic. Vanilla, ripe black cherries. Perfumed, oak-accented nose. Fleshy primary fruit flavors up front give way to silky tannins that progress through a dry finish. Intense and generous.

1994 Ethos Red, Columbia Valley $31. 90
Saturated cherry red with purple highlights. Medium-bodied. Highly extracted. Moderately tannic. Vanilla, ripe cherries, cassis, chocolate. Ripe chocolatey aromas lead a concentrated palate, with full, ripe flavors and fine-grained tannins on the finish. Impressively structured.

1994 Artist Series Red Meritage, Columbia Valley $50. 91
Dark crimson red with subtle purple highlights. Moderately full-bodied. Highly extracted. Moderately tannic. Toasted oak, brown spice, cassis, black fruits. A restrained toasty nose hints at richness that comes through on the palate. Fine-textured mouthfeel. Rich layered tannins taper through the finish. Big in all departments, with great structure.

1995 Artist Series Red Meritage, Columbia Valley $50. 94
Deep violet red. Moderately full-bodied. Moderately extracted. Moderately tannic. Cassis, mineral, oak spice. Supremely elegant aromas reveal a sumptuously textured, intense palate with a degree of persistence and length on the finish that shows its class. Very nice now, though this has all the elements to age further.

1994 Merlot, Columbia Valley $17. 87
Deep cherry red. Moderately full-bodied. Highly extracted. Quite tannic. Reminiscent of black fruits, tea. A solid mouthful with rich fruit accents under a layer of imposing tannins. Quite tough at present but structurally sound. This should age well.

1996 Merlot, Columbia Valley $18. 88
Bright, saturated ruby red. Subdued red fruit aromas. A lush attack leads a medium-bodied palate with lean tannins. The finish is flavorful and clean. A tasty effort in a lighter style, showing a bit of an edge to its tannins. Drink now.

1995 Merlot, Canoe Ridge Estate Vineyard, Columbia Valley $31. 90
Deep blackish ruby hue with brilliant clarity. Medium-bodied. Balanced acidity. Moderately extracted. Moderately oaked. Moderately tannic. Black fruits, vanilla, licorice. Pleasantly aromatic, with a lighter-styled palate and firm structure. Well balanced and finely wrought, though still a bit tight, with a lengthy finish nonetheless. Near-term cellaring might be helpful in resolving some scrappy tannins.

1994 Merlot, Cold Creek Vineyard, Columbia Valley $28. 92
Intense dark red with purple highlights. Full-bodied. Highly extracted. Heavily oaked. Moderately tannic. Reminiscent of cedar, pine, black fruits, tea. Deep, dark fruit and oak accents in the nose. Solid, dense palate with fruity depth and a firm but lengthy finish. Highly structured, though a bit tight for current enjoyment.

1995 Merlot, Horse Heaven Vineyard, Columbia Valley $31. 88
Very deep ruby red with a slight purplish cast. Medium-bodied. Balanced acidity. Moderately extracted. Mildly oaked. Mildly tannic. Minerals, red fruits, sweet herbs. Still a bit closed, with a touch of austerity on the palate. Elegant and well balanced, this is a solid table wine.

1994 Merlot, Indian Wells Vineyard, Columbia Valley $30. 90
Deep crimson color. Moderately full-bodied. Highly extracted. Moderately oaked. Moderately tannic. Reminiscent of black fruits, tea, chocolate. Silky entry with deep fruity flavors gives way to textured tannins through a lengthy, firm toasty finish. Elegant and generously proportioned, with enough structure to cellar well.

1995 Merlot, Indian Wells Vineyard, Columbia Valley $31. 85
Very deep blackish ruby hue. Medium-bodied. Balanced acidity. Highly extracted. Mildly oaked. Quite tannic. Minerals, red fruits. Quite closed and compact, with an angular feeling to the lighter-styled palate. Finishes with a wave of astringent tannins.

Scale: Superlative (96-100), Exceptional (90-95), Highly Recommended (85-89), Recommended (80-84), Not Recommended (Under 80)

234

1994 Merlot, Chateau Reserve, Columbia Valley $40. **96**

Very deep reddish purple. Full-bodied. Highly extracted. Moderately oaked. Quite tannic. Reminiscent of black fruits, licorice, tea, brown spice. Rich, brooding dark fruit nose. Solid, generously textured mouthfeel with great depth and full layered tannins through the finish. Substantial and structured. Though drinking nicely now, this could be cellared.

1995 Merlot, Chateau Reserve, Columbia Valley $42. **92**

Very deep ruby hue with brilliant clarity. Moderately full-bodied. Balanced acidity. Moderately extracted. Moderately oaked. Mildly tannic. Vanilla, red fruits, minerals. Still a bit reined-in aromatically, this youthful wine is lighter in style on the palate. Chalky tannins intrude on the palate, but the flavors expand through the finish. Mid-term cellaring should round it out and provide more complexity, though it is tasty now.

1995 Syrah, Reserve, Columbia Valley $28. **85**

Bright purple-red to the rim. Subdued earth and black fruit aromas show a subtle wood accent. A soft attack leads a moderately full-bodied palate showing velvety tannins. Lush, earthy finish. Interesting, but somewhat lacking in acidic grip. Drink now.

1995 Semillon, Late Harvest, Reserve, Columbia Valley $20. **87**

Deep bronzed golden hue. Full-bodied. Balanced acidity. Moderately extracted. Moderately oaked. Tropical fruits, pears, honey. Oak aromas, with a rich and viscous core of buttressing tropical fruit flavors. Luxuriant and velvety with a hint of acidity that keeps the sweetness in balance.

Chinook

1993 Merlot, Yakima Valley $21.50. **84**

Deep cherry red. Medium-bodied. Moderately extracted. Mildly tannic. Reminiscent of raspberries, dried herbs. Huge herb- and berry-scented nose. Ripe, fleshy fruit accent on the palate lingers through a soft finish. Very attractive now.

Claar

1997 Chardonnay, Columbia Valley $10.99. **87**

Brilliant yellow-gold. Heavy buttery aromas. A rich attack leads a full-bodied palate with broad, ripe apple flavors and full buttery qualities. This is a big, flavorful style with good acid balance. Very structured and tight, maybe further age will enhance it. Drink now or later.

1997 Dry Riesling, Columbia Valley $5.99. **81**

1997 White Riesling, Columbia Valley $5.99. **83**

Pale straw hue. Clean aromas of citrus zest and minerals. An off-dry entry leads a medium-bodied palate, with juicy acids and a quick finish. Drink now.

1997 Riesling, Botrytisized Ice Wine, Columbia Valley $29.99/375 ml. **90**

Brilliant pale amber hue. Forward spice and pear aromas. A rich entry leads a viscous, moderately full-bodied palate. Quite sweet, with rounded acidity. Polished and supple. Drink now.

Columbia Crest

1997 Chardonnay, Columbia Valley $9. **86**

Medium pale straw hue. Moderate aromas of butter, citrus, and oak spice. A crisp entry leads a medium-bodied palate with tangy fruit and brown spice flavors that linger on the finish. Nice texture and mouthfeel. Drink now.

1997 Chardonnay, Estate Series, Columbia Valley $14. **88**

Full yellow-gold. Aromatically complex with butterscotch and vanilla character. A smoky entry leads a moderately full-bodied palate with assertive smoke and toasty oak flavors that are well integrated with fruity, buttery character. Acids are balanced through the oak-spiced finish. Very stylish, layered, and complex.

1996 Chardonnay, Reserve, Columbia Valley $18.   88
Bright yellow-straw cast. Moderately full-bodied. Balanced acidity. Moderately extracted. Minerals, citrus. Crisp, subtly oaky aromas, and a ripe, generous mouthfeel. Shows lean flavors, with a hint of wood to the finish.

1996 Semillon-Chardonnay, Columbia Valley $8.   83
Pale straw hue. Moderately light-bodied. Balanced acidity. Moderately extracted. Citrus zest, minerals. Faint lemon zest aromas follow through on a light, crisp palate without a lot of fruit flavors.

1996 Sauvignon Blanc, Estate Series, Columbia Valley $9.   86
Pale yellow-gold. Medium-bodied. Balanced acidity. Moderately extracted. Mildly oaked. Smoke, butter, citrus. Soft and juicy, with a layer of mildly smoky oak flavors. Rounded, textured mouthfeel and lengthy finish.

1995 Cabernet Sauvignon, Columbia Valley $11.   83
Full ruby red. Medium-bodied. Moderately extracted. Moderately tannic. Cordial, minerals, oak spice. Ripe, jammy aromas follow through on the palate, with some firmness and spice on the finish.

1994 Cabernet Sauvignon, Estate Series, Columbia Valley $17.   89
Deep blood red. Medium-bodied. Moderately extracted. Mildly tannic. Brown spice, black fruits, minerals. Fleshy, ripe black fruit aromas follow through well on the palate. A lush entry turns dry, with minerally grip on the finish. Drinking very well now.

1995 Cabernet Sauvignon, Estate Series, Columbia Valley $21.   88
Deep brick red hue with a subtle browning rim. Ripe aromas show developed character. A rich entry leads a full-bodied palate with chewy black fruits and a dry anise-like finish with lingering chocolatey notes. Quite mature at present, though this can develop further. Drink now or later.

1994 Reserve Red, Columbia Valley $20.   89
Dark blood red with a garnet cast. Medium-bodied. Highly extracted. Quite tannic. Earth, brown spice, black tea, black fruits. Rich toasted oak nose. Concentrated spicy black fruit flavors, with rustic tannins on the finish. A little tough now; hopefully time will help.

1995 Reserve Red, Columbia Valley $22.   89
Saturated dark ruby red hue. Ripe, somewhat nutty, oak-influenced aromas. A firm attack leads a moderately full-bodied palate with dry tannins and focused fruit flavors finishing with a complex oak-spiced note. Drink now or later.

1996 Merlot, Columbia Valley $16.   89
Bright, deep ruby red to the rim. Generous vanilla and red fruit aromas show a forward oak accent. A lush attack leads a moderately full-bodied mouthfeel with firm tannins and a rounded, flavorful finish. Forward and quite drinkable. Drink now.

1994 Merlot, Estate Series, Columbia Valley $19.   88
Very deep ruby red to the rim with brilliant clarity. Moderately full-bodied. Balanced acidity. Highly extracted. Moderately oaked. Moderately tannic. Red fruits, brown spices. Fruit and wood nuances have intertwined to form a harmonious whole. Quite firmly structured, with a lash of tannin at the finish. Should mellow with mid-term (3–6 years) aging.

1995 Merlot, Estate Series, Columbia Valley $22.   90
Rich ruby red with a slight fade. Powerful spice, red fruit, and mineral aromas carry a prominent oak accent. A rich attack leads a supple, moderately full-bodied palate displaying velvety tannins. The finish is lengthy and flavorful. Generous and well rounded, with a nice balance between oak and fruit flavors. Drink within five years.

1996 Syrah, Reserve, Columbia Valley $22.   90
Bright, deep ruby red to the rim. Perfumed red fruit and vanilla aromas carry a generous oak accent. A soft attack leads a medium-bodied palate, with silky tannins and buoyant acidity. The finish is persistent and flavorful. Very modern in style, with a hedonistic and eminently drinkable personality. Drink now.

Scale: Superlative (96-100), Exceptional (90-95), Highly Recommended (85-89), Recommended (80-84), Not Recommended (Under 80)

Columbia Winery

1996 Chardonnay, Otis Vineyard, Yakima Valley $19. **91**

Bright yellow-straw cast. Moderately full-bodied. Full acidity. Moderately extracted. Moderately oaked. Brown spices, citrus, minerals. Aromatically complex, with a range of fruit, yeast, and wood influences. All are carried on a lean and vibrant frame that provides a refreshing and well-balanced finish.

1996 Chardonnay, Wyckoff Vineyard, Yakima Valley $19. **90**

Bright yellow-gold. Moderately full-bodied. Full acidity. Moderately extracted. Mildly oaked. Vanilla, citrus, minerals. Aromatically generous, with a firm core of citric flavors accented by judicious use of oak. Zesty and intense with a lengthy finish.

1998 Gewürztraminer, Yakima Valley $6. **86**

Bright straw hue. Generous spice and honeyed melon aromas. A rich entry leads a medium-bodied palate showing marked sweetness offset by crisp acidity. Clean, well-balanced finish. Drink now.

1996 Pinot Gris, Yakima Valley $10.99. **85**

Bright golden cast. Medium-bodied. Full acidity. Highly extracted. Minerals, grapefruit zest. Rather unyielding in aromatics, with a clean, racy, mildly bitter palate feel. A buttery note emerges in the finish.

1995 Semillon, Columbia Valley $9. **82**

1996 Semillon, Reserve Sur Lie, Columbia Valley $10.99. **80**

1995 Cabernet Franc, Red Willow Vineyard, David Lake Signature Series, Yakima Valley $20.99. **86**

Bright ruby cast. Moderately full-bodied. Full acidity. Moderately extracted. Mildly oaked. Moderately tannic. Earth, minerals. Lean and reserved, with a firm, minerally character. Quite linear through the vibrant finish. A solid table wine.

1996 Cabernet Franc, Red Willow Vineyard, avid Lake Signature Series, Yakima Valley $19. **86**

Bright ruby hue. Attractive candied cherry and spice aromas. A firm attack leads a medium-bodied palate that shows lean, gripping tannins. The finish is firm and angular. Tightly wound and focused, with a crisp, sturdy structure. Drink now or later. Can improve with more age.

1994 Cabernet Sauvignon, Otis Vineyard, David Lake Signature Series, Yakima Valley $23. **93**

Saturated blood red. Moderately full-bodied. Highly extracted. Moderately tannic. Cassis, mineral, spice. Intense and rich, with supple tannins and extraordinary purity of flavors that persist for a mile on the finish.

1995 Cabernet Sauvignon, Otis Vineyard, David Lake Signature Series, Yakima Valley $24. **83**

Pale ruby-red hue. Oak accents are very pronounced on the nose. A vibrant entry leads a medium-bodied palate with oak astringency dominating the flavors. Finishes with a note of bitterness. Drink now.

1994 Cabernet Sauvignon, Red Willow Vineyard, David Lake Signature Series, Yakima Valley $23. **91**

Deep cherry red with a bright rim. Medium-bodied. Highly extracted. Moderately tannic. Red berries, pomegranate. Exotic primary fruit aromas follow through on the palate, showing intensity that is matched by ultra-fine, dry tannins. Very silky.

1995 Cabernet Sauvignon, Red Willow Vineyard, David Lake Signature Series, Yakima Valley $29. **89**

Saturated violet hue. Anise and earth aromas show little fruit generosity. A firm entry leads a moderately full-bodied palate, with dry, powdery tannins through the finish. This seems rather tough at present, but will soften nicely.

1994 Cabernet Sauvignon, Sagemoor Vineyard, David Lake Signature Series, Columbia Valley $23.   88

Deep ruby red. Moderately full-bodied. Highly extracted. Moderately tannic. Cordial, black fruits, spice. Very ripe dark fruit aromas have a jammy note that follows through with very generous flavors and fine persistence. Tannins show a powdery quality.

1995 Cabernet Sauvignon, Reserve, Yakima Valley $15.   88

Deep ruby-violet hue with a subtle fade. Richly fruited aromas show classic cassis notes with generous oak accents. A rich entry leads a full-bodied palate with chewy fruit flavors and chunky, rich tannins. This is a very big wine with plenty of stuffing through a long flavorful finish. Drink within five years.

1994 Merlot, Columbia Valley $14.   88

Deep cherry color. Moderately full-bodied. Highly extracted. Moderately oaked. Moderately tannic. Reminiscent of black fruits, chocolate, tea. Rich berry-accented nose. Chewy, thick mouthfeel with a complex fleshy character on the palate, and some austere tealike tannins through the finish.

1994 Merlot, Red Willow Vineyard, David Lake Signature Series, Yakima Valley $23.   90

Bright reddish purple. Medium-bodied. Moderately extracted. Moderately oaked. Moderately tannic. Reminiscent of red fruits, minerals, toasted oak. Vibrant entry gives way to minerally undertones through the firm toasty finish. An elegant, structured style that should cellar well.

1995 Merlot, Red Willow Vineyard, David Lake Signature Series, Columbia Valley $23.   90

Deep blackish ruby hue. Medium-bodied. Full acidity. Moderately extracted. Mildly oaked. Mildly tannic. Red fruits, vanilla, minerals. Lighter in style and very well balanced. The core of flavor has a measure of complexity and a judicious oak accent. Well integrated, with a firm, angular finish. A solid table wine.

1996 Milestone Merlot, Red Willow Vineyard, David Lake Signature Series, Yakima Valley $24.   86

Bright ruby red with a slight fade. Attractive, high-toned wood, anise, and red fruit aromas show a judicious oak accent. A crisp attack leads a medium-bodied palate with firm tannins. Angular, flavorful finish. Relatively light in style, but tasty and well structured. Drink within five years.

1995 Pinot Noir, Washington $11.99.   81

1997 Pinot Noir, Washington $12.   81

1996 Syrah, Red Willow Vineyard, Yakima Valley $29.   87

Bright saturated ruby red to the rim. Clean mineral and red fruit aromas carry a very subtle oak accent. A firm attack leads a medium-bodied palate, with tannic grip. A snappy, compact finish. Quite modern in style and somewhat closed at present, but the balance bodes well for mid-term (3–6 years) aging. Drink now or later. Can improve with more age.

1998 Riesling, Cellarmaster's Reserve, Columbia Valley $7.   84

Pale straw hue. Modest appley aromas. A sweet, juicy entry leads a medium-bodied palate, with ripe, tangy flavors through the finish. Drink now.

Covey Run

1997 Chardonnay, Washington $9.   83

Pale gold. Zesty citrus aromas. A fruity, tart entry leads a moderately full-bodied palate with a rounded mouthfeel and concentrated, pure Chardonnay flavors lifted by good acids through the finish. Oak is subtle. Impressive flavors and structure. Drink now or later.

1996 Chardonnay, Reserve, Yakima Valley $13.   84

Full yellow-gold. Moderate aromas show a spicy oak accent. A crisp attack leads a medium-bodied palate with tart apple flavors that linger on the nutty finish. Drink now.

Scale: Superlative (96-100), Exceptional (90-95), Highly Recommended (85-89), Recommended (80-84), Not Recommended (Under 80)

1996 Chardonnay, Celilo Vineyard, Washington $25.　　　　**86**

Bright straw cast. Moderately full-bodied. Full acidity. Moderately extracted. Mildly oaked. Minerals, citrus, toast. Rather reserved in style, though well structured, with a weighty palate balanced by a crisp and zesty structure.

1998 Gewürztraminer, Washington $6.　　　　**82**

1997 Gewürztraminer, Celilo Vineyard, Washington $12.　　　　**85**

Bright straw hue. Lean, minerally aromas show an edge of residual sulfur that should disappear with a bit more bottle age. A lush entry leads a medium-bodied palate that has a slight hint of sweetness offset by bright acidity. The finish is spicy and flavorful. A clean wine. Drink now.

1996 Fumé Blanc, Columbia Valley $8.　　　　**86**

Medium straw cast. Medium-bodied. Balanced acidity. Moderately extracted. Dried herbs, citrus, minerals. Crisp herbal aromas have a wet wool note. Good grip and intensity on the palate, with a fine lengthy finish.

1995 Cabernet Sauvignon, Columbia Valley $12.99.　　　　**85**

Deep ruby red. Moderately full-bodied. Moderately tannic. Herbs, cordial. Cooked, herbal aromas lead a thick, solid mouthful of dry flavors, with precocious tannins coming through on the finish.

1996 Cabernet Sauvignon, Columbia Valley $12.99.　　　　**86**

Bright ruby-violet hue. Generously aromatic with a heavy oak accent and vibrant Cabernet fruits. A bright entry leads a moderately full-bodied palate with notes of bitterness and astringency lingering on the finish.

1996 Cabernet Sauvignon, Reserve, Columbia Valley $24.　　　　**86**

Saturated dark ruby hue. Rich chocolatey aromas have a dark fruity accent. A plush entry leads to a moderately full-bodied palate with rich chocolatey character that lingers though the long finish. Very oak accented, but this has flesh beneath.

1994 Cabernet Sauvignon, Whiskey Canyon Vineyard, Yakima Valley $28.　　　　**88**

Saturated red-garnet hue. Moderately full-bodied. Highly extracted. Moderately tannic. Black fruits, minerals. Mature aromas lead a weighty, dry palate, with grainy tannins lingering through the finish. This is showing mature flavors, but there is still plenty of life here.

1995 Malbec, Buoy Vineyard, Yakima Valley $16.　　　　**80**

1996 Cabernet-Merlot, Washington $10.　　　　**84**

Bright red-violet. Moderately light-bodied. Moderately extracted. Mildly tannic. Ripe berry fruits, vanilla. Bright berry fruit aromas lead a simple, crisp mouthful of similar flavors, with a hint of tannic bite for balance.

1995 Merlot, Columbia Valley $12.99.　　　　**83**

Deep ruby hue with brilliant clarity. Medium-bodied. Full acidity. Moderately extracted. Mildly oaked. Mildly tannic. Chocolate, minerals, red fruits. A light style with some complexity to its range of flavors. Quite crisp on the palate and a bit tart through the finish.

1994 Merlot, Reserve, Yakima Valley $23.　　　　**88**

Deep cherry red. Moderately full-bodied. Highly extracted. Reminiscent of black fruits, brown spice, minerals. Brooding dark fruit nose. Rich, ripe, and dense, with a chewy mouthfeel and ample supple tannins through the lengthy finish. Well structured, this should develop character with further age.

1995 Merlot, Reserve, Yakima Valley $23.　　　　**85**

Deep ruby red to the rim. Medium-bodied. Balanced acidity. Highly extracted. Mildly oaked. Moderately tannic. Red fruits, sweet herbs, vanilla. Aromatic and fairly complex, with a bit of an earthy, herbal streak. The palate is still tightly wound and compact, and chunky tannins rear up in the finish.

DeLille

1994 D2, Yakima Valley $22.   92

Full purple-tinged cherry red. Medium-bodied. Highly extracted. Mildly tannic.
Cassis, bramble fruits, red fruits. Inviting toasty aromas lead a focused palate with
good concentration of flavors and a lingering toasty finish. Superbly balanced, with
noble fine-grained tannins defining the finish.

1996 D2, Yakima Valley $24.   86

Bright violet-red hue. Aromatically restrained with clean, faintly herbal character.
A crisp entry leads to a medium-bodied palate with lighter berry fruit flavors and slight,
smoother tannins. Drink now.

1994 Chaleur Estate, Yakima Valley $32.   96

Dark black cherry with purple highlights. Moderately full-bodied. Highly extracted.
Quite tannic. Bittersweet chocolate, chalk, black cherries. Wonderfully deep black cherry
fruit flavors on the midpalate. Very impressive chalky, powdery tannins on the finish.
Very structured, this needs plenty of time. Youthful and vigorous.

1995 Chaleur Estate, Yakima Valley $34.   94

Deep red-violet. Moderately full-bodied. Highly extracted. Moderately tannic. Black fruits,
oak spice. Silky, ultrafine tannins leave a dry impression. Finely wrought and impressively
concentrated. This will be even better with some further cellar age.

1996 Chaleur Estate, Yakima Valley $38.   96

Semi-saturated dark ruby hue. Fleshy intensely fruity aromas have a chocolatey note. A
firm attack leads a moderately full-bodied palate with rich cassis and anise and chocolate
flavors. Tannins are well balanced, providing good grip on the finish. Drink now or later.

Dunham

1995 Cabernet Sauvignon, Columbia Valley $28.   93

Dark brick red. Moderately full-bodied. Highly extracted. Moderately tannic. Spice, black
fruits. Exotically spicy aromas show an oaky accent. Very full flavored and complex on the
palate, with notable intensity and depth. Long, long spicy finish.

E.B. Foote

1997 Chardonnay, Columbia Valley $12.   83

Pale yellow-gold. Tart apple aromas. A bright entry is followed by a medium-bodied
palate with crisp flavors that finish cleanly. Refreshing. Drink now.

1995 Cabernet Sauvignon, Columbia Valley $15.   87

Brick-ruby red. Medium-bodied. Moderately extracted. Moderately tannic. Black pepper,
dried herbs, black fruits. Jammy, herbal aromas lead a thick mouthfeel, with mineral and
herb flavors persisting.

1994 Cabernet Sauvignon, Cellar Reserve, Columbia Valley $32.   88

Opaque blood red. Moderately full-bodied. Highly extracted. Moderately tannic.
Chocolate, red fruits, earth. Very ripe to slightly overripe aromas lead a soft, viscous,
yet earthy palate with a deep black fruit character showing through. Low acid makes
for a very velvety mouthfeel, though the flavors finish dryly.

1996 Cabernet-Merlot, Columbia Valley $15.   82
1994 Merlot, Columbia Valley $12.   82
1995 Merlot, Columbia Valley $15.   84

Deep blackish ruby hue. Moderately light-bodied. Full acidity. Moderately extracted.
Mildly tannic. Chocolate malt, lacquer, plums. Extremely aromatic, with a very chocolatey
character and a mild oxidized note. Notably ripe fruit flavors come through on a lush
and velvety mouthfeel. Lengthy finish. Unusual but tasty.

Scale: Superlative (96-100), Exceptional (90-95), Highly Recommended (85-89),
Recommended (80-84), Not Recommended (Under 80)

Glen Fiona

1997 Syrah, Walla Walla Valley $35.   91

Opaque, saturated violet red. Intense sweet fruit and vanilla aromas, with a generous wood accent and a touch of heat. A lush attack leads a full-bodied palate showing grainy tannins. Rich, ripe finish. A thick, stuffed blockbuster style. Drink now or later. Can improve with more age.

Gordon Brothers

1997 Chardonnay, Columbia Valley $15.49.   81

1996 Cabernet Sauvignon, Columbia Valley $15.49.   88

Deep brick red. Medium-bodied. Moderately extracted. Moderately tannic. Mineral, black fruits, vanilla. Supple, well-rounded wine with juicy Cabernet fruit flavors and mineral notes on the finish. Very Claret-like.

1994 Tradition, Columbia Valley $19.99.   88

Deep ruby red. Medium-bodied. Moderately extracted. Mildly tannic. Red berry fruits, plums. Meaty, fleshy aromas are very inviting. A rounded, sumptuous palate shows soft, integrated tannins that linger through the finish. This reflects a high proportion of Merlot.

1994 Merlot, Columbia Valley $16.99.   87

Deep ruby with a slight garnet fade at the rim. Moderately full-bodied. Full acidity. Moderately extracted. Mildly oaked. Mildly tannic. Brown spices, red fruits. Pleasantly aromatic, with a nicely balanced, well-integrated palate feel. Solid though unobtrusive structure, and a dusty, mildly tannic finish.

Hedges

1997 Fumé Chardonnay, Columbia Valley $8.   84

Bright pale golden hue. Medium-bodied. Full acidity. Moderately extracted. Grassy lemon zest nose. Juicy flavors with a hint of sour apple dryness on the finish.

1997 Cabernet-Merlot, Washington $10.   81

1994 Red Mountain Reserve, Columbia Valley $30.   91

Opaque blackish red with purple highlights. Medium-bodied. Highly extracted. Moderately tannic. Black cherries, black tea. Concentrated black cherry flavors have a dry feel through the astringent finish. Impressive and structured, with solid tannins making it a little backward at present.

1995 Red Mountain Reserve, Columbia Valley $30.   89

Deep, opaque violet-red hue. Brooding chocolate, black fruit, and mineral aromas. A lush entry leads to a full-bodied palate with firm tannins. Rich, structured finish. Rather tough at present, but has the extract to outlast the tannins. Good for long-term cellaring.

1995 Three Vineyards, Columbia Valley $20.   90

Saturated, opaque red-purple. Moderately full-bodied. Highly extracted. Quite tannic. Black fruits, earth, minerals. Taut, angular, and tough to appreciate now. This has the structure and depth to cellar well.

Hogue

1997 Chardonnay, Columbia Valley $13.95.   86

Brilliant green-gold. Very pure fruit-centered aromas of green apples. A smooth entry leads a moderately full-bodied palate with pure Chardonnay flavors and very restrained vanilla oak notes. Acids are markedly crisp through the finish. Well structured. Drink now or later.

1997 Chardonnay, Barrel Select, Columbia Valley $8.95.   84

Brilliant yellow-gold. Ripe yellow apple and toasty oak aromas. A smooth entry leads a moderately full-bodied palate with creamy texture and lingering fruit and oak spice notes on the finish. Drink now or later.

1997 Chardonnay, Genesis, Sunnyside Vineyard, Yakima Valley $19.99.　89

Bright yellow-gold. Stylish aromas of wax and spice. A smooth entry leads a moderately full-bodied palate with lush, ripe flavors and well-integrated toasty nuances that persist through the finish. Well balanced, elegant, and refined.

1996 Semillon-Chardonnay, Columbia Valley $8.　86

Full golden straw hue. Medium-bodied. Balanced acidity. Moderately extracted. Nuts, figs, melon. Nutty aromas lead a surprisingly fresh-tasting palate, with an oily, glycerous mouthfeel and generous tropical flavors. Very concentrated.

1997 Fumé Blanc, Columbia Valley $8.　84

Pale platinum cast. Medium-bodied. Full acidity. Moderately extracted. Tart honeydew, citrus. High-toned fruity aromas lead a crisp palate that leaves the mouth refreshed. Not intensely flavorful but showing attractive aromatic character.

1996 Semillon, Columbia Valley $8.　86

Yellow-straw cast. Medium-bodied. Full acidity. Highly extracted. Tart kiwi, lemons, minerals. High-toned citrus aromas lead a bright, minerally palate. This straightforward style finishes cleanly with lingering juicy acids.

1994 Cabernet Franc, Genesis, Columbia Valley $15.　85

Bright ruby hue with a fade to the rim. Moderately full-bodied. Full acidity. Highly extracted. Moderately tannic. Minerals, red fruits. Lean and austere in style, with a firm structure. Finishes on a vibrant, earthy note.

1995 Cabernet Sauvignon, Columbia Valley $14.95.　83

Dark ruby with a fading rim. Muted aromas show a pickled herbal note. Shows a considerable American oak influence. A light entry leads to a medium-bodied palate with mild fruit sensations and some light bitterness through the finish. Drink now.

1994 Cabernet Sauvignon, Barrel Select, Columbia Valley $14.　87

Deep blood red. Medium-bodied. Moderately extracted. Mildly tannic. Black fruits, minerals, smoke. Crisp plummy flavors have a smoky accent, with clean herbal notes coming through on the finish. Drink now.

1995 Cabernet Sauvignon, Genesis, Champoux Vineyard, Columbia Valley $22.99.　92

Saturated violet-purple hue. Intensely rich dark fruit aromas with toasted oak accents. A firm entry leads to a full-bodied palate with deep, fleshy fruit flavors and rich tannins that coat the mouth. This needs much more time to resolve its youthful exuberance. Drink within five years.

1995 Cabernet Sauvignon, Reserve, Columbia Valley $30.　86

Bright violet-red hue. Crisp cassis and vanilla aromas show generous oak influence. A crisp entry leads to a moderately full-bodied palate with lively acids and balanced dry tannins. Showing a classic Cabernet structure. Drink now or later.

1997 Cabernet-Merlot, Columbia Valley $8.95.　80

1994 Merlot, Columbia Valley $15.　86

Ruby with a violet cast. Medium-bodied. Moderately extracted. Moderately oaked. Reminiscent of green tea, cigar box, minerals. Straightforward berry flavors up front, with solid tannins showing some green notes through the finish.

1996 Merlot, Barrel Select, Columbia Valley $14.95.　84

Bright, pale ruby red. Generous red fruit, mineral, and vanilla aromas show a slight oak accent. A ripe attack leads a medium-bodied palate with lean tannins and a lush, flavorful finish. Eminently drinkable, with ripe flavors and a clean, precise structure. Drink within five years.

1994 Merlot, Genesis, Columbia Valley $23.   **87**

Very deep ruby red with a slight garnet cast. Moderately full-bodied. Balanced acidity.
Highly extracted. Mildly oaked. Moderately tannic. Black fruits, sandalwood, licorice.
Still reined-in aromatically, this youthful wine is tightly wound and dense on the palate.
Deeply flavored and well balanced, with some unresolved tannins at the finish. Needs
some mid-term (3–6 years) aging to round itself out.

1996 Syrah, Genesis, Columbia Valley $15.   **86**

Bright saturated ruby red to the rim. Generous red fruit and spice aromas with a
prominent oak accent. A firm attack leads a medium-bodied palate showing astringent
tannins. Intense, flavorful finish. A firm, lean, and compact style. Drink now or later.
Can improve with more age.

Hoodsport

1997 Merlot, Yakima Valley $14.99.   **81**

Hyatt

1994 Cabernet Sauvignon, Reserve, Yakima Valley $32.   **87**

Garnet-cherry red. Medium-bodied. Moderately extracted. Moderately tannic. Herbs, oak
spice, red fruits. Lean, herbal-accented nose leads a concentrated palate, with tight red
fruit flavors and edgy tannins showing some authority on the finish. This should show
best with richer foods.

1995 Cabernet Sauvignon, Reserve, Yakima Valley $32.   **88**

Deep reddish purple. Medium-bodied. Highly extracted. Mildly tannic. Cassis, red
berries, minerals. A tight, high-toned nose reveals an angular, compact palate showing
youthful vibrancy. Some dry minerally undertones, with astringent tannins. Needs time
for optimum pleasure.

1994 Merlot, Yakima Valley $14.99.   **88**

Ruby red. Medium-bodied. Moderately extracted. Moderately oaked. Reminiscent of
black fruits, tea, minerals. Brooding dark fruit in the nose. A lean fruity style with some
austerity on the palate and reasonably firm tannins through the finish. Solid.

1994 Merlot, Reserve, Yakima Valley $29.99.   **90**

Ruby red. Moderately full-bodied. Moderately extracted. Heavily oaked. Moderately
tannic. Reminiscent of tea, dried herbs, black fruits. Brooding oak-accented aromas.
A solid, mouthfilling style with tightly wound flavors on the midpalate and a lengthy
austere finish.

Kestrel

1996 Chardonnay, Columbia Valley $22.   **93**

Bright yellow-gold. Outstanding aromas of butterscotch and ripe fruits. A toasty attack
leads a full-bodied palate with a lush texture and ripe fruit flavors. Exotic brown spice
comes through on the finish. Very stylish. Drink now or later.

1995 Cabernet Sauvignon, Columbia Valley $22.   **94**

Bright violet-purple hue. Aromas show complex oak influence with crisp black fruits.
A lively entrance leads to a moderately full-bodied palate with dry tannins covering the
fruit expression now. Time should help this, though this is highly structured and very
marked by complex oak spice. Drink now or later.

1996 Merlot, Columbia Valley $28.   **84**

Medium-dark ruby hue. Restrained very woody aromas. A firm entry leads a medium-
bodied palate with dull fruit flavors and a dry astringent finish. Rather lean, this does
not have the stuffing to improve. Drink now.

Kiona

1997 Chardonnay, Washington $11.   **83**

Dark straw cast. Moderately full-bodied. Balanced acidity. Moderately extracted. Minerals,
flint, butter. Shows a big minerally quality throughout. Ripe and rounded in the mouth
with a buttery texture moderated by crisp acids.

1997 Chardonnay, Reserve, Columbia Valley $19. **82**

1996 Cabernet Sauvignon, Washington $14.99. **86**

Bright purple-red. Medium-bodied. Moderately extracted. Moderately tannic. Sweet plums, black cherries, tobacco. Youthful appearance and aromas. Sweet, supple fruit flavors with good texture and mouthfeel. Dry, fine-grained tannins distinguish the finish.

1997 Cabernet Sauvignon, Washington $17.99. **87**

Saturated ruby hue. Ripe fruity aromas with a touch of vanilla oak. A soft entry leads to a medium-bodied palate with concentrated, fruit-forward character that fills the mouth. Finishes with soft, supple tannins. Drink now.

1995 Cabernet Sauvignon, Reserve, Yakima Valley $29.99. **92**

Saturated blood red. Moderately full-bodied. Highly extracted. Moderately oaked. Moderately tannic. Brown spice, sandalwood, licorice, earth. Rich, spicy aromas lead a concentrated, broad palate of spice flavors with sweet black fruit notes showing through a long finish. Very stylish, drinking well now.

1997 Cabernet-Merlot, Columbia Valley $9.99. **83**

Bright violet-red. Moderately light-bodied. Moderately extracted. Mildly tannic. Flowers, dried herbs. Engaging floral aromas lead a light-framed palate with bright floral flavors. Finishes with a hint of dry tannins.

1995 Merlot, Columbia Valley $18. **83**

Deep ruby color. Medium-bodied. Highly extracted. Moderately tannic. Reminiscent of ripe berries, brown spice, licorice. Fleshy berry aromas. Rich, expansive fruity palate with a mouthfilling character and some fine tannins on the lengthy finish. Would cellar well, although approachable now.

1996 Merlot, Washington $19.99. **82**

L'Ecole No. 41

1997 Chardonnay, Washington $19.50. **87**

Bright pale golden cast. Moderately full-bodied. Full acidity. Moderately extracted. Mildly oaked. Minerals, brown spices, butter. Generous aromas feature a judicious oak accent. Ripe and lush in the mouth, with zesty acidity providing balance to the finish.

1996 Semillon, Washington $13.50. **87**

Deep yellow-gold. Moderately full-bodied. Full acidity. Highly extracted. Figs, lemons, minerals, brown spice. An impressive array of spicy aromas leads an expansive palate held together by bright acids. Firm and concentrated, with a generous mouthfeel and understated oak accents.

1994 Cabernet Sauvignon, Columbia Valley $24. **90**

Dark blood red with subtle purple highlights. Medium-bodied. Highly extracted. Mildly tannic. Dill, tobacco, currants, black fruits. A very pronounced oak-accented nose follows through on the palate, with chewy, curranty black fruits on the midpalate. Full and long toasty finish. Very attractive.

1995 Cabernet Sauvignon, Columbia Valley $25. **94**

Saturated brick red. Moderately full-bodied. Highly extracted. Moderately oaked. Moderately tannic. Dill, coconut, black fruits. Extravagant spice aromas follow through on a densely flavored palate that has a surprisingly supple character, inviting current drinking.

1996 Cabernet Sauvignon, Columbia Valley $26. **90**

Saturated dark ruby with violet highlights. Aromatically distinctive with ripe aromas and distinctive woody accents. A rich entry leads a moderately full-bodied palate with a plush mouthfeel, and firm acidity. Well structured and intensely flavored.

1995 Cabernet Sauvignon, Windrow Vineyard, Walla Walla Valley $30. **86**

Deep red-violet. Moderately full-bodied. Highly extracted. Moderately tannic. Pepper, black fruits, earth. Generous and complex spice-accented aromas lead a supple, weighty mouthful of soft, fruity flavors that finish with some minerally intensity. Thick mouthfeel.

Scale: Superlative (96-100), Exceptional (90-95), Highly Recommended (85-89), Recommended (80-84), Not Recommended (Under 80)

1995 Cabernet Sauvignon-Merlot, Apogée, Pepper Bridge Vineyard,
Walla Walla Valley $30.   **93**

Bright red-violet. Medium-bodied. Moderately extracted. Moderately tannic. Coconut, spice, crisp berry fruits. Exotic, spicy, high-toned aromas lead a vibrant mouthful of fruit flavors, with supple tannins and oak spice notes lingering. Very silky and stylish.

1996 Cabernet Sauvignon-Merlot, Seven Hills Vineyard,
Walla Walla Valley $35.   **86**

Dark, saturated ruby-red hue. Full chocolate and dark fruit aromas with a distinctive, unusual note. A heavy entry leads a full-bodied palate with considerable weight and tart acids that make this angular and tough now.

1994 Merlot, Columbia Valley $22.   **92**

Deep ruby color. Medium-bodied. Moderately extracted. Moderately oaked. Moderately tannic. Reminiscent of black cherries, cedar, tobacco. Complex, deep nose. Rich, ripe fruity entry with complex toasty flavors and a minerally backbone through to a mild finish with grainy tannins. Very seductive and elegant.

1995 Merlot, Columbia Valley $24.   **92**

Very deep blackish ruby color. Medium-bodied. Balanced acidity. Moderately extracted. Moderately oaked. Mildly tannic. Brown spices, plums, dried herbs. Pleasantly aromatic and extremely flavorful, with a mile-long finish. The lush, inviting palate has a velvety texture and unobtrusive structure. Classic fruit and herbal flavors are intertwined with the judicious use of oak to make a complex and harmonious wine.

1996 Merlot, Columbia Valley $25.   **88**

Bright ruby red with a slight fade. Intense cedar and spice aromas show a dominant wood accent. A lush attack leads a moderately full-bodied palate with chunky, velvety tannins. Flavorful, spicy finish. Somewhat overpowered by its sweet wood flavors, but tasty nonetheless. Drink within five years.

Leonetti

1994 Cabernet Sauvignon, Columbia Valley $45.   **93**

Saturated dark black-cherry hue with purple highlights. Moderately full-bodied. Highly extracted. Moderately tannic. Toasted oak, dill, plums, earth, smoke. Full smoky, toasty oak nose has rich black fruit accents that follow through well on the palate. Rich, extracted flavors expand on the midpalate through a firm, deliciously toasty finish.

1995 Cabernet Sauvignon, Columbia Valley $45.   **90**

Saturated dark ruby hue. Richly aromatic with generous black fruit and marked oak spice. A silky entry leads a full-bodied palate with deep and complex flavors that persist through a long finish. Drink now.

Matthews

1996 Cabernet Sauvignon, Elerding Vineyard, Yakima Valley $35.   **94**

Saturated dark ruby hue. Moderately full-bodied. Highly extracted. Moderately tannic. Mint, chocolate, dark fruits. Broad, chocolatey aromas lead a concentrated, dry palate showing a core of lush fruit flavors, with firm Cabernet tannins clamping down on the finish. This needs more cellar time.

1995 Yakima Valley Red, Washington $28.   **88**

Bright cherry red. Medium-bodied. Moderately extracted. Mildly tannic. Vanilla, toasted oak, cherries. Inviting toasty nose. Straightforward crisp cherry flavors expand on the palate, with toasty oak flavors taking over on the finish. Well balanced and drinking nicely now.

1996 Cabernet Sauvignon-Cabernet Franc-Merlot, Yakima Valley Red,
Washington $35.   **84**

Deep ruby-red hue. Intense, unusual anise and mineral aromas carry a marked oak accent. A crisp entry leads to a spicy, medium-bodied palate with firm acidity and lean tannins. Angular, zesty finish. Unusual but interesting. Drink now.

Mountain Dome

NV Brut Rosé, Washington $16.   86

Deep salmon color. Full-bodied. Full acidity. Highly extracted. Cream, red fruits, toast. Attractive aromatics show complexity throughout. Ripe, racy, and intense in the mouth, with a firm structure and vibrant carbonation. A sturdy, weighty style.

1993 Brut, Columbia Valley $16.   87

Bright yellow-gold. Medium-bodied. Pears, yeast. Distinctive, mature aromas follow through on a leesy palate, with broad, very marked yeasty flavors that dominate through the finish.

Patrick M. Paul

1994 Cabernet Sauvignon, Columbia Valley $12.   88

Deep red brick color. Medium-bodied. Highly extracted. Moderately tannic. Black cherries, brown spice, toasted oak. Very dry oaky nose follows through on the palate. Compact and tightly wound, with solid astringency and very pronounced oak flavors complemented by rich black fruit accents. Not everyone's style.

1993 Merlot, Conner Lee Vineyards, Columbia Valley $12.   90

Deep cherry red. Moderately full-bodied. Highly extracted. Heavily oaked. Moderately tannic. Reminiscent of oak, black tea, black fruits. Very distinctive oak-accented aromas. The palate is concentrated and tightly wound, with a long, dry spicy finish. A very individualistic style that will appeal to those who like strong oak flavors.

Portteus

1995 Cabernet Sauvignon, Yakima Valley $30.   92

Saturated, opaque blood red. Moderately full-bodied. Highly extracted. Moderately tannic. Black fruits, chocolate, minerals. Outstanding spiced aromas lead a fleshy dark fruit entry that reveals plenty of supple, earthy flavors that linger through the finish. Very complex, with a fine expression of terroir.

1994 Cabernet Sauvignon, Reserve, Yakima Valley $26.   90

Opaque blood red with a purple rim. Moderately full-bodied. Highly extracted. Moderately tannic. Earth, oak spice, tar, coffee, black fruits. Rich oaky, brown spice aromas follow through on the palate. Has a nice rich center of dark fruits and earth, with oak coming through strongly on the finish. A generous style.

1994 Merlot, Yakima Valley $16.   89

Deep, dark red. Medium-bodied. Moderately extracted. Moderately oaked. Moderately tannic. Reminiscent of blackberries, brown spice. A ripe berry fruit nose leads an imposingly rich fruity entry with adequate firm tannins on the lengthy finish giving this solid appeal.

1995 Merlot, Yakima Valley $16.   90

Deep blackish ruby hue to the rim. Medium-bodied. Balanced acidity. Moderately extracted. Moderately oaked. Mildly tannic. Minerals, red fruits, cedar. Very well balanced, with a big range of complex flavors. Well-integrated, lush finish. Quite tasty.

1995 Merlot, Reserve, Yakima Valley $29.   91

Very deep blackish ruby hue. Medium-bodied. Balanced acidity. Moderately extracted. Heavily oaked. Mildly tannic. Pencil shavings, coffee, black fruits. Quite aromatic and largely wood driven, though quite attractive. Features a lush and harmonious core of flavors on the palate. Extremely well balanced through the lengthy finish.

1997 Syrah, Yakima Valley $20.   83

Bright garnet red with a slight fade. Pungent stewed fruit, herb, and mineral aromas. A soft attack leads a medium-bodied palate, with drying tannins. Tough, rather edgy finish. An unusual mix of very ripe flavors allied to an austere frame. Drink now.

Powers

1996 Chardonnay, Columbia Valley $10.   **82**

1996 Fumé Blanc, Columbia Valley $7.50.   **82**

1996 Cabernet Sauvignon, Washington $12.   **86**

Medium-dark violet red. Medium-bodied. Moderately extracted. Moderately tannic.
Cassis, minerals. Fleshy black fruit aromas. Wonderfully wrought, with plump fruit flavors
and generous fine-grained tannins not masking the pleasure.

1995 Cabernet Sauvignon, Mercer Ranch Vineyard, Columbia Valley $18.   **90**

Opaque red-purple. Moderately full-bodied. Highly extracted. Quite tannic. Minerals,
black fruits. Lush, fruity entry. Austere and tough, it has dense, fine-grained tannins
drying the finish. Shows fine weight, though the tannins are clamping down now.

1996 Cabernet-Merlot, Washington $12.   **86**

Deep red-purple. Moderately full-bodied. Highly extracted. Moderately tannic. Black
fruits. Big-shouldered and generous, with fleshy dark fruit flavors and chunky tannins.
No shy wallflower. Firm tannins will need some meaty accompaniment.

1995 Merlot, Columbia Valley $16.   **87**

Deep ruby hue with a garnet cast and brilliant clarity. Moderately light-bodied. Balanced
acidity. Moderately extracted. Moderately oaked. Mildly tannic. Sweet herbs, red fruits,
vanilla. Pleasantly aromatic, with a lighter-styled though lush mouthfeel. Red fruit flavors
are accented by light oak accents and an herbal streak. Complex lingering finish.

1996 Pinot Noir, Columbia Valley $9.   **80**

Preston Premium

1998 Gamay Beaujolais Rosé, Columbia Valley $8.   **82**

1994 Cabernet Sauvignon, Reserve, Columbia Valley $21.   **89**

Dark brick red. Medium-bodied. Moderately extracted. Moderately oaked. Mildly tannic.
Dill, bright red fruits, oak spice. American oak nose. Concentrated bright red fruit flavors
on entry follow through to a lengthy powdery finish showing fine dry tannins. Good
structure. Though drinking well now, this will be more attractive in a few years.

1995 Cabernet Sauvignon, Reserve, Columbia Valley $21.   **86**

Saturated, opaque brick red. Moderately full-bodied. Highly extracted. Moderately
tannic. Brown spice, black fruits. Strong impression of oak on the nose. Remarkably
intense and focused, with very elegant black fruit flavors and persistence on the finish.
Powdery tannins leave a dry sensation.

1994 Merlot, Preston Vineyard, Columbia Valley $10.   **85**

Garnet cherry color. Medium-bodied. Moderately extracted. Mildly tannic. Reminiscent
of red currants, dried herbs. Soft berry fruit flavors with mild tannins through the finish
make this easygoing and very drinkable.

1993 Merlot, Reserve, Columbia Valley $18.99.   **89**

Deep garnet cherry color. Medium-bodied. Moderately extracted. Moderately oaked.
Moderately tannic. Reminiscent of cherries, black tea, brown spice. An angular style with
forward cherry fruit on entry and some tight tannins on the finish. Nice now but could
withstand some short-term (1–2 years) cellaring.

1994 Merlot, Reserve, Columbia Valley $21.   **90**

Deep blackish red with a garnet cast. Medium-bodied. Balanced acidity. Moderately
extracted. Heavily oaked. Mildly tannic. Chocolate, cedar, coffee. Couldn't be more
aromatic and flavorful, but the flavors are largely wood driven. Nonetheless, this wine
is well balanced and lush, with a very lengthy finish. Quite seductive in its own way.

1995 Merlot, Western White Oak, Columbia Valley $16.   **87**

Very deep ruby red to the rim. Medium-bodied. Balanced acidity. Moderately extracted.
Moderately oaked. Mildly tannic. Red fruits, minerals, bacon. Still a little tight, with a
youthful character on the palate. Well balanced, with a juicy note of acidity to the finish.
Should open up quite nicely with near-term cellaring.

Quilceda Creek

1994 Cabernet Sauvignon, Washington $42.   91
Opaque violet red. Medium-bodied. Moderately extracted. Moderately tannic. Black
fruits, chocolate. Rich black fruit aromas lead a firm mouthful of flavors, with rich, dry
tannins featured on the finish. Concentrated, displaying sound structure and length.

1995 Cabernet Sauvignon, Washington $45.   93
Saturated violet-purple hue. Vanilla oak aromas have an oaky accent with cassis richness
showing. A bright entry leads to a full-bodied palate with lively acids and dry, powdery
tannins on the finish. Drink now or later.

Seth Ryan

1996 Cabernet Franc, Yakima Valley $14.81.   80

1994 Cabernet Sauvignon, Yakima Valley $25.93.   87
Opaque red-garnet hue. Moderately full-bodied. Highly extracted. Quite tannic. Black
fruits, oak spice. Aromas show a heavy wood influence. Tough, severe, dry tannins on the
finish make it hard to drink now. This has some rustic charm, and will develop in the
course of a few years.

1996 Jessica's Meritage, Columbia Valley $32.41.   85
Deep ruby hue with a violet rim. Medium-bodied. Balanced acidity. Moderately extracted.
Cherries, mineral, spice. Toasty, ripe, fruity aromas lead a bright, rounded palate with tart
flavors and a spicy oak finish that lingers.

Seven Hills

1995 Cabernet Sauvignon, Columbia Valley $20.   88
Dark ruby red. Medium-bodied. Balanced acidity. Moderately extracted. Mildly tannic.
Black fruits, sour cherry, oak spice. Supple, fleshy, and very well balanced, with the finish
showing soft tannins.

1995 Cabernet Sauvignon, Walla Walla Valley $24.   89
Bright cherry red with violet highlights. Medium-bodied. Highly extracted. Moderately
tannic. Pencil shavings, cassis, minerals. Classic, Claret-like aromas lead a bright, flavorsome mouthful with piercing fruit flavors and mineral snap.

1995 Cabernet Sauvignon, Klipsun Vineyard, Columbia Valley $24.   90
Opaque red-violet. Moderately full-bodied. Highly extracted. Quite tannic. Black fruits,
mineral, spice. Reserved, dark fruit aromas lead a tightly wound, well-stuffed palate, with
considerably dry, fine-grained tannins giving an assertive finish.

1994 Merlot, Columbia Valley $20.   85
Deep reddish purple. Medium-bodied. Moderately extracted. Moderately tannic.
Reminiscent of red fruits, black tea. Brooding fruity aromas reveal a tightly wound
center with concentrated flavors. This needs more time or good aeration.

1995 Merlot, Columbia Valley $20.   86
Very deep ruby red to the rim. Medium-bodied. Balanced acidity. Moderately
extracted. Mildly tannic. Cherries, black pepper, minerals. Fruit-driven aromatics
lead a lighter-styled palate showing vibrant acidity. Still a bit compact, with tannins
that grip down on the finish.

1994 Merlot, Seven Hills Vineyard, Walla Walla Valley $24.   90
Opaque purplish black hue. Moderately full-bodied. Highly extracted. Heavily oaked.
Moderately tannic. Reminiscent of black fruits, cedar, minerals. Heavily oak-accented
nose. Solid and tight on the palate, showing fine extraction and focus, but a little
attenuated on the finish. Needs more time in the cellar for optimum enjoyment.

1995 Merlot, Seven Hills Vineyard, Walla Walla Valley $24.　　　**90**

Deep ruby with a slight purplish cast and brilliant clarity. Moderately full-bodied. Balanced acidity. Highly extracted. Moderately oaked. Moderately tannic. Black fruits, dried herbs, minerals. Big and rich in style, showing a chunky, youthful texture. Complex and flavorful, with a wave of velvety tannins on the palate. Well balanced and finely extracted, this is a solid candidate for mid-term (3–6 years) to long-term (7–10 years) cellaring.

1995 Merlot, Klipsun Vineyard, Columbia Valley $24.　　　**93**

Deep, opaque blackish ruby hue with a purple cast. Full-bodied. Full acidity. Highly extracted. Heavily oaked. Quite tannic. Red fruits, vanilla. From its color to its flavor profile, this wine is solidly New World. Aromatic, with a rush of big oak-driven flavors and a dense core of ripe fruit. Despite its weight it is well balanced, and though the tannins are considerable, they have been finely extracted. Long-term cellaring should mellow it and bring out some complexity. A show wine, not for near-term drinking.

Silver Lake

1997 Chardonnay, Columbia Valley $11.99.　　　**84**

Brilliant yellow-gold. Ripe yellow apple aromas. A pure, fruity attack leads a medium-bodied palate that has rounded, concentrated fruit flavors with subtle oak notes. A very well-balanced, harmonious style. Drink now.

1997 Chardonnay, Reserve, Columbia Valley $15.99.　　　**83**

Full gold. Lean appley aromas. A firm attack leads a full-bodied palate with weighty mouthfeel and deeply oaky flavors. Finishes with a degree of alcohol warmth. Powerful, intense style.

1995 Cabernet Sauvignon, Columbia Valley $12.99.　　　**84**

Bright ruby hue with a subtle fade. Generously oak accented aromas. A crisp entry leads to a medium-bodied palate with bright berry fruits and lingering vanilla and oak spice. Very straightforward, lighter style.

1995 Cabernet Sauvignon, Reserve, Columbia Valley $17.99.　　　**87**

Saturated dark ruby hue. Fragrantly aromatic with a vanilla oak and cassis character. A firm entry leads to a full-bodied palate with well-integrated, silky tannins that linger on the finish. Rather well structured and well extracted, this will need some time.

1994 Cabernet Sauvignon, Hervé, Cuvée Selipsky,
Columbia Valley $24.99.　　　**83**

Bright garnet hue. Unusual, mature forest and stewed fruit aromas show a spicy oak accent. A firm entry leads to a full-bodied palate with big chewy tannins. Rich, intense finish. Unusual but interesting. Drink within five years.

1995 Merlot, Columbia Valley $12.99.　　　**81**

1995 Merlot, Reserve, Columbia Valley $17.99.　　　**83**

Rich garnet red. Generous cedar, red fruit, and mineral aromas. A lush attack leads a medium-bodied palate with austere tannins that provide grip. The finish is angular, though. Drink within five years.

Staton Hills

1997 Chardonnay, Washington $12.95.　　　**84**

Full yellow-gold. Very ripe, generously fruity aromas of peach and apple. A lush attack leads a full-bodied palate with tropical fruit flavors and well-balanced oak. The mouthfeel is opulent and the finish is smooth. Drink now.

1996 Fumé Blanc, Yakima Valley $8.95.　　　**83**

Bright pale straw hue. Medium-bodied. Balanced acidity. Moderately extracted. Dried herbs, lemons. Aromatically reserved, revealing a straightforward and delicate palate through to a warm finish.

1994 Cabernet Sauvignon, Columbia Valley $16. **89**

Dark ruby red hue. Generous spicy, oak accented aromas. A lean entry leads a moderately full-bodied palate with rich oak dominated flavors. Finishes in an angular manner with firm tannins and complex spicy flavors.

1995 Cabernet Sauvignon, Columbia Valley $15.95. **88**

Bright red-violet. Medium-bodied. Highly extracted. Moderately tannic. Black fruits, oak spice. Lush, fruity flavors with gentle oak spice and some fine-grained tannins giving authority to the finish. Probably better in a few years.

Ste. Chapelle

1997 Chardonnay, Reserve, Idaho $15. **83**

Pale straw hue. Elegant, smoky aromas. A juicy attack leads a medium-bodied palate with piercing acids and oak flavors coming to the fore. Interesting though not elegant cool climate Chardonnay style. Drink now.

1998 Johannisberg Riesling, Idaho $6. **83**

Pale platinum-straw hue. Muted aromas of minerals and citrus zest. A crisp attack leads a medium-bodied palate, with dry, zesty flavors and minerally firmness through the finish. Drink now.

1998 Dry Johannisberg Riesling, Idaho $6. **86**

Medium yellow-gold. Fresh aromas of crisp apples and herbs. A bright attack leads a medium-bodied palate, with crisp fruit flavors persisting on the finish. Very refreshing. Drink now.

Tefft

1994 Cabernet Sauvignon, Yakima Valley $25. **87**

Full crimson red. Medium-bodied. Moderately extracted. Mildly tannic. Black tea, cassis, cherries. Bright entry reveals a concentrated, angular palate with a firm finish. Still a little tightly wound; should be better in a few years.

1995 Cabernet Sauvignon, Yakima Valley $21.99. **89**

Opaque brick red. Moderately full-bodied. Highly extracted. Moderately tannic. Black fruits, minerals, spice. Dusty, spiced fruit aromas lead a full-flavored palate that has a degree of firmness and intensity that lingers through the finish. Still structured, though it is drinkable now.

NV Merlot, Columbia Valley $15. **87**

Deep ruby with a subtle garnet cast and brilliant clarity. Moderately full-bodied. Balanced acidity. Moderately extracted. Heavily oaked. Mildly tannic. Brown spices, red fruits, dill pickle. Quite aromatic, with a big oak overlay on the core of fruit flavors. Chewy on the palate, with some dusty tannins and a lengthy finish.

1994 Merlot, Winemakers Reserve, Yakima Valley $25. **92**

Deep reddish purple. Moderately full-bodied. Highly extracted. Quite tannic. Reminiscent of minerals, black fruit, tea. Dense, brooding aromatics. An imposing, slightly austere, but well-structured style with a solid minerally backbone and some warmth on the finish. Should evolve with cellaring.

Paul Thomas

1995 Chardonnay, Washington $7. **83**

Pale straw cast. Moderately full-bodied. Full acidity. Moderately extracted. Citrus, minerals. Crisp and reserved in a lean and racy style. Clean and refreshing through the finish.

1995 Cabernet Sauvignon, Reserve, Washington $14.99. **86**

Bright violet-ruby color. Medium-bodied. Moderately extracted. Mildly tannic. Red fruits, minerals, dried herbs. Well balanced, with bright, juicy acids and supple yet dry tannins lingering on the finish.

Scale: Superlative (96-100), Exceptional (90-95), Highly Recommended (85-89),
Recommended (80-84), Not Recommended (Under 80)

1996 Cabernet Sauvignon, Reserve, Columbia Valley $17.   84

Pale ruby hue with a subtle fade. Lighter attractive aromas show a oak accent. A supple entry leads a medium-bodied palate with spicy oak flavors that are well integrated. Harmonious and lengthy. Drink now.

1995 Merlot, Washington $10.50.   84

Bright reddish purple. Medium-bodied. Moderately extracted. Moderately oaked. Mildly tannic. Reminiscent of herbs, red fruits, brown spice. Lively, crisp red fruit palate with an attractive toasty finish. Quite fresh and forward in style.

1997 Riesling, Reserve, Columbia Valley $7.   81

Crimson Rhubarb Wine, Washington $5.99.   87

Brilliant faded pink. Moderately full-bodied. Full acidity. Highly extracted. Yeast, minerals, toast. Extremely fragrant, with a forward yeasty overtone that is almost Champagne-like. Full and round in the mouth, with a continuation of the yeasty flavors and vibrant acidity through the drying finish. Exotic.

Dry Bartlett Pear, Washington $7.99.   83

Bright yellow-straw cast. Moderately full-bodied. Low acidity. Moderately extracted. Minerals, stone fruits. Rather reserved in style, with a lush mouthfeel that lacks a bit of grip. Turns angular on the finish.

Raspberry Wine, Washington $7.99.   86

Bright ruby-garnet cast. Medium-bodied. Full acidity. Highly extracted. Raspberries, minerals. Extremely aromatic and quite pure, with a definite raspberry accent to the flavors throughout. Surprisingly firm on the palate, with sturdy acidity that makes for a lean, drying finish.

Walla Walla Vintners

1996 Washington State Red Cuvée, Washington $18.   87

Bright ruby with a subtly fading rim. Elegant oaky aromas with ripe berry fruit accents. A supple entry leads a medium-bodied palate with harmonious well-fruited flavors and a chocolatey, vanilla-accented finish. Supple and well balanced. Drink now.

Washington Hills

1997 Chardonnay, Columbia Valley $9.99.   83

Bright yellow-gold. Crisp yellow apple aromas. A bright attack leads a medium-bodied palate with clean fruity flavors and very subtle oak. Drink now.

1998 Gewürztraminer, Columbia Valley $6.   80

1996 Semillon-Chardonnay, Columbia Valley $7.99.   84

Bright yellow-gold. Medium-bodied. Full acidity. Moderately extracted. Dried herbs, kiwi. High-toned tropical aromas have an herbal twist leading juicy, vibrant flavors in a clean, fresh style.

1995 Cabernet Sauvignon, Columbia Valley $9.99.   86

Cherry-brick red with a slight fade on the rim. Medium-bodied. Moderately extracted. Moderately tannic. Berry fruits, minerals. Bright and juicy aromas follow through on the palate, with a fruit-forward entry that builds through the midpalate. Dry mineral and spice notes persist on the finish.

1997 Cabernet-Merlot, Columbia Valley $10.   81

1995 Merlot, Columbia Valley $12.99.   80

1997 Merlot, Varietal Select, Columbia Valley $11.   81

1998 Late Harvest White Riesling, Columbia Valley $8/375 ml.   88

Brilliant yellow-gold. Sweet peach and apricot aromas. A ripe, sweet entry leads a medium-bodied palate with off-dry, lush primary fruit flavors following through on the finish. Pure and quite concentrated. Drink now.

Waterbrook

1997 Chardonnay, Columbia Valley $10.   83

Bright yellow-straw hue. Mild yellow apple aromas. A juicy entry leads a medium-bodied palate with straightforward, clean fruity flavors and very subtle oak nuances. The finish is clean. Drink now.

1997 Sauvignon Blanc, Columbia Valley $13.   86

Medium straw cast. Moderately full-bodied. Balanced acidity. Moderately extracted. Mildly oaked. Vanilla, smoke, citrus. Subtle toasty oak aromas lead a generous mouthfeel, with bright smoky citrus flavors and a spicy warm finish. Has stuffing and character.

1997 Viognier, Columbia Valley $18.   86

Bright golden hue. Full-bodied. Balanced acidity. Highly extracted. Pears, apples, minerals. Pearlike aromas. Full, though lean and angular on the finish, with some powdery dryness.

1995 Cabernet Sauvignon, Columbia Valley $24.   92

Dark ruby red with violet highlights. Medium-bodied. Highly extracted. Moderately tannic. Cassis, spice, vanilla. Youthful, oak spice-dominated aromas lead a brisk, tightly wound palate displaying intense black fruit flavors and dusty, dry tannins.

1994 Merlot, Columbia Valley $19.99.   93

Opaque purple. Moderately full-bodied. Highly extracted. Moderately oaked. Moderately tannic. Reminiscent of plums, currants, toasted oak. Rich, ripe aromas. Deep, extracted fruity flavors with a firm minerally backbone to the palate give this length and structure in a feminine style. Drinkable now, it should cellar well.

1996 Merlot, Columbia Valley $22.   86

Bright garnet red. Generous spice aromas belie a wood-dominated character. A rounded attack leads a medium-bodied palate with crisp acidity and mild tannins. The finish is lush and spicy. A mellow, rounded, but well-balanced style. Drink now.

1995 Merlot, Reserve, Columbia Valley $32.   92

Deep blackish ruby color. Moderately full-bodied. Balanced acidity. Moderately extracted. Moderately oaked. Mildly tannic. Black fruits, brown spices, minerals. Pleasantly aromatic and relatively firm in style, with an angular presence on the palate. Fleshes out toward the lengthy finish. A tad restrained, but quite elegant.

Whidbey

1990 Port, Washington $12.99.   90

Black ruby hue with brick rim. Moderately full-bodied. Balanced acidity. Highly extracted. Moderately tannic. Medium sweetness. Reminiscent of mocha, dried plums, grenadine. Intensely concentrated and still youthful, with a lengthy palate of sweet-tasting fruit enlivened by tangy spice notes. Shows nice grip in the finish.

Andrew Will

1994 Cabernet Sauvignon, Washington $30.   90

Garnet-blood red. Medium-bodied. Highly extracted. Moderately tannic. Earth, brown spice, black fruits, cedar. Earthy, oak-accented nose. The rich, chewy black fruit palate has exotic toasty notes, with a lengthy dry finish. Austere and full flavored, with sound angular structure.

1996 Cabernet Sauvignon, Washington $32.   90

Opaque, saturated dark purple hue. Deep, brooding aromas of dark ripe fruits and vanilla oak. A rich entry leads a full-bodied palate with fabulous fruit intensity and soft, supple tannins that coat the mouth. Extravagantly generous and concentrated, though very approachable. Drink now.

1994 Cabernet Sauvignon, Reserve, Washington $40.   91

Opaque dark blood red. Moderately full-bodied. Highly extracted. Quite tannic. Black tea, earth, tart plums, minerals. Full earthy, oaky nose. A big dry palate with assertive grainy tannins make this wine very tight through the finish. Impressively structured. Needs time.

1995 Cabernet Sauvignon, Reserve, Washington $40.   93

Saturated violet purple. Moderately full-bodied. Highly extracted. Quite tannic. Cherry fruits, vanilla, minerals. Expressively aromatic, in a very youthful manner. Follows through as expected on the palate; very focused and tight, with bright cherry fruit flavors and astringent tannins through the finish. Impressively structured, it needs time.

1995 Sorella, Washington $40.   94

Deep violet red with an opaque cast. Moderately full-bodied. Balanced acidity. Moderately extracted. Moderately oaked. Moderately tannic. Black cherries, minerals, spice. Deep, minerally aromas follow through on a lush mouthfeel with mineral-rich flavors. Shows great grip and balance.

1996 Sorella, Washington $38.   92

Saturated purple-violet hue. Richly fruity aromas show ripe berry fruit and cassis character. Mouthfilling and fruit-forward flavors on entry lead a moderately full-bodied palate with softer, supple tannins on the finish. Big, fruity, and supple. Drink now or later.

1994 Merlot, Washington $25.   90

Very deep cherry red. Moderately full-bodied. Highly extracted. Quite tannic. Reminiscent of dried herbs, black fruit, toasted oak, minerals. Glycerous notes on the mouthfeel. The concentrated palate is focused by fine acidity and lengthy tannins, all of which give this real cellaring potential.

1995 Merlot, Washington $28.   90

Very deep blackish ruby hue. Moderately full-bodied. Balanced acidity. Moderately extracted. Moderately oaked. Mildly tannic. Leather, black fruits, chocolate. Fully flavored and rich, with an accent on oak. The core of flavors is dense and the finish is quite firm. A bit compact, it could use near-term to mid-term (3–6 years) aging to mellow it out a bit.

1996 Merlot, Washington $26.   86

Deep purple-red with a slight haze. Generous dill pickle and red fruit aromas show what seems to be a big American oak accent. A crisp attack is followed by a medium-bodied palate with juicy acidity and a bright finish. Somewhat light in style but tasty. Drink now.

1997 Merlot, Ciel du Cheval, Washington $30.   92

Deep, opaque purple-red. Restrained, embryonic black fruit, mineral, and spice aromas. A soft attack leads a moderately full-bodied palate with firm tannins. Big, tannic finish. A stuffed, extracted style that needs quite a bit more time. Good for long-term cellaring.

1996 Merlot, Klipsun, Washington $28.   90

Deep, opaque purple-red to the rim. Perfumed spice, chocolate, and red fruit aromas show a toasty oak accent. A lush entry leads a medium-bodied palate with fine grip and velvety tannins. Persistent, flavorful finish. Rounded and inviting. Drink now.

1997 Merlot, Klipsun, Washington $30.   90

Dark, opaque violet-red to the rim. Restrained spice and black fruit aromas show a subtle oak accent. A firm attack leads a moderately full-bodied, lush palate with robust, chunky tannins. Buoyant acidity makes for a vibrant, flavorful finish. Lots of stuffing—should open with age. Good for long-term cellaring.

1997 Merlot, Pepper Bridge, Washington $30.   91

Dark, opaque violet-red to the rim. Intense, perfumed floral red fruit aromas. A lean attack leads a medium-bodied palate with angular tannins. Vibrant, flavorful finish.

Exotically flavored, with excellent grip and style. Good for long-term cellaring.

1994 Merlot, Reserve, Washington $28.   **91**

Reddish garnet cast. Medium-bodied. Highly extracted. Heavily oaked. Quite tannic. Reminiscent of red fruits, herbs, minerals. An oak-accented nose leads a tightly wound, compact palate with some grainy tannins on the long, dry finish. Well stuffed, this should resolve further with time in the cellar.

1995 Merlot, Reserve, Washington $32.   **96**

Very deep blackish ruby hue. Moderately full-bodied. Balanced acidity. Moderately extracted. Moderately oaked. Mildly tannic. Black fruits, vanilla, minerals. This one is all about mouthfeel. Supple, velvety, and dense, yet perfectly balanced. Features a very precise core of complex fruit flavors buttressed by a firm but unobtrusive structure and well-integrated oak accents. Very attractive now and will improve with age.

1997 Merlot, Seven Hills, Walla Walla Valley $30.   **90**

Deep, opaque ruby red to the rim. Subdued, brooding spice and mineral aromas. A lush attack leads a moderately full-bodied palate with rich, velvety tannins, followed by a deep, rounded finish. Shows beautiful structure and extract, and should open quite well. Drink now or later. Can improve with more age.

Wilridge

1996 Cabernet Sauvignon, Klipsun Vineyards, Yakima Valley $38.   **84**

Saturated dark ruby hue. Richly fruity aromas show black cherry and cassis aromas with moderate oak accents. A rich entry leads a medium-bodied palate with fruit-forward flavors that fill the mouth. Tannins are supple and harmonious through the finish. Drink now or later.

1996 Melange, Yakima Valley $19.   **86**

Bright ruby-violet hue. Floral, violet scented aromas. A light entry leads to a medium-bodied palate with crisp fruit flavors and juicy fruit flavors. Very supple and juicy through the finish. Drink now.

1994 Merlot, Crawford Vineyard, Columbia Valley $19.   **87**

Opaque reddish purple. Moderately full-bodied. Moderately extracted. Moderately tannic. Reminiscent of red berries, dried herbs, minerals. Bright, lively red fruit entry with fine acidity, carrying though the midpalate into the finish. A very focused fruit-accented style with fine integrated tannins.

1994 Merlot, Klipsun Vineyards, Columbia Valley $19.   **85**

Opaque purple. Moderately full-bodied. Highly extracted. Moderately tannic. Reminiscent of cherry, tea, spice. Huge ripe berry aromas. Dense and concentrated berry fruit on the palate, with well-integrated soft tannins.

1996 Merlot, Klipsun Vineyards, Yakima Valley $32.   **82**

Woodward Canyon

1997 Chardonnay, Columbia Valley $30.   **87**

Deep yellow-straw cast. Moderately full-bodied. Balanced acidity. Highly extracted. Orange blossom, bread, minerals. Ripe and rounded, with subdued flavors and a weighty yet well-structured palate. The finish is firm and brightly acidic.

1997 Chardonnay, Reserve, Columbia Valley $35.   **89**

Brilliant yellow-gold. Rich buttery, fruity aromas are very stylish. A lush entry leads a moderately full-bodied palate with bright fruity flavors and a buttery mouthfeel. The finish is lengthy, with a touch of alcohol heat. Drink now.

1997 Riesling, Walla Walla County $9.   **86**

Bright pale golden hue. Aromas show a tropical, pithy character. Sweet and juicy on entry, with a medium bodied palate and an herbal note to the sweet flavors that linger on the finish. Features fine varietal character. Try with fresh fruit.

Scale: Superlative (96-100), Exceptional (90-95), Highly Recommended (85-89), Recommended (80-84), Not Recommended (Under 80)

254

1995 Cabernet Sauvignon, Artist Series, Canoe Ridge Vineyard, Washington $28.   **93**

Bright ruby red. Moderately light-bodied. Moderately extracted. Moderately tannic. Brown spice, minerals. Minerally, spicy aromas lead a firm mouthful of black fruit flavors heightened by bright acids. A degree of minerally intensity that showcases terroir.

1996 Cabernet Sauvignon, Artist Series, Canoe Ridge Vineyard, Columbia Valley $40.   **88**

Saturated dark ruby hue. Generously aromatic with ripe fruit and chocolate notes. Oak spice is very evident. A rich entry leads a moderately full-bodied palate with rich berry fruit flavors and supple, silky tannins. Very harmoniously balanced. Drink now.

1994 Cabernet Sauvignon, Captain Z.K. Straight, Columbia Valley $35.   **92**

Dark garnet red. Medium-bodied. Highly extracted. Moderately tannic. Plums, tobacco, cedar, earth, bitter chocolate. Solid, extracted black fruit flavors have many complex overtones. Assertive and full flavored, with a dry, well-defined finish showing some astringent tannins. Good structure.

1995 Cabernet Sauvignon, Old Vines, Columbia Valley $45.   **99**

Dark, opaque ruby cast. Moderately full-bodied. Moderately extracted. Quite tannic. Exotic spice, black fruits. Distinctively spicy aromas follow through on a concentrated palate showing precision and intensity. Very deep flavors are matched by supple but abundant tannins through the finish.

1994 Merlot, Columbia Valley $28.   **91**

Bright reddish purple. Moderately full-bodied. Moderately extracted. Moderately oaked. Moderately tannic. Reminiscent of raspberry, plum, tobacco. Rich, inviting aromatics lead a bright entry with a rich mouthfeel and chewy, supple tannins through the fine finish.

1995 Merlot, Columbia Valley $30.   **95**

Deep blackish ruby hue. Moderately full-bodied. Balanced acidity. Highly extracted. Mildly oaked. Moderately tannic. Chocolate, minerals, black fruits. Deeply flavored, with a brooding, complex core. Big and rich in texture, yet it maintains a sense of lightness. Well balanced and quite skillfully made, with a long finish. The velvety tannins will mellow with age.

1997 Merlot, Columbia Valley $30.   **90**

Medium ruby red with a fading rim. Very oak-accented aromas with bright fruity accents. A rich entry leads a moderately full-bodied palate with tightly wound fruit flavors and firm, dry tannins. Acids are bright.

Yakima River

1997 Lemberger, Sof Lem, Yakima Valley $9.   **85**

Pale ruby purple. Attractive spice and red fruit aromas carry a Rhone-like herbal overtone. A crisp entry leads a peppery, medium-bodied palate with a snappy, flavorful character. Soft through the finish. Drink now.

1994 Cabernet Sauvignon, Yakima Valley $15.   **87**

Cherry red with brick overtones and a pale rim. Medium-bodied. Moderately extracted. Mildly tannic. Tomato leaves, red fruits, dried herbs. Quite distinctive high-toned aromas lead a bright and juicy palate, but with solid astringency running through the finish. Leaning toward austerity, with clean acids keeping it lively.

1994 Cabernet Sauvignon, Winemakers Reserve, Yakima Valley $24.99.   **88**

Dark red with a subtle garnet cast. Medium-bodied. Highly extracted. Quite tannic. Black fruits, oak spice. Aromas show a degree of development, with very prominent oak spice. Bright black-fruit flavors are deluged under a wall of spice and tannins. Still hard edged, but well stuffed.

1997 Cabernet-Merlot, Yakima Valley $9.49.   81
1994 Merlot, Yakima Valley $15.   89

Deep ruby to the rim with a slight garnet cast. Moderately full-bodied. Balanced acidity. Highly extracted. Moderately oaked. Mildly tannic. Plums, minerals, licorice. Pleasantly aromatic, with a lush, mouthfilling character and good balance. Velvety tannins emerge at the finish.

1994 Merlot, Winemaker's Reserve, Yakima Valley $28.   90

Deep ruby with a garnet cast. Full-bodied. Full acidity. Highly extracted. Heavily oaked. Quite tannic. Cherry cordial, cinnamon, sweet herbs. Full throttled in every way, this is a firmly structured wine with big flavors to match. Fairly well balanced, with some drying tannins at the finish; it may dry out with age. In the meantime, it is a very interesting wine; attractive but not for everyday quaffing.

1995 Johns Vintage Port, Yakima Valley $16.   83

Deep ruby-garnet cast. Full-bodied. Full acidity. Highly extracted. Brown spices, black fruits, minerals. Carries a distinctive toasty oak note throughout. Quite flavorful, though full-throttled and somewhat fierce, with a marked hot quality. Drying through the finish, with very slight sweetness.

three

The Wines of Oregon

An Introduction: The Wines of Oregon

Oregon's wine industry is small and convivial. It is a cottage industry where the largest winery would be one of the Napa Valley's smaller operations on Highway 29. To put it into perspective there are single wineries in California that produce as much wine as all producers in the state of Oregon combined do. Unlike in France, however, Napoleon is not to blame for the way in which the industry has developed. There, in Burgundy, egalitarian succession laws introduced by the famous (or infamous depending on your particular cultural perspective) emperor led to the subdivision of the great wine estates among all heirs, not just the eldest male. Thus instead of a single Clos de Vougeot property of 124 acres, today there are no less than 77 proprietors of Clos de Vougeot, offering a bewildering array of labels.

Luckily, the situation in Oregon is actually the reverse. Pioneers such as David Lett of Eyrie, along with families like the Ponzis, Blossers, Eraths, and Adelsheims came along in the '60s and early '70s with idealistic dreams of cultivating fine wines in what was then very much a virgin territory. On a shoestring budget, their operations necessarily started small and have grown with widening public acclaim. The year 1979 ushered in a new age for the industry as Eyrie's 1975 Pinot Noir triumphed over several famous Burgundies in a Paris tasting sponsored by Gault-Millau. This so incensed the respected Burgundian negociant Robert Drouhin, that he restaged the tasting the following year in Beaune, with the same result.

Eighteen years later Mr. Drouhin's wine is at the head of the class, his Willamette Valley cuvée, Domaine Drouhin that is. The Drouhin's investment in what they believe to be Oregon's potential was followed by international vintners such as Laurent-Perrier and Brian Croser of Australia's Petaluma Winery. These investments have in turn opened several Californians' eyes to the possibilities, and suddenly Oregon is as dynamic and bustling with the exchange of ideas as any of the world's new viticultural regions. As the cross-pollination continues and new viticultural practices are translated to the vineyard, Oregon's wines will continue to improve. The embodiment of this is the International Pinot Noir Festival, held each summer in Oregon, where the world's producers get together to exchange ideas and information about the world's most fickle grape.

That grape is, indisputably, Oregon's signature varietal, and when people used to talk only of potential, they are now tasting the results. Oregon is unique in that, unlike any other potential Pinot Noir sites in the New World (but very much like Burgundy), it is possessed of a cool climate in which the warmer sites are sought out for viticulture. California and Australia, on the other hand, have warmer climates in which the coolest spots are sought out for the planting of Pinot Noir. In California, that coolness is usually provided by a blanket of fog from the Pacific Ocean, without which the production of Pinot Noir and many other grapes would be impossible. There is relative certainty in these areas that the fog will come, and in between the sun will shine, year in and year out. Very few of these vintages will ever be completely "washed out" by bad weather.

Oregon, however, is far more marginal, where it can be a genuine struggle to get the grapes ripe enough. Rain at harvest is a constant fear, and the vines themselves labor under a great deal of stress. In short, it is Pinot Noir heaven, and so enter the masochists. While Oregon will never be able to achieve great consistency in terms of the wine being very similar year in and year out, its highs such as those achieved in vintage years such as 1992 and 1994, for example, will be very high indeed. In off years, just as in Burgundy, it will be left to the individual producer to craft better wines than the vintage conditions might otherwise suggest. This can already be seen in the excellent wines produced by Oregon's top vintners in 1993 or 1995.

To the Pinot Noir fanatic this wide fluctuation in vintage is not all bad. To the contrary, each vintage is expressed quite differently, which in competent hands brings wines that are not better or worse but just different, and that difference can be half the fun. While the best 1993s are all silk and polish—a delight to drink now—the powerful 1994s are candidates for the cellar. Oregon most certainly does not display the sort of monotony in its vintages that some other regions have been accused of.

If it all sounds disarmingly like Burgundy, it is, and more than any other region in the United States, Oregon has the best chance of becoming America's "Golden Slope." As Robert Drouhin says when tasting Domaine Drouhin's wines, he wants to be able to say "if it is not Côte-de-Nuits, not Côte-de-Beaune, it must be Oregon." In somewhat cantankerous reference to the hundred or so producers of Pinot Noir in Oregon today, a certain producer sniffed that today only "20 or 30" were making truly serious wines. However, if Burgundy itself had only 20 or 30 producers to whom you could point to unknowingly on a shelf and say that the wine therein would be good, a number of wine writers would be put out of business.

Oregon at a Glance

Wines Reviewed:

235

Producers/Brands Represented:

61

Top 25 Oregon Pinot Noir Cuvées

Pinot Noir only ripens consistently (particularly in "off" vintages) in the most favorably situated Oregon vineyards. In such a climate, vineyard and cuvée designations on labels become very meaningful. Different vineyard locations—or microclimates—bring with them a range of factors such as slope, facing, or soil drainage that will result in fruit ripening at different times, or some vineyards being better able to cope with rain than others. Although buying Oregon Pinot Noir is not quite as fraught with peril as in Burgundy, it pays to know your cuvée designations. Below is a list of the top 25 Oregon Pinot Noir cuvées. These specific wines can usually be regarded as the best that Oregon will offer in Pinot Noir—year in and year out.

Adelsheim: *Elizabeth's Reserve*

Adelsheim: *Seven Springs Vineyard*

Bethel Heights: *Flat Block Reserve*

Beaux Frères: *Beaux Frères*

Chehelam: *Ridgecrest Vineyard*

Chehelam: *Rion Reserve*

Cristom: *Marjorie Vineyard*

Domaine Drouhin: *Laurene*

Domaine Serene: *Evanstead Reserve*

Elk Cove: *La Boheme*

Erath: *Weber Vineyard Reserve*

Evesham Wood: *Cuvée "J"*

Evesham Wood: *Temperence Hill Vineyard*

Oak Knoll: *Vintage Reserve*

Panther Creek: *Bednarik Vineyard*

Panther Creek: *Freedom Hill*

Ponzi: *Reserve*

St. Innocent: *Temperance Hill Vineyard*

St. Innocent: *Freedom Hill Vineyard*

St. Innocent: *O'Connor Vineyard*

Silvan Ridge: *Visconti Vineyard*

Silvan Ridge: *Eola Springs Vineyard*

Sokol Blosser: *Redland*

Willamette Valley Vineyards: *OVB*

Ken Wright Cellars: *Canary Hill*

Scale: Superlative (96-100), Exceptional (90-95), Highly Recommended (85-89), Recommended (80-84), Not Recommended (Under 80)

260

Reviews

Adelsheim

1995 Pinot Noir, Oregon $18.99.   **90**

Full crimson hue to a cherry-red rim. Medium-bodied. Moderately extracted. Moderately oaked. Moderately tannic. Jammy, earthy aromas. Smooth and harmonious, with great integration of flavors and depth on the palate. Very well balanced, with judicious tannins.

1994 Pinot Noir, Seven Springs Vineyard, Polk County $30.   **90**

Cherry red appearance. Medium-bodied. Moderately extracted. Moderately tannic. Reminiscent of berries, tar, dried herbs. Ripe berry fruit nose. Juicy berry fruit entry leads a firm finish with good tannins. A little dry on the finish, though this should resolve with further age.

Amity

1994 Pinot Noir, Willamette Valley $16.   **86**

Deep red color. Medium-bodied. Moderately extracted. Moderately oaked. Mildly tannic. Reminiscent of berries, raspberries, vanilla. Ripe, juicy style with vanilla oak flavors through the finish. Attractive and very drinkable.

1995 Pinot Noir, Oregon $12.   **82**

1995 Pinot Noir, Willamette Valley $16.   **82**

1995 Pinot Noir, Sunnyside Vineyard, Willamette Valley $18.   **86**

Pale pinkish red. Moderately light-bodied. Moderately extracted. Mildly oaked. Mildly tannic. Subtle floral aromas lead a crisp but lively palate of red fruits and minerals, with some richness on the midpalate and a subtle toasty finish.

1993 Pinot Noir, Winemakers Reserve, Willamette Valley $35.   **90**

Full dark red. Medium-bodied. Highly extracted. Moderately oaked. Moderately tannic. Rich black fruit with aromas of leather and earth. Full dry palate presence reveals tart black cherry flavors, with firm dry tannins throughout and a hint of toasty oak on a dry finish. Impressive structure. Needs some time.

Archery Summit

1996 Pinot Noir, Premier Cuvée, Oregon $35.   **81**

1996 Pinot Noir, Arcus Estate, Oregon $59.   **86**

Pale ruby cast. Medium-bodied. Full acidity. Moderately extracted. Moderately oaked. Mildly tannic. Sweet oak, minerals, red fruits. Forward aromas show generous sweet oak flavors. Light and lean in the mouth with racy acidity. Tasty and direct.

1996 Pinot Noir, Red Hills Estate, Oregon $59.   **84**

Pale dark ruby cast. Moderately full-bodied. Full acidity. Moderately extracted. Moderately oaked. Mildly tannic. Vanilla, minerals. Forward aromas carry a pleasant woody overtone. Light and lean in the mouth with a tight, minerally quality.

1996 Pinot Noir, Archery Summit Estate, Oregon $75.   **84**

Deep pale ruby cast. Moderately light-bodied. Full acidity. Subtly extracted. Mildly oaked. Moderately tannic. Minerals, brown spices. Aromatically reserved, showing a lean and minerally overtone. Light in the mouth with unyielding linear tannins in the finish.

Argyle

1994 Brut, Knudsen Vineyards, Willamette Valley $19.50.   **89**

Pale yellow-gold. Medium-bodied. Full acidity. Bread, citrus. Toasty, bready aromas have a firm citrus accent that follows well on the palate, with brisk, long citrus flavors that veer toward the lean side. The fine persistence is impressive.

Ashland

1995 Merlot, Rogue Valley $12.49.   **86**

Deep blackish ruby color. Medium-bodied. Full acidity. Moderately extracted. Mildly oaked. Mildly tannic. Red fruits, minerals. Flavorful and quite crisp in style, with acidity to the fore. Well balanced, with an angular, minerally finish.

Autumn Wind

1994 Pinot Noir, Reserve, Oregon $30.   **90**

Opaque dark red. Moderately full-bodied. Highly extracted. Moderately oaked. Moderately tannic. Reminiscent of black cherries, vanilla, licorice. Quite rich and chewy, with well-integrated, soft tannins through the finish. Generously proportioned style.

1996 Pinot Noir, Estate Reserve, Oregon $29.99.   **80**

Beaux Frères

1995 Pinot Noir, Yamhill County $50.   **90**

Dark crimson purple with an even fade. Moderately full-bodied. Highly extracted. Moderately oaked. Moderately tannic. A seductive monster. Very polished and rounded, with lots of supple tannins giving this great texture. Cherries, red plums, chocolate flavors up front. Approachable now, but best to cellar it for a few years.

1996 Pinot Noir, Yamhill County $54.   **82**

Benton Lane

1996 Pinot Noir, Oregon $15.   **86**

Bright cherry red. Medium-bodied. Moderately extracted. Mildly oaked. Mildly tannic. Earthy, brambly aromas lead a palate with black cherry flavors, and a peppery, spicy finish. Some dry tannins are evident, but are well balanced. Drinking nicely now.

1994 Pinot Noir, Reserve, Oregon $28.50.   **90**

Deep reddish purple. Moderately full-bodied. Highly extracted. Quite tannic. Reminiscent of brown spice, red fruits, minerals. A full and powerful style with a dense center of fruit and weighty tannins through the finish. Needs more time to resolve its big components and fine acidity.

1996 Pinot Noir, Reserve, Oregon $28.   **90**

Full ruby red with a light rim. Medium-bodied. Moderately extracted. Moderately oaked. Mildly tannic. Rounded, ripe cherry aromas lead a rich, glycerous mouthfeel that imparts a sense of smoothness through the finish. Herbal tea notes add complexity. Generous and balanced.

Bethel Heights

1996 Chardonnay, Reserve, Willamette Valley $17.   **81**

1994 Pinot Noir, Flat Block Reserve, Willamette Valley $24.   **89**

Deep reddish purple. Medium-bodied. Moderately extracted. Mildly tannic. Reminiscent of cherries, minerals, brown spice. Elegant nose, with a balanced and solidly structured palate through an oak-spice-accented finish.

1996 Pinot Noir, Flat Block Reserve, Willamette Valley $28.   **83**

Bright ruby purple. Medium-bodied. Full acidity. Moderately extracted. Mildly oaked. Mildly tannic. Vanilla, red fruits. Forward aromas carry a sweet oak accent. Lean and lively in the mouth, with subdued red fruit flavors. Crisp through the finish.

1995 Pinot Noir, Wadenswil Block Reserve, Willamette Valley $24.   **85**

Dark cherry red. Medium-bodied. Highly extracted. Moderately oaked. Moderately tannic. Roasted, medicinal nose. Distinctly austere, earthy notes lead a solid palate with black fruit hints and supple but dry tannins throughout. Austere style.

Scale: Superlative (96-100), Exceptional (90-95), Highly Recommended (85-89), Recommended (80-84), Not Recommended (Under 80)

Bridgeview

1997 Chardonnay, Oregon $5.99. **84**

Bright pale straw hue. Moderately light-bodied. Balanced acidity. Moderately extracted. Yellow apples. Simple fruity aromas lead a straightforward tart mouthful with a clean finish.

1997 Chardonnay, Blue Moon, Oregon $9.99. **80**

1997 Pinot Gris, Oregon $9.99. **86**

Dark straw color with a slight copper cast. Moderately full-bodied. Full acidity. Moderately extracted. Bananas, minerals. Quite aromatic, with a very ripe nose. Full and rich on the palate with lean acidity lending vibrancy to the rounded smoky finish.

1996 Merlot, Black Beauty, Paso Robles $17. **87**

Very deep purplish ruby hue with brilliant clarity. Medium-bodied. Balanced acidity. Moderately extracted. Heavily oaked. Mildly tannic. Chocolate, red fruits, sweet herbs. Quite aromatic, with complex flavors and a supple entry. Turns a little more angular and austere on the palate. Pleasant finish with good grip.

1995 Pinot Noir, Oregon $7.99. **84**

Cherry red with purple highlights. Medium-bodied. Moderately extracted. Mildly oaked. Mildly tannic. Reminiscent of ripe cherries, vanilla. Perfumed aromas. Bright cherry fruit and soft tannins make this forward and supple, though without great sophistication. Very quaffable.

1996 Pinot Noir, Oregon $10.99. **85**

Brilliant dark purple. Medium-bodied. Moderately extracted. Moderately tannic. Bright black fruit aromas lead a blackberry-flavored palate, with some dry tannins clamping down on the finish. Best with richer foods.

1997 Pinot Noir, Oregon $9.99. **81**

1995 Pinot Noir, Reserve, Oregon $15.99. **87**

Bright pinkish red. Medium-bodied. Moderately extracted. Moderately oaked. Moderately tannic. Vanilla and black cherry aromas lead maraschino cherry flavors on the palate, with attractive vanilla oak on the finish. Some astringent tannins dry the finish.

Broadley

1995 Pinot Noir, Reserve, Oregon $18. **88**

Bright reddish purple. Medium-bodied. Highly extracted. Moderately oaked. Moderately tannic. Full earthy aromas are quite powerful. Tightly wound red fruit flavors of cherry and raspberry up front. A strong mineral underlay keeps this dry and lean through the finish.

Callahan Ridge

1998 White Zinfandel, Umpqua Valley $7. **85**

Brilliant pale pink. Subdued mineral and candied berry aromas. A crisp entry leads a medium-bodied palate showing mild sweetness and a firm acidic cut. Tart, juicy finish. Drink now.

Chateau Benoit

1995 Chardonnay, Estate Reserve, Willamette Valley $18. **80**

1996 Chardonnay, Dijon Clone Reserve, Willamette Valley $35. **88**

Bright green-straw hue. Medium-bodied. Full acidity. Moderately extracted. Moderately oaked. Brown spice, citrus. Spicy, lemony aromas lead an angular yet concentrated palate with a lengthy finish. Quite structured and austere in nature.

1995 Pinot Noir, Estate, Willamette Valley $15. **80**

1994 Pinot Noir, Estate Reserve, Willamette Valley $25.   **92**

Opaque deep red. Moderately full-bodied. Highly extracted. Moderately oaked. Moderately tannic. Reminiscent of black cherries, minerals. Rich fruity entry with concentrated mineral notes follows through to a dry tannic finish. Very impressively proportioned, although a bit backward now for some palates. Has the stuffing to cellar.

1995 Pinot Noir, Estate Reserve, Willamette Valley $22.   **81**

1996 Sweet Marie, Willamette Valley $15/375 ml.   **84**

Brilliant bronze hue. Minerally aromas with a tropical fruit accent. A lush entry leads a very sweet, medium-bodied palate. Clean through the finish. Drink now.

Chehalem

1996 Pinot Gris, Reserve, Ridgecrest Vineyards, Willamette Valley $19.   **83**

Bright golden cast. Moderately full-bodied. Full acidity. Moderately extracted. Smoke, dried herbs. Quite aromatic, with full smoky flavors on the palate. Rich texture, though racy acidity balances the dry, flavorful finish.

1995 Pinot Noir, Three Vineyard, Willamette Valley $15.   **87**

Pale cherry red with a light rim. Moderately light-bodied. Moderately extracted. Moderately oaked. Mildly tannic. Lightly perfumed aromas of toasted oak and crisp red fruits. Elegant and lively mouthfeel. Slightly chocolatey flavors through the finish. Well balanced, drinking nicely now.

1996 Pinot Noir, Three Vineyard, Willamette Valley $18.   **85**

Bright pale ruby cast. Medium-bodied. Balanced acidity. Moderately extracted. Moderately oaked. Mildly tannic. Brown spices, red fruits. Forward aromas carry a hefty wood accent and a core of velvety berry flavors. Tasty, but lacks a bit for grip on the finish.

1995 Pinot Noir, Ridgecrest Vineyard, Willamette Valley $22.   **86**

Medium ruby red with a garnet cast . Medium-bodied. Moderately extracted. Moderately oaked. Mildly tannic. Full oak-accented aromas. An oaky palate with black cherry nuances and a crisp character. Some fruit persistence on the lingering toasty finish. Drinking nicely now.

1995 Pinot Noir, Rion Reserve, Willamette Valley $34.   **89**

Pale ruby red to a graduated light rim. Medium-bodied. Moderately extracted. Moderately oaked. Mildly tannic. Smoky cherry aromas lead a smooth, silky mouthfeel that reveals concentrated flavors and a rich texture. The tannins are mild but green tasting. This will be better with some bottle age.

1996 Pinot Noir, Rion Reserve, Ridgecrest Vineyard,
Willamette Valley $38.   **83**

Pale ruby-garnet cast. Moderately full-bodied. Low acidity. Moderately extracted. Moderately oaked. Mildly tannic. Brown spices, dried herbs, red fruits. Subdued aromas feature an herbal overtone and a generous oak accent. Lush and supple in the mouth, but low acidity makes for a flat finish.

Cooper Mountain

1997 Chardonnay, Willamette Valley $14.75.   **85**

Pale straw color. Medium-bodied. Full acidity. Moderately extracted. Apple, sweet lemon. Apple aromas lead a lively, juicy mouthful of flavors, with a clean finish that has some grip. Fresh, lively, and cleansing.

1996 Chardonnay, Reserve, Willamette Valley $19.75.   **88**

Bright gold-straw color. Moderately full-bodied. Full acidity. Highly extracted. Lemon, green apple, minerals. Attractive yeasty aromas. Bright acids bolster austere citrus flavors that grip the palate through the finish. Drinking well, with some mature notes.

Scale: Superlative (96-100), Exceptional (90-95), Highly Recommended (85-89), Recommended (80-84), Not Recommended (Under 80)

1997 Pinot Gris, Willamette Valley $14.75.   86

Bright straw hue. Medium-bodied. Full acidity. Moderately extracted. Minerals, flint.
Lean, crisp, and racy, with a sharp and tangy mouthfeel. Fleshes out with a bit of richness
through the finish. Will cut rich foods well.

1994 Pinot Noir, Estate, Willamette Valley $15.75.   87

Medium ruby color. Medium-bodied. Moderately extracted. Moderately tannic.
Reminiscent of tart cherries, minerals. Very firm acidity with some decent fruit extraction
gives this a firm palate presence. Although not hugely proportioned, it is well balanced,
and the acidity should allow it to improve further.

1995 Pinot Noir, Willamette Valley $13.   80

1994 Pinot Noir, Estate Reserve, Willamette Valley $29.75.   91

Dark red. Moderately full-bodied. Highly extracted. Moderately tannic. Reminiscent
of red fruits, brown spice, earth. A firm, structured style with a concentrated plummy,
fruity palate and impressive tannins through the finish. Tight, focused, and in need of
cellar age.

1995 Pinot Noir, Reserve, Willamette Valley $25.   88

Bright crimson purple. Medium-bodied. Moderately extracted. Moderately oaked. Mildly
tannic. Toasty black cherry aromas. Dried cherry flavors show some concentration. Quite
tight right now, this has some stuffing, although it is not particularly tannic.

Cristom

1996 Pinot Noir, Louise Vineyard, Willamette Valley $32.   88

Deep ruby-garnet cast. Moderately full-bodied. Balanced acidity. Moderately extracted.
Heavily oaked. Mildly tannic. Dried herbs, sandalwood, dill pickle. An aggressively herbal
nose leads a lush mouthfeel with a hefty oak accent. Supple though firm. Features a
lingering flavorful finish.

1994 Pinot Noir, Marjorie Vineyard, Willamette Valley $27.   92

Dark reddish purple. Moderately full-bodied. Highly extracted. Reminiscent of briar
fruits, minerals, earth. Chunky, concentrated fruit-accented style. Quite rich, with
a distinctive mineral note on the palate. Short- to medium-term cellaring should
benefit this.

1995 Pinot Noir, Marjorie Vineyard, Willamette Valley $27.   89

Bright crimson with a very subtle purple fade to the rim. Medium-bodied. Moderately
extracted. Mildly oaked. Moderately tannic. Herbal, earthy black fruit aromas play out
well on the palate, with dry, fine-grained tannins providing some grip through the finish.
Nice structure, suggesting it should develop well over the near term.

1996 Pinot Noir, Marjorie Vineyard, Willamette Valley $32.   90

Bright deep ruby hue. Moderately full-bodied. Balanced acidity. Moderately extracted.
Moderately oaked. Mildly tannic. Red fruits, minerals, vanilla. Ripe and lush, with an
aromatic interplay between fruit and wood flavors. Supple and generous in the mouth.
Lingering spicy finish.

1994 Pinot Noir, Mt. Jefferson Cuvée, Willamette Valley $17. 89

Ruby color. Medium-bodied. Moderately extracted. Mildly tannic. Reminiscent of
violets, black fruits, brown spices. A quite seductive, accessible style characterized by
good mouthfeel and nice concentrated black fruit on the palate. There is some mild
astringency on the finish. Drinking well now.

1995 Pinot Noir, Mt. Jefferson Cuvée, Willamette Valley $17. 85

Pale cherry red. Moderately light-bodied. Moderately extracted. Mildly oaked. Mildly
tannic. Faint earthy, meaty, barnyard aromas lead a delicate dry palate of dried red fruit
flavors through a finish with balanced fine-grained tannins. Quite a light style.

1996 Pinot Noir, Mt. Jefferson Cuvée, Willamette Valley $20. 82

1994 Pinot Noir, Reserv7e, Willamette Valley $27.   **92**

Bright red at the center with a purple-tinged rim. Moderately full-bodied. Highly extracted. Heavily oaked. Moderately tannic. Reminiscent of cranberry, leather, vanilla. Big leathery red fruit nose. Good center of red fruits well balanced by generous toasted oak flavors though the lengthy finish. Structured, generous, and drinking well now.

1995 Pinot Noir, Reserve, Willamette Valley $27.   **88**

Dark crimson, with an even fade on the rim. Medium-bodied. Moderately extracted. Moderately oaked. Mildly tannic. Green herbs and black cherry aromas lead a dark fruit entry with a bright character and lively acids. Some meaty notes linger through the finish, with fine-grained tannins. Well balanced, drinking nicely now.

1996 Pinot Noir, Reserve, Willamette Valley $30.   **84**

Pale ruby cast. Medium-bodied. Full acidity. Moderately extracted. Moderately oaked. Moderately tannic. Minerals, red fruits, spice. Aromatic yet lean, with a fragrant spicy quality and an angular mouthfeel. Finishes on the tough side.

Domaine Drouhin

1994 Pinot Noir, Oregon $30.   **89**

Bright reddish purple. Medium-bodied. Moderately extracted. Moderately oaked. Moderately tannic. Dry. Reminiscent of red fruits, minerals, cinnamon. Full, fruity aromatics lead a rich palate with rounded, mouthfilling flavors complemented by a minerally backbone through to a lengthy toasty finish. Approachable, though this has the structure to age.

1995 Pinot Noir, Oregon $28.   **88**

Deep ruby hue with a purple rim. Moderately full-bodied. Highly extracted. Moderately oaked. Moderately tannic. Reminiscent of red fruits, minerals, spice. A structured style with big balanced components, though it is rather closed and tight at present. Needs more time to come together.

1996 Pinot Noir, Oregon $33.   **86**

Pale ruby cast. Medium-bodied. Balanced acidity. Moderately extracted. Mildly oaked. Moderately tannic. Dried herbs, minerals, vanilla. Shows an attractive herbal edge throughout. Light in the mouth but balanced, with a lean finish that has grip.

1997 Pinot Noir, Oregon $33.   **81**

1994 Pinot Noir, Laurene, Willamette Valley $42.   **94**

Deep red with a bright purple rim. Moderately full-bodied. Highly extracted. Mildly oaked. Moderately tannic. Reminiscent of red fruits, vanilla, sweet herbs. A little closed aromatically but with dark, brooding aromas. Densely extracted flavors on the palate, with amazing focus and length. Extraordinary integration of flavors in this wine bodes well for its future.

1995 Pinot Noir, Laurene, Willamette Valley $45.   **91**

Dark crimson hue with an even fade. Medium-bodied. Moderately extracted. Moderately oaked. Moderately tannic. Undeveloped nose at present. Smooth, rich palate of soft red cherry flavors, with a toasty mocha note on a finish that shows good tannic grip.

1996 Pinot Noir, Laurene, Willamette Valley $48.   **89**

Bright ruby purple. Moderately full-bodied. Balanced acidity. Moderately extracted. Moderately oaked. Moderately tannic. Vanilla, red fruits. Attractive aromas are forward and clean, with ripe red fruits and a sweet oak accent. Shows some richness in the mouth and is finely balanced. Lean and angular through the flavorful finish.

Domaine Serene

1994 Pinot Noir, Reserve, Willamette Valley $20.   **90**

Bright reddish purple. Moderately full-bodied. Highly extracted. Moderately tannic. Reminiscent of ripe cherries, dried herbs, minerals. Bright, lively, lush fruit-accented style with a lengthy fruity finish complemented by soft tannins. Very elegant and long on the palate.

Scale: Superlative (96-100), Exceptional (90-95), Highly Recommended (85-89), Recommended (80-84), Not Recommended (Under 80)

1994 Pinot Noir, Evenstad Reserve, Willamette Valley $30.　　　**91**

Dense reddish purple. Moderately full-bodied. Highly extracted. Reminiscent of brown spice, red fruits, oak. A bright, lively, concentrated palate with lots of ripe red fruits. Quite structured but very accessible.

1995 Pinot Noir, Evenstad Reserve, Willamette Valley $33.　　　**93**

Pale crimson hue. Moderately light-bodied. Moderately extracted. Mildly oaked. Mildly tannic. Perfumed, floral aromas. Crisp and lively red fruit flavors have a juicy black cherry character, with a faintly sweet vanilla oak note lingering on the finish.

Duck Pond

1997 Chardonnay, Fries' Family Cellars, Columbia Valley $9.99.　　　**84**

Bright straw cast. Moderately full-bodied. Full acidity. Highly extracted. Apples, pears, yeast. Forward aromas carry a firmly defined fruit quality and a yeasty accent. Full and ripe in the mouth with spritzy acidity through the finish.

1997 Cabernet Sauvignon, Fries' Desert Wind Vineyard,
Columbia Valley $12.　　　**81**

1995 Pinot Noir, Willamette Valley $8.　　　**89**

Pale ruby hue with a light rim. Medium-bodied. Moderately extracted. Mildly oaked. Moderately tannic. Reminiscent of smoke, cranberries, ferrous minerals. Tart fruit palate with some astringent notes. Good acidity gives this some backbone through the minerally finish.

1996 Pinot Noir, Willamette Valley $8.　　　**80**

1994 Pinot Noir, Fries, Family Reserve, Willamette Valley $25.　　　**91**

Deep ruby color. Moderately full-bodied. Moderately extracted. Heavily oaked. Moderately tannic. Reminiscent of black fruits, raspberries, new oak. Big oaky presence on the palate giving flavors that are matched by dense and finely extracted fruit through the lengthy finish.

Elk Cove

1995 Pinot Noir, Yamhill County $17.　　　**80**

1994 Pinot Noir, Estate Reserve, Willamette Valley $25.　　　**89**

Pale ruby color. Medium-bodied. Moderately extracted. Mildly oaked. Moderately tannic. Reminiscent of oriental spice, cola, red cherries. Mouthfilling bright fruit with a touch of leanness through to a mildly astringent finish.

1994 Pinot Noir, La Boheme Vineyard, Willamette Valley $35.　　　**90**

Ruby red with a subtle haze. Moderately full-bodied. Highly extracted. Mildly oaked. Moderately tannic. Reminiscent of earth, oriental spices, red fruits. Big, with a racy mouthfilling character and excellent fruit definition carried by brisk acidity. A little young for current drinking but should do well in the cellar.

1996 Pinot Noir, Roosevelt, Oregon $40.　　　**86**

Bright dark ruby cast. Moderately full-bodied. Full acidity. Moderately extracted. Moderately oaked. Moderately tannic. Black fruits, minerals. Forward aromas feature a spicy overtone and a core of red fruit flavors. Lean and quite angular in the mouth, with a firm finish.

Eola Hills

1996 Chardonnay, Oregon $12.　　　**88**

Medium green-straw cast. Medium-bodied. Balanced acidity. Moderately extracted. Green apples, citrus fruits. Bright, crisp aromas lead a rounded, fruity mouthful with clean flavors persisting through the finish.

1996 Pinot Noir, Reserve, Oregon $20.　　　**84**

Pale ruby-garnet cast. Medium-bodied. Low acidity. Highly extracted. Mildly oaked. Moderately tannic. Minerals, wood, red fruits. Shows a slight green overtone in the nose. Firm and unyielding in the mouth, with an angular finish.

NV Late Harvest Sauvignon Blanc, Vin D'Or, Willamette Valley $15. **85**

Bronzed golden hue. Full-bodied. Full acidity. Highly extracted. Dried herbs, citrus. Sweet citrus aromas, with an amazingly sweet, viscous, and acidic palate. Impressive, but perhaps a bit much—only for the true sugar junkie.

Erath

1996 Chardonnay, Reserve, Willamette Valley $20. **80**

1997 Chardonnay, Reserve, Willamette Valley $20. **82**

1996 Chardonnay, Reserve, Niederberger Vineyard, Willamette Valley $50. **88**

Bright gold-straw color. Moderately full-bodied. Full acidity. Mildly oaked. Citrus, vanilla, brown spice. Rich, spicy aromas lead an impressively concentrated spicy mouthful of flavors, with a lingering, persistent finish. Has the structure to improve with a few more years of age.

1997 Chardonnay, Reserve, Niederberger Vineyard, Willamette Valley $50. **84**

Bright gold-straw color. Medium-bodied. Balanced acidity. Moderately extracted. Mildly oaked. Ripe apples, brown spice. Rounded and juicy, with clean, ripe Chardonnay fruit flavors accented by a hint of oak spice. Very forward and generous in character.

1997 Pinot Gris, Willamette Valley $12. **82**

1996 Pinot Noir, Willamette Valley $13. **82**

1993 Pinot Noir, Reserve, Willamette Valley $20. **89**

Medium ruby color with a garnet cast. Medium-bodied. Moderately extracted. Moderately oaked. Mildly tannic. Reminiscent of spice, ferrous minerals, mild raspberries. Rather dry, with pronounced wood flavors and lean, high-toned fruit through the finish. The sum of the parts is a subtle but acquired taste that works well with food.

1996 Pinot Noir, Reserve, Willamette Valley $27. **84**

Deep ruby red with a slight fade. Medium-bodied. Balanced acidity. Moderately extracted. Moderately oaked. Mildly tannic. Brown spices, minerals, red fruits. Forward aromas carry a big spicy overtone. Full in the mouth, though quite lean and structured. Flavorful through the finish.

1995 Pinot Noir, Vintage Select, Willamette Valley $19. **86**

Bright ruby red with a gradually lightening rim. Medium-bodied. Moderately extracted. Moderately oaked. Mildly tannic. Runs the gamut from smooth, harmonious pie cherry flavors with a mildly bitter edge, to chocolate and cinnamon flavors that linger through the finish.

1994 Pinot Noir, Weber Vineyard Reserve, Willamette Valley $25. **91**

Ruby color. Medium-bodied. Moderately extracted. Moderately oaked. Moderately tannic. Reminiscent of blackberries, earth, chocolate. Solid, rich black fruit palate with generous toasty flavors well integrated through to the lengthy finish. Drinking well now.

1997 Late Harvest White Riesling, Willamette Valley $9. **83**

Pale gold luster. Bright apple and mineral aromas. An off-dry attack leads a medium-bodied palate displaying smooth, pure fruity flavors. Acids are quite soft through the finish. Drink now.

1997 Late Harvest, Gewürztraminer, Willamette Valley $18/375 ml. **93**

Very deep copper-straw hue. Exotic aromas show an enticing, honeyed, bready quality. A rich entry leads a medium-bodied palate, with lots of sweetness and a lush, harmonious quality. Seems to have seen a good deal of botrytis. Very enticing. Drink now.

Evesham Wood
1994 Pinot Noir, Temperance Hill Vineyard, Willamette Valley $24.   **91**

Deep cherry red. Moderately full-bodied. Highly extracted. Reminiscent of blackberry, licorice, brown spice. Intense and deeply aromatic. A structured, big-shouldered style with impressive tannins through the finish. Nice oak notes are well balanced. Needs further cellar age.

Eyrie
1995 Pinot Noir, Willamette Valley $19.   **88**

Very pale garnet red. Moderately light-bodied. Moderately extracted. Moderately oaked. Moderately tannic. Perfumed, earthy, oriental spice box nose. A crisp, juicy palate shows soft red fruit flavors that are delicate though persistent through the finish. Lovely mouthfeel. Nice now.

1996 Pinot Noir, Willamette Valley $14.   **81**

Fiddlehead
1994 Pinot Noir, Willamette Valley $32.   **88**

Deep purplish red. Medium-bodied. Highly extracted. Moderately tannic. Reminiscent of raspberry, dried herbs. Bright youthful appearance. Concentrated berry fruit flavors on the palate give this a forward, fruit-driven character.

1995 Pinot Noir, Willamette Valley $32.   **88**

Medium cherry red. Medium-bodied. Moderately extracted. Moderately oaked. Mildly tannic. Sweet black fruit aromas reveal some jammy qualities on the palate. Cinnamon and chocolate flavors linger nicely on the finish.

Firesteed
1995 Pinot Noir, Oregon $9.99.   **87**

Pale cherry red with a light rim. Medium-bodied. Moderately extracted. Mildly tannic. Reminiscent of merde, dark fruits. Slightly Burgundian nose showing dark fruit. Rounded, elegant mouthfeel with a core of good red fruit through to a lengthy, fruity finish. Very accessible style.

1996 Pinot Noir, Oregon $9.99.   **81**

Flynn
1994 Pinot Noir, Estate, Willamette Valley $14.   **87**

Deep cherry red. Moderately full-bodied. Highly extracted. Moderately oaked. Moderately tannic. Reminiscent of cherries, black tea. A finely extracted, concentrated cherry fruit palate is well balanced by good astringent tannins through the finish. Impressive, but a little backward and tight at present.

Foris
1994 Cabernet Sauvignon, Klipsun Vineyard, Yakima Valley $19.   **88**

Opaque red-purple. Full-bodied. Highly extracted. Quite tannic. Black fruits. Dense, stuffed, and tightly wound at present. This has all the structural elements to age well, though is hard to appreciate now.

Girardet
1994 Pinot Noir, Barrel Select, Umpqua Valley $18.   **88**

Rich ruby appearance. Moderately full-bodied. Highly extracted. Moderately oaked. Moderately tannic. Reminiscent of briar fruits, vanilla. Pleasant aromas complement a clean, very concentrated berry palate with some mild astringency on the finish.

Henry Estate

1996 Chardonnay, Umpqua Valley $15. 89
Bright yellow-straw hue. Moderately full-bodied. Full acidity. Moderately oaked. Lime, vanilla, citrus. Spicy, oak-accented aromas lead a bright, racy mouthful, with concentrated flavors and impressive persistence through the finish.

1998 Gewürztraminer, Umpqua Valley $10. 84
Brilliant platinum hue. Subdued mineral and citrus aromas. A racy entry leads a medium-bodied palate, with aggressive acidity balancing ample richness. Clean, stylish finish. Drink now.

1998 Muller Thurgau, Umpqua Valley $8. 85
Bright straw hue. Ripe, spicy fruit cocktail aromas are quite generous. A sharp entry leads a light-bodied palate featuring tart acidity and a hint of sweetness. Intense and concentrated. Very clean, precise finish. Drink now.

1998 White Riesling, Umpqua Valley $8. 84
Very pale straw hue. Yellow apple aromas. A juicy entry leads a moderately light-bodied palate, with a good concentration of fruit flavors persisting through the finish. Drink now.

1997 Henry the IV, Umpqua Valley $20. 84
Brilliant purple-red hue. Lean earth, mineral, and black fruit aromas show a slight reductive note. A sharp attack leads to a moderately light-bodied palate with firm astringent tannins. Angular finish. A firm and austere style. Drink within five years.

1997 Merlot, Umpqua Valley $15. 82

1993 Pinot Noir, Barrel Select, Umpqua Valley $18. 87
Pale ruby hue. Medium-bodied. Moderately extracted. Mildly tannic. Rounded, balanced mouthfeel with some good glycerous notes. Though slightly lean in fruit flavors, it is a nice, relatively subtle style.

1994 Pinot Noir, Barrel Select, Umpqua Valley $24. 89
Dark cherry red with a purple cast. Medium-bodied. Moderately extracted. Moderately oaked. Moderately tannic. Vanilla oak and raspberry aromas are well expressed on the palate, with some intensity of fruit flavors and enough tannic grip to match.

1995 Pinot Noir, Barrel Select, Umpqua Valley $20. 86
Bright ruby purple. Moderately full-bodied. Balanced acidity. Moderately extracted. Moderately oaked. Mildly tannic. Carries a distinct hint of overripeness throughout. Ripe and flavorful in the mouth with a sense of richness. Sweet vanilla oak nuances play out in the finish.

1995 Pinot Noir, Umpqua Cuvée, Umpqua Valley $10. 85
Pale cherry red with purple highlights. Medium-bodied. Subtly extracted. Mildly oaked. Mildly tannic. Reminiscent of red berries, vanilla. A lighter style, with high-toned bright fruit and a balanced, mildly astringent finish. Highly quaffable.

1996 Pinot Noir, Umpqua Cuvée, Umpqua Valley $10. 80

1997 Pinot Noir, Umpqua Cuvée, Umpqua Valley $11. 81

Hinman

1998 Riesling, Willamette Valley $6.99. 81

1994 Pinot Noir, Oregon $10.99. 86
Bright reddish purple. Medium-bodied. Moderately extracted. Reminiscent of vanilla, cranberries, raspberries. Tart, lively palate with plenty of crisp fresh fruit and good astringency through the finish. Well integrated, with a seamless character.

1995 Pinot Noir, Oregon $11. 84
Bright reddish purple. Medium-bodied. Moderately extracted. Mildly oaked. Mildly tannic. Mild smoke and leather aromas. Simple but bright red cherry flavors have some fine-grained tannic grip through the finish.

Honeywood

NV Niagara, Oregon $7.50.   80

Grande Cranberry Wine, $7.50.   87

Brilliant pale red with a pinkish cast. Moderately full-bodied. Full acidity. Highly
extracted. Cranberries. Extremely fragrant, with a pure cranberry flavor throughout.
Full and intense on the palate, with sturdy acidity and a definite bitter note that balances
the sweetness. Fine.

Grande Peach Wine, $7.50.   88

Deep straw cast. Moderately full-bodied. Balanced acidity. Moderately extracted. Peaches.
Extremely aromatic, with a pungent nose that is pure peach essence. The flavors are well
translated onto the palate, and finish with some gentle sweetness. Pure and well crafted.

Red Currant Wine, Oregon $7.50.   88

Bright ruby-garnet cast. Moderately full-bodied. Full acidity. Highly extracted. Red fruits,
dried herbs, wood. Quite aromatic, with distinctive herbal overtones. The palate is full
throttled, with marked sweetness offset by a tart, juicy quality. Intense.

King Estate

1996 Chardonnay, Oregon $14.   81

1996 Chardonnay, Reserve, Oregon $18.   88

Medium yellow-gold. Smoky oak aromas. A vibrant attack leads a medium-bodied palate
with crisp, well-defined fruit flavors and rich oaky accents that persist through the finish.
Very well balanced, with good acid verve. This could improve over time. Drink now or
later.

1996 Pinot Gris, Oregon $13.   90

Bright yellow-straw cast. Moderately full-bodied. Full acidity. Moderately extracted.
Oranges, minerals, spice. Features a ripe nose, with a spicy accent to the fruit flavors.
Full and rich with vibrant acidity through the rounded, smoky finish.

1996 Pinot Gris, Reserve, Oregon $18.   82

1994 Cabernet Sauvignon, Oregon $30.   86

Bright ruby red hue. Generous sweet herb and red fruit aromas. A lean entry leads
to a medium-bodied palate with firm astringent tannins and a pronounced acidic cut.
Intense, structured finish. A clean and precise structure suggests a useful wine at the
table. Drink within five years.

1995 Pinot Noir, Oregon $18.   86

Pale ruby-garnet cast. Medium-bodied. Balanced acidity. Moderately extracted. Mildly
oaked. Mildly tannic. Vanilla, red fruits, minerals. Generous aromas feature a spicy oak
accent. Seamless and supple in the mouth, with a crisp finish.

1994 Zinfandel, Oregon $20.   87

Deep blackish ruby hue. Medium-bodied. Full acidity. Moderately extracted. Moderately
oaked. Mildly tannic. Brown spices, red fruits. Toasty oak aromas, with a core of vibrant
fruit flavors. Lighter on the palate, with sturdy acidity. Excellent grip and intensity, with
a balance that makes for easy drinking.

Kramer

1993 Pinot Noir, Estate, Willamette Valley $18.   84

Cherry red with a garnet cast. Moderately light-bodied. Subtly extracted. Mildly tannic.
Rather light in style with some dry wood notes through the finish. Certainly for current
drinking.

1992 Pinot Noir, Reserve, Willamette Valley $22.   85

Medium ruby red with a subtle garnet cast. Medium-bodied. Moderately extracted.
Reminiscent of red fruits, green tea, minerals. Has a solid center of crisp, mildly tart
fruit, with some astringent tannins through the finish.

La Garza

1996 Cabernet Sauvignon, Umpqua Valley $15.   84

Bright ruby purple. Medium-bodied. Full acidity. Moderately extracted. Mildly tannic. Cherries, minerals. Crisp and tart, with a lighter-styled palate and an unusual note to the flavors. Clipped, zesty finish.

1995 Cabernet Sauvignon, Reserve, Umpqua Valley $25.   82

Lange

1997 Chardonnay, Willamette Valley $16.   81

1996 Chardonnay, Reserve, Willamette Valley $20.   84

Pale straw hue. Medium-bodied. Full acidity. Moderately extracted. Citrus, minerals. Subtly oxidized aromas. Crisp, bright, austere citrus flavors emerge, though the mouthfeel is generous. Finishes on a lean, minerally note.

1994 Pinot Noir, Willamette Valley $18.   90

Deep red, nearly opaque appearance. Moderately full-bodied. Highly extracted. Moderately oaked. Moderately tannic. Reminiscent of bing cherries, licorice, minerals. Floral-scented nose. Generous and well-integrated flavors on the palate, with a creamy texture and a harmonious character. Very approachable now.

1996 Pinot Noir, Estate, Willamette Valley $40.   81

1994 Pinot Noir, Reserve, Willamette Valley $40.   93

Deep ruby color. Medium-bodied. Moderately extracted. Reminiscent of black fruits, earth, sweet herbs. Intriguing and complex earthy nose. Rich center of dark fruits with complex earthy flavors that are well integrated through the lengthy finish. Refined and graceful. Drinking nicely now but should be cellared for optimum pleasure.

1996 Pinot Noir, Reserve, Willamette Valley $20.   82

LaVelle

1996 Pinot Gris, Winter's Hill Vineyard, Oregon $13.   86

Deep yellow-straw cast. Moderately full-bodied. Full acidity. Moderately extracted. Tropical fruits, cream, minerals. Quite ripe and aromatic, with a sense of richness to the flavors. Vibrant acidity lends a cleansing note to the palate. Good grip and fine length on the finish.

1997 Riesling, Susan's Vineyard, Willamette Valley $8.   86

Medium gold luster. Classic Riesling aromas of petrol and tropical fruits. A lush entry leads a medium-bodied palate, with a fine glycerous mouthfeel and generous sweet fruit flavors. The finish has an oily note. A comparatively soft, medium-sweet style. Drink now.

Lorane Valley

1996 Pinot Noir, Oregon $10.   81

McKinlay

1995 Pinot Noir, Special Selection, Willamette Valley $32.50. 89

Dark crimson with an even fade to the rim. Medium-bodied. Moderately extracted. Moderately oaked. Mildly tannic. Herbaceous, with smooth red berry fruits. Good persistence of fruit flavors, with dried herbal notes lingering on the finish. Easy going and supple. Drinking well now.

Montinore

1996 Chardonnay, Winemaker's Reserve, Willamette Valley $17.99. 83

Bright straw cast. Medium-bodied. Full acidity. Moderately extracted. Minerals, citrus. Aromatically reserved, with a crisp and lively palate feel. Vibrant and zesty through the finish.

Scale: Superlative (96-100), Exceptional (90-95), Highly Recommended (85-89), Recommended (80-84), Not Recommended (Under 80)

1997 Pinot Gris, Willamette Valley $9.99. **86**

Platinum hue with a bright copper cast. Medium-bodied. Full acidity. Highly extracted. Blanched almonds, pears. Distinctive aromas lead an austere palate showing taut acids through a dry finish. Quite an assertive style that should partner with foods.

1995 Pinot Noir, Willamette Valley $10. **83**

Pale cherry red. Moderately light-bodied. Moderately extracted. Mildly oaked. Moderately tannic. Reminiscent of green herbs, tart cherries, earth. A lighter style, with some astringent tannins on the midpalate through the finish. Would suit those who like subtler, leaner styles.

1994 Pinot Noir, Winemaker's Reserve, Willamette Valley $14. **88**

Deep cherry red. Medium-bodied. Moderately extracted. Moderately oaked. Moderately tannic. Reminiscent of cherry fruit, earth, dried herbs. Quite solid on the palate, with ample acids, fruit, and tannins. Though a bit closed, it should resolve with some further age.

1995 Pinot Noir, Winemaker's Reserve, Willamette Valley $17.99. **87**

Bright pinkish red. Medium-bodied. Moderately extracted. Moderately oaked. Moderately tannic. Tart red cherry aromas have sage and thyme nuances. Focused, crisp cherry and raspberry flavors are supported by bright acids and mild but dry tannins, with subtle oak influences on the finish. Plenty of primary fruit flavors.

Mystic Mountain

1997 Chardonnay, Willamette Valley $16. **82**

Oak Knoll

1996 Chardonnay, Willamette Valley $14. **86**

Green-straw color. Medium-bodied. Balanced acidity. Moderately extracted. Lemon, apples. Zesty aromas lead a full-flavored palate with bright fruity flavors that finish with a note of sourness, making for an assertive style.

1996 Pinot Gris, Willamette Valley $13. **84**

Bright straw cast. Medium-bodied. Full acidity. Moderately extracted. Citrus zest, minerals. Bright, fresh, and racy in style with zesty acidity. Clean and crisp, if a tad unyielding in flavors. This does leave the palate refreshed.

1996 Pinot Gris, Vintage Reserve, Willamette Valley $17. **93**

Deep straw cast. Moderately full-bodied. Full acidity. Highly extracted. Flowers, oranges, minerals. Perfumed, pungent aromas reveal a wave of complex and exotic flavors. Extremely vibrant and zesty on the palate, with a lean, cleansing finish that is quite assertive.

1995 Pinot Noir, Willamette Valley $15. **87**

Pale cherry red with a light rim. Moderately light-bodied. Moderately extracted. Mildly tannic. Pungent leathery, earthy aromas. Lively, savory red cherry flavors have a meaty character that lingers through the finish. Well balanced, drinking nicely now.

1994 Pinot Noir, Silver Anniversary Reserve, Willamette Valley $20. **90**

Reddish purple. Medium-bodied. Moderately extracted. Moderately tannic. Reminiscent of red fruits, brown spice, vanilla. Bright concentrated fruit on the entry, with impressive full tannins through the finish. Quite angular and structured, it needs more time.

1994 Pinot Noir, Vintage Reserve, Willamette Valley $34. **91**

Dark black-cherry red. Medium-bodied. Highly extracted. Moderately oaked. Moderately tannic. Rich bramble fruit aromas lead a rich, flavorsome palate with a dry earthy backbone. Good tannic grip through the finish. Chewy and substantial, this has the structure to age well.

Frambrosia Raspberry Wine, Oregon $10/375 ml. **87**

Bright ruby-garnet cast. Medium-bodied. Full acidity. Moderately extracted. Raspberries. Pungent aromas of raspberries are translated well to the palate. Flavorful, though firmly structured, with vibrant acidity making for a lean finish with the slightest hint of sweetness.

Panther Creek

1994 Pinot Noir, Bednarik Vineyard, Willamette Valley $35.　　　**92**

Opaque blackish red with a full-colored rim. Full-bodied. Highly extracted. Heavily oaked. Quite tannic. Reminiscent of plums, black cherries, tar. Deep, brooding nose. Hugely thick, rich, and textured, with plenty of rich, heavy, well-integrated tannins. This has all the components in big proportions and should be cellared long term. Exotic.

1995 Pinot Noir, Bednarik Vineyard, Willamette Valley $27.99.　　　**88**

Full crimson hue to a graduated, lightening rim. Medium-bodied. Moderately extracted. Moderately oaked. Moderately tannic. Full, aromatic earth and black cherry nose. A solid dry palate shows plenty of toasty oak character and dry berry and pomegranate fruit flavors. Needs a little time to come together.

1995 Pinot Noir, Freedom Hill Vineyard, Willamette Valley $27.99.　　　**90**

Dark crimson purple. Moderately full-bodied. Highly extracted. Moderately oaked. Quite tannic. Earthy, bright red fruit aromas. Solid, tightly wound, austere, and dry through the tannic finish. Some generous red cherry flavors are lurking. Structurally impressive, this needs cellar time.

1995 Pinot Noir, Shea Vineyard, Willamette Valley $27.99.　　　**87**

Dark crimson with very subtle purple hints. Medium-bodied. Moderately extracted. Moderately oaked. Moderately tannic. Full, rich earthy nose. A solid dry palate with an austere black fruit accent, and earth and licorice through the finish. Sound structure, though this needs some time to soften.

1996 Pinot Noir, Winemaker's Cuvée, Oregon $33.　　　**83**

Bright ruby cast. Medium-bodied. Full acidity. Moderately extracted. Mildly oaked. Moderately tannic. Minerals, brown spices, red fruits. Aromatic and spicy, with a lean and intense mouthfeel. Angular and grippy, with a mildly astringent finish.

Ponzi

1994 Pinot Noir, Willamette Valley $18.　　　**89**

Deep cherry red fading to a purple rim. Moderately full-bodied. Highly extracted. Moderately tannic. Reminiscent of raspberry, vanilla, minerals. Highly extracted palate with a dense center of fruit, and impressive tight tannins through the finish. Needs more cellar time to resolve its big components.

1996 Pinot Noir, Willamette Valley $16.　　　**82**

1993 Pinot Noir, Reserve, Willamette Valley $26.99.　　　**92**

Deep ruby hue with slight fade to the rim. Medium-bodied. Moderately extracted. Mildly tannic. Reminiscent of minerals, red fruits, black tea. Quite aromatic and delicate in style, with a feminine grace. Well balanced and lengthy through the refined finish. This wine is attractive now and shows wonderful complexity.

1994 Pinot Noir, Reserve, Willamette Valley $35.　　　**92**

Nearly opaque reddish purple. Moderately full-bodied. Highly extracted. Moderately tannic. Reminiscent of red fruits, brown spices, minerals. Big, complex oak spice nose. A dense, firm style with well-integrated tannins and a tightly concentrated midpalate. Excellent lengthy finish. Needs more cellar time.

1995 Pinot Noir, 25th Anniversary Reserve, Willamette Valley $50.　　　**90**

Medium crimson hue to a pale garnet rim. Medium-bodied. Moderately extracted. Moderately oaked. Mildly tannic. A toasty nose leads caramelized cherry flavors, with mocha and spice notes through the finish. Quite angular, with bright acids. Well balanced and drinking nicely now.

Redhawk

1994 Pinot Noir, Vintage Select, Willamette Valley $15.　　　**84**

Ruby colored with a slight garnet cast. Medium-bodied. Moderately extracted. Mildly oaked. Moderately tannic. Reminiscent of earth, forest floor, tar. Earthy flavors with supple tannins on a lush, rounded palate.

Scale: Superlative (96-100), Exceptional (90-95), Highly Recommended (85-89), Recommended (80-84), Not Recommended (Under 80)

1994 Pinot Noir, Estate Reserve, Willamette Valley $25.   91

Deep red. Moderately full-bodied. Highly extracted. Moderately oaked. Moderately tannic. Reminiscent of black fruits, pepper, tar. Very aromatic black fruit with a hint of wood. Rich, ripe, chewy style with unusual but nice roasted meat flavors. Quite complex, with impressive extraction.

Rex Hill

1994 Pinot Noir, Willamette Valley $10.99.   87

Deep reddish purple. Moderately full-bodied. Highly extracted. Moderately oaked. Moderately tannic. Reminiscent of raspberries, vanilla, brown spice. Juicy fruit-accented style emphasizes generous layered red and black fruits through the toasty finish, with ample soft tannins. Very accessible now.

1996 Pinot Noir, Kings Ridge, Oregon $12.50.   81

1996 Pinot Noir, Limited Selection, Willamette Valley $18.   82

Siduri

1995 Pinot Noir, Oregon $30.   92

Deep ruby color. Moderately full-bodied. Moderately extracted. Moderately oaked. Mildly tannic. Reminiscent of vanilla, chocolate, black fruits. Rich textured style with well-integrated ripe tannins. Very supple but substantial through the finish. Generous oak flavors are well matched by impressive extraction.

1996 Pinot Noir, Oregon $34.   85

Cherry red with a pinkish purple cast. Medium-bodied. Moderately extracted. Moderately tannic. Soft and supple, with sweet cherry flavors and a lovely toasty accent throughout that gives this a very appealing mocha character. Very much defined by its toasty character. Drinking nicely now.

1997 Pinot Noir, Oregon $28.   82

Silvan Ridge

1995 Chardonnay, Oregon $13.   83

Brilliant yellow-gold. Oak-accented aromas show a bright fruity underlay. A vibrant attack leads a moderately full-bodied palate with crisp acids and short fruity flavors that finish with spicy, blanched almond notes. Showing early signs of age. Drink now.

1996 Chardonnay, Carolyn's Cuvée, Willamette Valley $22.   83

Full golden yellow. Very aromatic with a full oaky, nutty character. A rich entry leads a full-bodied palate with broad nutty flavors that finish quickly. This is showing mature character already. Drink now.

1996 Pinot Gris, Oregon $13.   84

Pale golden hue. Moderately full-bodied. Balanced acidity. Highly extracted. Minerals, earth, blanched almonds. Aromatically reserved, with a rich though lean palate feel. Features a mildly bitter note through the lengthy, nutty finish.

1996 Merlot, Rogue Valley $19.75.   81

1995 Merlot, Seven Hills Vineyard, Walla Walla Valley $28.   80

1994 Pinot Noir, Willamette Valley $19.   88

Dense, bright reddish purple. Moderately full-bodied. Highly extracted. Moderately tannic. Reminiscent of raspberries, cherries, vanilla. Ripe cherry fruit in the nose. Chewy, fruity style with plenty of integrated soft tannins on the palate through the finish. Could use short- to medium-term cellaring.

1995 Pinot Noir, Willamette Valley $19.   88

Bright purple-red. Medium-bodied. Moderately extracted. Moderately oaked. Moderately tannic. Toasty oak and bright fruity aromas lead an elegant, crisp red fruit and pomegranate palate with some intensity of flavors. Dry, oak-influenced finish. Needs a little time to come together.

1996 Pinot Noir, Eola Springs Vineyard, Willamette Valley $26.   **85**

Bright blackish ruby cast. Medium-bodied. Low acidity. Subtly extracted. Mildly tannic. Minerals, cherry cola. Aromatically reserved, with a very light palate feel. Crisp and zesty through the finish.

1995 Pinot Noir, Hoodview Vineyard, Willamette Valley $22.   **85**

Dark black-cherry red with purple highlights. Moderately full-bodied. Highly extracted. Moderately oaked. Moderately tannic. Floral, ripe aromas. Dry and vibrant, with tight red fruit flavors on the midpalate. Fine-grained tannins make the finish dry.

1994 Pinot Noir, Visconti Vineyard, Willamette Valley $26.   **88**

Bright cherry red. Medium-bodied. Moderately extracted. Moderately oaked. Moderately tannic. Reminiscent of black cherry, oak toast, brown spice. Bright cherry fruit nose. Bright fruit-accented entry with lively acidity and good toasty oak flavors through the finish. Approachable now but further time will allow the acids to settle.

1997 Gewürztraminer, Ice Wine, Bing Vineyard, Umpqua Valley $16/375 ml.   **89**

Deep yellow-gold. Exotic tropical fruit and sweet melon aromas jump from the glass. A lush entry leads a full-bodied, viscous palate with tons of sweetness. Rich, intense finish. Drink now.

1998 Early Muscat, Semi-Sparkling, Oregon $13.   **82**

Sineann

1996 Zinfandel, Old Vine, The Pines Vineyard, Columbia Valley $25.   **84**

Bright blackish purple. Medium-bodied. Full acidity. Moderately extracted. Moderately oaked. Mildly tannic. Green herbs, minerals, pepper. Quite aromatic, with an herbal complexity and toasty oak accents. Lighter styled and angular on the palate, with zesty acidity through an intense finish.

Sokol Blosser

1998 Muller-Thurgau, $14.95.   **85**

Brilliant green-straw hue, with a slight spritz. Ripe pear and fruit aromas. A crisp entry leads a light-bodied palate, with vibrant acidity and a hint of sweetness. Clean and well balanced. Drink now.

1994 Pinot Noir, Willamette Valley $17.   **89**

Bright cherry red. Medium-bodied. Moderately extracted. Mildly oaked. Mildly tannic. Reminiscent of red fruits, earth, mushrooms. Aromatically quite complex. Rich and balanced in the mouth. Well proportioned, with a fine lengthy finish. Very approachable now.

1995 Pinot Noir, Willamette Valley $15.   **87**

Medium cherry red with purple hints at the rim. Medium-bodied. Full acidity. Moderately extracted. Moderately oaked. Mildly tannic. Reminiscent of cranberries, cherries, vanilla. High-toned toasty cherry nose. Markedly high acidity on the palate give this wine presence and carries through the finish. Should be enough stuffing to cellar for a year and resolve the acidity.

1996 Pinot Noir, Willamette Valley $15.   **80**

1993 Pinot Noir, Redland, Willamette Valley $25.   **88**

Impressive deep cherry red. Medium-bodied. Moderately extracted. Moderately oaked. Moderately tannic. Reminiscent of brown spice, black fruits. Dry brown-spice scent in the nose. Well extracted and fairly weighty palate presence, although there are plenty of dry assertive flavors through the finish. This needs rich foods.

1994 Pinot Noir, Redland, Willamette Valley $35.   **92**

Deep, nearly opaque appearance. Medium-bodied. Highly extracted. Moderately oaked. Moderately tannic. Reminiscent of raspberries, cherries, spice cupboard. Hugely aromatic with spicy oak in the nose. Well extracted, lush, spicy palate with more finesse than power. Suitably high tannins and acidity for cellaring.

Scale: Superlative (96-100), Exceptional (90-95), Highly Recommended (85-89), Recommended (80-84), Not Recommended (Under 80)

1995 Pinot Noir, Redland, Yamhill County $35. **86**

Dark crimson hue with a purple cast. Medium-bodied. Highly extracted. Moderately oaked. Moderately tannic. Mildly leathery, bright plum aromas. A tart, minerally palate shows vibrant acids and intriguing austerity through the finish. Some tightly wound red fruit flavors might evolve with time.

St. Innocent

1995 Pinot Noir, Freedom Hill Vineyard, Willamette Valley $24.99. **91**

Dark crimson purple with an even fade to the rim. Medium-bodied. Highly extracted. Moderately oaked. Moderately tannic. Full complex aromas of earth, black cherries, plums. Outstanding long finish, with juicy black fruit flavors lingering through a solid earthy persistence. Quite dry, with fine-grained tannins in evidence. Nice now, but better in a few years.

1994 Pinot Noir, O'Connor Vineyard, Willamette Valley $32.50. **89**

Deep black cherry appearance. Moderately full-bodied. Highly extracted. Quite tannic. Reminiscent of bramble fruit, bacon, dry oak. Intense, chunky palate with impressive dry tannins through the finish. Quite complex and maybe too tough for some, but cellaring should resolve this.

1995 Pinot Noir, O'Connor Vineyard, Willamette Valley $19.99. **90**

Crimson with a purple-red fading rim. Medium-bodied. Moderately extracted. Moderately oaked. Moderately tannic. Floral violet hints. Bright brambly cherry flavors with full toasty brown spice accents through the finish. Still rather youthful and vigorous.

1996 Pinot Noir, O'Connor Vineyard, Willamette Valley $20. **85**

Pale dark ruby cast. Medium-bodied. Balanced acidity. Moderately extracted. Heavily oaked. Moderately tannic. Toasted coconut, minerals, sweet herbs. Quite aromatic, with a dominant sweet oak note. Light in style, yet quite firm, with an angular, minerally backbone.

1994 Pinot Noir, Seven Springs Vineyard, Willamette Valley $28.50. **90**

Deep reddish purple, nearly opaque. Moderately full-bodied. Highly extracted. Quite tannic. Reminiscent of brown spice, tar, roses. The Barolo of Willamette Valley Pinot Noirs. Dense and concentrated, with strapping tannins that clamp down on the finish. Difficult now but could well be worth the wait.

1994 Pinot Noir, Temperance Hill Vineyard, Willamette Valley $32.50. **92**

Deep, bright reddish purple. Medium-bodied. Moderately extracted. Moderately tannic. Reminiscent of blackberries, brown spice, leather. Brooding dark aromas. Very juicy black fruit with good clean astringent character through the very complex, lengthy finish. Much more forward than the O'Connor and Seven Springs bottlings.

Torii Mor

1995 Pinot Noir, Yamhill County $19. **88**

Pale cherry red. Medium-bodied. Moderately extracted. Reminiscent of tart raspberries, chocolate, toasted oak. Spicy fruit aromas lead a bright entrance with crisp, clean acidity carrying through the toasty finish.

1994 Pinot Noir, Reserve, Yamhill County $28. **93**

Deep reddish purple. Moderately full-bodied. Balanced acidity. Moderately extracted. Moderately oaked. Mildly tannic. Reminiscent of brown spice, black fruits, charred wood. Deep, finely extracted, and focused on the palate, with great acidity through a lengthy finish. Great finesse, elegance, and complexity.

Tualatin

1997 Riesling, Willamette Valley $8.50. **82**

1994 Pinot Noir, Estate Reserve, Willamette Valley $20. **90**

Bright red with purple highlights. Moderately full-bodied. Full acidity. Highly extracted. Mildly oaked. Moderately tannic. Reminiscent of sweet cherries, herbs, pine. Sweet fruit aromas. Ripe, juicy fruit on entry, with ample soft tannins well integrated with forceful

277

acidity carrying through to the finish. Should resolve with cellaring.

1995 Pinot Noir, Oregon $12.50.   85

Ruby appearance. Medium-bodied. Moderately extracted. Moderately oaked. Mildly tannic. Reminiscent of cherries, oak, toast. Pleasant fruity nose, with bright juicy fruit on the entry and soft tannins lingering through the finish.

1995 Pinot Noir, Founders' Reserve, Oregon $18.   89

Bright cherry red with purple highlights. Medium-bodied. Moderately extracted. Moderately oaked. Mildly tannic. Nice cherry-berry aromas with toasty oak notes. A substantial, textured mouthfeel reveals full bramble fruit and toasty oak flavors through the finish.

1996 Pinot Noir, Founders' Reserve, Oregon $28.   83

Pale ruby cast. Medium-bodied. Balanced acidity. Subtly extracted. Mildly oaked. Mildly tannic. Dried herbs, minerals, spice. Aromatically subdued, with a slight herbal bent. Light in the mouth, with a crisp, angular finish.

1994 Pinot Noir, OVB, Oregon $30.   89

Deep reddish purple. Medium-bodied. Highly extracted. Moderately oaked. Mildly tannic. Reminiscent of black cherries, chocolate. Ripe, brooding dark fruit aromas. Juicy fruit with integrated tannins and toasty oak flavors through the finish. Very approachable, but will probably cellar well for a few years.

1996 Pinot Noir, Whole Berry Fermented, Oregon $12.50.   80

1997 Pinot Noir, Whole Cluster Fermented, Oregon $14.99.   81

1994 Pinot Noir Port, Quinta Reserva, Oregon $18.   80

1997 Gewürztraminer, Late Harvest, Willamette Valley $12/375 ml.   82

1997 Semi-Sparkling Muscat, Willamette Valley $14.   80

Tyee

1993 Pinot Noir, Willamette Valley $13.50.   85

Cherry red appearance. Medium-bodied. Moderately extracted. Moderately tannic. Reminiscent of raspberries, vanilla. Crisp and juicy fruit on entry through to a brief finish. Very quaffable.

1996 Pinot Noir, Willamette Valley $17.95.   83

Pale ruby cast. Medium-bodied. Full acidity. Moderately extracted. Mildly oaked. Moderately tannic. Vanilla, red fruits, minerals. High-toned fruity aromas feature a sweet woody accent. Crisp and zesty in the mouth, with vibrant acidity making for a piercing finish.

Valley View

1994 Anna Maria Reserve, Rogue Valley $20.   86

Pale ruby-garnet cast. Medium-bodied. Full acidity. Moderately extracted. Moderately oaked. Mildly tannic. Spice, minerals. Features a hefty overlay of oak seasoning. Crisp, lean, and zesty in the mouth. Acidity provides an angular, juicy finish.

1995 Anna Maria Reserve, Rogue Valley $20.   81

1995 Merlot, Anna Maria, Rogue Valley $25.   83

Bright ruby red with a slight fade. Generous spice and cedar aromas show a dominant wood accent. A crisp attack leads a light-bodied palate with lean tannins. The finish is racy, with oak notes. A tasty quaffer. Drink now.

Van Duzer

1994 Pinot Noir, Eola Selection, Oregon $12.50.   87

Deep cherry red. Medium-bodied. Moderately extracted. Moderately oaked. Moderately tannic. Reminiscent of raspberries, vanilla. Big raspberry-vanilla nose leads a ripe, chewy palate with attractive toasted oak flavors through the finish. Very accessible style.

1997 Pinot Noir, Oregon $18.   82

Scale: Superlative (96-100), Exceptional (90-95), Highly Recommended (85-89), Recommended (80-84), Not Recommended (Under 80)

Willamette Valley Vineyards

1997 Chardonnay, Oregon $12.75.   **86**

Pale straw hue. Elegant vanilla and lemon aromas show a judicious oak influence. A lean entry is followed by a medium-bodied palate with crisp acidity. Delicate and well balanced through the finish. Drink now.

1996 Chardonnay, Founders' Reserve, Oregon $14.99.   **88**

Deep straw hue. Opulent cream, butter, and toast aromas carry a generous oak accent. A lush entry leads a moderately full-bodied palate with firm acidity. Full and flavorful, with admirable balance between wood and fruit. Drink now.

1996 Chardonnay, Estate, Dijon Clone, Oregon $21.99.   **90**

Yellow-straw color. Medium-bodied. Balanced acidity. Moderately extracted. Vanilla, pine, apples. Bright and juicy, with a rounded mouthfeel and fruit-centered flavors showing a subtle hint of oak seasoning. Complex and distinctive, with yeasty flavors lingering.

Witness Tree

1995 Pinot Noir, Willamette Valley $17.   **88**

Bright cherry red. Medium-bodied. Moderately extracted. Moderately oaked. Mildly tannic. Roasted walnut aromas. Smooth vanilla oak flavors with cherry pie accents through the finish. Lovely textured mouthfeel. Nice intensity and persistence.

Ken Wright Cellars

1995 Pinot Noir, Willamette Valley $18.49.   **83**

Medium crimson red with a pinkish cast. Moderately light-bodied. Moderately extracted. Moderately oaked. Mildly tannic. Straightforward dry cherry flavors with raspberry accents. Vanilla oak hints come through on the finish.

1995 Pinot Noir, Canary Hill Vineyard, Willamette Valley $24.99.   **90**

Bright cherry pink. Medium-bodied. Moderately extracted. Moderately oaked. Mildly tannic. Plenty of vanilla oak character complements sweet cherry flavors on the midpalate. Drinking nicely now, though tightly wound, with a lighter frame.

1995 Pinot Noir, Carter Vineyard, Willamette Valley $24.99.   **88**

Bright crimson pink. Medium-bodied. Moderately extracted. Mildly oaked. Mildly tannic. Straightforward bright cherry flavors expand on the palate and linger through a supple finish. This shows some youthful vigor.

four

The Wines
of New York State

An Introduction: The Wines of New York State

New York State has actually been an important center of wine production since the earlier days of the Republic. People might be surprised to hear that it always ranks near the top of the states (though still well behind California) in volume production. Much of that production comes from the western part of the state near Buffalo, on the eastern shore of Lake Erie in particular. Most of these wines are destined to become inexpensive "ports" or sparkling wines, the latter a New York State specialty with national recognition since the mid-19th century. As for premium table wines, however, production is far more limited and centered largely on the Finger Lakes or Long Island—two very different and distinctive wine regions that should not be lumped together.

The Finger Lakes

The Finger Lakes is the longer established of the two, and is centered on a series of thin, deep, long lakes in the west-central part of the state. The moderating influence of these waters and the warmth provided by east-facing hills allows the fragile grapevines to survive the region's harsh winters and to ripen grapes in the summer. As it is a cool grape-growing region, it is only fitting that it should specialize in white wines. Riesling in particular is where the Finger Lakes are beginning to establish a very solid reputation, but high quality, sophisticated sparkling wines are also appearing with more regularity.

Just as in Germany, where Riesling reaches its apex, the grapes struggle to ripen in the cool Finger Lakes climate and the hillsides and rivers make viticulture possible. It should not come as a surprise that German winemakers have been drawn here and winery names such as Wiemer or Frank attest to the fact. As the fortunes of Riesling have waned in the Chardonnay-besotten United States, it is abroad that many of these wines are leaving a mark. I was recently at a dinner with a large Belgian wine buyer in the French countryside when he amazed me by asking not about the latest glamour winery in Napa, but rather what my opinion was of Finger Lakes Riesling. He then proceeded to list all the best producers from the top of his head and retreated to his hotel room to procure a sample bottle he had been toting all around the Mosel the previous weekend (to bemused admiration, apparently).

U.S. consumers will eventually catch on to Riesling, and when they do the Finger Lakes will be shown to be the nation's finest Riesling appellation. At present, the wines are a steal, with some great bottles going for $10 and sometimes less. As with fine Riesling anywhere, these wines also age well, and I have been delighted by five- to ten-year-old examples that have developed that inimitable "petrolly" note that is the hallmark of a fine Riesling with some age. Though availability is somewhat limited, the best retailers around the country will carry some of the best examples. As a "house" wine, Finger Lakes Rieslings are astonishing values, particularly at a half or a third the price of many innocuous Chardonnays.

Long Island

As for Long Island, the peninsula that extends over a hundred miles from New York City east, into the Atlantic, the atmosphere and style of the wines couldn't

Scale: Superlative (96-100), Exceptional (90-95), Highly Recommended (85-89), Recommended (80-84), Not Recommended (Under 80)

282

be different. Centered near the end of the peninsula on the North Fork, about two hours from Times Square (traffic permitting), the twenty odd Long Island wineries bask in the relative warmth of the Atlantic Ocean and the Gulf Stream. This moderate climate makes it possible to ripen reds, and it is with red varietals that most of the wineries are expending much of their efforts.

Though warmer than the Finger Lakes, it is still fairly cool, and the resultant wines are not nearly as alcoholic or thick as their California cousins can be. Bordeaux lies just on the other shore and the geographic similarities between the regions have not gone unnoticed. Unlike Bordeaux, however, Long Island has a very young industry, having really only been founded in the '70s. As with any new wine industry, there is a learning curve where vintners must adapt to the peculiarities of the local climate and settle on styles and varietals.

The understandable desire to make "world class wines" in a hurry meant that a number of examples were over-made. Some wine makers confused full extract and hard tannins combined with inky colors and the concept of ageability as equating with greatness. However, much as the approach has lightened up in California, so it has also in Long Island. The pendulum is swinging back and most of the better Long Island wineries are finally beginning to hone in on a style that is more appropriate to the climate: balance and elegance, with moderate alcohol and sound acidity. Exciting examples of Merlot and Cabernet are to be found, with even the odd successful Pinot Noir. Chardonnay leads the way with whites, just as in every other corner of the world. Long Island's versions tend to be somewhat lighter in style, due to the climate, but oak is certainly in vogue. Long Island is certainly a region on the rise.

New York at a Glance

Wines Reviewed:

169

Producers/Brands Represented:

33

Reviews

Bauer

1998 Vidal Blanc, Niagara County $8.99.　　　　　　　　80

Bedell

1995 Chardonnay, North Fork of Long Island $11.99.　　　85

Deep, saturated straw hue. Generous mineral and cream aromas show a mature nutty accent. Supple and moderately full-bodied, with shy acidity. Lush finish. Drink now.

1995 Chardonnay, Reserve, North Fork of Long Island $14.99.　　　86

Deep yellow-straw hue. Complex, autolyzed, yeasty, smoky aromas. A firm attack leads a moderately full-bodied palate, with crisp acids. Firm and concentrated, with a phenolic edge to the finish. Drink now or later.

NV Main Road Red, New York $9.99.　　　　　　　　84

Deep, saturated purple-red hue. Generous red fruit, spice, and mineral aromas. A supple entry leads a moderately full-bodied palate. A soft, flavorful quaffer. Drink now.

1995 Cabernet Sauvignon, North Fork of Long Island $21.50.　　　85

Dark, saturated ruby purple. Brooding black fruit, licorice, and lacquer aromas. A firm entry leads a full-bodied palate, with a wave of grainy tannins. Big and rich, but very tight and tannic. Perhaps time will help, perhaps not. Mid-term cellar candidate (3–6 years).

1994 Cupola, North Fork of Long Island $25.　　　　　　88

Deep, saturated ruby red. Generous red fruit and mineral aromas. A firm attack leads a moderately full-bodied palate, with drying tannins. Reserved and balanced, with a hint of Bordeaux about it. Drink now.

1995 Cupola, North Fork of Long Island $27.50.　　　　　89

Dark, opaque ruby purple. Brooding mineral, black fruit, and smoke aromas carry a mild oak influence. A supple entry leads a full-bodied palate showing velvety tannins. Rich and flavor packed, but not tough. Drink now or later.

1995 Merlot, North Fork of Long Island $17.99.　　　　　86

Deep ruby purple to the rim. Generous black fruit and vanilla aromas show a marked wood accent. A firm entry leads a moderately full-bodied palate that has robust tannins. Full and rich, with an oaky finish. Drink now or later.

1995 Merlot, Reserve, North Fork of Long Island $27.50.　　　88

Opaque, saturated ruby purple. Powerful dark chocolate and black fruit aromas. A firm entry leads a brooding, full-bodied palate, with big, robust tannins. Thick and full-throttled. Needs time, but will probably always be aggressive. Mid-term cellar candidate (3–6 years).

NV Eis, New York $27.50/375 ml.　　　　　　　　90

Deep, brilliant amber hue. Powerful butterscotch, pineapple, and tropical fruit aromas. A firm entry lead a sharp, full-bodied palate that has tons of acidity. Thick and rich, yet showing a firm acidic cut that keeps the wine from cloying. A big Eiswein. Drink now or later.

NV Raspberry Wine, New York $9.99.　　　　　　　91

Saturated dark ruby red. Powerful, generous chocolate and raspberry aromas. A firm entry leads a fairly sweet, full-bodied palate. Rich and intense, with tons of flavor and fine length.

Bidwell

1996 Chardonnay, North Fork of Long Island $14.99.　　　84

Bright, saturated yellow-straw hue. Lean mineral and citrus aromas carry a toasty accent. A firm entry leads a moderately full-bodied palate showing crisp acidity. Vibrant and elegant. Drink now.

1996 Semi-Sweet Riesling, North Fork of Long Island $9.99.   **81**

1995 Cabernet Sauvignon, North Fork of Long Island $27.71.   **84**

Ruby-garnet hue with a slight fade. Cassis and chocolate aromas show an overripe note. A firm entry leads a moderately full-bodied palate, with drying tannins. Has convincing flavors on a lean frame. Drink now or later.

1995 Claret, North Fork of Long Island $34.99.   **85**

Ruby red with a slight fade. Shows cordial-like, overripe black fruit aromas. A firm entry leads a medium-bodied palate, with drying tannins. Very ripe, yet structured. Drink now or later.

1994 Merlot, North Fork of Long Island $19.99.   **80**

Casa Larga

1995 Cabernet Sauvignon, Finger Lakes $13.99.   **89**

Saturated red-purple. Moderately full-bodied. Highly extracted. Quite tannic. Ripe cherries, minerals, brown spice. Hints of overripe black fruits lead a firm palate of black fruit flavors with strong oak influences apparent. Hard-edged tannins clamp down on the finish.

1994 Pinot Noir, Finger Lakes $15.   **83**

Dark red. Medium-bodied. Moderately extracted. Mildly tannic. Austere herbaceous aromas with smoky tea accents. Dark fruit flavors are quite rich up front, with some dry tannin coming through on the finish.

Cayuga Ridge

NV Riesling, Cayuga Lake $9.50.   **83**

Very pale straw hue. Crisp aromas of tart peach and apple. A lively attack leads a medium-bodied palate, with juicy, tart peach flavors and a dry, minerally finish. Drink now.

Chateau Lafayette Reneau

1997 Chardonnay, Proprietor's Reserve, Finger Lakes $20.   **82**

1997 Johannisberg Riesling, Finger Lakes $9.99.   **81**

1997 Dry Riesling, Finger Lakes $9.99.   **84**

Very pale straw hue. Aromatically muted. A simple attack leads a moderately light-bodied palate, with attractive tart peach and herb flavors that linger on a fairly lengthy finish. Drink now.

1998 Pinot Noir Blanc, Finger Lakes $6.99.   **85**

Pale cherry-garnet hue with a slight spritz. Forward, pleasant berry aromas. A zesty entry leads a flavorful, medium-bodied palate. Crisp acids balance mild sweetness. Lengthy, clean, refreshing finish. Drink now.

1995 Cabernet Sauvignon, Finger Lakes $18.   **83**

Bright cherry red. Moderately light-bodied. Subtly extracted. Mildly tannic. Vanilla, red fruits. A lighter style, with bright acids and a quick finish. Shows very little typical Cabernet character, though tart acids and restrained balance make for a drinkable style.

1995 Cabernet Sauvignon, Owner's Reserve, Finger Lakes $20.   **86**

Bright cherry red with a pink rim. Medium-bodied. Highly extracted. Heavily oaked. Moderately tannic. Vanilla, cedar, red fruits. Aromas point to heavy use of oak, which is confirmed on the palate. Bright acids and astringency come through on the finish.

Duck Walk

1994 Merlot, Reserve, North Fork of Long Island $14.95.   **80**

1995 Merlot, Reserve, North Fork of Long Island $14.95.   **80**

1996 Blueberry Port, $12.95/375 ml.   **87**

Bright blackish purple. Moderately full-bodied. Balanced acidity. Moderately extracted. Mildly tannic. Black fruits, minerals, licorice. Pleasantly aromatic and fruit centered, with concentrated flavors on the palate, and a sense of lightness and balance throughout. Intense and clean, with an uplifting, angular finish.

Earle Estates

Blueberry Wine, $13.99.   **86**

Bright ruby purple. Medium-bodied. Full acidity. Moderately extracted. Blueberries, chocolate. Extremely aromatic, with a pure, fruit-accented quality. Exotically flavorful in the mouth, with vibrant acidity that lends a sense of balance to the sweetness in the finish.

Peach Perfection, $13.99.   **86**

Bright straw cast. Medium-bodied. Full acidity. Highly extracted. Peaches. Quite aromatic, with a forward, peachy quality. Sweet and round on the palate, with well-defined flavors. Spritzy acidity maintains a sense of balance and keeps the finish refreshing.

1996 Traditional Honey Mead, $13.99.   **80**

Chateau Frank

NV Celebre Cremant, Finger Lakes $10.   **83**

Bright green-straw cast. Moderately light-bodied. Full acidity. Citrus, tropical fruits. Forward fruity aromas lead a crisp and vibrant mouthfeel. Finishes with a touch of sweetness that will appeal to those who do not favor drier styles.

1991 Brut, Finger Lakes $15.   **88**

Medium straw color. Medium-bodied. Tropical fruits, citrus, smoke. Soft bready aromas. Elegant flavors have an impressively fruity center, with yeast complexity emerging on the finish.

1993 Blanc de Noirs, Finger Lakes $17.95.   **83**

Pale straw cast. Medium-bodied. Full acidity. Minerals, citrus peel. Aromatically reserved, with a lean and angular mouthfeel and plenty of citrus zest flavors through the crisp, vibrant finish.

Dr. Konstantin Frank

1997 Chardonnay, New York $10.95.   **82**

1998 Gewürztraminer, Limited Release, Finger Lakes $12.95.   **81**

NV Johannisberg Riesling, Salmon Run, New York $8.95.   **88**

Medium yellow-straw hue. Tropical fruit, ripe peach aromas. A flavorful attack leads a medium-bodied palate, with generous fruity flavors and a glycerous midpalate. Finishes smoothly with good persistence. Drink now.

1997 Semi-Dry Johannisberg Riesling, New York $9.95.   **84**

Medium yellow-straw hue. Pleasant aromas of minerals, apples, and herbs. A juicy, sweet entry leads a medium-bodied palate, with straightforward flavors and a hint of sour apple on the finish. An off-dry style. Drink now.

1997 Johannisberg Riesling, Dry, New York $9.95.   **82**

NV Cabernet, New York $14.95.   **83**

Bright violet-red. Medium-bodied. Moderately extracted. Mildly tannic. Violets, red berries, minerals. Floral, bright aromas lead a high-toned, fruity palate, with nice texture and a crisp, mineral-accented finish. Well balanced, drinking nicely now.

1995 Cabernet Sauvignon, Finger Lakes $22.   **86**

Full red-purple. Medium-bodied. Moderately extracted. Mildly tannic. Vanilla, minerals, red fruits. Primary fruit aromas indicate a fresh, youthful character that comes through on the palate. Finishes on the lean side; this is not built to age.

Scale: Superlative (96-100), Exceptional (90-95), Highly Recommended (85-89), Recommended (80-84), Not Recommended (Under 80)

286

1996 Cabernet Sauvignon, Old Vines, New York $22.　　　　**84**

Pale cherry red. Moderately light-bodied. Subtly extracted. Moderately oaked. Mildly tannic. Vanilla, red cherries. Candied fruit, floral aromas lead a lively vanilla-edged palate with a juicy finish. Crisp, lighter style.

1995 Pinot Noir, Finger Lakes $18.95.　　　　**86**

Medium cherry red. Medium-bodied. Moderately extracted. Mildly tannic. Faintly jammy red fruit aromas lead a crisp palate, with straightforward vague red fruit flavors through a mildly astringent finish. Nice weight and mouthfeel are a plus.

1996 Pinot Noir, Finger Lakes $18.95.　　　　**81**

1995 Johannisberg Riesling, Ice Wine, New York $29.95/375 ml.　　　　**90**

Brilliant amber hue. Generous caramel and spice aromas. A lush entry leads a viscous, full-bodied palate showing lean acids and lots of sweetness. Intense and stylish with great depth of flavor. Harmonious and pure. Drink now.

Glenora

1993 Blanc de Blancs, New York $12.99.　　　　**85**

Pale green-straw cast. Medium-bodied. Minerals, chalk, citrus zest. Reserved and elegant, with understated citrusy flavors. Balanced and lean, showing a judicious level of carbonation, a sense of roundness, and mild, sweet fruity notes on the finish.

NV Brut, New York $12.99.　　　　**86**

Pale gold. Moderately full-bodied. Ripe citrus, minerals. Full smoky, citrusy aromas lead a generously proportioned palate, with the accent on crisp fruit flavors. A substantial and rounded style.

1996 Chardonnay, Finger Lakes $13.99.　　　　**87**

Bright pale gold. Vibrant citrus aromas. Brightly acidic on the attack, with a medium-bodied palate and tart lemon flavors following cleanly through the finish. Impressively concentrated. A zesty, refreshing style that will work well with seafood. Drink now.

1996 Pinot Blanc, Finger Lakes $11.99.　　　　**80**

1998 Riesling, Finger Lakes $7.99.　　　　**83**

Pale straw hue. Mild aromas of minerals and stone fruits. A muted attack leads a moderately light-bodied palate showing straightforward fruit flavors that finish quickly. An off-dry style. Drink now.

1998 Dry Riesling, Finger Lakes $7.99.　　　　**84**

Pale straw hue. Perfumed aromas of yellow apples and herbs. A soft entry leads a medium-bodied palate, with crisp flavors and juicy acids on the finish. Drink now.

1995 Pinot Noir, North Fork of Long Island $11.99.　　　　**87**

Pinkish pale cherry red. Medium-bodied. Moderately extracted. Mildly tannic. Sweet raspberry aromas follow through on the palate, with lively acids to balance. Tannins are supple and balanced. An easy-drinking style.

1995 Cabernet Sauvignon, North Fork of Long Island $9.99.　　　　**83**

Deep cherry red with an even rim. Medium-bodied. Moderately extracted. Moderately oaked. Mildly tannic. Herbs, earth. Aromatically restrained, with an impression of austerity. Dry and earthy on the palate, with a minerally leanness that provides good grip on the finish, though faint bitterness persists.

1995 Cabernet Sauvignon, 20th Anniversary,
North Fork of Long Island $16.95.　　　　**83**

Bright cherry red with an even color to the rim. Medium-bodied. Moderately extracted. Moderately oaked. Moderately tannic. Minerals, black fruits. Austere aromas lead a juicy, bright palate, with black fruit flavors that turn very dry and lean through the finish. An angular style.

Goose Watch

1997 Merlot, Finger Lakes $16.50.   86

Bright violet red with a luminous cast. Bright, sweet, juicy aromas show violets and raspberries. A fresh, lively attack leads a medium-bodied palate with light but firm tannins. Very vibrant, fresh and youthful with zesty appeal. Drink now.

1997 Finale White Port, Finger Lakes $16.50/375 ml.   82

Gristina

1996 Chardonnay, North Fork of Long Island $11.99.   88

Rich yellow-straw hue. Forward tropical fruit and bread dough aromas. A supple entry leads a moderately full-bodied palate. Full yet crisp, with fine length. Drink now.

1995 Chardonnay, Andy's Field, North Fork of Long Island $21.99.   91

Rich yellow-straw hue. Fantastic tropical fruit and yeast aromas show a complex, leesy quality. A supple entry leads a full-bodied palate. Great intensity and complexity. Big, but well balanced. Drink now or later.

1997 Rosé of Cabernet, North Fork of Long Island $8.99.   85

Rich, brilliant raspberry pink. Reserved raspberry and bread dough aromas. A firm entry leads a full-bodied palate showing sharp acidity. Fruit centered, with a big bready finish. Drink now.

1996 Cabernet Sauvignon, North Fork of Long Island $15.99.   89

Deep ruby red with a slight fade. Generous cassis, mineral, and spice aromas show a gentle wood accent. A firm entry leads a moderately full-bodied palate, with drying tannins. Firm and intense, with a minerally finish. Drink now or later.

1993 Andy's Field Red, North Fork of Long Island $27.99.   90

Deep, saturated ruby purple. Powerful cassis, spice, and mineral aromas. A firm entry leads a full-bodied palate showing robust tannins. Highly extracted and intense. Accessible, but needs time. Mid-term cellar candidate (3–6 years).

1995 Merlot, North Fork of Long Island $14.99.   85

Dark, saturated ruby red. Black fruit and mineral aromas show a subtle oak accent. A firm entry leads a moderately full-bodied palate, with drying tannins. Sturdy and rich, with a tough-edged finish. Drink now or later.

1995 Pinot Noir, North Fork of Long Island $19.99.   86

Pale brick red. Powerful iron, spice, and red fruit aromas. A firm entry leads a medium-bodied palate, with drying tannins. Impressive aromatics; almost Burgundian. Drink now.

Hargrave

NV Chardonnay, Chardonette, North Fork of Long Island $6.99.   83

Bright straw hue. Lean mineral and melon aromas. A firm entry leads a crisp, medium-bodied palate. Zesty and angular. A clean, unoaked Chardonnay. Drink now.

1995 Chardonnay, Lattice Label, North Fork of Long Island $14.99.   85

Rich, saturated yellow-straw hue. Lean mineral and citrus aromas. A firm entry leads a moderately full-bodied palate that has crisp acidity. Firm and tight-fisted, with a phenolic edge to the finish. Drink now or later.

1997 Pinot Blanc, North Fork of Long Island $9.99.   84

Deep straw hue. Subdued melon, toast, and butter aromas. A supple entry leads a medium-bodied palate, with a lingering buttery finish. Clean and stylish, with Alsatian-type viscosity. Drink now.

1997 Cabernet Franc, North Fork of Long Island $14.99.   86

Bright cherry red with a slight fade. Generous herb, red fruit, and mineral aromas. A firm entry leads a medium-bodied palate, with drying tannins. Clipped, leafy finish. A lean Chinon style. Drink now.

1995 Pinot Noir, North Fork of Long Island $35.   **90**

Bright cherry-garnet hue with a slight fade. Powerful red fruit, mineral, and spice aromas show marked wood influence. A firm entry leads a moderately full-bodied palate, with drying tannins. Lengthy oak-tinged finish. Tasty and very stylish. Drink now or later.

Heron Hill

1997 Chardonnay, Ingle Vineyard, Proprietor's Reserve,
Finger Lakes $16.99.   **83**

Very pale straw hue. Smoky oak and citrus aromas. A zesty entry leads a medium-bodied palate with lean flavors that finish quickly with a note of oak spice. Rather shy on flavors, though clean and snappy. Drink now.

1996 Semi-Dry Riesling, Finger Lakes $8.49.   **83**

Pale straw hue. Lighter aroma of flowers and grapes. A crisp entry leads a light-bodied palate with brief mineral-accented flavors that finish quickly. A good match with shellfish. Drink now.

1997 Johannisberg Riesling, Ingle Vineyard, Finger Lakes $8.49.   **83**

Bright pale straw cast. Clean aromas of flowers and minerals. A juicy entry leads a medium-bodied palate, with white peach flavors that give way to a minerally finish. Lighter aperitif style. Drink now.

Hosmer

1997 Chardonnay, Cayuga Lake $12.   **84**

Bright straw cast. Medium-bodied. Full acidity. Highly extracted. Blanched almonds, minerals, butter. Aromatically reserved with a hint of oxidation that actually lends a sense of complexity. Ripe and rounded through the finish.

Raspberry Rhapsody, Finger Lakes $8.50.   **83**

Bright pale ruby cast. Medium-bodied. Balanced acidity. Moderately extracted. Red fruits. Rather reserved aromatically, with a lighter-styled though firmly structured palate feel. A hint of sweetness is balanced by angular acidity in the finish.

Hunt Country

1997 Seyval Blanc, Finger Lakes $6.99.   **80**

1997 Vidal Blanc, Ice Wine, Finger Lakes $24/375 ml.   **85**

Deep straw hue. Generous, earthy, honeyed melon aromas. A lean entry leads a sweet palate that has piercing acidity. Tart, intense finish. Drink now.

Jamesport

1997 Chardonnay, Cox Lane Vineyard, North Fork of Long Island $12.95.   **81**

Lamoreaux Landing

1997 Riesling, Dry, Finger Lakes $9.   **82**

1996 Cabernet Franc, Finger Lakes $14.   **82**

1995 Cabernet Sauvignon, Finger Lakes $18.   **82**

Laurel Lake

1996 Chardonnay, North Fork of Long Island $12.99.   **85**

Brilliant straw hue. Pleasant citrus, vanilla, and herb aromas. An acidic entry leads a crisp, moderately full-bodied palate. The finish is clipped and clean. Carries a bit of complexity, with a slight herbal edge. Drink now.

1995 Chardonnay, Reserve, North Fork of Long Island $13.99.   **86**

Luminous straw hue. Generous citrus, yeast, and mineral aromas. A firm entry leads a moderately full-bodied palate, with crisp acids. Firm and powerful, but restrained. Drink now.

NV Wind Song, North Fork of Long Island $7.99. **81**

NV Lake Rosé, North Fork of Long Island $9.99. **88**
Rich, saturated raspberry pink. Intense blackberry, citrus, and bread dough aromas.
A firm entry leads a moderately full-bodied palate, with crisp acids and a dry finish.
Shows some southern French overtones. Drink now.

1995 Cabernet Sauvignon, North Fork of Long Island $23.99. **88**
Brilliant cherry-garnet hue with a slight fade. Forward herb, mineral, and cassis aromas.
A firm entry leads a moderately full-bodied palate, with drying tannins, and a pure cassis
note to the finish. Balanced and well made. Drink now or later.

1996 Merlot, North Fork of Long Island $12.99. **85**
Bright cherry red with a slight fade. Subdued black cherry, dried herb, and mineral
aromas. A firm entry leads a crisp, medium-bodied palate that has drying tannins. Light
and stylish, and not overmade. Drink now.

Lenz

1992 "Cuvée" Sparkling Wine, North Fork of Long Island $19.99. **86**
Rich straw hue with fine bubbles. Pleasant cream, mineral, and earth aromas. A firm
entry leads a moderately full-bodied palate showing crisp acids. Rich and rounded, with
a sense of ripeness. Drink now.

1996 Chardonnay, Vineyard Selection, North Fork of Long Island $9.99. **85**
Rich yellow-straw hue. Subdued mineral, citrus, and butter aromas. A firm entry leads
a moderately full-bodied palate, with crisp acids. Vibrant and restrained. Drink now.

1995 Chardonnay, Barrel Fermented, North Fork of Long Island $24.99. **89**
Deep yellow-straw hue. Generous citrus, yeast, and butter aromas. A soft entry leads
a moderately full-bodied palate. Rich, rounded, and leesy, with a creamy mouthfeel.
Drink now.

1995 Gewürztraminer, North Fork of Long Island $10.99. **88**
Brilliant yellow-straw hue. Pleasant, classic lychee and flower aromas. A soft entry leads
a moderately full-bodied palate. Convincingly varietal, with an oily texture. Drink now.

1996 Blanc de Noir, North Fork of Long Island $7.99. **80**

1995 Cabernet Sauvignon, Estate, North Fork of Long Island $24.99. **90**
Deep ruby purple. Intense cassis, vanilla, and herb aromas. A supple entry leads a
moderately full-bodied palate, with velvety, plush, rounded tannins. Solid yet supple,
with fine balance. Drink now or later.

1997 Merlot-Cabernet, Vineyard Selection,
North Fork of Long Island $16.99. **86**
Deep, saturated ruby red. Pleasant red fruit and vanilla aromas carry a leafy accent. A soft
entry leads a medium-bodied palate showing velvety tannins. Fruit centered, with mild
oak accents. Drink now.

1995 Merlot, Estate, North Fork of Long Island $29.99. **89**
Deep, saturated ruby red. Generous raspberry and vanilla aromas show an integrated
oak accent. A supple entry leads a moderately full-bodied palate, with velvety tannins.
A rounded, softly extracted, harmonious style. Drink now or later.

1995 Pinot Noir, Estate, North Fork of Long Island $14.99. **84**
Bright ruby hue. Spice, mineral, and sour cherry aromas. A soft entry leads a moderately
light-bodied palate that shows drying tannins. Snappy finish. A crisp, lighter style, with
faint Pinot perfume. Drink now.

Macari

1997 Chardonnay, Stainless Steel, North Fork of Long Island $12. **84**
Bright straw hue. Clean mineral, herb, and citrus aromas. A firm entry leads a moderately full-bodied palate that has crisp acidity. Vibrant, with a slightly green finish. Drink now.

1996 Chardonnay, Barrel Fermented, North Fork of Long Island $14.   **88**

Deep yellow-straw hue. Forward spice, yeast, and banana aromas. A firm entry leads a moderately full-bodied palate. Full, lush, and complex, with a persistent yeasty finish. Drink now.

1997 Chardonnay, Barrel Fermented, North Fork of Long Island $17.   **93**

Deep yellow-straw hue. Fantastic vanilla, yeast, and cream aromas show an integrated oak influence. A supple entry leads a moderately full-bodied palate that features complex flavors. Lush, but powerful and lengthy. Drink now.

1997 Sauvignon Blanc, North Fork of Long Island $14.   **83**

Bright straw hue. Muted mineral and herb aromas. An acidic entry leads a medium-bodied palate, with crisp acidity. Zesty and straightforward. Drink now.

1997 Rosé d'Une Nuit, North Fork of Long Island $11.   **86**

Bright raspberry pink. Generous bread and red fruit aromas. A firm entry leads a moderately full-bodied palate, with a clean, lingering finish. Rich and rounded in a dry, Tavel-like style. Drink now.

1996 Merlot, North Fork of Long Island $20.   **90**

Bright ruby red. Pleasant dried herb, cedar, and cherry aromas show a generous wood accent. A supple entry leads a balanced, medium-bodied palate, with drying tannins. Lighter in style, but extremely flavorful and lengthy. Not overdone. Drink now.

Osprey's Dominion

NV Chardonnay, North Fork of Long Island $9.99.   **81**

1995 Chardonnay, North Fork of Long Island $11.99.   **83**

Rich straw hue. Mild citrus, vanilla, and butter aromas. A smooth entry leads a crisp, medium-bodied palate. Well balanced and clean through the finish. Drink now.

1996 Chardonnay, Reserve, North Fork of Long Island $25.   **84**

Deep yellow-straw hue. Generous apple, oak spice, and butter aromas. A firm entry leads a moderately full-bodied palate showing crisp acidity. Rich and full, with a lot of barrel influence. Drink now.

1997 Johannisberg Riesling, North Fork of Long Island $11.99.   **81**

1995 Cabernet Sauvignon, North Fork of Long Island $13.99.   **89**

Deep, saturated ruby red. Generous dried herb, mineral, and cassis aromas show mild oak influences. A soft entry leads a moderately full-bodied palate, with velvety tannins. Varietal and supple, with fine length. Drink now.

1996 Merlot, North Fork of Long Island $14.99.   **86**

Rich ruby hue with a slight fade. Generous raspberry and spice aromas. Medium-bodied, with silky tannins. Soft, smooth, and supple, with a lingering note of oak spice. Drink now.

1996 Pinot Noir, North Fork of Long Island $15.99.   **80**

NV Spice Wine, North Fork of Long Island $8.99.   **89**

Light garnet hue with a slight fade. Powerful cinnamon, spice, and berry aromas. A smooth entry leads a full-bodied palate, with a hint of sweetness and drying tannins. Rich, supple, extremely flavorful, and very tasty. Drink now.

Palmer

1997 Chardonnay, North Fork of Long Island $11.99.   **84**

Bright golden yellow. Mildly soured appley aromas. An angular attack leads a moderately full-bodied palate with crab apple flavors, but a generous mouthfeel. Rather awkward.

1996 Pinot Blanc, Estate, North Fork of Long Island $9.99.   **82**

1995 Cabernet Franc, Proprietor's Reserve,
North Fork of Long Island $15.   **80**

1995 Select Reserve Red, North Fork of Long Island $25.   **84**

Saturated purple-red. Medium-bodied. Highly extracted. Moderately tannic. Black cherry, licorice, earth. Solid black fruit-accented aromas lead a tightly wound palate with hard-edged tannins and lush, fruity flavors. Dry and angular through the finish, though not inaccessible now.

1995 Merlot, North Fork of Long Island $16.   **82**

1995 Merlot, Reserve, North Fork of Long Island $28.   **89**

Very deep blackish ruby hue. Moderately full-bodied. Balanced acidity. Highly extracted. Heavily oaked. Moderately tannic. Pencil shavings, cedar, black fruits, minerals. Oak driven on the nose, with a rich and extracted core of minerally fruit flavors. Firm in structure with grip to the tannins and a lengthy finish.

Paumanok

1997 Chardonnay, North Fork of Long Island $16.99.   **86**

Deep yellow-straw hue. Pleasant mineral, yeast, and bread aromas carry a toasty oak accent. A firm entry leads a moderately full-bodied palate. Rich and firmly structured. Should develop some complexities with a bit of age. Drink now or later.

1998 Chenin Blanc, North Fork of Long Island $12.   **84**

Rich yellow-straw hue. Pleasant citrus and mineral aromas. A firm entry leads a moderately full-bodied palate showing sharp acidity. The finish is firm and racy. Drink now.

1995 Cabernet Sauvignon, Grand Vintage, North Fork of Long Island $25. **90**

Dark, saturated ruby purple. Generous cassis, mineral, and mint aromas. A firm entry leads a full-bodied palate, with moderate but big tannins. The finish is concentrated and powerful. Very varietal and intense. Drink now or later.

1995 Assemblage, North Fork of Long Island $24.   **90**

Deep, saturated ruby purple. Generous mint, black fruit, and vanilla aromas show modest wood influence. A firm attack leads a moderately full-bodied palate, with big, velvety tannins. Full, rich, deep, and packed with flavor. Drink now or later.

1995 Merlot, Grand Vintage, North Fork of Long Island $22.   **88**

Deep, saturated ruby purple. Forward black fruit, dried herb, and mint aromas. A firm entry leads a full-bodied palate showing robust tannins. Extracted and thick, with a leafy edge. Tannins clamp down on the finish. Needs time. Mid-term cellar candidate (3–6 years).

1997 Sauvignon Blanc, Late Harvest,
North Fork of Long Island $29/375 ml.   **89**

Rich straw hue. Attractive honey, tropical fruit, and citrus aromas. A firm entry leads a moderately full-bodied palate, with lots of sweetness offset by crisp acids. Botrytized yet clean, with a good snap to the finish. Drink now.

Peconic Bay

1995 Chardonnay, Rolling Ridge, North Fork of Long Island $18.99. **86**

Deep straw cast. Moderately full-bodied. Balanced acidity. Highly extracted. Moderately oaked. Brown spices, bread, toast. Opulent and aromatic, with a big spicy overlay and a firm core of angular citric flavors. A big, intense style.

1996 Chardonnay, Sandy Hill, North Fork of Long Island $21.99. **82**

1995 Merlot, North Fork of Long Island $19.99.   **82**

1995 Merlot, Epic Acre, North Fork of Long Island $24.99.   **90**

Deep blackish ruby hue. Moderately full-bodied. Balanced acidity. Highly extracted. Mildly oaked. Moderately tannic. Black fruits, minerals. Quite deep and focused, with a full-scaled structure supported by real density of flavor. Flavorful and rich through a firm, velvety finish.

Pellegrini

1996 Chardonnay, North Fork of Long Island $12.99.   86

Bright golden cast. Medium-bodied. Balanced acidity. Moderately extracted. Pears, minerals, cream. Ripe and intense, with a rounded, creamy impression on the palate. Firm and flavorful through the finish.

1995 Cabernet Franc, North Fork of Long Island $23.   86

Brilliant ruby-red hue. Generous cedar, vanilla, and red fruit aromas. A crisp entry leads to a medium-bodied palate with firm, astringent tannins. Lean, angular finish. Rather tough at present, but should open with time. Drink within five years.

1995 Cabernet Sauvignon, North Fork of Long Island $15.99.   88

Deep, saturated purple-red hue. Intense vanilla and spice aromas show a dominant oak accent. A firm attack leads to a medium-bodied palate with grainy tannins. Lengthy, flavorful finish with solid acidic grip. Taut and stylish. Drink now or later.

1994 Encore, Vintner's Pride, North Fork of Long Island $23.99.   81

1995 Merlot, North Fork of Long Island $16.99.   88

Saturated dark ruby hue. Distinctive wood spice aromas. A firm attack leads a moderately full-bodied palate with firm, fine-grained tannins through a dry, lean finish. Shows underlying fruity character. Stylish and well balanced, with the stuffing and structure to improve over time.

Pindar

1994 Cuvée Rare Champagne, North Fork of Long Island $27.99.   88

Rich yellow-straw hue, with a fine, long-lasting bead. Generous mineral, white citrus, and dough aromas. A firm entry leads a crisp, moderately full-bodied palate. Lingering, vibrant finish. Rich and stylish, with a creamy texture. Drink now.

NV Long Island Winter White, North Fork of Long Island $7.99.   80

1997 Chardonnay, Peacock Label, North Fork of Long Island $10.99.   81

1996 Chardonnay, Reserve, North Fork of Long Island $12.99.   83

Rich, luminous straw hue. Generous mineral and dough aromas. A supple entry leads a medium-bodied palate. Lighter in style, with some richness to the finish. Drink now.

1996 Chardonnay, Sunflower Special Reserve,
North Fork of Long Island $16.99.   85

Deep yellow-straw hue. Generous mineral, cream, and dough aromas. A firm entry leads a moderately full-bodied palate showing crisp acids. Rich and firm, yet closed. Drink now or later.

1996 Viognier, North Fork of Long Island $19.99.   85

Deep yellow-straw hue. Unusual, sweaty, spicy aromas. A supple entry leads a medium-bodied palate. Shows some complexities, with a fat middle and a lean, minerally finish. Drink now.

1994 Cabernet Franc, North Fork of Long Island $12.99.   89

Light cherry red. Pleasant, perfumed sweet herb and spice aromas. A firm entry leads a medium-bodied palate, with drying tannins. Flavorful and angular, with good bite. Drink now or later.

1994 Cabernet Sauvignon, North Fork of Long Island $18.99.   85

Ruby red with a slight fade. Pleasant mineral, red fruit, and dried herb aromas. A firm entry leads a medium-bodied palate that shows drying tannins. Quite structured, with a lingering finish.

1993 Cabernet Sauvignon, Reserve, North Fork of Long Island $18.99.   86

Deep garnet hue. Mature and exotic forest, earth, and mineral aromas. A firm entry leads to a medium-bodied palate with lean, angular tannins. Sharp, flavorful finish. Showing lots of mature character on a very lean, somewhat austere frame. Will work well at the table. Drink now.

1994 Cabernet Sauvignon, Reserve, North Fork of Long Island $18.99.   **83**

Bright garnet hue. Generous cedar, herb, and mineral aromas show a degree of maturity and a marked oak accent. A soft attack leads to a medium-bodied palate with lean tannins. Angular, gripping finish. Interesting flavors, and not very intense. Drink now.

1995 Cabernet Sauvignon, Reserve, North Fork of Long Island $18.99.   **89**

Saturated, opaque ruby-purple hue. Reserved berry and mineral aromas. A firm entry leads to a moderately full-bodied palate with authoritative, lean tannins. Angular, cut finish. A tightly wound style that is rather ungenerous at present. Will always be austere, but should open with age. Drink now or later.

1997 Gamay, North Fork of Long Island $8.99.   **85**

Light cherry red with a slight fade. Sound mineral and red fruit aromas. A soft entry leads a moderately light-bodied palate that has crisp acids. Ripe, fruity, and generous. Drink now.

1993 Mythology, North Fork of Long Island $24.99.   **88**

Deep garnet-red hue. Perfumed brown spice, vanilla, and mineral aromas carry a marked oak accent. A lean attack leads to a medium-bodied palate with angular acidity and grippy tannins. Taut and well structured with an Italian-like edge. Firm, linear finish. Mature in flavor with a crisp structure that will work well at the table. Drink within five years.

1994 Mythology, North Fork of Long Island $24.99.   **88**

Full ruby red. Medium-bodied. Moderately extracted. Moderately tannic. Lead pencil, cranberries, earth. Attractive earthy nose has lead pencil qualities. The firm, dry, austere palate has great presence through a dry finish.

1995 Mythology, North Fork of Long Island $36.99.   **88**

Rich, saturated ruby red. Generous mineral, red fruit, and dried herb aromas. A firm entry leads a moderately full-bodied palate, with grainy tannins. Shows some leafy complexities. Finishes on a tough, lean note. Drink now or later.

1995 Merlot, North Fork of Long Island $18.99.   **84**

Deep, saturated ruby purple. Mild black fruit, mineral, and dried herb aromas. A firm entry leads a moderately full-bodied palate, with drying tannins. Firm and compact. A trifle mean through the finish. Drink now or later.

1995 Port, North Fork of Long Island $24.99.   **89**

Deep ruby red with a slight fade. Brooding berry and wood aromas carry a complex medicinal overtone. A firm entry leads a full-bodied, moderately sweet palate, with drying tannins. Full, rich, and ripe. Drink now or later.

1996 Johannisberg Riesling, Eiswein,
North Fork of Long Island $35/375 ml.   **86**

Deep yellow-straw hue. Generous tropical fruit, cream, and pineapple aromas. A supple entry leads a moderately full-bodied, sweet palate, with decent balancing acidity. Ripe and creamy. A tad fat. Drink now.

Prejean

1997 Gewürztraminer, Dry, Finger Lakes $12.   **80**

1997 Gewürztraminer, Semi-Dry, Finger Lakes $12.   **81**

Pugliese

1995 Blanc de Blanc Brut, North Fork of Long Island $15.99.   **80**

1995 Blanc de Noir, North Fork of Long Island $17.99.   **84**

Light pink, with a thin mousse and fine, long-lasting beads. Pleasant red fruit and mineral aromas. An acidic entry leads a sharp, medium-bodied palate. Steely and firm, with a quick fade. Drink now.

Scale: Superlative (96-100), Exceptional (90-95), Highly Recommended (85-89), Recommended (80-84), Not Recommended (Under 80)

294

1996 Sparkling Merlot, North Fork of Long Island $17.99.   **81**

1996 Chardonnay, Reserve, North Fork of Long Island $12.99.   **80**

1997 Cabernet Franc, North Fork of Long Island $13.99.   **84**

Bright ruby-garnet hue. Subdued mineral, red fruit, and herb aromas. A supple entry leads a medium-bodied palate, with velvety tannins. Flavorful and straightforward. Drink now.

1995 Merlot, Reserve, North Fork of Long Island $13.99.   **80**

1997 Sangiovese, North Fork of Long Island $13.99.   **88**

Bright raspberry pink. Intense, striking berry fruit and spice aromas. A supple entry leads a medium-bodied palate showing silky tannins. Generous, lush, and stylish. Lighter in style, but quite interesting. Drink now.

Port Bello, North Fork of Long Island $26.99.   **80**

Standing Stone

1997 Chardonnay, Finger Lakes $12.50.   **82**

1997 Cabernet Franc, Finger Lakes $15.50.   **81**

1996 Merlot, Finger Lakes $15.50.   **80**

Swedish Hill

1997 Cayuga White, Finger Lakes $6.99.   **82**

1997 Dry Riesling, Finger Lakes $9.99/.   **84**

Pale straw hue. Attractive aromas show peach and apricot character. A juicy, bright entry follows through on a medium-bodied palate, with tropical flavors well balanced by a citrus zest character on the finish. Drink now.

1997 Vidal Blanc, New York $7.99.   **84**

Very pale straw hue. Aromatically reserved, with tart citrus notes. A zesty entry leads a moderately light-bodied palate featuring clean flavors and a note of sweetness balanced by good acids. Drink now.

Ternhaven

1994 Cabernet Sauvignon, North Fork of Long Island $17.99.   **88**

Luminous garnet red with a slight fade. Pleasant black fruit, mineral, and spice aromas. A firm entry leads a medium-bodied palate that has drying tannins. A lighter style, but ripe, spicy, and very tasty through the finish. Drink now or later.

1995 Cabernet Sauvignon, North Fork of Long Island $15.99.   **90**

Dark, saturated ruby purple. Generous cassis, vanilla, and spice aromas show a hefty oak influence. A firm attack leads a moderately full-bodied palate, with drying tannins. Concentrated, persistent, and spicy. Drink now or later.

1994 Claret d'Alvah, North Fork of Long Island $18.99.   **89**

Bright ruby red with a slight fade. Pleasant red fruit, spice, and mineral aromas show a mild oak accent. A firm entry leads a medium-bodied palate, with drying tannins. The finish is well balanced, angular, and flavorful. Drink now or later.

1995 Claret d'Alvah, North Fork of Long Island $18.99.   **90**

Dark, saturated ruby purple. Generous cassis, mineral,·and spice aromas carry a marked wood accent. A firm entry leads a moderately full-bodied palate that shows robust tannins. Lingering, spicy finish. Firm and grippy. Drink now or later.

1996 Claret d'Alvah, North Fork of Long Island $17.99.   **85**

Rich, saturated ruby red. Generous, unusual red fruit and dill pickle aromas show hefty (American?) oak influence. A firm entry leads a medium-bodied palate, with drying tannins. Intense and austere through the finish. Drink now or later.

1994 Merlot, North Fork of Long Island $18.99. **88**

Luminous cherry red with a slight fade. Generous red fruit, mineral, and spice aromas show a fair amount of wood. A firm entry leads a medium-bodied palate, with drying tannins. Spicy and generous, with a tasty finish. Drink now.

1995 Merlot, North Fork of Long Island $19.99. **89**

Dark, saturated ruby purple. Generous sweet, herb, black cherry, and spice aromas jump from the glass. Shows a hefty wood accent and a slightly unusual overtone. A firm entry leads a full-bodied mouthfeel, with velvety tannins. Concentrated and intense. Should improve. Mid-term cellar candidate (3–6 years).

Treleaven

1997 Chardonnay, Cayuga Lake $11.99. **89**

Bright pale yellow. Interesting spicy, nutty aromas. A rich attack leads a medium-bodied palate with smooth texture and crisp apple flavors showing interesting spice through the finish. Rather distinctive.

five

The Wines of Virginia

An Introduction: The Wines of Virginia

Thomas Jefferson is one of this nation's better known wine-lovers. Never accused of turning down a good drink, he spent much of his time trolling around Europe, invariably sampling the local tipple. He brought back more than a passion for wine with him. An avid horticulturist, he set about trying to grow the great wine grapes of Europe in his back yard at Monticello. Today, modern-day residents of the Old Dominion have taken up the torch, and the state is a hot bed of wine production in the Mid-Atlantic. The most promising appellation? Monticello, the region around the bucolic town of Charlottesville with its Jefferson-designed university campus, which is nestled in the foothills of the Blue Ridge Mountains.

Though Virginian wines were well known in the early years of the 19th century, Prohibition was the final setback for an industry that had sputtered along for the previous hundred years. In recent times, however, the area has once again taken up winemaking, and it would seem that more and more new producers are jumping in with every passing year.

The notoriously long, hot summers are certainly capable of bringing all sorts of grapes to ripeness, but the intense humidity brings with it its own problems. This humidity is probably the biggest problem a modern-day Jeffersonian winemaker faces. It makes the region an attractive home to a number of bugs that like to munch on grapevines, but more seriously provides ideal conditions for rot in the vineyards—particularly later in the season when sugars have accumulated in the grapes. Virginia's viticulturists are a hardy lot, constantly combating nature's whims.

Given such difficulties, it may be surprising that Virginia actually makes some pretty good and occasionally outstanding wines. Reds are really its forte, with Bordeaux varietals seemingly the most popular. However, Virginia is also home to some of the nation's most experimental winemakers. Foremost among them would be Dennis Horton of Horton Vineyards, who has developed a national following for his Viognier and Rhône-style blends. The rapid-fire Mr. Horton seems to have just about every known grape variety planted, from Rkatsiteli, a little-known Eastern Mediterranean white, to a range of Portuguese table reds. If it's not there now it's because he's already tried it and ripped it out.

Then there is Barboursville, just down the road from Horton, an impressive estate owned by the Zonin family of Italy, one of that nation's larger wine producers. It would seem that Signore Zonin likes to fancy himself the country gentleman while riding around the property, surveying it on horseback, and no doubt cutting a dashing figure in the process. Less dashing perhaps, would be his winemaker Luca Paschina, an enologist from Alba in Piedmont who readily admits to being an awful horseman and who has come to look upon the owner's occasional visits with some trepidation because of it. Nonetheless, he is a better winemaker than equestrian, and has proceeded to add Italian specialties, such as Dolcetio and Pinot Grigio, to the line-up.

Scale: Superlative (96-100), Exceptional (90-95), Highly Recommended (85-89), Recommended (80-84), Not Recommended (Under 80)

What it all adds up to is an eclectic mix of young wineries that are each finding their own ways. As such, it is difficult to generalize about the wines, other than to say that they run the gamut. In some ways, that makes the region a lot of fun, as experimentation is sometimes rewarded. This makes it difficult to predict Virginia's future, but with characters like these, half the fun will no doubt be in getting there.

Reviews

Autumn Hill

1997 Chardonnay, Monticello $11. **81**

1997 Chardonnay, Barrel Select, Virginia $13. **81**

1993 Cabernet Sauvignon, Monticello $15. **84**

Opaque saturated color. Medium-bodied. Highly extracted. Moderately tannic. Earth, minerals, brown spice. Tough and reserved, with dry, earthy flavors and an impression of black fruits. Finishes in a dry, forceful manner, though the acids are low.

Barboursville

1997 Chardonnay, Monticello $12. **81**

1997 Chardonnay, Reserve, Monticello $15. **83**

Pale straw cast. Medium-bodied. Full acidity. Moderately extracted. Minerals, citrus. Lean, crisp, and zesty, with ripe citric flavors. A clean, easy-drinking style.

1997 Pinot Grigio, Monticello $13. **81**

1997 Sauvignon Blanc, Monticello $11. **81**

1995 Cabernet Sauvignon, Monticello $15. **86**

Blood red with an even fade to the rim. Medium-bodied. Moderately extracted. Moderately tannic. Mineral, vanilla, red fruits. A juicy, generous mouthfeel shows ripeness and tertiary flavors that are seamlessly woven with bright red fruits. Shows a nice acidic cut. Drinking well now.

1995 Cabernet Sauvignon, Reserve, Monticello $20. **83**

Bright pale ruby red with a fading rim. Moderately light-bodied. Moderately extracted. Mildly tannic. Cedar, red fruits, minerals. Crisp, minerally, and angular, with a wisp of dry tannins on the finish. A very tasty, rather lean style with a strong impression of new oak flavors.

Virginia at a Glance

Wines Reviewed:

94

Producers/Brands Represented:

26

1997 Dolcetto, Monticello $19.99.   **84**

Bright ruby cast. Moderately light-bodied. Full acidity. Moderately extracted. Mildly tannic. Dried herbs, earth, minerals. Shows distinctive and complex aromatics with a slight earthy edge. Lean and angular through the finish. Concentrated.

NV Octagon Red, Virginia $22.   **84**

Pale ruby red. Moderately light-bodied. Moderately extracted. Mildly tannic. Minerals, earth, cassis. Bright minerally aromas have a crisp fruity accent that follows through on the palate with a sense of elegance. The finish is bright, with an oak spice note. An Old World style.

1995 Pinot Noir, Monticello $14.99.   **87**

Dark red. Medium-bodied. Moderately extracted. Moderately oaked. Moderately tannic. Mildly herbaceous oak-accented aromas. Brisk, tart cherry flavors expand on the palate through a lingering, mildly astringent finish showing oak influence. Some substance, though short on finesse.

1997 Pinot Noir, Reserve, Monticello $19.99.   **81**

Breaux

1997 Chardonnay, Virginia $12.   **82**

1997 Chardonnay, Madeleine's, Virginia $15.   **84**

Bright yellow-straw cast. Medium-bodied. Balanced acidity. Moderately extracted. Pears, minerals, peaches. A fruit-forward style with ripe, generous flavors. Soft and lush in the mouth with just enough acidity to lend a sense of balance.

Chateau Morrisette

1997 Chardonnay, "M," Meadows of Dan, Virginia $14.   **86**

Bright yellow-gold. Clean yellow-apple aromas. A bright entry leads a medium-bodied palate with crisp citrus flavors that persist through the finish. No sign of oak. A very refreshing style.

Dashiell

1996 Chardonnay, Virginia $17.   **86**

Bright yellow-straw cast. Moderately full-bodied. Balanced acidity. Moderately extracted. Moderately oaked. Brown spices, citrus. Generous aromas feature ample wood seasoning and a zesty fruit component. Full but balanced and flavorful through the vibrant finish.

1997 Chardonnay, Virginia $17.   **86**

Bright yellow-gold. Clean aromas show subtle buttery and citrus notes and a slight nutty quality. A juicy entry leads a moderately full-bodied palate with fine texture and a smooth mouthfeel. Features clean citrus flavors with minimal oak influence. Drink now.

De Chiel

1997 Late Harvest Vidal Blanc, Montebello, Virginia $12/500 ml.   **82**

Dominion Wine Cellars

1996 Blackberry Merlot, Virginia $18.   **82**

1996 Raspberry Merlot, Virginia $19.   **85**

Deep ruby-garnet cast. Moderately full-bodied. Full acidity. Highly extracted. Mildly tannic. Stewed fruit. Carries a ripe fruit note to the flavors, and turns very puckering on the briskly tart berry finish.

Gray Ghost

1993 Cabernet Sauvignon, Virginia $25.   **81**

Horton

Stonecastle White, Orange County $8.   **82**

1997 Chardonnay, Orange County $15.   **83**

Pale straw cast. Medium-bodied. Full acidity. Moderately extracted. Mildly oaked. Brown spices, minerals. Restrained aromatics carry a subtle hint of oak. Crisp and lively in the mouth with an angular finish.

1997 Chardonnay, Reserve, Orange County $18.   **84**

Bright yellow-straw cast. Moderately full-bodied. Balanced acidity. Moderately extracted. Tropical fruits, flowers, minerals. Forward flavors show an unusual aromatic varietal quality. Big but crisp in the mouth, with a balanced finish that has grip.

1996 Cabernet Franc, Virginia $12.   **83**

Pale ruby-garnet hue. Moderately light-bodied. Full acidity. Moderately extracted. Moderately oaked. Mildly tannic. Brown spices, cedar, minerals. Shows an obvious oak influence in the nose. Light and crisp in the mouth, with an angular finish.

1995 Malbec, Virginia $15.   **81**

1995 Mourvedre, Orange County $12.50.   **81**

1995 Cotes d'Orange, Orange County $14.75.   **81**

1994 Stonecastle Red, Orange County $11.50.   **84**

Bright garnet red. Generous herb, red fruit, and cedar aromas show a hefty oak accent. A soft attack leads a medium-bodied palate that shows bright acidity and tannic grip. Fine structure and balance. Lengthy, spicy finish. Drink now.

1995 Vintage Port, Orange County $20.   **84**

Opaque blackish ruby hue. Full-bodied. Balanced acidity. Highly extracted. Brown spices, licorice, earth. A pungent style, with complex, rather unusual aromatics. Rich, round, and full on the palate, with just a hint of sweetness.

Ingleside Plantation

1995 Cabernet Franc, Virginia $11.99.   **84**

Bright ruby red with a garnet rim. Medium-bodied. Full acidity. Moderately extracted. Mildly oaked. Mildly tannic. Vanilla, cherries, minerals. Aromatically reserved, but juicy and flavorful on the palate, with a lean and angular finish.

NV Cabernet Sauvignon, Chesapeake Claret, Virginia $8.99.   **84**

Pale ruby-garnet hue with a fading rim. Moderately light-bodied. Full acidity. Moderately extracted. Mildly tannic. Earth, minerals, tart red fruits. Mature, stewed aromas are showing through, with an angular, minerally palate and gripping acids through the finish.

1994 Cabernet Sauvignon, Virginia $17.99.   **84**

Blood-garnet red with a fading rim. Medium-bodied. Moderately extracted. Mildly tannic. Earth, stewed fruits. Soft, earthy aromas lead a soft, mature-tasting palate, with gentle tannins through the finish.

1994 Cabernet Sauvignon, Special Reserve, Virginia $19.99.   **86**

Blood red with a garnet cast. Medium-bodied. Moderately extracted. Moderately tannic. Vanilla, dill, red fruits. Earth and herbal aromas dominate, with a dusty accent. Dry and lean on the palate, with chunky tannins showing some age and softness. Nicely mature, drinking well now.

1995 Cabernet Sauvignon, Special Reserve, Virginia $17.99.   **83**

Pale ruby hue with a subtle garnet rim. Medium-bodied. Moderately extracted. Mildly tannic. Cherries, vanilla. Soft minerally notes with red fruit accents are conveyed on the palate. Finishes with gentle oak spice and soft tannins. Drinking well now.

1997 Merlot, Virginia $14.99.   **86**

Bright violet hue. Generous aromas of vanilla and raspberries. A crisp attack leads a medium-bodied palate that is fleshy and fruit centered and shows velvety tannins. A forward, supple style with good varietal character. Drink now.

Jefferson

1997 Chardonnay, Monticello $9.99.   83
Bright green-gold. Medium-bodied. Balanced acidity. Moderately extracted. Butter, citrus. Aromatically reserved, with subtle fruit nuances and a decided buttery note. Crisp and lean through the finish.

1997 Chardonnay, Fantaisie Sauvage, Monticello $22.   86
Bright yellow-gold. Moderately full-bodied. Full acidity. Moderately extracted. Mildly oaked. Cream, tropical fruits, toast. Forward aromas show a fine interplay between fruit and yeast flavors, with a judicious oak accent. The finish is crisp and balanced.

1997 Chardonnay, Signature Series Reserve, Monticello $20.   84
Bright yellow-gold. Moderately full-bodied. Balanced acidity. Moderately extracted. Butter, minerals. Ripe aromas belie a forward buttery character. Big, but showing some balance in the mouth, with linear acidity through the finish.

1997 Cabernet Franc, Monticello $15.   81

1995 Cabernet Sauvignon, Monticello $18.   85
Black cherry red. Medium-bodied. Highly extracted. Moderately tannic. Black cherries, black fruits, tea. Rich aromas lead a solid, proportioned palate with concentrated fruity flavors and a weighty mouthfeel. Finishes with textured tannins.

1995 Meritage, Monticello $26.   86
Bright purple-red. Moderately light-bodied. Moderately extracted. Mildly tannic. Cherries, black tea, minerals. A mineral-accented nose show bright cherry fruit notes. Quite compact and dry on the palate, with grainy tannins coming through on the finish. Well balanced.

1997 Meritage, Monticello $28.   86
Bright cherry red hue with a slight fade. Forward and attractive mineral, berry, and vanilla aromas show a judicious oak accent. A lean attack leads to a medium-bodied palate with angular tannins and crisp acidity. Austere, structured finish. A taut and well defined style. Drink within five years.

1997 Merlot, Monticello $19.   88
Pale ruby-violet hue. Clean minerally, red fruit aromas. A crisp attack leads a medium-bodied palate with light but dry, firm tannins. The finish is clean and has a minerally note. Drink now.

Linden

1998 Riesling-Vidal, Virginia $13.   83
Brilliant straw hue with a slight spritz. Subdued earth and mineral aromas. A crisp entry leads a moderately light-bodied, lean palate that has forward fruit flavors. Racy finish with a hint of sweetness. Drink now.

1994 Cabernet Sauvignon, Virginia $16.   88
Bright, deep brick red. Medium-bodied. Moderately extracted. Mildly tannic. Earth, red fruits, licorice, brown spice. Austere spicy nose leads a solid earthy palate, with mouthfilling dry flavors that linger through the finish. Has a fine gout de terroir. Elegant, though not fruity in the least.

1995 Cabernet Sauvignon, Virginia $17.   84
Saturated, opaque blackish ruby hue. Unusual, high-toned anise and mineral aromas. A lean attack leads to a medium-bodied palate with firm, grippy tannins and shy acidity. Clipped, woody finish. Drink now.

1997 Late Harvest Vidal, Virginia $18/375 ml.   84
Deep straw hue. Earthy, toasty, sweet citrus aromas. A vibrant entry leads a medium-bodied palate showing moderate sweetness. Elevated acidity makes for a crisp, clean finish. Drink now.

Scale: Superlative (96-100), Exceptional (90-95), Highly Recommended (85-89),
Recommended (80-84), Not Recommended (Under 80)

Montdomaine

1993 Cabernet Sauvignon, Virginia $13.50.   **85**

Pale reddish purple. Medium-bodied. Moderately extracted. Mildly tannic. Faint black fruits, brown spice. Clean, somewhat austere style, with crisp fruity flavors on entry and a lengthy astringent finish. Not a whole lot of varietal character, but it has a good mouthfeel.

1993 Heritage, Virginia $15.   **89**

Dark blackish red. Medium-bodied. Moderately extracted. Mildly tannic. Black fruits, tobacco, dried herbs. Full dark fruit aromas have exotic tobacco and herbal notes. Almost fleshy flavors expand on the palate, with dry powdery tannins lingering on the finish. A complex melange of flavors.

Naked Mountain

1997 Chardonnay, Virginia $15.   **82**

1998 Riesling, Virginia $13.   **81**

1997 Cabernet Franc, Virginia $12.   **82**

1996 Cabernet Sauvignon, Virginia $15.   **86**

Dark ruby red with a subtle fade on the rim. Medium-bodied. Moderately extracted. Moderately oaked. Mildly tannic. Vanilla, brown spice, black fruits. A rounded, soft, sweet fruit-centered palate with a cedary, spicy overlay. Minerally dryness emerges on the finish. Well balanced, and drinking well now.

Oakencroft

1995 Cabernet Sauvignon, Monticello $14.   **86**

Deep ruby red with a brightening rim. Medium-bodied. Moderately extracted. Mildly tannic. Red fruits, brown spices, peanut. Spicy, aromatic nose leads an elegant palate with a cedary, minerally profile and juicy acids. Mature Claret style.

Oasis

NV Brut, Virginia $28.   **88**

Pale straw hue. Medium-bodied. Full acidity. Citrus, smoke, toast. Zesty, yeasty aromas show a degree of complexity that follows through on the palate and the finish. Very bright and citrus accented.

NV Celebration 2000 Brut Cuvée D'Or, Virginia $50.   **86**

Pale straw hue. Medium-bodied. Full acidity. Bread, dried herbs, citrus. Curious yet complex yeasty aromas lead concentrated flavors outlined with cutting acids and fine-beaded carbonation. A very distinctive style that will not appeal to everyone.

1995 Chardonnay, Virginia $18.   **81**

1998 Dry Gewürztraminer, Virginia $18.   **80**

1997 Semi-Dry Riesling, Virginia $18.   **88**

Deep yellow-gold. Very aromatic, with a full apple and petrol character. A flavorful attack leads a moderately full-bodied palate that has classic oily Riesling qualities. A solid food wine. Drink now.

1995 Cabernet Franc, Virginia $18.50.   **81**

1995 Cabernet Sauvignon, Virginia $19.50.   **80**

1997 Cabernet Sauvignon, Reserve, Virginia $19.50.   **81**

1997 Meritage, Virginia $38.50.   **84**

Pale garnet hue. Subdued herb and cedar aromas show a subtle oak accent. A soft attack leads to a moderately light-bodied palate with angular tannins and crisp acidity. Lengthy, smoke-tinged finish. Quite light in style but tasty and well structured. Drink now.

1995 Merlot, Virginia $24.50.   **80**

Prince Michel

1995 The Prince's Brut, Virginia $20.   **80**

1997 Chardonnay, Virginia $13.95.   **83**
Bright pale straw. Mild aromas of apple and pear show a clean varietal character.
A crisp entry leads a medium-bodied palate with bright, pure fruit flavors and a clean fin-
ish supported by crisp acids. A well-balanced, refreshing style. Drink now.

1997 Chardonnay, Barrel Select, Virginia $18.95.   **88**
Bright yellow-gold. Subtle oak aromas with ripe apple. A fruity attack leads a moderately
full-bodied palate with bright acids and fresh fruity flavors. Judiciously oaked, with a
lingering spicy finish. Drink now.

Rapidan River

1997 Gewürztraminer, Barrel Fermented, Virginia $18.95.   **82**

Rockbridge

1997 Chardonnay, Reserve, Virginia $15.   **86**
Deep yellow-gold. Ripe aromas show apple and butter. A bright entry leads a moderately
full-bodied palate with a rounded buttery mouthfeel and concentrated flavors. Finishes
with a note of alcohol warmth. A big, generous style. Drink now.

1997 St. Mary's Blanc, Virginia $8.   **80**

1997 Tuscarora White, Virginia $8.   **83**
Deep yellow-straw hue. Attractive candied pear and vanilla aromas. A rich entry leads a
moderately full-bodied palate, with mild sweetness offset by sturdy acidity. Crisp, flavorful
finish. Drink now.

1995 Cabernet, Virginia $14.   **83**
Bright violet-ruby hue. Medium-bodied. Moderately extracted. Mildly tannic. Spice,
minerals. Dusty, minerally aromas. Plenty of oak spice flavors emerge on the palate,
with light fruit flavors and a lean finish making for a more reserved style.

1996 Cabernet, Virginia $14.   **84**
Bright cherry red hue. Intense cranberry, cherry, and mineral aromas. A crisp attack
leads to a moderately light-bodied, fruit centered palate with soft tannins. Bright finish.
A straightforward quaffer. Drink now.

1997 Vidal Blanc, Late Harvest V d'Or, Virginia $15/375 ml.   **80**

Spotswood Trail

1997 Chardonnay, Ivy Creek, Monticello $15.   **83**
Bright yellow-gold. Moderately full-bodied. Balanced acidity. Moderately extracted.
Moderately oaked. Brown spices, tropical fruits. Forward aromas have a high degree of
ripeness and a hefty oak accent. Weighty and rich in the mouth with a hint of sweetness
through the finish.

Swedenburg

1995 Cabernet Sauvignon, Virginia $14.   **80**

Tarara

1997 Chardonnay, Virginia $12.99.   **83**
Bright straw cast. Medium-bodied. Balanced acidity. Moderately extracted. Minerals,
pears. Ripe, fruity aromas lead a straightforward, clean mouthfeel. The finish is soft.

1997 Sweet Vidal Blanc, Virginia $12.99/375 ml.   **80**

1997 Cabernet Franc, Virginia $13.99.   **81**

Scale: Superlative (96-100), Exceptional (90-95), Highly Recommended (85-89),
Recommended (80-84), Not Recommended (Under 80)

White Hall Vineyards

1997 Chardonnay, Virginia $12.   80

1997 Chardonnay, Reserve, Virginia $18.   89

Bright green-gold cast. Moderately full-bodied. Full acidity. Moderately extracted.
Moderately oaked. Smoke, brown spices, citrus. Ripe, forward aromas feature a generous
oak accent. Full smoky flavors open up on the palate, backed by crisp acidity through a
lengthy, flavorful finish.

1997 Cabernet Franc, Virginia $18.   84

Bright ruby with a garnet edge. Forward cedar and wood aromas. A firm entry leads to
a medium-bodied palate with grippy, angular tannins. Lean, firm finish. Showing some
substance. Drink now or later.

1997 Cabernet Sauvignon, Virginia $15.   81

NV Merlot, Lot 97, Virginia $12.99.   83

Medium ruby red with a subtle fade on the rim. Generous minerally, wood spice aromas.
A supple attack leads a medium-bodied palate that has crisp acids and moderate, soft
tannins. Drink now.

Williamsburg

NV Governor's White, American $6.49.   83

Bright straw hue. Reserved flower and mineral aromas. A lush entry leads a medium-
bodied palate, with crisp acidity. Rounded, flavorful finish. Stylish. Drink now.

NV James River White, American $6.49.   80

1997 Chardonnay, Vintage Reserve, Virginia $21.   81

1993 Gabriel Archer Reserve, Virginia $21.   85

Pale cherry red. Medium-bodied. Moderately extracted. Mildly tannic. Red fruit,
minerals, sun-dried tomatoes. Muted aromatics. The dry and dusty palate has some
sweet cherry hints and a solid minerally backbone. Subtle bitter hints on the finish.

1995 Merlot, Reserve, Virginia $18.   82

Willowcroft

1997 Chardonnay, Reserve, Virginia $13.   81

1996 Cabernet Franc, Virginia $16.   84

Bright ruby hue with a slight fade. Medium-bodied. Full acidity. Moderately extracted.
Heavily oaked. Mildly tannic. Menthol, minerals, brown spices. Quite aromatic, with
oak-driven flavors riding a lean and angular frame. Finishes with some snap.

Wintergreen

Raspberry Wine, Virginia $11.97/375 ml.   84

Bright ruby-garnet cast. Medium-bodied. Full acidity. Moderately extracted. Dried herbs,
minerals. Carries a big herbal note throughout. Lighter in style, with an angular finish
and a hint of sweetness.

six

Other U.S. Wines

An Introduction: Other U.S. Wines

Grape growing and winemaking is actually practiced all around the United States—some places more probable than others—but it's a big country with lots and lots of microclimates that make wine production possible in a range of locales. The most important centers tend to be in the Midwest, on the Great Lakes, in Missouri, and in the Southwest.

The Heartland

In the Midwest, there are small wine industries all around the Great Lakes, but particularly along Lake Erie and Lake Michigan. Both Ohio and Michigan boast a number of family wineries, capable of producing surprisingly good wines. The vines are usually planted near the lakes, where the moderating climactic influence of the water allows the vines to survive the brutally cold winters. Nonetheless, summers can be short and cool, and it is with white wines that the best results are achieved. As for Missouri, the heat of the southern heartland comes more into play, and a wider range of wines is produced. The industry is centered on Augusta, midway between Kansas City and St. Louis, and was largely pioneered by German settlers. The area remains true to its German heritage to this day, and has become a popular tourist destination. Perhaps unsurprisingly, given the summer heat, the region has made a name for itself by the production of convincing port-styled wines. This is not to pigeonhole area vintners, however, as truly exciting reds and even some decent whites are known to pop up every now and again.

The Southwest

Finally, though it may sound like more Texan bravado, the Southwest—from west Texas through New Mexico and even into Arizona—is actually capable of producing decent wines. The Texans are centered in the famous Hill Country west of Austin. The dry, hot, arid climate is perfect for grapevines, with little threat of inopportune freezes, problematic humidity, or rain at harvest. This makes for big, ripe—the uncharitable would add occasionally roasted—wines. The industry has really just gotten going, and there's lots of land out there, so it's difficult to make generalizations, but there are some promising reds being produced. The ubiquitous Chardonnay makes an appearance as well, confirming its well-deserved moniker as the "weed" of the wine world.

Chipotle and Champagne

Northern New Mexico, being high desert (New Mexicans like to point out that their state would be bigger than Texas if similarly flattened out), actually has a more variable climate than the Texas Hill Country. Wineries tend to be far flung, but the wines on the whole are amazingly convincing. Gruet, a sparkling wine firm based in Albuquerque, and founded by two Frenchmen from Champagne no less, must surely be among the most improbable wineries in the country. While their fellow countrymen have made major investments in California, these brothers took a detour. As with many stories such as this, there seems to have been a woman involved. At any rate, Gruet is one of the finest producers of sparkling wine in the country, and a favorite of adventurous restaurants from coast to coast. Albuquerque is also home to one of my favorite wine festivals in

Scale: Superlative (96-100), Exceptional (90-95), Highly Recommended (85-89), Recommended (80-84), Not Recommended (Under 80)

the world. The New Mexico Wine Fair is usually held on Labor Day weekend, right around the Route 66 festival and one of many ballooning events. With the spectacular mountain scenery, the sophisticated southwestern cuisine, and a glass of Gruet Blanc de Blancs, it is a wine experience like no other in the world.

Reviews

Ackerman (Iowa)
Apricot Wine, $6.50.   93

Very deep yellow-gold. Full-bodied. Full acidity. Highly extracted. Apricots, spice, mint. Complex and pungent aromatics have a botrytis-like edge. Full and viscous in the mouth, with marked sweetness balanced by razor-sharp acidity. Structured almost like an ice wine.

Blackberry Wine, $6.50.   85

Bright garnet cast. Full-bodied. Balanced acidity. Highly extracted. Red fruits, minerals. Forward and unusual aromatics lead to a ripe and viscous mouthfeel. Quite sweet, though an edge of acidity lends a sense of balance to the finish. Fine length.

Alba (New Jersey)
Red Raspberry Wine, $9.99/500 ml.   91

Light ruby-garnet cast. Full acidity. Highly extracted. Dried herbs, red fruits. Rather unusual aromatics lead a lighter-styled palate feel, with an extremely tart finish.

Bartlett (Maine)
Sweet Raspberry Wine,
Maine $9.99/375 ml.   91

Deep ruby-garnet cast. Moderately full-bodied. Full acidity. Highly extracted. Raspberries. Pleasantly aromatic, with a wave of pure raspberry flavors. Full in the mouth, with an overtone of sweetness balanced by tart acidity. Chocolate, anyone?

Coastal Apple & Pear Wine, $8.99.   87

Bright straw cast. Medium-bodied. Full acidity. Moderately extracted. Green apples, minerals. Pleasantly aromatic, with a well-defined wave of appley flavors. Lush but crisp in the mouth, with a slight hint of sweetness balanced beautifully by vibrant acidity. Well balanced and intense.

Other U.S. Wines at a Glance

Wines Reviewed:

144

Producers/Brands Represented:

39

Peach Wine, Semi-Dry, $11.99.   **85**
Deep yellow-gold. Moderately full-bodied. Full acidity. Highly extracted. Minerals, peaches. Features a rather unusual note on the nose that doesn't follow through to the palate. Firm and well-structured mouthfeel, with vibrant acidity balancing an overtone of sweetness and making for a dry finish.

Pear Wine, Dry, $9.99.   **81**

Pear Wine, French Oak Dry, $14.99.   **90**
Bright golden cast. Moderately full-bodied. Full acidity. Highly extracted. Mildly oaked. Pears, spices, minerals. Quite aromatic, with a very pure, pearlike note accented by well-integrated, spicy oak nuances. Mouthfilling and firm, with angular acidity and lengthy flavors. Intense and focused.

Wild Blueberry Wine, Oak Dry, $14.99.   **87**
Deep blackish ruby cast. Medium-bodied. Full acidity. Moderately extracted. Mildly tannic. Black fruits, dried herbs. Pleasantly aromatic, with a complex set of flavors. Firm and well structured in the mouth, with rather forceful acidity that makes for a drying finish. Flavorful and intense.

1994 Wild Blueberry Wine, Oak Dry, Winemakers Reserve, $21.99.   **93**
Very deep blackish ruby cast. Full-bodied. Balanced acidity. Highly extracted. Mildly oaked. Mildly tannic. Vanilla, cherry cordial, black fruits. Quite aromatic, with a distinctive spicy oak overlay to the deep core of dark fruit flavors. Firmly structured and well balanced, with a lengthy, intense finish.

Bell Mountain (Texas)
1995 Pinot Noir, Bell Mountain $12.   **80**

Biltmore (North Carolina)
NV Blanc de Blanc, North Carolina $16.99.   **81**

Chateau Biltmore 1995 Blanc de Blanc, North Carolina $24.99.   **81**

NV Chardonnay, American $14.99.   **86**
Bright straw cast. Medium-bodied. Balanced acidity. Moderately extracted. Mildly oaked. Vanilla, minerals, nuts. Forward aromas show an enticing leesy accent. Finishes in a lush and generous manner.

NV Merlot, American $13.99.   **81**

Cabernet Sauvignon, American $12.99.   **86**
Saturated brilliant red-purple. Medium-bodied. Highly extracted. Moderately oaked. Moderately tannic. Black cherries, minerals. Very expressive primary fruit aromas follow through on a lush entry that turns minerally and dry through the finish. Drinkable.

1997 Chateau Biltmore Cabernet Sauvignon, North Carolina $19.99.   **89**
Saturated purple. Moderately full-bodied. Highly extracted. Moderately tannic. Cassis, vanilla, licorice. Bright, spicy primary fruit aromas. Dense and saturated, with bright fruit flavors on entry that turn dry and lean through the finish. Better in a few years.

1997 Chateau Biltmore Vanderbilt Claret, North Carolina $19.99.

Boordy (Maryland)
1997 Seyval Blanc, Sur Lie Reserve, Maryland $8.50.   **80**

Cap Rock (Texas)
NV Sparkling Wine, American $12.99.   **86**
Bright yellow-straw hue. Medium-bodied. Tropical fruit, grass, minerals. Floral, grassy aromas follow through on the palate, with a decidedly grassy finish. Nonclassical flavors are refreshing and generous through the midpalate.

1997 Chardonnay, Texas $8.99.   **83**

Bright straw cast. Moderately full-bodied. Full acidity. Moderately extracted. Minerals, citrus. Aromatically reserved, with a steely and angular mouthfeel. Crisp and vibrant through the finish.

1997 Topaz Royale White, Texas $6.99.   **80**

1996 Cabernet Sauvignon, Texas $7.99.   **81**

1996 Cabernet Sauvignon, Reserve, Newsom Vineyard,
Texas High Plains $12.99.   **82**

Cedar Creek (Wisconsin)

1998 Semi-Dry Riesling, American $7.   **83**

Very pale straw. Lean aromas show a minerally, floral note. A juicy entry leads a medium-bodied palate, with bright apple flavors that linger on the finish. Decent flavor concentration. Drink now.

1997 Semi-Dry Vidal Blanc, American $7.   **81**

NV Cranberry Blush, American $7.   **87**

Saturated pale pinkish garnet hue. Intense sweet berry aromas leap from the glass. A crisp entry leads a zesty, medium-bodied palate that shows great acidic cut and a touch of sweetness. Juicy, flavorful finish. Drink now.

Chaddsford (Pennsylvania)

1997 Chardonnay, Pennsylvania $10.   **84**

Pale straw cast. Moderately light-bodied. Full acidity. Moderately extracted. Dried herbs, minerals. Forward herbal aromas lead a clean and snappy mouthfeel. Crisp and linear through the finish.

1995 Chardonnay, Philip Roth Vineyard, Pennsylvania $26.   **89**

Bright straw cast. Medium-bodied. Balanced acidity. Moderately extracted. Moderately oaked. Toasted coconut, minerals, citrus. Forward oak-accented aromas merge with firm minerally flavors in the mouth. Crisp and austere on the palate, with fine grip and intensity through the finish.

1995 Chardonnay, Stargazers Vineyard, Pennsylvania $24.   **84**

Bright yellow-gold. Moderately full-bodied. Full acidity. Moderately extracted. Moderately oaked. Brown spices, citrus, minerals. Carries a generous oak accent to a core of lean citric flavors. The flavors are ripe, though snappy and crisp through the finish.

1996 Cabernet Franc, Pennsylvania $18.   **86**

Bright ruby hue with a slight purple cast. Medium-bodied. Full acidity. Moderately extracted. Mildly oaked. Mildly tannic. Green vegetables, vanilla. Carries a big spicy oak streak, and shows an underlying core of underripe flavors. The summary effect is a lighter-styled, interesting wine, with a Loire-like flavor profile.

1995 Merican Red, Pennsylvania $29.99.   **83**

Ruby red with a lightening rim. Medium-bodied. Moderately extracted. Moderately tannic. Brown spice, earth. Lean, herbal aromas follow through on the palate, with bright acids and a minerally character that lingers on the finish. A reserved style with some bitter elements.

1997 Johannisberg Riesling, Sweet Late Harvest Style $18.   **83**

Pale straw hue. Subdued mineral and talc aromas. A rich entry leads a sweet, medium-bodied palate that has sturdy acidic balance. Straightforward, woolly finish. Drink now.

Chalet Debonné (Ohio)

1998 Riesling, Lake Erie $8.49.   **81**

1998 Riesling, Reserve, Grand River Valley $8.49.   **83**

Bright pale straw hue. Crisp citrus zest aromas. A vibrant entry leads a moderately light-bodied palate, with clean, mineral-edged flavors through the finish. Drink now.

Chateau Elan (Georgia)

Georgian-Style Port, American $22.   83

Deep blackish garnet cast. Medium-bodied. Balanced acidity. Moderately extracted. Peaches, blackberries, minerals. Extremely fragrant, with an unusual, high-toned fruit quality throughout. Lighter on the palate, with a sense of brightness through the finish. Interesting.

Chateau Grand Traverse (Michigan)

1996 Chardonnay, Barrel Fermented, Old Mission Peninsula $12.49.   83

Deep straw cast. Medium-bodied. Full acidity. Moderately extracted. Minerals, citrus. Aromas show subtle vanilla notes. Clean and focused, with an angular minerally mouthfeel. Crisp and zesty finish.

1996 Chardonnay, Reserve, Old Mission Peninsula $13.99.   84

Bright straw cast. Moderately full-bodied. Balanced acidity. Moderately extracted. Mildly oaked. Minerals, toast, brown spices. Forward aromas carry a pleasant oaky accent. Ripe and lush in the mouth with a snappy finish.

1997 Dry Johannisberg Riesling, Michigan $9.99.   81
1997 Semi-Dry Johannisberg Riesling, Michigan $9.99.   82
1997 Late Harvest Johannisberg Riesling, Michigan $12.49.   83

Medium gold-straw hue. Pear and apple aromas have mild herbal overtones. A vibrant entry leads a medium-bodied palate, with mild sweetness, stone fruit flavors, and a drying finish. Drink now.

1997 Dry Johannisberg Riesling, Select Harvest,
Old Mission Peninsula $12.49.   84

Medium yellow-straw cast. Varietally pure aromas of wax and minerals. A crisp entry leads a medium-bodied palate, with tart acids and an angular finish that shows a good persistence of dry flavors. This would be a good foil for lighter foods. Drink now.

1995 Merlot, Reserve, Old Mission Peninsula $23.99.   80
1995 Pinot Noir, Limited Release, Old Mission Peninsula $13.49.   81

Dos Cabezas (Arizona)

1997 Chardonnay, Reserve, Cochise County $18.   88

Deep yellow-gold. Full-bodied. Full acidity. Highly extracted. Oranges, cream, spice. Full and ripe, with an intense, weighty mouthfeel. Spritzy acidity lends a sense of buoyancy to the finish. A rich, flavorful style.

1997 Pinot Gris, Cochise County $14.95.   87

Deep yellow-gold. Moderately full-bodied. Balanced acidity. Moderately extracted. Moderately oaked. Toasted coconut, minerals, smoke. Oak is readily apparent on the nose and is joined by an exotic spicy note on the palate. Full and ripe, with richness tempered by acidity through a weighty, smoky finish.

1997 Petite Sirah, Cochise County $15.   87

Saturated dark purple. Moderately full-bodied. Highly extracted. Moderately tannic. Prunes, herbs. Complex, savory herb and fleshy fruit aromas. A silky mouthfeel has inky, rich black fruit that stands up to the tannic structure. This is drinking well now. A touch overripe.

Elk Run (Maryland)

1997 Chardonnay, Liberty Tavern Reserve, Maryland $15.   84

Deep yellow-gold. Aromas show a heavy buttery quality. A rich entry leads a full-bodied palate with a thick, glycerous mouthfeel and full buttery flavors. Fruit flavors are more subdued, though acids are in balance. A rich style. Drink now.

1998 Gewürztraminer, American $13.25.   81
1998 Johannisberg Riesling, American $12.   81

1997 Cabernet Franc, Maryland $15.   **82**

1997 Cabernet Sauvignon, Maryland $15.   **86**

Saturated ruby red hue. Intense, unusual anise and brown spice aromas show a big oak accent. A lean entry leads to a medium-bodied palate with firm grippy tannins and crisp acidity. Angular, flavorful finish. Drink now or later.

1997 Merlot, Maryland $18.   **84**

Saturated dark violet-ruby hue. Distinctively toasty aromas. A thick entry leads a moderately full-bodied palate with clunky, mean tannins. Rather inky and ungenerous through the finish. Drink now.

1997 Johannisberg Riesling, Vin de Jus Glacé, American $20/375 ml.   **80**

Fall Creek (Texas)

1997 Sauvignon Blanc, Texas $8.50.   **81**

1996 Meritus, Texas Hill Country $29.   **83**

Medium ruby red with a lightening rim. Medium-bodied. Moderately extracted. Moderately tannic. Cedar, red fruits, minerals. Very spicy, oak-driven aromas follow through on the palate, with a dry, lean character and a short finish.

Firelands (Ohio)

NV Riesling, Lake Erie $10.95.   **86**

Bright yellow-straw cast. Medium-bodied. Full acidity. Citrus, tropical fruits, minerals. Quite aromatic, with bright, Riesling-like flavors. Firm and frothy in the mouth, with refreshing acidity and a hint of sweetness to round things out.

1998 Gewürztraminer, Lake Erie $8.99.   **83**

Deep straw hue. Generous spicy aromas jump from the glass. A rich entry leads a fat, moderately full-bodied palate, with a bit of acidity through the finish that lends a sense of balance. Straightforward, tasty finish with a touch of sweetness. Drink now.

Fredericksburg Winery (Texas)

1997 Cabernet Sauvignon, Winecup, Texas $14.95.   **86**

Saturated dark ruby hue. Medium-bodied. Moderately extracted. Heavily oaked. Mildly tannic. Chocolate, spice, black fruits. Exotic toasted oak aromas show spicy complexity that comes through on the palate. Velvety, rich flavors are harmonious; despite the hefty oak accent, this does not turn too dry.

Good Harbor (Michigan)

1997 Semidry White Riesling, Leelanau Peninsula $8.   **88**

Rich golden hue. Deep, ripe tropical aromas. A rich entry leads a moderately full-bodied palate with a glycerous mouthfeel and a note of persistent fruit sweetness on the finish. Drink now.

Cherry Wine, Michigan $5.   **89**

Bright ruby red with a garnet tinge. Medium-bodied. Full acidity. Highly extracted. Black cherries. Pure and expressive aromatics are well translated onto the palate. Vibrant and racy, with tart acidity that balances a hint of sweetness in the finish. Flavorful and intense.

Grande River (Colorado)

1997 Chardonnay, Grand Valley $12.99.   **83**

Green-straw hue. Moderately full-bodied. Balanced acidity. Nuts, butter. Yeasty, faintly oxidized aromas. Soft nutty flavors emerge on a buttery mouthfeel with underlying lemon notes.

1996 White Meritage, Grand Valley $8.99.   **85**

Deep golden cast. Full-bodied. Low acidity. Moderately extracted. Vanilla, blanched almonds. Distinctive aromas lead a fat, viscous mouthfeel that concludes with marked dryness.

1996 Viognier, Grand Valley $19.99.   **84**
Bright golden hue. Moderately full-bodied. Balanced acidity. Moderately extracted.
Minerals, oranges, flowers. Aromatically reserved, with delicate though complex flavors
on the palate. Features fine length and intensity with solid grip.

1994 Grand Valley $12.99.   **88**
Deep brick red. Medium-bodied. Moderately extracted. Moderately tannic. Earth, brown
spice, leather, mint. Generous earthy, spicy nose. Astringent, earthy palate has plenty of
character and a mature flavor profile. Interesting and flavorful.

1995 Meritage, Grand Valley $12.99.   **81**

1996 Meritage, Grand Valley $12.99.   **86**
Bright cherry red hue. Perfumed spice, mineral, and red fruit aromas. A lean attack
leads to a medium-bodied palate with angular, grippy tannins and sturdy acidity. Crisp,
stylish finish. Drink now or later.

1996 Merlot, Grand Valley $11.99.   **87**
Bright ruby red to the rim. Powerful cedar, herb, and red fruit aromas show a big oak
accent. A firm attack leads a medium-bodied palate with solid tannins. Mouthwatering,
buoyant, flavorful finish. Well balanced and showing classic Merlot flavor complexities.
Drink within five years.

1996 Syrah, Grand Valley $15.99.   **84**
Bright purple-red hue. Forward overripe red fruit and mineral aromas. A smooth attack
leads a medium-bodied palate, with silky tannins. Supple, fruity finish. A pleasant
quaffing style. Drink now.

Gruet (New Mexico)

NV Blanc de Noirs, New Mexico $14.   **84**
Pale straw cast with a slight copper tinge. Moderately full-bodied. Full acidity. Fruit, citrus,
minerals. Carries a fruity overtone throughout. Lush and generous on the palate, with an
ample mouthfeel. Well balanced and flavorful, this would partner well with food.

NV Brut, New Mexico $14.   **83**
Medium yellow-straw hue. Medium-bodied. Full acidity. Minerals, citrus. Refined and
quite aromatic. Very full, fine-beaded carbonation with rounded, intense flavors that have
a spicy, toasty quality persisting through the finish. Very distinctive flavors.

1994 Blanc de Blancs, New Mexico $20.   **87**
Bright green-straw cast. Moderately full-bodied. Full acidity. Highly extracted. Smoke,
toast, minerals. Forward and attractive aromatics show a vibrant, toasty, smoky edge.
Firm and aggressive in the mouth, with zesty carbonation and a racy finish.

1997 Chardonnay, New Mexico $13.   **82**

Henke (Ohio)

NV Riesling, American $10.37.   **86**
Bright pale gold hue. Oily, tropical fruit aromas. A flavorful attack leads a medium-
bodied palate, with bright acids and classic oily, minerally Riesling flavors that linger
on the finish. Drink now.

1997 Seyval, Ohio River Valley $9.   **83**
Deep yellow-straw hue. Powerful smoke and vanilla aromas show a hefty oak accent.
A lush entry leads a medium-bodied palate that has a firm acidic edge. Rich. Rather
like a flashy, oak-dominated Chardonnay. Drink now.

1997 Vidal Blanc, Ohio River Valley $8.49.   **83**
Pale green-straw hue. Quite aromatic, with a grassy, grapefruit-flavored character. A juicy
entry leads a medium-bodied palate that has good flavor concentration and persistence
through the finish. Drink now.

Hermannhof (Missouri)

1997 Vignoles, Missouri $13.99.   80

Indian Creek (Idaho)

1997 Chardonnay, Idaho $9.95.   86

Pale green-gold. Aromatically restrained with subtle oak spice and citrus fruits. A juicy attack leads a medium-bodied palate with crisp, subtle fruit flavors well balanced by oak. A light, precise, cool climate style. Drink now.

1998 White Riesling, Idaho $6.95.   84

Bright pale platinum hue. Ripe, sweet apple aromas. A juicy entry leads a medium-bodied palate with moderately sweet flavors of ripe apples and peaches. The finish is clean. A softer, sweeter style. Drink now.

Kokopelli (Arizona)

1996 Cabernet Sauvignon, Arizona $9.   80
1995 Pinot Noir, Arizona $9.   80

L. Mawby (Michigan)

NV Blanc de Blanc Brut, Michigan $15.   84

Bright yellow-gold. Moderately full-bodied. Full acidity. Highly extracted. Cream, toast, butter. Ripe and opulent aromas are unusual, but complex. Firm and intense in the mouth, with aggressive carbonation and a flavorful finish.

NV Cremant Brut, Leelanau Peninsula $18.   86

Deep pale gold hue. Medium-bodied. Minerals, biscuits. Aromatically reserved, but well balanced and flavorful on the palate, with a sense of biscuity richness. Crisp through the finish.

NV Talisman Brut, Leelanau Peninsula $22.   87

Bright pale gold cast. Moderately full-bodied. Full acidity. Yeast, cream. Forward aromas show yeast-accented complexity. Full and rounded in the mouth, with judicious carbonation, this shows fine length and intensity.

Lonz (Ohio)

3 Islands American Ruby Port, $6.50.   86

Deep ruby with brick rim. Moderately full-bodied. Balanced acidity. Moderately extracted. Heavily oaked. Medium sweetness. Reminiscent of dried orange peel, vanilla, raisins. Richly textured, firmly structured on the palate, and layered with distinctive sweet, woody nuances.

Meier's (Ohio)

No. 44 American Ruby Port, $6.95.   86

Deep brickish garnet hue. Medium-bodied. Balanced acidity. Moderately extracted. Medium sweetness. Reminiscent of nuts, earth, coffee, cherries. Well focused and firmly textured, with sweet fruit nuances that play into the finish. Surprisingly well integrated for a "Port" of this price.

No. 44 Cream Sherry, $7.49.   80

Messina Hof (Texas)

1995 Cabernet Sauvignon, Barrel Reserve, Texas $9.99.   87

Bright brick red. Medium-bodied. Moderately extracted. Mildly tannic. Leather, brown spice, earth, dried fruits. Very aromatic leathery, spicy aromas have baked accents. Rich, solid mouthful of earthy flavors has a smoothly textured mouthfeel and a subtle lingering finish showing supple tannins.

Mount Pleasant (Missouri)

1996 Chardonel, Augusta $14. **88**

Bright straw hue. Attractive vanilla and spice aromas. A lush entry leads a medium-bodied palate with bright acidity and judicious oak. Rich, flavorful finish. Quite stylish. Drink now.

1997 Rayon d'Or, Missouri $14. **82**

1994 Cabernet Sauvignon, Augusta $35. **83**

Medium ruby red. Medium-bodied. Moderately extracted. Moderately oaked. Mildly tannic. Raspberry, cedar, toasted oak. Perfumed oak spice aromas follow through on a lighter-styled palate, with bright berry fruit flavors and mild tannins. Oak character is very prominent.

1994 Belle Yvonne, Missouri $50. **92**

Bright cherry red. Medium-bodied. Moderately extracted. Mildly tannic. Dill, brown spice, cherries. Hugely toasty oak nose leads a smooth, mellow palate with an extravagant oak character that persists through a long chocolatey, spicy finish. Very elegant and distinctive, though maybe not for everyone.

1994 Merlot, Augusta $45. **85**

Saturated dark ruby hue. Impressive chocolate and black fruit aromas show a heavy oak accent. A solid attack leads to a moderately full-bodied palate with dry gripping tannins and lively acids. Quite complex and chocolatey through the finish. The oak might be too much for some palates.

1994 Pinot Noir, Augusta $25. **83**

Pale garnet orange. Moderately light-bodied. Subtly extracted. Mildly tannic. A minerally, dusty nose leads a crisp, lean mouthful of flavors with a brief, dry finish.

JRL's Barrel Select Port, Augusta $11.95. **85**

Reddish brick hue with a distinctly browning rim. Medium-bodied. Highly extracted. Mildly tannic. Reminiscent of earth, dates, coffee. A caramelized coffee note runs through this. Though somewhat tawny in style, it still has plenty of stuffing.

1990 Port, Augusta, Missouri $18. **86**

Opaque blackish garnet cast. Moderately full-bodied. Low acidity. Highly extracted. Charred yeast, smoke, treacle. Features an odd charred note in the nose that is hard to overlook. Lean and drying through the finish. Strange.

1996 White Port, Augusta Missouri $25/375 ml. **86**

Deep straw cast. Moderately full-bodied. Balanced acidity. Moderately extracted. Blanched almonds, petrol, flowers. Quite aromatic and very traditional, with a touch of heat. Full, flavorful, and well balanced in the mouth, with a rounded, though not heavy, impression. Fresh, stylish, and convincing.

15 Barrel Tawny Port, Augusta $23.50. **88**

Bright pale amber. Medium-bodied. Full acidity. Moderately extracted. Medium sweetness. Reminiscent of golden raisins, toffee, pralines. Thick, slightly syrupy textured fruit is countered by a pleasant, acidic snap. Assertive dried fruit notes last well into the finish, accompanied by a pleasant warmth.

Tawny Port, Library Vol. V, Augusta Missouri $28. **85**

Bright orange-copper cast. Medium-bodied. Balanced acidity. Moderately extracted. Roasted nuts, caramel, brown spices. Pleasantly aromatic, with lush wood accents throughout. Rich and harmonious on the palate, with a well-balanced, lengthy finish.

1993 Vidal Blanc, Individual Berry Select, Augusta $30/375 ml. **85**

Very deep, tawny amber hue. Unusual, pungent, raisiny aromas show a spicy, woody quality. A rich entry leads a silky, medium-bodied palate with lots of sweetness. Exceptionally flavorful and forceful, like a spice bomb, but a bit off center. A love it or hate it style. Drink now.

Pend d'Oreille (Idaho)

1996 Chardonnay, Idaho $14.99.   81

1996 Cabernet Sauvignon, Idaho $15.99.   80

Sakonnet (Rhode Island)

1997 Chardonnay, Southeastern New England $15.95.   84

Pale yellow-straw hue. Lean citrus aromas. A bright attack leads a medium-bodied palate with pure citrus flavors and tart acids through the finish. Very fresh, pure style with no oak influence. Drink now.

1997 Gewürztraminer, Southeastern New England $14.95.   84

Bright yellow-straw hue. Aromatically subdued, with clean, minerally citrus flavors in the mouth. Medium-bodied and crisp, with vibrant acidity. Spicy, flavorful finish. Drink now.

1995 Pinot Noir, Southeastern New England $14.99.   81

St. Julian (Michigan)

1996 Chardonnay, Barrel Select, Michigan $12.95.   81

1997 Riesling, Michigan $11.99.   83

Pale green-straw hue. Crisp, tart fruit aromas. A vibrant entry leads a medium-bodied palate with white peach flavors and a note of glycerine on the mouthfeel. Finishes cleanly. Drink now.

1997 Seyval Blanc, Sweet Reserve, Lake Michigan Shore $6.50.   81

1997 Vidal Blanc, Sweet Reserve, Lake Michigan Shore $6.50.   83

Pale green-straw hue. Moderately aromatic with clean melon and citrus accents. A juicy entry leads a medium-bodied palate, with sweetness coming through on the finish. A straightforward off-dry style. Drink now.

1997 Vignoles, Michigan $9.50.   80

1995 Merlot, Lake Michigan Shore $20.   84

Deep blackish ruby hue. Medium-bodied. Full acidity. Highly extracted. Heavily oaked. Moderately tannic. Sour cherries, sweet herbs, vanilla. Aromatic, with a lean and austere palate feel that has up-front acidity. Mild astringency on the finish, but quite good length.

1995 Pinot Noir, Lake Michigan Shore $24.   86

Pale crimson hue. Moderately light-bodied. Moderately extracted. Mildly tannic. Vanilla oak aromas show crisp red berry accents with herbal nuances. Quite perfumed, with delicate flavors that have citrus acidity through the finish. Fresh style.

Catherman's Port, Michigan $12.   81

Solera Cream Sherry, Michigan $12.   88

Deep mahogany color with a slight greenish cast. Moderately full-bodied. Balanced acidity. Salted nuts, caramel, toffee. Shows attractive and authentic aromatics, with genuine complexity. Lush and sweet in the mouth, with a lengthy finish. Impressive.

Raspberry Champagne, Michigan $8.50.   88

Bright ruby-garnet cast with a slight fade. Medium-bodied. Full acidity. Highly extracted. Red fruits, minerals. Pleasantly aromatic, with gentle fruit overtones. Fully sparkling on the palate, with spritzy acidity balanced by a hint of sweetness. Flavorful and intense.

Ste. Chapelle (Idaho)

NV Brut, Idaho $7.99.   81

NV Johannisberg Riesling, Sparkling, Idaho $7.99.   84

Pale platinum cast. Moderately full-bodied. Full acidity. Highly extracted. Citrus peel, minerals. Pleasantly aromatic, with a firm and tart impression on the palate. Bright, angular, and citrusy through the finish.

1996 Chardonnay, Idaho $9.   **86**

Bright pale straw hue. Medium-bodied. Full acidity. Moderately extracted. Toasted oak, citrus. Austere minerally aromas lead a lean, angular palate punctuated by tart acidity. The mouthfeel has a rounded character, with a touch of smoky oak for complexity.

1996 Chardonnay, Canyon, Idaho $8.   **84**

Pale straw color. Moderately light-bodied. Balanced acidity. Moderately extracted. Tart apple, citrus. Faintly grassy, appley aromas lead straightforward, clean citrus flavors that linger on the finish.

1996 Fumé Blanc, Idaho $8.   **84**

Pale green-straw color Medium-bodied. Balanced acidity. Highly extracted. Grass, minerals, lemons. A very grassy, herbal nose reveals a flavorful palate that does not show primary fruit flavors. Finishes with authority.

1995 Cabernet Sauvignon, Washington $8.   **89**

Brick red. Medium-bodied. Moderately extracted. Moderately oaked. Moderately tannic. Candied red fruits, vanilla. Lean and taut, with elegant fruit flavors and drying tannins. A tougher style that is not built for cellaring, it will show best with food.

1995 Cabernet Sauvignon, Sagemoor's Dionysus Vineyard,
Washington $12.99.   **86**

Deep brick red. Medium-bodied. Moderately extracted. Moderately tannic. Black tea, earth, coconut. Dry and austere, this features drying tannins through the finish, with much primary fruit sensation.

Ste. Genevieve (Texas)

NV Sauvignon Blanc, Texas $4.99.   **86**

Pale yellow-gold, brilliant clarity. Medium-bodied. Balanced acidity. Moderately extracted. Lemons, limes, minerals. Smoky, citrusy aromas lead a fresh, lively palate that has fine flavors on the midpalate and good grip through the finish.

NV White Zinfandel, American $4.99.   **82**

NV Pinot Noir, Texas $8.99/1.5 L.   **83**

Bright violet red. Medium-bodied. Moderately extracted. Mildly tannic. Sweet cherries, blueberries. Attractive candied fruit aromas lead a ripe, fruity mouthful with the softest of tannins on the finish. Easy drinking, attractive.

Stone Hill (Missouri)

1997 Seyval, Missouri $9.99.   **82**

1997 Seyval, Barrel Fermented, Missouri $11.99.   **82**

1994 Estate Bottled Port, Hermann $23.99.   **83**

Saturated black cherry color. Moderately full-bodied. Highly extracted. Mildly tannic. Reminiscent of black cherries, earth, minerals. Expressive fruity aromas. Rich black fruit entry gives way to a solid minerally finish.

1997 Late Harvest Vignoles, Missouri $19.99/375 ml.   **85**

Deep copper hue. Exotic apricot and nutty nuances. A sweet entry leads a medium-bodied palate, with generous flavors and lean acidity. The finish is clean. Stylish and well balanced. Drink now.

Valley Vineyards (Ohio)

1997 Seyval, Ohio River Valley $7.75.   **86**

Bright straw hue. Generous spice and vanilla aromas. A rich entry leads a rounded, buttery palate that has balanced acidity. Harmonious and showy. Drink now.

1997 Semi-Sweet Vidal Blanc, Ohio River Valley $7.75.   **81**

Scale: Superlative (96-100), Exceptional (90-95), Highly Recommended (85-89), Recommended (80-84), Not Recommended (Under 80)

1997 Vidal Blanc, Ice Wine, Ohio River Valley $22/375 ml.   **85**
Bright yellow-straw hue. Toasty, buttery, honeyed aromas. A lush entry leads a medium-bodied palate featuring lots of sweetness. Spicy, rounded finish. Supple. Drink now.

Westport Rivers (Massachusetts)
1994 Brut RJR Cuvée, Southeastern New England $24.95.   **82**
1994 Blanc de Noir, Southeastern New England $28.95.   **87**
Very pale copper cast. Full-bodied. Full acidity. Highly extracted. Cream, yeast, toast. Attractive yeasty aromas lead a rich, ripe, racy palate feel. Intense and flavorful through the finish, showing excellent grip and length.

1992 Blanc de Blanc, Southeastern New England $34.95.   **84**
Bright yellow-straw cast. Medium-bodied. Full acidity. Lime zest, minerals. Aromatically reserved, with firm, zesty flavors and a steely mouthfeel. The finish is angular and flavorful.

1995 Chardonnay, Silver Label, Southeastern New England $14.95.   **81**
1997 Chardonnay, Silver Label, Southeastern New England $15.95.   **86**
Bright yellow-straw hue. Crisp citrus aromas. A very bright attack leads a medium-bodied palate with vibrant acids and tart fruit flavors. The oak influence is very subtle. Taut, pure, clean style that would be good with seafood. Drink now.

Wollersheim (Wisconsin)
NV White Riesling, American $7.   **84**
Pale straw hue. Mild aromas of apples and minerals. A sweet fruit attack leads a moderately light-bodied palate. Mild flavors finish quickly, leaving a subtle herbal impression. Drink now.

NV Dry Riesling, American $8.   **84**
Very pale straw hue. Clean, bright aromas of white peach and herbs. A juicy entry leads a medium-bodied palate, with juicy acids lingering on the finish. Very refreshing. Drink now.

NV Seyval Blanc, Prairie Fumé, American $8.   **83**
Bright platinum-straw hue. Lean, minerally aromas. A crisp entry leads a medium-bodied palate, with tart acidity offsetting a hint of sweetness. Finishes on an aggressive phenolic note. Shows some clean intensity. Drink now.

NV Seyval Blanc, River Gold, American $6.50.   **80**
1998 White Marechal Foch, Prairie Blush, Wisconsin $7.50.   **90**
Pale cherry hue with a slight fade and a gentle spritz. Generous berry, herb, and toast aromas. A crisp entry leads a medium-bodied palate that has lots of flavor and lean, mouthwatering acidity. Snappy, tasty finish. Very refreshing. Drink now.

1997 Pinot Noir, Cuvée 961, American $12.   **84**
Pale cherry red. Moderately light-bodied. Subtly extracted. Mildly tannic. Crisp fruits, minerals. Subtle tart berry aromas follow through to a crisp yet flavorful palate, with hints of oak spice lingering.

seven

The Wines of Canada

An Introduction: The Wines of Canada

Canada actually had a reasonably early start in North American winemaking. Sources claim Johann Schiller as being the father of the Canadian wine industry. Schiller was a German émigré who fought in the British army and took up winemaking on his discharge. Count Justin M. de Courtenay purchased his estate in 1864. De Courtenay, a man of letters, was certainly one of the earliest advocates of Canadian wines. He considered it feasible to produce Canadian wine the equal of, if not better than, those of Burgundy, and he told government ministers and officials of this view in his many letters. From his vineyards in Ontario he sent wine to be evaluated at a Paris exposition. The French tasters pronounced it to be similar to Beaujolais of that era, and commended it as worthy and *solide*, being of 13% alcohol in strength. Unfortunately this was not sufficient for the government to maintain his grant, so he ceased operation in 1878.

Subsequent to these early trials, indigenous "foxy" table grape varietals formed the backbone of grapes crushed for wine production in Canada until recently. Furthermore, World War I and 11 years of Prohibition have left a legacy of provincial control of alcoholic beverages that persists to this day. This Canadian wine of the past was frequently of dubious quality, often adulterated and fortified, and historically protected by steep tariffs.

Since the early '80s, Canadian winemaking has undergone a renaissance and small estate wineries are now creating a stir domestically and abroad. Canada, and particularly Ontario, has made international waves with its Icewines, and is producing serious table whites and reds from classic varieties and hybrids. In a short period of time Canada has developed a quality-minded commercial wine industry. The northerly location of Canada's wine-growing regions, the most important of which is the Niagara Peninsula, necessitates a preponderance of white varietals, which ripen more easily than reds.

As for popular whites, lean crisp Chardonnays are typical, though richer barrel fermented styles are also produced. Riesling is the most widely planted aromatic varietal and it renders a crisp lively style of wine. Gewürztraminer, Pinot Blanc, and sturdy hybrid varietals, are also widely planted.

Canada is not yet attracting international attention with its dry white wines in the manner that it is with its dessert wines. Because of its marginal climate, pioneering winemakers are still establishing its best vineyard locations. Very little dry white Canadian table wine is exported to the United States. Nonetheless, much palatable wine is produced, and it is well received on their domestic market. As things continue to improve and the industry continues to mature, certain sites and varietals will no doubt come to the fore, and Canadian whites will no doubt be seen with more regularity south of the border.

Dessert Styles

As for those dessert styles, Canada has slowly but surely been building a reputation as one of the world's most abundant and consistent producers of Icewine, a style of wine most closely associated with Germany. In Germany, Icewine is produced in miniscule quantities at astronomical prices; and even then, only in favorable years.

Most of Canada's Icewine is produced on the Niagara Peninsula, a cool growing region that can always count on a sustained cold spell in January to freeze Riesling or Vidal grapes on the vine. These grapes, when pressed in their frozen state, produce extraordinarily concentrated sweet wines with enough acidity to keep them fresh and uncloying. Given Canada's northerly latitude, other regions, particularly the Okanagan Valley in British Columbia, are also proving able to make outstanding Icewines. U.S. consumers have not yet been urged to seek these gems by the mainstream media; hence, these wines are not in widespread distribution. Devotees and enthusiasts will have to look to specialist wineshops in major markets.

Ontario and B.C.: The Canadian Wine Country

Ontario provides 85% of Canadian wine, and is by far the most important province for wine production in Canada. All the growing regions are within hailing distance of a climate-moderating body of lake water. The three designated viticultural areas are Pelee Island, Lake Erie North Shore, and the Niagara Peninsula.

Ontario is a cool climate growing region with an abundance of microclimates whose potential is still being explored and realized. As with the Finger Lakes in New York State, there is still a valid place for hybrid varietals such as Vidal and Seyval. It is a tricky business to get noble varietals such as Chardonnay to ripen consistently in every vintage. Further, reliable ripening of the classic red varietals is by no means guaranteed. Consequently, white varietals account for the bulk of plantings. However, excellent Merlots, Pinot Noirs, and some Cabernets can be produced in years such as 1991 and 1995 when these varietals do fully ripen. The vagaries of vintage are not at all unlike some European regions.

The conventional wisdom seems to be that, stylistically, Ontario winemakers are not seeking to, and indeed cannot, emulate full-blown Californian wines. They do, however, have an eye on subtlety and elegance. The pace is being set by boutique wineries in these regions, in marked contrast to the former pre-

Canada at a Glance

Wines Reviewed:

153

Producers/Brands Represented:

29

eminence of the old, long-established volume wine producers. The present emphasis is on quality as the provincial liquor board no longer has the liberty to protect Canadian wines by excessively marking up imported wines—a consequence of GATT protestations by European trade ministers.

The Okanagan Valley

British Columbia has four designated viticultural regions, of which the most important is the Okanagan Valley. Planted vineyard acreage is approximately a seventh of that in Ontario.

The Okanagan Valley is 100 miles long from north to south and is situated inland in the central southern part of B.C., north of the increasingly famous Columbia Valley in Washington State. Like much of Washington, the climate is great for the production of red wines toward the southern part, where conditions are semi-arid and irrigation is required. These distinct climactic conditions exist for about 15 miles at the very southern point of the valley. Germanic white varieties predominate toward the northern part of the valley where the nearby presence of lake water moderates the climate.

Virtually all wine production is consumed within the province, but the potential indicated by the best Merlots and Pinot Noirs from the Okanagan Valley is very promising in these early days of Canada's revamped wine industry, and already seem to at least rival the best reds produced in Ontario.

Reviews

Calona

1996 Chardonnay, Artist Reserve Series, Okanagan Valley $8.50.   **82**

1997 Chardonnay, Artist Series, Okanagan Valley $8.25.   **86**

Brilliant yellow-straw cast. Generous pleasant spice and vanilla aromas belie hefty wood treatment. A supple attack leads to a medium-bodied palate with balanced acidity through a persistent oaky finish. A clean, flavorful, oaky style. Drink now.

1995 Chardonnay, Private Reserve, Okanagan Valley $12.   **83**

Pale yellow-straw hue. Medium-bodied. Moderately extracted. Moderately oaked. Clean, simple apple and tart peach flavors have a nutty edge through the finish. Quite fresh, though not showing great concentration.

1996 Artist Reserve Series, Sovereign Opal, Okanagan Valley $6.25.   **80**

1996 Pinot Blanc, Artist Reserve Series Burrowing Owl Vineyard, Okanagan Valley $7.10.   **83**

Pale yellow. Medium-bodied. Moderately extracted. Sweet and tangy, with simple, light, floral fruit salad flavors. Quite juicy through the finish. Clean aperitif style.

1997 Pinot Blanc, Artist Series, Okanagan Valley $7.61.   **83**

Pale yellow straw. Clean, buttery aromas with a note of ripe citrus fruits. A bright entry leads a medium-bodied palate with a broad texture and attractive citrus flavors through the finish. Well balanced. Drink now.

1997 Pinot Gris, Artist Series, Okanagan Valley $6.97.   **83**

Very pale platinum-straw hue. Mild aromas show a hint of smoke and a note of citrus zest. Brightly acidic on the attack, leading a medium-bodied palate with clean flavors and minerally accent through the finish. Drink now.

1997 Fumé Blanc, Private Reserve, Okanagan Valley $9.50. 85

Pale brilliant straw hue. Subtle, clean bread dough and citrus aromas. Subtle wood treatment is apparent. A soft attack leads to a medium-bodied palate with balanced acidity. Smooth in character. Lingering flavorful finish. An ideal match for sole or delicate fish. Drink now.

1996 Semillon, Private Reserve, Burrowing Owl Vineyard, Okanagan Valley $10.70. 86

Medium straw color. Medium-bodied. Moderately extracted. Heavily oaked. Smoky vanilla aromas are very pronounced. The palate shows a heavy layer of toast and smoke, with supporting rounded citrus oil flavors. Quite exotic. Good with smoked foods, maybe.

1995 Optima, Private Reserve, Late Harvest, Botrytis Affected, Okanagan Valley $12.50/375 ml. 86

Brilliant yellow-gold. Medium-bodied. Moderately extracted. Nice floral, botrytized aromas lead a subtly sweet, almost grapey palate that concludes with a complex spicy finish.

1995 Ehrenfelser, Private Reserve, Late Harvest Botrytis Affected, Canada $21/375 ml. 90

Full orange-gold. Full-bodied. Low acidity. Pure honeyed apple aromas lead a thick, nectarous palate, with enormous concentration and sweetness making this a spectacular but cloying dessert in its own right.

Carriage House

1997 Chardonnay, Okanagan Valley $14. 84

Brilliant yellow-straw hue. Subdued cream and pear aromas. A firm attack leads to a medium-bodied palate with crisp acidity. Rich, rounded finish. Clean and refreshing, with a round character and no overt signs of oakiness. Drink now.

Cave Spring

1996 Chardonnay, Niagara Peninsula $9.95. 84

Pale straw cast. Moderately light-bodied. Moderately extracted. Moderately oaked. Aromas of pears and apples. Smooth, with a mildly glycerous mouthfeel and a buttery note. Some nutty nuances come through on the finish.

1997 Chardonnay, Niagara Peninsula $11.99. 81
1996 Dry Riesling, Niagara Peninsula $9.95. 80
1997 Riesling, Off Dry, Niagara Peninsula $7.99. 81
1997 Gamay, Niagara Peninsula $8.99. 84

Bright purple-red hue to the rim. Lean mineral and cranberry aromas. A sharp attack leads to a light-bodied palate with vibrant acidity. Clean, snappy finish. A refreshing quaffer. Drink now.

1997 Riesling, Indian Summer, Niagara Peninsula $16.99/375 ml. 88

Pale straw hue. Intense pineapple, ripe pear, and citrus aromas. A crisp attack leads to a medium-bodied palate with vibrant acidity and moderate sweetness. Finishes in a clean, citric manner. Refreshing. Drink now.

1997 Riesling, Icewine, Niagara Peninsula $48.99/375 ml. 95

Rich old gold hue. Generous butter, toffee, and tropical fruit aromas. A lush attack leads to a full-bodied palate with a lot of sweetness. Flavorful, lengthy, viscous finish. Opulent and intense. An impressively rich style of icewine. Drink now.

Cedar Creek

1995 Chardonnay, Okanagan Valley $13.95. 83

Pale silver-straw hue. Moderately light-bodied. Moderately extracted. Mildly oaked. Clean and fresh, with focused citrus flavors and a minerally backbone. Very straightforward and quaffable.

1995 Chardonnay, Reserve, Okanagan Valley $22.95.   **88**

Very pale silver-straw hue. Medium-bodied. Moderately extracted. Moderately oaked. Clean new oak aromas have a perfumed note. The palate is crisp, with focused citrus fruit flavors showing great definition. Vanilla oak flavors taper through the finish.

1995 Merlot, Reserve, Okanagan Valley $24.95.   **83**

Dark ruby red. Medium-bodied. Moderately extracted. Moderately oaked. Mildly tannic. Rich aromas of black fruits, earth, and toasted oak are followed by similar flavors on the palate. Very flavorsome, though not hugely structured. Rather short finish.

1995 Pinot Noir, Okanagan Valley $15.95.   **82**

1995 Riesling, Icewine, Okanagan Valley $49.95/375 ml.   **89**

Pale golden luster. Full-bodied. Hugely sweet and thick. Supersweet pear and apple flavors turn butterscotch-like on the finish. This is impressively sweet.

1995 Chardonnay, Reserve Icewine, Okanagan Valley $59.95/375 ml.   **90**

Pale golden luster. Full-bodied. Toasty, honeyed aromas. A smoky oak component adds complexity to the superrich apple and pear flavors that have a butter and caramel quality through the finish.

Colio

1995 Chardonnay, Lily Sparkling Wine, Ontario $8.   **83**

Pale yellow-straw cast. Medium-bodied. Moderately extracted. Mildly toasty nose with zesty notes leads a lemon zest palate with subtly toasty yeast flavors. Carbonation gives a frothy mouthfeel.

1996 Chardonnay, Lake Erie North Shore $8.   **81**

1996 Riesling-Traminer, Ontario $6.   **84**

Medium yellow-gold. Medium-bodied. Moderately extracted. Peach and grapefruit aromas follow through on a palate distinguished by a rounded mouthfeel with some weight.

1996 Vidal, Icewine, Ontario $20/375 ml.   **85**

Bright yellow. Medium-bodied. Aromas of sweet pears and apples follow through on a pure and concentrated palate with impressive levels of sweetness, though this is not a full-throttled style.

Gray Monk

1996 Gewürztraminer, Reserve, Okanagan Valley $10.95.   **87**

Very pale silver-straw cast. Medium-bodied. Moderately extracted. Perfumed faint lychee aromas are varietally suggestive. Lightly flavored palate, with simple floral accents and a clean finish. Delicate style with faithful aromatics.

1995 Pinot Auxerrois, Okanagan Valley $9.95.   **84**

Pale yellow-gold. Medium-bodied. Moderately extracted. Sweet peach blossom aromas lead a smooth, mildly glycerous mouthfeel, with stone fruit flavors lingering through the finish. Uncomplicated, clean, and easy drinking.

1995 Siegerrebe, Okanagan Valley $10.   **86**

Pale yellow-straw color. Medium-bodied. Moderately extracted. Attractively sweet lychee nut aromas play out on a smooth, rounded palate with a lingering sweet, spicy finish. Fruit cocktail. Highly quaffable.

1995 Pinot Blanc, Okanagan Valley $9.95.   **82**

1995 Pinot Gris, Okanagan Valley $10.95.   **80**

Harrow Estates

1996 Cabernet Franc, Lake Erie North Shore $7.   **81**

Hawthorne Mountain Vineyards

1996 Chardonnay, Okanagan Valley $9.95.   **81**

Scale: Superlative (96-100), Exceptional (90-95), Highly Recommended (85-89),
Recommended (80-84), Not Recommended (Under 80)

1996 Muscat-Ottonel, Okanagan Valley $7.95. **81**

1996 Riesling, Okanagan Valley $7.95. **80**

Hester Creek

1996 Pinot Blanc, Okanagan Valley $7.80. **82**

1996 Pinot Blanc, Grand Reserve, Okanagan Valley $9.25. **86**

Very pale straw hue. Medium-bodied. Moderately extracted. Floral tangerine aromas lead a crisp and spritzy palate, with an impression of faintly sweet fruit that lingers through the finish. Light but fresh, excellent as an aperitif or a shellfish accompaniment.

1996 Pinot Blanc, Signature Release, Okanagan Valley $10.50. **84**

Pale yellow-straw cast. Medium-bodied. Moderately extracted. Mildly oaked. Faintly toasty, smooth, malolactic mouthfeel has no rough edges. Nice crisp lemon flavors through the finish, with well-integrated oak notes.

1997 Cabernet Franc, Okanagan Valley $13. **84**

Bright pale brick-red hue. Forward herb and wood aromas show a marked oak influence. A firm attack leads to a medium-bodied palate with lean, drying tannins. Finish is rather oaky and tannic. Interesting flavors but seems to be drying out. Drink within five years.

1997 Merlot, Okanagan Valley $15. **82**

1997 Cabernet-Merlot, Okanagan Valley $14. **84**

Deep garnet-red hue. Forward iron, red fruit, and spice aromas show a generous oak accent. A crisp attack leads to a medium-bodied palate with grippy tannins and zesty acidity through a clean flavorful finish. A lively, clean, fruit-forward style.

1996 Late Harvest Trebbiano, Grand Reserve,
Okanagan Valley $12.80/375 ml. **88**

Brilliant golden luster. Moderately full-bodied. Moderately extracted. Rich tropical, spicy aromas have a honeyed quality. The palate shows juicy, sweet nectarine and peach flavors in abundance. Very well balanced, with no cloying character.

1997 Trebbiano, Reserve Late Harvest, Okanagan Valley $18/375 ml. **83**

Bright old gold hue. Subdued pear and apple aromas. A crisp attack leads to a medium-bodied palate with mild sweetness and zesty acidity through a clean, fruity finish. Straightforward and racy. Drink now.

1996 Pinot Blanc, Grand Reserve Icewine,
Okanagan Valley $28.50/375 ml. **89**

Brilliant yellow-gold. Medium-bodied. Full acidity. Sweet, crisp apple aromas lead a razor-sharp palate of green apple flavors with impressive sugar and acid levels. This might be better in a year or so when the acids have settled. Classic ice wine structure.

Hillebrand

1997 Trius Barrel Aged Icewine, Niagara Peninsula $50/375 ml. **86**

Rich old gold hue. Intense citrus, butter, and tropical fruit aromas. A lush attack leads to a moderately full-bodied palate with marked sweetness and just enough acidity to prevent this from excessive cloying through a plush, sweet finish. A very sweet style. Drink now.

Inniskillin Okanagan

1995 Merlot-Cabernet Franc, Dark Horse Vineyard,
Okanagan Valley $13.95. **85**

Bright ruby red. Moderately light-bodied. Moderately extracted. Mildly tannic. Black currant aromas lead crisp, high-toned cherry and licorice flavors that expand on the palate, with just a hint of tannin on the finish. Very easy drinking, with some classic flavors.

1995 Dark Horse Vineyard Meritage, Okanagan Valley $17.85. **86**

Full ruby red. Medium-bodied. Moderately extracted. Moderately oaked. Oak and black cherry aromas are well expressed on the palate through to a lingering dry finish. Shows enough structure to allow this to work with richer foods.

Jackson-Triggs

1997 Gewürztraminer, Proprietors' Reserve, Okanagan Valley $6.89.   **86**

Brilliant greenish straw hue. Generous lychee, pineapple, and spice aromas. A brisk attack leads to a moderately light-bodied palate with crisp acidity. Persistent flavorful finish. Well balanced and racy in a lighter style. Drink now.

1997 Pinot Blanc, Proprietors' Reserve, Okanagan Valley $6.90.   **82**

1996 Dry Riesling, Proprietors' Reserve, Okanagan Valley $6.90.   **86**

Luminous yellow-straw hue. Muted clean mineral and slate aromas. A firm attack leads to a medium-bodied palate with crisp acidity. Angular in character with a lingering flavorful finish. Showing the beginnings of a classic petrolly development. Drink now.

1997 Dry Riesling, Proprietors' Reserve, Okanagan Valley $6.90.   **82**

1997 Proprietors' Reserve Blanc de Noir, Okanagan Valley $6.46.   **86**

Brilliant raspberry-pink hue. Clean berry and mineral aromas. A crisp attack leads to a moderately light-bodied palate with zesty acidity. Sharp flavorful finish. A stylish dry Rosé. Drink now.

1996 Merlot, Proprietors' Reserve, Okanagan Valley $11.30.   **86**

Brilliant ruby red hue to the rim. Generous red fruit and mineral aromas carry a spicy oak accent. A firm attack leads to a medium-bodied palate with grippy, lean tannins. Angular, flavorful finish. A focused, well-cut style. Drink now or later. Can improve with more age.

1996 Riesling, Proprietors' Grand Reserve Ice Wine,
Okanagan Valley $44.07/375 ml.   **95**

Dark old gold hue. Powerful, complex honey, nut, and tropical fruit aromas. A ripe attack leads to a full-bodied palate with marked sweetness and angular acidity. Persistent, clean, complex finish. Well balanced and showing a range of flavors beyond the pineapple norm. Drink now or later. Can improve with more age.

1997 Riesling, Proprietors' Grand Reserve Ice Wine,
Okanagan Valley $44.07/375 ml.   **94**

Dark yellow-golden hue. Intense pineapple and honey aromas. A lush entry leads to a full-bodied palate with powerful sweetness balanced by piercing acidity. Sweet, zesty finish. Viscous and very sweet yet tart. A classic Icewine structure. Drink now.

1997 Riesling, Proprietors' Reserve Ice Wine,
Okanagan Valley $31.50/375 ml.   **89**

Dark golden-yellow hue. Pleasant tropical fruit and pineapple aromas. A viscous attack leads to a full-bodied palate with outrageous levels of sweetness. Thick, cloying finish. Hedonistic, but only for those with a real sweet tooth. Drink now.

Konzelmann

1996 Riesling, Niagara Peninsula $9.65.   **82**

1995 Dry Riesling, Late Harvest, Niagara Peninsula $10.95.   **85**

Bright yellow-gold. Medium-bodied. Full acidity. Highly extracted. Nice faintly petrol-accented nose shows good varietal character. The rich, rounded mouthfeel contrasts with the full, assertive tart citrus flavors that have a sense of depth.

1996 Vidal, Icewine, Niagara Peninsula $45.55/375 ml.   **90**

Dark gold. Moderately full-bodied. Highly extracted. Heavy, rich, honeyed aromas lead a tropical fruit palate, with a juicy character on entry that turns a little syrupy through the finish. Impressive, though only for drinking in small quantities.

Lake Breeze

1996 Pinot Blanc, British Columbia $9.   **82**

1996 Semillon, British Columbia $9.50.   **81**

Scale: Superlative (96-100), Exceptional (90-95), Highly Recommended (85-89),
Recommended (80-84), Not Recommended (Under 80)

Lang

1996 Gewürztraminer, Naramata $8.10.   **86**

Bright yellow-straw hue. Medium-bodied. Moderately extracted. Some weight and texture evident. If this is not varietally pure, it at least has some spicy character, with a juicy mouthfeel and nutty notes on the finish.

1995 Riesling, Icewine, British Columbia $33/375 ml.   **89**

Bright pale yellow. Medium-bodied. Moderately extracted. Honeyed pear and apple aromas lead a fresh, racy palate with plenty of sweet but pure flavors. Very clean on the finish. Acids are well matched to the sugar levels.

Magnotta

NV Moscato Superiore, $6.   **83**

Pale straw hue. Typical varietal aromas show a floral, fruity quality. A frothy, well carbonated entry leads a light-bodied palate with bright acids cutting through the residual sweetness. A crisp, quite dry style that remains fresh through the finish.

NV Rossana Blanc de Blancs, Canada $10.   **85**

Medium straw color. Medium-bodied. Highly extracted. Mildly oaked. Full smoky yeast and nutty, oaky aromas. Quite full-blown on the nose and palate, with some green apple fruit flavors in the background. Complex and interesting.

1997 Chardonnay, Barrel Fermented, Ontario $12.   **86**

Rich golden-yellow hue. Forward spice and vanilla aromas belie generous wood treatment. A firm attack leads to a moderately full-bodied palate and a lingering buttery finish. A rich but well-balanced style. An ideal match for lobster, crab, or any rich white fish. Drink now.

1997 Chardonnay, Chile International Series, Maipo Valley-Niagara $5.   **81**

1997 Chardonnay, Limited Edition, Ontario $9.   **81**

1995 Gewürztraminer, Limited Edition, Ontario $8.93.   **88**

Light yellow. Medium-bodied. Moderately extracted. Peach and apricot aromas lead a nutty, lychee-flavored palate that tapers to a lingering finish. Nice texture and mouthfeel give this extra appeal.

1996 Gewürztraminer, Limited Edition, Ontario $9.   **83**

Brilliant yellow-straw hue. Subtle clean mineral and citrus zest aromas. A crisp attack leads to a medium-bodied palate with firm acidity through a vibrant phenolic finish. Well structured but lacks somewhat for flavor intensity. Drink now.

1995 Gewürztraminer, Medium Dry, Ontario $6.39.   **83**

Medium straw color. Medium-bodied. Mildly sweet lychee and peach flavors give a fruit salad impression. Straightforward off-dry style.

1996 Gewürztraminer, Medium-Dry, Limited Edition, Ontario $9.   **86**

Brilliant green-gold hue. Clean and intense citrus zest and spice aromas. A soft attack leads to a moderately full-bodied palate with zesty acidity. Racy flavorful finish. Refreshing and varietally intense. Drink now.

1996 Pinot Gris, Special Reserve, Canada $7.10.   **80**

1997 Sauvignon Blanc, Chile International Series, Niagara-Maipo Valley $5.   **81**

1996 Sauvignon Blanc, Limited Edition, $9.   **83**

Deep, brilliant yellow-straw hue. Intense powerful dried herb and citrus aromas. A firm attack leads to a moderately full-bodied palate with crisp acidity. Quite lively through a clipped clean finish. Shows excellent varietal character but lacks a bit for intensity. Drink now.

1997 Cabernet Sauvignon, Chile International Series, Maipo Valley-Niagara $5.   **81**

1996 Cabernet Sauvignon, Limited Edition, Ontario $13.   **82**

1994 Cabernet Sauvignon, Special Reserve, Canada $7.10.   **83**

Dark cherry red. Medium-bodied. Moderately extracted. Mildly tannic. Good, varietally expressive black currant aromas lead a bright, dry, fruity palate with a minerally backbone that is highlighted by racy acids.

1997 Merlot, Chile International Series, Maipo Valley-Niagara $5.   **84**

Pale ruby-red hue with a fade to the rim. Unusual earth, herb, and mineral aromas. A firm attack leads to a moderately light-bodied palate with drying tannins through a clipped, crisp finish. Shows a particular (sulfur?) note to the nose that seems to blow off with aeration.

1991 Merlot, Limited Edition, Canada $12.50.   **87**

Cherry red with a subtly browning rim. Medium-bodied. Moderately extracted. Moderately oaked. Moderately tannic. Mature, developed aromas show great integration of oak and black fruits that are similarly expressed on the palate. The dry, lingering finish shows some earthy tannins and brown spice notes.

1995 Merlot, Limited Edition, Ontario $11.   **82**

1993 Merlot, Special Reserve, Canada $7.10.   **85**

Bright blood red. Medium-bodied. Moderately extracted. Mildly tannic. Crisp, bright acids carry flavors of cherries and red berry fruits through a minerally finish.

1994 Gran Riserva Red, Ontario $17.   **80**

1994 Gran Riserva Red, Canada $17.86.   **84**

Bright blood red. Medium-bodied. Moderately extracted. Moderately oaked. Moderately tannic. Plenty of concentrated crisp red cherry and berry fruit flavors dominate the palate, with a veneer of toasty oak that dries out the finish.

1991 Cabernet-Merlot, Limited Edition, Canada $11.07.   **82**

1995 Cabernet-Merlot, Limited Edition, Ontario $12.   **81**

1996 Millennium Red, Ontario $20.   **86**

Deep, opaque garnet-red hue. Powerful chocolate and spice aromas show a hefty oak influence. A supple attack leads to a moderately full-bodied palate with plush grippy tannins. Flavorful, well-structured finish. Stylish, weighty, and well balanced. Drink now or later. Can improve with more age.

1995 Syrah, Special Reserve, Canada $7.10.   **83**

Bright pale pinkish red. Moderately light-bodied. Moderately extracted. Mildly oaked. Crisp black and red fruit aromas lead a lively, fresh palate, with a juicy character and a hint of blackberries through a soft finish. Vanilla oak notes are well balanced. Easy-drinking style.

1994 Pinot Noir, Niagara Peninsula $7.10.   **85**

Cherry red center with a pale rim. Moderately light-bodied. Moderately extracted. A toasty, mature nose leads a very well-integrated palate with developed flavors of black cherries, earth, and leather. Quite supple and drinking well now.

1991 Pinot Noir, Limited Edition, Canada $11.79.   **87**

Medium brick-cherry red. Medium-bodied. Moderately extracted. Mildly tannic. Full, aromatic cherry and berry aromas lead a crisp, fruity palate showing good concentration of flavors, with great integration through a lingering finish.

1995 Pinot Noir, Limited Edition, Ontario $13.   **83**

Medium garnet-red hue with a slight fade. Restrained herb and red fruit aromas. A firm attack leads to a moderately light-bodied palate with lean tannins and crisp acidity through the sharp, clean finish. On the green side of the Pinot Noir spectrum, but refreshing. Drink now.

1995 Pinot Noir, Special Reserve, Canada $7.10.   **84**

Medium bright cherry red. Moderately light-bodied. Moderately extracted. Crisp, focused, juicy red cherry flavors on the palate taper to a fruity finish with soft, rounded tannins.

Passito Del Santo, Ontario $11.95/500 ml.   **80**

Framboise, Fortified Raspberry Dessert Wine, Ontario $11/500 ml.   **91**

Opaque ruby-red hue to the rim. Powerful cassis and raspberry aromas. A lush attack leads to a full-bodied palate with moderate sweetness and a hint of tannin. Flavorful, grippy finish. Balanced to drink by itself. Excellent for fireplace contemplation. Drink now.

1997 Vidal, Late Harvest, Niagara Peninsula $9/375 ml.   **83**

Rich old gold hue. Subdued, unusual hay, honey, and smoke aromas. A crisp attack leads to a medium-bodied palate with zesty acidity and marked sweetness. Sharp, flavorful finish. Solid, but lacks somewhat for intensity. Drink now.

1994 Vidal, Select Late Harvest, Ontario $10.70/375 ml.   **86**

Bright golden orange. Medium-bodied. Highly extracted. Faintly nutty, oxidized aromas lead sweet mandarin orange and apple flavors that are focused by crisp acids, keeping this fresh on the palate. Showing some maturity.

1997 Vidal, Icewine, Limited Edition, Niagara Peninsula $40/200ml.   **89**

Deep, brilliant copper-gold hue. Powerful honey, date, and citrus aromas. A racy attack leads to a moderately full-bodied palate with hefty sweetness offset by piercing acids. Persistent, flavorful, and sweet finish. Intense and well structured, this nectarous wine shows admirable balance. Excellent with fruit. Drink now or later. Can improve with more age.

1996 Vidal, Limited Edition Icewine, Niagara Peninsula $19.95/375 ml.   **90**

Dark golden luster. Full-bodied. Full acidity. Full pear and apple aromas lead a palate with impressive sweet fruit flavors and razor-sharp acidity to balance. This has a forceful presence on the palate. Well structured.

1996 Vidal, Sparkling Icewine, Ontario $50/375 ml.   **91**

Bright amber-gold hue with finely beaded, long lasting bubbles and a thin mousse. Powerful pineapple, honey, and citrus aromas. A zesty attack leads to a moderately full-bodied palate with marked sweetness shining through brisk carbonation. Flavorful, sweet, well-balanced finish. An exciting, well-crafted, and very tasty oddity. Excellent with chocolate. Drink now.

Mission Hill

1997 Chardonnay, Grand Reserve, Okanagan Valley $12.   **84**

Luminous golden-yellow hue. Subtle, clean spice and citrus aromas. A crisp attack leads to a medium-bodied palate with racy acidity through a snappy, vibrant finish. A clean and racy Chard with the slightest hint of wood-derived flavors. Drink now.

1997 Chardonnay, Private Reserve, Bin 88, Okanagan Valley $6.   **83**

Brilliant golden-yellow hue. Pleasant spice and vanilla aromas belie mild wood treatment. A firm attack leads to a full-bodied palate with aggressive acidity. Clean sharp finish. Well structured and youthful. Drink now or later. Can improve with more age.

1997 49 North White, Okanagan Valley $5.55.   **81**

1997 49 North Red, Okanagan Valley $5.55.   **82**

1996 Pinot Noir, Grand Reserve, Okanagan Valley $11.   **82**

1997 Pinot Noir, Private Reserve, Okanagan Valley $7.   **86**

Bright garnet-red hue to the rim. Subdued berry and mineral aromas. A firm attack leads to a medium-bodied palate with lean, drying tannins. Clipped, clean finish. Rather ungenerous, but refreshing. Drink now.

Pelee Island Winery

1996 Gewürztraminer, Ontario $6.99.   **80**

1995 Pinot Gris, Ontario $7.99.   **85**

Pale gold. Medium-bodied. Moderately extracted. The rounded mouthfeel has nice texture. Crisp flavors of tart peach and lemon fill the palate. This has some depth and a lingering finish.

1996 Seyval Blanc, Ontario $5.99.   **80**

Peller Estates

1996 Chardonnay, Okanagan Valley $11.99.   **84**

Very pale straw hue. Moderately light-bodied. Moderately extracted. Mildly oaked. Smooth vanilla oak aromas lead a clean citrus palate, with faint orange blossom notes lingering on the finish. Some oak accents are a plus. Very quaffable.

1997 Chardonnay, Founder's Series, Niagara Peninsula $10.   **88**

Dark golden-yellow hue. Subtle vanilla, cream, and spice aromas belie mild wood treatment. A soft attack leads to a medium-bodied palate with gentle acidity. Rich harmonious finish. Elegant and well balanced. Drink now.

1996 Pinot Blanc, Okanagan Valley $11.99.   **85**

Pale yellow-gold. Medium-bodied. Moderately extracted. Peach and melon aromas follow through well on a crisp, well-defined palate. Tart tropical fruit on the lingering finish. Smooth mouthfeel is a plus.

1996 Late Harvest Vidal, Limited Edition Founder's Series, Ontario $15/375 ml.   **83**

Brilliant golden-yellow hue. Powerful pineapple, honey, and citrus aromas. A soft attack leads to a medium-bodied palate with angular acidity and mild sweetness through a clean, vibrant finish. Tasty, but lacks real intensity. Drink now.

1997 Vidal, Icewine, Limited Edition Founder's Series, Niagara Peninsula $45/375 ml.   **91**

Deep old gold hue. Intense honey, smoke, and tropical fruit aromas. A luxuriant attack leads to a moderately full-bodied palate with marked sweetness and just enough acidity for balance. Rich, opulent, rounded finish. Well made and exotic. Drink now.

Pillitteri

1997 Chardonnay, Niagara Peninsula VQA $7.77.   **83**

Deep old gold hue. Powerful butter and spice aromas belie generous wood treatment. A soft attack leads to a full-bodied palate with adequate acidity through a lingering buttery finish. Rather blowsy but tasty. Drink up.

1997 Merlot, Niagara Peninsula VQA $11.97.   **83**

Bright ruby-red hue to the rim. Forward dried herb and mineral aromas. A crisp attack leads to a medium-bodied palate with lean tannins through a crisp, angular finish. Rather ungenerous, but refreshing. Drink now.

1997 Vidal Icewine, Niagara Peninsula VQA $29.97/375 ml.   **98**

Rich copper-gold hue. Powerful date, honey, and tropical fruit aromas. A lush attack leads to a moderately full-bodied palate with marked sweetness and balanced acidity. Sweet, lengthy, flavorful finish. Plush, well balanced, and hedonistic. Drink now.

1996 Vidal, Icewine, Niagara Peninsula $38/375 ml.   **86**

Brilliant deep gold. Moderately full-bodied. Full, ripe aromas are reminiscent of overripe pears. Sweet and nectarous, with a thick mouthfeel that gives a honeyed quality. Impressive, though a tad cloying.

Quails' Gate

1994 Chardonnay, Family Reserve, Okanagan Valley $15.   **86**

Bright yellow-straw hue. Medium-bodied. Moderately extracted. Heavily oaked. Rich, complex nutty aromas. Plenty of oak and mature yeasty flavors dominate the palate, though this is not hugely fruity. Smoky and complex, it will appeal to some palates and not to others.

1995 Old Vines Foch, Okanagan Valley $14.   **91**

Opaque dark purple. Medium-bodied. Highly extracted. Heavily oaked. Exotic, toasty new oak aromas lead a concentrated palate of chocolatey black fruit, with very smoky oak flavors that dominate through the finish. Tannins are quite soft but textured.

Scale: Superlative (96-100), Exceptional (90-95), Highly Recommended (85-89), Recommended (80-84), Not Recommended (Under 80)

1995 Pinot Noir, Okanagan Valley $12.   **80**

1995 Pinot Noir, Family Reserve, Okanagan Valley $15.   **85**

Dark ruby red. Medium-bodied. Moderately extracted. Moderately oaked. Mildly tannic. Rich toasty vanilla oak aromas lead a concentrated palate with red cherry flavors and plenty of vanilla oak notes throughout.

Reif Estate

1996 Late Harvest Riesling, Niagara Peninsula $8.40.   **85**

Pale yellow-gold. Medium-bodied. Moderately extracted. Sweet, faintly petrol-like aromas lead a mildly sweet peach and nectarine palate with a faint herbal backnote. Textured mouthfeel gives a sense of depth.

1996 Vidal, Late Harvest, Ontario $7.50.   **80**

1995 Cabernet Sauvignon, Niagara Peninsula $12.80.   **80**

1996 Vidal, Select Late Harvest, Ontario $13.60/375 ml.   **80**

1996 Vidal, Icewine, Niagara Peninsula $35.60/375 ml.   **91**

Deep golden luster. Moderately full-bodied. Full acidity. Highly extracted. Strong botrytis aromas lead a bright, high-toned palate of juicy sweet apple and apricot flavors. A forceful balance between acids and sugars gives this a classic Icewine structure. Distinguished by a long finish.

Southbrook Farms

NV Cassis, Canada $15/375 ml.   **96**

Deep purplish red. Moderately full-bodied. Big, pure sweet cassis aromas. The palate is packed with pure black currant flavors, with natural levels of sweetness and acidity giving this a mouthwatering finish. An outstanding example that has obvious dessert-matching potential.

NV Framboise, Canada $15/375 ml.   **93**

Deep raspberry red. Moderately full-bodied. Rich, heavy berry fruit aromas. Sensuous and silky, the sweet, fruity palate is just on the right side of cloying. Should provide outstanding pairings with chocolate desserts.

St. Hubertus

1996 Gamay Noir, Okanagan Valley $8.50.   **82**

1996 Pinot Meunier, Oak Bay Vineyard, Okanagan Valley $10.95.   **80**

Stoney Ridge

1995 Chardonnay, Lenko Vineyard, Niagara Peninsula $13.95.   **86**

Pale yellow-straw cast. Medium-bodied. Moderately extracted. Moderately oaked. Lovely nutty, toasty, yeasty aromas play out on a crisp, elegant palate, with a rounded, textured mouthfeel and a lingering toasty yeast finish.

1996 Vidal, Puddicombe Vineyard, Select Late Harvest,
Niagara Peninsula $14.25/375 ml.   **91**

Brilliant yellow-gold. Moderately full-bodied. Full acidity. An intense style, with great concentration of sweet, caramelized apple flavors that expand on the palate. Finishes with a persistent toffeelike note. Verging on cloying, but hugely impressive as a sipping dessert wine.

1996 Riesling-Traminer, Zimmerman Vineyard, Select Late Harvest,
Niagara Peninsula $14.25/375 ml.   **88**

Brilliant yellow-gold. Medium-bodied. Moderately extracted. Honeyed tropical fruit aromas lead a silky smooth palate of sweet, juicy peach and apricot flavors. Very pure and focused flavors through the finish. Glycerous, textured mouthfeel.

1995 Gewürztraminer, Icewine, Niagara Peninsula $35.95/375 ml.   **90**

Bright golden yellow. Moderately full-bodied. Highly extracted. Spicy aromas of nutmeg and tropical fruits follow through on an exotically flavored palate, with a juicy sweet character through the finish. Shows exotic complexity of flavors.

1996 Vidal, Icewine, Niagara Peninsula $28.95/375 ml.   **88**

Deep golden yellow. Full-bodied. Honeyed pear aromas lead a sweet and syrupy palate, with juicy fruit flavors on entry that turn thick through the finish. Nectarous, but only for drinking in small quantities.

1996 Riesling-Traminer, Icewine, Niagara Peninsula $35.95/375 ml.   **90**

Bright yellow-gold. Moderately full-bodied. Rich, sweet, honeyed aromas lead a succulently sweet palate of apple and apricot flavors through the finish. Aromatic varietal character is well defined and complemented by some spicy quality.

Strewn

1996 Chardonnay, Niagara Peninsula $9.95.   **83**

Very pale straw hue. Moderately light-bodied. Moderately extracted. Moderately oaked. A distinctive rich, yeasty nose comes through on the palate with a sense of weight. Quite substantial. Clean citrus flavors.

1996 Vidal, Icewine, Niagara Peninsula $45/375 ml.   **90**

Deep golden luster. Full-bodied. Rich honeyed aromas lead a viscous palate, with caramelized apple and peach flavors through the finish. Racy acids keep this from cloying. Classic Icewine structure.

Sumac Ridge

1993 Steller's Joy Brut, Okanagan Valley $12.95.   **89**

Pale straw cast. Medium-bodied. Moderately extracted. Rich Pinot Noir aromas lead a full, rounded mouthfeel with ripe flavors on a crisp palate. Has a similar flavor profile to a Pinot-rich Champagne. Soft bready notes add depth.

1996 Gewürztraminer, Private Reserve, Okanagan Valley $8.50.   **83**

Pale silver-straw hue. Medium-bodied. Moderately extracted. Tart and sweet citrus aromas, with a juicy, sweet lime zest palate. Long juicy finish. Shows some concentration and depth, though is not overburdened with varietal character.

1996 Pinot Blanc, Private Reserve, Okanagan Valley $9.95.   **82**

1995 Merlot, Okanagan Valley $11.95.   **83**

Dark ruby red. Medium-bodied. Moderately extracted. Mildly tannic. Decent rounded mouthfeel. Flavors of black fruits, licorice, oak spice, and earth that linger on the finish. Drinking well now.

1995 Pinot Noir, Private Reserve, Okanagan Valley $10.95.   **80**

1996 Pinot Blanc, Icewine, Okanagan Valley $19.95/375 ml.   **94**

Pale gold. Full-bodied. Full acidity. Superrich apple and tropical pineapple flavors are well focused through the finish by some piercing acids that give razor-sharp definition. This has the structure to develop further in the cellar.

Sunnybrook Farm

1997 Golden Peach Wine, Niagara $5.25.   **81**

1996 Spiced Apple Wine, Niagara $5.85.   **80**

Tinhorn Creek

1995 Merlot, Okanagan Valley $15.95.   **80**

1996 Pinot Noir, Okanagan Valley $13.95.   **86**

Bright cherry red with purple highlights. Moderately light-bodied. Moderately extracted. Moderately oaked. Mildly tannic. Racy, crisp cherry and blackberry flavors show good concentration, with bright acids highlighting the finish. Has a veneer of toasty oak.

1996 Kerner, Icewine, Okanagan Valley $39.50/375 ml.   **89**

Pale gold hue. Medium-bodied. Full acidity. Tinned fruit salad and honeyed apple flavors expand on the palate. Almost cloying on the finish, though juicy on the entry.

Best Canadian Producers

Canadian Red Wines

Premier Canadian Red Producers (***)
- Inniskillin Okanagan (Meritage)
- Jackson-Triggs (Merlot)
- Stoney Ridge
  (Cabernet Sauvignon, Merlot)
- Tinhorn Creek (Pinot Noir, Merlot)

Great Canadian Red Producers (**)
- Cedar Creek
  (Pinot Noir, Reserve Merlot)
- Lang Vineyards (Foch)
- Magnotta (Limited Edition Series)
- Sumac Ridge (Merlot)

Dependable Canadian Red Producers (Recommended)
Some producers placed in this third tier are new (or new to us) and may merit a higher placement in subsequent vintages. These producers are offset by an asterisk.
- Harrow Estates (Cabernet Franc)
- *Hawthorne Mountain (Merlot)
- *Hester Creek
  (Merlot, Cabernet Sauvignon)
- Mission Hill (Pinot Noir)
- *Pillitteri (Merlot)
- *Quails Gate (Foch, Pinot Noir)
- *Reif (Merlot)
- *St. Hubertus
- *Vineland (Pinot Noir)

Canadian White Wines

Premier Canadian White Producers (***)
- Stoney Ridge (Chardonnay)

Great Canadian White Producers (**)
- Calona (Chardonnay, Semillon)
- Cedar Creek (Chardonnay)
- Colio
- Jackson-Triggs
  (Gewürztraminer, Riesling)
- Konzelmann (Riesling)
- Mission Hill (Riesling)
- Peller Estates (Chardonnay)

Dependable Canadian White Producers (Recommended)
Some producers placed in this third tier are new (or new to us) and may merit a higher placement in subsequent vintages. These producers are offset by an asterisk.
- *Carriage House (Chardonnay)
- *Gray Monk (Gewürztraminer)
- *Lake Breeze (Semillon, Pinot Blanc)
- Magnotta (Limited Edition)
- Mission Hill (Chardonnay)
- Quails' Gate (Chardonnay)
- *Strewn (Chardonnay)
- Sumac Ridge (Gewürztraminer)

Canadian Dessert Wines

Premier Canadian Dessert Wine Producers (***)
- Calona (Late Harvest & Icewines)
- Jackson-Triggs (Grand Reserve Icewine)
- Magnotta (Limited Edition Icewine & Sparkling Icewine)
- Stoney Ridge
  (Select Late Harvest & Icewines)

Great Canadian Dessert Wine Producers (**)
- Cedar Creek (Icewine)
- Colio (Icewine)
- Hester Creek (Icewine)
- Hillebrand (Icewine)
- Jackson-Triggs
  (Proprietor's Reserve Icewine)
- Lang (Late Harvest & Icewines)
- Peller Estates (Icewine)
- Pillitteri (Icewine)
- Strewn Winery (Icewine)
- Sumac Ridge (Icewine)
- Tinhorn Creek (Icewine)

Dependable Canadian Dessert Wine Producers (Recommended)
Some producers placed in this third tier are new (or new to us) and may merit a higher placement in subsequent vintages. These producers are offset by an asterisk.
- *Cave Spring (Icewine)
- *Inniskillin (Icewine)
- *Kittling Ridge (Icewine)
- *Konzelmann (Icewine)
- *London Winery
  (Late Harvest & Icewines)
- *Mission Hill (Late Harvest & Icewines)
- *Reif Estate (Icewine)
- *Stonechurch (Icewine)
- *Strewn Winery (Icewine)
- *Vineland (Icewine)

Section Two: North America's Most Popular Varietals

eight

The Importance
of the
Appellation
to the Consumer

U.S. Wines: Why Is the Appellation (AVA) Important to the Consumer?

What does it mean to rate and review wines? A funny question one might think for people who engage in the effort on a daily basis, but an important one nonetheless. The point of such an exercise should be to provide the consumer with a frame of reference so that you can make informed buying decisions. On the face of it, this sounds simple enough, but the reality of the situation is a bit trickier.

On a monthly basis BTI produces the industry's largest and most comprehensive reviews of U.S. wines on a varietal by varietal basis. Five hundred Chardonnays, 500 Cabernets, 250 Merlots, and the list goes on. Confronted with page after page of names and numbers, the average consumer sets out to buy a bottle of Chardonnay. How is the decision made? I'll have an 89? Give me an 84? Hopefully some information can be gleaned from the tasting notes so that if one style of Chardonnay is preferred over another you will be steered in the right direction, but let's face it; the sheer number of choices has become bewildering.

Additionally, there just isn't that much truly bad wine being produced anymore. The rapid spread of modern winemaking technologies and their ready availability means that even at the least expensive end of the scale, very few wines will be deeply flawed or unpalatable. So then, gone are the early days of wine criticism, when I told you that wine A was bad, wine B was good, and therefore I recommend wine B. The reality is that in today's market the world is full of wine Bs.

We thus have to do more than provide a big list of ratings. We must describe what the wines in question are like in a way that will make sense to you. In order to do that they have to make sense to us first. This is why large categories such as Chardonnay require further subdivisions so that the information becomes more manageable and effective at the same time.

In U.S. categories, where we review over 200 wines of a specific varietal for a report, we taste the wines according to their geographic areas of origin and list them as such. We have been researching U.S. appellations in this manner since 1996 and believe that it is high time American wines were looked at through this rather European perspective. A number of factors have brought us to this conclusion.

It was only a short 20 years ago that the California wine industry was still coping with the devastating after-effects of Prohibition, trying to convince the world that it was an area capable of producing world-class wines. This was often done by holding comparative tastings between the best California wines and benchmarks from Bordeaux or Burgundy. So it was in the '80s as younger industries in Oregon, Washington, and even the East Coast struggled for public recognition by looking to have their wines compared with what had become California benchmarks. We think that at this point few will argue that wine-producing regions in such states as Oregon, Washington, New York, and Virginia are capable of producing world-class wines and sometimes do.

Whether we prefer this Willamette Valley Pinot Noir to that Carneros Pinot Noir might even be irrelevant, because these regions produce two very different versions of the varietal. There are differences between producers within these regions to be sure, but it is a fact that in general terms wines from the two areas just taste differently. If I prefer the style of wine produced in the Willamette and you prefer the style produced in Carneros, my preference becomes largely irrelevant for you. That's where the descriptive part comes in. We prefer to compare apples to apples, oranges to oranges, and then try to tell you what oranges and apples are like.

We attempt to give you more information, so that you can make your own decisions. This is done by highlighting key regions for specific varietals, making generalizations when we can, telling you when we can't, and trying to explain what makes the given area special. It is a long process, and one that has taken several hundred years in Burgundy or Bordeaux for instance, but what we should all be left with down the road is a better appreciation for the art of American viticulture. We will celebrate the differences, for it is these differences that make the world of wine interesting to begin with.

In order to facilitate this, we look at U.S. varietals as a whole according to their AVAs or American Viticultural Areas. The AVA system was adopted by the United States in the early '80s, in hopes of giving the consumer added information along the lines of the French AOC or Italian DOCG systems. Unlike these examples, however, an AVA comes without dictates about which varietals can be planted, yields, or even quality. Every bottle of American wine wears an AVA that tells the consumer where the grapes from which the wine was made came from.

If grapes were blended from various parts of California, the AVA would be California, and the bottle would reflect that. A blend of Napa and Sonoma grapes would be labeled North Coast. A blend of Sonoma AVAs, such as Dry Creek and Russian River Valley, would be labeled Sonoma County, while a wine coming solely from the Russian River will be labeled as such. Certainly the differences between larger or better-established appellations will be that much greater, but we also address the differences, for instance, between subregions within the Napa Valley, and what they might mean to you.

In the following chapters on North American wine styles the most popular varietals—Cabernet Sauvignon, Merlot, Pinot Noir, Zinfandel, and Chardonnay—contain extensive introductions and AVA information. These sections indicate those areas that particularly stand out for the given varietal, followed by a listing of highly recommended wines from that region, which are contained in this book. This means that instead of just looking for that 89-point Chardonnay with the tasting note that sounded intriguing, you might look for an Anderson Valley wine because you like Chardonnay that has firm acidity and makes an excellent aperitif, or maybe the area just sounds interesting. Either way it will be a more informed decision, and hopefully it will increase the chances that you will get what you are looking for.

nine

❧

North American Cabernet Sauvignon and Red Meritage

❧

An Introcuction: American Cabernet Sauvignon and Red Bordeaux Varietal Blends

In many respects the cradle of the resurgence of the American wine industry in the late 20th century was the Napa Valley. The decades of the '60s and '70s saw the rise of the boutique producers in the valley, and a worldwide reputation was rapidly achieved. The varietal with which that reputation was achieved was Cabernet Sauvignon. For years the measuring stick for world-class wine lay in the vineyards of Bordeaux, and as such it was with nothing short of shock that the wine world received the news that a California Cabernet had bested some of these Bordeaux benchmarks in Steven Spurrier's famous 1976 tasting. The revolution was launched, and in turn Napa served as a beacon for other emerging American wine regions. For many the concept of success in producing a great wine was synonymous with producing great Cabernet Sauvignon, and Napa itself had become a benchmark in this country.

Today the wine industries outside the North Coast, not only outside California but in other areas of the state as well, are maturing. They are discovering that producing world-class Cabernet no longer means trying to imitate Napa's wines, and instead they are learning how to deal with their own unique viticultural circumstances. To be sure, regional distinctions are emerging, and other areas are developing their own distinct reputations. Nonetheless, Napa still has much to offer in the way of trends.

Cabernet's Second Coming

Napa Cabernets have lightened up in recent years. After a period in the '70s and early '80s where many vintners thought the bigger the better, today's wine-makers have learned that wines don't need to be inaccessible in youth in order to age. Indeed, wines that are out of balance in youth don't magically come into balance with age. This realization has put Napa's vintners in the forefront with gentler winemaking techniques that emphasize the extraction of softer fruit tannins as opposed to harsh tannins. This has proven to be a real revolution. While critics were enamored of Napa's 1985 vintage, for instance, the tannic structure of many of those wines remains imposing to this day. Many of the wines were out of balance and it was assumed that the tannins would moderate with age. While it is true that the tannins have receded so have the other components in the wines. They are still by and large out of balance, as in many instances thick impressive tannic wines have merely turned into leaner, meaner tannic wines.

This decade has, so far, produced a string of great Cabernet vintages. The use of physiological ripeness and balance as guidelines, as opposed to high sugar levels alone, has made for a radical departure in style. Today's Napa Cabernets are still full-bodied, yet far better balanced than in years past. They are accessible in youth, yet show every indication of aging well. Time will tell, but in the meantime, regions such as the Santa Cruz Mountains and Washington State have followed Napa's lead and are applying these new vinification methods with zeal. The resultant wines are better than ever before, with only one caveat, price. While the quality is in the bottle, prices have jumped at amazing rates, and the best wines have become scarcer than ever. For the Cabernet collector, this

Scale: Superlative (96-100), Exceptional (90-95), Highly Recommended (85-89), Recommended (80-84), Not Recommended (Under 80)

may be good news, but for the Cabernet consumer, much of the category has unfortunately been taken off the everyday table.

Best U.S. Cabernet Producers

Premier U.S. Cabernet and Red Meritage Producers (***)

- S. Anderson (Richard Chambers Vineyard)
- Arrowood (Reserve Speciale)
- Beaulieu (Georges de la Tour)
- Beringer (Private Reserve and Single Vineyard Bottlings available only at the winery)
- Bernardus (Marinus)
- Cakebread (Reserve, Benchland, and Three Sisters)
- Cardinale
- Caymus (Napa Valley and Special Selection)
- Chimney Rock (Napa Valley, Reserve, and Elevage)
- Clos du Val (Reserve)
- Clos Pegase (Hommage)
- BR Cohn (Olive Hill)
- Cosentino (M. Coz Meritage)
- DeLille (Chaleur Estate)
- DeLoach (OFS)
- Diamond Creek (Volcanic Hill, Gravelly Meadow, Red Rock Terrace, and Lake)
- Dominus
- Dry Creek Vineyard (Reserve)
- Far Niente
- Ferrari Carano (Tresor)
- Fisher (Wedding and Lamb Vineyards)
- Flora Springs (Trilogy, Cypress Ranch, and Rutherford Reserve)
- Gallo Sonoma (Northern Sonoma Estate)
- Girard (Napa Valley and Reserve)
- Grace Family
- Grgich Hills (Napa Valley and Yountville Selection)
- Heitz (Martha's Vineyard)
- Hess Collection
- W. Hogue (The Terraces)
- Jarvis (Napa Valley, Reserve, and Lake William)
- Kathryn Kennedy (Santa Cruz Mountains)
- La Jota
- Laurel Glen
- L'Ecole No. 41 (Columbia Valley)
- Le Ducq (Meritage)
- Leonetti
- Merryvale (Profile and Reserve)
- Robert Mondavi (Reserve)

Cabernet at a Glance

Wines Reviewed:

941

Producers/Brands Represented:

397

Median Price:

$24

- Chateau Montelena (The Montelena Estate)
- Mount Veeder Winery (Napa Valley and Reserve)
- Niebaum-Coppola (Rubicon)
- Opus One
- Pahlmeyer
- Peju Province (Napa Valley and HB Estate)
- Joseph Phelps (Napa Valley, Backus, and Insignia)
- Pine Ridge (Stags Leap District, Howell Mountain, and Andrus)
- Plam
- Pride Mountain
- Quilceda Creek
- Ridge (Santa Cruz Mountains and Monte Bello)
- St. Clement (Howell Mountain and Orropas)
- St. Francis (Reserve)
- Chateau St. Jean (Reserve)
- Chateau Ste. Michelle (Horse Heaven, Cold Creek, and Artist Series Meritage)
- Shafer (Hillside Select and Stags Leap District)
- Signorello (Napa Valley and Founder's Reserve)
- Silverado (Limited Reserve)
- Silver Oak (Napa Valley and Alexander Valley)
- Spottswoode
- Stag's Leap Wine Cellars (Cask 23, Fay, and SLV)
- Stonestreet (Legacy)
- Waterbrook
- Whitehall Lane (Reserve)
- Andrew Will (Washington, Sorella, and Reserve)
- Woodward Canyon (Artist Series and Old Vines)

Great U.S. Cabernet and Red Meritage Producers (**)
- Adelaida (San Luis Obispo)
- Altamura
- S. Anderson (Stags Leap District)
- Anderson's Conn Valley Vineyards
- Apex
- Arrowood (Sonoma County)
- Barnard Griffin
- Barnett
- Benziger (Tribute, Reserve, and

Sonoma County)
- Beringer (Knights Valley and Alluvium)
- Byington (Smith Reichel and Bates Ranch)
- Cain (Cain Five)
- Cakebread (Napa Valley)
- Canoe Ridge Vineyard
- Chapellet
- Cinnabar
- Clos du Val
- Clos LaChance
- Clos Pegase (Napa Valley)
- Columbia Winery (Red Willow and Otis)
- Conn Creek (Anthology)
- Cooper-Garrod (Proprietor's Reserve and Santa Cruz Mountains)
- Corison
- Cosentino (Reserve and The Poet Meritage)
- Robert Craig (Affinity)
- Cuvaison (Napa Valley)
- Dalla Valle
- Dehlinger
- DeLille (D2)
- deLorimier (Mosaic)
- Dry Creek Vineyard (Sonoma County and Meritage)
- Dunn
- Gary Farrell
- Ferrari Carano (Sonoma County)
- Fisher (Coach Insignia)
- Thomas Fogarty
- Forman
- Franciscan (Oakville Estate and Magnificat)
- Freemark Abbey (Bosché and Sycamore)
- Gallo Sonoma (Stefani, Barelli Creek, and Frei Ranch)
- Geyser Peak (Reserve, Reserve Alexandre)
- Groth
- Harrison
- Hartwell
- Hedges (Red Mountain Reserve and Three Vineyards)
- Heitz (Trailside Vineyard)
- Hendry
- Herzog (Special Reserve)
- Robert Keenan
- Kendall-Jackson (Grand Reserve and Buckeye Vineyard)
- Kenwood (Artist Series and

Jack London)
- Kathryn Kennedy (Lateral)
- Kiona (Reserve)
- Kunde
- Lambert Bridge
- Langtry
- Lewis
- Liparita
- Louis M. Martini
  (Monte Rosso and Reserve)
- Merryvale (Napa Valley)
- Peter Michael (Les Pavots)
- Robert Mondavi (Napa Valley and SLD)
- Mount Eden (Santa Cruz Mountains and
  Old Vine Reserve)
- Oakville Ranch (Napa Valley and
  Roberts Blend)
- Paradigm
- Pine Ridge (Rutherford)
- Portteus
- Chateau Potelle (VGS and Napa Valley)
- Ravenswood (Pickberry and
  Rancho Salina)
- Martin Ray (Diamond Mountain, Santa
  Cruz Mountains, and Saratoga Cuvee)
- Richardson (Synergy and
  Horne Vineyard)
- St. Clement (Napa Valley)
- St. Francis (Sonoma County)
- Chateau St. Jean (Cinq Cepages)
- Chateau Ste. Michelle (Columbia Valley)
- Seavey
- Sierra Vista (Five Star Reserve)
- Silverado (Napa Valley)
- Simi (Reserve)
- Soquel (Partner's Reserve)
- Staglin
- Stag's Leap Wine Cellars (Napa Valley)
- Stonestreet (Alexander Valley)
- Swanson
- Titus
- Truchard
- Tulocay
- Viader
- Villa Mt. Eden (Signature Series)
- Von Strasser
- Whitehall Lane (Napa Valley)
- ZD

Dependable U.S. Cabernet and Red Meritage Producers (Recommended)

Some producers placed in this third tier are new (or new to us) and may merit a higher placement in subsequent vintages. These producers are offset by an asterisk.

- *Adelaida (Calitage)
- Atlas Peak
- Belvedere
- WB Bridgman
- Burgess
- *Cafaro
- Carmenet
- Cedar Mountain
- Cloninger
- Columbia Crest
- Columbia Winery (Sagemoor and Reserve)
- *Cornerstone
- *Douglass Hill
- *Dunham
- Estancia
- Fetzer
- Gordon Brothers
- Guenoc
- Hanna
- *Havens
- Helena View
- Hogue
- Jordan
- *Judd's Hill
- Kendall-Jackson (Vintners Reserve)
- *Kestrel
- *L'Ecole No. 41 (Seven Hills, Apogee, and Windrow)
- *Livingston
- *Lokoya (Diamond Mountain, Mount Veeder, and Rutherford)
- Markham
- *Matthews (Elerding Vineyard)
- *Neyers
- Pindar
- Powers
- Quail Ridge
- *Quintessa
- *Rancho Sisquoc
- Raymond
- *Rocking Horse
- Rosenblum
- St. Supery
- V. Sattui
- Sequoia Grove

- *Seven Hills
- Seth Ryan
- Simi (Napa Valley)
- Smith & Hook
- Sonoma Creek
- Chateau Souverain
- *Spring Mountain Vineyard
- Stags' Leap Winery
- Staton Hills
- Tefft
- Turnbull
- Villa Mt. Eden (Grand Reserve)
- Windsor
- *Woodside
- Yakima River

Ten Key Regions for American Cabernet Sauvignon and Red Bordeaux Varietal Blends

Napa Valley
Wines Reviewed: **323**
Median Price: **$30.00**

Napa is the nation's "grand cru" appellation, and Napa vintners have been nothing if not successful in marketing the valley as America's wine Eden. Geographically, the Napa Valley is reasonably contiguous, being 34 miles in length and between one and four miles in width from the town of Napa in the south to that of Calistoga in the north. It is an easy region in which to ripen grapes and consistently produces ripe full wines. The cool air from the San Pablo Bay, just north of San Francisco, moves from south to north, thus giving the southern area cooler average temperatures.

An imprecise but useful generalization would be that the cooler southern end is more favorable to white varieties and Pinot Noir while the further north one gets, the more red varietals one will encounter as the temperatures increase, with emphasis on Cabernet. This simplification does not account for the vagaries of soil types, microclimates, and vintners throughout the valley, and as such there are many exceptions to the rule. Nine sub-appellations have been created since the inception of the Napa Valley AVA in 1983 and these go some way toward addressing the differences in climate between some parts of the valley. With the hugely significant exception of Carneros, these sub-appellations are of more relevance to Cabernet than Napa's other darling, Chardonnay.

The coolest area just to the north of Carneros includes Yountville and the Oak Knoll District where a few Cabernets are to be found. Indeed, much of this region is cool enough to produce sparkling wines. Nonetheless, some well-known vintners are here; not the least of which is Dominus. A Yountville style would be hard to pin down as there are relatively few Cabernets and the differences have more to do with winemaking, but a safe generalization would be that the wines are not nearly as thick as those produced up the valley, and that they show a sense of elegance. Still at this cooler end of the valley, yet just to the east of Yountville, lies an extremely prominent appellation for fine Cabernet, the Stags Leap District.

Wine lovers have known for some time that Stags Leap is a special area, as evidenced since the early '70s by the wines of Warren Winiarski at Stag's Leap Wine Cellars. It is cooler than areas to the north, as the ocean winds that move up from the San Pablo Bay act as an air conditioner and moderate the heat of the afternoon that builds up on the bare rocks of the eastern mountains, which allow for the greater ripening potential than Yountville to the west. Those rocks also feature in the very different soil composition of the area. Over 95% of the soil is derived from volcanic rocks, which makes for a gravelly, well-drained, and less fertile environment than that featured in the Rutherford Bench. These factors combine to draw out the ripening process, affording a longer growing season and the possibility of greater physiological maturity than other regions of the valley floor. This translates into a particularly flavorful and supple style of Cabernet, often marked by red berry overtones.

North of Yountville and Stags Leap is the "American Medoc" for Cabernet, the triumvirate of Oakville, Rutherford, and St. Helena, from coolest to warmest, respectively. The names and wines read like a who's who of the wine industry, and this narrow belt of this narrow valley has become world famous. In this area, all factors have come together to make an ideal growing climate for red Bordeaux varietals, with Cabernet Sauvignon at the fore. Furthest to the cooler southern end of the belt, Oakville produces Cabernets of great ripeness and richness with a certain restrained elegance. It is also quite common to see a distinctive minty quality intermixed with the red and black fruit flavors. Rutherford, just to the north, shows Cabernet of marginally greater weight, with considerable depth and remarkably consistent black fruit flavors, while St. Helena Cabernet adds just another layer of weight.

Finally, at the top of the valley and often a good 20 or even 30 degrees warmer than the extreme southern end lies Calistoga. As one might expect, Calistoga Cabernet is big, rich, and ripe, with huge levels of extract. Nonetheless, the wines usually avoid the jammy, porty notes that can sometimes interject themselves into such warm climate wines. Indeed, one of the most difficult factors facing the Calistoga winemaker is managing the abundance of tannins that come naturally to these wines. As such, advances in the management of tannins that have been made in the last decade have helped Calistoga's wines to a great degree.

Highly Recommended Napa Valley Cabernet Sauvignon and Red Meritage

Napa Valley (General)
98 • Jarvis (CA) 1994 Cabernet Sauvignon, Napa Valley. $58.

97 • Jarvis (CA) 1993 Reserve, Cabernet Sauvignon, Napa Valley. $75.

97 • Beringer (CA) 1994 Private Reserve, Cabernet Sauvignon, Napa Valley. $75.

96 • Merryvale (CA) 1994 Profile, Napa Valley. $55.

94 • The Terraces (CA) 1994 Cabernet Sauvignon, Napa Valley. $49.99.

94 • Pahlmeyer (CA) 1995 Red, Napa Valley. $60.

94 • Jarvis (CA) 1996 Lake William, Napa Valley. $48.

94 • Cosentino (CA) 1995 M. Coz Meritage, Napa Valley. $75.

94 • Cakebread (CA) 1995 Benchland Select, Cabernet Sauvignon, Napa Valley. $75.

93 • Silverado (CA) 1994 Limited Reserve, Cabernet Sauvignon, Napa Valley. $50.

93 • Signorello (CA) 1995 Founder's Reserve, Cabernet Sauvignon, Napa Valley. $55.

93 • Signorello (CA) 1994 Founder's Reserve, Cabernet Sauvignon, Napa Valley. $55.

93 • Robert Mondavi (CA) 1995 Reserve, Cabernet Sauvignon, Napa Valley. $75.

93 • Le Ducq (CA) 1994 Meritage, Napa Valley. $99.

93 • Jarvis (CA) 1993 Cabernet Sauvignon, Napa Valley. $55.

93 • Hendry (CA) 1993 Block 8, Cabernet Sauvignon, Napa Valley. $22.

93 • Grgich Hills (CA) 1995 Cabernet Sauvignon, Napa Valley. $45.

93 • Cakebread (CA) 1995 Three Sisters, Cabernet Sauvignon, Napa Valley. $75.

92 • Signorello (CA) 1996 Founder's Reserve, Cabernet Sauvignon, Napa Valley. $75.

92 • Signorello (CA) 1995 Cabernet Sauvignon, Napa Valley. $30.

92 • Quail Ridge (CA) 1993 Volker Eisele Vineyard Reserve, Cabernet Sauvignon, Napa Valley. $39.99.

92 • Philippe-Lorraine (CA) 1996 Cabernet Sauvignon, Napa Valley. $18.50.

92 • Le Ducq (CA) 1993 Meritage, Napa Valley. $91.

92 • Jarvis (CA) 1993 Lake William, Napa Valley. $45.

92 • Conn Creek (CA) 1995 Anthology, Napa Valley. $44.

91 • Silverado (CA) 1994 Cabernet Sauvignon, Napa Valley. $22.50.

91 • Signorello (CA) 1996 Cabernet Sauvignon, Napa Valley. $35.

91 • Robert Mondavi (CA) 1995 Cabernet Sauvignon, Napa Valley. $21.

91 • Merryvale (CA) 1995 Reserve, Cabernet Sauvignon, Napa Valley. $30.

91 • Merryvale (CA) 1995 Profile, Napa Valley. $66.

91 • Joseph Phelps (CA) 1996 Cabernet Sauvignon, Napa Valley. $30.

91 • Grgich Hills (CA) 1994 Cabernet Sauvignon, Napa Valley. $30.

91 • Fisher (CA) 1995 Coach Insignia, Cabernet Sauvignon, Napa Valley. $25.

91 • Cakebread (CA) 1994 Reserve, Cabernet Sauvignon, Napa Valley. $50.

91 • Altamura (CA) 1995 Cabernet Sauvignon, Napa Valley. $40.

90 • ZD (CA) 1993 Reserve, Cabernet Sauvignon, Napa Valley. $45.

90 • William Hill (CA) 1994 Reserve, Cabernet Sauvignon, Napa Valley. $27.

90 • Signorello (CA) 1994 Cabernet Sauvignon, Napa Valley. $30.

90 • Robert Craig (CA) 1994 Affinity, Napa Valley. $33.

90 • Peter Michael (CA) 1994 Les Pavots Red, Knights Valley. $35.

90 • Joseph Phelps (CA) 1995 Cabernet Sauvignon, Napa Valley. $27.

90 • Joseph Phelps (CA) 1994 Cabernet Sauvignon, Napa Valley. $24.

90 • Hendry (CA) 1995 Block 8, Cabernet Sauvignon, Napa Valley. $24.

90 • Cosentino (CA) 1994 The Poet Meritage, Napa Valley. $30.

90 • Cosentino (CA) 1994 Reserve, Cabernet Sauvignon, Napa Valley. $40.

90 • Cakebread (CA) 1995 Cabernet Sauvignon, Napa Valley. $30.

90 • Beaulieu (CA) 1994 Tapestry Reserve, Napa Valley. $20.

89 • Villa Mt. Eden (CA) 1995 Grand Reserve, Cabernet Sauvignon, Napa Valley. $20.

89 • Thomas Fogarty (CA) 1996 Cabernet Sauvignon, Napa Valley. $25.

89 • Rutherford Ranch (CA) 1993 Cabernet Sauvignon, Napa Valley. $12.

89 • Rust Ridge (CA) 1995 Cabernet Sauvignon, Napa Valley. $24.

89 • Robert Mondavi (CA) 1994 Reserve, Cabernet Sauvignon, Napa Valley. $75.

89 • Robert Craig (CA) 1995 Affinity, Napa Valley. $35.

89 • Page Mill (CA) 1995 Macaire, Napa Valley. $32.

89 • Mayacamas (CA) 1992 Cabernet Sauvignon, Napa Valley. $30.

89 • Markham (CA) 1994 Cabernet Sauvignon, Napa Valley. $15.49.

89 • Livingston (CA) 1995 Stanley's Selection, Cabernet Sauvignon, Napa Valley. $24.

89 • Le Ducq (CA) 1995 Meritage, Napa Valley. $65.

89 • Le Ducq (CA) 1994 Sylviane, Cabernet Sauvignon, Napa Valley. $30.

89 • Judd's Hill (CA) 1995 Cabernet Sauvignon, Napa Valley. $28.

89 • Groth (CA) 1995 Cabernet Sauvignon, Napa Valley. $30.

89 • Freestone (CA) 1994 Cabernet Sauvignon, Napa Valley. $15.

89 • Cosentino (CA) 1995 The Poet Meritage, Napa Valley. $38.

89 • Chappellet (CA) 1995 Signature, Cabernet Sauvignon, Napa Valley. $24.

89 • Cafaro (CA) 1995 Cabernet Sauvignon, Napa Valley. $34.

89 • Beaulieu (CA) 1995 Tapestry Reserve, Napa Valley. $24.99.

88 • William Hill (CA) 1995 Reserve, Cabernet Sauvignon, Napa Valley. $27.

88 • Silverado (CA) 1995 Cabernet Sauvignon, Napa Valley. $25.

88 • Quail Ridge (CA) 1995 Volker Eisele Vineyard Reserve, Cabernet Sauvignon, Napa Valley. $40.

88 • Monticello (CA) 1994 Corley Reserve, Cabernet Sauvignon, Napa Valley. $35.

88 • Merryvale (CA) 1993 Profile, Napa Valley. $48.

88 • Markham (CA) 1995 Cabernet Sauvignon, Napa Valley. $19.

88 • Le Ducq (CA) 1995 Sylviane, Cabernet Sauvignon, Napa Valley. $30.

88 • Havens (CA) 1994 Bourriquot, Napa Valley. $28.

88 • Folie à Deux (CA) 1995 Reserve, Cabernet Sauvignon, Napa Valley. $22.

88 • Duckhorn (CA) 1994 Cabernet Sauvignon, Napa Valley. $35.

88 • Cosentino (CA) 1995 Reserve, Cabernet Sauvignon, Napa Valley. $40.

88 • Cakebread (CA) 1994 Cabernet Sauvignon, Napa Valley. $25.

88 • Beringer (CA) 1994 Cabernet Sauvignon, Knights Valley. $20.

87 • ZD (CA) 1994 Cabernet Sauvignon, Napa Valley. $30.

87 • Robert Mondavi (CA) 1994 Cabernet Sauvignon, Napa Valley. $22.

87 • Mirassou (CA) 1995 Harvest Reserve, Cabernet Sauvignon, Napa Valley. $17.95.

87 • Langtry (CA) 1994 Red Meritage, Napa Valley. $41.

87 • Folie á Deux (CA) 1995 Cabernet Sauvignon, Napa Valley. $18.

87 • Farella-Park (CA) 1994 Cabernet Sauvignon, Napa Valley. $28.

87 • Edgewood (CA) 1993 Cellarette Cuvée, Napa Valley. $22.50.

87 • Dunnewood (CA) 1994 Dry Silk, Cabernet Sauvignon, Napa Valley. $9.99.

87 • Clos du Val (CA) 1995 Cabernet Sauvignon, Napa Valley. $24.

87 • Clos du Val (CA) 1993 Cabernet Sauvignon, Napa Valley. $24.

86 • William Hill (CA) 1996 Cabernet Sauvignon, Napa Valley. $18.

86 • Vigil (CA) 1996 Valiente Claret, Napa Valley. $22.

86 • Vigil (CA) 1995 Valiente Claret, Napa Valley. $20.

86 • Stonegate (CA) 1995 Cabernet Sauvignon, Napa Valley. $18.

86 • Quail Ridge (CA) 1995 Cabernet Sauvignon, Napa Valley. $15.99.

86 • Monthaven (CA) 1995 Cabernet Sauvignon, Napa Valley. $9.99.

86 • Mirassou (CA) 1994 Harvest Reserve, Cabernet Sauvignon, Napa Valley. $17.95.

86 • Merryvale (CA) 1996 Hillside, Cabernet Sauvignon, Napa Valley. $18.

86 • Mayacamas (CA) 1993 Cabernet Sauvignon, Napa Valley. $38.

86 • Edgewood (CA) 1995 Cabernet Sauvignon, Napa Valley. $20.

86 • Beringer (CA) 1995 Appellation Collection, Cabernet Sauvignon, Knights Valley. $22.

86 • Beringer (CA) 1995 Alluvium Red, Knights Valley. $30.

85 • Stonehedge (CA) 1995 Cabernet Sauvignon, Napa Valley. $12.99.

85 • Ramspeck (CA) 1995 Cabernet Sauvignon, Napa Valley. $18.

85 • Quail Ridge (CA) 1994 Cabernet Sauvignon, Napa Valley. $14.99.

85 • Marcelina (CA) 1993 Cabernet Sauvignon, Napa County. $20.

85 • Hagafen (CA) 1995 Cabernet Sauvignon, Napa Valley. $20.

85 • Farella-Park (CA) 1995 Cabernet Sauvignon, Napa Valley. $32.

85 • Cosentino (CA) 1995 Cabernet Sauvignon, Napa Valley. $18.

Napa Valley (Calistoga)

95 • Fisher (CA) 1994 Lamb Vineyard, Cabernet Sauvignon, Napa Valley. $50.

93 • Cuvaison (CA) 1994 Cabernet Sauvignon, Napa Valley. $24.99.

93 • Clos Pegase (CA) 1994 Hommage Reserve, Cabernet Sauvignon, Napa Valley. $40.

92 • Fisher (CA) 1995 Lamb Vineyard, Cabernet Sauvignon, Napa Valley. $50.

92 • Chateau Montelena (CA) 1994 Montelena Estate, Cabernet Sauvignon,
Napa Valley. $85.

90 • Chateau Montelena (CA) 1993 Montelena Estate, Cabernet Sauvignon,
Napa Valley. $40.

89 • Guenoc (CA) 1995 Bella Vista Reserve, Cabernet Sauvignon, Napa Valley. $30.50.

89 • Clos Pegase (CA) 1995 Cabernet Sauvignon, Napa Valley. $22.99.

88 • Cuvaison (CA) 1995 Cabernet Sauvignon, Napa Valley. $.

87 • Chateau Montelena (CA) 1995 Calistoga Cuvée, Cabernet Sauvignon,
Napa Valley. $18.

85 • Helena View (CA) 1995 Tradition, Cabernet Sauvignon, Napa Valley. $38.

85 • Guenoc (CA) 1994 Bella Vista Reserve, Cabernet Sauvignon, Napa Valley. $30.50.

Napa Valley (St. Helena)

94 • St. Clement (CA) 1996 Oroppas, Napa Valley. $35.

94 • Spottswoode (CA) 1993 Cabernet Sauvignon, Napa Valley. $42.

94 • Plam (CA) 1995 Vintner's Reserve, Cabernet Sauvignon, Napa Valley. $30.

94 • Beringer (CA) 1993 Private Reserve, Cabernet Sauvignon, Napa Valley. $65.

93 • Spottswoode (CA) 1994 Cabernet Sauvignon, Napa Valley. $45.

92 • Spottswoode (CA) 1995 Cabernet Sauvignon, Napa Valley. $55.

92 • Spottswoode (CA) 1992 Cabernet Sauvignon, Napa Valley. $39.

91 • Louis Martini (CA) 1994 Reserve, Cabernet Sauvignon, Napa Valley. $18.

91 • Forman (CA) 1995 Cabernet Sauvignon, Napa Valley. $40.

90 • Titus (CA) 1994 Cabernet Sauvignon, Napa Valley. $22.

90 • St. Clement (CA) 1995 Oroppas, Napa Valley. $35.

90 • St. Clement (CA) 1994 Cabernet Sauvignon, Napa Valley. $25.

90 • Seavey (CA) 1993 Cabernet Sauvignon, Napa Valley. $28.

90 • Raymond (CA) 1995 Generations, Cabernet Sauvignon, Napa Valley. $50.

90 • Plam (CA) 1994 Vintner's Reserve, Cabernet Sauvignon, Napa Valley. $30.

90 • Flora Springs (CA) 1995 Cypress Ranch, Cabernet Sauvignon, Napa Valley. $40.

90 • Anderson's Conn Valley Vineyards (CA) 1994 Estate Reserve, Cabernet Sauvignon,
Napa Valley. $40.

89 • Neyers (CA) 1995 Cabernet Sauvignon, Napa Valley. $40.

89 • Newton (CA) 1995 Cabernet Sauvignon, Napa Valley. $36.99.

89 • Heitz (CA) 1992 Cabernet Sauvignon, Napa Valley. $20.

89 • Harrison (CA) 1994 Cabernet Sauvignon, Napa Valley. $33.

89 • Beaucanon (CA) 1994 Cabernet Sauvignon, Napa Valley. $14.

88 • Whitehall Lane (CA) 1996 Cabernet Sauvignon, Napa Valley. $22.

88 • V. Sattui (CA) 1995 Suzanne's Vineyard, Cabernet Sauvignon, Napa Valley. $22.50.

88 • Raymond (CA) 1994 Generations, Cabernet Sauvignon, Napa Valley. $35.

88 • Newlan (CA) 1995 Cabernet Sauvignon, Napa Valley. $20.

88 • Guenoc (CA) 1994 Beckstoffer IV Reserve, Cabernet Sauvignon,
Napa Valley. $40.50.

88 • Forman (CA) 1994 Cabernet Sauvignon, Napa Valley. $38.

88 • Conn Creek (CA) 1994 Anthology, Napa Valley. $44.

87 • St. Clement (CA) 1995 Cabernet Sauvignon, Napa Valley. $26.

87 • Raymond (CA) 1996 Reserve, Cabernet Sauvignon, Napa Valley. $23.

87 • Merryvale (CA) 1994 Cabernet Sauvignon, Napa Valley. $27.

87 • Cecchetti Sebastiani (CA) 1993 Cabernet Sauvignon, Napa Valley. $30.

87 • Burgess (CA) 1994 Vintage Selection, Cabernet Sauvignon, Napa Valley. $22.

86 • Van Asperen (CA) 1994 Signature Reserve, Cabernet Sauvignon, Napa Valley. $28.

86 • Raymond (CA) 1995 Reserve, Cabernet Sauvignon, Napa Valley. $20.

86 • Raymond (CA) 1994 Reserve, Cabernet Sauvignon, Napa Valley. $20.

86 • Heitz (CA) 1994 Cabernet Sauvignon, Napa Valley. $25.

86 • Heitz (CA) 1993 Cabernet Sauvignon, Napa Valley. $21.

86 • Guenoc (CA) 1995 Beckstoffer IV Reserve, Cabernet Sauvignon, Napa Valley. $40.50.

86 • Burgess (CA) 1995 Vintage Selection, Cabernet Sauvignon, Napa Valley. $24.

86 • Beaucanon (CA) 1996 Reserve, Cabernet Sauvignon, Napa Valley. $14.

86 • Beaucanon (CA) 1995 Cabernet Sauvignon, Napa Valley. $14.

86 • Anderson's Conn Valley Vineyards (CA) 1995 Estate Reserve, Cabernet Sauvignon, Napa Valley. $48.

85 • V. Sattui (CA) 1994 Suzanne's Vineyard, Cabernet Sauvignon, Napa Valley. $20.

85 • Buehler (CA) 1995 Estate, Cabernet Sauvignon, Napa Valley. $35.

Napa Valley (Rutherford)

95 • Peju Province (CA) 1995 Estate Bottled, Cabernet Sauvignon, Napa Valley. $55.

95 • Lokoya (CA) 1995 Cabernet Sauvignon, Rutherford, Napa Valley. $100.

95 • Caymus (CA) 1994 Special Selection, Cabernet Sauvignon, Napa Valley. $110.

94 • Pine Ridge (CA) 1994 Andrus Reserve, Napa Valley. $85.

94 • Peju Province (CA) 1994 H.B. Vineyard, Cabernet Sauvignon, Napa Valley. $55.

93 • Peju Province (CA) 1995 Cabernet Sauvignon, Napa Valley. $28.

93 • Niebaum-Coppola (CA) 1995 Rubicon, Rutherford, Napa Valley. $65.

93 • Flora Springs (CA) 1995 Trilogy, Napa Valley. $40.

93 • Fetzer (CA) 1994 Reserve, Cabernet Sauvignon, Napa Valley. $28.

93 • Caymus (CA) 1995 Cabernet Sauvignon, Napa Valley. $65.

92 • Whitehall Lane (CA) 1994 Morisoli Vineyard Reserve, Cabernet Sauvignon, Napa Valley. $36.

92 • Staglin (CA) 1995 Cabernet Sauvignon, Rutherford, Napa Valley. $42.50.

92 • Niebaum-Coppola (CA) 1994 Rubicon, Rutherford, Napa Valley. $65.

92 • Freemark Abbey (CA) 1994 Bosché Estate, Cabernet Sauvignon, Napa Valley. $44.

92 • Freemark Abbey (CA) 1992 Bosché Estate, Cabernet Sauvignon, Napa Valley. $27.99.

92 • Caymus (CA) 1994 Cabernet Sauvignon, Napa Valley. $35.

92 • Beaulieu (CA) 1995 Georges de Latour Private Reserve, Cabernet Sauvignon, Rutherford. $59.99.

92 • Beaulieu (CA) 1994 Georges de Latour Private Reserve, Cabernet Sauvignon, Rutherford. $50.

91 • V. Sattui (CA) 1994 Rosenbrand Family Reserve, Cabernet Sauvignon, Napa Valley. $60.

91 • Pine Ridge (CA) 1995 Andrus Reserve, Napa Valley. $85.

91 • Niebaum-Coppola (CA) 1992 Rubicon, Rutherford, Napa Valley. $45.

91 • Heitz (CA) 1993 Trailside Vineyard, Cabernet Sauvignon, Napa Valley. $48.

90 • Whitehall Lane (CA) 1995 Morisoli Vineyard Reserve, Cabernet Sauvignon, Napa Valley. $40.

90 • St. Supéry (CA) 1994 Cabernet Sauvignon, Napa Valley. $15.75.

90 • Quintessa (CA) 1995 Red, Rutherford. $75.

90 • Pine Ridge (CA) 1996 Cabernet Sauvignon, Rutherford, Napa Valley. $25.

90 • Pine Ridge (CA) 1995 Cabernet Sauvignon, Rutherford, Napa Valley. $24.

90 • Helena View (CA) 1992 Cabernet Sauvignon, Napa Valley. $20.

90 • Freemark Abbey (CA) 1992 Sycamore Vineyard, Cabernet Sauvignon, Napa Valley. $26.49.

90 • Flora Springs (CA) 1996 Trilogy, Napa Valley. $45.

90 • Flora Springs (CA) 1994 Trilogy, Napa Valley. $30.

89 • V. Sattui (CA) 1995 Preston Vineyard, Cabernet Sauvignon, Napa Valley. $27.

89 • V. Sattui (CA) 1995 Morisoli Vineyard, Cabernet Sauvignon, Napa Valley. $25.

89 • St. Supéry (CA) 1994 Meritage, Napa Valley. $40.

89 • Sequoia Grove (CA) 1995 Reserve, Cabernet Sauvignon, Napa Valley. $35.

89 • Freemark Abbey (CA) 1993 Sycamore Vineyard, Cabernet Sauvignon, Napa Valley. $28.99.

89 • Corison (CA) 1994 Cabernet Sauvignon, Napa Valley. $35.

88 • Staglin (CA) 1994 Cabernet Sauvignon, Rutherford, Napa Valley. $37.

88 • St. Supéry (CA) 1995 Meritage Red, Napa Valley. $40.

88 • Rocking Horse (CA) 1994 Garvey Family Vineyard, Cabernet Sauvignon, Rutherford. $25.

88 • Freemark Abbey (CA) 1994 Cabernet Sauvignon, Napa Valley. $19.99.

87 • Heitz (CA) 1992 Trailside Vineyard, Cabernet Sauvignon, Napa Valley. $48.

87 • Freemark Abbey (CA) 1995 Cabernet Sauvignon, Napa Valley. $24.

86 • V. Sattui (CA) 1994 Morisoli Vineyard, Cabernet Sauvignon, Napa Valley. $25.

86 • Sequoia Grove (CA) 1995 Cabernet Sauvignon, Napa Valley. $22.99.

86 • Helena View (CA) 1994 Cabernet Sauvignon, Napa Valley. $32.50.

86 • Heitz (CA) 1993 Bella Oaks Vineyard, Cabernet Sauvignon, Napa Valley. $28.

86 • Bell (CA) 1994 Baritelle Vineyard, Cabernet Sauvignon, Rutherford. $50.

85 • V. Sattui (CA) 1994 Preston Vineyard, Cabernet Sauvignon, Napa Valley. $30.

Napa Valley (Oakville)

99 • Opus One (CA) 1995 Oakville, Napa Valley Red. $100.

97 • Opus One (CA) 1992 Oakville, Napa Valley Red. $65.

96 • Opus One (CA) 1993 Oakville, Napa Valley Red. $85.

94 • Opus One (CA) 1994 Oakville, Napa Valley Red. $90.

93 • Joseph Phelps (CA) 1995 Backus Vineyard, Cabernet Sauvignon, Napa Valley. $70.

93 • Joseph Phelps (CA) 1994 Insignia, Napa Valley. $70.

93 • Heitz (CA) 1992 Martha's Vineyard, Cabernet Sauvignon, Napa Valley. $68.

92 • Joseph Phelps (CA) 1995 Insignia, Napa Valley. $75.

92 • Joseph Phelps (CA) 1994 Backus Vineyard, Cabernet Sauvignon, Napa Valley. $70.

92 • Girard (CA) 1995 Cabernet Sauvignon, Napa Valley. $28.

91 • Oakville Ranch (CA) 1994 Robert's Blend, Napa Valley. $45.

91 • Girard (CA) 1994 Reserve, Cabernet Sauvignon, Napa Valley. $40.

91 • Franciscan (CA) 1994 Oakville Estate, Magnificat Meritage, Napa Valley. $25.

91 • Far Niente (CA) 1995 Cabernet Sauvignon, Napa Valley. $70.

90 • Silver Oak (CA) 1994 Cabernet Sauvignon, Napa Valley. $65.

90 • Silver Oak (CA) 1993 Cabernet Sauvignon, Napa Valley. $50.

90 • Girard (CA) 1994 Cabernet Sauvignon, Napa Valley. $25.

90 • Franciscan (CA) 1994 Oakville Estate, Cabernet Sauvignon, Napa Valley. $17.

90 • Far Niente (CA) 1994 Cabernet Sauvignon, Napa Valley. $55.

90 • Dalla Valle (CA) 1993 Cabernet Sauvignon, Napa Valley. $40.

89 • Oakville Ranch (CA) 1995 Robert's Blend, Napa Valley. $45.

89 • Oakville Ranch (CA) 1995 Cabernet Sauvignon, Napa Valley. $35.

89 • Franciscan (CA) 1995 Oakville Estate, Magnificat Meritage, Napa Valley. $30.

88 • Turnbull (CA) 1995 Cabernet Sauvignon, Napa Valley. $20.

88 • Turnbull (CA) 1994 Cabernet Sauvignon, Napa Valley. $22.

87 • Swanson (CA) 1995 Alexis, Napa Valley. $40.

87 • Saddleback (CA) 1996 Cabernet Sauvignon, Napa Valley. $32.

87 • Robert Mondavi (CA) 1995 Oakville, Cabernet Sauvignon, Napa Valley. $27.

87 • Robert Mondavi (CA) 1994 Oakville, Cabernet Sauvignon, Napa Valley. $28.

87 • Oakville Ranch (CA) 1994 Cabernet Sauvignon, Napa Valley. $30.

86 • Swanson (CA) 1994 Cabernet Sauvignon, Napa Valley. $24.

86 • Franciscan (CA) 1995 Oakville Estate, Cabernet Sauvignon, Napa Valley. $17.

85 • Volker Eisele (CA) 1996 Cabernet Sauvignon, Napa Valley. $30.

85 • Volker Eisele (CA) 1995 Cabernet Sauvignon, Napa Valley. $30.

Napa Valley (Stags Leap District)

97 • Stag's Leap Wine Cellars (CA) 1995 Cask 23, Napa Valley. $120.

96 • Stag's Leap Wine Cellars (CA) 1994 Cask 23, Cabernet Sauvignon, Napa Valley. $100.

95 • Shafer (CA) 1994 Hillside Select, Cabernet Sauvignon, Stags Leap District, Napa Valley. $85.

95 • S. Anderson (CA) 1994 Richard Chambers Vineyard, Cabernet Sauvignon, Stags Leap District. $54.

95 • Pine Ridge (CA) 1996 Cabernet Sauvignon, Stags Leap District, Napa Valley. $40.

94 • Stag's Leap Wine Cellars (CA) 1995 SLV, Cabernet Sauvignon, Napa Valley. $70.

94 • Stag's Leap Wine Cellars (CA) 1995 Fay, Cabernet Sauvignon, Napa Valley. $70.

94 • Stag's Leap Wine Cellars (CA) 1994 Fay, Cabernet Sauvignon, Napa Valley. $50.

94 • S. Anderson (CA) 1995 Richard Chambers Vineyard, Cabernet Sauvignon, Stags Leap District. $65.

94 • Hartwell (CA) 1995 Sunshine Vineyard, Cabernet Sauvignon, Stags Leap District. $80.

94 • Chimney Rock (CA) 1996 Cabernet Sauvignon, Napa Valley. $30.

94 • Chimney Rock (CA) 1995 Reserve, Cabernet Sauvignon, Stags Leap District. $50.

93 • Stag's Leap Wine Cellars (CA) 1994 SLV, Cabernet Sauvignon, Napa Valley. $50.

93 • Shafer (CA) 1995 Cabernet Sauvignon, Stags Leap District, Napa Valley. $30.

93 • Shafer (CA) 1993 Hillside Select, Cabernet Sauvignon, Stags Leap District, Napa Valley. $60.

93 • Pine Ridge (CA) 1995 Cabernet Sauvignon, Stags Leap District, Napa Valley. $37.50.

92 • Clos du Val (CA) 1994 Reserve, Cabernet Sauvignon, Napa Valley. $53.

91 • Clos du Val (CA) 1993 Reserve, Cabernet Sauvignon, Napa Valley. $50.

90 • Shafer (CA) 1994 Cabernet Sauvignon, Stags Leap District, Napa Valley. $28.

90 • Chimney Rock (CA) 1995 Elevage, Stags Leap District. $50.

90 • Chimney Rock (CA) 1994 Reserve, Cabernet Sauvignon, Stags Leap District. $50.

90 • Chimney Rock (CA) 1994 Elevage, Stags Leap District. $40.

89 • Stag's Leap Wine Cellars (CA) 1995 Cabernet Sauvignon, Napa Valley. $26.

89 • Shafer (CA) 1996 Cabernet Sauvignon, Stags Leap District, Napa Valley. $35.

88 • Robert Mondavi (CA) 1995 SLD, Cabernet Sauvignon, Napa Valley. $27.

88 • Chimney Rock (CA) 1994 Cabernet Sauvignon, Napa Valley. $26.

86 • Stags' Leap Winery (CA) 1995 Cabernet Sauvignon, Napa Valley. $30.

86 • Pine Ridge (CA) 1994 Cabernet Sauvignon, Stags Leap District, Napa Valley. $35.

85 • Hartwell (CA) 1994 Sunshine Vineyard, Cabernet Sauvignon, Stags Leap District. $45.

Napa Valley (Yountville)

95 • Dominus (CA) 1995 Napanook Vineyard, Cabernet Sauvignon, Napa Valley. $95.

95 • Dominus (CA) 1994 Napanook Vineyard, Napa Valley. $75.

93 • Grgich Hills (CA) 1994 Yountville Selection, Cabernet Sauvignon, Napa Valley. $85.

89 • Rosenblum (CA) 1995 Holbrook Mitchell Trio, Napa Valley. $35.

88 • Dominus (CA) 1992 Napanook Vineyard, Napa Valley. $50.

88 • Charles Krug (CA) 1994 Vintage Selection, Cabernet Sauvignon, Napa Valley. $47.

87 • Rosenblum (CA) 1996 Holbrook Mitchell Trio, Napa Valley. $35.

87 • Rosenblum (CA) 1995 Hendry Vineyard, Reserve, Cabernet Sauvignon, Napa Valley. $40.

86 • Trefethen (CA) 1994 Cabernet Sauvignon, Napa Valley. $24.

85 • Charles Krug (CA) 1994 Peter Mondavi Family, Generations, Napa Valley. $30.

Napa Mountains

Wines Reviewed: **45**

Median Price: **$34**

The Napa Valley is indeed a valley. This means that there are mountains to be found on either side of the valley, and in these mountains, intrepid vintners are to be found toiling away. Though home to a range of sub-appellations, including Atlas Peak, Diamond Mountain, Howell Mountain, Spring Mountain, and Mount Veeder, these Napa mountain districts are still entitled to use the term Napa Valley on their labels. This point serves to illustrate the occasionally silly inadequacies of the AVA system.

Mountain viticulture is quite different from that to be found on the valley floor and an altogether better solution would have been to lump the mountain ranges surrounding the Napa Valley into a Napa Mountains appellation. Nonetheless, these subdistricts, led by Howell Mountain, are making a name for themselves, and connoisseurs in particular are gravitating to these long-lived, imposingly structured wines. As a whole they tend to be quite concentrated with a reputation for backwardness. That may be changing, however, as within the last few years new tannin management techniques have paid enormous dividends. The current crop of wines has actually become approachable virtually on release, while retaining a solid sense of structure that belies their mountain origins. Separate and distinct from the Napa Valley proper, these difficult to farm appellations will never become commercially sizable, but will continue to be of great importance at the quality end of the spectrum for years to come.

Highly Recommended Napa Mountains Cabernet Sauvignon and Red Meritage

Napa Mountains (Atlas Peak)

89 • Tulocay (CA) 1996 Cliff Vineyard, Cabernet Sauvignon, Napa Valley. $21.

88 • Atlas Peak Vineyards (CA) 1994 Cabernet Sauvignon, Atlas Peak, Napa Valley. $18.

87 • Tulocay (CA) 1994 Cliff Vineyard, Cabernet Sauvignon, Napa Valley. $22.

Napa Mountains (Diamond Mountain)

93 • Martin Ray (CA) 1995 Cabernet Sauvignon, Diamond Mountain, Napa Valley. $45.

93 • Diamond Creek (CA) 1995 Volcanic Hill, Cabernet Sauvignon, Napa Valley. $75.

93 • Diamond Creek (CA) 1995 Red Rock Terrace, Cabernet Sauvignon, Napa Valley. $75.

90 • Von Strasser (CA) 1994 Cabernet Sauvignon, Diamond Mountain, Napa Valley. $32.

90 • Diamond Creek (CA) 1994 Volcanic Hill, Cabernet Sauvignon, Napa Valley. $50.

89 • Lokoya (CA) 1995 Cabernet Sauvignon, Diamond Mountain, Napa Valley. $100.

88 • Diamond Creek (CA) 1994 Red Rock Terrace, Cabernet Sauvignon, Napa Valley. $50.

87 • Von Strasser (CA) 1995 Cabernet Sauvignon, Diamond Mountain, Napa Valley. $36.

Scale: Superlative (96-100), Exceptional (90-95), Highly Recommended (85-89), Recommended (80-84), Not Recommended (Under 80)

356

Napa Mountains (Howell Mountain)

97 • Pine Ridge (CA) 1996 Cabernet Sauvignon, Howell Mountain, Napa Valley. $40.

96 • La Jota (CA) 1996 15th Anniversary, Cabernet Sauvignon, Howell Mountain, Napa Valley. $58.

94 • Pine Ridge (CA) 1995 Cabernet Sauvignon, Howell Mountain, Napa Valley. $37.50.

93 • St. Clement (CA) 1995 Cabernet Sauvignon, Howell Mountain, Napa Valley. $45.

93 • La Jota (CA) 1995 Howell Mountain Selection, Cabernet Sauvignon, Howell Mountain, Napa Valley. $30.

92 • St. Clement (CA) 1994 Cabernet Sauvignon, Howell Mountain, Napa Valley. $45.

92 • Dunn (CA) 1993 Cabernet Sauvignon, Napa Valley. $35.

91 • Pine Ridge (CA) 1994 Cabernet Sauvignon, Howell Mountain, Napa Valley. $35.

91 • Cornerstone (CA) 1993 Beatty Ranch, Cabernet Sauvignon, Howell Mountain. $32.

89 • Viader (CA) 1993 Red, Napa Valley. $30.

87 • La Jota (CA) 1996 Howell Mountain Selection, Cabernet Sauvignon, Howell Mountain, Napa Valley. $34.

Napa Mountains (Mount Veeder)

95 • Mount Veeder Winery (CA) 1993 Reserve, Napa Valley. $40.

94 • Hess Collection (CA) 1993 Cabernet Sauvignon, Mount Veeder, Napa Valley. $20.

92 • Mount Veeder Winery (CA) 1995 Reserve, Napa Valley. $50.

92 • Hess Collection (CA) 1995 Cabernet Sauvignon, Mount Veeder, Napa Valley. $24.75.

92 • Chateau Potelle (CA) 1993 Cabernet Sauvignon, Mount Veeder, Napa Valley. $29.

91 • Mount Veeder Winery (CA) 1995 Cabernet Sauvignon, Napa Valley. $30.

91 • Hess Collection (CA) 1994 Cabernet Sauvignon, Mount Veeder, Napa Valley. $19.75.

89 • Chateau Potelle (CA) 1994 VGS, Cabernet Sauvignon, Mount Veeder, Napa Valley. $39.

87 • Lokoya (CA) 1995 Cabernet Sauvignon, Mount Veeder, Napa Valley. $100.

86 • Franus (CA) 1994 Cabernet Sauvignon, Napa Valley. $25.

Napa Mountains (Spring Mountain District)

98 • Pride Mountain (CA) 1996 Cabernet Sauvignon, Napa Valley. $29.99.

93 • Spring Mountain Vineyard (CA) 1993 Miravalle-Alba-Chevalier Red, Napa Valley. $28.

92 • Robert Keenan (CA) 1994 Hillside Estate, Cabernet Sauvignon, Spring Mountain District, Napa Valley. $24.

92 • Barnett (CA) 1995 Cabernet Sauvignon, Spring Mountain District, Napa Valley. $35.

91 • Cain (CA) 1994 Cain Five, Napa Valley. $50.

89 • Robert Keenan (CA) 1993 Hillside Estate, Cabernet Sauvignon, Spring Mountain District, Napa Valley. $23.

87 • Cain (CA) 1995 Cain Five, Napa Valley. $50.

87 • Barnett (CA) 1994 Cabernet Sauvignon, Spring Mountain District, Napa Valley. $35.

86 • Cain (CA) 1995 Cain Cuvee, Napa Valley. $22.

85 • Cain (CA) 1994 Cain Cuvee, Napa Valley. $19.

Sonoma County

Wines Reviewed: **159**

Median Price: **$24**

Trying to pin down a "Sonoma County style" for Cabernet is virtually hopeless. That being said it is important to point out why. Sonoma County is a designation used as a catchall for wines from the far more precise sub-appellations of the Russian River, Dry Creek, Alexander, and Sonoma Valleys, with many further divisions among them. Each area is unique and distinctive. What many producers choose to do, however, is blend wines from the various regions within the county and label accordingly. This is not necessarily a bad thing.

Following the Australian model, it makes perfect sense that if one were trying to make a balanced and well-rounded wine year in and year out, the best solution might be to blend from vineyards that share complimentary qualities. Alexander Valley grapes for richness, Russian River for acidity, and Dry Creek for intensity of fruit perhaps? The resultant wines are quite good and may even be more consistent, but the blending tends to mitigate the notion of terroir, and it is dangerous to attempt to pigeonhole Sonoma County wines as a whole because they are bound to be blended from different regions, in different proportions, and for different reasons. Despite this fact, three regions in particular within Sonoma have become known for the production of high-quality Cabernet: the Alexander, Sonoma, and Dry Creek Valleys.

The Alexander Valley is one of the most notable of the AVAs within Sonoma County for Cabernet. It features one of the warmest climates in Sonoma County, and as such, it is ideally suited to Bordeaux varietals. Although it is only some 18 miles from the ocean, the maritime influence is not what it is in, say, the Russian River Valley, as it is shielded by north-south mountain ranges. Alexander Valley Cabernets tend to be relatively rich, though without the weight one associates with Napa bottlings. Additionally, the acidity levels seem a shade more prominent. In this way, it might be fairly said that Alexander Valley Cabernet is somewhat of a bridge in style between Napa and Sonoma, taking some of the better attributes of each, with a telltale, supple, plummy, fruit-driven quality.

As for the Sonoma Valley, it sits at the southern end of Sonoma County, abutting the Carneros. The valley proper runs between the Mayacamas Mountains, which form the border with Napa, and Sonoma Mountain. As the valley opens up past Sonoma Mountain at the town of Glen Ellen, the climate changes from that in the southern end. The area as a whole is filled with wild and precipitous hills, which afford the vineyards ideal exposures to the sun. This, in combination with a lengthy growing season, moderate temperatures afforded by the cooling breezes of San Pablo Bay and the Petaluma Gap, and fertile though well-drained soils have made for a vine growing Eden. Sonoma Valley Cabernet tends to be quite extracted with exotically deep colors and black fruit aromas. This intensity of fruit character is the wine's hallmark, and despite the unusual level of extract, generally pronounced acidity lends a measure of balance.

As for the Dry Creek Valley, though a stone's throw from the Russian River and Alexander Valleys, it is unique. As usual, Sonoma County's tortured and eternally confusing geography is to blame. The natural boundaries of the valley, however, makes this an exceptionally tight and well-defined appellation. The Dry Creek parallels the Alexander Valley on the western side and drains into the Russian River. From the point where the Dry Creek meets the Russian River, it is a distance of about 16 miles to the point to the northwest where the Dry Creek Valley abruptly ends. Surrounded by mountains on three sides, with the only opening at the Russian River, there is no outlet for wind as in the Alexander Valley. Additionally, what fog that does enter from the Russian River Valley often comes in at night and burns off quickly during the day. Hence, temperatures are far warmer than in the Russian River Valley, particularly at the northern end. The valley is only two miles wide at its widest point, and the valley floor itself is quite narrow. Benchlands and hillsides dominate the region, and in the warmer northern end of the valley, red wine is king.

The Dry Creek area was largely settled in the late 19th century by Italian families, and as in other parts of Sonoma County, Zinfandel was the favored grape, interspersed with the usual blend of black varieties. Cabernet has taken root, however, and the resultant wines have that signature Dry Creek stamp, an exotic briar fruit character with crisp acidity. The wines are lighter in body than those from the Alexander or Sonoma Valleys, yet are well balanced and eminently drinkable.

Highly Recommended Sonoma County Cabernet Sauvignon and Red Meritage

Sonoma County (General)

94 • Ferrari-Carano (CA) 1993 Tresor Reserve, Sonoma County. $55.

94 • Chateau St. Jean (CA) 1992 Reserve, Cabernet Sauvignon, Sonoma County. $45.

93 • Gallo Sonoma (CA) 1994 Estate, Cabernet Sauvignon, Northern Sonoma. $54.99.

92 • Fisher (CA) 1994 Wedding Vineyard, Cabernet Sauvignon, Sonoma County. $50.

92 • Arrowood (CA) 1994 Réserve Spéciale, Cabernet Sauvignon, Sonoma County. $50.

91 • Simi (CA) 1994 Reserve, Cabernet Sauvignon, Sonoma County. $46.67.

91 • Ferrari-Carano (CA) 1994 Cabernet Sauvignon, Sonoma County. $28.

91 • Ferrari-Carano (CA) 1992 Reserve Red, Sonoma County. $47.

90 • Gallo Sonoma (CA) 1993 Estate, Cabernet Sauvignon, Northern Sonoma. $45.

90 • Ferrari-Carano (CA) 1993 Cabernet Sauvignon, Sonoma County. $22.50.

90 • Benziger (CA) 1995 Cabernet Sauvignon, Sonoma County. $16.

90 • Arrowood (CA) 1995 Cabernet Sauvignon, Sonoma County. $35.

89 • Windsor (CA) 1995 Shelton Signature Series, Cabernet Sauvignon, Sonoma County. $22.

89 • Rodney Strong (CA) 1994 Reserve, Cabernet Sauvignon, Northern Sonoma. $35.

89 • Rodney Strong (CA) 1993 Reserve, Cabernet Sauvignon, Northern Sonoma. $30.

89 • Marietta (CA) 1996 Cabernet Sauvignon, Sonoma County. $17.

89 • Chateau St. Jean (CA) 1995 Cinq Cépages, Cabernet Sauvignon, Sonoma County. $24.

89 • Chateau St. Jean (CA) 1994 Cinq Cépages, Cabernet Sauvignon, Sonoma County. $24.

89 • Benziger (CA) 1996 Cabernet Sauvignon, Sonoma County. $17.

88 • Windsor (CA) 1995 Private Reserve Meritage, Sonoma County. $20.

88 • Windsor (CA) 1994 Shelton Signature Series, Cabernet Sauvignon, Sonoma County. $21.

88 • Rodney Strong (CA) 1993 Alexander's Crown Vineyard, Cabernet Sauvignon, Northern Sonoma. $22.

88 • Chateau St. Jean (CA) 1994 Reserve, Cabernet Sauvignon, Sonoma County. $60.

88 • Chalk Hill (CA) 1994 Cabernet Sauvignon, Chalk Hill, Sonoma County. $26.

88 • Canyon Road (CA) 1995 Reserve, Cabernet Sauvignon, Sonoma County. $18.

87 • Wellington (CA) 1994 Mohrhardt Ridge Vineyard, Cabernet Sauvignon, Sonoma County. $15.

87 • St. Francis (CA) 1995 Cabernet Sauvignon, Sonoma County. $10.99.

87 • Gallo Sonoma (CA) 1994 Cabernet Sauvignon, Sonoma County. $12.

87 • Davis Bynum (CA) 1994 Eclipse, Sonoma County. $28.

87 • Alderbrook (CA) 1996 Cabernet Sauvignon, Sonoma County. $16.

86 • Windsor (CA) 1993 Private Reserve Meritage, Sonoma County. $22.

86 • Rodney Strong (CA) 1995 Cabernet Sauvignon, Sonoma County. $13.

86 • Rodney Strong (CA) 1995 Alexander's Crown Vineyard, Cabernet Sauvignon, Northern Sonoma. $24.

86 • Gary Farrell (CA) 1995 Hillside Selection, Cabernet Sauvignon, Sonoma County. $24.

85 • Windsor (CA) 1994 Signature Series, Cabernet Sauvignon, Sonoma County. $25.

85 • Corbett Canyon (CA) 1995 Reserve, Cabernet Sauvignon, Sonoma County. $10.

Sonoma County (Alexander Valley)

92 • Silver Oak (CA) 1993 Cabernet Sauvignon, Alexander Valley. $38.

91 • Stonestreet (CA) 1995 Legacy, Alexander Valley. $65.

91 • Stonestreet (CA) 1994 Legacy, Alexander Valley. $50.

91 • Silver Oak (CA) 1994 Cabernet Sauvignon, Alexander Valley. $45.

91 • Murphy-Goode (CA) 1994 Brenda Block, Cabernet Sauvignon, Alexander Valley. $30.

91 • Herzog (CA) 1995 Special Reserve, Cabernet Sauvignon, Alexander Valley. $25.99.

91 • Herzog (CA) 1994 Special Reserve, Cabernet Sauvignon, Alexander Valley. $26.69.

91 • Estancia (CA) 1994 Red Meritage, Alexander Valley. $18.

90 • Stonestreet (CA) 1994 Cabernet Sauvignon, Alexander Valley. $35.

90 • Korbel (CA) 1994 Cabernet Sauvignon, Alexander Valley. $18.99.

90 • Hanna (CA) 1995 Cabernet Sauvignon, Alexander Valley. $20.

90 • Gallo Sonoma (CA) 1994 Barrelli Creek Vineyard, Cabernet Sauvignon, Alexander Valley. $20.

90 • de Lorimier (CA) 1994 Mosaic Meritage, Alexander Valley. $20.

90 • Chateau Souverain (CA) 1994 Winemaker's Reserve, Cabernet Sauvignon, Alexander Valley. $30.

89 • Windsor (CA) 1994 Private Reserve, Cabernet Sauvignon, Alexander Valley. $20.

89 • Simi (CA) 1994 Cabernet Sauvignon, Alexander Valley. $19.

89 • Murphy-Goode (CA) 1995 Cabernet Sauvignon, Alexander Valley. $20.

89 • Kendall-Jackson (CA) 1994 Buckeye Vineyard, Cabernet Sauvignon, Alexander Valley. $24.

89 • Geyser Peak (CA) 1995 Reserve, Cabernet Sauvignon, Alexander Valley. $24.99.

89 • de Lorimier (CA) 1995 Mosaic Meritage, Alexander Valley. $24.

89 • Chateau Souverain (CA) 1995 Cabernet Sauvignon, Alexander Valley. $16.50.

89 • Byington (CA) 1994 Smith Reichel Vineyard, Cabernet Sauvignon, Alexander Valley. $18.

88 • Venezia (CA) 1996 Meola Vineyards, Cabernet Sauvignon, Alexander Valley. $19.99.

88 • Stonestreet (CA) 1995 Cabernet Sauvignon, Alexander Valley. $37.

88 • Murphy-Goode (CA) 1994 Murphy Ranch, Cabernet Sauvignon, Alexander Valley. $25.

88 • Kendall-Jackson (CA) 1995 Buckeye Vineyard, Cabernet Sauvignon, Alexander Valley. $27.

88 • Jordan (CA) 1994 Cabernet Sauvignon, Alexander Valley. $34.

88 • Geyser Peak (CA) 1995 Reserve Alexandre Meritage, Alexander Valley. $24.99.

88 • Geyser Peak (CA) 1994 Reserve, Cabernet Sauvignon, Alexander Valley. $28.

88 • Geyser Peak (CA) 1994 Reserve Alexandre Meritage, Meritage, Alexander Valley. $28.

88 • Clos du Bois (CA) 1995 Winemaker's Reserve, Cabernet Sauvignon, Alexander Valley. $50.

87 • Venezia (CA) 1995 Meola Vineyards, Cabernet Sauvignon, Alexander Valley. $20.

87 • Simi (CA) 1995 Cabernet Sauvignon, Alexander Valley. $22.

86 • Pedroncelli (CA) 1995 Morris Fay Vineyard, Cabernet Sauvignon, Alexander Valley. $13.

Scale: Superlative (96-100), Exceptional (90-95), Highly Recommended (85-89), Recommended (80-84), Not Recommended (Under 80)

86 • Iron Horse (CA) 1994 T-T Vineyards, Cabernet Sauvignon, Alexander Valley. $20.

86 • Estancia (CA) 1995 Red Meritage, Alexander Valley. $22.

86 • Chateau Souverain (CA) 1995 Winemaker's Reserve, Cabernet Sauvignon,
Alexander Valley. $35.

86 • Benziger (CA) 1995 Ash Creek Vineyards Reserve, Cabernet Sauvignon,
Alexander Valley. $25.

86 • Alexander Valley Vineyards (CA) 1996 Cabernet Sauvignon,
Alexander Valley. $17.50.

85 • Alexander Valley Vineyards (CA) 1995 Cabernet Sauvignon, Alexander Valley. $17.

Sonoma County (Dry Creek Valley)

94 • Dry Creek Vineyard (CA) 1995 Reserve, Cabernet Sauvignon, Dry Creek Valley. $27.

93 • Gallo Sonoma (CA) 1994 Frei Ranch Vineyard, Cabernet Sauvignon,
Dry Creek Valley. $18.

93 • Dry Creek Vineyard (CA) 1996 Cabernet Sauvignon, Dry Creek Valley. $18.75.

92 • Lambert Bridge (CA) 1994 Crane Creek Cuvée, Dry Creek Valley. $28.

91 • Gallo Sonoma (CA) 1993 Frei Ranch Vineyard, Cabernet Sauvignon,
Dry Creek Valley. $18.

90 • Windsor (CA) 1994 Private Reserve, Cabernet Sauvignon, Dry Creek Valley. $22.

90 • Michel-Schlumberger (CA) 1994 Cabernet Sauvignon, Dry Creek Valley. $20.

89 • Pezzi King (CA) 1995 Cabernet Sauvignon, Dry Creek Valley. $25.

89 • Belvedere (CA) 1995 Cabernet Sauvignon, Dry Creek Valley. $16.

89 • Belvedere (CA) 1994 Cabernet Sauvignon, Dry Creek Valley. $13.50.

88 • Peterson (CA) 1996 Bradford Mountain Vineyard, Cabernet Sauvignon,
Dry Creek Valley. $25.

88 • Pedroncelli (CA) 1996 Three Vineyards, Cabernet Sauvignon, Dry Creek Valley. $12.

88 • Pedroncelli (CA) 1995 Three Vineyards, Cabernet Sauvignon,
Dry Creek Valley. $12.50.

88 • Gallo Sonoma (CA) 1993 Stefani Vineyard, Cabernet Sauvignon,
Dry Creek Valley. $18.

88 • Dry Creek Vineyard (CA) 1995 Meritage, Dry Creek Valley. $25.

86 • Michel-Schlumberger (CA) 1993 Schlumberger Reserve, Cabernet Sauvignon,
Dry Creek Valley. $35.

86 • Michel-Schlumberger (CA) 1993 Cabernet Sauvignon, Dry Creek Valley. $19.50.

86 • Gallo Sonoma (CA) 1994 Stefani Vineyard, Cabernet Sauvignon,
Dry Creek Valley. $18.

85 • Lambert Bridge (CA) 1995 Crane Creek Cuvée, Dry Creek Valley. $32.

Sonoma County (Russian River Valley)

92 • De Loach (CA) 1993 OFS, Cabernet Sauvignon, Russian River Valley. $25.

90 • De Loach (CA) 1994 OFS, Cabernet Sauvignon, Russian River Valley. $27.50.

88 • Dehlinger (CA) 1995 Cabernet Sauvignon, Russian River Valley. $28.

87 • Davis Bynum (CA) 1994 Hedin Vineyard, Cabernet Sauvignon,
Russian River Valley. $24.

85 • Windsor (CA) 1994 River West Vineyard, Cabernet Sauvignon,
Russian River Valley. $18.

Sonoma County (Sonoma Mountain)

92 • Louis Martini (CA) 1994 Monte Rosso Vineyard Selection, Cabernet Sauvignon,
Sonoma Mountain. $30.

91 • Ravenswood (CA) 1995 Rancho Vineyards Red, Sonoma Mountain. $30.

91 • Benziger (CA) 1995 Tribute Red, Sonoma Mountain. $25.

90 • Ravenswood (CA) 1995 Pickberry Vineyards Red, Sonoma Mountain. $35.

90 • Laurel Glen (CA) 1995 Cabernet Sauvignon, Sonoma Mountain. $38.

90 • Laurel Glen (CA) 1994 Cabernet Sauvignon, Sonoma Mountain. $38.

90 • Benziger (CA) 1995 Reserve, Cabernet Sauvignon, Sonoma Mountain. $35.

89 • Sonoma Creek (CA) 1995 Van der Kamp Vineyard, Cabernet Sauvignon, Sonoma Mountain. $28.95.

88 • Benziger (CA) 1994 Tribute Red, Sonoma Mountain. $25.

Sonoma County (Sonoma Valley)

96 • St. Francis (CA) 1994 Reserve, Cabernet Sauvignon, Sonoma Valley. $30.

94 • Richardson (CA) 1996 Horne Vineyard, Cabernet Sauvignon, Sonoma Valley. $22.

94 • B.R. Cohn (CA) 1995 Olive Hill Vineyard, Cabernet Sauvignon, Sonoma Valley. $75.

93 • Kunde (CA) 1995 Cabernet Sauvignon, Sonoma Valley. $20.

92 • Sonoma Creek (CA) 1995 Reserve, Cabernet Sauvignon, Sonoma Valley. $17.95.

92 • Richardson (CA) 1996 Synergy, Sonoma Valley. $20.

92 • B.R. Cohn (CA) 1994 Olive Hill Vineyard, Cabernet Sauvignon, Sonoma Valley. $32.

91 • St. Francis (CA) 1995 Reserve, Cabernet Sauvignon, Sonoma Valley. $33.99.

91 • Sonoma Creek (CA) 1995 Rancho Salina Vineyard, Cabernet Sauvignon, Sonoma Valley. $28.95.

91 • Kenwood (CA) 1994 Jack London Vineyard, Cabernet Sauvignon, Sonoma Valley. $25.

91 • Carmenet (CA) 1993 Moon Mountain Estate Reserve Meritage, Sonoma Valley. $27.50.

90 • Kunde (CA) 1994 Cabernet Sauvignon, Sonoma Valley. $17.

90 • Kenwood (CA) 1995 Jack London Vineyard, Cabernet Sauvignon, Sonoma Valley. $25.

90 • Bartholomew Park (CA) 1996 Desnudos Vineyard, Cabernet Sauvignon, Sonoma Valley. $35.

89 • Sonoma Creek (CA) 1995 Meritage, Sonoma Valley. $17.95.

89 • Schug (CA) 1995 Heritage Reserve, Cabernet Sauvignon, Sonoma Valley. $40.

89 • Richardson (CA) 1995 Horne Vineyard, Cabernet Sauvignon, Sonoma Valley. $18.

89 • Ravenswood (CA) 1994 Rancho Salina Vineyards Red, Sonoma Valley. $30.

89 • Benziger (CA) 1995 Rancho Salina Vineyard, Cabernet Sauvignon, Sonoma Valley. $28.

88 • Kenwood (CA) 1995 Cabernet Sauvignon, Sonoma Valley. $18.

88 • Jessandra Vittoria (CA) 1995 Cabernet Sauvignon, Sonoma Valley. $30.

87 • Louis Martini (CA) 1995 Monte Rosso Vineyard Selection, Cabernet Sauvignon, Sonoma Valley. $35.

87 • Kenwood (CA) 1994 Cabernet Sauvignon, Sonoma Valley. $18.

87 • Gundlach Bundschu (CA) 1996 Rhinefarm Vineyards, Cabernet Sauvignon, Sonoma Valley. $24.

87 • Carmenet (CA) 1995 Moon Mountain Estate Reserve Meritage, Sonoma Valley. $40.

85 • Richardson (CA) 1994 Synergy, Sonoma Valley. $17.

85 • Kistler (CA) 1993 Kistler Vineyard, Cabernet Sauvignon, Sonoma Valley. $30.

Mendocino

Wines Reviewed: 12

Median Price: $18.50

Mendocino is the most northerly of California's wine-producing regions and as such it is far removed from the glamour and high society of the southern regions. It has four AVAs, of which Anderson Valley is the most significant and coolest, with its proximity to the coast giving a plentiful supply of cooling sea air along its length.

To the east of Anderson Valley runs the extreme northern section of the Russian

Scale: Superlative (96-100), Exceptional (90-95), Highly Recommended (85-89), Recommended (80-84), Not Recommended (Under 80)

River. It is along this stretch of water that the other vineyards of Mendocino County are to be found. Sea air does not have a significant impact in these inland regions and they do not exhibit the coolness found in the Anderson Valley.

Thus, it is here that red Bordeaux varietals are to be found. Though warmer than the coast, the region is still cool, and far cooler than the northern end of the Napa Valley, for instance. This makes for wines that, despite their deep color, feature flavors in the lighter red fruit spectrum of the grape. They are marked by well-balanced levels of acidity, and the tannins are by and large left in check.

Highly Recommended Mendocino Cabernet Sauvignon and Red Meritage

90 • Villa Mt. Eden (CA) 1995 Signature Series, Cabernet Sauvignon, Mendocino. $45.

90 • Villa Mt. Eden (CA) 1994 Signature Series, Cabernet Sauvignon, Mendocino. $50.

89 • Steele (CA) 1994 Cabernet Sauvignon, Anderson Valley. $28.

89 • Lolonis (CA) 1994 Private Reserve, Cabernet Sauvignon, Mendocino County. $25.

89 • Frey (CA) 1997 Butow Vineyards, Cabernet Sauvignon, Redwood Valley. $10.50.

88 • Yorkville (CA) 1995 Richard the Lion-Heart, Mendocino County. $20.

88 • Husch (CA) 1994 La Ribera Vineyard, Cabernet Sauvignon, Mendocino. $15.

86 • Windsor (CA) 1994 Private Reserve, Cabernet Sauvignon, Mendocino County. $22.

86 • Parducci (CA) 1995 Cabernet Sauvignon, Mendocino. $10.

86 • Husch (CA) 1996 Cabernet Sauvignon, Mendocino. $16.50.

Santa Cruz Mountains

Wines Reviewed: 30

Median Price: $25

Santa Cruz is certainly one of California's more improbable, dare one say impractical regions. This craggy, imposing, conifer-peaked range of mountains nestles along the southwestern side of the San Francisco Bay, encompassing the San Andreas fault and some of the Golden State's finest vineyard locations.

Specifics of climate, and hence resulting wine styles, can vary with altitude and aspect of vineyards, making sweeping generalizations or even gradual variations in character impossible to extrapolate. Rainfall and average temperature vary significantly with altitude, and sunshine hours will be dependent upon the specific vineyard orientation, with east-facing slopes being considerably warmer. However, given the mountainous terrain and the poverty of the shale-like soil, yields are ungratifyingly low, and viticulture is labor intensive. These factors alone account for the lack of corporate money and presence in the Santa Cruz Mountains, notwithstanding the ownership of Ridge Vineyards by a Japanese financial services company. It is an outpost of devoted amateurs and occasional eccentrics seeking focused seclusion.

The region mostly falls solidly into Region I (the coolest viticultural climate) on the UC Davis heat summation scale, with the warmest areas achieving Region II status (on a par with Russian River Valley). This puts it in a class of its own in California, as few other Region I/II areas can satisfactorily ripen Cabernet Sauvignon to the level of intensity seen here. Impeccable canopy exposure and low yields certainly play their role, but long slow ripening with plenty of sunshine hours on favorable east-facing slopes certainly is a major factor. Thus, Santa Cruz is actually a warmer area than it would appear at face value.

The region's greatest and most historic winery is Ridge Vineyards, whose Monte Bello Vineyard, at an elevation of over 2,000 feet, first planted in 1885, was one of the first vineyards to be established here. This hallowed and somewhat inaccessible, though magnificently situated terraced vineyard, produces some of the world's most highly sought after and longest lived Cabernets. The style is always deep, firm, and rich, but focused, with a great clarity of fruit flavors that maturity does not seem to blur. Paul Draper's Zen-like stewardship of this winery since 1969 has seen its reputation, and price, match its celestial elevation of 2,660 feet.

Making world-class wine is a labor of love when done at altitude in the Santa Cruz Mountains and this philosophy is not likely to change, even with the currently inflated prices of top Californian Cabernets. Developing terraced vineyards in remote mountainous regions will always be an expensive proposition and, combined with miserly low yields, will always be a deterrence to all but the most far-sighted of investors. After all, even on the Côte-Rôtie in France it is still more rewarding for some farmers to grow artichokes than Syrah.

Highly Recommended Santa Cruz Mountains Cabernet Sauvignon and Red Meritage

96 • Ridge (CA) 1993 Monte Bello, Cabernet Sauvignon, Santa Cruz Mountains. $55.

95 • Ridge (CA) 1994 Monte Bello, Santa Cruz Mountains. $65.

95 • Kathryn Kennedy (CA) 1994 Cabernet Sauvignon, Santa Cruz Mountains. $75.

94 • Mount Eden (CA) 1993 Old Vine Reserve, Cabernet Sauvignon, Santa Cruz Mountains. $35.

94 • Kathryn Kennedy (CA) 1995 Cabernet Sauvignon, Santa Cruz Mountains. $110.

94 • Cinnabar (CA) 1994 Saratoga Vineyard, Cabernet Sauvignon, Santa Cruz Mountains. $25.

93 • Ridge (CA) 1995 Cabernet Sauvignon, Santa Cruz Mountains. $22.

93 • Cooper-Garrod (CA) 1995 Cabernet Sauvignon, Santa Cruz Mountains. $28.

92 • Ridge (CA) 1995 Monte Bello, Santa Cruz Mountains. $70.

91 • Soquel (CA) 1995 Partner's Reserve, Cabernet Sauvignon, Santa Cruz Mountains. $40.

91 • Soquel (CA) 1994 Partner's Reserve, Cabernet Sauvignon, Santa Cruz Mountains. $40.

91 • Byington (CA) 1994 Twin Mountains, Cabernet Sauvignon, Santa Cruz Mountains. $14.50.

90 • Woodside (CA) 1993 Cabernet Sauvignon, Santa Cruz Mountains. $25.

90 • Thomas Fogarty (CA) 1996 Cabernet Sauvignon, Santa Cruz Mountains. $25.

90 • David Bruce (CA) 1996 La Rusticana d'Orsa, Santa Cruz Mountains. $32.

90 • David Bruce (CA) 1994 Reserve, Cabernet Sauvignon, Santa Cruz Mountains. $20.

90 • Cooper-Garrod (CA) 1994 Cabernet Sauvignon, Santa Cruz Mountains. $25.

90 • Clos La Chance (CA) 1994 Cabernet Sauvignon, Santa Cruz Mountains. $22.

89 • Martin Ray (CA) 1995 Cabernet Sauvignon, Santa Cruz Mountains. $25.

89 • Cooper-Garrod (CA) 1995 Proprietor's Reserve, Cabernet Sauvignon, Santa Cruz Mountains. $35.

89 • Byington (CA) 1993 Bates Ranch, Cabernet Sauvignon, Santa Cruz Mountains. $20.

88 • Mount Eden (CA) 1995 Old Vine Reserve, Cabernet Sauvignon, Santa Cruz Mountains. $39.99.

88 • Mount Eden (CA) 1995 Cabernet Sauvignon, Santa Cruz Mountains. $20.

88 • Bargetto (CA) 1995 Cabernet Sauvignon, Santa Cruz Mountains. $18.

87 • Cinnabar (CA) 1995 Saratoga Vineyard, Cabernet Sauvignon,

Santa Cruz Mountains. $25.

86 • Clos La Chance (CA) 1996 Cabernet Sauvignon, Santa Cruz Mountains. $22.

86 • Clos La Chance (CA) 1995 Cabernet Sauvignon, Santa Cruz Mountains. $21.

86 • Bargetto (CA) 1993 Bates Ranch, Cabernet Sauvignon, Santa Cruz Mountains. $18.

85 • Soquel (CA) 1994 Cabernet Sauvignon, Santa Cruz Mountains. $22.

Monterey

Wines Reviewed: **23**

Median Price: **$18**

Monterey has a considerable ocean breeze influence, giving it a distinctly cool growing climate at its closest point to the ocean in the Salinas Valley. Initial large plantings here during the 1970s in inappropriate locations gave this county a reputation for vegetal wines, as the vineyards exposed to the funneled sea breezes struggled to ripen red varietals. With more appropriate locations and a better understanding of microclimates, this region is now producing Chardonnay of the highest quality. Red wines have not been forgotten, however, just moved to more suitable locations.

First among these might be the Carmel Valley, although the Santa Lucia Highlands, in the form of the Smith & Hook Winery, is also showing promise. Though the Carmel Valley has similarly cool conditions as the rest of Monterey, it also has some very steep slopes that help in the ripening of Cabernet. The resultant wines are obviously cool climate in character, both lighter in body and lower in alcohol than their North Coast cousins are. Additionally, the wines often feature an herbal note that serves to add complexity when kept in check. Improved viticultural practices have now allowed vintners here to ripen red Bordeaux varietals with a certain measure of consistency, and the wines are showing continual improvement. Today, the Carmel Valley is producing Cabernet of outstanding quality, with the added benefit of having a very distinctive personality.

Highly Recommended Monterey Cabernet Sauvignon and Red Meritage

Monterey (General)

87 • Monterra (CA) 1996 Promise, Cabernet Sauvignon, Monterey County. $9.99.

87 • Lockwood (CA) 1994 Partners' Reserve, Cabernet Sauvignon, Monterey. $21.

87 • Jekel (CA) 1995 Sanctuary Estate Meritage, Monterey. $25.

87 • Cloninger (CA) 1994 Cabernet Sauvignon, Monterey. $13.

86 • Chateau Julien (CA) 1995 Private Reserve, Cabernet Sauvignon, Monterey County. $20.

85 • San Saba (CA) 1994 SSV, Cabernet Sauvignon, Monterey. $17.

85 • Mirassou (CA) 1993 Cabernet Sauvignon, Monterey County. $11.95.

Monterey (Carmel Valley)

91 • Bernardus (CA) 1994 Marinus, Carmel Valley. $28.

89 • Cloninger (CA) 1996 Quinn Vineyard, Cabernet Sauvignon, Carmel Valley. $14.

85 • Durney (CA) 1993 Cabernet Sauvignon, Carmel Valley. $20.

Monterey (Santa Lucia Highlands)

90 • Smith & Hook (CA) 1994 Masterpiece Edition, Cabernet Sauvignon, Santa Lucia Highlands. $35.

89 • Smith & Hook (CA) 1995 Cabernet Sauvignon, Santa Lucia Highlands. $18.

87 • Smith & Hook (CA) 1994 Cabernet Sauvignon, Santa Lucia Highlands. $18.

87 • Hahn Estates (CA) 1996 Red Meritage, Santa Lucia Highlands. $15.

86 • Smith & Hook (CA) 1995 Masterpiece Edition, Cabernet Sauvignon, Santa Lucia Highlands. $40.

Paso Robles

Wines Reviewed: **29**
Median Price: **$19**

Paso Robles is a large AVA without much ocean influence, making it a warm climate growing region, albeit with some cooler microclimates located toward the southwestern sector where sea air enters via the Templeton Gap. On the north it is bounded by Monterey County, with San Luis Obispo and Santa Barbara Counties to the south. Daytime temperatures are quite warm through the growing season and a high degree of ripeness is consistently achieved. These are conditions that emphatically make this red wine country, and Cabernet Sauvignon is the most widely planted varietal in the county.

Paso Robles Cabernet tends to be quite rich and ripe with deep berry and chocolate flavors. Occasionally the wines can veer into overripeness with some bottlings showing stewed flavors. As a younger region, Paso Robles is still in many respects finding its way, yet its unique physical attributes should continue to make for large-scaled, rustic leaning Cabernets with a greater sense of refinement in the years to come.

Highly Recommended Paso Robles
Cabernet Sauvignon and Red Meritage

89 • Martin Brothers (Renamed Martin & Weyrich, Spring 1999) (CA) 1995 Etrusco, Cabernet Sauvignon, Paso Robles. $18.

89 • Grey Wolf (CA) 1995 Barton Family Reserve Meritage, Paso Robles. $22.

88 • Justin (CA) 1994 Isosceles, Paso Robles. $32.50.

88 • Dover Canyon (CA) 1996 Ménage, Paso Robles. $28.

88 • Dover Canyon (CA) 1995 Ménage, Paso Robles. $22.

88 • Dark Star (CA) 1996 Cabernet Sauvignon, Paso Robles. $19.

87 • Grey Wolf (CA) 1994 Barton Family Reserve Meritage, Paso Robles. $19.

87 • Dark Star (CA) 1996 Ricordati, Paso Robles. $20.

86 • Pesenti (CA) 1996 Cabernet Sauvignon, Paso Robles. $15.

86 • Eberle (CA) 1996 Cabernet Sauvignon, Paso Robles. $20.

86 • Dover Canyon (CA) 1996 Cabernet Sauvignon, Paso Robles. $18.

86 • Castoro (CA) 1996 Cabernet Sauvignon, Paso Robles. $15.

86 • Carmody McKnight (CA) 1996 Cadenza, Paso Robles. $22.50.

85 • Castoro (CA) 1995 Cabernet Sauvignon, Paso Robles. $11.50.

Washington

Wines Reviewed: **123**
Median Price: **$23**

Washington State is a relative newcomer to the world of fine wines, but it has made as much progress in as little time as any region in the country. Luckily for the industry as a whole, two large wineries, Chateau Ste. Michelle and Columbia, have introduced consumers around the nation to the area's wines. Largely focusing on the production of high-quality wines at reasonable prices, the state's vintners have begun to firmly set their sights on the production of world-class products.

Geographically speaking, Washington is unlike any other viticultural area in the world. With virtually all the vineyards located in the rain shadow of the majestic Cascade Mountains, the area is in reality semi-arid. Only through irrigation with water from the mighty Columbia River and its tributaries can the area produce crops of any sort. Furthermore, virtually the entire Columbia Basin shares the same sand-based soil structure. This allows for something very rare in viticulture these days: vines planted on their own native rootstocks. Apparently, the root louse that causes *Phylloxera* doesn't travel very well in the sandy soils, and though it is endemic in some Washington vineyards, there is little alarm.

Eastern Washington is certainly a land of open skies and the region's volcanoes can be seen for hundreds of miles. This serves to illustrate the vastness of the region, and that region's potential. Of the possible vineyard sites, only a tiny fraction are actually planted. The biggest block to their development might be the brutal nature of the region's winters, which in February 1996 wiped out half of the state's production. Vines, however, are resilient things, and so are the area's vintners, who resumed full production in the 1997 harvest.

The AVA system in Washington is still underdeveloped, with a huge swath of land being entitled to use the Columbia Valley appellation. Smaller viticultural pockets such as the historic Yakima and Walla Walla Valleys should soon be augmented by the creation of new ones such as Canoe Ridge and Red Mountain.

Cabernet has been planted for some time in Washington, and in the last decade the region's winemakers have become quite adept at dealing with the varietal. Perhaps through their experience with Merlot, Washington winemakers have begun to ease up on the extraction of tannins, which so heavily marked bottlings from the mid '80s. Today, led by the boutique producers of the Walla Walla Valley, along with industry giants Chateau Ste. Michelle and Columbia, Washington Cabernet has taken on a new personality. Supple and brimming with character, the wines are still well structured with an emphasis on balanced acidity. Additionally, they tend to be a degree or two lower in alcohol than their California counterparts, making them quite a bit easier at the table. Today the top end of Washington Cabernet stands with California's best, and as production increases with the general level of quality, there is no doubt that Washington will earn a reputation not only in this country but also the world over.

Highly Recommended Washington Cabernet Sauvignon and Red Meritage

Washington/Columbia Valley (General)

99 • Woodward Canyon (WA) 1995 Old Vines, Cabernet Sauvignon, Columbia Valley. $45.

95 • Chateau Ste. Michelle (WA) 1995 Cold Creek Vineyard, Cabernet Sauvignon, Columbia Valley. $27.

94 • L'Ecole No. 41 (WA) 1995 Cabernet Sauvignon, Columbia Valley. $25.

94 • Kestrel (WA) 1995 Cabernet Sauvignon, Columbia Valley. $22.

94 • Chateau Ste. Michelle (WA) 1995 Horse Heaven Vineyard, Cabernet Sauvignon, Columbia Valley. $27.

94 • Chateau Ste. Michelle (WA) 1995 Artist Series Red Meritage, Columbia Valley. $50.

94 • Andrew Will (WA) 1995 Sorella, Washington. $40.

93 • Woodward Canyon (WA) 1995 Artist Series, Canoe Ridge Vineyard, Cabernet Sauvignon, Washington. $28.

93 • Quilceda Creek (WA) 1995 Cabernet Sauvignon, Washington. $45.

93 • Leonetti (WA) 1994 Cabernet Sauvignon, Columbia Valley. $45.

93 • Dunham (WA) 1995 Cabernet Sauvignon, Columbia Valley. $28.

93 • Andrew Will (WA) 1995 Reserve, Cabernet Sauvignon, Washington. $40.

92 • Woodward Canyon (WA) 1994 Captain Z.K. Straight, Cabernet Sauvignon, Columbia Valley. $35.

92 • Waterbrook (WA) 1995 Cabernet Sauvignon, Columbia Valley. $24.

92 • Hogue (WA) 1995 Genesis, Champoux Vineyard, Cabernet Sauvignon, Columbia Valley. $22.99.

92 • Andrew Will (WA) 1996 Sorella, Washington. $38.

91 • Quilceda Creek (WA) 1994 Cabernet Sauvignon, Washington. $42.

91 • Hedges (WA) 1994 Red Mountain Reserve, Columbia Valley. $30.

91 • Chateau Ste. Michelle (WA) 1994 Artist Series Red Meritage, Columbia Valley. $50.

91 • Barnard Griffin (WA) 1996 Cabernet Sauvignon, Columbia Valley. $16.95.

91 • Andrew Will (WA) 1994 Reserve, Cabernet Sauvignon, Washington. $40.

90 • Seven Hills (WA) 1995 Klipsun Vineyard, Cabernet Sauvignon, Columbia Valley. $24.

90 • Powers (WA) 1995 Mercer Ranch Vineyard, Cabernet Sauvignon, Columbia Valley. $18.

90 • Leonetti (WA) 1995 Cabernet Sauvignon, Columbia Valley. $45.

90 • L'Ecole No. 41 (WA) 1996 Cabernet Sauvignon, Columbia Valley. $26.

90 • L'Ecole No. 41 (WA) 1994 Cabernet Sauvignon, Columbia Valley. $24.

90 • Hedges (WA) 1995 Three Vineyards, Columbia Valley. $20.

90 • Chateau Ste. Michelle (WA) 1996 Cabernet Sauvignon, Columbia Valley. $16.

90 • Chateau Ste. Michelle (WA) 1995 Cabernet Sauvignon, Columbia Valley. $16.

90 • Chateau Ste. Michelle (WA) 1994 Ethos Red, Columbia Valley. $31.

90 • Canoe Ridge Vineyard (WA) 1995 Cabernet Sauvignon, Columbia Valley. $22.

90 • Apex (WA) 1994 Cabernet Sauvignon, Columbia Valley. $35.

90 • Andrew Will (WA) 1996 Cabernet Sauvignon, Washington. $32.

90 • Andrew Will (WA) 1994 Cabernet Sauvignon, Washington. $30.

89 • Ste. Chapelle (ID) 1995 Cabernet Sauvignon, Washington. $8.

89 • Staton Hills (WA) 1994 Cabernet Sauvignon, Columbia Valley. $16.

89 • Preston Premium (WA) 1994 Reserve, Cabernet Sauvignon, Columbia Valley. $21.

89 • Hedges (WA) 1995 Red Mountain Reserve, Columbia Valley. $30.

89 • Columbia Crest (WA) 1995 Reserve Red, Columbia Valley. $22.

89 • Columbia Crest (WA) 1994 Reserve Red, Columbia Valley. $20.

89 • Columbia Crest (WA) 1994 Estate Series, Cabernet Sauvignon, Columbia Valley. $17.

89 • Apex (WA) 1995 Cabernet Sauvignon, Columbia Valley. $35.

88 • Woodward Canyon (WA) 1996 Artist Series, Canoe Ridge Vineyard, Cabernet Sauvignon, Columbia Valley. $40.

88 • W.B. Bridgman (WA) 1994 Cabernet Sauvignon, Columbia Valley. $15.

88 • Staton Hills (WA) 1995 Cabernet Sauvignon, Columbia Valley. $15.95.

88 • Seven Hills (WA) 1995 Cabernet Sauvignon, Columbia Valley. $20.

88 • Patrick M. Paul (WA) 1994 Cabernet Sauvignon, Columbia Valley. $12.

88 • Matthews (WA) 1995 Yakima Valley Red, Washington. $28.

88 • Gordon Brothers (WA) 1996 Cabernet Sauvignon, Columbia Valley. $15.49.

88 • Gordon Brothers (WA) 1994 Tradition, Columbia Valley. $19.99.

Scale: Superlative (96-100), Exceptional (90-95), Highly Recommended (85-89), Recommended (80-84), Not Recommended (Under 80)

88 • E.B. Foote (WA) 1994 Cellar Reserve, Cabernet Sauvignon, Columbia Valley. $32.

88 • Columbia Winery (WA) 1994 Sagemoor Vineyard, David Lake Signature Series, Cabernet Sauvignon, Columbia Valley. $23.

88 • Columbia Crest (WA) 1995 Estate Series, Cabernet Sauvignon, Columbia Valley. $21.

88 • Caterina (WA) 1995 Wahluke Slope Vineyard Reserve, Cabernet Sauvignon, Columbia Valley. $32.

87 • W.B. Bridgman (WA) 1995 Cabernet Sauvignon, Columbia Valley. $13.99.

87 • Walla Walla Vintners (WA) 1996 Washington State Red Cuvée, Washington. $18.

87 • Silver Lake (WA) 1995 Reserve, Cabernet Sauvignon, Columbia Valley. $17.99.

87 • Kiona (WA) 1997 Cabernet Sauvignon, Washington. $17.99.

87 • Hogue (WA) 1994 Barrel Select, Cabernet Sauvignon, Columbia Valley. $14.

87 • E.B. Foote (WA) 1995 Cabernet Sauvignon, Columbia Valley. $15.

87 • Caterina (WA) 1995 Cabernet Sauvignon, Columbia Valley. $19.

87 • Barnard Griffin (WA) 1995 Cabernet Sauvignon, Washington. $16.95.

87 • Arbor Crest (WA) 1995 Cameo Reserve, Cabernet Sauvignon, Washington. $13.

86 • Washington Hills (WA) 1995 Cabernet Sauvignon, Columbia Valley. $9.99.

86 • W.B. Bridgman (WA) 1996 Cabernet Sauvignon, Columbia Valley. $14.

86 • Ste. Chapelle (ID) 1995 Sagemoor's Dionysus Vineyard, Cabernet Sauvignon, Washington. $12.99.

86 • Preston Premium (WA) 1995 Reserve, Cabernet Sauvignon, Columbia Valley. $21.

86 • Powers (WA) 1996 Cabernet-Merlot, Washington. $12.

86 • Powers (WA) 1996 Cabernet Sauvignon, Washington. $12.

86 • Paul Thomas (WA) 1995 Reserve, Cabernet Sauvignon, Washington. $14.99.

86 • Kiona (WA) 1996 Cabernet Sauvignon, Washington. $14.99.

86 • Hogue (WA) 1995 Reserve, Cabernet Sauvignon, Columbia Valley. $30.

86 • Covey Run (WA) 1996 Reserve, Cabernet Sauvignon, Columbia Valley. $24.

86 • Covey Run (WA) 1996 Cabernet Sauvignon, Columbia Valley. $12.99.

85 • Seth Ryan (WA) 1996 Jessica's Meritage, Columbia Valley. $32.41.

85 • Covey Run (WA) 1995 Cabernet Sauvignon, Columbia Valley. $12.99.

85 • Chateau Ste. Michelle (WA) 1994 Cabernet Sauvignon, Columbia Valley. $16.

Washington (Yakima Valley)

96 • DeLille (WA) 1996 Chaleur Estate, Yakima Valley. $38.

96 • DeLille (WA) 1994 Chaleur Estate, Yakima Valley. $32.

94 • Matthews (WA) 1996 Elerding Vineyard, Cabernet Sauvignon, Yakima Valley. $35.

94 • DeLille (WA) 1995 Chaleur Estate, Yakima Valley. $34.

93 • Columbia Winery (WA) 1994 Otis Vineyard, David Lake Signature Series, Cabernet Sauvignon, Yakima Valley. $23.

92 • Portteus (WA) 1995 Cabernet Sauvignon, Yakima Valley. $30.

92 • Kiona (WA) 1995 Reserve, Cabernet Sauvignon, Yakima Valley. $29.99.

92 • DeLille (WA) 1994 D2, Yakima Valley. $22.

91 • Columbia Winery (WA) 1994 Red Willow Vineyard, David Lake Signature Series, Cabernet Sauvignon, Yakima Valley. $23.

90 • Portteus (WA) 1994 Reserve, Cabernet Sauvignon, Yakima Valley. $26.

89 • Tefft (WA) 1995 Cabernet Sauvignon, Yakima Valley. $21.99.

89 • Columbia Winery (WA) 1995 Red Willow Vineyard, David Lake Signature Series, Cabernet Sauvignon, Yakima Valley. $29.

88 • Yakima River (WA) 1994 Winemakers Reserve, Cabernet Sauvignon, Yakima Valley. $24.99.

88 • Hyatt (WA) 1995 Reserve, Cabernet Sauvignon, Yakima Valley. $32.

88 • Foris (OR) 1994 Klipsun Vineyard, Cabernet Sauvignon, Yakima Valley. $19.

88 • Covey Run (WA) 1994 Whiskey Canyon Vineyard, Cabernet Sauvignon, Yakima Valley. $28.

88 • Columbia Winery (WA) 1995 Reserve, Cabernet Sauvignon, Yakima Valley. $15.
87 • Yakima River (WA) 1994 Cabernet Sauvignon, Yakima Valley. $15.
87 • Tefft (WA) 1994 Cabernet Sauvignon, Yakima Valley. $25.
87 • Seth Ryan (WA) 1994 Cabernet Sauvignon, Yakima Valley. $25.93.
87 • Hyatt (WA) 1994 Reserve, Cabernet Sauvignon, Yakima Valley. $32.
86 • Wilridge (WA) 1996 Melange, Yakima Valley. $19.
86 • DeLille (WA) 1996 D2, Yakima Valley. $24.

Washington (Walla Walla Valley)

93 • L'Ecole No. 41 (WA) 1995 Apogée, Pepper Bridge Vineyard, Cabernet Sauvignon-Merlot, Walla Walla Valley. $30.
89 • Seven Hills (WA) 1995 Cabernet Sauvignon, Walla Walla Valley. $24.
86 • L'Ecole No. 41 (WA) 1996 Seven Hills Vineyard, Cabernet Sauvignon-Merlot, Walla Walla Valley. $35.
86 • L'Ecole No. 41 (WA) 1995 Windrow Vineyard, Cabernet Sauvignon, Walla Walla Valley. $30.

Virginia

Wines Reviewed: 27
Median Price: $18

Thomas Jefferson's dreams of producing high quality *Vinifera* wines in his home state look to be becoming a reality. Even if his early efforts to establish vineyards around Charlottesville failed due to the intervention of the *Phylloxera* louse, his foresight in choosing suitable locations has been vindicated by the fact that this same area is at the forefront of the viticultural renaissance in the Old Dominion.

The vast majority of all vineyards are now in the service of *Vinifera* varietals such as Chardonnay and Cabernet Sauvignon. The state has six AVAs: Monticello, Northern Neck George Washington Birthplace, Shenandoah Valley, Eastern Shore, North Fork of Roanoke, and Rocky Knob, but the vintners themselves are still learning about the region's qualities, and the area as a whole is probably best dealt with in generalities. The newness of the industry makes it difficult to come to authoritative conclusions about differences in style among the various viticultural areas, however, the hotbed of production at the moment is centered around Charlottesville where the Monticello AVA resides.

To this point Virginia Cabernet has been somewhat variable, with solid efforts standing side by side with those that are still finding their way. Virginia presents a range of problems to the winegrower, not least among them the famous southern humidity, yet research and experience are allowing quality conscious producers to overcome these problems. As the process unfolds, some of the better efforts from producers such as Piedmont and Linden give reason to keep a careful eye on Virginia as an up-and-coming producer of quality Cabernet.

Highly Recommended Virginia Cabernet Sauvignon and Red Meritage

89 • Montdomaine (VA) 1993 Heritage, Virginia. $15.
88 • Linden (VA) 1994 Cabernet Sauvignon, Virginia. $16.
86 • Oakencroft (VA) 1995 Cabernet Sauvignon, Monticello. $14.
86 • Naked Mountain (VA) 1996 Cabernet Sauvignon, Virginia. $15.
86 • Jefferson (VA) 1997 Meritage, Monticello. $28.
86 • Jefferson (VA) 1995 Meritage, Monticello. $26.

Scale: Superlative (96-100), Exceptional (90-95), Highly Recommended (85-89), Recommended (80-84), Not Recommended (Under 80)

86 • Ingleside Plantation (VA) 1994 Special Reserve, Cabernet Sauvignon, Virginia. $19.99.

86 • Barboursville (VA) 1995 Cabernet Sauvignon, Monticello. $15.

85 • Williamsburg (VA) 1993 Gabriel Archer Reserve, Virginia. $21.

85 • Montdomaine (VA) 1993 Cabernet Sauvignon, Virginia. $13.50.

85 • Jefferson (VA) 1995 Cabernet Sauvignon, Monticello. $18.

Long Island, New York
Wines Reviewed: **30**
Median Price: **$20.25**

When speaking about New York Cabernet, one is almost exclusively talking about wines from Long Island. As an appellation, Long Island extends nearly 120 miles out into the Atlantic Ocean from New York City. Only 15 miles or so wide, the island is split into two long fingers divided by the Peconic Bay near the town of Riverhead, 70 miles from the East River. Known as the North and South Forks, this end of the island is where viticulture has taken hold. The South Fork is synonymous to many with the Hamptons, New York's answer to Malibu, and the area is home to a few vineyards. The majority, however, are in the more rural and pastoral North Fork, which at only five miles wide and 35 miles long is all but surrounded by water.

At present there are about 20 wineries in the area, all but two of which are relatively small. It is still a very young industry with the earliest wineries dating from the 1970s, but expansion has been swift as the area has a laundry list of natural attributes. While the more established upstate New York viticultural areas have a more extreme climate that favors white *Vinifera* varietals, Long Island has the ability to ripen red varieties such as Cabernet and Merlot. The warmer climate is a function of the more southerly latitude, the fact that the vineyards are nearly surrounded by the moderating influence of the Atlantic, and that they are shielded from extreme freezes by warm moist winds that blow in from the Carolinas in the fall and winter. Additionally, there is the enviable position of being a stone's throw from one of the largest markets for fine wines in the world, New York City.

As for Long Island Cabernet, many of the wines bear a resemblance to Bordeaux or Washington, in that they feature more restrained levels of alcohol and higher acidity levels than their California counterparts. In many ways, today's wines remind one of similar efforts from Washington ten or even 15 years ago. It may just be that the area's winemakers are a bit behind in the winemaking curve that California and Washington vintners have set, and Long Island will claim its place in the upper echelon in the near future. As was the case with Washington (and Oregon's Pinot Noir) in the 1980s, the potential is certainly there.

Highly Recommended Long Island
Cabernet Sauvignon and Red Meritage

90 • Ternhaven (NY) 1995 Claret d'Alvah, North Fork of Long Island. $18.99.

90 • Ternhaven (NY) 1995 Cabernet Sauvignon, North Fork of Long Island. $15.99.

90 • Paumanok (NY) 1995 Grand Vintage, Cabernet Sauvignon, North Fork of Long Island. $25.

90 • Paumanok (NY) 1995 Assemblage, North Fork of Long Island. $24.

90 • Lenz (NY) 1995 Estate, Cabernet Sauvignon, North Fork of Long Island. $24.99.

90 • Gristina (NY) 1993 Andy's Field Red, North Fork of Long Island. $27.99.

89 • Ternhaven (NY) 1994 Claret d'Alvah, North Fork of Long Island. $18.99.

89 • Pindar (NY) 1995 Reserve, Cabernet Sauvignon, North Fork of Long Island. $18.99.

89 • Osprey's Dominion (NY) 1995 Cabernet Sauvignon, North Fork of Long Island. $13.99.

89 • Gristina (NY) 1996 Cabernet Sauvignon, North Fork of Long Island. $15.99.

89 • Bedell (NY) 1995 Cupola, North Fork of Long Island. $27.50.

88 • Ternhaven (NY) 1994 Cabernet Sauvignon, North Fork of Long Island. $17.99.

88 • Pindar (NY) 1995 Mythology, North Fork of Long Island. $36.99.

88 • Pindar (NY) 1994 Mythology, North Fork of Long Island. $24.99.

88 • Pindar (NY) 1993 Mythology, North Fork of Long Island. $24.99.

88 • Pellegrini (NY) 1995 Cabernet Sauvignon, North Fork of Long Island. $15.99.

88 • Laurel Lake (NY) 1995 Cabernet Sauvignon, North Fork of Long Island. $23.99.

88 • Bedell (NY) 1994 Cupola, North Fork of Long Island. $25.

86 • Pindar (NY) 1993 Reserve, Cabernet Sauvignon, North Fork of Long Island. $18.99.

86 • Lenz (NY) 1997 Vineyard Selection, Merlot-Cabernet, North Fork of Long Island. $16.99.

85 • Ternhaven (NY) 1996 Claret d'Alvah, North Fork of Long Island. $17.99.

85 • Pindar (NY) 1994 Cabernet Sauvignon, North Fork of Long Island. $18.99.

85 • Bidwell (NY) 1995 Claret, North Fork of Long Island. $34.99.

85 • Bedell (NY) 1995 Cabernet Sauvignon, North Fork of Long Island. $21.50.

Scale: Superlative (96-100), Exceptional (90-95), Highly Recommended (85-89), Recommended (80-84), Not Recommended (Under 80)

Top Wines

99 • Woodward Canyon (WA) 1995
Old Vines, Cabernet Sauvignon,
Columbia Valley. $45.

99 • Opus One (CA) 1995 Oakville,
Napa Valley Red. $100.

98 • Pride Mountain (CA) 1996
Cabernet Sauvignon,
Napa Valley. $29.99.

98 • Jarvis (CA) 1994 Cabernet Sauvignon,
Napa Valley. $58.

97 • Stag's Leap Wine Cellars (CA) 1995
Cask 23, Napa Valley. $120.

97 • Pine Ridge (CA) 1996 Cabernet
Sauvignon, Howell Mountain,
Napa Valley. $40.

97 • Opus One (CA) 1992 Oakville, Napa
Valley Red. $65.

97 • Jarvis (CA) 1993 Reserve, Cabernet
Sauvignon, Napa Valley. $75.

97 • Beringer (CA) 1994 Private Reserve,
Cabernet Sauvignon,
Napa Valley. $75.

96 • Stag's Leap Wine Cellars (CA) 1994
Cask 23, Cabernet Sauvignon,
Napa Valley. $100.

96 • St. Francis (CA) 1994 Reserve,
Cabernet Sauvignon,
Sonoma Valley. $30.

96 • Ridge (CA) 1993 Monte Bello,
Cabernet Sauvignon, Santa Cruz
Mountains. $55.

96 • Opus One (CA) 1993 Oakville,
Napa Valley Red. $85.

96 • Merryvale (CA) 1994 Profile,
Napa Valley. $55.

96 • La Jota (CA) 1996 15th Anniversary,
Cabernet Sauvignon, Howell
Mountain, Napa Valley. $58.

96 • DeLille (WA) 1996 Chaleur Estate,
Yakima Valley. $38.

96 • DeLille (WA) 1994 Chaleur Estate,
Yakima Valley. $32.

95 • Shafer (CA) 1994 Hillside Select,
Cabernet Sauvignon, Stags Leap
District, Napa Valley. $85.

95 • S. Anderson (CA) 1994 Richard
Chambers Vineyard, Cabernet
Sauvignon, Stags Leap District. $54.

95 • Ridge (CA) 1994 Monte Bello,
Santa Cruz Mountains. $65.

95 • Pine Ridge (CA) 1996 Cabernet
Sauvignon, Stags Leap District,
Napa Valley. $40.

95 • Peju Province (CA) 1995 Estate
Bottled, Cabernet Sauvignon, Napa
Valley. $55.

95 • Mount Veeder Winery (CA) 1993
Reserve, Napa Valley. $40.

95 • Lokoya (CA) 1995 Cabernet
Sauvignon, Rutherford,
Napa Valley. $100.

95 • Kathryn Kennedy (CA) 1994
Cabernet Sauvignon,
Santa Cruz Mountains. $75.

95 • Fisher (CA) 1994 Lamb Vineyard,
Cabernet Sauvignon,
Napa Valley. $50.

95 • Dominus (CA) 1995 Napanook
Vineyard, Cabernet Sauvignon,
Napa Valley. $95.

95 • Dominus (CA) 1994 Napanook
Vineyard, Napa Valley. $75.

95 • Chateau Ste. Michelle (WA) 1995 Cold
Creek Vineyard, Cabernet Sauvignon,
Columbia Valley. $27.

95 • Caymus (CA) 1994 Special Selection,
Cabernet Sauvignon,
Napa Valley. $110.

ten

North American Merlot

An Introduction: North American Merlot

Merlot is becoming a big business. In a very short period of time Cabernet's second sister has been introduced to the consuming public on a grand scale, and they like what they have seen so far. Easier to pronounce, made for earlier drinking, and softer than Cabernet Sauvignon, Merlot is quickly becoming the nation's red wine of choice. The news media has talked about the promise of Viognier and continues to trot out and dust off the "Rhône Rangers" as the perennial next big thing, but Merlot has quietly and systematically begun to break the tyranny of Cabernet. Someone hit the ignition switch a couple years back and no one seems to have noticed, except the buying public.

While all this may sound rosy, it poses certain problems when trying to assess the varietal on a regional basis. Quite frankly, with so many new Merlot vineyards coming on line, and the temptation for vintners to stretch yields to meet the seemingly insatiable demand, there is a certain sameness to much of the Merlot currently on the market. Until a vineyard reaches a certain age (purists would argue ten years or so at the least), it is hard to get a picture of what type of quality one might ultimately expect. Additionally, huge swaths of California's Central Valley and other areas that one generally wouldn't associate with Bordeaux varietals are being planted with the grape, largely to make wine to compete in the fighting varietal market.

Merlot has been produced for some time, however, in the cradle of California viticulture, Napa and Sonoma. It is here that, unsurprisingly, the best California Merlots are to be found, and correspondingly, some of the most suitable growing conditions. California, however, is not the entire story. For the last several years, Washington State has produced Merlots that stand with the best in the country, and in great years such as 1992 and 1994 has produced the *best* Merlots in the country. If you like Merlot and you haven't tried Washington's version, it's time for a quick trip to your favorite retailer. Often described as two-thirds Bordeaux, one-third California, Washington Merlot is supple and accessible, yet well structured and possessed of sound acidity with more subtle alcohol levels than many California wines. This makes them particularly successful with food while not overpowering when being consumed without. Finally, New York's Long Island has been working with Merlot for a decade or more and some early signs have been promising.

In the most general terms, Merlot of world-class quality is being produced in only a handful of areas such as these. Even the fickle Pinot Noir, despite what are theoretically far-greater growing restrictions, is planted in a wider range of locations. Much of this is probably due to the newness of many plantings, but with its rise in popularity, the varietal will certainly be planted in many more areas, some successfully and others not. For now, however, the consumer looking for the best Merlots in the nation should look to the wines from Napa, Sonoma, and Washington. Fortunately, as the benchmarks, these regions also have developed styles that are separate and distinct.

Scale: Superlative (96-100), Exceptional (90-95), Highly Recommended (85-89), Recommended (80-84), Not Recommended (Under 80)

Best U.S. Merlot Producers

Premier U.S. Merlot Producers (***)

- S. Anderson (Reserve)
- Arrowood
- Beringer (Bancroft Ranch)
- Chateau St. Jean (Reserve)
- Chateau Ste. Michelle
- Flora Springs (Windfall Vineyard)
- L'Ecole No. 41
- Leonetti
- Matanzas Creek
- Pahlmeyer
- Pine Ridge (Carneros)
- Plam
- Rutherford Hill (Reserve)
- Silverado
- St. Francis (Reserve)
- Stag's Leap Wine Cellars
- Waterbrook
- Whitehall Lane (Leonardini Reserve)
- Andrew Will
- Woodward Canyon

Great U.S. Merlot Producers (**)

- Apex
- Barnard Griffin
- Benziger
- Davis Bynum
- Cafaro
- Canoe Ridge Vineyard
- Chateau St. Jean (Sonoma County)
- Clos du Val
- Clos Pegase
- Columbia Crest
- Columbia Winery
- Cosentino
- Cuvaison
- Duckhorn
- Fisher
- Franciscan
- Gary Farrell
- Hyatt
- Lambert Bridge
- Lockwood
- MacRostie
- Newton
- Oakville Ranch
- Robert Pecota (Steven Andre Vineyard)
- Joseph Phelps

Merlot at a Glance

Wines Reviewed:

383

Producers/Brands Represented:

240

Median Price:

$20

- Philippe-Lorraine
- Pine Ridge (Crimson Creek)
- Portteus
- Preston Premium
- Rancho Sisquoc
- Rodney Strong
- Rosenblum
- Seven Hills
- Shafer
- St. Francis (Sonoma County)
- Swanson
- Ternhaven
- Whitehall Lane (Napa Valley)
- Wildhurst

Dependable U.S. Merlot Producers (Recommended)

Some producers placed in this third tier are new (or new to us) and may merit a higher placement in subsequent vintages. These producers are offset by an asterisk.

- *Antares
- Bargetto
- Bedell
- *Byington
- Caterina
- *Chappellet
- Cinnabar
- Covey Run
- Crichton Hall
- Estancia
- Farella-Park
- Ferrari-Carano
- *Fetzer (Bonterra)
- *Gainey
- Gallo-Sonoma
- Geyser Peak
- Gordon Brothers
- Havens
- Hogue
- *Jarvis
- Jekel
- Chateau Julien
- *Justin
- Kendall-Jackson
- Kenwood
- Kiona
- Kunde
- J. Lohr
- Lolonis

- *Macari
- Markham
- Merryvale
- Robert Mondavi
- *Monticello
- *Neyers
- *Niebaum Coppola
- Palmer
- *Fess Parker
- *Peju
- *Powers
- *Ravenswood
- Rombauer
- *Charles Shaw
- Robert Sinskey
- Chateau Souverain
- St. Clement
- Stags' Leap Winery
- Sterling
- Stonestreet
- *Tefft
- Voss
- *Wellington
- Wild Horse
- Windsor
- Yakima River

Five Key Regions for American Merlot

Washington
Wines Reviewed: **99**
Median Price: **$21.50**

"Washington State is making world-class Merlot." So says Chateau Ste. Michelle winemaker Mike Januik, and his sentiments are being echoed not only by neighboring winemakers but by many in the news media as well. Since the 1992 vintage, the finest Washington Merlots have been competitive with the best in the country and in outstanding vintages such as 1994 they can be *the* best. How have Washington Merlots become this good?

Good vintages have surely helped, but the revolution has been fermenting for some time. Quite simply, the vineyards of eastern Washington are worlds apart from the established coastal appellations of California and Oregon. Separated from the ocean by two mountain ranges, including the towering Cascades, rainfall is sparse. Averaging six to ten inches a year, the landscape is semi-desert, with the mighty Columbia River providing the lifeblood, as with much agriculture in the West, water for irrigation. Precisely regulated drip irrigation serves for most producers, meaning water at regular intervals, in the right quantities, and at the right times. The arid climate also makes for long, hot, and sunny summer days with correspondingly cool night temperatures. This allows even and reliably ripened grapes in most years with a remarkably high level of acidity given the ripeness achieved.

Are there other factors, perhaps something even more obvious? "Yes," responds Januik, "Most of Washington's vineyards are planted on their own rootstocks, not grafted native rootstocks which are almost universally used elsewhere in the hopes of thwarting *Phylloxera*." This element further distinguishes the area from those to the south, and has long been rumored a great benefit for those lucky enough to possess such vineyards. The potential benefits also outweigh the risks, in that Washington's vineyards are not as densely packed as those in California, and the *Phylloxera* louse has difficulty navigating through Washington's largely sandy soils.

The 1992 vintage proved to be a turning point for high-end wines from this part of the world, but wineries such as Ste. Michelle, Columbia, and Hogue have been turning out high-quality wines that have flown off retailers' shelves for some time. It is probable that this initial commitment to quality *and* value, which generated a large and profitable industry, has come full circle and allowed the proliferating boutique wineries such as Leonetti, Waterbrook, and L'Ecole No. 41 to move right into a market that has already been cut out for the state's wines. They now reside on the shelves alongside their large-scaled neighbors who are increasingly setting their sights on making world-class wines; and, at the moment, Merlot is driving the bus.

The AVA system in Washington is still underdeveloped, with a huge swath of land entitled to use the Columbia Valley appellation, however, there are more precise areas that have shown some distinctive characteristics. As mentioned before, Washington Merlot is often thought of as being one-part California and two-parts Bordeaux, with the same lushness, yet firmer acidity than California versions, being a hallmark. Generally speaking, Yakima Valley Merlots tend to be a bit more structured than those from other areas, with a tendency to tougher tannins. This may be due in part to the tastes of the area's winemakers, but is a feature of the wines nonetheless. A subregion in the area, Red Mountain, shows wines that are even deeper, with high levels of extract, as exemplified by Kiona and Hedges.

On the opposite end of the scale is Walla Walla, with its string of boutique wineries. Lush and endearing with a heavy reliance on oak seasoning, the Merlots of Leonetti, Waterbrook, L'Ecole No. 41, Patrick M. Paul, and the like are highly coveted and eminently accessible. It must be noted that this also has much to do with winemaking, as many of these wineries' bottlings utilize grapes grown outside the vastly underdeveloped Walla Walla Valley.

Finally, further west down the Columbia River lies the micro-appellation of Canoe Ridge, a 1,000-foot hill rising from the riverbanks and looking out over the barren scrubland on the Oregon side. Named by the explorers Lewis and Clark during their famous 19th century expedition through the area, the hill resembles an overturned canoe. It is jointly owned, in its entirety, by Chateau Ste. Michelle, and the Canoe Ridge Winery, a member of the prestigious Chalone family of wineries. Planted only in the late '80s, it would be an understatement to say that the initial releases have shown promise. They are already some of the best Merlots in the state *and* the country. Lying somewhere between Yakima and Walla Walla in style, Canoe Ridge shows attractive fruit, while being relatively elegant and restrained. The wines are also blessedly devoid of harsh tannins.

The scary part of all this good news is that this is a young industry that is still feeling its way. The wines are going to get even better at the top end. More important, industry leaders such as Ste Michelle and Columbia have undergone aggressive and exhaustive research programs in conjunction with Washington universities. This has allowed them to answer many questions about the regional peculiarities of grape growing in Washington itself, as opposed to relying on information from the University of California at Davis, which is more often than not designed for the California industry. What they have learned is being shared with the state's other growers and promises a shoring up of quality from top to bottom. At the moment there is a high level of cooperation between vintners, as the market for Washington wines has so far seemed unlimited, and that bodes very well for the industry in the near future. In short, with regards Merlot, Washington is at present the most exciting spot in the country.

Highly Recommended Washington Merlot

96 • Chateau Ste. Michelle (WA) 1994 Chateau Reserve, Merlot, Columbia Valley. $40.

96 • Andrew Will (WA) 1995 Reserve, Merlot, Washington. $32.

95 • Woodward Canyon (WA) 1995 Merlot, Columbia Valley. $30.

93 • Waterbrook (WA) 1994 Merlot, Columbia Valley. $19.99.

93 • Seven Hills (WA) 1995 Klipsun Vineyard, Merlot, Columbia Valley. $24.

92 • Waterbrook (WA) 1995 Reserve, Merlot, Columbia Valley. $32.

92 • Tefft (WA) 1994 Winemakers Reserve, Merlot, Yakima Valley. $25.

92 • L'Ecole No. 41 (WA) 1995 Merlot, Columbia Valley. $24.

92 • L'Ecole No. 41 (WA) 1994 Merlot, Columbia Valley. $22.

92 • Chateau Ste. Michelle (WA) 1995 Chateau Reserve, Merlot, Columbia Valley. $42.

92 • Chateau Ste. Michelle (WA) 1994 Cold Creek Vineyard, Merlot, Columbia Valley. $28.

92 • Barnard Griffin (WA) 1994 Reserve, Merlot, Columbia Valley. $24.

92 • Apex (WA) 1995 Merlot, Columbia Valley. $40.

92 • Apex (WA) 1994 Merlot, Columbia Valley. $28.99.

92 • Andrew Will (WA) 1997 Ciel du Cheval, Merlot, Washington. $30.

91 • Woodward Canyon (WA) 1994 Merlot, Columbia Valley. $28.

91 • Portteus (WA) 1995 Reserve, Merlot, Yakima Valley. $29.

91 • Andrew Will (WA) 1997 Pepper Bridge, Merlot, Washington. $30.

91 • Andrew Will (WA) 1994 Reserve, Merlot, Washington. $28.

90 • Yakima River (WA) 1994 Winemaker's Reserve, Merlot, Yakima Valley. $28.

90 • Woodward Canyon (WA) 1997 Merlot, Columbia Valley. $30.

90 • St. Clement (WA) 1995 Merlot, Columbia Valley. $22.

90 • Seven Hills (WA) 1995 Seven Hills Vineyard, Merlot, Walla Walla Valley. $24.

90 • Seven Hills (WA) 1994 Seven Hills Vineyard, Merlot, Walla Walla Valley. $24.

90 • Preston Premium (WA) 1994 Reserve, Merlot, Columbia Valley. $21.

90 • Portteus (WA) 1995 Merlot, Yakima Valley. $16.

90 • Patrick M. Paul (WA) 1993 Conner Lee Vineyards, Merlot, Columbia Valley. $12.

90 • Hyatt (WA) 1994 Reserve, Merlot, Yakima Valley. $29.99.

90 • Columbia Winery (WA) 1995 Red Willow Vineyard, David Lake Signature Series, Merlot, Columbia Valley. $23.

90 • Columbia Winery (WA) 1994 Red Willow Vineyard, David Lake Signature Series, Merlot, Yakima Valley. $23.

90 • Columbia Crest (WA) 1995 Estate Series, Merlot, Columbia Valley. $22.

90 • Chateau Ste. Michelle (WA) 1995 Canoe Ridge Estate Vineyard, Merlot, Columbia Valley. $31.

90 • Chateau Ste. Michelle (WA) 1994 Indian Wells Vineyard, Merlot, Columbia Valley. $30.

90 • Canoe Ridge Vineyard (WA) 1994 Merlot, Columbia Valley. $18.

90 • Barnard Griffin (WA) 1995 Reserve, Merlot, Columbia Valley. $26.95.

90 • Andrew Will (WA) 1997 Seven Hills, Merlot, Walla Walla Valley. $30.

90 • Andrew Will (WA) 1997 Klipsun, Merlot, Washington. $30.

90 • Andrew Will (WA) 1996 Klipsun, Merlot, Washington. $28.

90 • Andrew Will (WA) 1995 Merlot, Washington. $28.

90 • Andrew Will (WA) 1994 Merlot, Washington. $25.

89 • Yakima River (WA) 1994 Merlot, Yakima Valley. $15.

89 • Preston Premium (WA) 1993 Reserve, Merlot, Columbia Valley. $18.99.

89 • Portteus (WA) 1994 Merlot, Yakima Valley. $16.

89 • Columbia Crest (WA) 1996 Merlot, Columbia Valley. $16.

89 • Caterina (WA) 1994 Merlot, Columbia Valley. $16.

89 • Canoe Ridge Vineyard (WA) 1995 Merlot, Columbia Valley. $18.

89 • Barnard Griffin (WA) 1997 Ciel du Cheval Vineyard, Merlot, Columbia Valley. $39.

88 • L'Ecole No. 41 (WA) 1996 Merlot, Columbia Valley. $25.

88 • Hyatt (WA) 1994 Merlot, Yakima Valley. $14.99.

88 • Covey Run (WA) 1994 Reserve, Merlot, Yakima Valley. $23.

88 • Columbia Winery (WA) 1994 Merlot, Columbia Valley. $14.

88 • Columbia Crest (WA) 1994 Estate Series, Merlot, Columbia Valley. $19.

88 • Chateau Ste. Michelle (WA) 1996 Merlot, Columbia Valley. $18.

88 • Chateau Ste. Michelle (WA) 1995 Horse Heaven Vineyard, Merlot, Columbia Valley. $31.

88 • Caterina (WA) 1996 Merlot, Columbia Valley. $18.

88 • Canoe Ridge Vineyard (WA) 1996 Merlot, Columbia Valley. $19.

87 • Wilridge (WA) 1994 Crawford Vineyard, Merlot, Columbia Valley. $19.

87 • Tefft (WA) NV Merlot, Columbia Valley. $15.

87 • Preston Premium (WA) 1995 Western White Oak, Merlot, Columbia Valley. $16.

87 • Powers (WA) 1995 Merlot, Columbia Valley. $16.

87 • Hogue (WA) 1994 Genesis, Merlot, Columbia Valley. $23.

87 • Gordon Brothers (WA) 1994 Merlot, Columbia Valley. $16.99.

87 • Chateau Ste. Michelle (WA) 1994 Merlot, Columbia Valley. $17.

87 • Barnard Griffin (WA) 1995 Merlot, Washington. $16.95.

87 • Apex (WA) 1996 Merlot, Columbia Valley. $35.

86 • Waterbrook (WA) 1996 Merlot, Columbia Valley. $22.

86 • Seven Hills (WA) 1995 Merlot, Columbia Valley. $20.

86 • Hogue (WA) 1994 Merlot, Columbia Valley. $15.

86 • Columbia Winery (WA) 1996 Red Willow Vineyard, David Lake Signature Series, Milestone Merlot, Yakima Valley. $24.

86 • Andrew Will (WA) 1996 Merlot, Washington. $26.

85 • Wilridge (WA) 1994 Klipsun Vineyards, Merlot, Columbia Valley. $19.

85 • W.B. Bridgman (WA) 1995 Merlot, Columbia Valley. $14.99.

85 • Seven Hills (WA) 1994 Merlot, Columbia Valley. $20.

85 • Preston Premium (WA) 1994 Preston Vineyard, Merlot, Columbia Valley. $10.

85 • Covey Run (WA) 1995 Reserve, Merlot, Yakima Valley. $23.

85 • Chateau Ste. Michelle (WA) 1995 Indian Wells Vineyard, Merlot, Columbia Valley. $31.

Napa Valley

Wines Reviewed: 81

Median Price: $26

In the Napa Valley Cabernet is king. So runs the conventional wisdom anyway, but the reality is much more complicated. When speaking of the Napa Valley for appellation purposes, one is talking about a very diverse region capable of producing a wide range of varietals. From the downright chilly southern end of the valley to the semi-tropical northern end, from the heights of the mountains to the fog-banked valley floor, the Napa Valley is capable of growing almost anything.

Cabernet, however, is what brought the valley into the international limelight some 20 years ago. Though grown successfully in a number of spots, many of the premier Cabernets come from a small area in the center of the valley known as the Rutherford Bench. This is important when thinking about the less-established Merlot varietal. Though introduced as a stand-alone by Sterling nearly 30 years ago, the grape until quite recently was used, as in Bordeaux, as a blending component to soften Cabernet, or as a more significant component of a Meritage-style blend.

With the explosion of popularity Merlot has enjoyed, Napa's vintners have rapidly reassessed the varietal. In Bordeaux, Merlot generally prefers slightly cooler conditions than Cabernet, and if one applies this lesson to the Napa Valley and follows the cooler temperature gradients south from the Rutherford Bench, you just might land smack in the middle of the Stags Leap District. By coincidence, or maybe it is not a coincidence at all, this is the home to what seems to be some of the more promising Merlot vineyards in the valley, with a disproportionate level of representation on the list of key producers.

S. Anderson, Silverado, Shafer, Stag's Leap Wine Cellars, Clos du Val: the names are a veritable who's who of great Merlot producers.

Wine lovers have known for some time that Stags Leap is a special area, as evidenced since the early '70s by the wines of Warren Winiarski at Stag's Leap Wine Cellars. It is cooler than areas to the north, as the ocean winds that move up from San Pablo Bay act as an air conditioner and moderate the heat of the afternoon, which builds up on the bare rocks of the eastern mountains. Those rocks also feature in the very different soil composition of the area. Over 95% of the soil is derived from volcanic rocks, which makes for a gravelly, well-drained, and less fertile environment than the Rutherford Bench. These factors combine to draw out the ripening process, affording a longer growing season and the possibility of greater physiological maturity than other regions of the valley floor.

This translates into a particularly flavorful and supple style of Merlot, often marked by subtle minty overtones. The prowess of the region's winemakers and the scarcity of poor vintages also make for consistent wines, which still manage to reflect the subtle differences from one growing season to the next. Saying that Stags Leap may be positioning itself as the Rutherford Bench of Merlot, however, is not to exclude many excellent Merlots from other parts of the valley, just as exceptional Cabernet is made in a range of areas within the overall appellation.

A primary example might be Howell Mountain. Since its recent introduction, Beringer's Bancroft Ranch bottling has generated a great deal of consumer and critical interest. Big, firm, ripe, deep, and rich, the adjectives pour forth, and belie the wine's mountain origins. Merlot, however, throws a new dimension into the traditional Howell Mountain equation: aging potential with earlier approachability. While the monumental Cabernets from Napa mountain producers such as Dunn, Diamond Creek, or Pahlmeyer are usually well balanced and age quite well, they are rarely if ever accessible in their youths. Indeed, a debate has raged for some time about how to soften the mountain fruit or whether one would want to at all, as fans of the style think the proposal to be sacrilege.

Beringer's Bancroft Ranch may portend an interesting compromise: full throttle depth and intensity indicative of mountain fruit, with the tannins naturally softened by a less tannic varietal. This could well lead to a growing sub-genre of Napa Merlot, just as with Cabernet, utilizing the region's distinctive mountain fruit. The results, however, might be even more spectacular, as the varietal may prove itself easier to keep in balance than Cabernet. Napa's various mountain vineyards, including examples in the western range exemplified by Newton and Hess, just might be where some of the most significant developments in Napa Merlot could be seen in the near future.

Highly Recommended Napa Valley Merlot

94 • S. Anderson (CA) 1996 Reserve, Merlot, Stags Leap District. $40.

94 • Silverado (CA) 1995 Merlot, Napa Valley. $22.50.

94 • Rutherford Hill (CA) 1996 Reserve, Merlot, Napa Valley. $44.

93 • Whitehall Lane (CA) 1995 Leonardini Vineyard Reserve, Merlot, Napa Valley. $36.

93 • Plam (CA) 1995 Vintner's Reserve, Merlot, Napa Valley. $25.

93 • Flora Springs (CA) 1995 Windfall Vineyard, Merlot, Napa Valley. $32.

92 • Whitehall Lane (CA) 1996 Leonardini Vineyard Reserve, Merlot, Napa Valley. $40.

92 • Niebaum-Coppola (CA) 1995 Francis Coppola Family Wines, Merlot, Napa Valley. $32.

92 • Flora Springs (CA) 1996 Windfall Vineyard, Merlot, Napa Valley. $40.

92 • Cosentino (CA) 1996 Reserve, Merlot, Napa Valley. $34.

92 • Beringer (CA) 1994 Bancroft Ranch, Merlot, Howell Mountain. $45.

91 • Swanson (CA) 1995 Merlot, Napa Valley. $24.

91 • Philippe-Lorraine (CA) 1996 Merlot, Napa Valley. $21.

91 • Neyers (CA) 1996 Merlot, Napa Valley. $28.

90 • Rutherford Hill (CA) 1995 Reserve, Merlot, Napa Valley. $40.

90 • Peju Province (CA) 1995 Merlot, Napa Valley. $35.

90 • Oakville Ranch (CA) 1995 Merlot, Napa Valley. $35.

90 • Monticello (CA) 1994 Corley Reserve, Merlot, Napa Valley. $28.

90 • Merryvale (CA) 1995 Reserve, Merlot, Napa Valley. $32.

90 • Le Ducq (CA) 1994 Sylviane, Merlot, Napa Valley. $30.

90 • Joseph Phelps (CA) 1995 Merlot, Napa Valley. $26.

90 • Duckhorn (CA) 1995 Merlot, Napa Valley. $28.

90 • Duckhorn (CA) 1993 Merlot, Howell Mountain, Napa Valley. $30.

90 • Cosentino (CA) 1996 Merlot, Oakville, Napa Valley. $60.

90 • Beringer (CA) 1995 Bancroft Ranch, Merlot, Howell Mountain. $50.

89 • Voss (CA) 1995 Merlot, Napa Valley. $20.

89 • S. Anderson (CA) 1995 Reserve, Merlot, Stags Leap District. $32.

89 • Shafer (CA) 1996 Merlot, Napa Valley. $32.

89 • Shafer (CA) 1995 Merlot, Napa Valley. $28.

89 • Robert Keenan (CA) 1996 Merlot, Napa Valley. $30.

89 • Pine Ridge (CA) 1996 Crimson Creek, Merlot, Napa Valley. $25.

89 • Niebaum-Coppola (CA) 1996 Merlot, Napa Valley. $32.

89 • Markham (CA) 1995 Reserve, Merlot, Napa Valley. $38.

89 • Joseph Phelps (CA) 1996 Merlot, Napa Valley. $30.

89 • Fisher (CA) 1996 RCF Vineyard, Merlot, Napa Valley. $30.

89 • Charles Krug (CA) 1994 Reserve, Merlot, Napa Valley. $21.50.

89 • Chappellet (CA) 1996 Merlot, Napa Valley. $22.

89 • Audubon (CA) 1996 Hopper Creek Vineyard, Merlot, Napa Valley. $20.

88 • Whitehall Lane (CA) 1996 Merlot, Napa Valley. $22.

88 • Whitehall Lane (CA) 1995 Merlot, Napa Valley. $20.

88 • Stag's Leap Wine Cellars (CA) 1994 Merlot, Napa Valley. $26.

88 • Markham (CA) 1995 Merlot, Napa Valley. $18.

88 • Farella-Park (CA) 1995 Merlot, Napa Valley. $24.

88 • Duckhorn (CA) 1996 Merlot, Napa Valley. $32.

88 • Cakebread (CA) 1995 Merlot, Napa Valley. $28.50.

88 • Cafaro (CA) 1995 Merlot, Napa Valley. $30.

87 • Stags' Leap Winery (CA) 1995 Merlot, Napa Valley. $28.

87 • St. Clement (CA) 1994 Merlot, Napa Valley. $24.

87 • Robert Pecota (CA) 1995 Steven Andre Vineyard, Napa Valley. $25.

87 • Robert Mondavi (CA) 1995 Merlot, Napa Valley. $26.

87 • Newton (CA) 1996 Merlot, Napa Valley. $32.

87 • Flora Springs (CA) 1995 Merlot, Napa Valley. $16.

86 • Sterling (CA) 1995 Merlot, Napa Valley. $14.

86 • Robert Pecota (CA) 1996 Steven Andre Vineyard, Merlot, Napa Valley. $29.

86 • Robert Mondavi (CA) 1996 Merlot, Napa Valley. $26.

86 • Merryvale (CA) 1996 Reserve, Merlot, Napa Valley. $32.

86 • Markham (CA) 1996 Merlot, Napa Valley. $19.

Scale: Superlative (96-100), Exceptional (90-95), Highly Recommended (85-89),
Recommended (80-84), Not Recommended (Under 80)

86 • Le Ducq (CA) 1995 Sylviane, Merlot, Napa Valley. $30.

86 • Jarvis (CA) 1996 Merlot, Napa Valley. $46.

86 • Crichton Hall (CA) 1996 Merlot, Napa Valley. $26.

85 • Beaulieu (CA) 1994 Merlot, Napa Valley. $12.99.

Sonoma County Merlot

Wines Reviewed: **43**

Median Price: **$20**

As mentioned earlier, trying to pin down a "Sonoma County style" for Merlot is virtually hopeless. That being said it is important to point out why. Sonoma County is a designation used as a catchall for wines from the far more precise sub-appellations of the Russian River, Dry Creek, Alexander, and Sonoma Valleys, with many further divisions among them. Each area is unique and distinctive. What many producers choose to do, however, is blend wines from the various regions within the county and label accordingly. This is not necessarily a bad thing.

Aside from the Sonoma Valley, which is covered later, Merlots that specifically come from the Dry Creek and Russian River Valleys are of particular note. These regions are generally cool with the exception of the northern end of Dry Creek. Thus, within each valley, there is a band that has similar climactic conditions that allow for the ripening of high-quality Merlot. In the Russian River Valley, this band is to the east, further from the ocean and past some of the state's best Pinot Noir vineyards. In the Dry Creek Valley the prime locations are toward the southern cooler end of the valley. The wines themselves are marked by an abundant fruity quality and soft, lush personalities.

Finally, the Merlots that come from Sonoma Mountain at the southern end of the county deserve a special mention. Rising out of the Sonoma Valley, the Sonoma Mountain vineyards are over 1,000 feet off the valley floor, in wild and rugged terrain. Benziger's Merlot exemplifies the style and shares more in common with Napa's mountain Merlots than with those in the Sonoma Valley proper. The wines are rich, ripe, and rugged with perhaps more charisma than their seemingly better-behaved Napa mountain soul mates.

Highly Recommended Sonoma County Merlot

Sonoma County (General)

97 • Chateau St. Jean (CA) 1994 Reserve, Merlot, Sonoma County. $55.

92 • St. Francis (CA) 1996 Merlot, Sonoma County. $23.99.

92 • Benziger (CA) 1995 Reserve, Merlot, Sonoma County. $32.

90 • Windsor (CA) 1995 Shelton Signature Series, Merlot, Sonoma County. $23.50.

89 • St. Francis (CA) 1995 Merlot, Sonoma County. $18.

89 • Quatro (CA) 1996 Merlot, Sonoma County. $12.

89 • Kenwood (CA) 1995 Merlot, Sonoma County. $20.

89 • Byington (CA) 1995 Bradford Mountain, Merlot, Sonoma County. $20.

88 • Windsor (CA) 1996 Shelton Signature Series, Merlot, Sonoma County. $24.50.

88 • Rodney Strong (CA) 1996 Merlot, Sonoma County. $16.

88 • Lambert Bridge (CA) 1996 Merlot, Sonoma County. $20.

88 • Estancia (CA) 1996 Merlot, Sonoma County. $14.

88 • Chateau St. Jean (CA) 1996 Merlot, Sonoma County. $18.

87 • Gallo Sonoma (CA) 1996 Merlot, Sonoma County. $11.

86 • Windsor (CA) 1995 Private Reserve, Merlot, Sonoma County. $18.

86 • Gary Farrell (CA) 1995 Ladi's Vineyard, Sonoma County. $22.

85 • Fetzer (CA) 1995 Barrel Select, Merlot, Sonoma County. $13.99.

Sonoma County (Alexander Valley)

91 • Clos du Bois (CA) 1995 Selection, Merlot, Alexander Valley. $20.

89 • Hanna (CA) 1995 Merlot, Alexander Valley. $21.

89 • de Lorimier (CA) 1996 Merlot, Alexander Valley. $18.

88 • Geyser Peak (CA) 1996 Reserve, Merlot, Alexander Valley. $32.

86 • Clos du Bois (CA) 1996 Merlot, Alexander Valley. $20.

85 • Trentadue (CA) 1994 Merlot, Alexander Valley. $18.

Sonoma County (Dry Creek Valley)

88 • Belvedere (CA) 1996 Merlot, Dry Creek Valley. $16.

87 • Peterson (CA) 1996 Merlot, Dry Creek Valley. $22.50.

86 • Belvedere (CA) 1995 Preferred Stock, Merlot, Dry Creek Valley. $24.

Sonoma County (Russian River Valley)

91 • Gary Farrell (CA) 1996 Merlot, Russian River Valley. $22.

90 • Rosenblum (CA) 1995 Lone Oak Vineyard, Merlot, Russian River Valley. $20.

89 • Mietz (CA) 1995 Merlot, Sonoma County. $21.

89 • Davis Bynum (CA) 1995 Laureles Estate Vineyard, Merlot, Russian River Valley. $24.

88 • Louis Martini (CA) 1995 Reserve, Merlot, Russian River Valley. $18.

Sonoma Valley

Wines Reviewed: 11
Median Price: **$25.00**

"I ride over my beautiful ranch. Between my legs is a beautiful horse. The air is wine. The grapes on a score of rolling hills are red with autumn flame. Across Sonoma Mountain, wisps of sea fog are stealing. The afternoon sun smolders in the drowsy sky. I have everything to make me glad I am alive." So wrote Jack London of the vineyard that now bears his name and fruit for Kenwood Vineyards, in the Sonoma Valley. Little did he know that he might have been surveying what would become California's Pomerol, a tiny super-appellation with a brilliant affinity for Merlot.

As an appellation, Sonoma Valley sits at the southern end of Sonoma County, abutting the Carneros. The valley proper runs between the Mayacamas Mountains, which form the border with Napa, and Sonoma Mountain. As the valley opens up past Sonoma Mountain at the town of Glen Ellen, the climate changes from that in the southern end. It is here, and more precisely between the town of Kenwood and Santa Rosa, that a combination of factors has come together to make for a Merlot growing Eden. A lengthy growing season, moderate temperatures afforded by the cooling breezes of the San Pablo Bay and the Petaluma Gap, and fertile though well-drained soils are the area's hallmark.

Unlike virtually all other California sites, the valley's potential for Merlot was realized almost 30 years ago. As early as 1971, Joseph T. Martin, a furniture store owner, sold his share in that business and bought a 100-acre prune and walnut orchard near Kenwood. He established 90 acres of vineyards, including plantings of Merlot. Miller later went on to build the St. Francis Winery. St. Francis was one of the varietal's earliest proponents, and produced a stand-alone Merlot bottling from the outset.

Today, other notable Merlot producers include Matanzas Creek, Kenwood, and Wellington, with others almost certain to follow their successes. Matanzas Creek in particular has drawn attention to the region with its Journey project, a stated attempt to produce no less than one of the world's greatest Merlots. Using draconian selection and impeccable vinification methods, they have certainly succeeded in producing a world-class wine. Is the wine worth the $155 price tag, however? The question is almost irrelevant, because it is made in such limited quantities, and there will always be collectors to snap such rarities up. Rather, the wine was produced to make a point, and that point has been duly noted. This part of the Sonoma Valley will be a force in American Merlot for years to come.

Sonoma Valley Merlot has overtones of tobacco with a slight herbal quality, which reminds one of the varietal's character as seen in Bordeaux. Complex and aromatic, the wines are not the blockbusters that some Napa Valley Merlots can be. Rather, there is a certain restraint, evidenced even by show wines such as the Journey. Balance and finesse take precedence over a core of red fruit flavors, which still evoke the wine's California origins. These qualities combine to make for a very intriguing style of Merlot indeed.

Highly Recommended Sonoma Valley Merlot

94 • Matanzas Creek (CA) 1994 Journey, Merlot, Sonoma Valley. $155.

94 • Bartholomew Park (CA) 1996 Alta Vista Vineyards, Merlot, Sonoma Valley. $32.

93 • St. Francis (CA) 1995 Reserve, Merlot, Sonoma Valley. $33.99.

93 • St. Francis (CA) 1994 Reserve, Merlot, Sonoma Valley. $29.

89 • Wellington (CA) 1995 Merlot, Sonoma Valley. $16.

89 • Kenwood (CA) 1995 Massara, Merlot, Sonoma Valley. $25.

89 • Kenwood (CA) 1995 Jack London Vineyard, Merlot, Sonoma Valley. $25.

89 • Gundlach Bundschu (CA) 1996 Rhinefarm Vineyards, Merlot, Sonoma Valley. $21.

88 • Matanzas Creek (CA) 1996 Merlot, Sonoma Valley. $47.

88 • Castle (CA) 1996 Merlot, Sonoma Valley. $18.

86 • Kunde (CA) 1997 Merlot, Sonoma Valley. $17.

Long Island, New York

Wines Reviewed: **20**

Median Price: **$19**

Long Island extends nearly 120 miles out into the Atlantic Ocean from New York City. Only 15 miles or so wide, the island is split into two long fingers divided by the Peconic Bay near the town of Riverhead, 70 miles from the East River. Known as the North and South Forks, this end of the island is where viticulture has taken hold. The South Fork is synonymous to many with the Hamptons, New York's answer to Malibu, and the area is home to a few vineyards. The majority, however, are in the more rural and pastoral North Fork, which at only five miles wide and 35 miles long is all but surrounded by water.

At present there are about 20 wineries in the area, all but two of which are relatively small. It is still a very young industry with the earliest wineries dating from the 1970s, but expansion has been swift as the area has a laundry list of natural attributes. While the more established upstate New York viticultural areas have a more extreme climate that favors white *Vinifera* varietals, Long Island has the ability to ripen red varieties such as Cabernet and Merlot. The warmer climate is a function of the more southerly latitude, the fact that the vineyards are nearly surrounded by the moderating influence of the Atlantic, and that they are shielded from extreme freezes by warm moist winds that blow in from the Carolinas in the fall and winter. Additionally, there is the enviable position of being a stone's throw from one of the largest markets for fine wines in the world, New York City.

As for Long Island Merlot, there is no doubt that the area's vintners can ripen the grapes, and that they are of sufficiently high quality to make very good wines. The winemaking in many instances, however, is still finding its way. The wines often tend to be quite tannic and extracted, bordering on toughness. It would be questionable whether many of the current releases would blossom with age. As California vintners have been learning since the 1980s, bigger doesn't always mean better, and wines that are out of balance in youth don't gain balance with age.

It is almost as if the area is still trying too hard to make world-class wines, instead of making world-class *Long Island* wines. It is hard to say what form Long Island Merlot will eventually evolve into. That being said, many of the wines do bear a resemblance to Bordeaux or Washington State, in that they feature more restrained levels of alcohol and higher acidity levels than their California counterparts. In many ways, today's wines remind one of similar efforts from Washington ten and 15 years ago. It may just be that the area's winemakers are a bit behind in the winemaking curve that California and Washington vintners have set, and Long Island will claim its place in the upper echelon in the near future. As was the case with Washington (and Oregon's Pinot Noir) in the 1980s, the potential is certainly there.

Highly Recommended Long Island Merlot

90 • Peconic Bay (NY) 1995 Epic Acre, Merlot, North Fork of Long Island. $24.99.

90 • Macari (NY) 1996 Merlot, North Fork of Long Island. $20.

89 • Ternhaven (NY) 1995 Merlot, North Fork of Long Island. $19.99.

89 • Palmer (NY) 1995 Reserve, Merlot, North Fork of Long Island. $28.

89 • Lenz (NY) 1995 Estate, Merlot, North Fork of Long Island. $29.99.

88 • Ternhaven (NY) 1994 Merlot, North Fork of Long Island. $18.99.

88 • Pellegrini (NY) 1995 Merlot, North Fork of Long Island. $16.99.

88 • Paumanok (NY) 1995 Grand Vintage, Merlot, North Fork of Long Island. $22.

88 • Bedell (NY) 1995 Reserve, Merlot, North Fork of Long Island. $27.50.

86 • Osprey's Dominion (NY) 1996 Merlot, North Fork of Long Island. $14.99.

86 • Bedell (NY) 1995 Merlot, North Fork of Long Island. $17.99.

85 • Laurel Lake (NY) 1996 Merlot, North Fork of Long Island. $12.99.

85 • Gristina (NY) 1995 Merlot, North Fork of Long Island. $14.99.

Scale: Superlative (96-100), Exceptional (90-95), Highly Recommended (85-89), Recommended (80-84), Not Recommended (Under 80)

Top Wines

97 • Chateau St. Jean (CA) 1994 Reserve, Merlot, Sonoma County. $55.

96 • Chateau Ste. Michelle (WA) 1994 Chateau Reserve, Merlot, Columbia Valley. $40.

96 • Andrew Will (WA) 1995 Reserve, Merlot, Washington. $32.

95 • Woodward Canyon (WA) 1995 Merlot, Columbia Valley. $30.

94 • Silverado (CA) 1995 Merlot, Napa Valley. $22.50.

94 • S. Anderson (CA) 1996 Reserve, Merlot, Stags Leap District. $40.

94 • Rutherford Hill (CA) 1996 Reserve, Merlot, Napa Valley. $44.

94 • Pine Ridge (CA) 1996 Merlot, Carneros. $35.

94 • Matanzas Creek (CA) 1994 Journey, Merlot, Sonoma Valley. $155.

94 • Bartholomew Park (CA) 1996 Alta Vista Vineyards, Merlot, Sonoma Valley. $32.

93 • Whitehall Lane (CA) 1995 Leonardini Vineyard Reserve, Merlot, Napa Valley. $36.

93 • Waterbrook (WA) 1994 Merlot, Columbia Valley. $19.99.

93 • St. Francis (CA) 1995 Reserve, Merlot, Sonoma Valley. $33.99.

93 • St. Francis (CA) 1994 Reserve, Merlot, Sonoma Valley. $29.

93 • Seven Hills (WA) 1995 Klipsun Vineyard, Merlot, Columbia Valley. $24.

93 • Ridge (CA) 1996 Monte Bello Ridge, Merlot, Santa Cruz Mountains. $40.

93 • Plam (CA) 1995 Vintner's Reserve, Merlot, Napa Valley. $25.

93 • Flora Springs (CA) 1995 Windfall Vineyard, Merlot, Napa Valley. $32.

92 • Whitehall Lane (CA) 1996 Leonardini Vineyard Reserve, Merlot, Napa Valley. $40.

92 • Waterbrook (WA) 1995 Reserve, Merlot, Columbia Valley. $32.

92 • Tefft (WA) 1994 Winemakers Reserve, Merlot, Yakima Valley. $25.

92 • St. Francis (CA) 1996 Merlot, Sonoma County. $23.99.

92 • Niebaum-Coppola (CA) 1995 Francis Coppola Family Wines, Merlot, Napa Valley. $32.

92 • Lockwood (CA) 1995 Partners' Reserve, Merlot, Monterey County. $24.

92 • L'Ecole No. 41 (WA) 1995 Merlot, Columbia Valley. $24.

92 • L'Ecole No. 41 (WA) 1994 Merlot, Columbia Valley. $22.

92 • Flora Springs (CA) 1996 Windfall Vineyard, Merlot, Napa Valley. $40.

92 • Cosentino (CA) 1996 Reserve, Merlot, Napa Valley. $34.

92 • Chateau Ste. Michelle (WA) 1995 Chateau Reserve, Merlot, Columbia Valley. $42.

92 • Chateau Ste. Michelle (WA) 1994 Cold Creek Vineyard, Merlot, Columbia Valley. $28.

92 • Beringer (CA) 1994 Bancroft Ranch, Merlot, Howell Mountain. $45.

92 • Benziger (CA) 1995 Reserve, Merlot, Sonoma County. $32.

92 • Barnard Griffin (WA) 1994 Reserve, Merlot, Columbia Valley. $24.

92 • Apex (WA) 1995 Merlot, Columbia Valley. $40.

92 • Apex (WA) 1994 Merlot, Columbia Valley. $28.99.

92 • Andrew Will (WA) 1997 Ciel du Cheval, Merlot, Washington. $30.

eleven

❧

North American Pinot Noir

❧

An Introduction: American Pinot Noir

For many (admittedly mad) vintners in various remote locations around the world, Pinot Noir is the Holy Grail. No other wine is so ephemeral, such an enigma. Great Pinot combines an extraordinary bouquet of spice, fruits, and earth, with a sense of lightness, sometimes bordering on frailty, in the mouth. Pinot Noir can indeed be a sensuous if sometimes fleeting experience. While the Cabernet Sauvignon of Bordeaux is all power and weight, Pinot Noir is the epitome of grace and elegance. Accordingly, vignerons in Bordeaux tend to concern themselves with structure. If the wine feels right in the mouth, the bouquet, with time, will inevitably work itself out. In Burgundy, vignerons try to get that all-important bouquet, and having accomplished that, feel that the mouthfeel cannot help but follow suit. Frankly, Pinot Noir is a tougher proposition.

It seems almost fitting then, that Pinot Noir just might be the world's most difficult grape to grow. Maddening and often disheartening, Pinot Noir has been the ruin of more than a few well-intentioned vintners, and it may be just that legacy that has attracted a new breed of individualistic pioneers to relatively remote places like Oregon or California's South Central Coast. While Burgundy has long been the undisputed home of the world's great Pinot Noirs, no other location in the Old World has shown much promise with the grape. Despite some token success here and there, countries with centuries of grape growing tradition, such as Spain and Italy, have had very little success. The initial reason for this is climate. Pinot Noir will not make quality wines in warm climates. Indeed, on the widely recognized heat summation scale that vintners use, Pinot Noir will almost invariably need to be grown in the coolest climate. Still, cooler temperatures alone will not guarantee success, for the fickle grape reacts viciously to many other factors.

Thus, the regions in which the grape can even hope to be grown are very few indeed, and even then it is often on the margins, where all factors will need to come together frequently at precisely the right time for a vintage to be great. Burgundy has been the benchmark, yet Burgundians themselves can often expect no more than two "great" vintages a decade. While Chardonnay has turned into the world's darling, a chameleon of a grape that can make at least decent wines in a huge range of locations, Pinot Noir is the exact opposite. Yet, for the vintner, or wine drinker, who has caught the bug, nothing else will suffice.

I have a theory as to why people are prepared to spend such amazing sums, while often being disappointed, in the search for great Pinot Noir, whether they are making it or drinking it. Pinot Noir is like nirvana, the seventh chakra, and only the select few will ever get there. When one first develops an interest in wine, it is often through the introduction of something white or rosé that has a bit of sweetness such as White Zinfandel or Riesling. Then the tastes turn drier as the budding wine drinker finds that drier whites such as Chardonnay are better at the dinner table, and are viewed as being more "sophisticated." Once a taste for dryness is achieved, the next step is red, and for many the bigger the taste the better. The subtlety is not as important as the power and confidence that a Bordeaux or California Cabernet can engender. Many wine drinkers stop here, but sometimes the dedicated Cabernet fanatic has his interest piqued by something else: the exotic nature of a great Pinot Noir, its grace and finesse, and how

Scale: Superlative (96-100), Exceptional (90-95), Highly Recommended (85-89), Recommended (80-84), Not Recommended (Under 80)

difficult an experience it often is to repeat. The bug has bitten and the fanatic has been born, often looking down his nose a bit at his Bordeaux drinking cousins.

Needless to say, a driven core of New World winemakers have been bitten and are searching high and low for the new Cote d'Or. Unlike Chardonnay, which sometimes seems to be sprouting up in every corner of the country, Pinot Noir is successful in only a few pockets, as its failure was mercifully swift and unequivocal in other areas. When talking about terroir, or the factors that differentiate a wine from Carneros and a wine from Oregon's Willamette Valley, Pinot Noir is probably the world's best vehicle. It is the varietal that most readily reflects its origins in the way it tastes, smells, and looks. Though the race has just begun (most U.S. experience with Pinot Noir is less than twenty years old), it is already possible to discern regional distinctions, and possible even to look at our crystal ball to see what scenarios the future might bring for those brave few who have taken up the search for wine's Holy Grail.

Best U.S. Pinot Noir Producers

Premier U.S. Pinot Noir Producers (***)
- Adelsheim
- Au Bon Climat
- Beringer (Stanly Ranch)
- Bernardus
- Calera
- Carneros Creek
- David Bruce
- Dehlinger
- Domaine Drouhin
- Domaine Serene
- Gary Farell
- Panther Creek
- Ponzi
- Robert Mondavi (Reserve)
- Rochioli
- Sanford
- Signorello
- St. Innocent
- Williams Selyem

Pinot Noir at a Glance

Wines Reviewed:
417

Producers/Brands Represented:
196

Median Price:
$20

Great U.S. Pinot Noir Producers (**)

- Babcock
- Benton Lane
- Benziger
- Bouchaine
- Byington
- Byron
- Cambria
- Chalone
- Chimere
- Clos La Chance
- Cosentino
- Cristom
- Domaine Carneros
- Elkhorn Peak
- El Molino
- Etude
- Evesham Wood
- Fiddlehead
- Thomas Fogarty
- Foxen
- Gainey
- Hartford Court
- Kalin
- Macrostie
- Morgan
- Mount Eden
- Oak Knoll
- Paraiso Springs
- Stephen Ross
- Saintsbury
- Schug
- Sokol Blosser
- Steele
- Torii Mor
- Bethel Heights
- Castle
- Chateau St. Jean
- Chateau Souverain
- Claudia Springs
- Clos du Val
- Cooper Mountain
- Davis Bynum
- De Loach
- Edmeades
- Edna Valley Vineyard
- Erath
- Eyrie
- Fetzer
- *Foley
- *Hargrave
- Kendall-Jackson
- La Crema
- *Laetitia
- *Martinelli
- Meridian
- Newlan
- *Nichols
- Fess Parker
- *Siduri
- Silvan Ridge
- Rodney Strong
- Talley
- Tulocay
- Wild Horse
- Willamette Valley Vineyards
- *Ken Wright Cellars
- ZD

Dependable U.S. Pinot Noir Producers (Recommended)

Some producers placed in this third tier are new (or new to us) and may merit a higher placement in subsequent vintages. These producers are offset by an asterisk.

- Acacia
- Adelaida
- *Anderson's Conn Valley Vineyards
- Archery Summit
- Argyle
- Beaux Frères

Scale: Superlative (96-100), Exceptional (90-95), Highly Recommended (85-89), Recommended (80-84), Not Recommended (Under 80)

Five Key Regions for American Pinot Noir

Oregon

Wines Reviewed: 152
Median Price: **$22**

Oregon Pinot Noir has come as close as that of any region outside Burgundy to what purists adore about this tricky grape. Indeed, this grape variety alone has put Oregon on the international wine map through the efforts of small producers who have taken a similar challenge as vignerons in Burgundy. That challenge is to ripen these notoriously fickle red grapes in a cool climate.

Oregon offers a marginal climate for ripening red wine grapes. Its finest appellations are sandwiched between the Coast Ranges to the west and the Cascades to the east. These appellations are subjected to a marked maritime influence of low cloud and rain that flow over the green crests of the Coast Range mountains.

Unlike California, there are no swathes of vineyards carpeting valley floors and walls. In Oregon slopes have to be carefully chosen, if they are to have any chance of ripening Pinot Noir. Oregon's finest vineyards are dotted throughout the wine-producing areas on southeast- and southwest-facing slopes, to get the maximum of precious sunlight hours.

The three principal appellations of Oregon are the Willamette Valley, the Umpqua Valley, and the Rogue Valley, which are stretched from north to south between the mountains of the Coastal Ranges and Cascades. In these appellations, Burgundy's celebrated red grape variety is the mainstay of the Oregon wine industry. The Willamette Valley is the most important and largest appellation for Pinot Noir, and it grows the grapes for most of Oregon's finest wines.

Oregon Pinot Noir is generally richer than Burgundy—the grapes can often accumulate more sugar—but usually is lighter than California. At its best it comes closer to encapsulating the magical perfume and texture of Pinot Noir than does California, and of course, it is a great deal less heady, rarely exceeding 13% alcohol by volume.

Vintage variation is a fact of life in many great regions, and Oregon is no exception. When the weather gods are smiling, as they were in 1994, sumptuously rich Pinot Noirs can be produced by virtually all producers. The 1995, 1996, and 1997 vintages are more mixed in that all experienced some rain around the harvest, though those wineries that held their nerve, or were lucky, still triumphed in difficult conditions. The year 1998 has been proclaimed a potentially outstanding vintage for Oregon Pinot Noir and these wines are eagerly anticipated by devoted Pinotophiles.

Oregon Pinot Noir is not inexpensive, and weighs in at between $20 and $40 per bottle. Then again, no serious attempt to make Pinot Noir will come very cheaply.

Highly Recommended Oregon Pinot Noir

94 • Domaine Drouhin (OR) 1994 Laurene, Pinot Noir, Willamette Valley. $42.
93 • Torii Mor (OR) 1994 Reserve, Pinot Noir, Yamhill County. $28.

93 • Lange (OR) 1994 Reserve, Pinot Noir, Willamette Valley. $40.

93 • Domaine Serene (OR) 1995 Evenstad Reserve, Pinot Noir, Willamette Valley. $33.

92 • St. Innocent (OR) 1994 Temperance Hill Vineyard, Pinot Noir, Willamette Valley. $32.50.

92 • Sokol Blosser (OR) 1994 Redland, Pinot Noir, Willamette Valley. $35.

92 • Siduri (OR) 1995 Pinot Noir, Oregon. $30.

92 • Ponzi (OR) 1994 Reserve, Pinot Noir, Willamette Valley. $35.

92 • Ponzi (OR) 1993 Reserve, Pinot Noir, Willamette Valley. $26.99.

92 • Panther Creek (OR) 1994 Bednarik Vineyard, Pinot Noir, Willamette Valley. $35.

92 • Cristom (OR) 1994 Reserve, Pinot Noir, Willamette Valley. $27.

92 • Cristom (OR) 1994 Marjorie Vineyard, Pinot Noir, Willamette Valley. $27.

92 • Chateau Benoit (OR) 1994 Estate Reserve, Pinot Noir, Willamette Valley. $25.

91 • St. Innocent (OR) 1995 Freedom Hill Vineyard, Pinot Noir, Willamette Valley. $24.99.

91 • Redhawk (OR) 1994 Estate Reserve, Pinot Noir, Willamette Valley. $25.

91 • Oak Knoll (OR) 1994 Vintage Reserve, Pinot Noir, Willamette Valley. $34.

91 • Evesham Wood (OR) 1994 Temperance Hill Vineyard, Pinot Noir, Willamette Valley. $24.

91 • Erath (OR) 1994 Weber Vineyard Reserve, Pinot Noir, Willamette Valley. $25.

91 • Duck Pond (OR) 1994 Fries Family Reserve, Pinot Noir, Willamette Valley. $25.

91 • Domaine Serene (OR) 1994 Evenstad Reserve, Pinot Noir, Willamette Valley. $30.

91 • Domaine Drouhin (OR) 1995 Laurene, Pinot Noir, Willamette Valley. $45.

91 • Cooper Mountain (OR) 1994 Estate Reserve, Pinot Noir, Willamette Valley. $29.75.

90 • Tualatin (OR) 1994 Estate Reserve, Pinot Noir, Willamette Valley. $20.

90 • St. Innocent (OR) 1995 O'Connor Vineyard, Pinot Noir, Willamette Valley. $19.99.

90 • St. Innocent (OR) 1994 Seven Springs Vineyard, Pinot Noir, Willamette Valley. $28.50.

90 • Ponzi (OR) 1995 25th Anniversary Reserve, Pinot Noir, Willamette Valley. $50.

90 • Panther Creek (OR) 1995 Freedom Hill Vineyard, Pinot Noir, Willamette Valley. $27.99.

90 • Oak Knoll (OR) 1994 Silver Anniversary Reserve, Pinot Noir, Willamette Valley. $20.

90 • Lange (OR) 1994 Pinot Noir, Willamette Valley. $18.

90 • Ken Wright Cellars (OR) 1995 Canary Hill Vineyard, Pinot Noir, Willamette Valley. $24.99.

90 • Elk Cove (OR) 1994 La Boheme Vineyard, Pinot Noir, Willamette Valley. $35.

90 • Domaine Serene (OR) 1994 Reserve, Pinot Noir, Willamette Valley. $20.

90 • Cristom (OR) 1996 Marjorie Vineyard, Pinot Noir, Willamette Valley. $32.

90 • Benton Lane (OR) 1996 Reserve, Pinot Noir, Oregon. $28.

90 • Benton Lane (OR) 1994 Reserve, Pinot Noir, Oregon. $28.50.

90 • Beaux Freres (OR) 1995 Pinot Noir, Yamhill County. $50.

90 • Autumn Wind (OR) 1994 Reserve, Pinot Noir, Oregon. $30.

90 • Amity (OR) 1993 Winemakers Reserve, Pinot Noir, Willamette Valley. $35.

90 • Adelsheim (OR) 1995 Pinot Noir, Oregon. $18.99.

90 • Adelsheim (OR) 1994 Seven Springs Vineyard, Pinot Noir, Polk County. $30.

89 • Willamette Valley Vineyards (OR) 1995 Founders' Reserve, Pinot Noir, Oregon. $18.

89 • Willamette Valley Vineyards (OR) 1994 OVB, Pinot Noir, Oregon. $30.

89 • St. Innocent (OR) 1994 O'Connor Vineyard, Pinot Noir, Willamette Valley. $32.50.

89 • Sokol Blosser (OR) 1994 Pinot Noir, Willamette Valley. $17.

89 • Ponzi (OR) 1994 Pinot Noir, Willamette Valley. $18.

89 • McKinlay (OR) 1995 Special Selection, Pinot Noir, Willamette Valley. $32.50.

89 • Henry Estate (OR) 1994 Barrel Select, Pinot Noir, Umpqua Valley. $24.

Scale: Superlative (96-100), Exceptional (90-95), Highly Recommended (85-89), Recommended (80-84), Not Recommended (Under 80)

89 • Erath (OR) 1993 Reserve, Pinot Noir, Willamette Valley. $20.

89 • Elk Cove (OR) 1994 Estate Reserve, Pinot Noir, Willamette Valley. $25.

89 • Duck Pond (OR) 1995 Pinot Noir, Willamette Valley. $8.

89 • Domaine Drouhin (OR) 1996 Laurene, Pinot Noir, Willamette Valley. $48.

89 • Domaine Drouhin (OR) 1994 Pinot Noir, Oregon. $30.

89 • Cristom (OR) 1995 Marjorie Vineyard, Pinot Noir, Willamette Valley. $27.

89 • Cristom (OR) 1994 Mt. Jefferson Cuvee, Pinot Noir, Willamette Valley. $17.

89 • Chehalem (OR) 1995 Rion Reserve, Pinot Noir, Willamette Valley. $34.

89 • Byington (CA) 1995 Pinot Noir, Willamette Valley. $20.

89 • Bethel Heights (OR) 1994 Flat Block Reserve, Pinot Noir, Willamette Valley. $24.

88 • Witness Tree (OR) 1995 Pinot Noir, Willamette Valley. $17.

88 • Torii Mor (OR) 1995 Pinot Noir, Yamhill County. $19.

88 • Sokol Blosser (OR) 1993 Redland, Pinot Noir, Willamette Valley. $25.

88 • Silvan Ridge (Or) 1995 Pinot Noir, Willamette Valley. $19.

88 • Silvan Ridge (OR) 1994 Visconti Vineyard, Pinot Noir, Willamette Valley. $26.

88 • Silvan Ridge (OR) 1994 Pinot Noir, Willamette Valley. $19.

88 • Panther Creek (OR) 1995 Bednarik Vineyard, Pinot Noir, Willamette Valley. $27.99.

88 • Montinore (OR) 1994 Winemaker's Reserve, Pinot Noir, Willamette Valley. $14.

88 • Ken Wright Cellars (OR) 1995 Carter Vineyard, Pinot Noir, Willamette Valley. $24.99.

88 • Girardet (OR) 1994 Barrel Select, Pinot Noir, Umpqua Valley. $18.

88 • Fiddlehead (OR) 1995 Pinot Noir, Willamette Valley. $32.

88 • Fiddlehead (OR) 1994 Pinot Noir, Willamette Valley. $32.

88 • Eyrie (OR) 1995 Pinot Noir, Willamette Valley. $19.

88 • Domaine Drouhin (OR) 1995 Pinot Noir, Oregon. $28.

88 • Cristom (OR) 1996 Louise Vineyard, Pinot Noir, Willamette Valley. $32.

88 • Cristom (OR) 1995 Reserve, Pinot Noir, Willamette Valley. $27.

88 • Cooper Mountain (OR) 1995 Reserve, Pinot Noir, Willamette Valley. $25.

88 • Broadley (OR) 1995 Reserve, Pinot Noir, Oregon. $18.

87 • Van Duzer (OR) 1994 Eola Selection, Pinot Noir, Oregon. $12.50.

87 • Sokol Blosser (OR) 1995 Pinot Noir, Willamette Valley. $15.

87 • Rex Hill (OR) 1994 Pinot Noir, Willamette Valley. $10.99.

87 • Panther Creek (OR) 1995 Shea Vineyard, Pinot Noir, Willamette Valley. $27.99.

87 • Oak Knoll (OR) 1995 Pinot Noir, Willamette Valley. $15.

87 • Montinore (OR) 1995 Winemaker's Reserve, Pinot Noir, Willamette Valley. $17.99.

87 • Henry Estate (OR) 1993 Barrel Select, Pinot Noir, Umpqua Valley. $18.

87 • Flynn (OR) 1994 Estate, Pinot Noir, Willamette Valley. $14.

87 • Firesteed (OR) 1995 Pinot Noir, Oregon. $9.99.

87 • Cooper Mountain (OR) 1994 Estate, Pinot Noir, Willamette Valley. $15.75.

87 • Chehalem (OR) 1995 Three Vineyard, Pinot Noir, Willamette Valley. $15.

87 • Bridgeview (OR) 1995 Reserve, Pinot Noir, Oregon. $15.99.

86 • Sokol Blosser (OR) 1995 Redland, Pinot Noir, Yamhill County. $35.

86 • King Estate (OR) 1995 Pinot Noir, Oregon. $18.

86 • Hinman (OR) 1994 Pinot Noir, Oregon. $10.99.

86 • Henry Estate (OR) 1995 Barrel Select, Pinot Noir, Umpqua Valley. $20.

86 • Erath (OR) 1995 Vintage Select, Pinot Noir, Willamette Valley. $19.

86 • Elk Cove (OR) 1996 Roosevelt, Pinot Noir, Oregon. $40.

86 • Domaine Drouhin (OR) 1996 Pinot Noir, Oregon. $33.

86 • Chehalem (OR) 1995 Ridgecrest Vineyard, Pinot Noir, Willamette Valley. $22.

86 • Benton Lane (OR) 1996 Pinot Noir, Oregon. $15.

86 • Archery Summit (OR) 1996 Arcus Estate, Pinot Noir, Oregon. $59.

86 • Amity (OR) 1995 Sunnyside Vineyard, Pinot Noir, Willamette Valley. $18.

86 • Amity (OR) 1994 Pinot Noir, Willamette Valley. $16.

85 • Willamette Valley Vineyards (OR) 1995 Pinot Noir, Oregon. $12.50.

85 • Tyee (OR) 1993 Pinot Noir, Willamette Valley. $13.50.

85 • St. Innocent (OR) 1996 O'Connor Vineyard, Pinot Noir, Willamette Valley. $20.

85 • Silvan Ridge (OR) 1996 Eola Springs Vineyard, Pinot Noir, Willamette Valley. $26.

85 • Silvan Ridge (OR) 1995 Hoodview Vineyard, Pinot Noir, Willamette Valley. $22.

85 • Siduri (OR) 1996 Pinot Noir, Oregon. $34.

85 • Kramer (OR) 1992 Reserve, Pinot Noir, Willamette Valley. $22.

85 • Henry Estate (OR) 1995 Umpqua Cuvee, Pinot Noir, Umpqua Valley. $10.

85 • Cristom (OR) 1995 Mt. Jefferson Cuvee, Pinot Noir, Willamette Valley. $17.

85 • Chehalem (OR) 1996 Three Vineyard, Pinot Noir, Willamette Valley. $18.

85 • Bridgeview (OR) 1996 Pinot Noir, Oregon. $10.99.

85 • Bethel Heights (OR) 1995 Wadenswil Block Reserve, Pinot Noir, Willamette Valley. $24.

California's South Central Coast

Wines Reviewed: **40**
Median Price: **$24.50**

As one drives south, and south, and south from San Francisco, logic would follow that the climate would be correspondingly warmer. In general terms this is true, but when you finally make it down to Santa Barbara you find out that the immediate area is, in fact, downright chilly. It has to do with a quirk of nature and California's tortured geology. Between Alaska and the Strait of Juan de Fuca at South America's southern tip, the coastal mountain ranges have a north-south orientation, effectively blocking the maritime influence of the Pacific, but for the few gaps to be found here and there.

The valleys and mountains around Santa Barbara, however, have an east-west orientation, which ushers in the cool Pacific air. Were it not for this, we would be discussing the area's affinity for Port. In several small valleys near the coast in San Luis Obispo and Santa Barbara Counties, however, the conditions have all come together for the production of world class Pinot Noir. Two vineyards in particular, "Bien Nacido" and "Sanford & Benedict," are among the very finest Pinot Noir sites in the state and supply many of the top producers. Additionally, since there are subtle differences again between fruit from the Edna, Arroyo Grande, and Santa Maria Valleys, it is quite common to see producers blend their Pinot Noirs with a range of sources.

Generally, however, the area produces wines that are exceedingly generous in their fruit characters, from lighter cherry to plum flavors, but rarely if ever with the overripe aspects common to warmer climates. The intriguing varietal characters that are found in Pinot Noir often complement this forcefulness of fruit. It is often described as a subtle stemminess or gamey quality that adds a tremendous amount of complexity to the bouquet and avoids the simple red cherry spectrum of the grape. In very broad terms and specific examples notwithstanding, it is this area that at the moment often produces the state's most complex examples of Pinot Noir.

Highly Recommended
South Central Coast Pinot Noir

94 • Cambria (CA) 1996 Reserve, Pinot Noir, Santa Maria Valley. $42.

93 • Laetitia (CA) 1996 Laetitia Vineyard, Pinot Noir, San Luis Obispo County. $29.

93 • Byron (CA) 1996 Pinot Noir, Santa Maria Valley. $18.

92 • Au Bon Climat (CA) 1996 Piccho and Rincon, Pinot Noir, Arroyo Grande Valley. $40.

91 • Steele (CA) 1995 Bien Nacido Vineyard, Pinot Noir, Santa Barbara County. $34.

91 • Laetitia (CA) 1996 Les Galets Vineyard, Pinot Noir, San Luis Obispo County. $29.

90 • Sanford (CA) 1995 Pinot Noir, Santa Barbara County. $20.

90 • Nichols (CA) 1996 Cottonwood Canyon Vineyard, Pinot Noir, Santa Barbara County. $33.

90 • Fess Parker (CA) 1995 American Tradition Reserve, Pinot Noir, Santa Barbara County. $28.

90 • Au Bon Climat (CA) 1996 Sanford & Benedict Vineyard, Pinot Noir, Santa Ynez Valley. $35.

89 • Gainey (CA) 1996 Limited Selection, Pinot Noir, Santa Maria Valley. $28.

89 • Foxen (CA) 1995 Sanford & Benedict Vineyard, Pinot Noir, Santa Ynez Valley. $28.

89 • Foley (CA) 1997 Santa Maria Hills Vineyard, Pinot Noir, Santa Maria Valley. $32.

89 • Cambria (CA) 1995 Julia's Vineyard, Pinot Noir, Santa Maria Valley. $27.

89 • Babcock (CA) 1997 Pinot Noir, Santa Barbara County. $20.

88 • Whitcraft (CA) 1996 Bien Nacido Vineyard, Pinot Noir, Santa Maria Valley. $34.99.

88 • Meridian (CA) 1996 Coastal Reserve, Pinot Noir, Santa Barbara County. $20.

88 • Fetzer (CA) 1995 Bien Nacido Vineyard Reserve, Pinot Noir, Santa Barbara County. $24.

87 • York Mountain Winery (CA) 1994 William Cain Vineyard, Pinot Noir, San Luis Obispo County. $14.

87 • Stephen Ross (CA) 1996 Bien Nacido Vineyard, Pinot Noir, Santa Maria Valley. $24.

87 • Norman (CA) 1995 William Cain Vineyard, Pinot Noir, Paso Robles. $18.

87 • Gary Farrell (CA) 1996 Bien Nacido Vineyard, Pinot Noir, Santa Barbara County. $28.

87 • Foley (CA) 1996 Santa Maria Hills Vineyard, Pinot Noir, Santa Maria Valley. $25.

86 • Stephen Ross (CA) 1996 La Colline Vineyard, Pinot Noir, Arroyo Grande Valley. $20.

86 • Stephen Ross (CA) 1996 Edna Ranch, Pinot Noir, Edna Valley. $22.

86 • Laetitia (CA) 1996 Reserve, Pinot Noir, San Luis Obispo County. $18.

86 • Fess Parker (CA) 1996 American Tradition Reserve, Pinot Noir, Santa Barbara County. $26.

86 • Byron (CA) 1994 Reserve, Pinot Noir, Santa Barbara County. $24.

86 • Babcock (CA) 1996 Pinot Noir, Santa Ynez Valley. $30.

85 • Santa Rita Creek (CA) 1995 Pinot Noir, Paso Robles. $14.50.

85 • Meridian (CA) 1997 Pinot Noir, Santa Barbara. $14.

85 • Fess Parker (CA) 1996 Pinot Noir, Santa Barbara County. $18.

85 • Au Bon Climat (CA) 1996 La Bauge Au-Dessus, Pinot Noir, Santa Barbara County. $25.

Russian River Valley

Wines Reviewed: **30**
Median Price: **$29**

The Russian River Valley is an exceedingly beautiful part of Sonoma County, only miles from the cooling waters of the Pacific. It is carved by the Russian River as it flows south from Mendocino, through the Alexander Valley, and into the Pacific. Because of its proximity to the ocean and the natural funnels for sea air that are provided by the river and the Petaluma Gap to the south, the climate is frequently very chilly. In the western parts nearest the ocean, there is a sub-appellation, the Green Valley, in which conditions are so cool that some of California's most noted sparkling wines are produced there by Iron Horse, Gloria Ferrer, and Korbel.

The area has a long viticultural history and the Korbel Cellars in particular date to 1886. Pinot Noir has long been important to the region and most of the vineyards upon which the area's reputation has been made were planted in the early '70s. The Allen, Rochioli, and Olivet Lane vineyards are of particular distinction and their fruits have the good fortune of being vinified by some of the state's best winemakers. Gary Farrel, Rochioli, Dehlinger, and Williams Selyem all are making stunning Pinot Noirs with grapes from one or all of these vineyards.

Because of the coolness of the climate, the growing season is quite long with the early ripening Pinot Noir generally being harvested in mid-September. This, in combination with the well-established vineyards, the proclivity of the climate, and superior winemaking has resulted in some of the country's best Pinot Noirs to date.

There is indeed a very distinct Russian River style. It is marked by a penetrating depth of flavor. The wines tend to brooding and concentrated flavors that remind the taster of vibrant and piercing crushed raspberries or blackberries. They are exceedingly pure and direct with deep colors. The gamey leathery edge that one might find in the South Central Coast is less frequent here, but the wines are typically more concentrated, focused, and fruit driven. Additionally, the winemaking is more even, with a great consistency from top to bottom. If the South Central Coast at its best someday might emulate wines from the Côte-de-Nuits, the Russian River is already producing wine that has more than a passing resemblance to the Côte-de-Beaune. If you are a fan of exotically pure, fruit-driven Pinot Noir, look no further.

Highly Recommended
Russian River Valley Pinot Noir

92 • David Bruce (CA) 1995 Reserve, Pinot Noir, Russian River Valley. $26.

91 • Davis Bynum (CA) 1995 Limited Edition, Pinot Noir, Russian River Valley. $28.

90 • Stonestreet (CA) 1995 Pinot Noir, Russian River Valley. $30.

90 • Gary Farrell (CA) 1995 Allen Vineyard, Pinot Noir, Russian River Valley. $40.

90 • David Bruce (CA) 1996 Pinot Noir, Russian River Valley. $.

89 • Signorello (CA) 1996 Martinelli Vineyard, Pinot Noir, Russian River Valley. $45.

89 • Rochioli (CA) 1995 Pinot Noir, Russian River Valley. $34.99.

89 • Gary Farrell (CA) 1995 Rochioli Vineyard, Pinot Noir, Russian River Valley. $50.

89 • Cosentino (CA) 1996 Pinot Noir, Russian River Valley. $50.

88 • Signorello (CA) 1995 Martinelli Vineyard, Pinot Noir, Russian River Valley. $48.

88 • Martinelli (CA) 1996 Martinelli Vineyard, Pinot Noir, Russian River Valley. $25.

88 • Kenwood (CA) 1995 Olivet Lane, Pinot Noir, Russian River Valley. $22.

88 • Hartford Court (CA) 1996 Arrendell Vineyard, Pinot Noir, Russian River Valley. $42.

88 • Gary Farrell (CA) 1996 Pinot Noir, Russian River Valley. $22.50.

87 • Hartford Court (CA) 1995 Arrendell Vineyard, Pinot Noir, Russian River Valley. $34.

86 • Rochioli (CA) 1996 Pinot Noir, Russian River Valley. $35.

86 • Patz & Hall (CA) 1996 Pinot Noir, Russian River Valley. $30.

86 • Moshin (CA) 1995 Pinot Noir, Russian River Valley. $16.

86 • Davis Bynum (CA) 1996 Limited Edition, Pinot Noir Limited Edition, Russian River Valley. $28.

Carneros

Wines Reviewed: 52

Median Price: $26

Carneros sits just north of the shores of San Pablo Bay, a northern extension of San Francisco Bay, and is divided between Napa and Sonoma Counties. The division is purely political, and from a viticultural standpoint Carneros stands alone, separate and distinct from Napa or Sonoma, and is one of California's most homogenous and best-conceived AVAs.

Like other areas that are showing promise for Pinot Noir, Carneros, or more properly Los Carneros, has a chilly climate. It is moderated by the waters of the bay, and the maritime fogs and winds. The late afternoon winds in particular, are notorious in their strength as they race from the bay and the Petaluma Gap to the warmer inland valleys. Indeed, recent research has shown that the winds may have an effect even beyond the temperature. It has been shown that in response to high winds a grapevine will slow or shut down the photosynthetic process in order to avoid dehydration. This additional stress coupled with the lengthy growing season should bode well for Pinot Noir.

The results, however, though competent, have not usually been as exciting as one might expect. Carneros Pinot Noir tends to wind up in the delicate red cherry-flavored end of the spectrum with little of the exotic notes that make great Pinot Noir so thrilling. To date, most of the wines have been very correct, but somehow lacking that extra dimension.

Suspicion has been directed to the clones of Pinot Noir that were originally planted. Mainly the product of UC Davis, these clones may be more suited to viticultural regions that don't share the more marginal climate of Carneros. These questions are being addressed, and Francis Mahoney of Carneros Creek has been in the forefront of research in this area. In a classic example of the maddening properties of Pinot Noir, Mahoney is in the final phase of a three-part clonal selection program that he began in 1975! With the arrival of *Phylloxera* in the area, perhaps the more unfortunate aspects of having to replant will be offset by a greater understanding of how new Pinot Noir clones will help to boost Carneros Pinot to the forefront. To be sure Pinot Noir from Mahoney and some other producers are beginning to show those added dimensions that have proven so elusive, and the next few years may see a revolution in Carneros Pinot Noir.

Highly Recommended Carneros Pinot Noir

93 • Beaulieu (CA) 1996 Reserve, Pinot Noir, Carneros. $30.

92 • Signorello (CA) 1995 Las Amigas Vineyard, Pinot Noir, Carneros. $48.

92 • Bouchaine (CA) 1994 Reserve, Pinot Noir, Carneros. $27.

91 • Signorello (CA) 1996 Los Amigas Vineyard, Pinot Noir, Carneros. $45.

91 • Saintsbury (CA) 1995 Reserve, Pinot Noir, Carneros. $28.

91 • MacRostie (CA) 1995 Reserve, Pinot Noir, Carneros. $25.

91 • Beringer (CA) 1995 Stanly Ranch, Pinot Noir, Los Carneros, Napa Valley. $30.

90 • Robert Mondavi (CA) 1996 Reserve, Pinot Noir, Napa Valley. $36.

90 • ZD (CA) 1995 Pinot Noir, Carneros. $24.

89 • Robert Mondavi (CA) 1995 Reserve, Pinot Noir, Napa Valley. $31.

89 • Schug (CA) 1995 Heritage Reserve, Pinot Noir, Carneros. $30.

89 • Richardson (CA) 1996 Sangiacomo Vineyard, Pinot Noir, Carneros. $19.

89 • Etude (CA) 1995 Pinot Noir, Carneros. $33.50.

89 • Chateau St. Jean (CA) 1995 Durell Vineyard, Pinot Noir, Carneros. $30.

89 • Castle (CA) 1997 Sangiacomo Vineyard, Pinot Noir, Los Carneros. $30.

89 • Buena Vista (CA) 1995 Grand Reserve, Pinot Noir, Carneros. $26.

88 • Robert Mondavi (CA) 1995 Pinot Noir, Napa Valley. $18.

88 • Robert Mondavi (CA) 1995 Pinot Noir, Carneros. $26.

88 • MacRostie (CA) 1995 Pinot Noir, Carneros. $17.75.

88 • Carneros Creek (CA) 1996 Pinot Noir, Carneros. $18.

87 • Domaine Chandon (CA) 1996 Pinot Noir, Carneros. $28.95.

87 • Cuvaison (CA) 1995 Eris, Pinot Noir, Carneros. $18.99.

87 • Crichton Hall (CA) 1995 Pinot Noir, Napa Valley. $25.

87 • Castle (CA) 1997 Durell Vineyard, Pinot Noir, Los Carneros. $30.

87 • Beaulieu (CA) 1995 Reserve, Pinot Noir, Carneros. $29.95.

87 • Acacia (CA) 1995 Pinot Noir, Carneros. $16.

86 • Saintsbury (CA) 1996 Reserve, Pinot Noir, Carneros. $34.

86 • Domaine Carneros (CA) 1995 Pinot Noir, Carneros. $20.

86 • Cosentino (CA) 1996 Pinot Noir, Carneros. $30.

85 • Clos du Val (CA) 1995 Pinot Noir, Carneros. $20.

California's Mount Harlan and Chalone

Wines Reviewed: **6**
Median Price: **$35**

Though not really in the same spirit as the aforementioned larger viticultural areas, it would be impossible to discuss the state of American Pinot Noir without addressing the extraordinary "micro-appellations" of Chalone and Mt. Harlan. Both appellations are in the Gavilan Mountain Range above and between the Monterey and San Benito AVAs east of Monterey. It is one of the few areas in California with limestone-based soils. Additionally, both are essentially single winery AVAs with extraordinary histories.

Mount Harlan is the home of Calera, the winery founded by California's current day Pinot Noir guru, Josh Jensen. His vineyards are at an altitude of 2,200 feet, and despite some reports to the contrary from journalists who have never actually been to the area, Mt. Harlan provides the cool temperatures and long growing season favored by Pinot Noir. Indeed, the average annual temperature is between 58 and 60 degrees Fahrenheit.

The vineyards were established in 1974 after an exhaustive search for the limestone soils that were similar to those Jensen remembered from working the 1970 vintage at Burgundy's Domaine de la Romanée-Conti. What the limestone means in Burgundy is good drainage, which is important in an area prone to inopportune rainfall. What it has meant on Mt. Harlan, an area with very little rainfall, is a draconian yield. This was especially true in the early days when Jensen was driving water up the side of Mt. Harlan by truck.

His winemaking philosophy is completely non-interventionist, with the centerpiece being an eight-story gravity flow winery, which allows him to go from grape to bottle without mechanical handling. Jensen relies on wild yeasts and never filters his wines. Additionally, being a true "terroirist" he has divided his Pinot Noir holdings into four separate and distinct vineyards. Reed, Jensen, Selleck, and Mills are vinified and bottled separately, providing a fascinating opportunity to taste and compare. The range is complemented by a pleasant, though quite different, Central Coast bottling, which allows him to stay in business.

To say the single vineyard Mt. Harlan Pinot Noirs are exotic would be an understatement. They are incredibly concentrated with outrageous bouquets, yet on the palate they display a sense of lightness. They are wines that are exceedingly difficult to compare to other Pinot Noirs, and one is left inevitably with the conclusion that they are not Côte-de-Nuits, not Côte-de-Beaune, but Mt. Harlan. If you are passionate about Pinot Noir, the wines of Calera cannot be missed.

As for Chalone, the vineyards are located some 30 miles as the crow flies further down the Gavilan Range, and are exceedingly remote. At about 1,650 feet they are above the fog line, and the vineyard is made all the more impressive by the dramatic backdrop of the jagged mountains of the Pinnacles National Monument.

The area was originally planted by a Frenchman in 1919, and the holdings were extended in 1946. Chalone's reserve Pinot Noir is crafted from these 1946 plantings and accordingly shows all the concentration one would expect. A tiny winery was constructed in 1960 by some amateur enthusiasts, and was subsequently purchased by Richard Graff, a Harvard music graduate who had been studying at UC Davis. The first release of Chalone was in 1969 and the property is now a publicly held corporation in a coalition with several wineries, including Carmenet, Acacia, and Canoe Ridge in Washington.

Chalone's Pinot Noirs are built for the long haul, and made in a very elegant and restrained style. Though not bursting at the seams with varietal intensity, their track record in the cellar is unquestionable. These are wines for contemplation, and are correspondingly difficult to evaluate in their youth. After several years of age the wines tend to open up with a minerally complexity accented by soft floral notes. Along with Calera, these wines stand out as being quite separate and distinct from the rest of California's Pinot Noirs, and deserve a place in any well-stocked cellar.

Highly Recommended Mount Harlan and Chalone Pinot Noir

95 • David Bruce (CA) 1996 Pinot Noir, Chalone. $32.

94 • David Bruce (CA) 1995 Pinot Noir, Chalone. $32.

91 • Calera (CA) 1995 Selleck, Twentieth Anniversary Vintage, Pinot Noir, Mount Harlan. $38.

88 • Chalone (CA) 1993 Reserve, Pinot Noir, Chalone . $35.

86 • Calera (CA) 1994 Mills, Pinot Noir, Mount Harlan. $35.

86 • Calera (CA) 1994 Jensen, Pinot Noir, Mount Harlan. $38.

Top Wines

95 • **David Bruce (CA) 1996 Pinot Noir, Chalone. $32.**

94 • **Domaine Drouhin (OR) 1994 Laurene, Pinot Noir, Willamette Valley. $42.**

94 • **David Bruce (CA) 1995 Pinot Noir, Chalone. $32.**

94 • **Cambria (CA) 1996 Reserve, Pinot Noir, Santa Maria Valley. $42.**

93 • **Torii Mor (OR) 1994 Reserve, Pinot Noir, Yamhill County. $28.**

93 • **Lange (OR) 1994 Reserve, Pinot Noir, Willamette Valley. $40.**

93 • **Laetitia (CA) 1996 Laetitia Vineyard, Pinot Noir, San Luis Obispo County. $29.**

93 • **Edmeades (CA) 1996 Pinot Noir, Anderson Valley. $20.**

93 • **Domaine Serene (OR) 1995 Evenstad Reserve, Pinot Noir, Willamette Valley. $33.**

93 • **Byron (CA) 1996 Pinot Noir, Santa Maria Valley. $18.**

93 • **Beaulieu (CA) 1996 Reserve, Pinot Noir, Carneros. $30.**

92 • **St. Innocent (OR) 1994 Temperance Hill Vineyard, Pinot Noir, Willamette Valley. $32.50.**

92 • **Sokol Blosser (OR) 1994 Redland, Pinot Noir, Willamette Valley. $35.**

92 • **Signorello (CA) 1995 Las Amigas Vineyard, Pinot Noir, Carneros. $48.**

92 • **Siduri (OR) 1995 Pinot Noir, Oregon. $30.**

92 • **Ponzi (OR) 1994 Reserve, Pinot Noir, Willamette Valley. $35.**

92 • **Ponzi (OR) 1993 Reserve, Pinot Noir, Willamette Valley. $26.99.**

92 • **Panther Creek (OR) 1994 Bednarik Vineyard, Pinot Noir, Willamette Valley. $35.**

92 • **David Bruce (CA) 1995 Reserve, Pinot Noir, Russian River Valley. $26.**

92 • **Cristom (OR) 1994 Reserve, Pinot Noir, Willamette Valley. $27.**

92 • **Cristom (OR) 1994 Marjorie Vineyard, Pinot Noir, Willamette Valley. $27.**

Scale: Superlative (96-100), Exceptional (90-95), Highly Recommended (85-89), Recommended (80-84), Not Recommended (Under 80)

404

92 • Chateau Benoit (OR) 1994 Estate
Reserve, Pinot Noir,
Willamette Valley. $25.

92 • Bouchaine (CA) 1994 Reserve,
Pinot Noir, Carneros. $27.

92 • Au Bon Climat (CA) 1996 Piccho and
Rincon, Pinot Noir,
Arroyo Grande Valley. $40.

91 • Steele (CA) 1995 Bien Nacido
Vineyard, Pinot Noir,
Santa Barbara County. $34.

91 • St. Innocent (OR) 1995 Freedom Hill
Vineyard, Pinot Noir,
Willamette Valley. $24.99.

91 • Signorello (CA) 1996 Los Amigas
Vineyard, Pinot Noir, Carneros. $45.

91 • Saintsbury (CA) 1995 Reserve,
Pinot Noir, Carneros. $28.

91 • Redhawk (OR) 1994 Estate Reserve,
Pinot Noir, Willamette Valley. $25.

91 • Oak Knoll (OR) 1994 Vintage
Reserve, Pinot Noir, Willamette
Valley. $34.

91 • Nichols (CA) 1996 Pisoni Vineyard,
Pinot Noir, Monterey County . $42.

91 • MacRostie (CA) 1995 Reserve,
Pinot Noir, Carneros. $25.

91 • Laetitia (CA) 1996 Les Galets
Vineyard, Pinot Noir, San Luis Obispo
County. $29.

91 • Evesham Wood (OR) 1994
Temperance Hill Vineyard,
Pinot Noir, Willamette Valley. $24.

91 • Erath (OR) 1994 Weber Vineyard
Reserve, Pinot Noir, Willamette
Valley. $25.

91 • Duck Pond (OR) 1994 Fries Family
Reserve, Pinot Noir,
Willamette Valley. $25.

91 • Domaine Serene (OR) 1994
Evenstad Reserve, Pinot Noir,
Willamette Valley. $30.

91 • Domaine Drouhin (OR) 1995
Laurene, Pinot Noir,
Willamette Valley. $45.

91 • Davis Bynum (CA) 1995 Limited
Edition, Pinot Noir,
Russian River Valley. $28.

91 • David Bruce (CA) 1996 Pinot Noir,
Central Coast. $16.

91 • David Bruce (CA) 1994 Estate
Reserve, Pinot Noir, Santa Cruz
Mountains. $35.

91 • Cooper Mountain (OR) 1994 Estate
Reserve, Pinot Noir, Willamette
Valley. $29.75.

91 • Claudia Springs (CA) 1996 Reserve,
Pinot Noir, Anderson Valley. $18.

91 • Calera (CA) 1995 Selleck, Twentieth
Anniversary Vintage, Pinot Noir,
Mount Harlan. $38.

91 • Beringer (CA) 1995 Stanly Ranch,
Pinot Noir, Los Carneros, Napa
Valley. $30.

twelve

❧

North American Zinfandel

❧

An Introduction: American Zinfandel

Old Vine Zinfandel: King of the California Reds?

The great wine-growing regions of the world tend to have one thing in common. Their reputations are often inextricably linked to a single varietal. Merlot and Cabernet in Bordeaux, Burgundian Pinot Noir, Tuscan Sangiovese, German Riesling, or Australian Shiraz—the pairings are evocative to wine lovers and often say something about the regions themselves. It is almost possible to taste the sunny Mediterranean character of Sangiovese, the elegance of Bordeaux, or the epic proportions and brash fruitiness of an Australian Shiraz. What then is the quintessential California wine?

The Ups and Downs of Zinfandel

The last quarter century has seen the renaissance of a wine industry that was decimated by Prohibition, and for most, the Holy Grail has been Cabernet Sauvignon. In a rush to show the world that California could once again produce world-class wines, winemakers looked to Europe for a measuring stick, and that stick was firmly planted in the great vineyards of Bordeaux. Meeting with critical acclaim, and, more important, consumer acceptance, vintners rushed to plant Cabernet, followed in short order by Chardonnay, Pinot Noir, and Merlot. Indeed, these are world-class wines, and well deserved of their growing international reputations, but they came at a price, and that price was often a very part of California's viticultural heritage.

For the previous hundred years, Zinfandel had been the king of California reds. In 1884 it accounted for 40 percent of all the state's grapevines, but the grand old vineyards increasingly fell victim to modern economics and changing trends. Replaced by more popular varietals, attacked by *Phylloxera*, or succumbing to senility and neglect, old Zinfandel vineyards have been under siege. Fortunately, a small band of dedicated producers, coupled with a near-fanatical cult following, have continued to hold out, and against all odds, the pendulum just might be poised to swing back.

Zinfandel Strikes Back

So just what is it about these old vineyards that is helping to put Zinfandel back on the map? The consensus seems to be that a vineyard reaches a qualitative peak between 25 and 50 years of age. Because of Prohibition, there are relatively few old vineyards in California. Of the state's 350,000 acres of *Vinifera*, fewer than three percent are over 50 years of age. The vast majority of these are devoted to Zinfandel. While the percentage of Cabernet vineyards exceeding even 25 years of age is minute, it is quite possible to sample the fruits of a fully mature Zinfandel vineyard, often at half the price.

In addition, old vineyards inherently produce less fruit. This factor provides a natural limit on the vine's tendency to overproduce. Though a problem if quantity is the ultimate goal, it is an essential factor in the production of high quality wines. Since the price of Cabernet has risen so precipitously in the last few years, it has once again become economical for vintners to produce wine from shy-yielding old Zinfandel vineyards, and winemakers are scouring the state looking for the odd parcel of vines. Also, the vintners have learned how well

Scale: Superlative (96-100), Exceptional (90-95), Highly Recommended (85-89), Recommended (80-84), Not Recommended (Under 80)

some of the old methods of pruning and farming these vineyards have worked, and are seeking to apply these principles to more and more new plantings.

Drink Your Zin!

When it comes to the appeal of Zinfandel, Paul Draper, winemaker and C.E.O. of Ridge Vineyards has summed it up best. He says, "From day one, Zinfandel has so much forward fruit that it's sensual to drink right away. Its appeal is immediate, whereas Cabernet needs time to develop. You can have a very sensual experience with Cabernet, but you can have a comparable experience with young Zinfandel, which is why, in a restaurant, I'd be more likely to order a Zinfandel than a Cabernet."

Sacrilegious though it may sound, the best releases of Zinfandel are flatly outperforming many of the more highly touted Cabernets. In our tastings of current release Zinfandel's high percentages are rated 90 points or above. This percentage is often shockingly high. Indeed, at this point on the market it is virtually impossible to find many bad bottles of Zinfandel. In addition to the renewed efforts of some of California's best winemakers, recent vintages have gone from strength to strength. More varied, more accessible, and often more interesting, the current crop of Zinfandel's are on a roll and less expensive than Cabernet to boot. So then, the quintessential California wine? If one could capture the essence of the Golden State in a glass, it would most certainly contain a hearty, warming, and self-assured measure of Zinfandel.

Best U.S. Zinfandel Producers

Premier U.S. Zinfandel Producers (***)

- Chateau Potelle (VGS)
- Cline
- De Loach (OFS)
- Gary Farrell
- Lamborn Family Vineyards
- Martinelli
- Ravenswood
- Ridge
- Rocking Horse
- Rosenblum

Zinfandel at a Glance

Wines Reviewed:
209

Producers/Brands Represented:
132

Median Price:
$18

- St. Francis
- Steele
- Storybook Mountain (Reserve)
- Turley
- Wellington

Great U.S. Zinfandel Producers (**)

- Adelaida
- Benziger
- Robert Biale
- Bogle
- David Bruce
- Castle
- Chateau Potelle
- Davis Bynum
- De Loach
- De Rose
- Edmeades
- Ferrari-Carano
- Franciscan
- Frog's Leap
- Gallo Sonoma
- Grgich Hills
- Hartford Court
- Hendry
- Hop Kiln
- Kenwood
- Kunde
- Lambert Bridge
- Limerick Lane
- Lolonis
- Marietta
- Nalle
- Portteus
- Renwood
- Richardson
- Saucelito Canyon
- Scheutz Oles
- Sierra Vista
- Signorello
- Sineann
- Sobon
- Storybook Mountain
- Truchard
- Windsor

Dependable U.S. Zinfandel Producers (Recommended)

Some producers placed in this third tier are new (or new to us) and may merit a higher placement in subsequent vintages. These producers are offset by an asterisk.

- Alderbrook
- Beringer
- Brutocao
- Burgess
- *Claudia Springs
- Clos du Val
- Creston
- *Deaver
- *Dickerson
- Dry Creek Vineyard
- Eberle
- *Edmunds St. John
- Fanucchi
- Fetzer
- Folie à Deux
- Green & Red
- *Grey Wolf
- Haywood
- Herzog
- *Jackson Valley Vineyards
- Karly
- Kendall-Jackson
- *Markham
- Louis M. Martini
- Martini & Prati
- McIlroy
- Meeker
- Meridian
- Mission View
- Newlan
- *Niebaum Coppola
- Oakville Ranch
- Pedroncelli
- Pesenti
- *Pezzi King
- Preston
- Rafanelli
- River Run
- Sonora
- *Sparrow Lane
- *Storrs
- Rodney Strong
- Joseph Swan
- *The Terraces
- Titus
- Topolos
- *Tria
- *Valley of the Moon
- Villa Mt. Eden
- Voss
- *Wildhurst

Five Key Regions for American Zinfandel

Sonoma Valley

Wines Reviewed: **16**
Median Price: **$23**

Sonoma County is great Zinfandel country. That has long been the common wisdom, and by all measure of results that is the truth. Three of the top five appellations are all within Sonoma County, and each displays a distinct style. That fact is a testament to the diversity of growing regions within the county. The Sonoma, Russian River, and Dry Creek Valleys, however, each share a distinctive fruit-forward character about their Zins, which tends to separate them from other great Zin-producing areas such as the Napa Valley or Amador County. Of the three areas, the Sonoma Valley has played the most historic role.

As an appellation, Sonoma Valley sits at the southern end of Sonoma County, abutting the Carneros. The valley proper runs between the Mayacamas Mountains, which form the border with Napa and Sonoma Mountain. As the valley opens up past Sonoma Mountain at the town of Glen Ellen, the climate changes from that in the southern end. The area as a whole is filled with wild and precipitous hills that afford the vineyards ideal exposures to the sun. This, in combination with a lengthy growing season, moderate temperatures afforded by the cooling breezes of San Pablo Bay and the Petaluma Gap, and fertile though well-drained soils have made for a vine-growing Eden.

These attributes were not lost on 19th century author, Jack London, who owned a ranch in the area and commented that "the grapes on a score of rolling hills are red with autumn flame." Many of those vineyards, as was quite typical of the time, were planted with Zinfandel, and often accompanied by a field blend of Petite Sirah, Carignane, or even Alicante Bouchet. Some of the younger vineyards about which London wrote are even bearing fruit today, and that is a key to the greatness of Sonoma Valley Zinfandel. St. Francis, Wellington, Ravenswood, Kunde, and others have bottlings of Zin sourced all or in part from vineyards better than 100 years old, while many other vineyards are 50 years and older. Monte Rosso, Old Hill, Cooke, and Pagani: these and other famous Sonoma Valley Zinfandel vineyards read like pages from California's viticultural history; and now that Zinfandel is once again receiving its proper due, wine-makers have begun to dote on these vineyards and there has been an explosion in rare vineyard-designated bottlings.

As for the overall style of Sonoma Valley Zin, the age of the vineyards and their composition once again figure prominently. Though varying from vintner to vintner, Sonoma Valley Zin tends to be rich, ripe, and heavily extracted with impressive coloring. Some of that coloring and extraction is often lent by the small percentages of Petite Sirah and other grapes that are common to the valley's Zin vineyards, while the age of these vineyards leads to smaller and more intense crops. Yields of one to two tons to the acre and sometimes less are not uncommon. The region's sunny climate, and the cool nights in particular, help to concentrate the fruit while retaining acidity for balance. This makes for wines such as the St. Francis Pagani Vineyard and others that may be upward of 15% alcohol, yet still maintain a sense of balance, and rarely come across as being overripe. This is a marked difference from the porty notes that are common to similarly scaled wines from warmer places such as Amador County. Finally, as for winemaking, though small barrel aging is common, it is quite rare to come across a wood dominated or even a heavily toasted "claret style" Zin, as is so often found in the Napa Valley to the east. Rich, deep, and brooding with dark fruit flavors, yet balanced and crisp, that's Sonoma Valley Zin in a nutshell.

Highly Recommended
Sonoma Valley Zinfandel

95 • St. Francis (CA) 1996 Pagani Vineyard Reserve, Zinfandel, Sonoma Valley. $28.

95 • Rosenblum (CA) 1996 Samsel Vineyard, Maggie's Reserve, Zinfandel, Sonoma Valley. $28.

95 • Ravenswood (CA) 1996 Monte Rosso, Zinfandel, Sonoma Valley. $24.

91 • Ridge (CA) 1995 Pagani Ranch, Late Picked 100 Year Old Vines, Zinfandel, Sonoma Valley. $22.

91 • Ravenswood (CA) 1996 Old Hill Vineyard, Zinfandel, Sonoma Valley. $26.

90 • Valley of the Moon (CA) 1995 Zinfandel, Sonoma Valley. $25.

87 • Haywood (CA) 1995 Rocky Terrace, Los Chamizal Vineyard, Zinfandel, Sonoma Valley. $25.

86 • Louis Martini (CA) 1993 Heritage Collection, Zinfandel, Sonoma Valley. $12.

86 • Kenwood (CA) 1995 Zinfandel, Sonoma Valley. $15.

86 • Kenwood (CA) 1995 Upper Weise Ranch, Zinfandel, Sonoma Valley. $20.

85 • Coturri (CA) 1996 P. Coturri Family Vineyards, Zinfandel, Sonoma Valley. $23.

Russian River Valley

Wines Reviewed: 18
Median Price: $20

The Russian River Valley in Sonoma County has a long viticultural history and today it is known widely for world class Pinot Noir. This is understandable given the coolness of the climate. Accordingly, the production of fine Zinfandel's in the area might sound strange, as the grape is generally associated with much warmer climates such as Amador and the northern end of the Napa Valley. Such is the versatility of Zinfandel that it can produce great wines in a wide range of locations. Additionally, the Russian River bottlings tend to be quite distinctive in reflection of their cool climate origins.

Due to the cold, the growing season is extremely long with the Zinfandel harvest generally occurring in mid to late October. This extended "hang time" allows for an extreme degree of physiological ripeness that concentrates the region's typically vibrant fruit flavors. Meanwhile, the coolness of the climate keeps acidity levels up and balances the opulence of the fruit nicely. The wines, in a flavor profile not totally dissimilar to the region's Pinot Noirs, display a vibrant piercing crushed raspberry and blackberry flavor. They are quite pure and focused in character, even when they reach higher alcohol levels. Finally, as with the Sonoma Valley, most winemakers seem content to use oak seasoning judiciously, preferring to let that spectacularly pure Russian River fruit shine through.

Again like Sonoma Valley, the Russian River is well endowed with many turn-of-the-century vineyards, and attention has been refocused on them in the wake of Zinfandel's resurrection. No one is more indicative of this trend than De Loach. In 1995 they bottled five vineyard-designated Zins in addition to their regular bottlings. These vineyards were planted between 1895 and 1934. Best illustrating the changing economics and perceptions of Zinfandel, however, is the fact that the fruit from these vineyards was used to make De Loach's *white* Zinfandel until 1990. Today, the lucky consumer who is able to secure a few bottles will be rewarded with a fascinating tour of Russian River Zin.

Highly Recommended
Russian River Valley Zinfandel
96 • Martinelli (CA) 1996 Jackass Vineyard, Zinfandel, Russian River Valley. $25.

94 • Ravenswood (CA) 1996 Wood Road Belloni, Zinfandel, Russian River Valley. $24.

94 • De Loach (CA) 1996 Barbieri Ranch, Zinfandel, Russian River Valley. $20.

93 • De Loach (CA) 1996 Saitone Ranch, Zinfandel, Russian River Valley. $20.

93 • De Loach (CA) 1996 OFS, Zinfandel, Russian River Valley. $27.50.

91 • Martinelli (CA) 1997 Louisa & Giuseppe, Zinfandel, Russian River Valley. $18.

90 • Martini & Prati (CA) 1996 Reserve, Zinfandel, Russian River Valley. $18.

89 • Signorello (CA) 1996 Zinfandel, Russian River Valley. $25.

89 • De Loach (CA) 1996 Papera Ranch, Zinfandel, Russian River Valley. $20.

88 • Limerick Lane (CA) 1996 Collins Vineyard, Zinfandel, Russian River Valley. $24.

86 • Topolos (CA) 1995 Piner Heights, Zinfandel, Russian River Valley. $16.50.

86 • McIlroy (CA) 1996 Porter-Bass Vineyard, Zinfandel, Russian River Valley. $18.

86 • De Loach (CA) 1996 Zinfandel, Russian River Valley. $18.

86 • De Loach (CA) 1996 Pelletti Ranch, Zinfandel, Russian River Valley. $20.

Napa Valley
Wines Reviewed: **34**
Median Price: **$18**

When speaking of the Napa Valley for appellation purposes, one is talking about a very diverse region capable of producing a wide range of varietals. From the downright chilly southern end of the valley to the semi-tropical northern end, from the heights of the mountains to the fog-banked valley floor, the Napa Valley is capable of growing almost anything. Though Zinfandel can thrive, at least theoretically, in conditions as diverse as the Russian River Valley or Amador County, it should come as no surprise that its plantings in the Napa Valley are far more limited. Frankly, with the astronomical prices that Oakville, Rutherford, or St. Helena Cabernet have reached, why bother with Zinfandel?

These areas produce some of the world's best Cabernet and the vast majority of Zin vineyards that lasted into the Cabernet boom of the 1980s have long since been dug up and replanted with Cabernet. Nonetheless, Zinfandel continues to thrive in the mountain ranges on either side of the valley proper, and at the very northern tip of the valley in Calistoga. Additionally, with the second coming of Zinfandel in the last few years, it is starting to pop up again in the portfolios of many of the valley's better-known vintners, most of whom had retired the varietal, at least in its red manifestation, years ago. Unfortunately, many of these producers have been forced to source their fruit from newly established vineyards that are often outside the Napa Valley proper.

Some vintners, however, have continued to carry the torch. Ravenswood and Rosenblum, as in other areas of California, have been able to ferret out some spectacular vineyards, while wineries such as Lamborn, Sky, and Storybook Mountain have against all odds, and probably their bankers' advice, chosen to specialize in Napa Valley Zinfandel. Storybook Mountain is probably the best-known Napa estate Zin specialist, and deservedly so. Purchased as a long defunct winery in 1976 by Dr. J. Bernard Seps, a Stanford history professor otherwise known as Jerry, Storybook Mountain was re-established as a vineyard after lengthy consultations with the legendary enologist Andre Tchelistcheff, among others. Considering the clay loam soil and mountainside topography, it was most certainly red wine country, and Dr. Seps threw himself headlong into Zinfandel. Since then he has spent the last 20 years being not only the Napa Valley's foremost Zinfandel producer but also its most tireless promoter.

His wines are typical of the Napa Valley style; one that is separate and distinct from Sonoma's various appellations as well as Amador County. In short the Napa Valley seems to be the primary home of the often talked about "claret style" of Zinfandel. Napa's Zins tend to exhibit a certain restraint, with more tightly wound characters. Oak aging also tends to play a greater part in the wines, particularly when compared to Sonoma bottlings. Napa Valley Zins are often vinified in much the same manner as the valley's Cabernets—hence the claret moniker. Nonetheless, these wines are well made and would certainly appeal to the fan of California Bordeaux varietals. The wines are like well-behaved versions of other California Zins, where the outrageous fruit forward or porty characters of the grape are usually downplayed. Indeed, this may make Napa Zin easier to deal with at the table, but the real Zinfandel fanatic will often lament that claret style Zinfandels have had too much of their ebullient fruit characters, or "Zinniness" if you will, covered up and domesticated.

Highly Recommended Napa Valley Zinfandel

95 • Turley (CA) 1996 Hayne Vineyard, Zinfandel, Napa Valley. $35.

95 • Rosenblum (CA) 1996 White Cottage Vineyard, Zinfandel, Howell Mountain. $21.

94 • Rocking Horse (CA) 1996 Lamborn Vineyard, Zinfandel, Howell Mountain. $18.

93 • Lamborn Family (CA) 1995 The French Connection, Unfiltered, Zinfandel, Howell Mountain, Napa Valley. $22.50.

92 • Markham (CA) 1995 Zinfandel, Napa. $16.

91 • Ravenswood (CA) 1996 Dickerson Vineyard, Zinfandel, Napa Valley. $24.

91 • Chateau Potelle (CA) 1995 VGS, Zinfandel, Mount Veeder, Napa Valley. $35.

90 • Storybook Mountain (CA) 1995 Eastern Exposures, Zinfandel, Napa Valley. $19.50.

90 • Sparrow Lane (CA) 1996 Reserve, Beatty Ranch, Zinfandel, Howell Mountain. $25.

89 • V. Sattui (CA) 1995 Zinfandel, Howell Mountain, Napa Valley. $18.

89 • Hendry (CA) 1995 Block 7, Zinfandel, Napa Valley. $18.

88 • Signorello (CA) 1994 Zinfandel, Napa Valley. $25.

88 • Schuetz Oles (CA) 1996 Korte Ranch, Zinfandel, Napa Valley. $18.

88 • Rosenblum (CA) 1996 Reserve, Hendry Vineyard, Zinfandel, Napa Valley. $22.

88 • Ridge (CA) 1995 York Creek, Zinfandel, Spring Mountain. $22.

88 • Niebaum-Coppola (CA) 1996 Edizione Pennino, Zinfandel, Napa Valley. $26.

87 • Stonehedge (CA) 1995 Zinfandel, Napa Valley. $14.99.

87 • Signorello (CA) 1995 Zinfandel, Napa Valley. $25.

87 • Robert Mondavi (CA) 1996 Zinfandel, Napa Valley. $18.

87 • Monthaven (CA) 1995 Zinfandel, Napa Valley. $9.99.

86 • V. Sattui (CA) 1995 Suzanne's Vineyard, Zinfandel, Napa Valley. $16.75.

86 • Turley (CA) 1995 Moore "Earthquake" Vineyard, Zinfandel, Napa Valley. $35.

86 • Rust Ridge (CA) 1996 Zinfandel, Napa Valley. $18.

86 • Edgewood (CA) 1995 Zinfandel, Napa Valley. $14.

Scale: Superlative (96-100), Exceptional (90-95), Highly Recommended (85-89),
Recommended (80-84), Not Recommended (Under 80)

414

Dry Creek Valley

Wines Reviewed: 12
Median Price: $16

The Dry Creek Valley, though a stone's throw from the Russian River and Alexander Valleys, is unique. As usual Sonoma County's tortured and eternally confusing geography is to blame. The natural boundaries of the valley, however, make this an exceptionally tight and well-defined appellation. The Dry Creek parallels the Alexander Valley on the western side and drains into the Russian River. From the point where the Dry Creek meets the Russian River, it is about 16 miles to the northwest where the Dry Creek Valley abruptly ends. Surrounded by mountains on three sides, with the only opening being at the Russian River, there is no outlet for wind as in the Alexander Valley. Additionally, what fog does enter from the Russian River Valley often comes in at night and burns off quickly during the day. Hence, temperatures are far warmer than in the Russian River Valley, particularly at the northern end. The valley is only two miles wide at its widest point, and the valley floor itself is quite narrow. Benchlands and hillsides dominate the region, and in the warmer northern end of the valley, red wine is king.

The Dry Creek area was largely settled in the late 19th century by Italian families, and as in other parts of Sonoma County, Zinfandel was the favored grape, interspersed with the usual blend of black varieties. First planted in the 1880s, some of these vineyards have miraculously survived to this day. None of Dry Creek's old vineyards are more famous than one, however. That vineyard (actually a collection of three vineyards) is known as Lytton Springs, and it is easily one of the greatest vineyards, of any varietal, in the country. The oldest sections of the vineyard are better than 100 years of age but the wine was first bottled by Ridge Vineyards in 1972. Since that time, the wine has enjoyed cult status, and stood defiantly through Zinfandel's darker days. It was this wine that opened the eyes of the world to the quality of Zinfandel from the Dry Creek Valley, and paved the way for Zin specialists such as Nalle. In 1991 and 1995, Ridge purchased two of the three parcels of vineyards that comprise the Lytton Springs bottling, and in 1993 dropped the word Zinfandel from the label altogether, in deference to the field blend that contains a significant dollop of Petite Sirah with a touch of Grenache. The resultant wines are beautifully balanced and complex, with a penetrating, though not overwhelming depth of flavor, the classic Dry Creek profile.

In describing a general style for Dry Creek Valley Zinfandel, it is probably easiest to first explain what it is not. Dry Creek's Zins are not as deep and extracted as Sonoma Valley's. They are not as racy or fruity as their Russian River neighbors are, nor are they as restrained or as oak influenced as examples from the Napa Valley. Finally, they are not as big and rustic as the wines from Amador. What's left, in a word, is balance. Dry Creek Zinfandel comes across as being almost elegant while retaining that beautiful core of brambly fruit without which a Zinfandel would be lost. Dry Creek Zins don't shout at you, but stand out as having a bit of everything, in a very enticing package. As such, they are wines of undeniably broad appeal.

Highly Recommended Dry Creek Valley Zinfandel

92 • Ridge (CA) 1996 Lytton Springs, Zinfandel, Dry Creek Valley. $25.

91 • Rosenblum (CA) 1996 Rockpile Vineyard, Zinfandel, Dry Creek Valley. $22.

91 • Lambert Bridge (CA) 1996 Zinfandel, Dry Creek Valley. $20.

90 • Pedroncelli (CA) 1996 Mother Clone, Special Vineyard Selection, Zinfandel, Dry Creek Valley. $12.

89 • Tria (CA) 1996 Zinfandel, Dry Creek Valley. $18.

86 • Pedroncelli (CA) 1996 Pedroni-Bushnell Vineyard, Single Vineyard Selection, Zinfandel, Dry Creek Valley. $13.

86 • Nalle (CA) 1996 Zinfandel, Dry Creek Valley. $20.

Amador County

Wines Reviewed: **21**

Mean Price: **$15**

Amador County is a historic part of California in the western foothills of the Sierra Mountains. It is here that the gold rush began in 1848 and by 1870 more than 100 wineries were operating in the area, servicing the miners' enological needs. Of those 100 wineries, only one has survived through the trials and tribulations of a century of California viticulture. That winery is now known as Sobon Estate. Luckily, several of the original plantings of Zinfandel fared better than the wineries and are bearing fruit today. Indeed, the Grand-Pere Vineyard, which was planted in 1868 and is currently bottled by Renwood, is reputed to be the oldest vineyard in the state. Since 1973, there has been a new influx of wineries, and the region's modern day reputation has been staked largely on Zinfandel, which accounts for two-thirds of Amador's plantings.

Climatically and physically, Amador County is miles away from the coastal appellations of California. It sits on the eastern edge of the great Central Valley, and the cooling influence of the ocean is only present in the form of afternoon breezes. This makes for a very warm climate, which is mitigated largely by planting at the higher elevations of the Sierra foothills. The principal AVA within Amador, the Shenandoah Valley, is planted around the 1,000 foot line, while another, Fiddletown, is between 1,500 and 2,500 feet. Nonetheless, day-time temperatures in the ripening season are consistently between 80 and 100 degrees Fahrenheit, and the resulting fruit tends to gather a great deal of tannin and intensity.

Amador County Zins tend to be big and rustic, often with a distinctive stewed fruit character that has port like overtones. The wines can divide tasters, and some find them overwhelming. Traditionalists and Zin fanatics, however, will see the wines' charms, and vineyard-designated bottlings from some of the historic plantings are rapidly becoming cult items. What can be said with certainty, however, is that Amador County Zinfandel is one of the nation's most distinctive and individual styles of wine.

Scale: Superlative (96-100), Exceptional (90-95), Highly Recommended (85-89), Recommended (80-84), Not Recommended (Under 80)

Highly Recommended Amador County Zinfandel

93 • Sierra Vista (CA) 1996 Reeves Vineyard, Zinfandel, El Dorado. $15.

89 • Deaver (CA) 1994 Old Vines, Zinfandel, Amador County. $12.99.

87 • Folie à Deux (CA) 1996 Eschen Vineyard Old Vine, Zinfandel, Fiddletown. $22.

86 • Sierra Vista (CA) 1996 Herbert Vineyard, Zinfandel, El Dorado. $15.

86 • Shenandoah Vineyards (CA) 1996 Vintners Selection, Zinfandel, Shenandoah Valley. $15.

86 • Madroña (CA) 1996 Reserve, Zinfandel, El Dorado. $16.

86 • Granite Springs (CA) 1995 Zinfandel, El Dorado. $11.50.

86 • Folie à Deux (CA) 1996 Old Vine, Zinfandel, Amador County. $18.

86 • Deaver (CA) 1995 Zinfandel, Amador County. $15.

Top Wines

97 • Cline (CA) 1996 Big Break Vineyard, Zinfandel, Contra Costa County. $24.

96 • Martinelli (CA) 1996 Jackass Vineyard, Zinfandel, Russian River Valley. $25.

95 • Turley (CA) 1996 Hayne Vineyard, Zinfandel, Napa Valley. $35.

95 • Steele (CA) 1996 Catfish Vineyard, Zinfandel, Clear Lake. $18.

95 • St. Francis (CA) 1996 Pagani Vineyard Reserve, Zinfandel, Sonoma Valley. $28.

95 • Rosenblum (CA) 1996 White Cottage Vineyard, Zinfandel, Howell Mountain. $21.

95 • Rosenblum (CA) 1996 Samsel Vineyard, Maggie's Reserve, Zinfandel, Sonoma Valley. $28.

95 • Rosenblum (CA) 1996 Annette's Reserve, Rhodes Vineyard, Zinfandel, Redwood Valley. $20.

95 • Ridge (CA) 1996 Dusi Ranch, Zinfandel, Paso Robles. $25.

95 • Ravenswood (CA) 1996 Monte Rosso, Zinfandel, Sonoma Valley. $24.

95 • Cline (CA) 1996 Live Oak Vineyard, Zinfandel, Contra Costa County. $24.

94 • St. Francis (CA) 1996 Old Vines, Zinfandel, Sonoma County. $20.

94 • Rocking Horse (CA) 1996 Lamborn Vineyard, Zinfandel, Howell Mountain. $18.

94 • Ravenswood (CA) 1996 Wood Road Belloni, Zinfandel, Russian River Valley. $24.

94 • De Loach (CA) 1996 Barbieri Ranch, Zinfandel, Russian River Valley. $20.

93 • Steele (CA) 1996 Du Pratt Vineyard, Zinfandel, Mendocino. $20.

93 • Sierra Vista (CA) 1996 Reeves Vineyard, Zinfandel, El Dorado. $15.

93 • Lamborn Family (CA) 1995 The French Connection, Unfiltered, Zinfandel, Howell Mountain, Napa Valley. $22.50.

93 • De Loach (CA) 1996 Saitone Ranch, Zinfandel, Russian River Valley. $20.

93 • De Loach (CA) 1996 OFS, Zinfandel, Russian River Valley. $27.50.

92 • Turley (CA) 1996 Old Vines, Zinfandel, California. $30.

92 • Steele (CA) 1996 Pacini Vineyard, Zinfandel, Mendocino. $16.

92 • Ridge (CA) 1996 Lytton Springs, Zinfandel, Dry Creek Valley. $25.

92 • Ridge (CA) 1995 Geyserville, Zinfandel, Sonoma County. $22.

92 • Markham (CA) 1995 Zinfandel, Napa. $16.

91 • Rosenblum (CA) 1996 Rockpile Vineyard, Zinfandel, Dry Creek Valley. $22.

91 • Rosenblum (CA) 1996 Harris Kratka Vineyard, Zinfandel, Alexander Valley. $22.

91 • Ridge (CA) 1995 Pagani Ranch, Late Picked 100 Year Old Vines, Zinfandel, Sonoma Valley. $22.

91 • Ravenswood (CA) 1996 Old Hill Vineyard, Zinfandel, Sonoma Valley. $26.

91 • Ravenswood (CA) 1996 Dickerson Vineyard, Zinfandel, Napa Valley. $24.

91 • Martinelli (CA) 1997 Louisa & Giuseppe, Zinfandel, Russian River Valley. $18.

91 • Lambert Bridge (CA) 1996 Zinfandel, Dry Creek Valley. $20.

91 • Gary Farrell (CA) 1996 Old Vine Selection, Zinfandel, Sonoma County. $22.50.

91 • David Bruce (CA) 1995 Ranchita Canyon Vineyard, Zinfandel, Paso Robles. $15.

91 • Cline (CA) 1996 Bridgehead Vineyard, Zinfandel, Contra Costa County. $24.

91 • Chateau Potelle (CA) 1995 VGS, Zinfandel, Mount Veeder, Napa Valley. $35.

Scale: Superlative (96-100), Exceptional (90-95), Highly Recommended (85-89), Recommended (80-84), Not Recommended (Under 80)

thirteen

❧

North American Red Rhône Varietals

❧

In Introduction: Who in the World Are the Rhône Rangers?

The Rhône Rangers are a hearty band of U.S. vintners who have been planting and promoting lesser-known varietals from France's Rhône Valley as opposed to the chocolate and vanilla of the wine world: Cabernet and Chardonnay. Instead, they sing the praises of wines such as Syrah, Mourvedre, Grenache, and Carignane. Syrah and Mourvedre tend to be full-bodied, rich, and flavorful reds while Grenache and Carignane tend to the lighter side of the spectrum. Additionally, we have included Petite Sirah. Although not technically a Rhône varietal (its origins are a matter of dispute), Petite Sirah, like Zinfandel, has become a California original. Often made from plots planted at the turn of the century, California's best Petite Sirahs often outperform the more hyped (but younger) plantings of Syrah. Rich, tannic, and dense, Petite Sirah is a real mouthful, and offers one of the best values in California wine today.

Best U.S. Red Rhône Producers

Premier U.S. Red Rhône Varietal Producers (***)
- Alban (Grenache, Syrah)
- Bonny Doon (Le Cigare Volant)
- David Bruce (Petite Sirah)
- Cambria (Syrah)
- Cline (Mourvedre, Carignane)
- Columbia Crest (Syrah)
- Dehlinger (Syrah)
- Edmunds St. John (Syrah)
- La Jota (Petite Sirah)
- Marietta (Blend, Syrah)
- Joseph Phelps (Le Mistral, Syrah)
- Ridge (Mataro, Petite Sirah)
- Stags' Leap Winery (Petite Sirah)
- Thackrey (Syrah, Petite Sirah)

Red Rhône Varietals at a Glance

Wines Reviewed:

132

Producers/Brands Represented:

87

Median Price:

$18

Scale: Superlative (96-100), Exceptional (90-95), Highly Recommended (85-89), Recommended (80-84), Not Recommended (Under 80)

Great U.S. Red Rhône Varietal Producers (**)

- Bogle (Petite Sirah)
- Cline (Syrah)
- Columbia (Syrah)
- Concannon (Petite Sirah)
- Curtis (Syrah)
- Edmunds St. John (Mourvedre, Les Cotes Sauvages)
- Fess Parker (Syrah)
- Fife (Petite Sirah, Max Cuvee)
- Geyser Peak (Shiraz)
- McDowell (Syrah)
- Qupe (Syrah)
- Renwood (Syrah)
- Sierra Vista (Syrah)
- Stag's Leap Wine Cellars (Petite Sirah)
- Swanson (Syrah)

Dependable U.S. Red Rhône Varietal Producers (Recommended)

Some producers placed in this third tier are new (or new to us) and may merit a higher placement in subsequent vintages. These producers are offset by an asterisk.

- *Beaulieu (Ensemble, Syrah)
- *Bonterra (Syrah)
- WB Bridgman (Syrah)
- *Fetzer (Syrah, Petite Sirah)
- Foppiano (Petite Sirah)
- *Fox Hollow (Shiraz)
- Guenoc (Petite Sirah)
- *Hogue (Genesis)
- Horton (Stonecastle Red, Cotes d'Orange, Syrah, Mourvedre)
- Jory (Red Zeppelin, Mano Nera)
- *Kathryn Kennedy (Syrah)
- *LinCourt (Syrah)
- *McCrea (Syrah)
- *Orfila (Syrah)
- *Kent Rasmussen (Petite Sirah, Syrah)
- *Ravenswood (Icon)
- *Rockland (Petite Sirah)
- Rosenblum (Petite Sirah, Mourvedre, Carignane)
- *Santa Barbara Winery (Syrah)
- *Shooting Star (Grenache)
- *Signorello (Petite Sirah, Syrah)
- *Stillman Brown (Petite Sirah)
- *Tablas Creek (Tablas Hills Cuvée Rouge)
- Trentadue (Carignane)
- *Villa Mt. Eden (Syrah)
- *Voss (Syrah)
- *Wellington (Syrah, Alicante Bouschet)

Highly Recommended "Rhône Rangers"

Carignane

91 • Cline (CA) 1996 Ancient Vines, Carignane, Contra Costa County. $18.

89 • Windsor (CA) 1996 Carignane, Mendocino County. $10.

87 • Trentadue (CA) 1995 Carignane, Sonoma County. $12.

86 • River Run (CA) 1996 Wirz Vineyard, Carignane, Cienega Valley. $15.

Cinsault

86 • Castle (CA) 1997 Cinsault, Dry Creek Valley. $19.

Grenache

92 • Alban (CA) 1996 Alban Estate Vineyard, Grenache, Edna Valley. $29.

Mourvedre

95 • Cline (CA) 1996 Small Berry Vinyard, Mourvedre, Contra Costa. $28.

93 • Cline (CA) 1996 Ancient Vines, Mourvedre, Contra Costa County. $18.

88 • Ridge (CA) 1997 Bridgehead, Mataro, Contra Costa County. $.

86 • Wild Horse (CA) 1996 James Berry Vineyard, Mourvedre, Paso Robles. $16.

86 • Rosenblum (CA) 1997 Chateau La Paws, Côte du Bone, Mourvedre, Contra Costa County. $9.50.

Petite Sirah

92 • Bogle (CA) 1997 Petite Sirah, California. $10.

90 • Stags' Leap Winery (CA) 1995 Petite Sirah, Napa Valley. $22.

90 • Ridge (CA) 1996 York Creek, Petite Sirah, Spring Mountain, Napa Valley. $.

88 • Signorello (CA) 1996 110 Year Old Vines, Petite Sirah, Napa Valley. $25.

88 • Geyser Peak (CA) 1996 Winemaker's Selection, Petite Sirah, Alexander Valley. $20.

88 • David Bruce (CA) 1997 Petite Syrah, Central Coast. $16.

87 • Edmeades (CA) 1996 Eagle Point Vineyard, Petite Sirah, Mendocino. $20.

87 • Dos Cabezas (AZ) 1997 Petite Sirah, Cochise County. $15.

86 • Windsor (CA) 1996 Petite Sirah, North Coast. $12.

85 • David Bruce (CA) 1997 Ranchita Canyon, Petite Sirah, Paso Robles. $18.

Syrah

97 • Thackrey (CA) 1995 Orion, Old Vines Rossi Vineyard, Syrah, St. Helena, Napa Valley. $45.

95 • Thackrey (CA) 1996 Orion, Old Vines Rossi Vineyard, St. Helena, Napa Valley. $60.

95 • Thackrey (CA) 1993 Orion, Old Vines Rossi Vineyard, Syrah, St. Helena, Napa Valley. $30.

94 • Thackrey (CA) 1994 Orion, Old Vines Rossi Vineyard, St. Helena, Napa Valley. $30.

93 • Signorello (CA) 1996 Syrah, Napa Valley. $30.

93 • Kathryn Kennedy (CA) 1996 Maridon Vineyard, Syrah, Santa Cruz Mountains. $38.

93 • Edmunds St. John (CA) 1996 Syrah, California. $18.

92 • Qupé (CA) 1996 Bien Nacido Hillside Estate, Syrah, Santa Barbara County. $35.

92 • Beaulieu (CA) 1995 Signet Collection, Syrah, Dry Creek Valley. $25.

92 • Alban (CA) 1996 Reva Syrah, Edna Valley. $23.

91 • Glen Fiona (WA) 1997 Syrah, Walla Walla Valley. $35.

91 • Dehlinger (CA) 1996 Goldridge Vineyard, Syrah, Russian River Valley. $28.

91 • Dehlinger (CA) 1995 Syrah, Russian River Valley. $35.

91 • Bonterra (CA) 1996 Syrah, Mendocino County. $25.

90 • LinCourt (CA) 1996 Syrah, Santa Barbara County. $14.

90 • Columbia Crest (WA) 1996 Reserve, Syrah, Columbia Valley. $22.

89 • Qupé (CA) 1996 Bien Nacido Reserve, Syrah, Santa Barbara County. $25.

89 • Marietta (CA) 1996 Syrah, California. $16.

89 • Kent Rasmussen (CA) 1996 Ramsay Reserve, Syrah, Napa Valley. $20.

89 • Fess Parker (CA) 1996 American Tradition Reserve, Rodney's Vineyard, Syrah, Santa Barbara County. $30.

89 • Cambria (CA) 1996 Tepusquet Vineyard, Syrah, Santa Maria Valley. $18.

89 • Alban (CA) 1996 Lorraine, Syrah, Edna Valley. $29.

88 • Zaca Mesa (CA) 1996 Zaca Vineyards, Syrah, Santa Barbara County. $20.

88 • W.B. Bridgman (WA) 1997 Syrah, Columbia Valley. $18.

88 • Voss (CA) 1995 Shiraz, Napa Valley. $16.

88 • Swanson (CA) 1996 Syrah. $40.

88 • Meridian (CA) 1996 Syrah, Paso Robles. $14.

88 • J. Lohr (CA) 1996 South Ridge, Syrah, Paso Robles. $14.

88 • Fess Parker (CA) 1996 Syrah, Santa Barbara County. $18.

87 • Geyser Peak (CA) 1996 Reserve, Shiraz, Sonoma County. $32.

87 • Curtis (CA) 1996 Ambassador's Vineyard, Syrah, Santa Ynez Valley. $18.

87 • Columbia Winery (WA) 1996 Red Willow Vineyard, Syrah, Yakima Valley. $29.

87 • Beaulieu (CA) 1996 Signet Collection, Syrah, North Coast. $25.

86 • Wild Horse (CA) 1996 James Berry Vineyard, Syrah, Paso Robles. $18.

86 • Seven Peaks (CA) 1996 Shiraz, Paso Robles 1.6% rs. $16.

86 • Richardson (CA) 1997 Syrah, Sonoma Valley. $22.50.

86 • R.H. Phillips (CA) 1996 EXP, Syrah, Dunnigan Hills. $12.

86 • Paraiso Springs (CA) 1996 Syrah, Santa Lucia Highlands. $22.50.

86 • Monterra (CA) 1996 Syrah, Monterey County. $9.99.

86 • Michel-Schlumberger (CA) 1996 Syrah, Coastal California. $20.

86 • Kendall-Jackson (CA) 1996 Vintner's Reserve, Syrah, California. $16.

86 • Kendall-Jackson (CA) 1995 Grand Reserve, Syrah, California. $20.

86 • Hogue (WA) 1996 Genesis, Syrah, Columbia Valley. $15.

86 • Geyser Peak (CA) 1996 Shiraz, Sonoma County. $16.

86 • Fox Hollow (CA) 1996 Shiraz, California. $8.99.

86 • Domaine de la Terre Rouge (CA) 1996 Sentinel Oak Vineyard, Pyramid Block, Syrah, Shenandoah Valley. $25.

86 • Cline (CA) 1996 Syrah, Caneros. $18.

85 • McDowell (CA) 1997 Syrah, Mendocino. $12.

85 • Chateau Ste. Michelle (WA) 1995 Reserve, Syrah, Columbia Valley. $28.

Rhône Varietal Blend

92 • Joseph Phelps (CA) 1996 Le Mistral, California. $25.

90 • Qupé (CA) 1996 Los Olivos Red Cuvee, Ibarra, Young, and Stolpman Vineyards, Santa Barbara County. $18/375 ml.

90 • Bonny Doon (CA) 1996 Le Cigare Volant, California. $22.

90 • Beaulieu (CA) 1996 Ensemble, Signet Collection, California. $25.

88 • Tablas Creek (CA) 1996 Tablas Hills Cuvée Rouge, Paso Robles. $19.99.

88 • Fife (CA) 1996 Max Cuvee, Napa Valley. $30.

87 • Beaulieu (CA) 1996 Beauzeaux, Signet Collection, California. $20.

86 • Thackrey (CA) NV Pleiades VII Old Vines Red, California. $28.

85 • Mount Palomar (CA) 1996 Rey Sol Le Mediterrane Old Vines Selection Red, South Coast. $10.

85 • Curtis (CA) 1997 Heritage, Old Vines Red, California. $10.

fourteen

❦

North American Red Italian Varietals

❦

An Introduction: What About These New-Wave Italian Varietals?

Red Italian Varietals at a Glance

Wines Reviewed:

49

Producers/Brands Represented:

42

Median Price:

$18

In the nineteenth century California had a great deal of Charbono and Barbera planted. This was in great part due to the Italian heritage of many of the area's winemakers. These men were no fools. They planted varietals that grew well in California's Italianesque climate, and made pleasant everyday wines. While today's producers of Barbera and Charbono are a direct link to that lineage, Italy's glamour grapes, Sangiovese and Nebbiolo, are being planted with ever increasing frequency

The beauty of Sangiovese in particular is its diversity. In its Tuscan home it produces not only simple Chianti but also powerful Brunellos and innovative "Super Tuscan" blends. With as much clonal diversity as Pinot Noir (quite a bit indeed), Sangiovese can be made into a wide variety of wines. From lighter-styled reds with a food friendly streak of edgy acidity, to Cabernet enhanced cellar candidates, California Sangiovese should offer a lot to vintner and consumer alike. Surprisingly, however, the results have so far been spotty.

As for Nebbiolo, the jury is still out. Notoriously difficult to grow, the wines produced thus far in California have ranged from brutal to decent but overpriced. At no time has Piedmont seemed in danger. There has, however, been signs of life on the horizon. Martin Brothers' 1994 Nebbiolo "Vecchio" from the Central Coast was the first Nebbiolo that we have tasted from California that was actually a dead ringer for a solid Barolo (it's all in the bouquet—that unmistakable yet rarely seen "tar and roses" aroma). A fluke perhaps, but Martin Brothers (renamed Martin & Weyrich in Spring '99) has been working with the grape since the mid '80s and has recently been finding more and more success with some of their other Italianesque bottlings, such as their now consistently excellent Moscato d'Asti knock-off, Allegro. Perhaps it's a bit early to say that Nebbiolo, like Sangiovese, is showing signs of taking off, but remember Sangiovese itself has come a long way in five years. After all, stranger things have happened.

Best U.S. Red Italian Varietal Producers

Premier U.S. Italian Varietal Producers (***)

• Altamura (Sangiovese)
• Chameleon (Barbera, Sangiovese)
• Ferrari Carano (Siena)
• Shafer (Firebreak)
• Staglin (Stagliano)
• Swanson (Sangiovese)
• Venge (Sangiovese)

Great U.S. Italian Varietal Producers (**)

• Adelaida (Sangiovese)
• Bella Vista (Dolcetto, Sangiovese)
• Cambria (Sangiovese)
• Castelletto (Sangiovese)
• Cosentino (Sangiovese, Nebbiolo)
• Eberle (Barbera)
• Estancia (Sangiovese)
• Montevina (Barbera, Sangiovese)
• Kent Rasmussen (Dolcetto)
• Renwood (Barbera)
• Venezia (Sangiovese)

Dependable U.S. Italian Varietal Producers (Recommended)

Some producers placed in this third tier are new (or new to us) and may merit a higher placement in subsequent vintages. These producers are offset by an asterisk.

• *Acorn (Dolcetto, Sangiovese)
• *Babcock (Sangiovese)
• Barboursville (Barbera)
• Beaulieu (Sangiovese)
• *Benziger (Sangiovese)
• *Bonterra (Sangiovese)
• *Byington (Nebbiolo)
• *Chappellet (Sangiovese)
• *Coturri (Sangiovese)
• *Duckhorn (Paraduxx)
• *Fife (Barbera, Charbono, Sangiovese)
• Flora Springs (Sangiovese)
• *Thomas Fogarty (Sangiovese)
• *Forest Glen (Sangiovese)
• Justin (Nebbiolo)
• Martin Brothers (Nebbiolo)
• Martini & Prati (Barbera)
• Robert Mondavi (Barbera, Sangiovese)
• *Pugliese (Sangiovese)
• Rabbit Ridge (Barbera)
• *Rutherford Hill (Sangiovese)
• Sebastiani (Barbera)
• *Silverado (Sangiovese)
• Trentadue (Sangiovese)

Highly Recommended American-Italian Reds

Barbera

89 • Chameleon (CA) 1996 Barbera, Amador County. $14.

87 • Terra d'Oro (CA) 1995 Montevina, Barbera, Amador County. $18.

87 • Louis Martini (CA) 1994 Heritage Collection, Barbera, Lake County. $12.

Dolcetto

87 • Acorn (CA) 1996 Alegria Vineyards, Dolcetto, Russian River Valley. $18.

Sangiovese

91 • Thomas Fogarty (CA) 1996 Estate Reserve, Sangiovese,
Santa Cruz Mountains. $27.50.

91 • Rutherford Hill (CA) 1995 21st Anniversary, Sangiovese, Napa Valley. $30.

90 • Staglin (CA) 1996 Stagliano, Sangiovese, Rutherford, Napa Valley. $35.

90 • Altamura (CA) 1994 Sangiovese, Napa Valley. $28.

90 • Adelaida (CA) 1995 Sangiovese, San Luis Obispo County. $24.

89 • Trentadue (CA) 1995 Sangiovese, Alexander Valley. $18.

89 • Chappellet (CA) 1995 Sangiovese, Napa Valley. $22.

88 • Pugliese (NY) 1997 Sangiovese, North Fork of Long Island. $13.99.

88 • Chameleon (CA) 1996 Sangiovese, North Coast. $16.

87 • Terra d'Oro (CA) 1995 Montevina, Sangiovese, Amador County. $16.

87 • Obester (CA) 1995 20th Anniversary, Sangiovese, Mendocino County. $13.95.

87 • Forest Glen (CA) 1996 Sangiovese, California. $9.99.

87 • Amador Foothill Winery (CA) 1995 Sangiovese, Shenandoah Valley. $12.

86 • Venge (CA) 1996 Penny Lane Vineyard, Sangiovese, Oakville, Napa Valley. $20.

86 • Iron Horse (CA) 1995 T-bar-T Vineyards, Sangiovese, Alexander Valley. $16.

86 • Deaver (CA) 1996 Sangiovese, Amador County. $16.

86 • Cambria (CA) 1996 Tepusquet Vineyard, Sangiovese, Santa Maria Valley. $18.

86 • Atlas Peak Vineyards (CA) 1995 Reserve, Sangiovese, Atlas Peak, Napa Valley. $24.

86 • Albertoni (CA) 1996 Sangiovese, California. $13.99.

85 • Venezia (CA) 1996 Alegria Vineyards, Sangiovese, Russian River Valley. $19.99.

85 • Folie à Deux (CA) 1996 Sangiovese, Amador County. $16.

85 • Babcock (CA) 1996 Eleven Oaks, Sangiovese, Santa Ynez Valley. $18.

Italian Varietal Blends

93 • Duckhorn (CA) 1995 Paraduxx, Napa Valley. $20.

87 • Shafer (CA) 1995 Firebreak, Napa Valley. $27.

86 • Hidden Cellars (CA) 1996 Sorcery Red, Mendocino. $28.

86 • Ferrari-Carano (CA) 1995 Siena, Sonoma County. $28.

Scale: Superlative (96-100), Exceptional (90-95), Highly Recommended (85-89),
Recommended (80-84), Not Recommended (Under 80)

fifteen

North American Cabernet Franc, Malbec, and Petit Verdot

An Introduction: What about U.S. Cabernet Franc, Malbec, and Petit Verdot?

Cabernet Franc is very closely related to Cabernet Sauvignon and, indeed, it is widely presumed that Cabernet Franc is just a well-established mutation of Cabernet Sauvignon. It is ideally suited to cooler climates as it buds and ripens earlier than Cabernet Sauvignon. Additionally, it is less susceptible to poor weather during harvest. In the Medoc and Graves region of Bordeaux, where it typically constitutes about 15% of the final blend, it is seen as a measure of insurance against poor Cabernet Sauvignon or Merlot weather. Cabernet Franc used to be planted almost as widely as Cabernet Sauvignon in Bordeaux well into the '60s, but Cabernet Sauvignon had swung into such favor that 20 years later it had twice the acreage of Cabernet Franc. Cabernet Franc tends to be lighter in color and tannins than Cabernet Sauvignon, with an earlier maturing character. On Bordeaux's Right Bank, Cabernet Franc has a stronger foothold, and is best known as the dominant grape in the blend for the famed chateau, Cheval Blanc. In the Loire it is the most widely planted red varietal where it yields lighter wines, with distinct herbal overtones. U.S. Cabernet Francs are still largely in the experimental stage and there is a huge spectrum of interpretations, from heavy Napa wines to lighter styles from the East Coast.

Malbec is a rarely planted varietal in Bordeaux, which yields a wine of great color if sometimes it is somewhat short on flavor. It can be tricky to grow as it is susceptible to a range of vineyard diseases. Nonetheless, it has taken hold in Argentina, where it produces a rich rustic wine. In the United States there is very little planted, but some early efforts have proven to be promising.

Petit Verdot, on the other hand, can yield a wine of great depth and personality. It has fallen from favor in Bordeaux, however, as it ripens later than Cabernet Sauvignon and hence only in the best of years. This might

Cabernet Franc, Malbec, and Petit Verdot at a Glance

Wines Reviewed:

65

Producers/Brands Represented:

57

Median Price:

$18

bode well for the varietal in California, which has no such ripening problems, and indeed some of the early efforts with the grape have been surprisingly excellent, with solid structure, deep color, and exotic aromatics. Of all three varieties in California, Petit Verdot just may be the one to watch in the long run.

Best U.S. Cabernet Franc, Malbec, and Petit Verdot Producers

Premier U.S. Cabernet Franc, Malbec, and Petit Verdot Producers (***)

- Benziger Imagery Series (Cabernet Franc, Petit Verdot, & Malbec)
- Jarvis (Cabernet Franc)

Great U.S. Cabernet Franc, Malbec, and Petit Verdot Producers (**)

- Columbia Winery (Red Willow Cabernet Franc)
- Chateau Ste. Michelle (Cold Creek Vineyard Cabernet Franc)
- Helena View (Cabernet Franc)

Dependable U.S. Cabernet Franc, Malbec, and Petit Verdot Producers (Recommended)

Some producers placed in this third tier are new (or new to us) and may merit a higher placement in subsequent vintages. These producers are offset by an asterisk.

- Ahlgren (Cabernet Franc)
- Badger Mountain (Cabernet Franc)
- Barboursville (Cabernet Franc)
- Carmenet (Cabernet Franc)
- *Chappellet
- Clos du Bois (Cabernet Franc)
- Cosentino (Cabernet Franc)
- Gainey (Limited Selection Cabernet Franc)
- Geyser Peak (Cabernet Franc, Petit Verdot, & Malbec)
- Guenoc (Cabernet Franc & Petit Verdot)
- Horton (Cabernet Franc & Malbec)
- Jekel (Cabernet Franc, Petit Verdot, & Malbec)
- Justin (Cabernet Franc)
- Kendall-Jackson (Cabernet Franc)
- *Niebaum Coppola (Cabernet Franc)
- *Peju Province (Cabernet Franc & Petit Verdot)
- *Pride Mountain (Cabernet Franc)
- Quail Ridge (Cabernet Franc)
- *Signorello (Cabernet Franc)
- *Waterbrook (Cabernet Franc)

Highly Recommended Cabernet Franc, Malbec, and Petit Verdot

Cabernet Franc

93 • Jarvis (CA) 1996 Cabernet Franc, Napa Valley. $44.

90 • Signorello (CA) 1995 Cabernet Franc, Napa Valley. $35.

90 • Niebaum-Coppola (CA) 1996 Cabernet Franc, Napa Valley. $20.

89 • Pride Mountain (CA) 1996 Cabernet Franc, Sonoma County. $25.

89 • Pindar (NY) 1994 Cabernet Franc, North Fork of Long Island. $12.99.

89 • Benziger (CA) 1996 Imagery Series, Rancho Salina & Blue Rock Vineyards, Cabernet Franc, Sonoma County. $22.

89 • Ahlgren (CA) 1996 Bates Ranch, Cabernet Franc, Santa Cruz Mountains. $18.

88 • Cosentino (CA) 1996 Cabernet Franc, Napa Valley. $25.

87 • Midnight Cellars (CA) 1995 Crescent, Cabernet Franc, Paso Robles. $15.

87 • Hagafen (CA) 1996 Cabernet Franc, Napa Valley. $18.

86 • Yorkville (CA) 1996 Rennie Vineyard, Cabernet Franc, Mendocino County. $14.

86 • Pellegrini (NY) 1995 Cabernet Franc, North Fork of Long Island. $23.

86 • Kendall-Jackson (CA) 1995 Buckeye Vineyard, Cabernet Franc, Alexander Valley. $20.

86 • Hargrave (NY) 1997 Cabernet Franc, North Fork of Long Island. $14.99.

86 • Gainey (CA) 1996 Limited Selection, Cabernet Franc, Santa Ynez Valley. $20.

86 • Columbia Winery (WA) 1996 Red Willow Vineyard, David Lake Signature Series, Cabernet Franc, Yakima Valley. $19.

86 • Columbia Winery (WA) 1995 Red Willow Vineyard, David Lake Signature Series, Cabernet Franc, Yakima Valley. $20.99.

86 • Chappellet (CA) 1996 Cabernet Franc, Napa Valley. $24.

86 • Chaddsford (PA) 1996 Cabernet Franc, Pennsylvania. $18.

85 • Mission View (CA) 1995 Cabernet Franc, Paso Robles. $13.50.

85 • Hogue (WA) 1994 Genesis, Cabernet Franc, Columbia Valley. $15.

Malbec

85 • Geyser Peak (CA) 1996 Winemaker's Selection, Malbec, Alexander Valley. $20.

Petite Verdot

86 • Geyser Peak (CA) 1996 Winemaker's Selection, Petite Verdot, Alexander Valley. $20.

sixteen

North American Chardonnay

American Chardonnay

Chardonnay is the world's most recognized and requested white wine, so much so that it has effectively become a cliché. This popularity is further exaggerated in the United States where Chardonnay has become synonymous with white wine. Why is Chardonnay so popular? First and foremost, Chardonnay is not only capable of producing some of the world's greatest white wines, but also it grows virtually anywhere. It is a straightforward wine to produce.

Chardonnay is made at all price points but has also reached the pinnacle of quality in many nations and several continents, not only in its native France. Chardonnay simply has mass flavor appeal. Other varietals may present more distinctive personalities: Sauvignon Blanc with its aggressive herbal flavors and gripping acidity; Gewürztraminer filling the nose and palate with hints of rose-water and spice; or Viognier in its wildly exotic, unctuous manifestations. Chardonnay strikes the proverbial middle chord that translates to universal magnetism and a marketer's dream.

In the last decade or so Chardonnay has become the most popular white wine in the United States. This has led to massive plantings of the varietal, and there are now better than a thousand different bottlings produced in every vintage. From Massachusetts to Arizona, and most everywhere in between, Chardonnay has taken root. Differences in both style and price are as much, if not more, a product of winemaking decisions than of location. This is not to say that fruit from cool states such as Oregon does not differ from that of California's hot Central Valley. Chardonnay, perhaps more than any other variety, is the wine-maker's equivalent of a blank white canvas.

Left to its own devices, Chardonnay is simple, fresh, and clean with fruit ranging in flavors from apple and pear in cooler regions to tropical fruit notes in hot climates. The winemaker's decision to use oak or not greatly impacts both flavor and price. Oak barrels are very expensive. Chardonnay is often left on its lees, the sediment precipitated during fermentation. This imparts a toasty bread-like flavor. This process, which is sometimes indicated on the label as "Sur Lie," takes time and time equals money. A major contributor to flavor is the use of a secondary fermentation known technically as "malolactic fermentation." This secondary fermentation is bacteria-induced and creates no additional alcohol. Instead, it converts one kind of acid, *malic*, which is found in Granny Smith apples, to another softer acid, *lactic*, which is found in milk. In addition to acid conversion, malolactic fermentation creates a natural compound called diacetyl. Diacetyl is used by margarine producers to make their product taste like butter. It does the same for Chardonnay. Again this process takes time, which, as we know, in turn equals money. Chardonnay tends to ride out vintage difficulties fairly well, and outside of Oregon's notoriously fickle weather it usually offers a modicum of consistency, particularly in California. Recently, however, the West Coast has had some difficult Chardonnay vintages.

Difficult Vintages?

Craig Williams, the well-respected winemaker of Napa Valley stalwart Joseph Phelps refers to the challenging nature of the '96 harvest with mention of "heat spikes that rendered the sugar/acid/flavor balance between vineyards as highly variable." He goes on to say that "although many excellent wines have been produced from the '96 vintage, it was not a year where quality was consistent throughout." The results of our tastings of '96 Chardonnays from California bear this out. Through rigorous selection and a bit of luck, many producers made fine wines, while a number of others had difficulty maintaining acid levels. Across the board, the '96 Chardonnays are accessible in youth, with ripe and generous characters that won't take well to bottle age. The 1997s will be a definite step up in quality.

As for the Northwest, while 1994 was excellent and 1995 was sound in Oregon, 1996 and 1997 have proven to be even more difficult than California's '96. Combating rain and a lack of ripeness, better Oregon vintners were at least able to make attractive zesty wines, but we will have to wait for future vintages to see a repeat of the knockout 1994s. The 1998 vintage should be just the ticket, as vintners are talking about a replay of 1994. Luckily, Washington fared much better than Oregon in 1996, and a number of outstanding wines were produced.

What has all this meant for price? Not much, as prices are still creeping upward. Fortunately, the increases have been nowhere near the magnitude of those experienced in Cabernet, Merlot, or Pinot Noir, but the average bottle of U.S. Chardonnay will still set you back about $18.

Chardonnay and Food

In regards to pairing Chardonnay with food, pricey and flashy Chardonnay, from California glamour appellations, tends to be fat and rich, with plenty of oak, butter, and spice. On their own these wines are interesting, if heavy. With food they can be clumsy, dominating, and largely incompatible. Cooler climate Chardonnays are often more restrained, with clean fruit balanced by crisp acidity. These wines work with a great deal of dishes from fish to fowl. Crisp, "simplistic" Chardonnay also works well as an aperitif, stimulating the palate rather than drowning it.

❧

Chardonnay at a Glance

Wines Reviewed:
599

Producers/Brands Represented:
376

Median Price:
$18

Best U.S. Chardonnay Producers

Premier U.S. Chardonnay Producers(***)

- Arrowood (Cuvée Michel Berthoud)
- Au Bon Climat (Various Bottlings)
- Beringer (Private Reserve and Sbragia)
- Chateau Potelle (VGS)
- Chateau Ste. Michelle (Reserve and Vineyard designated bottlings)
- Columbia Winery (Wyckoff and Otis Vineyards)
- Gary Farrell
- Ferrari-Carano (Alexander Valley, Reserve, and Tre Terre)
- Fisher (Whitney's Vineyard)
- Franciscan (Cuvée Sauvage)
- Gallo-Sonoma (Estate)
- Guenoc (Genevieve Magoon)
- Hanzell
- Jarvis
- Kistler
- Lewis Cellars
- Matanzas Creek
- Mer et Soleil
- Peter Michael
- Robert Mondavi (Reserve)
- Mount Eden Vineyards
- Newton
- Patz and Hall
- Joseph Phelps (Ovation)
- Qupe
- Ridge
- Rombauer
- San Saba Vineyard
- Shafer (Red Shoulder Ranch)
- Signorello (Founder's Reserve and Hope's Cuvée)
- Stag's Leap Wine Cellars (Reserve and Beckstoffer)
- Talbott

Great U.S. Chardonnay Producers(**)

- Adelaida
- Apex
- Arrowood (Sonoma County)
- Beaucanon
- Bernardus
- Beringer
- David Bruce (Estate Reserve)
- Byington
- Byron (Reserve)
- Calera
- Cambria
- Chalk Hill
- Chalone Vineyard
- Chateau Montelena
- Chateau Potelle
- Chateau St. Jean (Robert Young, Belle Terre, and Durell)
- Chateau Ste. Michelle
- Cinnabar
- Columbia Winery
- Cooper Mountain
- Crichton Hall
- Cronin
- Cuvaison
- Dehlinger
- De Loach (OFS)
- Domain Hill and Mayes
- Edmeades
- El Molino
- Eola Hills
- Far Niente
- Fisher (Coach Insignia)
- Thomas Fogarty (Estate Reserve)
- Franciscan (Napa Valley)
- Gainey
- Gallo-Sonoma (Stefani and Laguna Ranch)
- Grgich Hills
- Gristina (Andy's Field)
- Hess
- Jory (Lion Oaks Ranch)
- Kendall-Jackson
- La Crema
- Landmark
- Laurier
- L'Ecole No. 41
- J. Lohr
- Merryvale
- Robert Mondavi (Carneros, Napa Valley)
- Morgan
- Oakville Ranch
- Paraiso Springs
- Fess Parker
- Peju Province
- Joseph Phelps
- Plam
- Qupe

Scale: Superlative (96-100), Exceptional (90-95), Highly Recommended (85-89), Recommended (80-84), Not Recommended (Under 80)

- Rochioli
- Rosenblum
- Sanford
- Santa Barbara Winery
- Signorello (Napa Valley)
- Silverado
- Simi (Reserve)
- Sonoma-Cutrer
- Sonoma-Loeb
- St. Clement
- St. Francis (Reserve)
- Stag's Leap Wine Cellars
- Steele
- Swanson
- Mark West
- Wild Horse
- Wildhurst
- Woodward Canyon

Dependable U.S. Chardonnay Producers (Recommended)

Some producers placed in this third tier are new (or new to us) and may merit a higher placement in subsequent vintages. These producers are offset by an asterisk.

- Anapamu
- *Babcock
- Barnard Griffin
- Benziger
- *Burgess
- Byron
- Camelot
- Canoe Ridge Vineyard
- Carmenet
- *Chappellet
- Chateau Morrisette
- Chateau Woltner
- Clos La Chance
- Clos Pegase
- Cobblestone
- *Cristom
- *Curtis
- Dry Creek Vineyard (Reserve)
- Elkhorn Peak
- Gloria Ferrer
- Flora Springs
- *Foley
- Forest Glen
- Foxen

- Guenoc
- Harrison
- *Hartford Court
- Horton
- Joullian
- Kalin
- Robert Keenan
- *Kestrel
- *Lambert Bridge
- *Long
- *Macari
- MacRostie
- *Martinelli
- *Peter McCoy
- *McCrea
- McIlroy
- Meridian
- *Monticello
- Murphy-Goode
- *Neyers
- *Nichols
- *Niebaum-Coppola
- *Fess Parker
- *Pezzi King
- *Piedmont
- Pine Ridge
- *Ramey
- *Rancho Zabaco
- Martin Ray (Mariage)
- Stephen Ross
- Saintsbury
- Schug
- Sterling
- *Storrs
- Talley
- *Testarossa
- Marimar Torres
- Treleaven
- *Truchard
- *Venezia
- Villa Mt. Eden
- Waterbrook
- Willamette Valley Vineyards
- ZD

10 Key Regions for American Chardonnay

Napa Valley

Wines Reviewed: **90**
Median Price: **$22.00**

Napa is the nation's "grand cru" appellation, and Napa vintners have been nothing if not successful in marketing the valley as America's wine Eden. Geographically, the Napa Valley is reasonably contiguous, being 34 miles in length and between one and four miles in width from the town of Napa in the south to that of Calistoga in the north. It is an easy region in which to ripen grapes and consistently produces ripe full wines. The cool air from San Pablo Bay, just north of San Francisco, moves from south to north, giving the southern area cooler average temperatures.

An imprecise but useful generalization would be that the cooler southern end is more favorable to white varieties and Pinot Noir while the further north one gets the more red varietals one will encounter as the temperatures increase, with emphasis on Cabernet. This simplification does not account for the vagaries of soil types, microclimates, and vintners throughout the valley, and as such there are many exceptions to the rule. Nine sub-appellations have been created since the inception of the Napa Valley AVA in 1983, and these go some way toward addressing the differences in climate between some parts of the valley. With the hugely significant exception of Carneros, these sub-appellations are of more relevance to Cabernet than Chardonnay.

In style Napa Valley Chardonnays tend typically to be rich and ripe with an appealing fatness that makes them very accessible when young. They are generally made in relatively full-blown styles with more than a passing resemblance to Australian show wines, albeit with firmer structures. Though the winemaking runs the gamut, there is a definite tendency to endow the wines with a solid measure of oak. If you want a wine that will stand up to rich poultry or seafood dishes look no further, but those seeking a crisp aperitif style may want to look elsewhere. A number of wines listed here, however, may be sourced all or in part from the Napa subregion of Carneros. These wines tend to be in a lighter style (see Carneros, two sections forward). In the end, quality is universally high, and very few disappointing wines will carry the Napa AVA.

Highly Recommended Napa Valley Chardonnay

94 • Newton (CA) 1997 Chardonnay, Napa County. $25.
94 • Franciscan (CA) 1996 Oakville Estate, Cuvée Sauvage, Chardonnay, Napa Valley. $30.
94 • Ferrari-Carano (CA) 1995 Reserve, Chardonnay, 87% Napa County, 13% Sonoma County. $34.
94 • Beringer (CA) 1996 Sbragia-Limited Release, Chardonnay, Napa Valley. $35.
93 • Signorello (CA) 1997 Hope's Cuvée, Chardonnay, Napa Valley. $60.
92 • Robert Mondavi (CA) 1996 Reserve, Chardonnay, Napa Valley. $30.
92 • Peju Province (CA) 1997 Chardonnay, Napa Valley. $18.
92 • Cuvaison (CA) 1996 Reserve, Chardonnay, Napa Valley. $.
92 • Beringer (CA) 1997 Private Reserve, Chardonnay, Napa Valley. $36.
91 • Patz and Hall (CA) 1997 Chardonnay, Napa Valley. $30.
91 • Franciscan (CA) 1995 Oakville Estate, Cuvée Sauvage, Chardonnay, Napa Valley. $30.

91 • Clos La Chance (CA) 1997 Chardonnay, Napa Valley. $17.

91 • Chappellet (CA) 1997 Signature Estate, Chardonnay, Napa Valley. $26.

90 • Stag's Leap Wine Cellars (CA) 1996 Reserve, Chardonnay, Napa Valley. $37.

90 • Signorello (CA) 1996 Hope's Cuvée, Chardonnay, Napa Valley. $60.

90 • Signorello (CA) 1996 Founder's Reserve, Chardonnay, Napa Valley. $45.

90 • Peter Michael (CA) 1996 "Clos du Ciel," Chardonnay, Napa County. $38.

90 • Peter McCoy (CA) 1996 Clos de Pierres, Chardonnay, Knights Valley. $39.

90 • Lewis Cellars (CA) 1997 Reserve, Chardonnay, Napa Valley. $34.99.

90 • Jarvis (CA) 1996 Reserve, Chardonnay, Napa Valley. $48.

90 • Jarvis (CA) 1996 Chardonnay, Napa Valley. $38.

90 • Beringer (CA) 1996 Private Reserve, Chardonnay, Napa Valley. $30.

89 • Venezia (CA) 1997 Regusci Vineyards, Chardonnay, Napa Valley. $20.

89 • Signorello (CA) 1997 Chardonnay, Napa Valley. $30.

89 • Peter Michael (CA) 1996 "Belle Côte," Chardonnay, Knights Valley. $42.

89 • Patz and Hall (CA) 1997 Carr Vineyard, Chardonnay, Mount Veeder. $42.

89 • Joseph Phelps (CA) 1996 Ovation, Chardonnay, Napa Valley. $40.

89 • Hess Collection (CA) 1996 Chardonnay, Napa Valley. $15.

89 • Elkhorn Peak (CA) 1997 Fagan Creek Vineyard, Chardonnay, Napa Valley. $18.

89 • Cosentino (CA) 1997 "The Sculptor" Reserve, Chardonnay, Napa Valley. $30.

89 • Chateau Potelle (CA) 1996 VGS, Chardonnay, Mount Veeder, Napa Valley. $38.

89 • Beaucanon (CA) 1997 Reserve, Chardonnay, Napa Valley. $12.

88 • Sterling (CA) 1997 Chardonnay, Napa Valley. $15.

88 • Raymond (CA) 1996 Generations, Chardonnay, Napa Valley. $27.

88 • Peju Province (CA) 1997 HB Vineyard, Chardonnay, Napa Valley. $26.

88 • Niebaum-Coppola (CA) 1997 Chardonnay, Napa Valley. $20.

88 • Monticello (CA) 1996 Wild Yeast Corley Reserve, Chardonnay, Napa Valley. $32.50.

88 • Grgich Hills (CA) 1997 Chardonnay, Napa Valley. $30.

88 • Flora Springs (CA) 1997 Reserve, Chardonnay, Napa Valley. $24.

88 • Edgewood (CA) 1997 Chardonnay, Napa Valley. $18.

88 • Crichton Hall (CA) 1996 Chardonnay, Napa Valley. $22.

88 • Chappellet (CA) 1997 Estate, Chardonnay, Napa Valley. $17.

87 • Robert Mondavi (CA) 1996 Chardonnay, Napa Valley. $19.

87 • Monthaven (CA) 1997 Chardonnay, Napa Valley. $9.99.

87 • Hagafen (CA) 1997 Reserve, Chardonnay, Napa Valley. $18.

87 • Cosentino (CA) 1997 Chardonnay, Napa Valley. $18.

87 • Beaucanon (CA) 1997 Jacques de Coninck, Chardonnay, Napa Valley. $30.

86 • William Hill (CA) 1997 Reserve, Chardonnay, Napa Valley. $20.

86 • William Hill (CA) 1997 Chardonnay, Napa Valley. $14.50.

86 • V. Sattui (CA) 1997 Carsi Vineyard, Chardonnay, Napa Valley. $18.

86 • Stags' Leap Winery (CA) 1997 Chardonnay, Napa Valley. $21.

86 • S. Anderson (CA) 1997 Chardonnay, Stags Leap District. $22.

86 • St. Supéry (CA) 1996 Dollarhide Ranch, Chardonnay, Napa Valley. $12.50.

86 • Pine Ridge (CA) 1997 Knollside Cuvée, Chardonnay, Napa Valley. $17.50.

86 • Parducci (CA) 1996 Carneros Bighorn Ranch, Reserve, Chardonnay,
Napa Valley. $20.

86 • Franciscan (CA) 1997 Oakville Estate, Chardonnay, Napa Valley. $15.

86 • Far Niente (CA) 1997 Chardonnay, Napa Valley. $40.

86 • Chateau Montelena (CA) 1996 Chardonnay, Napa Valley. $29.

86 • Beringer (CA) 1996 Chardonnay, Napa Valley. $15.

86 • Atlas Peak Vineyards (CA) 1997 Chardonnay, Atlas Peak, Napa Valley. $16.

85 • Oakville Ranch (CA) 1996 ORV, Chardonnay, Oakville. $32.

85 • Merryvale (CA) 1996 Reserve, Chardonnay, Napa Valley. $30.

Sonoma County

Wines Reviewed: **99**
Median Price: **$20**

Sonoma County as an AVA is twice the size of the Napa Valley. It is generally cooler and somewhat more complex as a region than Napa, encompassing six major AVAs and their sub-appellations as well as the two large umbrella AVAs of Northern Sonoma and Sonoma Coast. These AVAs go some way toward defining the different styles of wine within the county. With the exception of Carneros, straddled across Napa Valley and Sonoma County, and with its own identity, it is difficult to easily determine a consistent style throughout the region. Most producers blend from different sub-appellations throughout the county and thus label with the Sonoma County designation.

The Russian River Valley is one of the most notable of the AVAs within Sonoma County. A distinctly maritime climate with cooling sea winds and the influence of the Russian River itself all combine to give cooler growing conditions that produce leaner styles of Chardonnay in general, as exemplified by Sonoma-Cutrer, Gary Farrell, and De Loach. An indication of the climactic leanings of the area is that much of the Chardonnay in Russian River is used in the production of sparkling wine. This will indicate wines that are very crisp and focused with solid acidity. Some Russian River bottlings, accordingly, are best when held for a year or two.

On the other hand, the Alexander Valley is one of the warmest climate AVAs in Sonoma County, and as such, much of its Chardonnay production is destined toward "county" designated blends. Although it is only some 18 miles from the ocean, the maritime influence is not what it is in the Russian River Valley, and the Alexander is actually a much more important producer of varietals such as Cabernet and even Zinfandel. At the high end of production, the style of Alexander Valley could be described as lush, rich, and tropical.

Overall, Sonoma County Chardonnay can reach great heights, and at the very top might be even more exciting than Napa bottlings, but the wines as a whole are much more variable. They tend to be higher in acidity than Napa Chardonnays, with firmer structures, and are accordingly less approachable in youth. Without question, high end Sonoma Chardonnay shows best at the table when paired with foods.

Highly Recommended Sonoma County Chardonnay

Sonoma County (General)

94 • Gallo Sonoma (CA) 1996 Estate, Chardonnay, Northern Sonoma. $38.

92 • Sonoma-Cutrer (CA) 1996 Les Pierres, Chardonnay, Sonoma County. $29.99.

92 • Arrowood (Ca) 1996 Réserve Spéciale, Cuvée Michel Berthoud, Chardonnay, Sonoma County. $38.

91 • St. Francis (CA) 1997 Reserve, Chardonnay, Sonoma County. $22.99.

91 • Sonoma-Cutrer (CA) 1996 The Cutrer, Chardonnay, Sonoma County. $27.99.

91 • Pezzi King (CA) 1997 Chardonnay, Sonoma County. $21.

91 • La Crema (CA) 1997 Cold Coast Vineyards, Chardonnay, Sonoma Coast. $19.

91 • Domaine Laurier (CA) 1996 Reserve, Chardonnay, Sonoma County. $16.

90 • Dry Creek Vineyard (CA) 1997 Reserve, Chardonnay, Sonoma County. $20.

Scale: Superlative (96-100), Exceptional (90-95), Highly Recommended (85-89), Recommended (80-84), Not Recommended (Under 80)

442

89 • Paradise Ridge (CA) 1997 Barrel Select, Nagasawa Vineyard, Chardonnay, Sonoma County. $17.95.

89 • Hartford Court (CA) 1996 Seascape Vineyard, Chardonnay, Sonoma Coast. $35.

89 • Fisher (CA) 1997 Whitney's Vineyard, Chardonnay, Sonoma County. $40.

88 • Simi (CA) 1995 Reserve, Chardonnay, Sonoma County. $29.

88 • Laurier (CA) 1996 Chardonnay, Sonoma County. $15.

88 • Landmark (CA) 1996 Damaris Reserve, Chardonnay, Sonoma County. $32.

88 • Lambert Bridge (CA) 1997 Chardonnay, Sonoma County. $18.

87 • Rodney Strong (CA) 1996 Chalk Hill Vineyard Reserve, Chardonnay, Northern Sonoma. $24.

87 • Dry Creek Vineyard (CA) 1997 Chardonnay, Sonoma County. $16.

86 • Simi (CA) 1996 Chardonnay, Sonoma County. $17.

86 • Martinelli (CA) 1996 Charles Ranch, Chardonnay, Sonoma Coast. $30.

86 • Chalk Hill (CA) 1996 Chardonnay, Chalk Hill, Sonoma County. $28.

Sonoma County (Alexander Valley)

93 • Ferrari-Carano (CA) 1996 Chardonnay, Alexander Valley. $21.

92 • Chateau St. Jean (CA) 1996 Robert Young Vineyard, Chardonnay, Alexander Valley. $24.

90 • Geyser Peak (CA) 1996 Reserve, Chardonnay, Alexander Valley. $23.

89 • Murphy-Goode (CA) 1996 Island Block Reserve, Chardonnay, Alexander Valley. $24.

89 • Huntington (CA) 1997 Cairns Cuvée, Chardonnay, Alexander Valley. $16.

86 • Venezia (CA) 1996 Big River Ranch, Chardonnay, Alexander Valley. $19.99.

86 • de Lorimier (CA) 1996 Chardonnay, Alexander Valley. $16.

86 • Clos du Bois (CA) 1997 Calcaire Vineyard, Chardonnay, Alexander Valley. $18.

Sonoma County (Dry Creek Valley)

88 • Pedroncelli (CA) 1997 F. Johnson Vineyard, Chardonnay, Dry Creek Valley. $13.

86 • Gallo Sonoma (CA) 1996 Stefani Vineyard, Chardonnay, Dry Creek Valley. $18.

Sonoma County (Russian River Valley)

95 • Martinelli (CA) 1996 Gold Ridge, Chardonnay, Russian River Valley. $20.

94 • Gary Farrell (CA) 1996 Allen Vineyard, Chardonnay, Russian River Valley. $28.

93 • Rochioli (CA) 1995 Estate, Chardonnay, Russian River Valley. $25.

92 • Zabaco (CA) 1996 Chardonnay, Russian River Valley. $14.

89 • Murphy-Goode (CA) 1996 J&K Murphy Vineyard Reserve, Chardonnay, Russian River Valley. $24.

89 • Mark West (CA) 1996 Chardonnay, Russian River Valley. $15.

89 • Joseph Swan (CA) 1997 Estate Vineyard, Chardonnay, Russian River Valley. $22.50.

88 • Gallo Sonoma (CA) 1997 Chardonnay, Russian River Valley. $14.

87 • Gallo Sonoma (CA) 1996 Laguna Ranch Vineyard, Chardonnay, Russian River Valley. $20.

87 • Chateau Souverain (CA) 1996 Winemaker's Reserve, Chardonnay, Russian River Valley. $20.

86 • Windsor (CA) 1996 Preston Ranch, Private Reserve, Chardonnay, Russian River Valley. $14.

86 • Windsor (CA) 1996 Barrel Fermented, Private Reserve, Chardonnay, Russian River Valley. $15.

86 • Herzog (CA) 1996 Special Reserve, Chardonnay, Russian River Valley. $19.99.

85 • Windsor (CA) 1996 Private Reserve Estate, Chardonnay, Russian River Valley. $20.

85 • Rutz (CA) 1996 Dutton Ranch, Chardonnay, Russian River Valley. $30.

Sonoma County (Sonoma Valley)

94 • Matanzas Creek (CA) 1995 Journey, Chardonnay, Sonoma Valley. $95.

88 • Steele (CA) 1996 Parmlee-Hill Vineyard, Chardonnay, Sonoma Valley. $26.

88 • Matanzas Creek (CA) 1996 Chardonnay, Sonoma Valley. $30.

87 • Kunde (CA) 1996 Wildwood Vineyard, Chardonnay, Sonoma Valley. $20.

86 • Kunde (CA) 1996 Kinneybrook Vineyard, Chardonnay, Sonoma Valley. $20.

Carneros

Wines Reviewed: **40**

Median Price: **$24**

Carneros has an identity quite distinct from either the Napa Valley or Sonoma County. The cool and windy climate has a strong maritime influence with winds racing from the San Pablo Bay and through the Petaluma Gap on the Sonoma Coast. Cool foggy mornings are the norm here.

Arguably, typical Carneros Chardonnay is among the easier styles of California wines to pick out in blind tastings. The style is characterized by lean, tart, crisp apple flavors and many are quite understated when young. These wines are often not at their best in extreme youth and better examples can develop tertiary nutty qualities with some bottle age. A sizable proportion of the region's Chardonnay, as much as a third, is used for high-quality sparkling wine production.

Carneros is not the home to many wineries, but supplies grapes to wineries outside its boundaries. Indeed, most Chardonnays from wineries in the Napa Valley proper are produced with Carneros fruit. This is further testament to the fact that this district produces some of the nation's best examples of the varietal.

Highly Recommended Carneros Chardonnay

94 • Shafer (CA) 1997 Red Shoulder Ranch, Chardonnay, Carneros, Napa Valley. $35.

93 • Shafer (CA) 1996 Red Shoulder Ranch, Chardonnay, Carneros, Napa Valley. $30.

92 • Patz & Hall (CA) 1997 Hyde Vineyard, Chardonnay, Carneros. $36.

91 • Truchard (CA) 1996 Chardonnay, Carneros, Napa Valley. $24.

91 • Steele (CA) 1996 Durell Vineyard, Chardonnay, Carneros. $26.

91 • Ramey (CA) 1996 Hyde Vineyard, Chardonnay, Carneros, Napa Valley. $45.

89 • St. Clement (CA) 1997 Abbots Vineyard, Chardonnay, Carneros, Napa Valley. $20.

89 • Cuvaison (CA) 1997 Chardonnay, Carneros. $.

88 • Chateau St. Jean (CA) 1996 Durell Vineyard, Chardonnay, Carneros. $24.

87 • Stag's Leap Wine Cellars (CA) 1996 Beckstoffer Ranch, Chardonnay, Napa Valley. $30.

87 • Rombauer (CA) 1997 Chardonnay, Carneros. $25.75.

87 • Adastra (CA) 1996 Chardonnay, Carneros, Napa Valley. $22.

86 • Schug (CA) 1997 Chardonnay, Carneros. $18.

86 • Schug (CA) 1996 Heritage Reserve, Chardonnay, Carneros. $25.

86 • Salmon Creek (CA) 1996 Chardonnay, Los Carneros, Sonoma County. $16.

86 • Foxridge (CA) 1997 Chardonnay, Carneros. $9.99.

86 • Ehlers Grove (CA) 1997 Winery Reserve, Chardonnay, Carneros, Napa Valley. $30.

86 • Bouchaine (CA) 1996 Chardonnay, Carneros. $18.

86 • Benziger (CA) 1996 Chardonnay, Carneros. $13.

86 • Anderson's Conn Valley Vineyards (CA) 1996 Fournier Vineyard, Chardonnay, Carneros. $40.

85 • Neyers (CA) 1997 Chardonnay, Carneros. $27.99.

85 • Liparita (CA) 1997 Chardonnay, Carneros. $24.

Monterey

Wines Reviewed: 33

Median Price: $16

Surprise, Surprise...In several of the last few vintages the highest percentage of outstanding Chardonnay within any given area in the country has come from Monterey and its surrounding appellations.

Monterey has a considerable ocean breeze influence, giving it a distinctly cool growing climate at its closest point to the ocean in the Salinas Valley. Initial large plantings here during the 1970s in inappropriate locations gave this county a reputation for vegetal wines, as the vineyards exposed to the funneled sea breezes struggled to ripen red varietals. With more appropriate locations and a better understanding of microclimates, this region is now producing Chardonnay of the highest quality. Our tastings reveal that Monterey often turns in the highest proportion of 'excellent' Chardonnays, and although this is hardly a scientific measurement, it is clearly a sign that something very exciting is happening with Chardonnay in this region.

The most notable of the sub-appellations farther from the coast are Arroyo Secco, Chalone, and the Santa Lucia Highlands. Most producers are choosing to use the Monterey designation on their bottlings, but it is reasonable to assume that in time these AVAs will gain stronger identities in their own right, as more producers will choose to use the more specific AVA designation on their label. The style of top-notch Monterey Chardonnay is not a statement of outright power but more often ripeness of flavors allied to balance and refinement with excellent acidity. Mirassou exemplifies the style perfectly with their consistently excellent but value-conscious Chardonnays that are made with fruit sourced from the Arroyo Secco AVA. These are wines that can be enjoyed by themselves or right through the meal.

Highly Recommended Monterey Chardonnay

93 • San Saba (CA) 1997 Chardonnay, Monterey. $20.

91 • Talbott (CA) 1996 Cuvée Cynthia, Chardonnay, Monterey. $45.

91 • Morgan (CA) 1996 Reserve, Chardonnay, Monterey. $25.

91 • J. Lohr (CA) 1997 Riverstone, Chardonnay, Monterey. $14.

90 • Talbott (CA) 1995 Diamond T Estate, Chardonnay, Monterey. $45.

89 • Paraiso Springs (CA) 1997 Chardonnay, Santa Lucia Highlands. $16.

89 • Chalone (CA) 1996 Reserve, Chardonnay, Chalone. $45.

88 • Joullian (CA) 1996 Chardonnay, Monterey. $15.50.

88 • Chalone (CA) 1997 The Pinnacles, Chardonnay, Chalone. $31.

88 • Chalone (CA) 1996 Chardonnay, Chalone. $27.

88 • Bernardus (CA) 1996 Chardonnay, Monterey County. $18.

87 • Testarossa (CA) 1996 Chardonnay, Chalone Appellation, Monterey County. $29.

86 • Wente (CA) 1996 Riva Ranch Reserve, Chardonnay, Arroyo Secco, Monterey. $16.

86 • Shale Ridge (CA) 1997 Chardonnay, Monterey. $9.99.

86 • Raymond (CA) 1997 Chardonnay, Monterey. $13.

86 • Monterra (CA) 1997 San Bernabé Ranch, Chardonnay, Monterey County. $8.99.

86 • Lockwood (CA) 1997 Chardonnay, Monterey. $14.99.

86 • Heartswood (CA) 1995 Private Reserve, Chardonnay, Monterey. $9.99.

86 • Guglielmo (CA) 1997 Private Reserve, Chardonnay, Monterey County. $14.

85 • Jekel (CA) 1997 FOS Reserve, Chardonnay, Monterey. $22.

85 • Kendall-Jackson (CA) 1996 Paradise Vineyard, Chardonnay, Arroyo Seco. $18.

California's South Central Coast

Wines Reviewed: **54**
Median Price: **$20**

The southerly location of the South Central Coast and the associated heat is mitigated in pockets with cooler microclimates created by the access of cool sea air through river valleys leading to the ocean. With coolness being dictated by access to sea air, it follows that a variety of different growing conditions exist. The more northerly county of San Luis Obispo is divided into four AVAs: Paso Robles, York Mountain, Edna Valley, and Arroyo Grande. Paso Robles is a large AVA without much ocean influence, making it a warm climate growing region with some cooler microclimates located toward the southwestern sector where the sea air enters via the Templeton Gap. Edna Valley and Arroyo Secco are further south and closer to the ocean, giving them cooler maritime climates and a more natural association overall with the Chardonnay vines that dominate both appellations. Indeed, both AVAs are also a source of premium sparkling wine grapes supplied to a number of wineries.

Santa Barbara has a cool climate for grape growing thanks to the cool ocean air that moves along the Santa Maria Valley. Just how cool a given area might be is dictated by its distance along the valley from the ocean. This region produces some of the finest Chardonnays of the South Central Coast as exemplified by bottlings from Au Bon Climat. At their best these wines have the richness of Napa but with more finesse and fine acidity to match. The style of winemaking, however, is often quite flashy, with a heavy reliance on toasty oak. These are wines, like Napa's, which pair well with richer dishes.

A little further southwards in Santa Barbara the Santa Ynez Valley provides slightly warmer growing conditions, but westwards along the river toward the ocean are some excellent cooler microclimates that are ideally suited to Burgundian varietals such as Pinot Noir and Chardonnay. Longoria and Babcock are two such wineries that produce fine Santa Ynez bottlings.

Highly Recommended South Central Coast Chardonnay

98 • Foley (CA) 1997 Barrel Select, Chardonnay, Santa Barbara County. $28.

95 • Foley (CA) 1997 Bien Nacido Vineyard, Chardonnay, Santa Maria Valley. $24.

94 • Foley (CA) 1996 Barrel Select, Chardonnay, Santa Barbara County. $25.

93 • Villa Mt. Eden (CA) 1996 Signature Series, Bien Nacido Vineyard, Chardonnay, Santa Maria Valley. $30.

93 • Qupé (CA) 1997 Bien Nacido Vineyard, Chardonnay, Santa Barbara County. $18.

93 • Au Bon Climat (CA) 1997 Alban Vineyard, Chardonnay, Edna Valley. $35.

91 • Steele (CA) 1996 Bien Nacido Vineyard, Chardonnay, Santa Barbara County. $26.

90 • Stephen Ross (CA) 1997 Bien Nacido Vineyard, Chardonnay, Santa Maria Valley. $20.

90 • Seven Peaks (CA) 1997 Reserve, Chardonnay, Edna Valley. $16.

90 • Santa Barbara Winery (CA) 1996 Reserve, Chardonnay, Santa Ynez Valley. $24.

90 • Qupé (CA) 1996 Bien Nacido Reserve, Chardonnay, Santa Barbara County. $25.

89 • Meridian (CA) 1996 Coastal Reserve, Chardonnay, Edna Valley. $15.

89 • LinCourt (CA) 1997 Chardonnay, Santa Barbara County. $14.

89 • Fess Parker (CA) 1997 American Tradition Reserve, Marcella's Vineyards, Chardonnay, Santa Barbara County. $24.

89 • Baileyana (CA) 1997 Chardonnay, Edna Valley. $17.

89 • Au Bon Climat (CA) 1997 Chardonnay, Santa Barbara County. $18.

89 • Au Bon Climat (CA) 1996 Le Bouge D'à Côte, Chardonnay, Santa Barbara County. $19.

88 • Villa Mt. Eden (CA) 1997 Grand Reserve, Bien Nacido Vineyard, Chardonnay, Santa Maria Valley. $18.

88 • Stephen Ross (CA) 1997 Edna Ranch, Chardonnay, Edna Valley. $18.50.

88 • McKeon-Phillips (CA) 1996 Reserve, Chardonnay, Santa Barbara County. $21.33.

88 • Fess Parker (CA) 1997 American Tradition Reserve, Chardonnay, Santa Barbara County. $22.

88 • Cambria (CA) 1996 Reserve, Chardonnay, Santa Maria Valley. $36.

87 • Talley (CA) 1997 Chardonnay, Arroyo Grande Valley. $22.

87 • Nichols (CA) 1996 Paragon Vineyard, Chardonnay, Edna Valley. $32.

87 • Gainey (CA) 1996 Limited Selection, Chardonnay, Santa Barbara County. $28.

87 • Fess Parker (CA) 1997 Chardonnay, Santa Barbara County. $16.

86 • Rosenblum (CA) 1997 Chardonnay, Edna Valley. $23.

86 • Nichols (CA) 1997 Edna Ranch Vineyard, Chardonnay, Edna Valley. $32.

86 • Laetitia (CA) 1996 Reserve, Chardonnay, San Luis Obispo County. $18.

86 • Justin (CA) 1997 Reserve, Chardonnay, Paso Robles. $18.

86 • Cottonwood Canyon (CA) 1994 Barrel Select, Chardonnay, Santa Barbara County. $29.

86 • Adelaida (CA) 1996 Chardonnay, San Luis Obispo County. $21.

85 • Testarossa (CA) 1997 Chardonnay, Santa Maria Valley. $26.

85 • Sanford (Ca) 1997 Chardonnay, Santa Barbara County. $18.

85 • Kendall-Jackson (CA) 1996 Camelot Vineyard, Chardonnay, Santa Maria Valley. $19.

85 • Harmony (CA) 1997 Chardonnay, San Luis Obispo County. $14.50.

Mendocino

Wines Reviewed: 14

Median Price: $18

Mendocino is the most northerly of California's wine-producing regions and as such it is far removed from the glamour and high society of the southern regions. It has four AVAs, of which Anderson Valley is the most significant and coolest with its proximity to the coast giving a plentiful supply of cooling sea air along its length. As is so often the pattern this is also sparkling wine country with Roederer Estate and Scharfenberger sourcing their Chardonnay from here. Unblended Chardonnays from this region show all the character of cool climate wines with bright acidity bolstering clean styles without heavy oak treatment. These wines are the Chablis of California—an ideal way to start a meal or quaff without food.

To the east of Anderson Valley runs the extreme northern section of the Russian River. It is along this stretch of water that other vineyards of Mendocino County are associated. Sea air does not have a significant impact on the other growing areas of Mendocino that are farther inland and hence they do not exhibit the coolness found in the Anderson Valley. Fetzer has a major presence along the Russian River in Mendocino and produces consistently reliable Chardonnay from their extensive plantings in the region.

Highly Recommended Mendocino Chardonnay

89 • Jepson (CA) 1996 Chardonnay, Mendocino County. $15.

89 • Edmeades (CA) 1996 Chardonnay, Anderson Valley. $18.

88 • Lolonis (CA) 1996 Private Reserve, Chardonnay, Redwood Valley, Mendocino. $25.

88 • Indigo Hills (CA) 1997 Chardonnay, Mendocino County. $11.

88 • Fetzer (CA) 1996 Reserve, Chardonnay, Mendocino County. $20.

87 • Husch (CA) 1996 Special Reserve, Chardonnay, Anderson Valley. $22.

86 • Steele (CA) 1996 Du Pratt Vineyard, Chardonnay, Mendocino County. $26.

Washington

Wines Reviewed: **42**

Median Price: **$14.50**

The AVA system in Washington is still underdeveloped, with a huge swath of land being entitled to use the Columbia Valley appellation. Smaller viticultural pockets such as the historic Yakima and Walla Walla Valleys should soon be augmented by the creation of new ones, such as Canoe Ridge and Red Mountain. With Chardonnay it makes more sense to treat Washington in general terms, but with varietals that show more stylistic variation, such as Merlot and Cabernet, there is more variation within the state, and hence more in-depth coverage in those chapters.

As for Chardonnay, it is certainly a widely planted and produced varietal. Washington Chardonnay tends to be well structured with solid acidity, due to the very cool desert nights and a lengthy growing season. Winemaking, though variable, tends to be a bit lighter handed with regard to oak treatment, allowing for a harmonious style built on finesse. There are exceptions, and some winemakers in the Walla Walla area have a tendency to swing for the fences. When Washington Chardonnay is good, it is very good, but quality on the whole can still be somewhat variable, as would be expected of such a new region. Nonetheless, it is one of the nation's most exciting viticultural areas and developments should prove quite interesting.

Highly Recommended Washington Chardonnay

93 • Kestrel (WA) 1996 Chardonnay, Columbia Valley. $22.

92 • Chateau Ste. Michelle (WA) 1996 Indian Wells Vineyard, Chardonnay, Columbia Valley. $26.

91 • Columbia Winery (WA) 1996 Otis Vineyard, Chardonnay, Yakima Valley. $19.

90 • Columbia Winery (WA) 1996 Wyckoff Vineyard, Chardonnay, Yakima Valley. $19.

90 • Chateau Ste. Michelle (WA) 1996 Cold Creek Vineyard, Chardonnay, Columbia Valley. $26.

90 • Apex (WA) 1997 Chardonnay, Columbia Valley. $17.99.

89 • Woodward Canyon (WA) 1997 Reserve, Chardonnay, Columbia Valley. $35.

89 • Hogue (WA) 1997 Genesis, Sunnyside Vineyard, Chardonnay, Yakima Valley. $19.99.

89 • Chateau Ste. Michelle (WA) 1996 Reserve, Chardonnay, Columbia Valley. $31.

88 • Columbia Crest (WA) 1997 Estate Series, Chardonnay, Columbia Valley. $14.

88 • Columbia Crest (WA) 1996 Reserve, Chardonnay, Columbia Valley. $18.

88 • Chateau Ste. Michelle (WA) 1996 Canoe Ridge Estate Vineyard, Chardonnay, Columbia Valley. $28.

88 • Canoe Ridge Vineyard (WA) 1997 Chardonnay, Columbia Valley. $14.

88 • Bookwalter (WA) 1997 Vintner's Select, Chardonnay, Washington. $18.

88 • Barnard Griffin (WA) 1997 Chardonnay, Washington. $12.95.

87 • Woodward Canyon (WA) 1997 Chardonnay, Columbia Valley. $30.

87 • L'Ecole No. 41 (WA) 1997 Chardonnay, Washington. $19.50.

87 • Claar (WA) 1997 Chardonnay, Columbia Valley. $10.99.

86 • W.B. Bridgman (WA) 1997 Chardonnay, Columbia Valley. $10.99.

86 • Hogue (WA) 1997 Chardonnay, Columbia Valley. $13.95.

86 • Covey Run (WA) 1996 Celilo Vineyard, Chardonnay, Washington. $25.

86 • Columbia Crest (WA) 1997 Chardonnay, Columbia Valley. $9.

86 • Chateau Ste. Michelle (WA) 1996 Chardonnay, Columbia Valley. $14.

86 • Caterina (WA) 1997 Chardonnay, Columbia Valley. $15.

86 • Bookwalter (WA) 1997 Chardonnay, Columbia Valley. $8.

86 • Barnard Griffin (WA) 1996 Reserve, Chardonnay, Columbia Valley. $17.95.

Oregon
Wines Reviewed: **24**
Median Price: **$17.50**

Though sometimes lumped together with Washington, its neighbor to the north, Oregon is in fact as different from that area as is possible. In diametrical opposition, Oregon's vineyards are largely planted in the cool and rainy river valleys south of Portland. There is a considerable marine influence, and consequently a reliance on cool climate varietals such as Chardonnay, Pinot Noir, and Pinot Gris. Furthermore, it is largely a cottage industry, with over a hundred tiny producers, and no huge winery to bring forth the message.

Pinot Noir has already achieved greatness in many Oregon vineyards, but, confusingly, Chardonnay seems to have lagged behind somewhat. Lately many Oregon winemakers have come to the realization that this may be in large part due to the fact that most of the Chardonnay vineyards were planted with a clone of the grape imported from California, and better adapted to that state's much hotter climate. Oregon's climate shares more in common with that of Burgundy and growers are rushing to experiment with a greater variety of Burgundian clones. Early results have been promising.

The resulting wines can be quite complex with high levels of acidity and solid structures. Due to its marginal climate, Oregon, unlike California, has wide vintage swings. In some ways, this makes things more interesting as a particular vineyard's wine will have a markedly different character from year to year. The year 1994 was among the best, if not the best, Oregon vintage in the last decade, and the Pinot Noirs in particular are stunning. Subsequent vintages have been somewhat more problematic, but 1998 appears to be a fantastic vintage waiting in the wings. Though still quite youthful, Oregon is beginning to come into its own for Chardonnay and clonal improvements should help to paint a very different picture in years to come.

Highly Recommended Oregon Chardonnay

90 • Willamette Valley Vineyards (OR) 1996 Estate, Dijon Clone, Chardonnay, Oregon. $21.99.

89 • Henry Estate (OR) 1996 Chardonnay, Umpqua Valley. $15.

88 • Willamette Valley Vineyards (OR) 1996 Founders' Reserve, Chardonnay, Oregon. $14.99.

88 • King Estate (OR) 1996 Reserve, Chardonnay, Oregon. $18.

88 • Erath (OR) 1996 Reserve, Niederberger Vineyard, Chardonnay, Willamette Valley. $50.

88 • Eola Hills (OR) 1996 Chardonnay, Oregon. $12.

88 • Cooper Mountain (OR) 1996 Reserve, Chardonnay, Willamette Valley. $19.75.

88 • Chateau Benoit (OR) 1996 Dijon Clone Reserve, Chardonnay, Willamette Valley. $35.

86 • Willamette Valley Vineyards (OR) 1997 Chardonnay, Oregon. $12.75.

86 • Oak Knoll (OR) 1996 Chardonnay, Willamette Valley. $14.

85 • Cooper Mountain (OR) 1997 Chardonnay, Willamette Valley. $14.75.

New York
***Wines Reviewed:* 34**
***Median Price:* $13**

The wine regions of New York State are all toward the cooler end of the spectrum in climactic terms. With the state's cold winters the moderating presence of water is a necessity for the successful growing of vinifera grapes. The two regions of significance in this respect are the Finger Lakes and the North Fork of Long Island.

The Finger Lakes, south of Lake Ontario, are comprised of a series of narrow but very deep lakes. The most important are Cayuga Lake, Seneca Lake, and Keuka Lake. The vineyards are situated on hills by the lakes that angle the sun's warmth onto the grapes. With the severity of winter always posing a risk to the noble grape varieties, hybrid varieties such as Seyval Blanc and Vignoles are also grown in abundance here.

Much of the Chardonnay goes toward the production of premium sparkling wine. The styles of Chardonnay tend toward the delicate and lean end of the spectrum. The finest examples display a European sense of refinement and elegance and make natural partners to shellfish and seafood. Such wines often carry the label of Dr. Konstantin Frank, one of the region's top producers, founded by a Russian immigrant who was one of the first to exploit the potential of the area for quality wine production.

As for Long Island, the North Fork of Long Island AVA perfectly describes its location in its own title. It is markedly warmer than the Finger Lakes. The principal factors behind this are its more southerly location, the surrounding waters of the Atlantic Ocean, and the warm air that moves up from southern states during the winter. Vinifera varieties grow more easily here, even Cabernet Sauvignon and Merlot. Relative to the Finger Lakes, the Chardonnay styles are a tad richer although they are as yet more variable. Long Island is still a very new region, but early signs have been encouraging, and further developments should prove to be quite interesting.

Highly Recommended New York Chardonnay
93 • Macari (NY) 1997 Barrel Fermented, Chardonnay, North Fork of Long Island. $.

91 • Gristina (NY) 1995 Andy's Field, Chardonnay, North Fork of Long Island. $21.99.

89 • Treleaven (NY) 1997 Chardonnay, Cayuga Lake. $11.99.

89 • Lenz (NY) 1995 Barrel Fermented, Chardonnay, North Fork of Long Island. $24.99.

88 • Macari (NY) 1996 Barrel Fermented, Chardonnay, North Fork of Long Island. $14.

88 • Gristina (NY) 1996 Chardonnay, North Fork of Long Island. $11.99.

87 • Glenora (NY) 1996 Chardonnay, Finger Lakes. $13.99.

86 • Pellegrini (NY) 1996 Chardonnay, North Fork of Long Island. $12.99.

86 • Peconic Bay (NY) 1995 Rolling Ridge, Chardonnay, North Fork of Long Island. $18.99.

Scale: Superlative (96-100), Exceptional (90-95), Highly Recommended (85-89), Recommended (80-84), Not Recommended (Under 80)

450

86 • Paumanok (NY) 1997 Chardonnay, North Fork of Long Island. $16.99.

86 • Laurel Lake (NY) 1995 Reserve, Chardonnay, North Fork of Long Island. $13.99.

86 • Bedell (NY) 1995 Reserve, Chardonnay, North Fork of Long Island. $14.99.

85 • Pindar (NY) 1996 Sunflower Special Reserve, Chardonnay,
   North Fork of Long Island. $16.99.

85 • Lenz (NY) 1996 Vineyard Selection, Chardonnay, North Fork of Long Island. $9.99.

85 • Laurel Lake (NY) 1996 Chardonnay, North Fork of Long Island. $12.99.

85 • Hargrave (NY) 1995 Lattice Label, Chardonnay, North Fork of Long Island. $14.99.

85 • Bedell (NY) 1995 Chardonnay, North Fork of Long Island. $11.99.

Virginia
Wines Reviewed: 25
Median Price: $15

Thomas Jefferson's dreams of producing high-quality vinifera wines in his home state look to be becoming a reality. Even if his early efforts to establish vineyards around Charlottesville failed due to the intervention of the *Phylloxera* louse, his foresight in choosing suitable locations has been vindicated by the fact that this same area is at the forefront of the viticultural renaissance in the Old Dominion.

The styles of Chardonnay emerging in Virginia seem much more rooted in Europe than the West Coast of the United States, with higher acidity levels and a pleasant affinity for the table. Use of oak varies from subtle to occasionally overbearing. In Virginia Chardonnay is usually more competent than exciting. It is with red wines, particularly Bordeaux varietals, that Virginia is making its clearest statements so far.

Highly Recommended Virginia Chardonnay

89 • White Hall Vineyards (VA) 1997 Reserve, Chardonnay, Virginia. $18.

88 • Prince Michel (VA) 1997 Barrel Select, Chardonnay, Virginia. $18.95.

86 • Rockbridge (VA) 1997 Reserve, Chardonnay, Virginia. $15.

86 • Jefferson (VA) 1997 Fantaisie Sauvage, Chardonnay, Monticello. $22.

86 • Dashiell (VA) 1997 Chardonnay, Virginia. $17.

86 • Dashiell (VA) 1996 Chardonnay, Virginia. $17.

86 • Chateau Morrisette (VA) 1997 "M," Meadows of Dan, Chardonnay, Virginia. $14.

Top American Chardonneys

98 • Foley (CA) 1997 Barrel Select, Chardonnay, Santa Barbara County. $28.

95 • Martinelli (CA) 1996 Gold Ridge, Chardonnay, Russian River Valley. $20.

95 • Foley (CA) 1997 Bien Nacido Vineyard, Chardonnay, Santa Maria Valley. $24.

94 • Shafer (CA) 1997 Red Shoulder Ranch, Chardonnay, Carneros, Napa Valley. $35.

94 • Newton (CA) 1997 Chardonnay, Napa County. $25.

94 • Mer et Soleil (CA) 1993 Chardonnay, Central Coast. $30.

94 • Matanzas Creek (CA) 1995 Journey, Chardonnay, Sonoma Valley. $95.

94 • Gary Farrell (CA) 1996 Allen Vineyard, Chardonnay, Russian River Valley. $28.

94 • Gallo Sonoma (CA) 1996 Estate, Chardonnay, Northern Sonoma. $38.

94 • Franciscan (CA) 1996 Oakville Estate, Cuvée Sauvage, Chardonnay, Valley. $30.

94 • Foley (CA) 1996 Barrel Select, Chardonnay, Santa Barbara County. $25.

94 • Ferrari-Carano (CA) 1995 Reserve, Chardonnay, 87% Napa County, 13% Sonoma County. $34.

94 • Beringer (CA) 1996 Sbragia-Limited Release, Chardonnay, Napa Valley. $35.

93 • Villa Mt. Eden (CA) 1996 Signature Series, Bien Nacido Vineyard, Chardonnay, Santa Maria Valley. $30.

93 • Storrs (CA) 1997 Ben Lomond Mountain, Chardonnay, Santa Cruz Mountains. $24.

93 • Signorello (CA) 1997 Hope's Cuvée, Chardonnay, Napa Valley. $60.

93 • Shafer (CA) 1996 Red Shoulder Ranch, Chardonnay, Carneros, Napa Valley. $30.

93 • San Saba (CA) 1997 Chardonnay, Monterey. $20.

93 • Rochioli (CA) 1995 Estate, Chardonnay, Russian River Valley. $25.

93 • Qupé (CA) 1997 Bien Nacido Vineyard, Chardonnay, Santa Barbara County. $18.

93 • Mer et Soleil (CA) 1995 Chardonnay, Central Coast. $35.

93 • Mer et Soleil (CA) 1994 Chardonnay, Central Coast. $31.99.

93 • Macari (NY) 1997 Barrel Fermented, Chardonnay, North Fork of Long Island.

93 • Kestrel (WA) 1996 Chardonnay, Columbia Valley. $22.

93 • Ferrari-Carano (CA) 1996 Chardonnay, Alexander Valley. $21.

93 • Au Bon Climat (CA) 1997 Alban Vineyard, Chardonnay, Edna Valley. $35.

92 • Zabaco (CA) 1996 Chardonnay, Russian River Valley. $14.

92 • Sonoma-Cutrer (CA) 1996 Les Pierres, Chardonnay, Sonoma County. $29.99.

92 • Robert Mondavi (CA) 1996 Reserve, Chardonnay, Napa Valley. $30.

92 • Ridge (CA) 1996 Chardonnay, Santa Cruz Mountains. $25.

92 • Peju Province (CA) 1997 Chardonnay, Napa Valley. $18.

92 • Patz & Hall (CA) 1997 Hyde Vineyard, Chardonnay, Carneros. $36.

92 • Mer et Soleil (CA) 1996 Chardonnay, Central Coast. $34.99.

92 • Guenoc (CA) 1997 "Unfiltered" Reserve, Genevive Magoon Vineyard, Chardonnay, Guenoc Valley. $30.

92 • Cuvaison (CA) 1996 Reserve, Chardonnay, Napa Valley.

92 • Chateau Ste. Michelle (WA) 1996 Indian Wells Vineyard, Chardonnay, Columbia Valley. $26.

92 • Chateau St. Jean (CA) 1996 Robert Young Vineyard, Chardonnay, Alexander Valley. $24.

92 • Beringer (CA) 1997 Private Reserve, Chardonnay, Napa Valley. $36.

92 • Arrowood (Ca) 1996 Réserve Spéciale, Cuvée Michel Berthoud, Chardonnay, Sonoma County. $38.

Scale: Superlative (96-100), Exceptional (90-95), Highly Recommended (85-89), Recommended (80-84), Not Recommended (Under 80)

452

seventeen

꽃

Sauvignon Blanc, White Meritage, and Semillon

꽃

Sauvignon Blanc at a Glance

Wines Reviewed:
102

Producers/Brands Represented:
89

Median Price:
$10

White Meritage at a Glance

Wines Reviewed:
15

Producers/Brands Represented:
15

Median Price:
$16

Semillon at a Glance

Wines Reviewed:
11

Producers/Brands Represented:
10

Median Price:
$10

What Is American Sauvignon Blanc?

Sauvignon Blanc is widely planted in the United States, and produces a wine in two broadly different styles following two different examples. In France (from whence the varietal emigrated) it is grown widely in the Loire and Bordeaux. In Bordeaux it is barrel fermented and produces a ripe, rich wine that is not unlike a Chardonnay with a bit more snap. The vast majority of U.S. wines are vinified in this style. In the Loire, however, Sauvignon is often left out of barrel and the varietal is allowed to show its aggressive herbal side and brisk acidity. One of the world's great wine styles, Sancerre (and more recently New Zealand, which has "out Sancerred" Sancerre) can be a shock to the uninitiated, but many who do try it are smitten. Thus, U.S. wineries have tended to shy away from this latter manifestation, though some such as Voss, have made it into a specialty. Rumblings are being heard that more producers may choose to follow the latter path. Only time will tell.

Best U.S. Sauvignon Blanc Producers

Premier U.S. Sauvignon Blanc Producers (***)
- Cain (Musque)
- Chalk Hill
- Ferrari Carano (Reserve)
- Murphy-Goode (The Deuce & Reserve)
- Matanzas Creek
- Robert Mondavi (I-Block)
- Rochioli
- Spottswoode
- Voss

Great U.S. Sauvignon Blanc Producers (**)
- Benziger
- Cakebread
- Chateau St. Jean (La Petite Etoile)
- Duckhorn
- Ferrari Carano
- Gainey (Limited Selection)

Scale: Superlative (96-100), Exceptional (90-95), Highly Recommended (85-89), Recommended (80-84), Not Recommended (Under 80)

- Grgich Hills
- Iron Horse
- Kendall Jackson
- Merryvale
- Robert Mondavi (Fumé Blanc Reserve)
- Murphy Goode
- Sanford
- Stag's Leap Wine Cellars
- Waterbrook

Dependable U.S. Sauvignon Blanc Producers (Recommended)

Some producers placed in this third tier are new (or new to us) and may merit a higher placement in subsequent vintages. These producers are offset by an asterisk.

- Beringer
- *Calaghan
- DeLoach
- *Dos Cabezas
- Dry Creek Vineyards
- *Estancia
- *Foley
- William Hill
- Kenwood (Reserve)
- Markham
- *Peter Micheal (L'Apres-Midi)
- Morgan
- Robert Pepi
- Chateau Ste. Michelle
- Simi
- St. Clement

Highly Recommended Blanc Sauvignon

95 • Voss (CA) 1997 Sauvignon Blanc, Napa Valley. $12.50.

94 • Estancia (CA) 1996 Pinnacles, Fumé Blanc, Monterey County. $10.

94 • Cain (CA) 1996 Musque, Ventana Vineyard, Sauvignon Blanc, Monterey. $16.

93 • Murphy-Goode (CA) 1996 The Deuce, Fumé II, Alexander Valley. $24.

93 • Foley (CA) 1996 Sauvignon Blanc, Santa Barbara County. $14.

93 • Chalk Hill (CA) 1996 Sauvignon Blanc, Chalk Hill, Sonoma County. $19.

92 • Robert Mondavi (CA) 1995 To-Kalon Vineyard I Block, Fumé Blanc, Napa Valley. $50.

92 • Murphy-Goode (CA) 1996 Reserve, Fumé, Alexander Valley. $16.50.

91 • St. Supéry (CA) 1997 Dollarhide Ranch, Sauvignon Blanc, Napa Valley. $9.90.

91 • Peter Michael (CA) 1996 L' Apres-Midi, Sauvignon Blanc, Napa County. $20.

91 • Matanzas Creek (CA) 1996 Sauvignon Blanc, Sonoma County. $18.

90 • Cakebread (CA) 1996 Sauvignon Blanc, Napa Valley. $14.

90 • Beringer (CA) 1996 Sauvignon Blanc, Napa Valley. $9.

90 • Benziger (CA) 1996 Fumé Blanc, Sonoma County. $10.

89 • Spottswoode (CA) 1996 Sauvignon Blanc, Napa Valley. $18.

89 • Robert Mondavi (CA) 1994 To-Kalon Vineyard Reserve, Fumé Blanc, Napa Valley. $20.

89 • Merryvale (CA) 1996 Sauvignon Blanc, Napa Valley. $17.

89 • Chateau Potelle (CA) 1996 Sauvignon Blanc, Napa Valley. $11.

88 • Stonegate (CA) 1996 Sauvignon Blanc, Napa Valley. $9.50.

88 • Husch (CA) 1996 La Ribera Vineyard, Sauvignon Blanc, Mendocino. $10.50.

88 • Chateau St. Jean (CA) 1996 La Petite Etoile Vineyard, Fumé Blanc, Russian River Valley. $13.

87 • Robert Mondavi (CA) 1995 To-Kalon Vineyard Reserve, Fumé Blanc, Napa Valley. $22.

87 • Renaissance (CA) 1997 Sauvignon Blanc, North Yuba. $10.

87 • Grgich Hills (CA) 1996 Fumé Blanc, Napa Valley. $18.

87 • Dry Creek Vineyard (CA) 1996 Reserve, Fumé Blanc, Dry Creek Valley. $15.75.

87 • Domaine Napa (CA) 1996 Fumé Blanc, Napa Valley. $9.99.

86 • Waterbrook (WA) 1997 Sauvignon Blanc, Columbia Valley. $13.

86 • Ste. Genevieve (TX) NV Sauvignon Blanc, Texas. $4.99.

86 • Rutherford Vintners (CA) 1995 Barrel Select, Fumé Blanc, North Coast. $8.99.

86 • Rochioli (CA) 1997 Sauvignon Blanc, Russian River Valley. $16.

86 • Raymond (CA) 1996 Valley Reserve, Sauvignon Blanc, Napa Valley. $11.

86 • Murphy-Goode (CA) 1997 Fumé Blanc, Sonoma County. $11.50.

86 • Kenwood (CA) 1996 Reserve, Sauvignon Blanc, Sonoma Valley. $15.

86 • Dunnewood (CA) 1996 Coastal Series, Vintner's Select, Sauvignon Blanc, Mendocino. $5.99.

86 • Covey Run (WA) 1996 Fumé Blanc, Columbia Valley. $8.

86 • Columbia Crest (WA) 1996 Estate Series, Sauvignon Blanc, Columbia Valley. $9.

86 • Canyon Road (CA) 1997 Sauvignon Blanc, California. $6.99.

86 • Arbor Crest (WA) 1996 Sauvignon Blanc, Washington. $7.25.

85 • Temecula Crest (CA) 1997 Sauvignon Blanc, Temecula. $9.95.

85 • Page Mill (CA) 1997 French Camp Vineyard, Sauvignon Blanc, San Luis Obispo. $11.

85 • Morgan (CA) 1997 Sauvignon Blanc, Sonoma-Monterey. $13.

85 • Calona (Canada) 1997 Private Reserve, Fumé Blanc, Okanagan Valley. $9.50.

What Is White Meritage?

Meritage was the term (chosen in a contest...no kidding) given to U.S. wines made from a traditional blend of Bordeaux style varietals that can vary from year to year. The red meritage category, a blend of Cabernet Sauvignon, Merlot, Cabernet Franc, etc. is better known, as wines such as Opus One and Dominus have caught the public's fancy. There is a white side to the meritage coin, however. White Meritage refers to a blend of Sauvignon Blanc and Semillon, which is then barrel fermented. The rich rounded flavors of Semillon are used to round out the snappy and vibrant Sauvignon, while the barrel aging adds

a layer of oaky complexity. The resultant wines are a bit like Chardonnays that are not quite as round in the mouth and tend to be more firmly structured with a sturdy vibrant finish.

Best U.S. White Meritage Producers

Premier White Meritage Producers (***)

• Carmenet (Paragon Vineyard)
• Yorkville (Eleanor of Aquitaine)

Great White Meritage Producers (**)

• Benziger (Tribute)
• Cardinale (Royale)
• Cosentino (The Novelist)
• Flora Springs (Soliloquy)
• Guenoc (Langtry)
• Merryvale (Vignette)
• Venezia

Dependable White Meritage Producers (Recommended)

Some producers placed in this third tier are new (or new to us) and may merit a higher placement in subsequent vintages. These producers are offset by an asterisk.

• Beringer (Alluvium)
• Concannon (Assemblage)
• deLorimier (Spectrum)
• Hidden Cellars (Alchemy)
• Simi (Sendal)

Highly Recommended Meritage

93 • Merryvale (CA) 1996 Vignette, Napa Valley. $22.

91 • Cardinale (CA) 1996 Royale, California. $20.

91 • Benziger (CA) 1995 Tribute White, Sonoma Mountain. $17.

87 • Langtry (CA) 1996 White Meritage, Guenoc Valley. $21.

86 • Yorkville (CA) Eleanor of Aquitaine, Randle Hill Vineyard, Mendocino. $16.

Scale: Superlative (96-100), Exceptional (90-95), Highly Recommended (85-89), Recommended (80-84), Not Recommended (Under 80)

456

86 • Carmenet (CA) 1996 Reserve White Meritage, Paragon Vineyard, Edna Valley. $15.

85 • Simi (CA) 1995 Sendal, Sonoma County. $20.

85 • Grande River (CO) 1996 White Meritage, Grand Valley. $8.99.

What Is American Semillon?

Semillon is best known as the blending grape used with Sauvignon Blanc in Bordeaux. It is bottled alone however in Australia, and increasingly in the United States. Several Washington vintners in particular seem to have shown interest in the varietal. In the United States it produces a medium-bodied, lush wine that has distinctive figgy flavors and often features a yeasty note. It tends to be fairly rich and lower in acidity. As such, it makes a good match with poultry or rich seafood dishes. The best examples are seriously underpriced and make for excellent value.

Best U.S. Semillon Producers

Premier Semillon Producers (***)

• Brutocao
• Signorello
• Yorkville

Great Semillon Producers (**)

• Clos du Val
• Columbia Winery
• Kendall Jackson
• L'Ecole No. 41
• Windsor

Dependable Semillon Producers (Recommended)

Some producers placed in this third tier are new (or new to us) and may merit a higher placement in subsequent vintages. These producers are offset by an asterisk.

• Amador Foothill Winery
• Columbia Crest
• *Rosenblum
• Chateau Ste. Michelle

Highly Recommended Semillon

89 • Fenestra (CA) 1996 Semillon, Livermore Valley. $9.50.

87 • Signorello (CA) 1996 Semillon, Napa Valley. $20.

87 • L'Ecole No. 41 (WA) 1996 Semillon, Washington. $13.50.

86 • Hogue (WA) 1996 Semillon, Columbia Valley. $8.

86 • Calona (Canada) 1996 Private Reserve, Burrowing Owl Vineyard, Semillon, Okanagan Valley. $10.70.

86 • Amador Foothill Winery (CA) 1996 Semillon, Shenandoah Valley. $9.

eighteen

Riesling, Gewürztraminer, and Chenin Blanc

Riesling at a Glance

Wines Reviewed:
64

Producers/Brands Represented:
48

Median Price:
$9

Gewürztraminer at a Glance

Wines Reviewed:
38

Producers/Brands Represented:
33

Median Price:
$10

Chenin Blanc at a Glance

Wines Reviewed:
11

Producers/Brands Represented:
9

Median Price:
$9

What about American Riesling?

Riesling is widely grown throughout the United States. Indeed, most regions sport at least some bottlings of this noble German variety. U.S. Riesling is uniformly inexpensive, often representing good value. In general character these wines are cheerful, trading on their fresh, exuberant tropical flavors and absence of oak seasoning. Cooler California climates such as Monterey, Washington, Oregon, and the Finger Lakes in New York tend to supply the best examples of U.S. Riesling. These wines are rarely earthy, nor do they show the classic "petrol" aromas and vibrant acidity that characterizes German Rieslings. Rather, they tend to be early drinking quaffers, and a good alternative to those tiring of Chardonnay.

Best U.S. Riesling Producers

Premier U.S. Riesling Producers (***)
• Jekel
• Mirassou
• Paraiso Springs
• Hermann J. Wiemer

Great U.S. Riesling Producers (**)
• Argyle
• Concannon
• Covey Run
• Fetzer
• Dr. Konstantin Frank
• Gainey
• Glenora
• Hogue
• Indian Creek
• Kiona
• J. Lohr
• Kendall-Jackson
• Peconic Bay
• Standing Stone
• Ventana
• Washington Hills

Scale: Superlative (96-100), Exceptional (90-95), Highly Recommended (85-89), Recommended (80-84), Not Recommended (Under 80)

Dependable U.S. Riesling Producers (Recommended)

Some producers placed in this third tier are new (or new to us) and may merit a higher placement in subsequent vintages. These producers are offset by an asterisk.

- *Amity
- Bonny Doon
- Chateau St. Jean
- Chateau Ste. Michelle
- Columbia Crest
- Columbia Winery
- Durney
- Eola Hills
- Firestone
- Freemark Abbey
- Geyser Peak
- *Good Harbor
- LaVelle
- *Fess Parker
- V. Sattui
- St. Julian
- Windsor

Highly Recommended Riesling

90 • Paraiso Springs (CA) 1997 Riesling, Santa Lucia Highlands. $9.

89 • Firestone (CA) 1997 Riesling, Santa Barbara County 1.67% rs. $7.

88 • Oasis (VA) 1997 Semi-Dry Riesling, Virginia 2% rs. $18.

88 • Good Harbor (MI) 1997 Semidry White Riesling, Leelanau Peninsula 2% rs. $8.

88 • Fetzer (CA) 1997 Johannisberg Riesling, California 2.93% rs. $6.99.

88 • Dr. Konstantin Frank (NY) NV Salmon Run, Johannisberg Riesling, New York. $8.95.

86 • Woodward Canyon (WA) 1997 Riesling, Walla Walla County. $9.

86 • V. Sattui (CA) 1998 Dry Johannisberg Riesling, Napa Valley. $11.25.

86 • Ste. Chapelle (WA) 1998 Dry Johannisberg Riesling, Idaho. $6.

86 • LaVelle (OR) 1997 Susan's Vineyard, Riesling, Willamette Valley 2.4% rs. $8.

86 • Kendall-Jackson (CA) 1997 Vintner's Reserve, Johannisberg Riesling, California 2.42% rs. $11.

86 • Jackson-Triggs (Canada) 1996 Proprietors' Reserve, Dry Riesling, Okanagan Valley 1.26% rs. $6.90.

86 • Henke (OH) NV Riesling, American 1.75% rs. $10.37.

86 • Hagafen (CA) 1998 Johannisberg Riesling, Napa Valley 2.6% rs. $12.

85 • Reif Estate (Canada) 1996 Late Harvest Riesling, Niagara Peninsula 4% rs. $8.40.

85 • Konzelmann (Canada) 1995 Late Harvest, Dry Riesling, Niagara Peninsula. $10.95.

85 • Concannon (CA) 1997 Johannisberg Riesling, Arroyo Seco-Monterey 3% rs. $9.95.

What about American Gewürz?

Gewürztraminer is most closely associated with Alsace, where it reaches its enological apex in late harvest form— in styles that vary from dry to very sweet. U.S. Gewürztraminer rarely achieves the intensity of varietal character found in wines from Alsace, nonetheless there are numerous delicious dry examples to be found.

Cooler regions in California often yield the best results for Gewürztraminer, in circumstances where this variety can ripen late and produce distinctive clove and lychee-like varietal flavors. Cool climate Oregon and even the Finger Lakes of New York also have a number of producers of good dry Gewürztraminer that will often be characterized by fresh acidity and a leaner style.

Best U.S. Gewürztraminer Producers

Premier U.S. Gewürztraminer Producers (***)
- Adler Fels

Great U.S. Gewürztraminer Producers (**)
- Alderbrook
- Bouchaine

- Cosentino
- De Loach
- Thomas Fogarty
- Stonestreet
- Windsor

Dependable U.S. Gewürztraminer Producers (Recommended)

Some producers placed in this third tier are new (or new to us) and may merit a higher placement in subsequent vintages. These producers are offset by an asterisk.

- Apex
- Bargetto
- Chateau St. Jean
- *Claiborne & Churchill
- Concannon
- Dr. Konstantin Frank
- *Eola Hills
- Fetzer
- Geyser Peak
- Handley
- Husch
- Lazy Creek
- *Lenz
- *Martinelli
- Montinore
- *Mosby
- Navarro
- *Joseph Phelps
- *Chateau Ste. Michelle
- Snoqualmie
- *Treleaven

Highly Recommended Gewürztraminer

93 • Martinelli (CA) 1997 Gewürztraminer, Russian River Valley. $12.

92 • Adler Fels (CA) 1997 Gewürztraminer, Sonoma County. $11.

89 • Thomas Fogarty (CA) 1997 Gewürztraminer, Monterey. $12.50.

88 • Stonestreet (CA) 1997 Gewürztraminer, Anderson Valley. $16.

88 • Magnotta (Canada) 1995 Limited Edition, Gewürztraminer, Ontario. $8.93.

88 • Lenz (NY) 1995 Gewürztraminer, North Fork of Long Island. $10.99.

87 • Paraiso Springs (CA) 1997 Gewürztraminer, Santa Lucia Highlands. $9.

87 • Gray Monk (Canada) 1996 Reserve, Gewürztraminer, Okanagan Valley. $10.95.

86 • Magnotta (Canada) 1996 Medium-Dry, Limited Edition, Gewürztraminer, Ontario 2% rs. $9.

86 • Lang (Canada) 1996 Gewürztraminer, Naramata 1.1% rs. $8.10.

86 • Jackson-Triggs (Canada) 1997 Proprietors' Reserve, Gewürztraminer, Okanagan Valley 1.18% rs. $6.89.

86 • Husch (CA) 1998 Gewürztraminer, Anderson Valley. $11.

86 • Forest Ville (CA) 1997 Gewürztraminer, California 2.88% rs. $5.99.

86 • Columbia Winery (WA) 1998 Gewürztraminer, Yakima Valley 3% rs. $6.

85 • Covey Run (WA) 1997 Celilo Vineyard, Gewürztraminer, Washington. $12.

What about American Chenin Blanc?

Chenin Blanc is almost as widely planted in California as Chardonnay, but most of these vines are confined to the Central Valley where they produce undistinguished generic white wines from high yielding vineyards. The typical U.S. style of Chenin is rather fruitier and lacking the "sweaty" note that characterizes many French Loire examples. Only a handful of producers in California persist with making world-class dry Chenin Blancs from low yielding vines in prime vineyard locations that have not yet been planted with ubiquitous Cabernet and Chardonnay vines. The best, however, can offer fine value for money.

Scale: Superlative (96-100), Exceptional (90-95), Highly Recommended (85-89), Recommended (80-84), Not Recommended (Under 80)

462

Best U.S. Chenin Blanc Producers

Premier U.S. Chenin Blanc Producers (***)

- Chappellet (Old Vine Cuvée)
- Chalone
- Ventana

Great U.S. Chenin Blanc Producers (**)

- Chappellet
- Covey Run
- Dry Creek Vineyard
- Husch
- Kiona
- William Wheeler

Dependable U.S. Chenin Blanc Producers (Recommended)

Some producers placed in this third tier are new (or new to us) and may merit a higher placement in subsequent vintages. These producers are offset by an asterisk.

- *Arciero
- *Columbia Winery
- *Durney
- Pine Ridge

Highly Recommended Chenin Blanc

88 • Chappellet (CA) 1997 Old Vine Cuvée, Special Select White Wine, Napa Valley. $14.

86 • Weinstock (CA) 1998 Contour, Clarksburg. $8.95.

85 • Chappellet (CA) 1997 Dry Chenin Blanc, Napa Valley. $11.

84 • Robert Pecota (CA) 1998 Dry Chenin Blanc, Monterey County. $11.

84 • Paumanok (NY) 1998 Chenin Blanc, North Fork of Long Island. $12.

84 • Husch (CA) 1998 Chenin Blanc, Mendocino 2% rs. $8.50.

84 • Chalone (CA) 1996 Reserve, Chenin Blanc, Chalone. $20.

83 • Kendall-Jackson (CA) 1997 Vintner's Reserve, Chenin Blanc, California 2.1% rs. $11.

83 • Callaway (CA) 1998 Chenin Blanc, California. $7.50.

82 • Weinstock (CA) 1997 Contour, Clarksburg. $8.95.

81 • Bookwalter (WA) 1998 Chenin Blanc, Washington 3.3% rs. $6.

nineteen

❧

North American New Wave Whites: Viognier, Pinot Gris, and Pinot Blanc

❧

An Introduction: New Tastes in U.S. Whites?

Quibble not, Chardonnay is the nation's most popular white wine. It is, in fact, synonymous with white wine, having officially supplanted the misused term "chablis" (lower case intended) some time ago. Like its red counterpart Cabernet, however, there are some rumblings. As they say, familiarity breeds contempt, and while the world of white wine has as yet to find its Merlot in shining armor (nor even a Pinot Noir or Syrah for that matter), there are growing indications that the "cutting edge" of the wine consuming public is proving ever more receptive to at least the occasional Chardonnay alternative. Some of the hottest white wines, for both winemakers and consumers, include Viognier, Pinot Gris, and Pinot Blanc. Viognier in particular has taken off not only in the United States, but in many areas around the world. Where plantings were once confined to a small corner of the northern Rhône Valley, the grape can now be found in Australia, South Africa, Chile, the Languedoc, and Virginia to name but a few. As winemakers in emerging areas try to figure out what goes best and where, Viognier, in a remarkably short period of time, has been added to the arsenal.

The winemaking behind Viognier is a topic of debate, and as expected, wineries have embraced a wide range of vinification techniques. Viognier, in its Condrieu manifestation, is fat and lush, with a honeyed, tropical fruit-accented bouquet and lower levels of acidity. As such, it does not age well and is almost always best consumed within two or three years of the vintage. In the United States, unlike Condrieu, some Viogniers are being made like Chardonnays, with a heavy reliance on oak. Unfortunately, the varietal usually doesn't possess the structure of Chardonnay, and as a result the oak can become overwhelming. Those versions that have largely been fermented in stainless steel seem to better preserve the grape's natural attributes—a lush mouthfeel and an exotic natural bouquet. Oaked or not, U.S. Viognier, like Condrieu, is best consumed early, as some of the better releases from the last year or two have already begun to fall apart. For all its richness, this can still be a wine for many seasons. Its lighter manifestations are ideal as summer wines, consumed as aperitifs, or served with seafood, while heftier versions can ward off winter's chill.

Certain areas have chosen to take a pass on Viognier and chart new directions (some but not all dictated by climate), For instance, savvy marketers have taken an Austrian leaning white from the cooler northern alpine vineyards of Italy and created a sensation. Clean, crisp, and vibrant, that wine is Italian Pinot Grigio, made from a varietal that has accordingly gained an unexpected measure of cachet. Vintners in Oregon have taken notice, and while their Pinot Gris (the French and English synonym) was originally thought of as a "cash flow" wine that simply had an affinity for their chilly climate, it has begun to take on a life of its own. Some Oregon producers have reported that the demand for Pinot Gris has outstripped that for their Chardonnays, and it has been confirmed that the variety as a whole is selling briskly. The Pacific Northwest is an area of the country awash with regional pride and Pinot Gris has been looked on locally with a great deal of affection, following the success of Oregon Pinot Noir and the Bordeaux varietals of Washington.

Finally, though associated with Alsace, the "Pinot Blanc" often planted in the United States, and more specifically in California, is actually believed to be

Scale: Superlative (96-100), Exceptional (90-95), Highly Recommended (85-89), Recommended (80-84), Not Recommended (Under 80)

466

Melon (may-lon). Melon's origins actually lie in Burgundy where it was seen as a lesser alternative to Chardonnay. However, it is now more prevalent in the Loire, where it is bottled as Muscadet. Many U.S. Pinot Blancs have the flinty attributes of Muscadet, especially when they are fermented in stainless steel (no malolactic) and without wood aging. Others, however, use the full treatment, with some or full malolactic and lots of oak. This style is prevalent in the wines of Monterey in particular. On the whole, U.S. Pinot Blancs range from tart orchard fruit flavors with crisp acidity and racy mouth feels, to those with more lushness and viscosity. Pinot Blanc works well at the table in its "Chardonnay-like" Monterey versions, while lighter U.S. Pinot Blancs, like Muscadets, work well as an aperitif or with shellfish. As always, tasting notes will provide a good indication of the style in which the wine was made.

Best U.S. New Wave White Producers

Premier U.S. New Wave White Producers (***)
• Alban (Viognier, Roussanne)
• Cline (Marsanne)
• Joseph Phelps (Viognier)

Great U.S. New Wave White Producers (**)
• Beringer (Viognier)
• Bonterra (Viognier)
• Calera (Viognier)
• Chalone (Pinot Blanc)
• Chateau St. Jean (Pinot Blanc)
• Eberle (Viognier)
• Eyrie (Pinot Gris)
• Hinman (Pinot Gris)
• Horton (Viognier, Marsanne)
• Kunde (Viognier)
• Laetitia (Pinot Blanc)
• Lockwood (Pinot Blanc)
• J. Lohr (Pinot Blanc)
• Mirassou (Pinot Blanc)
• Oak Knoll (Pinot Gris)
• Paraiso Springs (Pinot Blanc)
• Fess Parker (Viognier)
• Silvan Ridge (Pinot Gris)
• Steele (Pinot Blanc)
• Twin Brook (Pinot Gris)

New Wave Whites at a Glance

Wines Reviewed:
69

Producers/Brands Represented:
59

Median Price:
$14

Dependable U.S. New Wave White Producers (Recommended)

Some producers placed in this third tier are new (or new to us) and may merit a higher placement in subsequent vintages. These producers are offset by an asterisk.

- *Bell (Viognier)
- Benziger (Viognier, Pinot Blanc)
- *Bernardus (Marsanne)
- Byron (Pinot Gris)
- Cooper Mountain (Pinot Gris)
- *DeRose (Viognier)
- *Dos Cabezas (Pinot Gris)
- *Eola Hills (Pinot Gris)
- Iron Horse (Viognier)
- *Karly (Marsanne)
- King Estate (Pinot Gris)
- McDowell (Viognier)
- *La Famiglia di Robert Mondavi (Pinot Gris)
- *Morgan (Marsanne)
- Mount Palomar (Rousanne, Viognier)
- Preston (Viognier)
- Renwood (Viognier)
- *Rosenblum (Viognier)
- Saddleback (Pinot Blanc)
- *Smith & Hook (Viognier)
- Sobon (Viognier, Roussanne)
- *Sunstone (Viognier)
- Villa Mt. Eden (Pinot Blanc)
- Wild Horse (Pinot Blanc)

Highly Recommended New Wave Whites

Pinot Blanc

88 • Laetitia (CA) 1996 Reserve, Pinot Blanc, San Luis Obispo County. $17.

88 • Laetitia (CA) 1996 La Colline Vineyard Designated Reserve, Pinot Blanc. $25.

87 • Byron (CA) 1996 Pinot Blanc, Santa Maria Valley. $16.

86 • Saddleback (CA) 1997 Pinot Blanc, Napa Valley. $13.50.

86 • Hester Creek (Canada) 1996 Grand Reserve, Pinot Blanc, Okanagan Valley. $9.25.

85 • Peller Estates (Canada) 1996 Pinot Blanc, Okanagan Valley. $11.99.

85 • Murphy-Goode (CA) 1996 Pinot Blanc, Sonoma County. $13.50.

Pinot Gris

93 • Oak Knoll (OR) 1996 Vintage Reserve, Pinot Gris, Willamette Valley. $17.

90 • King Estate (OR) 1996 Pinot Gris, Oregon. $13.

88 • Martini & Prati (CA) 1996 Vino Grigio, California. $12.50.

87 • Dos Cabezas (AZ) 1997 Pinot Gris, Cochise County. $14.95.

87 • Bargetto (CA) 1997 Pinot Grigio, Central Coast. $15.

86 • Montinore (OR) 1997 Pinot Gris, Willamette Valley. $9.99.

86 • LaVelle (OR) 1996 Winter's Hill Vineyard, Pinot Gris, Oregon. $13.

86 • La Famiglia di Robert Mondavi (CA) 1996 Pinot Grigio, California. $16.

86 • Cooper Mountain (OR) 1997 Pinot Gris, Willamette Valley. $14.75.

86 • Callaway (CA) 1997 Pinot Gris, Temecula. $12.

86 • Bridgeview (OR) 1997 Pinot Gris, Oregon. $9.99.

85 • Pelee Island Winery (Canada) 1995 Pinot Gris, Ontario. $7.99.

85 • Columbia Winery (WA) 1996 Pinot Gris, Yakima Valley. $10.99.

Viognier

91 • Rosenblum (CA) 1997 Viognier, Santa Barbara County. $15.

91 • Fess Parker (CA) 1996 Viognier, Santa Barbara County. $22.

90 • Joseph Phelps (CA) 1996 Vin du Mistral, Viognier, Napa Valley. $28.

89 • De Rose (CA) 1996 Viognier, Cienega Valley. $15/375 ml.

87 • Smith & Hook (CA) 1996 Viognier, Arroyo Seco. $18.

87 • Glen Ellen (CA) 1995 Expressions, Viognier, San Benito County. $11/375 ml.

87 • Beringer (CA) 1996 Viognier, Napa Valley. $25.

86 • Waterbrook (WA) 1997 Viognier, Columbia Valley. $18.

86 • Iron Horse (CA) 1997 Viognier, Alexander Valley. $18.

Scale: Superlative (96-100), Exceptional (90-95), Highly Recommended (85-89), Recommended (80-84), Not Recommended (Under 80)

468

85 • Pindar (NY) 1996 Viognier,
North Fork of Long Island. $19.99.

85 • Calera (CA) 1997 Viognier,
Mount Harlan. $30.

Other Whites

93 • Mount Palomar (CA) 1996
Castelletto, Cortese, Temecula. $16.

91 • Cline (CA) 1996 Marsanne,
Los Carneros. $20.

89 • La Famiglia di Robert Mondavi (CA)
1996 Tocai Friulano, California. $18.

88 • Mount Pleasant (MO) 1996
Chardonel, Augusta. $14.

88 • Robert Pepi (CA) 1997 Malvasia
Bianca, Central Coast. $14.

87 • Mount Palomar (CA) 1997
Rey Sol Le Mediterrane Blanc,
Temecula. $16.

86 • Rosenblum (CA) 1996 Semillon-
Chardonnay, Livermore Valley. $11.

86 • Zaca Mesa (CA) 1996 Zaca Vineyards,
Roussanne, Santa Barbara County.
$16.50.

86 • Mount Palomar (CA) 1997 Rey Sol,
Roussane, Temecula. $18.

86 • Hogue (WA) 1996 Semillon-
Chardonnay, Columbia Valley. $8.

85 • Windsor (CA) 1998 Late Harvest,
Murphy Ranch, Muscat Canelli,
Alexander Valley 4.2% rs. $13.50.

85 • Sokol Blosser (OR) 1998
Muller-Thurgau. $14.95.

85 • Henry Estate (OR) 1998 Muller
Thurgau, Umpqua Valley 2% rs. $8.

twenty

North American Sparkling Wines

An Introduction: What about American Bubbly?

Ahh sparkling wines. At the base of many a party, sparkling wines are seen as an indispensable celebratory ingredient. In recent years, however, the French original, Champagne, has become dauntingly expensive. Enter the U.S. alternative. At the very top end of the quality spectrum U.S. bubbly has become good enough to compete with mass market Champagne, and often at a fraction of the price. U.S. sparklers tend to be fruitier in flavor and feature less of the complex yeasty notes that belie a quality Champagne. The very best producers offer wines in the $20 range and even less, making them exceptional value when compared to comparable Champagnes.

Best U.S. Sparkling Wine Producers

Premier U.S. Sparkling Wine Producers (***)
• Argyle
• Domaine Carneros (Le Rêve)
• Equinox
• Iron Horse
• J. Wine Co.
• Roederer Estate
• Scharffenberger
• Schramsberg

Great U.S. Sparkling Wine Producers (**)
• S. Anderson
• Domaine Carneros
• Domaine Chandon
• Codorniu
• Gloria Ferrer
• Glenora
• Gruet
• Handley
• Mumm Cuvée Napa
• Piper-Sonoma

Sparkling Wines at a Glance

Wines Reviewed:

86

Producers/Brands Represented:

46

Median Price:

$19

Dependable U.S. Sparkling Wine Producers (Recommended)

Some producers placed in this third tier are new (or new to us) and may merit a higher placement in subsequent vintages. These producers are offset by an asterisk.

- *Falconer
- Chateau Frank
- Robert Hunter
- Jepson
- *Laetitia
- L. Mawby
- *Maxus
- Mountain Dome
- *Paradise Ridge
- Pindar
- Domaine Ste. Michelle
- Tribaut
- Wente
- Westport Rivers
- Windsor

Highly Recommended Sparkling Wines

Brut

93 • Roederer Estate (CA) 1992 L'Ermitage, Anderson Valley. $35.

92 • Iron Horse (CA) 1989 Brut LD, Sonoma County Green Valley. $45.

92 • Gloria Ferrer (CA) 1989 Carneros Cuvée Brut, Carneros. $28.

91 • Schramsberg (CA) 1992 J.Schram, Napa Valley. $65.

91 • Maxus (CA) 1991 English Cuvée, California. $29.99.

91 • Domaine Carneros (CA) 1993 Brut, Carneros. $19.

90 • Maxus (CA) 1991 Brut, California. $19.99.

90 • J Wine Co. (CA) 1994 J Brut, Sonoma County. $28.

90 • Iron Horse (CA) 1993 Brut, Sonoma County. $23.50.

90 • Equinox (CA) NV Harmony Cuvée Brut, Santa Cruz Mountains. $27.

89 • Roederer Estate (CA) NV Brut, Anderson Valley. $17.

89 • Iron Horse (CA) 1993 Vrais Amis, Sonoma County. $28.

89 • Iron Horse (CA) 1993 Russian Cuvée, Sonoma County. $23.50.

89 • Domaine Chandon (CA) 1998 25th Anniversary Reserve Cuvée, Napa County. $24.

89 • Argyle (OR) 1994 Brut, Knudsen Vineyards, Willamette Valley. $19.50.

88 • Pindar (NY) 1994 Cuvée Rare Champagne, North Fork of Long Island. $27.99.

88 • Oasis (VA) NV Brut, Virginia. $28.

88 • Laetitia (CA) 1993 Elegance Brut, California. $23.

88 • Gloria Ferrer (CA) 1990 Royal Cuvée Brut, Vintage Reserve, Carneros. $20.

88 • Domaine Chandon (CA) NV Brut Cuvée, Napa County. $18.

88 • Chateau Frank (NY) 1991 Brut, Finger Lakes. $15.

87 • Piper Sonoma (CA) NV Brut, Sonoma. $14.

87 • Mumm Cuvée Napa (CA) NV Brut Prestige, Napa Valley. $15.95.

87 • Mountain Dome (WA) 1993 Brut, Columbia Valley. $16.

86 • Oasis (VA) NV Celebration 2000 Brut Cuvée D'Or, Virginia. $50.

86 • Lenz (NY) 1992 "Cuvée" Sparkling Wine, North Fork of Long Island. $19.99.

86 • Glenora (NY) NV Brut, New York. $12.99.

86 • Cap Rock (TX) NV Sparkling Wine, American. $12.99.

85 • Folie à Deux (CA) 1993 Fantaisie Brut, Napa Valley. $18.

Blanc de Blancs

93 • Domaine Carneros (CA) 1992 Le Reve, Blanc de Blancs, Carneros. $35.

92 • Schramsberg (CA) 1994 Blanc de Blancs, Napa Valley. $26.

92 • Iron Horse (CA) 1990 Blanc de Blancs LD, Sonoma County, Green Valley. $45.

92 • Equinox (CA) 1992 Cuvée de Chardonnay, Blanc de Blanc, Santa Cruz Mountains. $33.

91 • Iron Horse (CA) 1991 Blanc de Blancs, Sonoma County. $30.

90 • Falconer (CA) 1983 Blanc de Blancs RD, San Luis Obispo County. $19.95.

Scale: Superlative (96-100), Exceptional (90-95), Highly Recommended (85-89), Recommended (80-84), Not Recommended (Under 80)

474

87 • Gruet (NM) 1994 Blanc de Blancs,
New Mexico. $20.

86 • Tribaut (CA) NV Blanc de Blancs
Brut, California. $9.

85 • Glenora (NY) 1993 Blanc de Blancs,
New York. $12.99.

Blanc de Noirs

91 • Schramsberg (CA) 1992 Blanc de
Noirs, Napa Valley. $27.

90 • Piper Sonoma (CA) NV Blanc de
Noir, Sonoma. $15.

88 • Mumm Cuvée Napa (CA) NV Blanc
de Noir, Napa Valley. $15.95.

87 • Westport Rivers (MA) 1994
Blanc de Noir, Southeastern
New England. $28.95.

86 • Gloria Ferrer (CA) NV Blanc de
Noirs, Carneros. $15.

86 • Domaine Chandon (CA) NV Blanc de
Noirs, Carneros. $18.

85 • Robert Hunter (CA) 1992 Brut de
Noirs, Sonoma Valley. $25.

Brut Rosé

92 • Roederer Estate (CA) NV Brut Rosé,
Anderson Valley. $21.

90 • Maxus (CA) 1991 Midnight Cuvée,
California. $19.99.

90 • Iron Horse (CA) 1993 Brut Rosé,
Sonoma County. $28.

87 • Laetitia (CA) 1993 Elegance Brut
Rosé, San Luis Obispo County. $23.

86 • Mountain Dome (WA) NV Brut Rosé,
Washington. $16.

Other Sparkling Wines

89 • Sumac Ridge (Canada) 1993 Steller's
Joy Brut, Okanagan Valley. $12.95.

87 • L. Mawby (MI) NV Talisman Brut,
Leelanau Peninsula. $22.

86 • L. Mawby (MI) NV Cremant Brut,
Leelanau Peninsula. $18.

86 • Firelands (OH) NV Riesling, Lake
Erie. $10.95.

85 • Magnotta (Canada) NV Rossana
Blanc de Blancs, Canada. $10.

twenty-one

North American Rosé

An Introduction: What about American Rosé?

U.S. Rosés cover a multitude of variations on a subtle theme. Colors vary from barely perceptible pink tinges to full blown cranberry hues. They are rarely vinified with the lavish expense of premium wines, and they can be made from a wide array of red grape varieties. By definition they are not usually very varietally expressive, and as such can be made from almost any grape that can add some color. A favorite is Zinfandel, which for many years has been the mainstay of California blush wines. At the lower end of the spectrum, Rosés, frequently bearing the White Zinfandel tag, can have rather faint flavors, sometimes obvious sweetness, and an occasional lack of acidity. At their best, U.S. Rosés made from noble varietals are fresh and fruity, sporting much more character and color than French Rosés. Italian and Rhône varietals often yield the best results in California, sometimes even with a touch of oak seasoning.

Best U.S. Rosé Producers

Premier U.S. Rosé Producers (***)
• Paraiso Springs (Baby Blush)
• Swanson (Rosato of Sangiovese)

Great U.S. Rosé Producers (**)
• Cosentino (Tenero Rosa)
• McDowell (Grenache Rosé)
• Pedroncelli (Zinfandel Rosé)
• Joseph Phelps (Vin du Mistral Rosé)
• Sanford (Vin Gris de Pinot Noir)
• Sobon (Rhone Rosé)
• Wollersheim (Prairie Blush)
• Les Vieux Cepages (Ronfleur)

Dependable U.S. Rosé Producers (Recommended)
Some producers placed in this third tier are new (or new to us) and may merit a higher placement in subsequent vintages. These producers are offset by an asterisk.

• *Beaulieu (Solaris & Pinot Noir de Vin Gris)
• *Beringer (Rosé de Saignee)
• Cakebread (Rosé)

Rosé at a Glance

Wines Reviewed:
43

Producers/Brands Represented:
40

Median Price:
$7.50

- Concannon (Righteously Rosé)
- *Curtis (Syrah Rosé)
- De Loach (White Zinfandel)
- *La Famiglia di Robert Mondavi (Rosato Sangiovese)
- *Peju (Provence)
- Preston (Gamay Rosé)
- *Thornton (Grenache Rosé)
- *Treleaven (Saumon Blush)

Highly Recommended Rosé Wines

92 • Pedroncelli (CA) 1998 Vintage Selection, Zinfandel Rosé, Sonoma County. $8.

90 • Wollersheim (WI) 1998 Prairie Blush, White Marechal Foch, Wisconsin 1.8% rs. $7.50.

90 • Thornton (CA) 1998 Collins Ranch, Grenache Rosé, Cucamonga Valley 1.45% rs. $7.99.

89 • Beringer (CA) 1997 Rosé de Saignée, California. $16.

88 • Sobon (CA) 1997 Rhone Rose, Shenandoah Valley. $9.

88 • Laurel Lake (NY) NV Lake Rosé, North Fork of Long Island. $9.99.

88 • Curtis (CA) 1997 Syrah Rosé, Santa Ynez Valley. $8.

87 • Swanson (CA) 1998 Rosato, Sangiovese, Napa Valley. $14.

87 • Cedar Creek (WI) NV Cranberry Blush, American 2.9% rs. $7.

86 • Peju Province (CA) 1997 Provence-A California Table Wine, California 1.1% rs. $16.50.

86 • Montevina (CA) 1997 Rosato, Nebbiolo, Amador County 1.7% rs. $7.50.

86 • Macari (NY) 1997 Rosé d 'Une Nuit, North Fork of Long Island. $11.

86 • Jackson-Triggs (Canada) 1997 Proprietors ' Reserve Blanc de Noir, Okanagan Valley 1.15% rs. $6.46.

85 • Yakima River (WA) 1997 Sof Lem, Lemberger, Yakima Valley. $9.

85 • Gristina (NY) 1997 Rosé of Cabernet, North Fork of Long Island. $8.99.

85 • Chateau Lafayette Reneau (NY) 1998 Pinot Noir Blanc, Finger Lakes 2.5% rs. $6.99.

85 • Callahan Ridge (OR) 1998 White Zinfandel, Umpqua Valley 4% rs. $7.

Scale: Superlative (96-100), Exceptional (90-95), Highly Recommended (85-89), Recommended (80-84), Not Recommended (Under 80)

480

twenty-two

❧

North American Fortified Wines

❧

An Introduction: American Fortified Wines

Fortified wines, those inevitable after dinner elixirs, have been a part of the American wine industry since its inception. Indeed, the early American taste for fortified wines was well documented, as the signing of the declaration of independence was toasted with a round of Madeira, and it, along with Port and Sherry, was the preferred drink of the Eastern aristocracy well into our own century. That the native industry should strive to compete for this market was only natural.

As in much of the wine-producing New World, vintners took a run at Sherry (and do to this day), but the results on the whole pale, often quite literally, to the Spanish original. Port, however, has been an altogether more satisfying experience. While the climate and soil of Jerez have not been duplicated elsewhere, the broiling heat and unique winemaking practices of the Douro have proven much easier to replicate, perhaps nowhere more so than in California's Amador County and San Joaquin Valley.

Beyond California, Port-style wines are being made in much of the country. As might be expected a certain measure of heat helps, and the most successful examples have come from warm states such as Missouri. As the saying goes a little residual sugar can cover up a multitude of sins, but the Missouri Ports of producers such as Stone Hill and Mount Pleasant truly stand on their own merits, and have proven as consistently competent as many California versions.

Best U.S. Fortified Wine Producers

Premier U.S. Fortified Wine Producers (***)
- Beaulieu (Muscat)
- Bonny Doon (Cassis, Framboise)
- Cedar Mountain (Port)
- Guenoc (Port)
- Ficklin (Port)
- Quady (Muscat, Port)

Fortified Wines at a Glance

Wines Reviewed:
61

Producers/Brands Represented:
43

Median Price:
$18

Great U.S. Fortified Wine Producers (**)

- Beringer (Port)
- Geyser Peak (Port)
- Mount Pleasant (Port)
- Pindar (Port)
- Stone Hill (Port)
- Whidbey (Port)
- Windsor (Port)

Dependable U.S. Fortified Wine Producers (Recommended)

Some producers placed in this third tier are new (or new to us) and may merit a higher placement in subsequent vintages. These producers are offset by an asterisk.

- *Duck Walk (Port)
- Horton (Port)
- Justin (Port)
- Pesenti (Port)
- *Prager (Port)
- Rosenblum (Muscat, Port)
- *St. Amant (Port)
- St. Julian (Sherry)
- Sonora (Port)
- Trentadue (Port)
- *Twin Hills (Port)

Highly Recommended Fortified Wines

93 • Quady (CA) 1990 Vintage Starboard, Amador County 10.6% rs. $21.50.

92 • Ficklin (CA) 10 Year Old Tawny Port, California 9.5% rs. $22.

92 • Cedar Mountain (CA) 1996 Vintage Port, Amador County 10% rs. $19.50.

91 • Quady (CA) 1993 LBV Port, Amador County 8.18% rs. $12.

91 • Ficklin (CA) 1988 Vintage Port, California 9% rs. $25.

90 • Whidbey (WA) 1990 Port, Washington 9.8% rs. $12.99.

90 • Quady (CA) 1989 Frank 's Vineyard Vintage Starboard, California 10.4% rs. $19.

89 • Twin Hills (CA) Zinfandel Port, Lot XCII, Paso Robles 5% rs. $25.

89 • Quady (CA) Batch 88 Starboard, California 11.1% rs. $11.50.

89 • Quady (CA) 1990 Frank 's Vineyard Vintage Starboard, California 10.2% rs. $19.

89 • Prager Winery & Port Works (CA) Noble Companion 10 Year Old Tawny Port, Napa Valley 8.4% rs. $45.

89 • Pindar (NY) 1995 Port, North Fork of Long Island. $24.99.

88 • Trentadue (CA) 1994 Petite Sirah Port, Alexander Valley 8.6% rs. $20.

88 • St. Julian (MI) Solera Cream Sherry, Michigan 17% rs. $12.

88 • Prager Winery & Port Works (CA) 1993 Royal Escort LBV Port, Petite Sirah, Napa Valley 5.5% rs. $38.50.

88 • Mount Pleasant (MO) 15 Barrel Tawny Port, Augusta 8.5% rs. $23.50.

88 • Beringer (CA) 1994 Port of Cabernet Sauvignon, Napa Valley 10.29% rs. $20.

87 • Guenoc (CA) 1994 Vintage Port, California 9.7% rs. $25.

87 • Geyser Peak (CA) 1995 Henry 's Reserve Shiraz Port, Alexander Valley. $15/375 ml.

87 • Duck Walk (NY) 1996 Blueberry Port 10% rs. $12.95/375 ml.

86 • Sonora Winery & Port Works (CA) 1994 Vintage Port, Sierra Foothills 8.5% rs. $16/500 ml.

86 • Mount Pleasant (MI) 1996 White Port, Augusta Missouri 10.5% rs. $25/375 ml.

86 • Mount Pleasant (MI) 1990 Port, Augusta, Missouri 11.1% rs. $18.

86 • Meier 's (OH) No. 44 American Ruby Port 8.3% rs. $6.95.

86 • Lonz (OH) 3 Islands American Ruby Port 9.9% rs. $6.50.

86 • Justin (CA) 1996 Obtuse, Paso Robles 15% rs. $22.50.

86 • Ficklin (CA) Tinta Port, California 8.5% rs. $12.

85 • Windsor (CA) Rare Port, California 11.9% rs. $13.

85 • St. Amant (CA) 1995 Vintage Port, Amador County 7% rs. $28.

85 • Mount Pleasant (MO) JRL 's Barrel Select Port, Augusta 6.75% rs. $11.95.

Scale: Superlative (96-100), Exceptional (90-95), Highly Recommended (85-89), Recommended (80-84), Not Recommended (Under 80)

484

85 • Mount Pleasant (MI) Tawny Port,
  Library Vol. V, Augusta Missouri
  10.9% rs. $28.

85 • Dominion Wine Cellars (VA) 1996
  Raspberry Merlot,
  Virginia 18.5% rs. $19.

twenty-three

North American Dessert Wines

An Introduction: American Dessert Wines

Most American dessert wines are late harvest or botrytised styles, which means that the sugars are concentrated in the grapes allowing for a sweet and often viscous wine. These methods are applied to many varietals around the country, but broadly speaking, there are two major styles. The first involves Sauvignon Blanc and/or Semillon and is modeled on the famous sweet wines from the Sauternes district of Bordeaux. Most are botrytised and then aged in oak barrels to add an overlay of luxuriant oaky flavors. Semillon achieves a rich, figgy sort of personality while Sauvignon tends to have a bit more acidity and comes across as being not quite so lush. They are sometimes bottled individually but often work best in combination for this style of wine.

Beyond the Sauternes style, U.S. producers make late harvest or "Icewines" from aromatic varietals such as Riesling, Gewürztraminer, Chenin Blanc, and Muscat. These wines often emulate classic European styles such as Piemontese Moscato, German Trockenbeerenausleses, and Alsatian Vendange Tardives. California provides the vast majority of the late harvest dessert wines, blessed as it is with a dry, lengthy harvesting season. Washington State has a suitable climate for making high-quality Icewine from naturally frozen late harvested grapes, as does New York and other northern tier states. With a labor-intensive production process, these wines will always be more expensive then dry table wines, but they often represent considerable value when compared to imported French and German alternatives.

Canada has slowly but surely been building a reputation as one of the world's most abundant and consistent producers of Icewine, a style of wine most closely associated with Germany. In Germany, Icewine is produced in miniscule quantities at astronomical prices; and even then, only in favorable years. Most of Canada's Icewine is produced on the Niagara Peninsula, a cool growing region that can always count on a sustained cold spell in January to freeze Riesling or Vidal grapes on the vine. These grapes when pressed in their frozen state produce extraordinarily concentrated sweet wines with enough acidity to keep them fresh and uncloying. Given Canada's northerly latitude, other regions, namely, the Okanagan Valley in British Columbia, are also proving able to make outstanding Icewines. U.S. consumers have not yet been urged to seek these gems by the mainstream media; hence, these wines are not in widespread distribution. Devotees and enthusiasts will have to look to specialist wineshops in major markets. A separate list of Canadian Best Producers for dessert wines is on page 335.

Best U.S. Dessert Wine Producers

Premier U.S. Dessert Wine Producers (***)
• Beringer (Special Select Johannisberg Riesling & Nightingale)
• Callaway (Sweet Nancy)
• Chappellet (Moelleux Chenin Blanc)
• Dolce
• Freemark Abbey (Edelwein Gold)
• Grgich Hills (Violetta)
• Swanson (Late Harvest Semillon)

Great U.S. Dessert Wine Producers (**)

- Alderbrook (Late Harvest Muscat de Frontignan)
- Bonny Doon (Vin de Glacière)
- Chateau St. Jean (Belle Terre Vineyards, Special Select Riesling)
- De Loach (Late Harvest Gewürztraminer)
- de Lorimier (Lace)
- Elk Cove (Ultima Riesling)
- J. Lohr (Late Harvest Johannisberg Riesling)
- Joseph Phelps (Eisrebe)
- Martin Brothers (Moscato Allegro)
- Newlan (Late Harvest Johannisberg Riesling)
- Quady (Orange Muscat & Black Muscat)
- Silvan Ridge (Various Late Harvest and Icewines)

Dependable U.S. Dessert Wine Producers (Recommended)

Some producers placed in this third tier are new (or new to us) and may merit a higher placement in subsequent vintages. These producers are offset by an asterisk.

- Amity (Select Cluster Riesling)
- *Apex (Icewine)
- *Bedell (Eis)
- *Chalk Hill (Botrytised Semillon)
- *Chateau Grand Traverse (Icewine)
- Chateau Ste. Michelle (Late Harvest/Icewine Riesling)
- Elk Cove (Ultima Gewürztraminer)
- Ferrari-Carano (Eldorado Gold)
- *Dr. Konstantin Frank (Riesling Icewine)
- Geyser Peak (Late Harvest Riesling)
- Jekel (Late Harvest Riesling)
- *Kendall-Jackson (Late Harvest Chardonnay)
- *Martinelli (Muscat Alexandria)
- *Navarro (Late Harvest Cluster Select Riesling)
- Robert Pecota (Moscato d'Andrea)
- Renaissance (Late Harvest Riesling)
- *Santa Barbara Winery (Late Harvest Sauvignon Blanc)
- *Voss (Botrytis Sauvignon Blanc)

Dessert Wines at a Glance

Wines Reviewed:

107

Producers/Brands Represented:

78

Median Price:

$30 ($15/375ml. Bottles)

Scale: Superlative (96-100), Exceptional (90-95), Highly Recommended (85-89), Recommended (80-84), Not Recommended (Under 80)

Outstanding Dessert Wines

97 • Dolce (CA) 1995 Late Harvest Dessert Wine, Napa Valley 10% rs. $50/375 ml. Cellar Selection.

95 • Beringer (CA) 1994 Nightingale, Private Reserve, Botrytized Sauvignon Blanc-Semillon, Napa Valley 17.1% rs. $22/375 ml.

93 • Erath (OR) 1997 Late Harvest, Gewürztraminer, Willamette Valley 19.5% rs. $18/375 ml.

93 • Ackerman (IA) Apricot Wine 9% rs. $6.50. Best Buy.

92 • Chateau St. Jean (CA) 1995 Belle Terre Vineyards, Special Select Late Harvest, Johannisberg Riesling, Alexander Valley 18.1% rs. $25/375 ml.

92 • Apex (WA) 1997 Ice Wine, Gewürztraminer, Columbia Valley 16.7% rs. $35/375 ml.

91 • Stoney Ridge (Canada) 1996 Puddicombe Vineyard, Select Late Harvest, Vidal, Niagara Peninsula 13.5% rs. $14.25/375 ml.

91 • Magnotta (Canada) Framboise, Fortified Raspberry Dessert Wine, Ontario 18% rs. $11/500 ml.

91 • Bartlett (ME) Sweet Raspberry Wine, Maine 11% rs. $9.99/375 ml.

91 • Alba (NJ) Red Raspberry Wine 13% rs. $9.99/500 ml.

90 • Martinelli (CA) 1997 Jackass Hill, Muscat Alexandria, Russian River Valley. $18/375 ml.

90 • Grgich Hills (CA) 1995 Violetta, Late Harvest, Napa Valley 11% rs. $40/375 ml.

90 • Dr. Konstantin Frank (NY) 1995 Ice Wine, Johannisberg Riesling, New York 22% rs. $29.95/375 ml.

90 • Claar (WA) 1997 Botrytisized Ice Wine, Riesling, Columbia Valley 23% rs. $29.99/375 ml.

90 • Calona (Canada) 1995 Private Reserve, Late Harvest Botrytis Affected, Ehrenfelser, Canada. $21/375 ml.

90 • Bonny Doon (CA) 1997 Muscat Vin de Glacière, California 19.3% rs. $15/375 ml.

90 • Bedell (NY) NV Eis, New York. $27.50/375 ml.

90 • Beaulieu (CA) NV Muscat de Beaulieu, California 12% rs. $10.99/375 ml.

Icewine

98 • Pillitteri (Canada) 1997 Vidal Icewine, Niagara Peninsula VQA 19.8% rs. $29.97/375 ml.

95 • Jackson-Triggs (Canada) 1996 Proprietors' Grand Reserve Ice Wine, Riesling, Okanagan Valley 26.4% rs. $44.07/375 ml.

95 • Cave Spring (Canada) 1997 Icewine, Riesling, Niagara Peninsula 21% rs. $48.99/375 ml.

94 • Sumac Ridge (Canada) 1996 Icewine, Pinot Blanc, Okanagan Valley 26.75% rs. $19.95/375 ml. Cellar Selection.

94 • Jackson-Triggs (Canada) 1997 Proprietors' Grand Reserve Ice Wine, Riesling, Okanagan Valley 24.9% rs. $44.07/375 ml.

91 • Reif Estate (Canada) 1996 Icewine, Vidal, Niagara Peninsula 19.5% rs. $35.60/375 ml.

91 • Peller Estates (Canada) 1997 Icewine, Limited Edition Founder's Series, Vidal, Niagara Peninsula 20% rs. $45/375 ml.

91 • Magnotta (Canada) 1996 Sparkling Icewine, Vidal, Ontario 18% rs. $50/375 ml.

90 • Strewn (Canada) 1996 Icewine, Vidal, Niagara Peninsula 20% rs. $45/375 ml.

90 • Stoney Ridge (Canada) 1996 Icewine, Riesling-Traminer, Niagara Peninsula 19.5% rs. $35.95/375 ml.

90 • Stoney Ridge (Canada) 1995 Icewine, Gewürztraminer, Niagara Peninsula 21% rs. $35.95/375 ml.

90 • Magnotta (Canada) 1996 Limited Edition Icewine, Vidal, Niagara Peninsula 19% rs. $19.95/375 ml.

90 • Konzelmann (Canada) 1996 Icewine, Vidal, Niagara Peninsula 18.5% rs. $45.55/375 ml.

90 • Cedar Creek Estate (Canada) 1995 Reserve Icewine, Chardonnay, Okanagan Valley 32% rs. $59.95/375 ml.

twenty-four

North American Fruit Wines

An Introduction: American Fruit Wines

We have extolled the virtues of traditionally made American fruit wines for some years now, and this year shall be no different, as the category is full of well-made and downright excellent wines. Perhaps most surprising is the fact that some of the best wines are actually made in dry table styles.

"It's about time dry fruit wines got some attention," declares winemaker Bob Bartlett happily. Indeed, Bartlett's blueberry wines, made from Maine berries, continue to be quite a rarity. Unlike the sweet dessert styles made by most fruit wine producers, Bartlett's top blueberry cuvée is dry and aged up to 18 months in 100% new French oak. Deep and exotic, with an extraordinary fragrance and a supple structure, this wine has proven to be one of the nation's great wine secrets, year after year. Those looking for fruity blueberry juice need not apply. It resembles sweet, fresh blueberries about as much as Cabernet resembles sweet, fresh grapes.

New French oak for fruit wines is rare because it is both risky and expensive, but Bartlett believes his wines are worth it. Hand-picked low bush blueberries, which are smaller and juicier than the high bush blueberries found in supermarkets, are crushed in a conventional grape crusher, then cold fermented on the skins. The wines are also from a single patch (Bartlett's Blueberry Monopole?). Some sugar must be added to bring alcohol levels up, but there is no residual sweetness in the final product.

Bartlett has often had to fight to get his products released. When he and his wife started making fruit wines in 1981, new state legislation had to be written to allow them to sell from their winery. Bartlett wrote that law and got it sponsored. He has also tried to get permission to put vintage dates on his labels (the fruit for his wines is often from a single vintage, and yes there is vintage variation). An implacable BATF won't allow it, however, ruling that vintages can only apply to grapes.

Fruit Wines at a Glance

Wines Reviewed:

21

Producers/Brands Represented:

9

Median Price:

$9

"What about vintage cars?" laughs Bartlett, amused but also angered by the pointless restriction.

Bartlett makes only fruit wines, some of which are sweet, but his dry wines are his pride and joy. In addition to the blueberry wines, he produces white pear and apple wines, and has introduced a mead. The dry table wines are, like most grape-based wines, often at their best with food. "It's really exciting to match these wines with food," Bartlett says, "because there's no history, no precedent." He suggests serving the blueberry wine with Italian dishes or grilled lamb, and the pear wine with smoked fish. A tasty thought indeed.

Best U.S. Fruit Wine Producers

Premier U.S. Fruit Wine Producers (***)
• Bargetto (Chaucer's)
• Bartlett
• St. Julian (Raspberry Champagne)

Great U.S. Fruit Wine Producers (**)
• Hosmer
• Paul Thomas

Dependable U.S. Fruit Wine Producers (Recommended)
Some producers placed in this third tier are new (or new to us) and may merit a higher placement in subsequent vintages. These producers are offset by an asterisk.

• *Ackerman
• *Alba
• *Bedell
• Earle Estates
• *Good Harbor
• *Honeywood
• Hoodsport
• Nashoba Valley Winery
• Wildwood Cellars
• *Wintergreen

Highly Recommended Fruit Wines

96 • Southbrook Farms (Canada) NV Cassis, Canada 16% rs. $15/375 ml.

93 • Southbrook Farms (Canada) NV Framboise, Canada 16% rs. $15/375 ml.

93 • Bartlett (ME) 1994 Wild Blueberry Wine, Oak Dry, Winemakers Reserve. $21.99.

91 • Bedell (NY) NV Raspberry Wine, New York. $9.99.

90 • Bartlett (ME) Pear Wine, French Oak Dry. $14.99.

89 • Good Harbor (MI) Cherry Wine, Michigan. $5. Best Buy.

88 • Honeywood (OR) Red Currant Wine, Oregon. $7.50. Best Buy.

88 • Honeywood (OR) Grande Peach Wine. $7.50. Best Buy.

87 • Paul Thomas (WA) Crimson Rhubarb Wine, Washington 1.2% rs. $5.99. Best Buy.

87 • Honeywood (OR) Grande Cranberry Wine. $7.50. Best Buy.

87 • Bartlett (ME) Wild Blueberry Wine, Oak Dry. $14.99.

87 • Bartlett (ME) Coastal Apple & Pear Wine 1.4% rs. $8.99.

86 • Paul Thomas (WA) Raspberry Wine, Washington 3.6% rs. $7.99. Best Buy.

86 • Earle Estates (NY) Peach Perfection 5% rs. $13.99.

86 • Earle Estates (NY) Blueberry Wine 3% rs. $13.99.

85 • Bartlett (ME) Peach Wine, Semi-Dry 4.5% rs. $11.99.

Scale: Superlative (96-100), Exceptional (90-95), Highly Recommended (85-89), Recommended (80-84), Not Recommended (Under 80)

Brand Index

Brand Index

A

B

C

505

T

V

W

Bibliography

Bibliography

Baldy, Marian W. 1997. *The University Wine Course*. San Francisco, Calif.: The Wine Appreciation Guild.

Boulton, Roger B., Vernon L. Singleton, Linda F. Bisson, Ralph E. Kunkee. 1996. *Principles and Practices of Winemaking*. New York: Chapman and Hall.

Clarke, Oz. 1991. *Oz Clarke's New Classic Wines*. New York: Simon and Schuster.

_____. 1995. *Oz Clarke's Wine Atlas*. London: Little, Brown and Company.

Gladstones, John. 1997. *Viticulture and Environment*. Adelaide, South Australia: Winetitles.

Halliday, James. 1991. *Wine Atlas of Australia and New Zealand*. North Ryde, New South Wales: Angus and Robertson.

_____. 1993. *Wine Atlas of California*. New York: Viking.

Hanson, Anthony. 1995. *Burgundy*. London: Faber and Faber.

Johnson, Hugh, and James Halliday. 1992. *The Vintner's Art*. New York: Simon and Schuster.

Macaluso, Roberto. 1994. *La vite ed il vino nella provincia Granda*. Brescia: Edizione Internazionale.

Meredith, Ted Jordan. 1990. *Northwest Wine*. Kirkland, Wash.: Nexus Press.

Morton, Lucie T. 1985. *Winegrowing in Eastern America*. Ithaca, N.Y.: Cornell University Press.

Robinson, Jancis. 1994. *The Oxford Companion to Wine*. Oxford: Oxford University Press.

Vine, Richard P., Ellen M. Harkness, Theresa Browning, and Cheri Wagner.1997. *Winemaking*. New York: Chapman and Hall.

Winkler, A.J., James A. Cook, W.M. Kliewer, and Lloyd A. Lider. 1974. *General Viticulture*. Los Angeles: University of California Press.

The authoritative
buying guide
to wine, beer,
and spirits.

■ Before You Buy

Tastings

≈ The Journal of The Beverage Testing Institute ≈